The Nazi Movement in Baden, 1920-1945

The Nazi Movement in Baden, 1920-1945

Johnpeter Horst Grill

The University of North Carolina Press *Chapel Hill*

© 1983 The University of North Carolina Press

Manufactured in the United States of America

Library of Congress Cataloging in Publication Data

Grill, Johnpeter Horst, 1943-
    The Nazi movement in Baden, 1920-1945.

        Bibliography: p.
        Includes index.
        1. Nationalsozialistische Deutsche Arbeiter-Partei.
Gau Baden--History. 2. Nationalsozialistische Deutsche
Arbeiter-Artei--History. 3. Baden (Germany)--Politics and
government. I. Title.
DD253.4.B3G74 1983   324.243038'094346   82-14483
ISBN 0-8078-1472-5

Publisher's Note

The University of North Carolina Press in consultation
with the author has chosen to publish this book in its
present form in order to achieve necessary economies.

To Deborah, Michael, Brenda, and my parents

Contents

Contents : ix

Maps

TABLE

Preface

This study grew out of my University of Michigan dissertation, which was directed by Professor Gerhard L. Weinberg. It examines the relationship between the polymorphic NSDAP and the long-term völkisch activists who controlled the Gau offices. This book is based largely on unpublished party and state records. I am indebted to the staffs of the Library of Congress, the National Archives, the Leo Baeck Institute in New York City, the Institut für Zeitgeschichte in Munich, the Stadtarchiv in Karlsruhe, the Staatsarchiv Freiburg, the Generallandesarchiv Karlsruhe, and the Berlin Document Center.

In particular, Helmut Weber and Frau Köckert of the Generallandesarchiv Karlsruhe provided me with valuable and untiring assistance. Mr. Weber also arranged an interview with Walter Köhler, the former deputy Gau leader and minister president of Baden. I owe the greatest debt to Professor Gerhard L. Weinberg, who supervised my dissertation and prepared me for serious archival research. I am also grateful for his continued interest in this project.

Without the financial support obtained during the summers of 1977, 1978, and 1980 from the Office of Research and Graduate Studies of Mississippi State University, this book would have taken much longer to complete. My colleagues Glover Moore and Harold Snellgrove proofread the manuscript, and Roy Scott offered valuable advice and constant encouragement. My work-study student, Debra Randle, and Mrs. Linda Hilton typed the manuscript.

List of Abbreviations

AfB   Amt für Beamte
       (Office for Civil Servants)

AfK   Amt für Kommunalpolitik
       (Office for Municipal Affairs)

AHS   Adolf-Hitler-Schule
       (Adolf Hitler Schools)

CdZ   Chef der Zivilverwaltung
       (Chief of Civil Administration)

C. V. Zeitung Central-Verein Zeitung
       (Central-Verein Newspaper)

DAF   Deutsche Arbeitsfront
       (German Labor Front)

DAI   Deutsches Ausland-Institut (Stuttgart)
       (German Foreign Institute)

DDP   Deutsche Demokratische Partei
       (German Democratic party)

DHV   Deutschnationaler Handlungsgehilfenverband
       (German National Union of Commercial Employees)

DNVP   Deutschnationale Volkspartei
       (German National People's party)

DVFB   Deutschvölkische Freiheitsbewegung
       (German Völkisch Freedom Movement)

DFVP   Deutschvölkische Freiheitspartei
       (German Völkisch Freedom Party)

DVP	Deutsche Volkspartei (German People's party)
DVRP	Deutschvölkische Reichspartei (German Völkisch Reich party)
EHD	Elsässische Hilfsdienst (Alsatian Auxiliary Service)
GSA	Gauschulungsamt (Gau Indoctrination Office)
HJ	Hitler-Jugend (Hitler Youth)
KPD	Kommunistische Partei Deutschlands (Communist party of Germany)
NSBO	Nationalsozialistische Betriebszellenorganisation (National Socialist Organization of Factory Cells)
NSDAP	Nationalsozialistische Deutsche Arbeiterpartei (National Socialist German Workers' party)
NSDFB	Nationalsozialistische Deutsche Frontkämpferbund (NS German Front Fighters League)
NSDStB	NS-Deutscher Studentenbund (National Socialist Student Association)
NSF	NS-Frauenschaft (National Socialist Women's League)
NSFB	Nationalsozialistische Freiheitspartei (National Socialist Freedom Party)
NSKK	NS-Kraftfahrerkorps (National Socialist Motor Corps)
NSV	NS-Volkswohlfahrt (National Socialist Welfare Organization)
OR	Opferring (Alsatian Probationary Association)
PL	Politischer Leiter (Party Cadre Functionary)

PO	Politische Organisation (Political Cadre Organization)
RAD	Reichsarbeitsdienst (National Labor Service)
RJF	Reichsverband Jüdischer Frontkämpfer (National League of Jewish Veterans)
RM	Reichsmark (German Mark)
RPA	Rassenpolitischeamt (Racial Political Office)
SA	Sturmabteilung (Storm Troopers)
SNN	Strassburger Neueste Nachrichten (Strassburg Newspaper)
SPD	Sozialdemokratische Partei Deutschlands (Social Democratic party of Germany)
SS	Schutzstaffel (Protection Squads)
VKPD	Vereinigte Kommunistische Partei Deutschlands (United Communist party of Germany)
WHW	Winterhilfswerk (Winter Relief Organization)

The Nazi Movement in Baden, 1920–1945

Introduction

This is a case study of the history of National Socialism in
Baden from its origins in Pforzheim and Mannheim in 1920/21
to its total collapse amidst the ruins of the Third Reich in
1945. In recent years several works have focused on the
local and regional origins of the Nazi party and on the evolution of various party affiliates and organizations both before
and after 1933. But except for Orlow's massive study of the
national party from 1919 to 1945, most of these works accept
the existence of an artificial time barrier--1933. They
examine either the party's pre-1933 history or its function
and structure after the Nazi seizure of power. This study,
by contrast, traces the evolution and function of the party
from 1920 to 1945 in one of German's most liberal states.
Between 1925 and 1945 Gau Baden was led by a single Gau leader,
Robert Wagner, who guided the small völkisch movement to power
and ultimately to complete defeat. In 1940 Wagner even became
the chief of civil administration in Alsace, allowing him the
opportunity to export National Socialism and at the same time
to increase greatly the influence of Gau Baden in Nazi Germany.[1]

This continuity permits an examination of the role of the
völkisch true believer before and after the Nazis seized power
and facilitates a study of the impact these party activists
had on Baden society during periods of Nazi stagnation, growth,
and triumph. Between 1919 and 1932 Baden was governed by a

majority coalition that supported the republic. During much
of this period Baden also had a Socialist minister of interior
who closely supervised political extremism on the left and
the right. Nevertheless, by July 1932 a majority of Baden
voters rejected the republic and cast votes for the Nazis,
the Communists, and the German National People's party (DNVP).
Several critical questions present themselves. How and why
was the Nazi party able to capture a substantial percentage
of Baden voters by 1932 and how did the population of Baden
react to Nazi rule after 1933? Specifically, how important
was the Gau party in the seizure and maintenance of power by
Hitler?

The state of Baden, fifth in size among the German states
in 1919, emerged from the First World War with an area of
15,070 square kilometers and a population of 2,208,507. Only
a few Baden enclaves in Württemberg, Hesse, the Prussian district of Hohenzollern, and Switzerland, and several enclaves
in Baden from these states, affecting less than 4,000 people,
distracted from the unity of the state of Baden. The Rhine
River provided a natural frontier in the south and in the west.
Baden's western neighbor across that stream was Alsace, which
after 1918 was under French administration. To the northwest
and north were the Bavarian Palatinate and Hesse; Württemberg
and the Prussian district of Hohenzollern were on the eastern
border. In the south, along the Rhine and Lake Constance,
Baden shared a common border with Switzerland. Baden is divided into two major geographic regions. The lowlands are
concentrated in the Rhine Valley and constitute 20 percent of
the total land area of the state. The eastern highlands con-
sist of the Black Forest in south and central Baden and the
Odenwald in the northeast.[2]

Baden's average population density of 153 people per square
kilometer was the highest in southern Germany. It varied significantly from 306 persons per square kilometer along the
northern Rhine Valley to 72 people per square kilometer in the
Black Forest. North of Karlsruhe were more towns and cities.
There the average population of a community exceeded 1,000,
and 25 percent of the entire population of Baden lived
in the four northern urban centers of Karlsruhe, Mannheim,
Pforzheim, and Heidelberg. Mannheim was the industrial center
of Baden; Karlsruhe was the administrative center of the state.
In southern Baden the average population of a community varied
between 200 and 500, and in the Black Forest it dropped to
below 50. The major urban centers in the south were Freiburg,
Konstanz, and Lörrach. Baden's 16 urban centers with populations over 10,000 held 36.4 percent of the state's population.
Only five of these towns (of which four were in northern Baden)
had populations over 70,000. At the same time 36.3 percent of
the state's population lived in communities having less than
2,000 residents.[3]

Compared to other southern German states, Baden was ori-
ented more toward industry and commerce. In 1925 industry
provided a livelihood for 39.6 percent of Baden's population
while agriculture and forestry supported 28.2 percent. Trade
and commerce followed with 15.9 percent, and the administration
and bureaucracy provided a living for 4.9 percent. In terms
of the working force, 35.6 percent were employed in industry,
33.8 percent in agriculture (and forestry), 13 percent in
trade and commerce, and 3.7 percent in the bureaucracy and
administration.[4]

Of the forty administrative districts of Baden in 1925,
five were predominantly industrial and thirteen others reflected

substantial industrial characteristics. Trade and commerce
dominated thirteen districts, especially Karlsruhe, Mannheim,
Freiburg, Offenburg, and Heidelberg. Most of Baden's industrial districts were located in the northern part of the state
between the river Murg and the river Neckar and in southern
Säckingen and Lörrach. Northern Baden was 43 percent industrial and only 18 percent agricultural. In southern Baden
agriculture occupied 38 percent of the population, and industry furnished a livelihood for only 34 percent of the inhabitants.[5]

Factories employing more than 20 workers existed in 479
communities in Baden in 1925. A total of 2,408 factories
employed 251,130 workers, who represented 10.9 percent of the
population. One-third of these workers were employed in the
three urban centers of Mannheim, Pforzheim, and Karlsruhe.
Mannheim had the largest and most complex industrial enterprises. The districts of Wiesloch, Säckingen, Pforzheim,
Weinheim, and Lörrach employed the highest percentages of
industrial workers in relation to the total population. In
Säckingen, for example, 21.2 percent of the population was
employed in industry.[6]

Northeastern and southeastern Baden were predominantly
rural as were several districts along the Upper Rhine (see
Map 1). In eighteen of the forty administrative districts
of Baden in 1925, at least half of the population was directly
dependent on agriculture. Agriculture and forestry provided
a livelihood for 653,248 people or 28.2 percent of the population. In addition, 222,999 persons were part-time farmers
who also pursued a variety of trades or worked in factories.
The state's rural population was one of the densest in Germany,
with an average of forty-seven people per 100 hectares (260

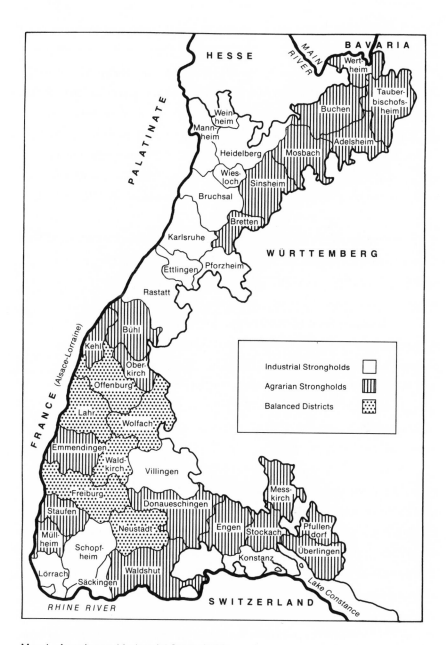

Map 1. *Agrarian and Industrial Strongholds*

acres). For Germany as a whole the figure was only thirty-one
persons per 100 hectares. The average farm in Baden consisted
of only 3.8 hectares. By the 1920s the constant fragmentation
of family plots had produced a large number of marginal farms,
many under two hectares in size.[7]

The marginal farmers with less than two hectares occupied
60 percent of the state's farms. They were concentrated in
the Rhine Valley between the district of Mannheim and the
district of Rastatt. But over one-third of these "farmers"
pursued, as their major professions, occupations in factories
or commercial enterprises. Another 17 percent were artisans
and owners of small businesses. Only 26 percent of all farms
under two hectares were operated by full-time farmers. The
second type of farm in Baden ranged between two and five hectares and made up 32.8 percent of Baden's agricultural units.
Full-time farmers maintained 80 percent of these farms in the
Rhine Valley between the districts of Bühl and Lörrach and
along the foothills of the Black Forest and the Odenwald.
Viniculture, tobacco, and livestock specialization occupied
these farmers. Finally the "healthy rural middle class" of
Baden with farms between five and twenty hectares was strongest
in the foothills of the Black Forest and Odenwald. These farmers, who raised livestock and grew wheat, had a well-devel-
oped comparative system for acquiring goods and marketing
products. Estates and large farms over twenty hectares accounted for less than 2 percent of the units in Baden but held
38.47 percent of the agricultural land surface. The large
estates (over 100 hectares) were owned predominantly by the
state, communities, or corporate bodies rather than landlords.[8]

In Baden, 58.5 percent of the population were Catholics,
and 38.7 percent were Protestants. Only 2.9 percent of the

inhabitants of Baden claimed adherence to the various minority
religions, ranging from the Mennonites to the Jews (see Map 2).
In 1925 the 24,064 Jews accounted for 1.1 percent of the state's
population, which was slightly above the German average of .9
percent. Sixty-eight percent of all of Baden's Jews lived in
the six districts of Mannheim, Heidelberg, Pforzheim, Karlsruhe,
Freiburg, and Konstanz. Of the forty districts of Baden,
twenty-eight had an overwhelming Catholic majority and twelve
had a clear Protestant majority. Protestant strength was concentrated in northern Baden between the districts of Karlsruhe
and Weinheim and in the northeastern rural areas. Isolated
Protestant strength was located along the Rhine in the rural
districts of Kehl, Emmendingen, and Müllheim, and in industrial Lörrach. Catholicism was strongest in southeastern and
central Baden and in several northern districts like Wiesloch,
Buchen, and Tauberbischofsheim. Many of these districts had
Catholic majorities of over 90 percent of the total population.[9]

Baden provides both an appropriate and important area
for an investigation of the evolution of the Nazi party. The
state's diverse socioeconomic and religious conditions were
similar to those of Germany as a whole. In addition, the clear
economic and religious differences between many of Baden's
districts (Amtsbezirke) permit an examination of the appeal
of the party to specific socioeconomic and religious segments
of society. Baden is also important because National Socialism evolved and eventually prospered in this state, despite
the fact that Catholics and Socialists cooperated politically
and dominated the state government until the eve of the collapse of the republic. This hostile political environment did
little, however, to stifle grassroots Nazi activities during

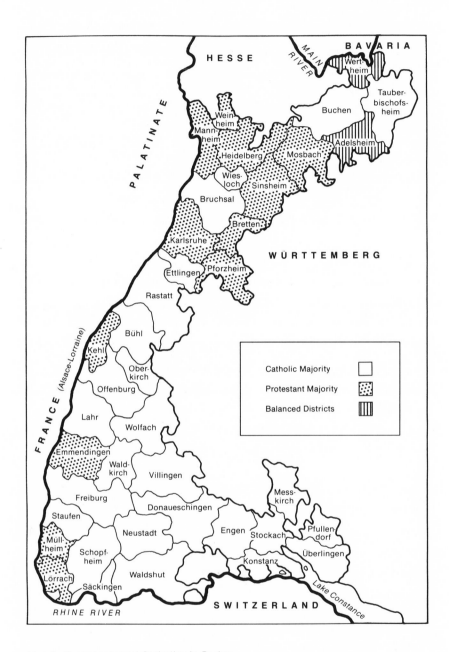

Map 2. *Protestants and Catholics in Baden*

the early years of the republic. By 1928 the Baden party had established itself with a major electoral breakthrough in the state's rural, Protestant areas.

1 The Revolution and the Radical Right in Baden, 1918-1923

THE REVOLUTION AND LEFTIST UPRISINGS

The region of Baden in the present state of Baden-Württemberg
was a separate state before the total collapse of 1945. Baden
was welded into a unified state in southwestern Germany during
the long reign of the Margrave Karl Friedrich (1746-1811) and
it quadrupled its size during the Napoleonic period by absorbing a hodgepodge of ecclesiastical and secular territories.
The settlement at Vienna in 1815 recognized the new Grand
Duchy of Baden, and in 1819 the Counts of Hochberg were approved as the legal heirs to the throne. This Protestant dy-
nasty brought Baden into the German Empire in 1871 and also
witnessed the collapse of the monarchical structure in Germany
and Baden in November 1918.[1]

The new Grand Duke Karl Ludwig Friedrich (1811-18) granted
a constitution in 1818 that "placed Baden at the head of constitutionalism in Germany."[2] During much of the nineteenth
century the National Liberals dominated the bureaucracy and
the political process, then in 1904 an act of the legislature
provided for secret and direct election to the lower house.
With this constitutional reform Baden became the most democratic state in Germany. But this change also threatened the
Liberals' political domination since they now faced increasing
competition from the Socialists and the Catholic Center party.

The growth of the latter represented the greatest danger to
the "Liberal legacy" of the nineteenth century. Consequently,
the Liberals formed an election alliance with the Socialists
that was directed against the Center party. The Baden Socialists in return defied their national leadership and voted for
the Baden budget in 1910. Before the war, the liberal Baden
minister of interior, Baron Johann von Bodman, "favored progressive social legislation and he espoused the cause of the
Social Democrats despite opposition from the Baden Grand Duke."[3]

After 1904 Baden's political scene was dominated by these
three major blocs. The Center party, representing the Catholics, formed electoral alliances with the conservative forces
in Baden (which included the League of Farmers). The Catholics
could neither tear down the school laws passed by the Liberals
during the nineteenth century nor form a government. Nevertheless, through the establishment of associations and a press
and the activism of the clergy, they "maintained a high level
of Catholic consciousness in both urban and rural areas."[4]
The Liberal camp articulated the varied views of the National
Liberals, Progressives, Democrats, and National Socialists.
On the eve of the war, the National Liberals in Baden were
guided by Edmund Regmann, who was willing to work with the
Socialists "in the hope of awaking a feeling of responsibility
to the idea of the state . . . and a warmer involvement in
the (state's) fate."[5] Finally, the Socialists represented
the growing labor class in Baden's industrial areas.

Between 1905 and 1913 the Liberals' popular vote decreased
from 35.5 percent to 33 percent, while the Catholic-Conservative
bloc declined from 46.5 percent to 44 percent of the total
vote. The Socialists, reflecting the gradual modernization
of Baden, increased their popular following from 17 to 22

percent of the vote. Although the Great Coalition broke down
in Baden in 1913, politics on the eve of the war was characterized by moderation.[6] On 21 October 1913, the last prewar state
elections were held in Baden. The Socialists won a plurality
of the vote in five electoral districts (Karlsruhe, Mannheim,
Pforzheim, and the county districts Mannheim-Weinheim and
Karlsruhe-Ettlingen), while the Liberals obtained a plurality
only in the northern district of Heidelberg and in the southern
electoral district of Schopfheim-Lörrach-Müllheim. In the district of Emmendingen-Lahr, the Liberals shared leadership with
the Catholics, with both winning 42.5 percent of the vote. The
Center party won a clear majority in eleven districts and a
plurality in eleven others. The Center party's strength was
concentrated in the southern Catholic districts and (in combination with the Conservatives) in northeastern Baden. These
electoral results reflected, on the whole, the economic and
religious divisions of Baden.[7]

Baden's moderate political structure received its greatest test during the World War. By 1917 and early 1918, proposals for greater democratization were introduced in the
Baden legislature. Events moved rapidly in October 1918.
Publications such as the _Politischer Rundbrief_ appeared in
Karlsruhe that demanded a people's state, international cooperation, and freedom and justice for all. In the middle of the
same month, a Socialist state conference prepared another program for democratization, which it also made available to
the bourgeois parties. Finally, by the end of October unrest
broke out among workers in Mannheim.[8] Four years of warfare
had helped to undermine even the most liberal government in
Germany.

The revolution in Baden in late 1918 was a political

upheaval influenced primarily by events in Karlsruhe and
Mannheim. The political demands of party leaders in Karlsruhe,
combined with the pressures from the Mannheim soviets, over-
turned the liberal monarchy without bloodshed. On 2 November
1918, the government of Baden yielded to the political pressures
and announced its plan to initiate a bill for a proportional
election law. But by then events in Germany and in Baden were
overtaking the Karlsruhe government. On 7 November Ludwig
Marum, a Socialist leader in Karlsruhe, published an article
in the Volksstimme in which he demanded immediate democratization and questioned whether the liberal minister of interior,
Baron Johann von Bodman, could carry out the necessary reforms.
The catalyst that brought events in Baden to a political climax
was the activism of the Mannheim Socialists, who demanded more
rapid democratization. The Mannheim party local sent its
representative and leader Anton Geiss to Karlsruhe to demand
the resignation of the government. In the morning of 9 November, Geiss and representatives from the National Liberal, Progressive, and Center parties visited Bodman to inform him
that Mannheim would erupt if he did not resign. Bodman promised to call the state legislature into session within a week
to deal with these demands.[9]

The government's actions did not prevent the appearance
of Soldiers' Soviets in Mannheim on 9 November. In the evening
of the same day, the Kaiser's abdication was announced in
Karlsruhe's newspapers and immediately caused the appearance
of mass gatherings under the guidance of agitators from the
new Independent Socialist party. Although Soldiers' Soviets
were formed in all urban centers of Baden, contemporary observers like Hugo Marx of Heidelberg testified to the lack of
real disturbances even in Mannheim. To ensure this trend and

to capture the revolutionary movement, the mayors of Mannheim and Karlsruhe established Welfare Committees in which all of the parties were represented. The following day, the Karlsruhe Soviets and the Welfare Committee established a new provisional government, which received de facto recognition from Bodman while the final form of government was left to a future state convention. In Karlsruhe on 10 November, a crowd of predominantly young men entertained themselves by tearing insignias from the shoulders of officers and soldiers, but, according to one observer, fewer than one thousand adults listened with moderate enthusiasm to the proclamation of the new government.[10]

Isolated soviets in Lörrach and Offenburg still opposed the parliamentary solution, but the majority of Baden's soviets clearly supported the political settlement. The Baden Assembly of Soviets rejected a vague millennium and demanded instead the creation of a framework for the "next generation in Germany." The only violence occurred in Karlsruhe on 12 November 1918, when a drunken sailor, Heinrich Klumpp, a native of Karlsruhe with a sordid past that included a jail term for embezzlement in 1913, led a group of soldiers to the royal residence, causing the court to flee from Karlsruhe. More important, on 14 November the provisional government, under pressures from the soviets of Mannheim and Karlsruhe, proclaimed the Free Peoples' Republic of Baden but left the final form of the government up to the National Assembly, which was scheduled to be elected on 5 January 1919.[11]

All parties, except for the Conservatives, were represented in the new provisional government. Unlike most other German states, Baden refrained from forming a simple Socialist alliance in November 1918. The Majority Socialists received five ministries, including the presidency, while the Independent

Socialists occupied two positions. Two ministries each were allocated to the Center party and the Democrats. This broad coalition actually was not very revolutionary, since the National Liberals, Progressives, and Socialists had cooperated in a Great Coalition before 1913. The real difference was that the Center party joined the coalition in November 1918. Heinrich Köhler, a future minister president, and Gustav Trunk, the first minister in charge of securing the supply of food, were the only two important members of the Center party in Karlsruhe in November 1918. Köhler used his influence to ensure the incorporation of the Catholics in the provisional government. His motive was pragmatic, for Köhler wanted to stop the revolution in Baden, even if it required cooperation with the Socialists. Later in life he noted, "I remember exactly how I shuddered at my first thoughts of a collaboration with the Social Democratic party."[12]

The National Assembly of Baden was elected on 5 January 1919, by 88.1 percent of the eligible voters. The Center party emerged as the strongest party with 36.6 percent of the vote, followed closely by the Socialist party with 32.1 percent and the Democratic party with 22.8 percent. The new German National People's party, which was strongest in the north and northeast of the state, and the Independent Socialist party represented the political extremes on the right and the left with only 7 percent and 1.7 percent of the votes, respectively. Since the Independent Socialists failed to win a seat in the Assembly, their representatives withdrew from the government, leaving only the "Weimar Coalition" composed of Socialists, Democrats, and the Center party to govern Baden until 1929. Baden was also the first state in Germany to adopt a new constitution on 12 March 1919, which the voters approved by plebiscite in April.

The same plebiscite also recognized the National Assembly as
the state legislature until the first state election in October
1921.[13]

The constitution, which granted suffrage to all Baden
citizens who had reached the age of twenty, set up a unicameral
legislature, which was elected for four years. The legislature
in turn selected the ministers and the state president of
the government. In November 1918, eleven ministers constituted
the provisional government, but by 1925 the ministries had
been reduced to four, although frequently only three ministers
occupied the ministries of Interior, Culture and Education
(and Justice), and Finance. Since the coalition partners controlled the legislature, they also controlled the ministries.
A small circle of political leaders dominated these positions.
For example, Josef Schmitt of the Center party was minister
of education (1925–28), minister of finance (1927–31), and
minister of justice (1931–33), while Adam Remmele, a Social
Democrat whom the Nazis despised particularly, was state
president (1922 and 1927), minister of interior (1919–28),
minister of education (1928–30), and minister of justice (1929–
31). Between 1919 and 1924 the state presidency rotated
among the three coalition partners. After 1924, however, the
Center party occupied the post, except for 1927, when the
Socialist Remmele was minister president.[14]

After 1920, Baden experienced a proliferation of parties
and the emergence of extremist groups on the left and right,
along with the decline of the Democratic party throughout
Germany. Seven political parties took part in the election
of June 1920; in May 1928, seventeen political parties, ranging from socioeconomic interest groups to religious parties,
participated in the national election. But until 1929, the

Weimar Coalition remained in power in Baden, controlling sixty-one of the eighty-six seats of the state legislature in 1921 and fifty of the sixty-one seats during the 1925-29 legislative period. After 1929 the Center party and the Socialists, who formed a government without the Democrats, still dominated fifty-two of the eighty-eight seats. In 1931, Baden made its first turn to the right by admitting the German People's party to the government. But not until November 1932 did majority government end in the state after the Socialists withdrew from the coalition, leaving the government with only forty-one of the eighty-eight legislative seats. The fact remains, however, that until 1932 the clear majority of the voters were represented in the government by parties that supported the republic.[15]

Despite the peaceful transition from a monarchy to a democratic republic in 1918 and the subsequent stability of the Weimar Coalition in Baden, a few perceptive observers rapidly shed their initial optimism. The failure of the 1918 revolution in Baden to change the fundamental structure of the civil service, the judiciary, the economy, and the military was characteristic of all German states. Naturally, representatives from the political left and some democrats in Baden noticed this trend as early as 1918. Some like Karl Bittle, the editor of Politischer Rundbrief, had argued in October 1918 for a democratic republic based on justice and freedom for all. One year later he had joined the Communist party, escaped to Württemberg, and become disillusioned with German workers, whom he accused of being too phlegmatic and too little committed to class consciousness to carry out a real German revolution. Others like Hugo Marx, a Jewish jurist employed in Mannheim in 1921, observed that the judicial representatives

in Mannheim were not only frequently anti-Semitic but also
very cool toward the new democratic order.[16] Prophetically,
one observer in Baden, who began writing a history of the
November revolution in his native state in late 1918, noted
his doubts in 1920 that the Baden population was mature enough
to cope with the greater freedom and would be able to break
the "chains" of the bureaucracy and of the military establishment.[17]

After 1918, Baden did witness the growth of such organized right-wing parties as the German National People's Party
and the Landbund (Agrarian League) which rejected the new
pluralistic and democratic society by clinging to pre-1918
social and political images. The state also saw the appearance of numerous radical völkisch groups ranging from the
Schutz- und Trutzbund to the Nazi party. Although right-wing
political parties and völkisch groups, gradually and persistently, helped to undermine support for the republic, between
1919 and 1923 these groups never played a critical or even
dangerous role. The government of Baden and particularly the
Socialist minister of interior, Adam Remmele, simply did not
tolerate open, potentially dangerous, extreme right-wing political activities.

Much more dangerous to the stability of the new democracy
in Baden during the immediate post-war years were the various
extreme left-wing uprisings and disturbances that occurred in
all parts of the state. Some of this urban unrest was motivated by economic pressures, and some was a labor response to
right-wing outrages such as the murder of prominent national
political figures like Walther Rathenau (June 1922) and Matthias
Erzberger (August 1921). But most important in terms of generating fear among the various components of the urban and rural

middle class were the Communist attempts between 1919 and
1923 to undermine the stability of the republic whenever the
opportunity arose. In general, mass public political activism
and intimidation between 1919 and 1923 were dominated by the
left.

This did not mean that Remmele tolerated left-wing violence. In fact, he was adamant in his opposition to these
disturbances, particularly if Communists were involved. In
early 1919, he directed the government's district representatives to monitor the activities of "Bolsheviks" and Spartacists who might attempt to disturb the Constituent National
Assembly.[18] But Remmele was faced with the almost total un-
reliability of the Baden militia in 1918/19. For example, in
early 1919 the Spartacists in Mannheim with the help of many
young men responded to the murder of the Independent Socialist
leader Kurt Eisner in Munich by breaking into the jails, free-
ing hundreds of prisoners, and burning the files of the criminal
police, while the militia (Volkswehr) stood by idle. As a
response, Remmele called for the creation of volunteer battalions staffed with people who had at least six months of
combat experience. Although representatives of the right
welcomed the proposed crackdown on the Bolsheviks and Spartacists, they agitated against recruitment among workers.[19]
This illustrates the deep gulf that separated the right from
the new government. Although the government in Baden was
adamant in its opposition to the left-wing violence as early
as 1919, it could do little to expurgate the traditional anti-
labor prejudice of the political right.

Remmele was effective, however, in preventing Communist
coups and in controlling the various uprisings that plagued
Baden between 1919 and 1923. The Kapp Putsch in Berlin in

March 1920 led to extreme left-wing responses in Mannheim.
Revolutionary workers went beyond the government's peaceful
resistance to the Berlin reactionaries by setting up soviets
in five major factories. Remmele, who clearly saw the dangers
of this volatile situation, wanted the problem defused before
the soviets added salary demands to their political aims and
consequently won the support of most workers. In the end, the
failure of the mass of workers to support the soviets was
crucial, since the Baden military commander told the government
in late March 1920 that he did not have enough troops to take
Mannheim by force.[20]

Remmele continued to use labor to combat potential Communist Putsches. In late March 1920, he urged the use of labor
unions and Christian workers' organizations to control such
uprisings, if necessary by force. He ordered the press to
emphasize the deep division between the Socialist ministers
and the Communists, no doubt to let the workers know that the
Socialist members of the Baden government did not support the
Communists.[21] By May 1920, the Baden government was self-confident enough to disregard the warnings of the Stuttgart military commander of an impending Communist Putsch. The unrest
that did occur in July and August 1920, in places like Karlsruhe
and St. Georgen in southern Baden, began as protests over the
cost of living. In Karlsruhe mobs plundered warehouses; and
in St. Georgen a large mass of workers, incensed by the high
price of meat, confiscated five animals, butchered them, and
then disbursed the meat at a price well below the market value.
In both cases, the authorities were able to restore order quickly.[22]

Between 1921 and late 1923, the Baden government was faced
repeatedly with similar crises. In all cases the government

was able to contain the violence and in particular to control
the Communists. After the 1920 disorders were brought under
control, the Baden papers again were full of reports in early
1921 of impending Communist uprisings. In addition, the government captured Communist circulars which indicated that the
Communists were organizing for some type of antirepublican
action. Actually, the Communist uprising of March 1921 did not
have a great impact on Baden. It was confined to a minor mob
action in Mannheim that resulted in a few casualties. Not
until late 1923 did the Communists play a major role in a Baden
uprising.[23] The largest disturbances in 1921 and 1922 resulted
from mass labor demonstrations against right-wing excesses.

The biggest upheaval in 1921 came as a reaction to the
murder of Matthias Erzberger, the former national minister of
finance. In Heidelberg alone, a mass rally of workers and
Socialist students composed of almost seven thousand people
protested the "monocled reaction" and the "swastika wearers"
by going on a rampage. The mob tore down monarchical insignias from the buildings and statues and even destroyed the
windows of the Badische Post, a paper that reflected the views
of the German People's party. In 1922 the drama was repeated
after the murder of Walther Rathenau, the German foreign
minister, by right-wing extremists. Again organized labor
demonstrated in northern and southern Baden in July 1922
against these flagrant attacks on the public. In Singen,
a community in southern Baden, workers went to the villa of
the factory director Pulsen. After the mob had pillaged the
villa, it proceeded to the home of a retired army officer,
Major Scherer. When Scherer shot at the workers who were
stealing food, a Communist worker killed the major. Similarly
in Mosbach on 4 July, workers from the Amilin and Soda factory

broke into the residence of the Freiherr Franz von Gemmingen
to show their disapproval of the "old order."[24] Shocked by
these events, Baden's industrial interests naturally sought
help from the government. Several days after the Singen demon-
stration, representatives from industrial concerns of southern
Baden were sent to Karlsruhe to plead for protection.[25]

The greatest shock to industry, and the largest uprising
involving Communist agitators, occurred in Upper Baden between
14 September and 23 September 1923. The echoes from this
conflict were heard as far north as Heidelberg. Between fifteen hundred and two thousand workers had been concentrated
in a construction project in the Weil-Leopoldshöhe area. In
early 1923, a Communist became the shop leader of these workers.
On 14 September, a committee of factory workers, with the support of the local Communists, called a general strike to voice
economic grievances. After the government sent special police
forces to Lörrach, real violence broke out. The workers forced
factory owners of the surrounding area to march with them to
Schopfheim as hostages. In Schopfheim and Lörrach, the mob
beat and mishandled factory owners and a Kaufmann, Adolf Meyer,
who was known as a Lörrach "fascist chieftain." Some of the
more violent Communists who committed these acts were very
young, unemployed men who had joined the Communist party only
a month or two earlier. Once again the government of Baden
was able to gain control, particularly after the national Communist leadership called an end to the violence.[26]

Again, however, the Baden middle classes and the industrial interests were frightened. For example, the League of
the Clock Industry of the Donaueschingen area in early October
1923 complained to the government about the disturbances and
pleaded for protection.[27] The government may have been able

to control the extreme left-wing violence but it could not
erase the growing suspicions of the middle classes. After
all, between 1919 and 1923 open mass political violence was
the preserve of the left and of outraged labor. These activities only confirmed the anti-Weimar attitude of a political
right that was regaining its own momentum and confidence.
These postwar disturbances also helped to fuel the fire of
suspicion and enmity of those segments of Baden society that
could not accept the military defeat of 1918.

THE RECHTSBLOCK IN BADEN

Frustration produced by the military collapse combined with
fear of social revolution to generate the first signs of organized right-wing resistance in democratic Baden. Between 1919
and 1928, the dominant political right in Baden, both in terms
of voting patterns and recognition by political observers, was
represented by the German National People's party (DNVP) and
the Agrarian League (Landbund). These two parties reflected
the fears and frustrations of urban and rural middle classes
who could accept neither the 1918 defeat nor the subsequent
political and social modernization. The DNVP, an alliance of
conservative and racist forces, had emerged in 1919 to participate in elections to the Constituent Assembly and won 7 percent of the total vote in Baden. By 1920, the party won 12
percent of the vote. Its strength lay in northern Baden, particularly in the Protestant rural districts where the party
won between 19 and 40 percent of the vote in the 1920 election.
In addition, the Nationalists were strong in the Protestant,
rural districts along the Rhine between Kehl and Müllheim.

In 1921, for the first time, the DNVP faced competition from
the Landbund. The Agrarian League was also strongest in the
rural, Protestant districts of northern and southeastern Baden.
In the state election of 1921 the Landbund was able to harness
8.3 percent of the total vote. In 1925, the DNVP and Landbund
united to form a Rechtsblock (coalition of the right) in Baden
and succeeded in winning 12.2 percent of the vote in the state
election of that year. Only after 1928 was this Rechtsblock
replaced by a stronger political party on the right, the National Socialist German Workers' party (NSDAP).[28]

The DNVP did not appear in reaction to the left-wing
urban and rural violence that plagued Baden between 1919 and
1923. Instead, it represented elements in Baden that could
not accept defeat and revolution, elements that had opposed
the Socialists and liberal forces prior to the World War by
allying themselves with the Catholic Center party during elections. Before 1914, this alliance had worked best in the
northern and especially in the northeastern rural districts
of Baden. In 1919, the DNVP emerged relatively strong in
these districts, and only later in 1920 did the Nationalists
make noticeable inroads in Protestant southwestern districts.
It is important to remember that the Nationalists of Baden
rejected the republic from the very beginning. One DNVP election leaflet, which circulated in January 1919, defended the
monarchy, stressed the party's support for Christianity and
private property, and demanded protection for farmers and
control of cartels. Finally, the leaflet engaged in "respectable" anti-Semitism while advocating strong support for Germanism (Deutschtum). Extreme nationalism, suspicion of large
industry, and distrust of republicanism thus characterized
the party's mentality as early as 1919/20.[29]

The political left and in fact members of the coalition
government in Baden naturally distrusted both the DNVP and,
before the appearance of the Landbund, the German People's
party (DVP). For example, during the Kapp Putsch, the state's
representatives collaborated with the government coalition
partners (Democrats, Socialists, and Center party) and even
with the Independent Socialists to ensure that the Kapp Putsch
would not have an impact in Baden. Regional governments in
Baden prepared plans that called for organized labor and militia resistance in case of a Kapp Putsch in Baden. Preparations
were also made to cut lines of communications with Karlsruhe
should "reactionaries" gain control of the Baden capital.
When the Nationalists and DVP representatives of Konstanz
protested their exclusion from the discussion and even declared
that they represented the "order-loving" bourgeoisie, the
state commissioner for the region of Konstanz reminded them
of Kapp's close ties with the rightist parties.[30] During
subsequent disturbances in Baden, labor and left-wing agitators
continued to focus on the Nationalists and even the DVP as
enemies of the republic. This attack only increased the determination of these middle-class parties to warn against the
dangers of socialization and communization during election
campaigns and to depict themselves as saviors of the Mittelstand
from the chaos.[31]

The importance of the Nationalists in Baden (and after
1921 of the Landbund and the Nationalists) was twofold. First,
in terms of the sociopolitical climate the Rechtsblock of 1921
was strongest in all Baden districts where the NSDAP did best
in the July 1932 election. The only exceptions were Oberkirch,
a Catholic district, and Donaueschingen, where the Landbund
voters returned to the Center party. For example, the Rechts-

block in 1921 won 49 percent of the vote in the district of
Kehl, 46 percent in the district of Bretten, and 48.6 percent
in the district of Wertheim. In July 1932, the Nazi party
won 58.7 percent of the vote in the district of Kehl, 55.5
percent in the district of Bretten, and 51.2 percent in the
district of Wertheim. Since the revolution of 1918 did not
really change the basic political socialization process in
Baden, the Rechtsblock's values were instilled in the postwar
generation of the urban and rural Protestant middle classes.
The "new voters" who flocked to the Nazi party by July 1932
had been produced by this environment. Even in the most democratic state of Germany the pattern was familiar. First, the
Nationalists emerged in 1919 to combat the new democratic
order. Then beginning in 1920 with the collapse of the
"middle," the German Democratic party simply continued to lose
voters to the urban and rural right-wing political parties.
The second importance of the Nationalists and the Landbund
for the subsequent evolution of the Nazi party in Baden was
that many Nazi activists started their political careers in
either the DNVP or the Landbund or both. For example, Walter
Buch of Karlsruhe, the future Nazi party court director, wrote
for the Badische Wochenzeitung, a paper published by a DNVP
city councilman, and he was a DNVP candidate in the 1921 election. This list could be expanded to include the racist Arnold
Ruge and the future deputy Gau leader of Baden, Walter Köhler.[32]
Both in terms of generating a pool of potential voters and
in stimulating and sheltering numerous early Nazi activists,
the Baden DNVP and the Landbund contributed substantially
toward the destruction of the democratic order in Baden.

THE VÖLKISCH MOVEMENT

Although historians have debated the nature and significance
of National Socialism's ideology without producing a uniformly acceptable definition, few would deny that it was a völkisch
movement. Völkisch is perhaps best translated as a "racist
populism" composed of anti-Semitism, intolerant nationalism,
and a rejection of modernity. These various trends had thrived
already before 1919 in large part because certain segments
of German society had been unwilling or unable to accept Germany's modernization. After 1918, the representatives of
modernity--Jews, Socialists, and middle-class democrats--seemed
to have triumphed completely. Added to this was the overriding
fact that Germany had lost the war after years of suffering.
The Nationalists had organized in 1918/19 to combat these
trends on the political level. The völkisch activists organized to combat political modernity outside the formal political
theater. Many of the future leading Nazi activists in Baden
received their political baptism in this milieu of völkisch
currents between 1919 and 1923. A barometer to measure the
intensity of this völkisch activism after 1918 was anti-Semitism. The Jew as the symbol of political and social modernity
became the focus of radical antirepublicanism and antimodernism. Long before they joined the Nazi party, many Baden Nazis
had been enthusiastic anti-Semites. As George L. Mosse has
pointed out, anti-Semitism "provided much of the cement for
this (völkisch) thought and gave it a dynamic it might otherwise have lacked."[33]

This venom was poured on 1.1 percent of the population in
Baden. Over half of the 23,909 inhabitants of Baden who claimed
Judaism as their religious preference lived in the four cities

of Mannheim, Karlsruhe, Freiburg, and Heidelberg. In all four
cities organized anti-Semitism appeared as early as 1919. But
anti-Semitism was also strong in the rural areas of the state,
particularly where economic modernization had destroyed the
social homogeneity of the community. Since Baden's Jews were
very prominent in the professions, trade, and finance, anti-
Semitism was reinvigorated by economic conflicts. The 3,386
Jews of Karlsruhe, for example, represented 2.3 percent of the
city's population but provided 26 percent of the doctors and
40 percent of the lawyers. In particular, the völkisch activists in Baden resented the two Jewish ministers of the
revolutionary government in 1918, Ludwig Marum (Justice) and
Ludwig Haas (Interior).[34]

Anti-Semitic leaflets and anti-Semitic tirades appeared
in various parts of Baden in early 1919. Teachers even received anti-Semitic literature from northern Germany. The
spread of anti-Semitism in Baden in both print and word among
a wide circle of the population caused Minister of Interior
Adam Remmele to order his district representatives to monitor
the trend and most importantly to prevent violence to Jews.[35]
Students were in the forefront of the anti-Semitic movement
in Baden. When the Jewish professor Max Mayer was called to
the Technical University in Karlsruhe in the winter of 1919/20,
the students declared a strike. According to the students, one
position in the chemistry department was already occupied by
a Jewish professor, and they announced that they would not
accept another. As a result, Professor Mayer declined to accept the position. Similarly, several years later the medical
students of the University of Freiburg provided the NS
Student League with more votes than any other university department. The fact that 40 percent of the Jewish students of

Freiburg studied medicine, no doubt, reinvigorated the anti-
Semitism of the medical students.[36]

The Völkischer Beobachter of Munich eagerly focused on
Baden's anti-Semitism long before the Nazis acquired this
völkisch paper. On 29 December 1919, the paper published
the letter of Eugen Mayer, a businessman in Donaueschingen in
southern Baden, to Julius Rosenau, a Jewish merchant in Frankfurt. Mayer, apparently irritated over a business dispute
with Rosenau, denounced all "greedy Jews." He blamed them for
Germany's misfortune during the war and suggested that the
whole "Jewish tribe" be flogged across Germany's borders.
Another letter to the Völkischer Beobachter in April 1920
had been sent by the Karlsruhe local of the Schutz- und Trutzbund to the Baden government. This letter accused Jews of
exploiting the German people during and after the war and
charged that they were still obtaining preferential treatment
during Jewish holidays in order to obtain certain kinds of
nourishments. Most important, the Karlsruhe Schutz- und
Trutzbund warned that if such conduct did not cease, the
Gentile population of Baden would lose its patience.[37]

Arnold Ruge provides an important example of a völkisch
activist in Baden after 1918 who had formed the basis of his
political and social philosophy long before the German defeat
in the war or the urban disturbances after 1919. Born in
Görlitz, Silesia, on 1 January 1881, to a Reichsbank director,
Ruge was the great nephew of the "1848 democrat" Arnold Ruge.
After having studied classical philology and philosophy in
Heidelberg, Ruge earned a Ph.D. and subsequently became a
lecturer at the University of Heidelberg. In 1904/5 he apparently still rejected the students' anti-Semitism and even
wrote articles for the Frankfurter Zeitung. He may have

become an anti-Semite because a Jewish professor was promoted before him.[38] In any case, by 1911 Ruge had taken up the cause of antimodernism and antifeminism, which led him to a violent anti-Semitism. In 1911, he published a pamphlet that lashed out against egalitarianism and materialism. The work maintained that German universities depended for their academic excellence on "masculine rigorism." This was being undermined by feminism since with the admission of women the quality of the lectures had declined. During the same period, Ruge became involved in a nasty dispute with the Women's Movement in Heidelberg and in particular with Marianne Weber, the wife of the famous sociologist Max Weber. In the end Ruge simply accused the movement of being led by Jews and sterile or unmarried women. During the war Ruge continued his antifeminism by arguing that men must dominate economic, military, and political affairs and that women should limit themselves to the kitchen and to nursing and breeding. In 1917 the German League against Women Emancipation even urged Ruge to write a petition for the creation of a women's university to allow the exclusion of women from German universities.[39]

Ruge emerged from the war (in which he did not participate) with his anti-Semitism and antiliberalism reinvigorated. As a major anti-Semitic spokesman in Heidelberg in late 1919 he established contacts with the Schutz- und Trutzbund, the most extreme anti-Semitic völkisch organization in Germany. Finally, when Ruge attacked Jews on 22 November 1919, at the yearly celebration of the Ruperto Carola in Heidelberg, the Baden minister of education, responding in part to pleas from the Jewish community, initiated disciplinary procedures that caused Ruge to lose his teaching position in June 1920. This did not, of course, stop Ruge's anti-Semitic tirades. Instead,

Ruge became involved with most major antirepublican forces
in Baden. He was a member of the DNVP until 1920 and an active member of the Schutz- und Trutzbund until May 1922. His
völkisch activism even caused him to come to the attention of
Dietrich Eckart, who devoted space to the Baden anti-Semite
in the Völkischer Beobachter.[40]

In May 1922 Ruge also began issuing his own journal,
which he published in Heidelberg. In this journal, Deutsche
Wohlfahrt, he insulted the major democratic and republican
forces in Germany. Eventually the Baden government banned
the journal for six months. Ruge, however, only shifted his
activities to Munich in early 1923.[41] There he came in contact not only with the Nazis but with such völkisch organizations as the Bund Blücher. A persistent bickerer and quar-
reler, Ruge broke with most organized political groups after
becoming involved in a series of personal clashes. Finally,
in 1923 the Bavarian government sentenced him to prison for
his role in the death of a student who had been killed following one of Ruge's speeches, extolling the need to "clean
house." In the summer of 1924 the völkisch true believer
emerged from prison and returned to Baden to play again an
active part in organized völkisch activism.[42]

Völkisch activists like Ruge illustrate the continuity
of prewar antimodernism and the potential grassroots support
for an organized völkisch movement in Baden. Most important,
Ruge's activities were not unique in postwar Germany. Between
1920 and 1922 over one hundred völkisch, anti-Semitic organizations emerged in various parts of Germany, all rejecting
the republic. The most influential and largest völkisch
group in Baden (and Germany) and one that had attracted Ruge
as early as 1919 was the German Racist League for Defense and

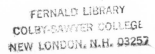

Attack (Schutz- und Trutzbund). In November 1922, the national commissioner for the supervision of public order concluded that the Schutz- und Trutzbund was the "largest, most active and influential anti-Semitic union in Germany." The roots of this league lay in the efforts of the Pan-German League to fight the liberalization of Germany during 1918/19 by using anti-Semitism as the mass force against the new parliamentary trend. The constitution of the Bund promised to fight "for the moral rebirth of the German Volk. It considers the pernicious and destructive influence of Jewry to be the main cause of the defeat and the removal of this influence to be necessary for the political and economic recovery of Germany, and for the salvation of German Kultur." The Bund's strength of 25,000 members in December 1919 expanded to around 160,000, organized in 600 locals, by July 1922 when the organization was disbanded by government decree. The nature of the Bund's activities can be seen by its distribution of over 70 million propaganda items in 1920 alone, many with swastika mastheads.[43]

In Baden, the Pan-German League tried to recoup its losses as early as May 1919 when it circulated leaflets to its members that denounced materialism and the revolution and lamented the loss of German values. Although the members of the league met twice a week, the revolution's momentum still intimidated the right in early 1919 since members were advised to disseminate propaganda by word of mouth. By November 1919 a local of the Schutz- und Trutzbund had been established in Karlsruhe which presented lectures on the "Jewish Problem" and distributed leaflets that identified Karlsruhe's Jewish shops.[44] In May 1920, the local of Karlsruhe published its program. The Bund demanded the reconstruction of the German fatherland and the resurgence of völkisch feeling. Most important, it proposed the destruction of everything that was not German. Of the seven demands of the platform, three were outright anti-Semitic, ranging from a demand for the expulsion of Eastern Jews to a plea to cleanse German culture of Jewish influence. Three other demands were more subtle in their anti-Semitism, focusing on banks, war profiteers, and usurers. Only one declaration, on securing the supply of food, was non-racial in intent. Anti-Semitism was the real imperative of the movement. In March 1920, Ruge gave a speech as a Schutz- und Trutzbund agitator in Karlsruhe in which he declared that Jews must disappear from the face of the earth. One month later the Karlsruhe local sent a letter to the government of Baden warning that the patience of the non-Jewish population of Baden was reaching its limit. These themes were also articulated by other Baden locals of the Bund in public rallies and in print.[45]

By 1920 the Schutz- und Trutzbund was the most important völkisch league in Baden. Gradually efforts were made to unite the various locals. In the spring of 1921, the first Gau Baden Day of the organization was held. It was attended by members, local leaders, and the national representatives, Landrat von Hertzberg and Alfred Roth. The Baden league also had a Gau leader, Karl Ernst, a druggist and native of Schwetzingen in northern Baden. Finally, by early 1922, the Baden Bund could rely on a state business manager to handle the voluminous paperwork. Unlike the Nazi party in Baden at this time, the Bund had a state organization and a relatively large member-ship for a völkisch organization before 1923. In September 1920, the local of Heidelberg had already 380 members which was much larger than the membership of the Nazi party in that town before 1928. The membership might have been even higher

had the entrance fee of 3 RM and the monthly fee of 1 RM not
been such a barrier to potential members. In 1921, the Baden
Gau even proposed to set membership fees at 5 RM per month
despite the fact that the movement attempted to bring the
workers back to the bosom of the nation. The local of
Karlsruhe, for example, called a membership meeting on 16
May 1920, to discuss the theme, "What Is Communism?" The answer given, as reported by the Völkischer Beobachter, was that
Jews had destroyed a basically sound idea.[46] But membership
fees and fees for meetings were much too high to attract a
mass labor following even if labor had been susceptible to
this violent völkisch anti-Semitism.

Despite the Baden Bund's initial strength, it declined
after 1921 because of internal divisions and a government
crackdown which banned the Schutz- und Trutzbund's public
activities. Such notorious Bund members of Baden as Philipp
Lenard, a Nobel Prize winner in physics, and the professional
anti-Semite Ruge rejected the centralism of the Bund's national
leadership. They lashed out at the national leader Alfred
Roth, and accused him of incompetence and of furthering dangerous centralism.[47] This was followed after the murder of
Walther Rathenau in the summer of 1922 by the Baden government's attack on the Bund. Adam Remmele defended the dissolution of the Schutz- und Trutzbund in Baden in a letter to the
German supreme court on 26 August 1922, arguing that the Bund
had engaged in a systematic hate campaign against the "Jewish
part of the German population." When subsequent völkisch
groups appeared in Baden in late 1922 and early 1923, Remmele
again banned them by accusing them of being continuations of
the outlawed anti-Semitic Bund.[48]

The importance of the Bund to the subsequent growth of

the Nazi party was crucial. First, unlike many paramilitary
leagues in Germany after the war, the Bund attempted to organize
a national völkisch organization. In addition, the most active members of the Bund joined the NSDAP and became Nazi
activists. Most important, the majority of the early Nazi
locals grew out of local Schutz- und Trutzbund organizations
or were sponsored initially by Bund locals. After the Bund
was outlawed in the summer of 1922, its national leadership
directed the members to join the Nazi party. In Baden, for
example, many urban and even rural Nazi locals grew out of
Schutz- und Trutzbund locals. In Mannheim the first organized
presentation of Nazi ideas occurred in a Bund meeting. Ernst
Ulshöfer, a Nazi activist from Stuttgart, was invited on 28
January 1920 to present the program of the NSDAP to the members of the Mannheim Schutz- und Trutzbund. According to the
Bund's leadership, the invitation was extended to allow the
membership to hear all available German völkisch ideas. In
other instances, whole locals of the Bund in Baden were converted to National Socialism. This was the case in Liedolsheim,
a small rural community outside of Karlsruhe. A local of the
Bund had emerged in this community in 1920; by the summer of
1923 most of these members had joined the Nazi party.[49]

The Schutz- und Trutzbund also produced a significant
number of leading Nazis in Baden. Gau Baden's Schutz- und
Trutzbund business leader, Walter Buch, joined the Nazi party
in 1922 and actively campaigned for Hitler's party in Baden
in 1923. Buch eventually became chairman of the Nazi party's
national court (Uschla). Another important future Nazi leader
in Baden who had been active in both the DNVP and the Schutz-
und Trutzbund before 1923 was Walter Köhler. This future
deputy Gau leader of the Nazi party, who was born on 30

September 1894, in Weinheim, was the son of a small businessman. After Köhler served an apprenticeship in a bank, he
joined the army and participated in the First World War until
he was captured in 1916 by the English. After 1918, he returned to his father's trade and colonial wares business and
became active in right-wing political activities. In 1924,
after becoming impatient with the lack of activism of the DNVP,
he turned to the Nazi party and founded a local in his native
community. A final example was Albert Roth, the future Nazi
party's rural expert in Baden, who was born in 1893 in rural
Liedolsheim. After the war, he returned to his native community as a farmer and became active in most of the right-wing
activities ranging from the Landbund to the Schutz- und
Trutzbund. In July 1923 he traveled to Munich with some
of his völkisch friends and joined the Nazi party. All of
these former Bund members who became Nazi activists remained
in the NSDAP until 1945.[50]

In addition to important future Nazi activists like
Köhler and Roth, many other Bund members made the transition
from the Schutz- und Trutzbund to the Nazi party even if they
did not remain with the Hitler movement until 1945. Hermann
Kettner, the leader of the Mannheim Schutz- und Trutzbund who
arranged the first organized Nazi propaganda meeting in that
city, joined the NSDAP by May 1922. Even after the Nazi party
was banned by Remmele in the summer of 1922, former Bund members in Baden continued to flock to the Hitler movement. Most
of these converts came from the lower middle class, although
a few like the engineers Hermann Kettner and Hermann Krumm
were representatives of the professional middle class. The
Bund brought few industrial workers to the Nazi party despite
its publicized desire to win the worker back to völkisch
German nationalism.[51]

PARAMILITARY ORGANIZATIONS

In addition to the Schutz- und Trutzbund and the various other
racist bands active in Baden after 1918, one of the most important incubators of future Nazi activists was the Free Corps
or paramilitary organization. This was generally true for all
parts of Germany where the various paramilitary organizations
played an active part in attempting to undermine the republic.
Although the paramilitary organizations in Baden could not
openly defy the democratic order, since the Socialist minister
of interior kept a watchful eye on them, many future Nazi
activists experienced organized völkisch activism first in a
paramilitary unit. Indeed, many of the concepts or programs
articulated by these paramilitary groups, with the sole exception of monarchism, could have passed as National Socialism's
standard themes.[52]

The government of Baden had no sympathies or tolerance
for paramilitary organizations even during the peak of the
leftist disturbances. For example, in March 1919, the government rejected an offer of help from the Freiburg Academic
Deutschbund to fight the Spartacists. One year later, again
during leftist disturbances, the democratic government of
Baden rejected the army's pleas to sign up more short-term
volunteers because the Baden ministers considered such a move
politically unwise.[53]

Despite the government's attitude, several covert paramilitary organizations appeared in Baden after 1918. Many of
these organizations, and especially their leaders and activists,
were intertwined. One important example of the role and program of a military adventurer in democratic Baden after 1918,
and one who played a major role in the Nazi party between 1929
and 1933, is provided by Otto Wagener, who directed the German

Legion in Karlsruhe. Born in 1888 in Durlach, Baden, Wagener
grew up in a solid middle-class home. His father was the director of a sewing-machine factory in Karlsruhe. After high
school, Otto Wagener selected a military career. During the
war, he became a general staff officer. This promising military career was destroyed by the defeat of 1918. As chief of
staff of the German Legion in the Baltic area, Wagener became
involved in a series of postwar military adventures in the
Baltic region, in Silesia, and in the Ruhr. After his return
to Baden, Wagener was imprisoned briefly in Karlsruhe in early
1920 to prevent him from supporting the Kapp Putsch. After
his release, he became the factory director of his father's
firm (Heid und Neu). He also assumed the leadership of the
German Legion in Karlsruhe with the expressed purpose of continuing the work of the Kurland legion in Baden.[54]

The aim of this organization, according to a bulletin
issued in August 1920, was to fight Bolshevism and the Entente.
For this purpose Baden (like Bavaria and Württemberg) needed
a strong volunteer force. The Legion, according to the official bulletin, rejected all class and confessional divisions,
but it also denied emphatically that it represented National
Bolshevism. One month later the Legion of Karlsruhe published
a clear view of its reactionary platform, a platform that
could have been issued by the Nazis with the sole exception
of the monarchical political solution. The program of the
Legion pointed out that traditionally the problem of overpopulation had been solved by emigration. Since the nineteenth
and early twentieth centuries, however, industrialization had
provided a false solution to overpopulation because the cities
only produced the "Fourth Estate," which was the feeding ground
for Marxism. The solution was simple to the Legion. Since

the German state by nature had a social conscience (and only
the Jew was liberal), the Legion planned to limit the concentration of people in urban centers, control the growth of
unbound fortunes, help workers, and provide education for all
economic levels by establishing corporate chambers to handle
diverse economic groups. For cultural and moral issues, a
Reich bishop would be selected. The corporate chamber and
the bishop were assigned the task of electing an upper house,
which would be in charge of finances, the army, and laws.
Finally, a Reich regent would be selected for life to handle
foreign affairs. Clearly the program of the German Legion in
Baden was a nostalgic attempt to turn the clock back to a
preindustrial world of alleged harmony, directed by a substitute monarch.[55]

Wagener was also tied to another paramilitary group, the
Baden Orgesch, which the Baden minister of interior, Remmele,
considered the most dangerous of all of the völkisch and right-
wing bands in Baden before 1923. In fact, Wagener was its
deputy state leader (the Baden government called it Organization
Damm) until February or March 1921. He invited national leaders of the Orgesch like General Oskar von Watter, its treasurer,
to address the German Legion in Baden.[56] This again reveals
the close inter-relationship between the various völkisch and
para-military groups in Baden after the war.

The organization Escherich or Orgesch appeared first in
Bavaria in 1919 in an effort of the urban and rural Bavarian
middle classes to combat the left. After the Munich Soviets,
the specter of Bolshevism was a living nightmare for many
Bavarians. The Bavarian Christian Farmers' League actively
promoted the organization, which was under the guidance of
the Bavarian Forstrat Escherich. On a larger scale the

Escherich organization, as it expanded beyond Bavaria, was part of Germany's "home guard" system. Escherich was also able to establish a cooperative system with North German groups and even obtain Reichswehr training and weapons. After protests from the Inter-Allied Military Commission in late 1920, the national Orgesch organization finally disbanded in May 1921. Beneath the surface, however, Orgesch activities continued, and many of the weapons obtained from the Reichswehr were simply hidden.[57]

In Baden's rural areas leftist leaflets had appeared in 1919 that threatened farmers with fire if they continued to charge high prices for their products. In response to the potential danger from the extreme left, two developments occurred in Baden. First, the Baden minister of interior established an organization called the Technische Nothilfe for both urban and rural areas. In case of a Communist uprising, these units would help to continue the basic operations of the utilities and government until order could be reestablished.[58] Second, was the secret appearance of the Orgesch or Organization Damm mentioned above. Although the Baden government had outlawed the Orgesch in the fall of 1920, it functioned covertly until the summer of 1921 when the government finally discovered its existence.[59] Already by the summer of 1920, the Baden Orgesch had an elaborate organization that included district leaders. By early 1921, the organization grew and even included a youth section, which developed the shooting skills of the young members.[60]

Despite Wagener's position of deputy leadership, apparently the Orgesch never had a state leader. When the police discovered the organization in the summer of 1921, there was only a committee of three retired military officers: a major

Alfred Krause, a captain Otto Hauck, and a lieutenant Hans
Thummel. There were also leaders for the three major subdivisions of Baden (north, center, and south), all again former
military officers who had been active in paramilitary activities after 1918. For example, the leader of the center, Captain
Friedrich Wilhelm von Wins of Ettlingen, had been active in
the militia of Silesia and in various other paramilitary organizations. Later he found his way to the Nazi party (with
a low membership number of 3,169) and became a German Labor
Front leader.[61]

It was certainly significant that so many of the more
active Baden Orgesch leaders came from peripheral areas of
Germany or from abroad. Damm had military service in Latin
America. One of his assistants was born in Rosario, Argentina,
and others were natives of Metz. Several important Baden
leaders came from the eastern borderlands, and particularly
from such "German" outposts as Dorpat and Riga. Many of these
men had experienced the postwar upheavals in the East and had
belonged to a variety of anti-Bolshevik Free Corps like the
Estonian Baltic battalion. One Baden activist even wrote
articles reflecting news about the Baltic circle.[62]

Most of the Baden Orgesch members who later made the
transition to the Nazi party referred to their Orgesch membership as Damm membership. Although Damm was never the head of
the Baden Orgesch but only a regional leader, he was one of
the most important Orgesch activists in Baden, both in terms
of recruiting members and in continuing activities even after
the government crackdown in 1921. Damm was born on 25 February
1886 in Koburg to the wife of a medical doctor. He served in
the German army between 1906 and 1913 and then marketed his
military skills in Paraguay until the outbreak of the Great

War. Damm rose to the position of captain during the war and
then remained active in the Free Corps movement in the Baltic
until March 1920. In the summer of 1920 he returned to Baden
and joined the Orgesch to protect the Reich and private property
and to prevent a Communist Putsch. In his private letters
to his relatives in Argentina, Damm revealed that his aim was
to prepare for a future war of revenge. And even during police interrogations in 1921, he admitted that Germany must
hide as many weapons as possible to prepare for at least a
small-scale war should the enemies attempt to occupy Germany.[63]

Damm's feelings of revenge were shared by many of the
more active Orgesch members of Baden. But even more important in winning converts, particularly in Baden's rural areas,
was the organization's antileftist agitation. This appeal
helped to convince "respectable" people to support the movement, people who had no intentions of supporting right-wing
Putsches. In rural areas in northeastern Baden, converts to
the Organization Damm in September 1920 claimed to have experienced the activities of the "reds" in the urban center after
the war. They demanded now that the Bürgertum protect itself.
Martin Forster, a member of Damm and the local Landbund leader of Rohrbach in the district of Heidelberg, made it clear
that the purpose of the Orgesch was to fight Communists and
to protect the rural communities. Many converts were established members of society who really feared social upheavals.[64]

Damm appealed to their fears in all of his recruiting
drives. For example, in late 1920 he went to Schefflenz,
Schopfheim, to address community leaders and specifically
promised protection against Communist plunder in the countryside. In the Wiesental area in southern Baden, near industrial strongholds, farmers came at night to Hermann Neiking,

the local Orgesch leader, to plan "protection" schemes from leftist dangers. Neiking was a medical student who had been a member of a Catholic student fraternity. After serving in the war, he belonged to an academic defense organization in Münster, which helped quell unrest in the industrial areas of Westphalia. Neiking, in fact, admitted his strong dislike of industrial workers, although he claimed to admire the miners.[65] Given these fears of the left in Baden, it was little wonder that the government in 1921 found that "respectable" members of society from civil servants and teachers to farmers and estate owners belonged to the organization. One court official (Landgerichtsrat Frommherz) even published articles for the organization in various newspapers.[66]

These fears were exploited by the Orgesch leadership for financial gains and funds. In January 1921, the national treasurer of the Orgesch, retired general von Watter, addressed a meeting in Heidelberg. He agreed to advance the Baden organization funds for administrative tasks, but in return the Baden Orgesch had to raise 5 million RM. The Baden leaders were told to appeal to industry, banks, agriculture, and commerce by telling them that their contributions amounted to an insurance against theft and plunder by the reds. The Orgesch would protect private property.[67]

The Baden Orgesch created a committee of fifteen men to attract money from industry and commerce. In northern Baden, the businessman (Fabrikant) Hermann Stachelhaus of Mannheim was in charge of the collection drive. In central Baden, the bank director Nikolai of Karlsruhe handled the fund drive, while in southern Baden the Kaufmann Viktor Himmelsbach of Freiburg approached industry for help. Stachelhaus, a retired officer, was born on 19 December 1869, in Mühlheim. He was

also the co-owner of shipyard (<u>Reederei</u>) Stachelhaus and
Buchloh of Mannheim. After the war, he had been a leader of
the militia of Mannheim and even financed volunteers for the
struggle in Upper Silesia in 1921. Viktor Himmelsbach was
only a Kaufmann employed by the firm Himmelsbach in which his
father was a partner. This Freiburg firm was a major lumber
company, which had been founded in 1846 in Oberweier and then
established itself in Freiburg by 1900. After 1914, the three
directors of the firm were Josef and Oskar Himmelsbach and
Friedrich Jäckle. Despite police reports that the Orgesch obtained money from "high finance" and industry, there is no
evidence that the largest Baden firms were actively involved
in the collection drives. The name of Daimler Benz, for example, never appeared even in the police reports. Instead,
small and medium-size businesses like the Stachelhaus shipyard and the lumber firm in Freiburg were in the forefront
of the Orgesch movement in Baden.[68]

The Baden Orgesch, however, obtained and spent much more
money than the Nazi party could before and for a long time
after 1923. Robert Kessler, one of Damm's associates, testified that the Orgesch leaders of Baden each received as much
as 1,500 RM a month for expenses. As late as 1928, the Nazi
party of Baden only had a monthly salary obligation of around
1,000 RM. Also between April and May 1921, the Orgesch leader of northern Baden, von Wins, received 18,000 RM from
Stachelhaus and another 1,000 RM from a Rastatt bank. During
the same period, Wins spent about 18,500 RM. And Freiburg
Orgesch leader Hermann Neiking did not hesitate to request
24,000 RM in order to recruit students for Upper Silesia.[69]
These figures do not reveal massive contributions from the
great industrialists of Baden, but they do testify to the

substantial support the Orgesch received in Baden from people
who were afraid of the leftist dangers to private property.

The Baden government's attack on the Orgesch was successful in destroying the effectiveness of the organization even
if court cases had to be dropped in December 1921 because the
members of the Baden Orgesch had joined before membership
in this organization was officially banned.[70] Damm attempted
to continue his work by organizing a substitute organization
called Südwestdeutscher Zeitungsdienst. According to Damm,
this would be a correspondence bureau which would "feed" national propaganda to the press. Although the Zeitungsdienst's
headquarters were in Württemberg, the organization was intended
to serve Baden, Württemberg, and Hesse. Damm wanted his delegates to use the bourgeois papers to fight the alleged threat
of Bolshevism. He recruited collaborators in the countryside
who were charged with the dual tasks of gathering information and obtaining the cooperation of the local press. The
strength of the Südwestdeutscher Zeitungsdienst in Baden was
clearly in northern and northeastern rural districts. A list
of October 1921 reveals that farmers, clerks, lawyers, and
professionals dominated the membership in the districts of
Mosbach, Eberbach, Sinsheim, and Adelsheim. Even in southern
Baden, Damm in late 1922 appealed to farmers and the Mittelstand of the small communities. This emphasis on the rural
population was not surprising, since Damm's collaborator in
Württemberg was Wilhelm Mayer, an active Landbund leader. The
rural population would provide, so at least Damm argued, the
force to resist the Marxists at home and the French across the
Rhine.[71]

Damm was reactionary in politics and economics. The
Baden police in late 1922 discovered a secret Denkschrift

(position paper) that Damm had prepared in May 1922. His plan called for the persistent expansion of the organization in the countryside until 1928, when the French would dare to stay only in German cities. According to the plan, in June 1930 the government in Berlin would be overthrown and an all-out attack would be launched against the French. Finally, by the end of 1931 a plebiscite would vote overwhelmingly (95 percent) for a new monarchy, and an emperor would be selected on 5 January 1932.[72] Damm was really a monarchist who could not accept the defeat of Germany or the revolution in politics in 1918. But the Baden government never gave him the chance to develop his new organization. The Zeitungsdienst was outlawed in January 1923, and Damm left Baden for Württemberg to establish still another right-wing organization. Remmele continued his vigilance, and after 1923 Damm was never again able to play a significant public role in Baden.[73]

One reason Remmele considered the Damm organization so dangerous was the fact that Damm was connected with the stashing of illegal weapons in Baden. In fact, the Orgesch was discovered in Baden in the summer of 1921 after the police had unearthed weapons first in February/March and then in May/June 1921 in northern and southern Baden. These illegal weapons also illustrated the close connection between the army and the paramilitary units in southern Germany, and particularly in Württemberg. This neighboring state protected the paramilitary activists who committed illegal acts in Baden and then returned to Württemberg. For example on 25 February 1921, the Baden police discovered weapons on the estate of von Bodman, a DNVP activist in the district of Stockach. The political left in Baden immediately took the government to task and warned that the Orgesch was much more dangerous than most

people imagined. The government, however, pointed out that
the culprit responsible for the weapons, officer Fritz Keller,
had returned to Stuttgart on 26 February. The government of
Württemberg refused to cooperate with Baden since it wanted
to protect the information that the former Württemberg militia
had stashed many of its weapons to keep them out of the hands
of the Entente.[74]

More important in terms of stirring the emotions of the
left and republican forces in Baden was the discovery of
weapons in Osterburken in the district of Adelsheim after an
anonymous informant provided the police with the necessary
information. Apparently in early April 1921, Württemberg
had sent troops on their way to put down Communist disturbances in Sängerhausen through Osterburken. On their return
to Württemberg, Oskar Dirlewanger, a student in Mannheim but
a resident of Stuttgart, convinced the train station clerk in
Osterburken to store some weapons to keep them from the French.
This was supported not only by the station clerk, who was a
member of a Catholic club, but also by the mayor and a Democratic city council member. The patriotic atmosphere made
it possible during the postwar era to obtain the support of
moderate "respectable" members of society for such illegal
activities. And the more extreme right in Baden (and in other
German states) took advantage of this atmosphere. The aim
of people like Dirlewanger (who joined the Nazi party in 1923)
was not only to resist the French but also to destroy the
republic.[75]

The Osterburken affair produced vociferous political com-
mentaries. The Communists attacked the "Socialist Pigs" who
allegedly were now afraid of the Orgesch, while the Socialist
paper Volksfreund denounced the reactionaries and the Orgesch.

Even the Karlsruher Zeitung, which was used by the government
for official announcements, ran a copy of the Volksfreund
article, which had severely admonished the government for the
Osterburken affair. When the Baden Statepresident reprimanded
the Karlsruher Zeitung, its editor replied that criticism was
needed since too many prosecutors and judges were still reactionaries.[76] On the other hand, the Baden Nationalists in
the Landtag pointed to alleged Communist threats and made it
clear that they had more respect for those who hid the weapons
than for the informants who revealed them. Similarly, the
Badische Post, the organ of the DVP, ran an article on "poor
Germany," which was castrating itself. The paper also claimed
that Damm had sent it a letter in which he maintained that
the weapons were not intended to be used against the republic
but only against the enemies across the Rhine. Even some
Center party supporters who opposed right-wing rhetoric were
sympathetic toward the principle of hiding weapons from the
former enemies.[77]

The Baden government's response to the Osterburken affair
was swift. It arrested the station clerk and issued warrants
for the arrest of Damm, Dirlewanger, and others involved in
the weapon stashing. Individual complicity was not difficult
to establish after Damm's collaborator, Robert Kessler, admitted to the police that Damm had arranged the affair with the
intent of eventually distributing the weapons in Baden.[78] On
the other hand, it was much more difficult to prosecute the
offenders since Württemberg did not cooperate and the army
made it an issue of national security. For example, the German army's Peace Commission in Stuttgart wrote its Karlsruhe
branch to advise the press to be cautious when reporting the
discovery of weapons because to do so might endanger national

interests. Remmele completely rejected this and pointed out
that the press in Baden could not be influenced. Instead, he
suggested that the Peace Commission put an end to the free
flow of weapons in Württemberg.[79]

The Baden government knew that the security police chief
of Württemberg, Paul Hahn, was involved in the weapons affair.
Hahn, a member of the Social Democratic party and a veteran
officer of the First World War, had organized antirevolutionary
combat forces in Württemberg as early as 1918/19. To prevent
further friction between Baden and Württemberg, the Baden
Statepresident urged Reichs Chancellor Joseph Wirth, a fellow
Badenese and dedicated republican, to set up a conference
between the two states. Württemberg informed Wirth and Baden
that its militia had in fact disbursed its weapons along rail
lines in 1920 to keep them out of the hands of the Entente.
To pursue the matter, according to Stuttgart, would only aid
the enemy.[80] In the end, the Reich commissar for disarmament,
State Secretary Peters, came to southern Germany in September
1921 to give the Baden government a more detailed summary of
the problem. Peters pointed out that such cases as Osterburken
occurred frequently in Germany. When he took office, no one
could tell him how much the troops had left behind or sold
after 1918. In response to the French demand for one and one-
half million guns, the Germans planned to give the Entente only
old, worn-out field guns and hide the new weapons for the
German police and army. As a result of this policy, admitted
Peters, overzealous people hid weapons in various places, including Osterburken and Stockach, Baden. These weapons belonged
to the German army units stationed in Stuttgart. Peters made
it clear that to preserve the Reich's interests, any trial of
the Baden culprits should not reveal this practice by the German

military. The Baden cabinet in October 1921 decided to allow
the state prosecutor to determine whether charges would be
filed against the people involved in the Osterburken affair.
Although the cases were dropped, Remmele had succeeded in
eliminating the Orgesch from Baden.[81]

The impact of the Orgesch on the political constellation
of Baden was minimal. It never attempted a Putsch or a public move against the government. But the Baden Orgesch illustrates the prevailing fear of social revolution and the accompanying frustration over the military defeat even in democratic
Baden. During this period many supporters of Damm and many
who hid weapons from the French were respectable members of
society, not völkisch activists. But many of the future Nazi
activists in Baden obtained their political baptism in the
Damm organization. One of the strongest supporters of Damm
in Baden, who found his way to the Nazi party, was the former
Gau leader of the Schutz- und Trutzbund.[82] To name only two
more examples of Damm members who became Nazi activists, Hans
Knab of Eberbach became Kreisleiter of Pforzheim, and Bruno
Wiesener became the founder of the Hitler Youth in Pforzheim.
Both had belonged to the Damm organization and to the Nazi
party before November 1923.[83]

Although many Baden Nazis in 1923 were still members of
the Damm organization, Munich warned Baden party members in
early 1923 to separate themselves from the monarchist Damm.
Walter Buch, for example, a party member and friend of Damm,
disassociated himself from the Damm organization since Damm
was only a soldier and "nothing more."[84] Despite this break
between the Nazi party and the Damm organization, many Badenese who joined the NSDAP after 1925 had belonged to Damm's
movement. In some rural districts of northeastern Baden, the

Damm organization continued in one form or another and future
Nazis like the Kreisleiter of Überlingen, Gustav Robert Oexle,
or the local leader of Tiefenbach, Sinsheim, were members of
one of these "Damm" subterfuges in the 1920s. Only at the end
of the 1920s did they join the Nazi party.[85]

   In addition to Damm and the Schutz- und Trutzbund, the
other important paramilitary organization in Baden that prepared future Nazi activists was the Bund Oberland. This organization had evolved from the Free Corps Oberland, and it
collaborated with Hitler in the Kampfbund in 1923. Its strength
was concentrated in Bavaria and Upper Silesia, but the Bund
also had members and locals in Baden. In Baden, the Bund was
organized well enough in 1923 to have regional representatives.
One of these regional Bund leaders, Karl Gropp of Mannheim,
led the preparations in Mannheim for the anticipated Putsch of
November 1923.[86] Even more important was the fact that the
Bund in Baden prepared several future Nazi Kreisleiters like
Konrad Glas of Emmendingen and Franz Kerber of Freiburg.
Although Glas did not join the Nazi party until 1928 and
Kerber did not become a member until 1929, both had been ac-
tive members of the Bund Oberland. Both had been völkisch
activists before they joined the Hitler movement.[87]

   The importance of the various paramilitary and völkisch
organizations in Baden for the development of future Nazi
activists was vital. In many ways, the Damm organization
and the Schutz- und Trutzbund allowed frustrated Badenese
to escape the political socialization process after 1918 which
eventually might have caused them to accept the republic.
These organizations also helped to perpetuate the fears of
social revolution and the frustrations produced by military
defeat. This occurred despite the fact that the state of Baden

was ruled by a government coalition which supported the republic. And even Remmele's persistent surveillance of right-wing
activism could not destroy the hard core of völkisch true
believers. The paramilitary and völkisch groups in Baden
never threatened the security of the state before 1925. They
did, however, represent a tumor that became malignant under
the impact of deteriorating economic conditions.

2 The Nazi Party in Baden, 1920-1923

Before November 1923, the Nazi party in Baden represented
only a small minority within the right-wing camp. Overshadowed by the Nationalists and the Landbund, and until 1922 by
the Schutz- und Trutzbund, the early Nazi party was important,
however, for two reasons. First, it clearly demonstrated
that National Socialism was not merely a Bavarian episode
but rather a German phenomenon. Even in this democratic state,
underlying socioeconomic and political tensions combined with
the frustrations produced by the revolution and the military
defeat to create a völkisch movement as early as 1919. Second,
the Nazi party members of Baden who joined before November
1923 staffed many of the more important state and party posts
there after 1933.

It was not surprising that right-wing radicals in Baden
and other parts of Germany looked to Munich and Hitler after
1919. The German Workers' party established in Munich in the
beginning of 1919 gradually gained recognition among rightist
circles in Munich after Hitler began to appeal to a broader
audience by holding major public rallies in 1920. The party's
new activism, Hitler's dynamic personality, and the party's
appeal to win workers back to völkisch nationalism spread the
fame of the NSDAP across the borders of Bavaria. Important,

too, was the fact that Munich after 1920 became a haven for right-wing groups and activists. A coup in March 1920 overthrew the Social Democratic government and initiated a right-wing administration under Gustav Kahr. It was only natural for Baden's völkisch activists to look to Munich for inspiration and adulation, particularly in communities where Munich natives were working or visiting.[1]

Beginning in 1920, individuals in Baden, especially in such large urban centers as Pforzheim and Mannheim, established contacts with Munich and the Nazi party. Then near the end of 1921 Schutz- und Trutzbund locals in small rural towns like Liedolsheim began to correspond with the Nazi leadership in Munich.[2] At the same time, Munich and particularly the Völkischer Beobachter, even before it came under the control of the NSDAP, took notice of völkisch events in the democratic stronghold of southern Germany. In early 1920, the paper urged Munich students to emulate the anti-Semitic campaigns of those students who had opposed the nomination of a Jewish professor to a position with the Technical University of Karlsruhe. After the Nazis gained control of the Völkischer Beobachter, the paper naturally continued to show interest in the right-wing activities of democratic Baden. Commenting on a major Schutz- und Trutzbund activity in Baden in early 1921, the Völkischer Beobachter noted the Bund meeting "again reveals the fast and evergrowing development of the völkisch movement in Baden."[3]

The Nazi party expanded outside Munich on 18 April 1920 by creating a local in Rosenheim, Bavaria. By 8 May, another Nazi local had been established in Stuttgart by members of the local Schutz- und Trutzbund. This local, which received official recognition on 4 June, played an active and crucial part in disseminating National Socialism in southwestern Germany between 1920 and 1923. Indeed, several Baden Nazis joined the party first in Stuttgart. For example, as an eighteen-year-old, Walter Jourdan traveled to Stuttgart in the summer of 1921 and came into contact with the Nazi party, which he promptly joined.[4] In addition, the Stuttgart Nazis assisted in founding the first two Baden locals in Pforzheim and Mannheim, major industrial centers with half of the population dependent on industry. The common theme articulated by the early Baden and Stuttgart Nazis in both cities was the need to win the workers back to the national cause. In both cities, former Socialists and Communists who became Nazi activists in 1920/21 played an important part in the party's leadership before 1923, despite the fact that the bulk of the Nazi converts came from the lower middle class.[5]

The first Baden local of the Nazi party was established in Pforzheim on 28 October 1920. The Stuttgart local, no doubt, played an important part in spreading National Socialism to Pforzheim. Some documents list Ernst Ulshöfer, one of the founders of the Stuttgart local, as the leader of Pforzheim's Nazi party in 1921 and show Pforzheim as part of the Landesverband Württemberg. However, Pforzheim, like most communities where National Socialism took root before 1925, had a strong, native grassroots völkisch movement.[6] Without discounting the agitation of Ulshöfer in Baden, the initiative in the formation of the Nazi party in Pforzheim was taken by the sixty-year-old mechanic Heinrich Wittmann, who had been an active member of the Socialist party before the war. Wittmann gathered about seventy anti-Semitic and völkisch activists, ranging from the university-educated Gymnasium teacher Herbert Kraft to the rootless young drifter Bruno

Wiesener. In his introductory address, which was reported
by the Völkischer Beobachter on 21 November 1920, Wittmann
justified the formation of a new party on the grounds that
the German worker had never had a real workers' party. The
workers had been unorganized and dispersed. The aim of the
new party in Pforzheim, according to Wittmann, was to resur-
rect German völkisch thought, particularly among the workers,
and to remove the influence of the Jews.[7] Unlike Damm, the
new Baden Nazi party did not promise protection from the "reds"
but instead pledged to work for the conversion of the workers
to a völkisch socialism.

The first public meeting of the Pforzheim local, on 1
January 1921, was directed by Wittmann. The guest speaker
was Ernst Ulshöfer, a mechanic who was born in Heidelberg on
21 April 1884, and who became an itinerant agitator, first for
the Syndicalists and then for the Communists. After being
converted to National Socialism in 1920, he became an active
Nazi speaker in southwestern Germany and even in Munich.
Ulshöfer's speech to the Pforzheim local was entitled "National
or International Socialism" and focused on the alleged harm
that internationalism had done to the workers. When Ulshöfer
turned to the Jewish issue and then tied it to all of Germany's
ills, he received enthusiastic applause.[8]

This appeal to the national, völkisch feelings of the
worker, combined with vehement attacks on Jews, was the most
persistent theme presented at successive meetings of the
Pforzheim local (and for that matter of most urban locals of
Baden before 1923). Unlike the more traditional right-wing
groups such as the Orgesch and the Landbund, these early urban
Nazis believed that Germany's revival could be achieved through
the conversion of the workers to völkisch nationalism. For

example, Fritz Todt, the future minister of armaments and
munitions, was one of the early Pforzheim converts to National
Socialism. He was born in 1891 in Pforzheim and studied engineering at the Technical University of Karlsruhe. Todt
first heard of Hitler in the fall of 1921. By January 1923,
he was a party member and actively engaged in the support of
the Nazi movement. According to his testimony in March 1924,
he was most impressed by the National Socialist workers who
respected their engineer superiors and were always willing
to work ten or twelve hours a day.[9] No doubt, like many early
Nazi converts Todt was attracted by the concept of reviving
Germany's strength through the energies of the workers, and
all of this without the cost of a real socioeconomic revolution.

The second Baden local originated in Mannheim, a city
plagued by disturbances after November 1918. The Mannheim
Soviets had forced the moderate Socialist party leaders to
assume the responsibilities of power in November 1918 and
then demanded the resignation of the grand duke. Unemployment councils had also pressured large retail stores to contribute goods to the unemployed and needy. In early 1919,
the brother of Adam Remmele proclaimed a soviet republic in
Baden and initiated a regime that lasted only from a Saturday
to the following Monday. Further difficulties occurred in
June 1919 because of high food prices, compounded by fears of
an impending French invasion. Little wonder that the Schutz-
und Trutzbund was so active in Mannheim in its attempts to
convert workers to a völkisch nationalism, which promised
to bring social peace without changing the basic social patterns.[10]

The first Nazi address in Mannheim delivered to an

organized völkisch group was presented by Ernst Ulshöfer,
the Stuttgart Nazi leader, on 28 January 1921. According to
an account published in the Völkischer Beobachter, the leader
of the Mannheim Schutz- und Trutzbund, the engineer Hermann
Kettner, invited Ulshöfer to Mannheim because the membership
of the Bund wanted to hear all German völkisch views. Ulshöfer
presented the same theme in Mannheim that he had articulated
in Pforzheim. He pointed out that nationalistic and socialistic sentiments represented a natural union; völkisch concepts provided the cement. Ulshöfer and the sponsors of the
meeting wanted to convince the worker to renounce the internationalism of Marxism by offering him a right-wing movement
with a "social conscience." This message was really no different from what the Schutz- und Trutzbund had argued as
early as 1919/20. While Ulshöfer was a worker, most of the
other participants in the meeting listed in the Völkischer
Beobachter were members of the professional middle class.
The participation of an engineer, a chemist, and an actor
simply reflected the general social profile of the Schutz-
und Trutzbund in Mannheim. At the conclusion of the meeting,
these Bund leaders urged other Schutz- und Trutzbund members
to adopt the program of the NSDAP and to send their inquiries
to Ulshöfer in Stuttgart.[11]

Ulshöfer played a much more active role in Mannheim
than in Pforzheim. By 4 February 1921, a local of the Nazi
party had been established in Mannheim under the provisional
leadership of a local Bund activist, an engineer. Although
Ulshöfer was active in Mannheim's party affairs, he did not
become local leader officially until May 1922. Mannheim
became a key local for Munich, and Anton Drexler, the founder
of the German Workers' party, even called it "Landesleitung

Mannheim." But the Nazi local made little progress at first
in the largest urban center of Baden, and as late as January
1922 the Völkischer Beobachter admitted that only a few party
members belonged to the Mannheim local. According to the
Völkischer Beobachter, only gradually in early 1922 was the
party able to establish itself in Mannheim, the "Jerusalem
on the Rhine." Every Monday evening, the party held a membership meeting in a local pub. By early 1922, the local also
established a special business section and it acquired Ernst
Ulshöfer as resident local leader. During the first half of
1922, important national party figures like Gottfried Feder,
Hermann Esser, Julius Streicher, Wilhelm Frick, and Arthur
Dinter visited the Mannheim local. Its major activities, as
reported in the Völkischer Beobachter, included the distribution of anti-Semitic literature, fighting battles with the
Communists, and the general attempt to spread the völkisch
message to the workers.[12]

The Mannheim party's activism was reflected in the conversion of new party members, although the size of the membership remained modest. The original membership roll of the
Mannheim local lists 178 members who joined between 13 April
and 28 August 1922. Most of these members lived in Mannheim,
Heidelberg, and Ludwigshafen. Only a few gave their home
addresses as Renchen, Tiengen, Bruchsal, Wilhelmshaven, and
even Lampertsheim, Hesse. The number of new members listed
for any given day ranged from three on 13 April to eight on
5 May. Although the document is not complete, it does at
least reveal a profile of the Mannheim converts before 1923.
The party in Baden's largest urban center included all social
groups but it was predominantly a male and lower-middle-class
organization. Only two women and five unskilled workers were

members of the Mannheim local in 1922. Perhaps no more than
20 percent of the local's membership came from the professional
middle class.[13]

The party made particularly little headway among the industrial workers of Mannheim, both in terms of membership and
propaganda drives. In one meeting on 6 April 1922, Ulshöfer
addressed a hall full of workers. Accusing France of desir-
ing hegemony in Europe, he urged Germany not to fulfill the
terms of the Versailles Treaty. After the speech, three
Communists spoke to the assembled workers and then led them
from the hall singing the "International." On another occasion, Hermann Esser came to Mannheim to lead a rally. When
he attempted to speak, the workers who had arrived early to
occupy the seats created so much noise that the gathering
had to be disbanded. Then the workers assaulted the leading
Nazis in the hall. This caused the Mannheim local to urge
its members to join the Storm Troopers since the party was
operating in a hostile environment.[14]

The fact that several party activists in Mannheim, and
throughout Baden, were former Communists or Socialists did
not help the party win significant labor support. Ulshöfer,
the local leader of Mannheim, was a mechanic and former Communist; so too was one of the Schutz- und Trutzbund members
who participated in the meeting that introduced National
Socialism to Mannheim. Richard Cordier, who was praised by
Munich in January 1922 as an excellent agitator, was a former
Marxist. A native of Saarbrücken, Cordier had belonged to
the Zentralverband der Angestellten, a white-collar employees'
organization, until he became implicated in a financial scan-
dal. Then he made his way to various other political movements, including the Independent Socialists. In Mannheim,

Cordier appeared first as a Communist agitator and only then was converted to National Socialism. "Communists" like Cordier, however, had little appeal for Baden's workers. In Baden, he was known as an opportunist and even called a scoundrel by the Socialist paper Volksstimme.[15]

Similar conversions of such "political drifters" occurred in other parts of Baden. In Weinheim, the young Walter Jourdan had belonged to a Marxist youth organization before joining the Nazi party in the summer of 1921 while visiting Stuttgart. In addition, one of the earliest members of the Nazi local of Freiburg, the master shoemaker Franz Tritschler, and one of the party's activists in northeastern Baden, Erwin Würth, had belonged to the Socialist party. Würth was a member of the SPD between 1919 and 1920, and Tritschler led a Socialist union in Freiburg until 1922.[16] These "leftist" Nazis, however, were the exception rather than the rule in terms of the total party membership in Baden both before and after 1923. They represented both young drifters like Cordier and more established members of the Socialist subculture like Wittmann who were converted to völkisch nationalism during the war. None of these early converts were industrial workers. The lack of appeal to labor was reflected in March 1922 when the Völkischer Beobachter expressed the hope that soon all members of society would be represented in the Baden party.[17]

The establishment of Nazi locals in Pforzheim and Mannheim in 1920/21 occurred through a combination of local initiative and stimuli emanating from both Stuttgart and Munich. Since organized National Socialism in Baden between 1920 and 1922 was very much an urban phenomenon, Munich promptly directed its attention to the urban centers of the state. In March

1922 the Völkischer Beobachter urged its readers in Karlsruhe
to send their addresses to Hugo Kromer, a party activist in
Karlsruhe, for the purpose of creating a local. By June
1922, the Nazis of Karlsruhe had done so and were holding
regular weekly meetings. The local leader was Hugo Kromer,
a sculptor and native of Strassburg. Kromer, who was born in
1896, left Alsace in 1918 and settled in Karlsruhe, where he
soon gravitated toward the völkisch movement, particularly
the Schutz- und Trutzbund.[18] In other large Baden towns where
no locals existed before 1923, converts joined the party organizations of neighboring towns. Or in the case of Freiburg
the Völkischer Beobachter urged its readers in that community
to send their addresses to Munich to allow for more coordination. During the first half of 1922 the Baden party expanded
to almost every major town even though in some cases no locals
were created. Groups in such towns were very small, often
numbering no more than five or ten followers. The largest
urban locals in Baden existed in the northern part of the
state in Mannheim, Karlsruhe, and Pforzheim, besides Freiburg,
also an important Nazi center. There was no central leadership or organization to coordinate these locals. After July
1922, it became even more difficult for Munich to provide
leadership and guidance since Baden banned the Nazi party.[19]

SMALL-TOWN AND RURAL LOCALS

In addition to these urban Nazi locals and activities that
attempted to convert the worker to völkisch nationalism, there
was another current of organized National Socialism in Baden
before November 1923. By that year the party had also estab-

lished itself in Baden's smaller towns and rural communities.
Right-wing, _völkisch_, and paramilitary activities were well
established in many small and rural communities of Baden after
1918. Damm had campaigned against the "red" terror, and
several DNVP meeting halls were decorated with swastikas long
before the Nazi locals were established in these small communities. Many rural and small communities articulated their
dissatisfaction with the new order, although they did not
create Nazi locals until 1926/27.[20] But already by 1922/23,
"rural" and small-town Nazis had organized several strongholds
in Baden.

Why should the rural and small-town resident of Baden
have been interested in a movement that called itself "National
Socialism" and appealed to workers? First, many small communities where Nazi locals emerged in 1922/23 had been introduced to the "outside world" by the war. After serving in the
war, young farmers and artisans were no longer satisfied that
traditional conservatism could solve Germany's problems.
Second, in many rural communities economic modernization had
broken down the homogeneity of rural conservatism and traditionalism. For example, in 1925 only 100,000 out of a total
of 255,000 factory workers in Baden resided in large urban
centers while the rest lived in rural communities (_Landgemein-
den_). Half of these workers were employed in small factories
in the "rural" communities, and the other half who lived in
the _Landgemeinden_ commuted to work in the large cities. In
such rural and small communities in Baden, the early Nazi
converts came from the radicalized "traditional right,"
which appealed not only to farmers but also to workers in
an attempt to revive the _völkisch_ strength of Germany.[21]

Two revealing examples of how National Socialism evolved

in a small town and a rural community of Baden before November
1923 are provided by the communities of Eberbach and
Liedolsheim, both located in northern Baden. These communities became strongholds of National Socialism after 1925.
Eberbach was in 1924 a small Protestant town of 6,299 people
near Heidelberg. Before the war, with the exception of 1909-
13 when a Socialist represented Eberbach and the rural district of Heidelberg, the area was dominated by the National
Liberals. Even during a period of Socialist representation,
the National Liberals were not impotent since this was the
period of the Great Coalition. After 1918 the largest industry
in Eberbach was the Odin firm, which employed fewer than 500
workers. In 1926, the town employed about 2,000 workers and
artisans of whom one-fourth lived outside of Eberbach. One
reflection of the political climate in the community is revealed by the election of May 1924 when the völkisch won almost 12 percent of the vote and the Marxists gathered 30.5
percent. The rest of the votes went to the middle-class parties and the Catholic Center party.[22]

National Socialism in Eberbach, unlike the large urban
centers, emerged from the traditional right and was supported
by small businessmen, artisans, and even civil servants. For
the most part participants were solid, if not leading, members
of society; many even belonged to a respectable Stammtisch.
National Socialism was first introduced to the youth group
of the DNVP, which, like the adult DNVP, met regularly once
a week for discussion sessions. In one of these meetings,
a Kaufmann from Munich, Christian Spindler, reported on Hitler
and his movement in Munich. The report came to the attention
of the regular DNVP membership, and shortly converts were
won for Hitler from both the young and the older Nationalists

of Eberbach. The early members who joined the Munich local
by 1923 ranged from a former "Black Reichswehr" member to a
respectable high-school teacher. Typical of the small businessmen who flocked to the party was Hans Knab. Knab, who also
played a major role as a local and district party leader after
1925, was born in 1887 in Eberbach. He attended but never
graduated from high school. Although he listed his father's
occupation as Fabrikant and his own as Kaufmann, both he and
his father operated and owned one of Eberbach's three quarries. After serving in the Great War, Knab returned to his
native community and became active in the Organization Damm
and the DNVP before joining the Nazi party in 1923. A marginal businessman with a limited education and a long involvement in right-wing politics, Knab was important enough in
December 1924 to be put on the election slate of the National
Socialist Freedom party in Baden.[23]

Liedolsheim on the other hand was one of those rural
communities near Karlsruhe where social homogeneity had broken down because of gradual economic change. In many small
rural communities like Liedolsheim, the farms were too small
to support a family. Farmers who obtained jobs in factories
in Karlsruhe (which was only twelve miles away) or in other
nearby towns were introduced to new political and social philo-
sophies and in particular to Marxism. This collapse of social
cohesion, combined with the effects of the war, accelerated
the growth of völkisch nationalism in the countryside. This
was especially true of communities like Liedolsheim which were
predominantly Protestant and still had a substantial population of full-time farmers. In Liedolsheim 44 percent of all
farms were over two hectares compared to only 15 percent for
the district of Karlsruhe as a whole. Farmers with less than

two hectares of land were prime candidates for urban jobs and eventually even Marxism. In Liedolsheim there were many marginal farmers, but on the whole the community still had a substantial percentage of full-time farmers who made an adequate living from the land and resented the urban world.[24]

In Liedolsheim and in many similar communities in northern and central Baden, völkisch nationalism appeared as early as 1919. In fact, the farmers in this area were already so actively anti-Semitic and radical in 1919 that Adam Remmele, in an address to a Socialist party conference, warned about the dangers of "Bolshevism" among farmers. This rural activism resulted from a combination of forces that included a strong reaction against the loss of social homogeneity, frustrations associated with the defeat of 1918, and the farmers' resentment of government controls on agriculture. In 1919, these feelings were translated into DNVP votes. In the district of Karlsruhe, for example, many farmers and rural artisans in communities like Liedolsheim voted heavily for the DNVP even as early as January 1919. This was long before the promulgation of the Treaty of Versailles and the disintegration of the "middle" in 1920.[25]

After 1933 the Gau Baden party paper Der Führer referred to Liedolsheim as the "Munich of Baden." Indeed, the three founding fathers of the Nazi local in Liedolsheim, Robert Roth, Albert Roth, and August Kramer, remained active in the party until 1945. All held important party posts after the party reemerged in Baden in 1925. In particular, Albert Roth became Gau Baden's most successful rural agitator after 1925. Before 1923, however, the real guiding spirit of the völkisch activists in Liedolsheim was Robert Roth, a native of that community. Roth, who was born in 1891, attended public school

and a trade school and then became a master carpenter in 1909.
According to his own account, he became interested in politics during the war. In fact, his captain directed him to
Fritsch's Hammer, a völkisch, anti-Semitic publication. Conversations with his captain and the literature allegedly influenced Roth to such a degree that he began to take racial mea-
surements while stationed in northern France. Returning home
to his native community after the war, he organized an athletic
club and a "Reading club for Race and German Volkstum."[26]

Together with Albert Roth (who was not related to Robert
directly), Robert Roth formed a local of the Schutz- und Trutzbund in 1920. Albert, a farmer and local Landbund leader,
was born in Liedolsheim on 10 September 1893. This future
activist of the Nazi party and enthusiastic advocate of the
concept of "racial leaders" was discharged from the army in
April 1917 because of severe near-sightedness.[27] These two
Roths came in contact with another völkisch activist, August
Kramer, the future Gau propaganda and Gau organization leader
after 1925. Kramer, the third member of the Liedolsheim leadership, was born in Lahr on 19 October 1900. He served in
the army only between June and December 1918. After the war
he became an elementary schoolteacher but could not find a
job until 1922. Instead, he was employed by the Ministry of
Culture as a "helper" in 1921/22. Kramer was first introduced to Hitler's views while visiting Munich in 1922 as a
member of a hiking club. After returning to Baden and obtaining a teaching position in Linkenheim, he joined the Nazi
party. In constant trouble with the authorities because of
his völkisch activism, he was transferred to Liedolsheim,
where he joined the Roths, who had also been introduced to
National Socialism by this time.[28]

In July 1923, these three men, along with several other
people from Liedolsheim, traveled to Munich to participate in
a Turnfest (a meeting for calisthenics enthusiasts). Like
most völkisch athletes who attended the meeting in Munich,
the Liedolsheim representatives also went to hear Hitler speak.
In addition, they met Hitler personally. During an interview
that allegedly lasted an hour, the völkisch activists from
Liedolsheim pleaded with Hitler to come to Baden or send one
of his associates. Hitler declined because the Nazi party
was outlawed in Baden after July 1922 and because he claimed
that he could not spare a single man in Bavaria. Despite
Hitler's rejection, many of the Liedolsheim athletes, including Kramer and the Roths, formally joined the NSDAP local
of Munich before returning to Baden.[29] Actually, this was
only a formality for most of the Liedolsheim natives since
they had been quite active in the Nazi movement in Baden as
early as 1922.

THE COVERT NSDAP

By the summer of 1922, the Socialists in Baden increasingly
focused attention on the activities of the state's Nazis.
For example, on 12 June 1922, the Socialists introduced an
official question in the Landtag that directed attention to
the public activities and particularly the anti-Semitism of
the Nazis in the district of Mannheim. The Socialist spokesman in the state legislature declared that the Nazi party
was an appendage of the DNVP and that both used racism to
divert the population from the real exploiters, the capitalists.
Following the murder of Rathenau, the Baden government on 4

July 1922 outlawed the Nazi party locals in Baden and imposed
a penalty of from three months to five years in prison for
offenders.[30] Subsequently, as new völkisch organizations
appeared, Remmele moved against all signs of völkisch revival.
By January 1923, six major völkisch groups, ranging from the
Nazi party to the League of National Soldiers, had been outlawed in Baden. Remmele was adamant in his anti-völkisch
crusade, and his special political police force kept a constant vigil on Nazi and völkisch activities and organizations.
By recording the activities of known Nazis, the police could
move against various organizations that attempted to escape
police detection by subterfuge.[31]

The constant vigilance of the political police led authorities to discover a dozen Nazi organizations in nine different
Baden communities from Karlsruhe in north-central Baden to
Lörrach in the south. Most of the Nazi locals or organizations
were detected in the major urban centers, but a few were found
in small rural communities. In all cases, Nazis had been active between December 1922 and April 1923 by distributing leaflets and discussing National Socialism in closed meetings.
Following these discoveries, Remmele put pressure on the state's
Ministry of Justice to expedite the cases and obtain convic-
tions. By the summer of 1923, several Nazis in Baden were
convicted and sentenced to the minimum term of three months'
imprisonment.[32] Remmele's enthusiastic anti-völkisch campaign continued unabated. Rallies were monitored and in some
cases banned when their völkisch nature became obvious. In
addition, the Baden police prohibited known völkisch agitators
from addressing meetings in Baden.[33]

The Baden government's crackdown on Nazi agitators and
völkisch activists was complicated by two problems. First,

the Bavarian government and police were generally uncooper-
ative with Baden authorities in cases involving the extradi-
tion of Munich Nazis who had been active in Baden before returning to Munich.[34] More important was the fact that the
Nazi leadership of Munich advised Baden Nazis or potential
Nazis to join the Munich local in order to circumvent
Karlsruhe's ban on Nazi locals in Baden. This worked well
for the Baden converts. Although courts accepted Baden's
ban of Nazi locals, and the German Oberreichsanwalt (prosecutor) supported Baden's prosecution of Nazis who belonged
to the Munich local but lived in Baden, the Supreme Court
in Leipzig lifted the sentences that had been imposed on
several Baden Nazis who had joined the Munich local. In its
ruling the Leipzig court pointed out that Baden's ban of the
Nazi locals in July 1922 had not specifically outlawed membership in Munich.[35]

Courts in Baden also ruled against the prosecution of
alleged Baden Nazis when the government could not prove that
actual Nazi locals had been established in specific Baden
communities. Remmele, of course, was outraged, and he attacked Baden's judges for showing too much leniency to the
right. This only alienated more of the conservative judges
from the government's anti-Nazi crusade.[36] In addition,
there is evidence that some Baden police officers who had to
arrest local Nazis actually sympathized with them. One police officer in Pforzheim even informed the Nazis he was arresting that he supported their cause.[37]

Although the Baden government did not officially ban
membership in non-Baden locals until November 1923, it maintained a close surveillance of Nazi activities between the
summer of 1922 and November 1923. Nazi and völkisch activism,

however, continued and spread to all parts of Baden until by
1923 there were eighteen official Nazi locals in Baden.[38] To
circumvent police surveillance, the Nazis used various subterfuges, ranging from advertisements in the Völkischer
Beobachter that called for the formation of "reading clubs"
to small-caliber-rifle clubs and "Germanic" holiday celebrations. Some Nazi activists even attempted to bring völkisch
individuals together in an organizational framework by establishing the Deutschvölkische Freiheitspartei (DVFP) in
Karlsruhe in February 1923. This local included representatives from the former Schutz- und Trutzbund, the disbanded
Nazi local, and from the Union of Nationalistic Soldiers.
In March 1923, the group was even addressed by the Nazi activist Walter Buch. In that same month Remmele moved against
the organization and banned it.[39] This did not deter further
völkisch activities, particularly during the summer and fall
of 1923 when the nation was in the grips of massive inflation
and turmoil. By June 1923, Walter Buch reported that the
party was making good progress in Karlsruhe through the efforts of several young and energetic Nazi activists.[40]

Munich played an important part in the cultivation of
National Socialism in Baden. In many communities Nazi activities were either introduced or stimulated by residents of
Munich who were in Baden for business reasons. In St. Georgen,
for example, a man living in Munich but apparently working
in Baden collected the dues from the local Nazis who were
members of the Munich local. In Pforzheim young Karl Hensler
was told by party authorities in Munich to join and recruit
members for the Munich local. By September 1923, he was col-
lecting membership dues. In addition, Badenese came into
contact with National Socialism when they visited Munich

during the Turnfest of 1923. This had played a part in the
evolution of National Socialism in Liedolsheim and Eggenstein.
After returning from the Munich Turnfest in the summer of 1923,
several Eggenstein residents held discussion sessions with
Nazis from neighboring Liedolsheim.[41] Munich made no attempt
to hide the fact that Nazis were active in Baden after July
1922. The Völkischer Beobachter admitted the existence of
locals and party members in Baden, and Baden Nazis sent articles to the Völkischer Beobachter that were published in the
paper's section "Aus der Bewegung" and signed by the "Nazis
of Baden." In September 1923, this paper concluded with
satisfaction that the movement in Baden was advancing despite
arrests and harassment.[42]

There was also, as the letters of Walter Buch have already demonstrated, an active correspondence between Munich
and the Baden Nazis or sympathizers. In 1923, this exchange
was particularly strong between Munich and northern Baden
towns like Mannheim, Heidelberg, Karlsruhe, Pforzheim, and
Bruchsal, although other regions of Baden also participated.[43]
Munich exchanged letters with both locals and individual Nazis
in Baden. Hitler's personality as the "unifying myth" was
already quite apparent in the adulation he received on the
occasion of his birthday in April 1923. Kurt Gottgaul, a
party member in Mannheim, wrote Hitler a birthday greeting
on 19 April 1923, urging him to remember that even outside
of Bavaria numerous fellow Germans were close to him. In
the name of Hitler's followers in Mannheim, Gottgaul promised to endure persecution, arrest, and even confiscation of
party funds, and to continue to fight to free the fatherland
from dishonor and disgrace.[44]

To circumvent police supervision, the Nazis of Baden

resorted to several methods in communicating with Munich.
Ernst Ulshöfer, the local leader of Mannheim, wrote to Hitler
in 1923 by sending the letters to a Miss Steininger in Munich,
who in turn was to deliver them to Hitler personally. On occasion Ulshöfer traveled to Munich to discuss urgent issues directly with Hitler. Other Baden Nazis like Wilhelm Zimmermann
of Karlsruhe gave Munich a secret address that Munich was to use
for party correspondence.[45] In general, the lines between
Nazi activists in Baden and Munich remained open and active.

The dominant theme and motivating force of the Nazi activists in Baden during these early years was anti-Semitism.
This was as true in Karlsruhe as it was in a small community
like St. Georgen. One activist who took part in a Nazi meeting
in Karlsruhe in April 1923 told the police that he participated because he thought that there were too many Jews in
Baden.[46] In addition to anti-Semitism, the Nazi activists
appealed to workers and farmers despite the fact that many
of these activists came from the lower middle class. In
Karlsruhe, for example, the supporters of Hitler in December
1922 distributed literature to the workers of a major machine
shop. Other Karlsruhe Nazis (like the former Socialist Erwin
Würth) went to the rural northeast and with the help of party
members who were farmers appealed to the rural population.[47]

One of the most interesting meetings in Baden that was
sponsored by the Nazis and illustrates the party's dual appeal
to farmers and workers occurred in Liedolsheim. Under the
guise of a Schlageter celebration, the "athletic club" of
Liedolsheim sponsored a major völkisch meeting, which brought
together Nazis and völkisch activists from various communities of northern and central Baden. The meeting on 22 July
1923, which was attended by about three hundred people from

Liedolsheim, Karlsruhe, Heidelberg, Pforzheim, and other surrounding communities, commemorated the death of the native
Badenese Albert Leo Schlageter, who had been executed by the
French. August Kramer had also invited all non-Marxist parties and clubs of Liedolsheim to take part in the commemoration. The rhetoric focused on the evils of Versailles and
the Jews, and it stressed the need to rescue Germany from the
"Jewish materialistic world view" by returning to völkisch
ideas. The various speakers also called for the liberation
of the workers from the alien Marxist ideology. Capital was
not rejected, only Mammonism. In fact, one speaker even reminded the audience that capital was necessary to allow industry to function and to create jobs and was not really harmful
as long as Jews did not control it. Another agitator who
praised the farmer as the true representative of German culture was greeted with lively applause. After the speeches
the Karlsruhe Nazi Willi Worch urged the participants to parade through the streets of Liedolsheim. Symbolically, before
the crowd dispersed, an old Reich navy flag, displaying the
swastika in one corner, was donated to the Liedolsheim hosts.[48]

In addition to the steady communication between Baden
Nazis and Munich, there also existed an important correspondence between Munich and notable right-wing sympathizers in
Baden. This type of exchange reveals who was interested in
Hitler in Baden and what themes articulated by the Nazis appealed to this audience in Baden. It also reveals that the
impact of the Nazi party in Baden ranged far beyond the narrow and small party membership. For example, a lieutenant
colonel Wilhelm Tellenbach of Baden-Baden carried on an active
correspondence with Munich between May and September 1923.
In one letter dated 31 May 1923, he urged Hitler to expand

his activities and influence to other German states. Tellenbach
wanted an audience with Hitler, no doubt, to suggest how the
movement could best expand in Baden.[49]

One of the more "illustrious" Nazi sympathizers in Baden
was Philipp Lenard of Heidelberg, a Nobel Prize winner in
physics. Born in 1862 in Pressburg, Hungary (modern Bratislava,
Czechoslovakia) to ethnic German parents, Lenard went to Germany in 1883 to study physics. After having earned a Ph.D. in
physics from the University of Heidelberg, he began a fruitful career as a teacher and scientist, which culminated in
winning a Nobel Prize and a position in Heidelberg. A vituperous supporter of the German war efforts between 1914 and
1918, he became a violent anti-Semite and Pan-German nationalist. In addition, after 1918 he experienced both economic
hardship, since he had invested heavily in war bonds, and the
death of his son, which may have resulted in part from malnu-
trition. Finally, Lenard continued his battle against modern
physics and the representative of this trend, the Jew Albert
Einstein. By 1922, he was a rabid anti-Semite and antirepublican. On 27 June 1922, he refused to honor Rathenau's death,
which had been declared a state holiday by the Baden government, because the former foreign minister had been a Jew. On
that day a Heidelberg union leader and the Socialist student
leader Karl Mierendorff, with the aid of workers, patrolled
the streets to make sure no one was working. A crowd of about
five hundred workers gathered in front of Lenard's Institute
and attempted to induce the well-known rightist leader to
honor the day. When someone finally poured water from a
window of the Institute, the crowd stormed the building, beat
up a student, and forced Lenard to come to the local union
hall. The anti-Semitic, <u>völkisch</u> professor was finally rescued

and taken into protective custody after Hugo Marx, a Jewish
prosecutor from Heidelberg, addressed the mob and calmed emotions.[50]

Lenard continued to be an outspoken right-wing activist,
although he did not join the Nazi party until 1937. As a
member of the Pan-German League he wrote a letter to his friend
Johannes Stark, another Nobel Prize winner in physics and
völkisch activist. In this letter of 27 September 1923, Lenard
urged closer collaboration between the Pan-Germans and Nazis.
After all, argued Lenard, both the Nazi party and the Pan-Germans supported anti-Semitism, and neither was connected with
any political party that engaged in "idle chatter." Lenard
also felt that the Pan-German League could free itself sufficiently from capitalistic influences to cooperate with the
völkisch movement. On the same day Lenard also dispatched a
letter to Heinrich Class, the head of the Pan-German League.
The physicist greeted the reappearance of the Alldeutsche
Blätter, the Pan-German publication, on 22 September 1923,
but he noted also with disappointment that no reference was
made to an entente between the Pan-Germans and Nazis. Lenard
reminded Class that this could only add to the disintegration
of the völkisch movement. Most important, according to Lenard,
if Bavaria set in motion a march on Berlin (instead of pursuing separatism), then the Pan-German League should be prepared to put itself at the disposal of the movement that would
overthrow the republic. Had the Alldeutsche Blätter announced
an agreement between Class and Hitler, Lenard argued, then
this could have been implemented more readily.[51]

Lenard's political imperative was a völkisch, anticapitalistic nationalism that looked for its sociopolitical ideals in
the preindustrial past. His correspondence also reveals that

by 1923 Hitler's movement was clearly perceived by such Baden sympathizers as a _völkisch_, antirepublican movement rather than a variant of "National Bolshevism." Reflecting Hitler's prestige, Stark sent Lenard's letter to Munich because he wanted the "leader" to find encouragement in the esteem and recognition of such an important man.[52]

PARTY MEMBERSHIP

Given the growing prestige of the Nazi party in certain _völkisch_ circles in Baden, who actually joined the Baden party between 1920 and 1923? Although no detailed membership list of the Baden party has survived, enough sources are available to reveal at least some of the social characteristics and something about the size of the party before November 1923. By 1923 Baden had eighteen locals, located mostly in the northern and north-central districts. The membership of these locals varied from 18 in the rural community of Helmsheim to 178 in Mannheim, the largest local in Baden by the summer of 1922. After July 1922, it became more difficult for the outlawed party to recruit members.[53] Even during September and October 1923 when converts flocked to the Hitler movement, in part because of the disastrous inflation, only 3 percent of an available list of 4,000 new members came from Baden. For a comparison, Württemberg (where the Nazis could operate more freely) claimed twenty-eight locals by May 1923. The total membership of eighteen of these locals, including one of the largest (Stuttgart) in southern Germany, was only 2,934. In view of these statistics it seems most unlikely that the Baden party had more than 1,500 to 2,000 members by November 1923.[54]

Four major sources provide some information about 25 percent of the Baden party's pre-Putsch membership. One document that lists the members who joined Hitler's party between September and October 1923 reveals the names of about 130 converts from all parts of Baden. There is also a membership file of the Mannheim local, dated 28 August 1922, which lists 178 names. A third document gives the names of 108 Baden party members who had joined by 1923 and were still active in 1933. Finally, various police and court reports of 1922/23 provide information on the activities and occupations of almost 100 Nazi activists from all parts of Baden. Excluding duplicates, these lists furnish information on about 500 Baden party members.[55]

In regard to sex, age, and geographic origin, the lists clearly show a young, male-dominated political movement that was strongest in northern Baden, particularly between the districts of Rastatt and Mannheim/Heidelberg. About 85 percent of all party members on these lists joined or were active in this region. The party was especially strong in the districts of Mannheim, Heidelberg, Karlsruhe, Bruchsal, and Rastatt. In southern Baden, the party was very active in urban centers like Freiburg, Lörrach, and Konstanz, although small towns and rural communities were also represented. Both in northern and southern Baden the party was strongest in the urban areas where the party attempted to capture the support of labor. The party also had a few very strong rural locals in some of these urban districts before November 1923. In general, after 1925 the party structure expanded from this core first to the northeast and then after 1928/29 to the south.

The police and court records before 1924 do not reveal

a single female Nazi party activist, and only six women appear
in the other sources. This is not surprising since by November
1923 only 4.4 percent of all Nazi party members in Germany
were women. In terms of age, the great majority of the 500
members listed were between the ages of twenty-two and thirty-
three. In fact, almost two-fifths of all of these members were
born in and after 1900. Many of the younger members joined
in late 1923 when economic and social conditions provided
a fertile soil for the growth of völkisch activism. But the
more "established" völkisch activists and the ones who stayed
with the Nazi movement were not a roving, rootless Lumpenproletariat.

The list of 500 party members shows representatives from
all social classes. Perhaps 4 percent of this group were
former Marxists who rediscovered völkisch nationalism during
and immediately after the war. This was particularly true of
the urban Nazi activists like Ernst Ulshöfer and Richard Cordier
of Mannheim who had belonged to the Communist party. Similarly, the presiding officer of the Pforzheim local, Wittmann,
had been a lifelong member of the SPD, while Franz Tritschler,
one of the founding fathers of the Freiburg local, had led a
Socialist union. These examples can be repeated for many
other Nazi locals of Baden before 1923. But none of these
"Marxists" was really an industrial worker. Wittmann was a
mechanic, Tritschler was a master shoemaker, and Erwin Würth
of Karlsruhe (who had campaigned in rural Sinsheim) was a
Kaufmann. Some had belonged to the SPD all their lives,
whereas others, like the young Walter Jourdan from Weinheim
who joined the Nazi party in Stuttgart in 1921, had been members of Socialist youth clubs.[56]

It is clear, however, that the manual worker (Handarbeiter)

who appeared in these documents was really a skilled worker
or artisan and not an industrial worker. About 23 percent of
the party members listed on the four documents were artisans,
craftsmen, or skilled workers. Most of these converts had
belonged to a right-wing club or party rather than a Marxist
party. For example, the skilled workers and brewers of the
Schremmp brewery in Karlsruhe represented a Nazi stronghold.
But brewers and Nazi activists like Peter Riedner (a future
Gau treasurer) and Willi Worch (a future Kreisleiter of Karlsruhe) had been supporters of <u>völkisch</u> nationalism from the
beginning of their political careers. Others like Franz
Moraller, a young watch repairman in Karlsruhe who worked in
his father's shop, received political baptism only through
the Nazi party in 1923. Although the Baden party attracted
a few unskilled workers (3.5 percent), its success in converting the industrial class from Marxism to <u>völkisch</u> nationalism, apart from a few Marxist converts who were not even
industrial workers, was minimal.[57]

The solid middle class and the professionals accounted
for only 6 percent of the 500 members. Only in the industrial
and academic centers of Mannheim and Heidelberg did the percentage rise to almost 10 percent of the membership. The
party membership in Mannheim included a doctor, a factory
director, and, according to Werner Maser, the young noble
Otto von Waldstein. In addition the Jewish prosecutor Hugo
Marx of Heidelberg, who worked in Mannheim, noted that some
judicial representatives of Mannheim (like the <u>Landgerichtsrat</u>
Heinrich Bammesberger) either joined the Nazi party or were
very sympathetic toward it.[58] Most of these representatives
of the solid middle class did not play an important part in
the Baden party both before and after 1923. Two important

exceptions to this generalization were Herbert Kraft of Pforzheim and Oskar Hüssy of Säckingen. Both joined the party before November 1923, and both remained loyal to Hitler until
1945. Kraft was born in 1886 in Heidelberg and received a
thorough international education. After the war he became
involved with a paramilitary organization and right-wing politics in Pforzheim, where he was a professor in a local Gymnasium. Hüssy, who was born in 1903 in Säckingen, was obviously
much younger than Kraft. He encountered National Socialism
first as a student in Munich in 1922 and after his return to
Baden he founded the Nazi local of Säckingen in the summer of
1923. Although Hüssy's father was part owner of one of the
largest textile factories in Baden, which employed over five
hundred workers, Oskar did not become director of this factory
until 1929. In 1923, Oscar Hüssy was just another right-wing
student who was attracted to Hitler. Both Kraft and Hüssy
assumed important party posts before 1933.[59]

The largest social group represented on all four lists,
and the one that provided the most numerous individual bio-
graphies, was the urban, white-collar, lower middle class.
Many of these men assumed leading party posts after 1925 (and
1933). Before November 1923, however, many of the lower-middle-class representatives still played only a modest role in
the party structure. This group, which included public schoolteachers like August Kramer (the future Gau organization leader) and white-collar employees like Hermann Röhn (the future
deputy Gau leader), accounted for 17 percent of the total
membership of the sample reflected in the four sources. Most
were young men who were born around 1900 and had some kind of
training or job. But they were not rooted or well established
in society. Röhn, for example, joined the Reichswehr in October

1922, and August Kramer lost his teaching position in the summer of 1923.[60] The most extreme example of the rootless drifter was Fritz Plattner. He was born in 1901 in Karlsruhe and experienced military service only at the very end of the war. As a postal worker he became active in the Christian white-collar union movement. After holding a series of different jobs between 1920 and 1922, Plattner joined the Nazi party in Mannheim in 1922.[61] Most of the urban white-collar and lower-middle-class converts did not fit Plattner's pattern of constant drift. But neither did they have well-established careers or families.

Another category that was claimed by 31 percent of the 500 party members included people who were white-collar employees, unemployed, and those who were "in between jobs." The term Kaufmann cannot simply be translated as clerk or salesman since it could mean drifter (Fritz Plattner), terminated teacher (August Kramer), small machine factory owner (Karl Berkmüller), insurance clerk (Hermann Röhn) and even quarry owner (Hans Knab). Most of these people had only a limited education, and all were really part of the white-collar, lower middle class. Many of the leading Gau and district party posts after 1925 (and 1933) were occupied by these Kaufmänner. This included the Deputy Gau leader, the Gau organization leader, the Gau Hitler Youth leader, the Gau's German Labor Front leader, and the head of the Gestapo in Karlsruhe. If one combines the white-collar Nazis, the artisans, craftsmen, and the skilled workers with the Kaufmänner, then almost three-fourths of the 500 Nazis in the sample must be classified as members of the urban lower middle class.[62]

By late 1923, the Nazi party in Germany and in Baden had also penetrated the countryside. In fact, by the autumn of

1923 over half of the new party recruits came from rural areas.
Most of these converts were rural artisans, craftsmen, and
skilled workers, although some peasants also joined the party.
In Baden, only 7 percent of the 500 Nazis were actual farmers.
But in some communities like Liedolsheim, the percentage was
not only higher but the farmers were also closely tied to the
rural artisans and craftsmen. For example, in Liedolsheim five
families contributed the bulk of the early Nazi converts. The
Seiths were all farmers, while the Seitz, Gobelbecker,
Zimmermann, and Roth families were composed of rural artisans,
craftsmen, skilled workers, and farmers. These small farmers
and rural artisans who belonged to the DNVP and Landbund represented one segment of Liedolsheim's society while the marginal
farmer who worked in a factory and supported Marxism delin-
eated the other major social division of Liedolsheim.[63]

The rural component of the Baden party before November
1923 was still a subordinate part of the total membership.
Most Nazis in Baden lived in the major urban centers, and
Munich clearly focused on these centers. In addition, newspapers in Baden still portrayed Hitler as an opponent of farmers. For example, the business manager of the Landbund of
central Baden asked for an interview with Hitler in October
1923 to discover how the Nazi party stood vis-à-vis agriculture. The farm leader desired the interview "so that he could
tell the farmers in their meetings in all frankness that Hitler
was not opposed to them." This letter clearly reveals that
most farmers in Baden were still confused about the position
of National Socialism on agriculture, even if the right-wing
ideology of the Nazis appealed to them. The roots of the subsequent Nazi expansion into the countryside, however, were
well established by 1923. The Landbund leader of Liedolsheim,

Albert Roth, who represented the small Protestant farmers around
Karlsruhe, reemerged in 1925 to lead the party's rural offensive. This was so successful that by early 1929 one observer
concluded that the Nazi party of Baden was the heir to the
Landbund.[64]

These generalizations apply, of course, only to about 25
percent of the Gau's membership before November 1923. But
there is no reason to assume that these 500 Baden Nazis were
peculiar and that observations based on them could not be
applied to the total membership of the party in Baden during
this period. Völkisch activists from all social classes and
all geographic areas joined the Baden party by 1923. But on
the whole, the Baden party was a male-dominated movement that
was strongest among the lower middle classes of Baden's urban
areas, particularly in northern and central Baden.

One of the four sources provides more than just information about the social structure of the 1923 Baden party membership. There is also a list of 108 members who joined the
party by 1923 and were still active in 1933. These were the
true völkisch believers who remained with the Hitler movement
out of real conviction. This list must be slightly adjusted.
First, there was no information on about 5 percent of the members listed. Second, some party members who joined by 1923
and remained active in the party after 1925 do not appear
on the list because they left either the state or the party
shortly before 1933. Hans Knab, for example, joined the party
in 1923 but was expelled in 1930 for disobedience. He was,
however, admitted to the party again in 1934 and even became
a Kreisleiter.[65] Next, it should be noted that four of the
members listed on the document were active in the party in
1923 outside of Baden.[66] Finally, about seven important

Baden Nazis who were party members in 1923 do not appear on
the 1923/33 list.[67] Despite these limitations and reserva-
tions, this list does provide information about at least one
hundred long-term völkisch true believers in Baden.

The obvious conclusion that one can draw from this list
is that most of the Baden Nazis who had joined the party by
1923 did not remain in the party after 1925 (or by 1933).
Only about 7 percent of all pre-Putsch Baden Nazis remained
in the party until 1933. Most probably dropped out of the
party after November 1923. The second most important conclusion one can draw from the 1923/33 list is that about 30
percent of these activists assumed leading party and state
posts after 1933. This was the obvious result of longevity,
since in 1923 only about 8 percent of these men held key party
positions.

In terms of geography the north and areas around Karlsruhe
were represented most profusely. Of the twenty-five communities listed only five were south of Rastatt: urban Freiburg,
Konstanz, Säckingen, Lörrach, and rural Hagnau in the district
of Überlingen. In terms of relative percentage, the greatest
continuity of membership occurred in small towns like Eberbach
and rural communities like Liedolsheim. For example, only
17 percent of the party members came from Mannheim, whereas
Liedolsheim provided 15 percent of the long-term activists.
The Mannheim members, however, could not have represented more
than 5 percent of the 1923 membership. The Liedolsheim groups,
on the other hand, accounted for about 75 percent of the original membership. All of these small communities, with the
exception of Ziegelhausen, which was 56 percent Catholic, were
clearly Protestant towns where the social cohesion of the
völkisch activists provided a bond that was absent in the large

urban centers.

In terms of age and occupation, these activists resemble
the other 500 members. The list reflected a male-dominated
(only one woman was listed) lower-middle-class membership.
Over 85 percent of all members were born between 1893 and
1905. The Kaufmänner led the list with 23 percent of the membership. They were followed by artisans (21 percent), farmers
(17 percent), white-collar employees (10 percent), civil servants (9 percent), and skilled workers and craftsmen (8 percent). The professionals and solid middle class were represented by only 5 percent of the membership. It was not until
after 1928/29 that more Gebildete and professionals joined
the Nazi party and assumed leading posts.

In terms of leadership positions, the farmers and skilled
workers and craftsmen played important roles in the Baden
party before 1933. After 1933, both groups were overshadowed
by professional party activists who called themselves Kaufmänner. In reality, this meant völkisch activists who were
"floating white-collar employees" or only marginally employed.
The Gau Hitler Youth leader was trained as a newspaper apprentice; the Gau leader of the German Labor Front until 1936 was
everything from a postal helper to an unemployed Nazi activist;
the Gau propaganda leader was a salesman and the Gau organization leader was a former teacher. All called themselves
Kaufmänner. They were not tied down to a job or career like
the farmers or the artisans and skilled workers. Instead,
they could engage in full-time party work by occupying some
of the leading Gau party posts. Robert Wagner, the Gau leader, relied on full-time völkisch activists to staff his positions. After all, he was also a mobile, full-time Nazi activist who had lost his career and future in November 1923.[68]

THE CRISIS OF 1923

The French occupation of the Ruhr and the subsequent economic difficulties in 1923 provided fertile soil for the growth of political extremism in Baden, to both the left and right of the political spectrum. Throughout the first half of 1923, unions, Socialist papers, and Communist agitators in Baden warned about alleged illegal Nazi activities. In some parts of Baden, union leaders reported Nazi activities (a term they applied freely to Nazis and "bourgeois fascists") to the authorities, and in southern Baden Communists even patrolled the streets of Tiengen to prevent an alleged Nazi meeting in April 1923. The political left in Baden in 1923 warned of the "Hitlerbanden," and the Communists of Mannheim, in particular, called for the creation of a proletarian security force to cope with the Nazi danger.[69]

The economic and social tensions finally erupted in southern Baden during the fall of 1923 with a series of major disturbances. Clashes between Communists and DNVP youth groups occurred in that part of Baden in early September. Much more dangerous to the republic were the labor demonstrations that broke out spontaneously on September 12 but were quickly supported by the local and state Communists. Jails were stormed in Lörrach, employers were mishandled and forced to contribute economic aid, and a general strike was declared in Schopfheim. Although young workers attempted to carry the strike to the major urban centers of southern Baden, the police established order by 20 September. The general strike collapsed, and the Communists of southern Baden, who had not even been supported by the national party leadership, had to capitulate. Only a few isolated centers continued to collect weapons for apparent plans to continue the revolt.[70]

The basic underlying cause for these disturbances was the deteriorating economic situation. Even small rural communities like Rust in south-central Baden were affected. Rust was 96 percent Catholic and had no strong völkisch movement. Yet, on 20 September, farmers and people who had leased land in order to engage in agriculture disarmed the police and engaged in a mass protest against the economic conditions. They also demanded an improvement in their land contracts. There is no evidence that the Nazis played a part in these disturbances. Instead the community's political life was dominated by the Center party, although the Communists in May 1924 did win some protest votes.[71]

Considering the disturbances in late 1923, the role of the Nazis in Baden was modest. The party registered its first casualty when Dr. Winter was killed in a clash between Nazis and Communists in Steinen, and Paul Jansen of Mannheim launched a hand-grenade attack on the stock market of Mannheim.[72] Much more active were the traditional right-wing organizations. Fear of Communist plunder in the countryside had produced various local paramilitary organizations in southern Baden. The military in Stuttgart again provided these local defense clubs with weapons. A lieutenant Gustav Dürrstein from the army unit in Donaueschingen gave machine guns to a Dr. Montfort, who in turn distributed them to various factory and firm directors. Montfort was a member of the Treudeutsch Vereinigung Oberrhein, which had been formed in 23 August 1923 in Schönau. Not only had this organization been visited by Damm, but Montfort admitted to the police that he had recruited members for the Nazi party. In addition, the future Gau leader of the Nazi party in Baden, Robert Wagner, who was stationed as a

lieutenant in Villingen, was actively engaged in supplying the
right with weapons. As in 1921, the Baden minister of interior
protested to the Reichswehr minister and he scolded the military for its involvement. And as in 1921, the military argued
that the weapons were intended for the maintenance of public
order, and, of course, the military also warned that the Entente
must not find out about these weapons. The weapons were Reichswehr arms that had been hidden in order to keep them from the
French. Despite Remmele's protests, the case was eventually
dropped.[73]

Although the Nazis of Baden had not planned a Putsch in
September 1923 or even organized well to counteract the activities of the Communists, many Badenese who were attracted to
the Hitler movement began to focus on the military potential of the Nazi party. Individual Nazis participated in
local defense clubs, and Montfort apparently used the clubs
to recruit actively for the party. Many potential converts
began to refer to Hitler's movement as a military organization. This is clearly shown in the correspondence between
Munich and Baden in 1923. In Pforzheim, Herbert Kraft
even arranged local military exercises that were to be used
against the French. In Karlsruhe, students of the Technical
University told Munich that they were ready for a four-week
training course for "infantry recruits." Some Badenese frankly wrote to Munich that they wanted to join "Hitler's army."[74]
Munich had to be very reserved about sending SA paraphernalia
to Baden or training hordes of Baden volunteers. The national
party leadership did, however, on occasion invite Baden Nazis
to come to Munich (at party expense) to report on conditions
in Baden.[75]

In fact, the situation in Baden was quite unfavorable

for a potential Nazi revolt despite the support of sympathizers
like Lenard of Heidelberg. The actual Hitler Putsch in Munich
on 8/9 November 1923 did produce some minor echoes in Baden.
The response, however, was neither well organized nor successful. According to party accounts (which are not very trust-
worthy), Fritz Plattner gathered one hundred men to storm the
Baden ministries as soon as news of the successful revolt
reached Baden; the Eberbach SA marched to Heidelberg, and the
Mannheim Bund Oberland organized for the march on Munich. All
of these plans were comic opera operations which had no chance
of success. Instead, a major disturbance in Mannheim was produced not by the Nazis but by young unemployed men who plundered shops.[76]

The Nazi plans were totally unrealistic because Baden
was governed by a "Weimar Coalition" and not a reactionary
clique. Karlsruhe supported Berlin and Berlin's efforts to
defuse the volatile situation, at home and abroad.[77] When
the Baden minister president received a telegram from Gustav
Stresemann in the morning of 9 November 1923, which appealed
for help, he made it clear that Baden would support Berlin
and the constitution. The Karlsruhe government banned all
paramilitary organizations, and it cut mail, telephone, and
rail connections with Bavaria. The government also published
a notice in the Karlsruher Zeitung of the impending arrest
of leading Baden Nazis. On 9 November 1923, State President Heinrich Köhler addressed the state legislature and emphasized Baden's loyalty to the Reich and the republican constitution. Köhler warned that any attempted Putsch in Baden could
and would be crushed. The police promptly implemented Köhler's
policy by arresting most of the known Nazi leaders in Baden,
both in large urban centers like Mannheim and Pforzheim and

in small communities like Liedolsheim. The Baden Nazis who had struggled hard under government restrictions between July 1922 and November 1923 now had to pay the final price for Hitler's mistake in Munich.[78]

3 National Socialism in Baden, 1924-1928, Revival and Organization

THE DEUTSCHE PARTEI

After 1933, leading Baden Nazis recalled the period immediately following the failure of the Munich Putsch as a time of disillusionment and temporary rejection of all forms of political activities.[1] Although the Nazis in Baden must have been greatly disappointed after November 1923, individual völkisch activists continued to agitate for the "cause." Even more important was the fact that after the attempted Putsch Baden witnessed the emergence, for the first time, of an organized völkisch political party, the Deutsche Partei. By 1924, this party had a statewide organization and even a Gau leader. In effect, the failure of 1923 forced the völkisch and Nazi activists in Baden to form a more permanent and elaborate organization, which took part in elections.

Until the emergence of the Deutsche Partei in January 1924, the völkisch political scene of Baden was characterized by disorganization and the appearance of many different völkisch clubs and movements. The police used its detailed file on active völkisch and right-wing agitators to initiate numerous searches and arrests. In order to ensure the destruction of Hitler's movement in Baden, the state's security officials moved against all groups and organizations that either displayed swastikas or marched about the countryside on weekends.[2]

The authorities were effective enough in November and December 1923 to crush all attempts by former Nazis to reestablish the party, or a substitute, but they could not destroy individual allegiance to the völkisch cause.

The young, lower-middle-class Nazis, particularly in Baden's urban centers, continued to cling to their völkisch ideology with tenacious conviction. In Karlsruhe, the police arrested and interrogated several young völkisch activists in December 1923. All were violently anti-Semitic and extremely laudatory of Hitler. One young Kaufmann admitted frankly that he would join Hitler's party immediately if it were not illegal.[3] Another, Robert Rützler, was arrested by the police on 1 December 1923, after he appeared in a Karlsruhe cafe, wearing a swastika and distributing Nazi leaflets. As early as late November, Rützler had posted on houses leaflets that warned workers against the alleged attempts of Jews, Nationalists, and Catholic political leaders to reestablish the monarchy now that Hitler, the leader of the German workers with a social conscience, had been betrayed. Rützler's friend Franz Moraller also admitted to the police that he liked the NS Worker's party and that he was particularly attracted by Hitler's anti-Semitism. Both Rützler and Moraller denied that they belonged to the illegal Hitler party but admitted membership in the völkisch Deutscher Herold. These two young völkisch activists, twenty-one and twenty, were employed by their fathers' businesses. Although they were not drifters, they were not well established, both in life and in business. The Völkische Jugend, founded in January 1924 in Karlsruhe (and subsequently in other urban centers), gathered many such young activists. Later, the Völkische Jugend evolved into the Schlageterbund, the forerunner of the Baden SA.[4]

After January 1924, a marked increase of völkisch activism became noticeable in the urban centers of Baden. Some former urban Nazis joined such paramilitary organizations as the Rossbach League; others became members of more traditional "Fatherland clubs" before they found their way back to the Nazi party in 1927/28. Many younger activists like Moraller were attracted by the völkisch youth clubs and athletic organizations whose members, the Baden police noted in the summer of 1924, spent their time marching in formation. In August of the same year the Völkische Jugend was strong enough to hold a major meeting in Karlsruhe.[5] Numerous völkisch organizations appeared, and disappeared just as quickly, in 1924. Among them, anti-Semitism was always a common denominator.[6]

In many rural and small communities, völkisch activism also reappeared by early 1924. In Merchingen young activists wore swastikas to the local Turnverein, and in Diedesheim (Mosbach) völkisch youths beat up supporters of the republic. These young activists were anti-Semitic, and they violently opposed the republic. For the most part, they were rural or small-town artisans, craftsmen, Kaufmänner, and farmers who found their way to the Nazi party after 1924. In addition, there were also former Nazis like Erwin Würth who became active again in the rural communities of northeastern Baden in early 1924.[7]

Of particular importance was the continuation of völkisch activities in Liedolsheim. In this community the social cohesion of the pre-1923 activists was strong enough to allow for the collective continuation of völkisch activism and eventually of National Socialism. One of the first signs of the reemergence of völkisch activism appeared in February 1924 when a group of Liedolsheim schoolchildren was discovered on

the schoolgrounds, displaying swastikas and engaging in "military exercises." After the local school board (in a vote of
six to three) recommended punishment for these actions, the
parents, older brothers, and other relatives of the children,
who were determined to reverse the decision, descended on the
mayor and the other local authorities. Most of these outraged
relatives were related through marriage. All were young men
between the ages of twenty-five and twenty-seven, and many of
these farmers and rural artisans were members of the local
Landbund and the DNVP. They had never accepted the republic,
and many had belonged to the Nazi party as early as 1923.
After 1924 these activists established again a major Nazi
stronghold in the countryside of the district of Karlsruhe.[8]

The former Nazis and völkisch activists of Baden must
have been encouraged by the court decisions of 1924 that reversed many cases against Baden Nazis who had been convicted
and fined in 1923. The Socialist papers bitterly denounced
the legal profession's "reactionism," and the minister of interior also attacked the leniency of the judges who dealt
with right-wing political crimes.[9] The right in turn organized a major rally in July 1924 in Pforzheim, which was attended by all of the patriotic leagues and organizations of the
area to protest the minister of interior's constant offensive
against "patriotic" meetings and organizations.[10] Indeed,
Remmele, who could not control the judicial authorities, did
move against Nazis and völkisch activists who held public
positions. In 1924, several teachers and policemen were discharged because of their völkisch activities.[11] These developments, however, did little to discourage the völkisch true
believer.

The first Baden party to emerge in early 1924 that repre-

sented a statewide völkisch organization and a continuation
of the Nazi party was the Deutsche Partei. Although left-
wing papers noted the Deutsche Partei's first state conference in Freiburg on 20 January 1924, and even called it a
Nazi conference, Remmele permitted the party to exist apparently because it had an inoffensive name and its behavior
was proper.[12] The leader of the party was a lawyer, Erwin
Müller, who was the first Gau leader of a Baden völkisch party. Müller was born on 1 October 1876 in Bauersbach, Bretten,
and practiced law in Karlsruhe. By his own admission, he
was apolitical until March 1919 when he joined the Independent
Socialist party, allegedly to enlighten the workers about the
"nonsense" of Marxism. Dissatisfied with the Independent
Socialists, Müller turned to the SPD and finally to the Nazi
party. There is no evidence, however, that Müller played a
major role in the NSDAP before November 1923.[13]

The party gradually established a structure in 1924 that
included district and local leadership positions. Many of
the leaders of the Deutsche Partei had been active in the Nazi
party in 1923. The major Nazi urban leaders of Mannheim,
however, did not return to the Deutsche Partei, and many urban leaders with "leftist" Nazi backgrounds (like Ulshöfer and
Cordier) disappeared from the völkisch scene in Baden after
1923. In addition, the "leftist" Nazi leaders of Pforzheim
did not return to the fold until after 1928. Until the fall
of 1924 the district positions of the Deutsche Partei were
dominated by professionals, especially lawyers and dentists.
Many of the southern völkisch leaders of the party ended up
in the Deutschvölkische Freiheitspartei (DVFP) in 1925. Despite this shift in urban leadership patterns, the party's
themes in 1924 had not changed. The party appealed to anti-

Semitism and attempted to convert both workers and farmers.
In order to solve Germany's problems, the Deutsche Partei demanded a corporative solution for socioeconomic issues.[14]

The Deutsche Partei was particularly active in communities with populations between two thousand and sixteen thousand. Many Nazi (and völkisch) activists of 1923 who lived
in these communities remained active and maintained closer
political and even social ties than the Nazis of the large
urban centers. Most of these men were natives of the communities where they were politically active. For the most part,
they were employed and many belonged to such "respectable"
social organizations as the Stammtisch. For example, Hans
Knab of Eberbach had participated in the Nazi party in 1923.
In 1924, he belonged to the Deutsche Partei and subsequently
to the Völkisch Block and the NSFP (Nationalsozialistische
Freiheitspartei). Knab and the Eberbach Nazis were visited
by a variety of völkisch speakers in 1924, including the
future Gau leader of Baden, Robert Wagner. The Deutsche Partei was established in Eberbach on 14 April 1924 with thirty-
four members, of whom nine were below the age of twenty. Many
of these early activists, including Knab, joined the Nazi party in 1925.[15]

In addition to the revival of old Nazi locals like those
in Eberbach and Liedolsheim, locals of the Deutsche Partei also
emerged in several new communities. Most of the new centers
were based on solid right-wing traditions and activities. In
Weinheim, a town with a population of sixteen thousand, Walter
Köhler left the DNVP and joined the Deutsche Partei in 1924.
A native of Weinheim, Köhler was the son of a small businessman. After participating in the war, he returned to his father's trade and colonial wares business and became active in

the DNVP. According to Köhler, the future deputy Gau leader
and minister president of Baden, he left the traditional right
(DNVP) because he felt that it was too lethargic; he was look-
ing for action. Under Köhler's leadership the Deutsche Partei
was converted into a Nazi local as soon as the party became
legal again in Baden in early 1925. Similarly, in the small
communities of Weingarten and Eggenstein in the district of
Karlsruhe, the Deutsche Partei emerged from a solid right-wing
tradition that included the Landbund and the DNVP. At the same
time, these communities with fewer than five thousand people
had had enough economic modernization to experience the growth
of Marxist parties, which undoubtedly helped to mobilize the
native right-wing forces. In Eggenstein, Ludwig Griesinger,
who was born in 1897 and had served in the army during the
war, had participated in völkisch activities as early as 1923.
After taking part in the Munich Turnfest of 1923, Griesinger
came into contact with the Liedolsheim Nazis. Griesinger,
like Knab and Köhler, was not a rootless unemployed drifter.
Knab owned a quarry, Köhler was employed in his father's im-
port business, and Griesinger owned a small construction firm.
All of these men belonged to the lower middle class, but they
had enough social standing in their communities to attract
a following. In the large urban centers, this type of stable
völkisch infrastructure did not exist. But in both cases
völkisch activists who railed against Jews and the republic
and who appealed to workers and peasants had reemerged by
1924.[16]

The various völkisch forces in Baden were able to test
the popularity of their views in the national election of
May 1924. In April, they united in the Völkisch Soziale Block
to pursue a common election campaign. Two-thirds of the can-

didates of the Block came from southern Baden, particularly from the districts of Lörrach and Waldshut. The remaining candidates lived in the districts of Rastatt and Mannheim. Half of these men were professionals (lawyers and a dentist), one was a Kaufmann, one an artisan (weaver), but only one was a metalworker. There were no farmers on the list, and the workers from the major northern urban centers were not represented. The only worker was from the southern community of Tiengen in the district of Waldshut. One candidate, Helmut Klotz, even lived in Munich. The election slate was clearly dominated by southern völkisch activists who were either professionals or white-collar employees. Although some of these candidates had belonged to the Nazi party in 1923, most of them selected the DVFP after the völkisch movement split in early 1925.[17]

The results of the election on May 4 reflected the aftermath of the Ruhr crisis and the catastrophic inflation that had plagued Baden during 1923 (see Map 3). The völkisch forces of Baden emerged with 4.8 percent of the vote. Despite the Block's large number of southern candidates, the strongest völkisch districts were in northern urban and rural districts, reaching 13.9 percent in the city of Bruchsal and 12.8 percent of the total vote in the rural district of Bretten. In southern Baden only the rural Protestant district of Müllheim and the industrial district of Lörrach provided the Völkisch Block with higher percentages of the vote than for the state as a whole. The party did especially well in Baden cities with populations over ten thousand. Although only 39 percent of the state's votes were cast in these cities, the völkisch party obtained 47.9 percent of its votes in these urban centers. In addition, the völkisch were very strong in rural Protestant communities, especially around Karlsruhe. The urban middle

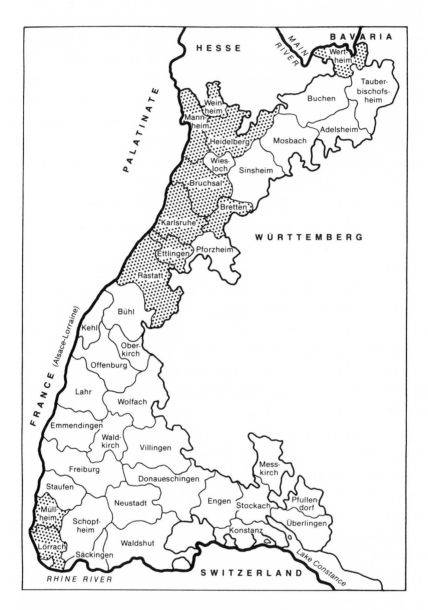

Map 3. *Reichstag Election: May 1924*

Völkischsozialer Block Strongholds: Districts with over 4.8% of the vote

classes that were affected by the inflation and the rural, Protestant voters who had rejected the republic as early as 1919 flocked to the völkisch party. The Socialists and the Nationalists, however, discounted the importance of the völkisch votes. With fewer than 5 percent of the total vote, the Völkisch Block was obviously not going to play a significant political role.[18]

After the election, the Deutsche Partei became more visible in Baden. In July it began to organize one of the largest "patriotic" meetings in Baden in 1924. After considerable hesitation, Remmele finally gave permission to the Deutsche Partei to organize a Deutsche Tag as long as anti-Semitism was controlled. On 12 October (a Sunday) about two thousand people arrived by train in Bruchsal. They represented a variety of völkisch and nationalistic organizations, ranging from the Deutsche Partei to the Wehrwolf, Wikingbund, Frontkriegerbund, and the Mannheim youth organization of the DNVP. The pre-1923 Baden Nazis were well represented, with Liedolsheim sending a band, Franz Moraller reading an anti-Semitic poem, and Heinrich Wippermann leading the Bruchsal local of the Deutsche Partei. In the morning of 12 October 1924, the local leaders of the participating völkisch groups met to discuss various matters, including the problem of election debts. Then the ceremonies to honor the war dead were introduced with speeches that attacked the Treaty of Versailles and Jews. The future Gau leader of Baden who had served in the army as an officer and who represented the veterans' club of Karlsruhe, Robert Wagner, described the alleged stab in the back and promised that in time the "criminals" would be swept away.[19]

The Deutsche Partei finally ran into difficulties when it attempted to transform itself into the NSFP. This party

had emerged on the Reich level as early as July 1924 when
Gregor Strasser, Erich Ludendorff, and Albrecht von Graefe
merged the Nazi party and the DVFP. In September 1924, the
organ of the Deutsche Partei of Baden, the Völkischer Kämpfer,
finally called itself Kampfblatt of the NSFP. This was too
much for Remmele, and he proceeded to move against the new
party paper. Müller circumvented the government's attack by
publishing a substitute entitled Wahrheit ("Truth"). The
paper was first issued on 25 October 1924 and distributed to
party members and subscribers of the Völkischer Kämpfer. Some
papers were also available for public sale. Müller had planned
to use one hundred thousand copies of the paper in the Reichstag election campaign of November/December 1924, but financial difficulties cut the supply to only five thousand copies.
The paper attacked Jews and Mammonism and called for the union
of all "producers." Significantly, the Wahrheit declared that
Hitler was and would remain the spiritual leader of the movement.[20]

The party's election slate in December included again
representatives from the various völkisch groups in Baden.
Hans Knab had been active in the NSDAP in 1923, Friedrich
Berlinger of Durlach was the Gau leader of the paramilitary
Frontkriegerbund but did not join the Nazi party until 1927,
Kurt Bürkle was the district leader of the DVFP of Baden-Baden,
and Walther Haas, the future Gau leader of the DVFP, fought
the Nazis as late as 1929. Unlike the election slate of May,
two-thirds of the candidates in December came from northern
districts. In fact, none of the May candidates remained on
the ticket. The pre-1923 Nazis were better represented, and
the list included farmers but no lawyers or doctors. The
lower-middle-class image of the December group was clear.

Many of the professionals who had been on the May election
slate (but were now excluded) joined the Nazi party's rival
in 1925--the DVFP.[21]

The major völkisch rival to the NSFP in Baden in December
1924 was the Deutschvölkische Reichspartei (DVRP), which was
led by Arnold Ruge, the Heidelberg anti-Semite, and supported
by Robert Roth of Liedolsheim. Ruge had broken with the Nazi
party (but not Hitler) in 1923 when he claimed that "scum"
had gathered around Hitler in Munich. Ruge also claimed that
the Nazi party had betrayed the true völkisch and anticapitalistic imperatives by allying itself with the DNVP.[22] After
his release from prison, Ruge returned to Baden and continued
in the summer of 1924, as he freely boasted, his fight against
Jewry. In Baden, he made contacts with some of the dissident
Nazis who opposed the NSFP's leadership. Ruge and Karlsruhe
Nazis like Willi Worch campaigned in the countryside of Karlsruhe, including Liedolsheim. Apparently they converted Robert
Roth during the summer of 1924.[23]

Both völkisch parties suffered from a general decline of
right-wing radicalism during the December election (see Map 4).
This resulted in large part from the improving economic and
political conditions. In addition, the DNVP and the Landbund
absorbed most of the right-wing votes in the urban and rural
areas of Baden, winning 8.5 percent and 5.9 percent of the
vote, respectively. The NSFP emerged as the strongest splinter
party with 1.9 percent of the vote. Ruge's movement won only
.3 percent of the vote. With minor exceptions, both parties
did best in northern Baden. The greatest decline of völkisch
strength occurred in the urban centers of Baden, especially
in the largest cities like Karlsruhe, Mannheim, Pforzheim,
and Freiburg. Only in medium-sized cities of northern Baden

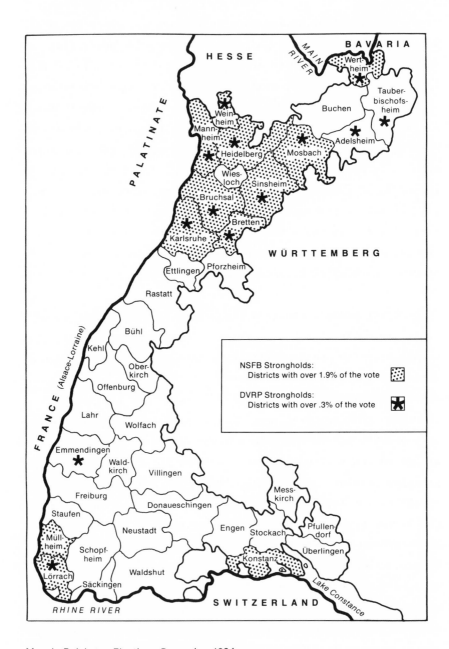

Map 4. *Reichstag Election: December 1924*

(with the exception of Konstanz in the south), where the völk-isch parties were well organized, did they win substantial votes. Both parties also appealed to some of the rural Protestant communities of northern Baden where völkisch traditions were strong. Despite these isolated successes, however, the organ of the DNVP, the Badische Zeitung, was absolutely right when it noted the shrinking völkisch strength. Both parties were insignificant in Baden's political life, attracting only 22,565 votes from a total of almost one million. This mere 2.2 percent of the vote had no real impact on the political constellation in Baden.[24] These völkisch votes do, however, reveal a small but persistent völkisch pool in democratic Baden. It was this "pool" that produced the Nazi activists before and after 1924.

Müller frankly admitted the NSFP's failure in the election. In a circular issued after the election and distributed to his district and local leaders, he blamed the lack of organization and völkisch cooperation for the weak electoral showing of the NSFP in Baden. And Müller reminded his leaders that this weak showing only "hurt Hitler." The Baden leader pointed out that the movement needed a press to spread its message, but it had lacked sufficient money (200 RM) to issue even a special election leaflet. Müller also blamed the völkisch Reichstag delegates for failing to push for an organization or guild for the German Kaufmannstand that would provide a link between the producer and the consumer. To plan for the future, Müller scheduled a state leadership conference for 11/12 January 1925, in Karlsruhe.[25] Müller never succeeded in uniting the völkisch forces in Baden. In early 1925, the völkisch parties divided into several hostile groups. Within months, a new leader emerged in Baden who gathered the northern Nazis and

organized them into an effective party. Müller's career had
ended with the December election.

ROBERT WAGNER

The man who emerged in 1925 as the new Gau leader of the Nazi
party in Baden and who held the office until 1945 was born on
13 October 1895 in rural Lindach in northeastern Baden. Robert
Wagner had only a grade-school education and training in a
teacher's seminar before he volunteered for military service
in August 1914. According to his commanding officer, Wagner
was a solid and heroic young lieutenant. He first experienced
the German collapse when confronted by a mutiny in Valenciennes,
which was led by the nephew of Friedrich Ebert, the future
Socialist president of the new German republic. After the
armistice, Lieutenant Wagner saw further disturbances in
Mannheim and Karlsruhe, which reinforced his antirepublicanism.[26] He gave vent to these feelings after he was sent to
Meiningen, Thuringia, by hiding weapons from the Allied Control Commission during 1921/22. The young officer was arrested by the left-wing government and only the intervention
of the minister of defense saved Wagner from a trial. Instead,
he was sent back to Baden, where he became again involved in
right-wing activities while stationed in Villingen.[27] By
1923, he was totally alienated from the republic. Unlike
many young officers who had emerged from the war, however,
Wagner still had a potential career in the army.

   After service at Villingen, he was sent to the Infantry
School of Munich; there he first encountered National Socialism in the fall of 1923 while attending a Hitler rally. Even

more important in converting Wagner to Hitler's cause was
his discovery, while visiting General Erich Ludendorff, that
the World War I hero supported the Nazi leader with apparent
enthusiasm. Wagner's antirepublican conspiratorial career
culminated on 8 November 1923, when Ludendorff's stepson,
Lieutenant Pernet, called Wagner to the headquarters of the
conspiratorial Kampfbund to instruct him to lead the students
of the Infantry School to the beer hall in Munich where Hitler
planned to stage his Putsch. With the failure of the Putsch
on 9 November 1923, Wagner's future as an officer disappeared
and during the subsequent trial he was sentenced to one year
and one month imprisonment.[28] The war and the revolution had
changed Wagner's life drastically. Without the war he would
probably have become just another public schoolteacher in
Baden. The Great War removed him from civilian society and
the traditional, conservative environment of his native Lindach.
The defeat and the revolution in 1918 alienated him from the
mainstream of society. The failure of the Putsch in November
1923 destroyed his army career and caused him to become a
full-time völkisch agitator in his native state.

    After serving in jail only a few days, Wagner in late
summer of 1924 returned to Baden, unemployed, with no pros-
pects and only limited help from his old regimental comrades.
He first settled in southern Baden, where he had been stationed in 1923, and attended closed right-wing rallies in
Donaueschingen and Villingen. Then in October 1924, he participated in the Deutsche Tag in Bruchsal as a representative
of the Karlsruhe veterans organization (Frontkriegerbund).
Finally, on 17 October 1924, he registered with the police
of Karlsruhe, the Schlageterbund.[29] This was an important
step for Wagner. He had traveled throughout Baden and

addressed völkisch groups in late 1924 with speeches about
Hitler. But in Karlsruhe, Wagner had made contact with the
young völkisch activists who had formed the Völkische Jugend.
In addition, he won the support of Nazis like Peter Riedner
and Willi Worch of Karlsruhe who had opposed the NSFP leadership of Baden in 1924. With the support of these Karlsruhe
activists, Wagner first established his leadership position
and at least a base for his power. Despite Wagner's control
of the Schlageterbund, he was still not important enough in
late 1924 to be put on the NSFP's election slate.[30]

In February 1925, Wagner traveled to Munich and obtained
Hitler's mandate to establish officially a Nazi party in
Baden. After returning to Karlsruhe, Wagner invited various
völkisch leaders and former Nazis to attend a conference.
About sixty people came on 25 March 1925. After Wagner informed them of Hitler's decision, most of the participants
joined the new Nazi party with only a minority choosing the
new DVFP.[31] According to Franz Moraller, a close associate
of Wagner, the Nazi party was totally ignored by the public.
Wagner issued a pamphlet on 15 April 1925, calling for the
creation of the NSDAP in Baden in order to demonstrate that
Badenese could also contribute to the fight against "Jewish
Marxist rule." Three days later, he followed this appeal
with a notice in the Völkischer Beobachter, announcing that
the Baden minister of interior had lifted the ban on the
NSDAP and calling for the rebuilding of the party.[32]

Remmele permitted the reestablishment of the Baden NSDAP
because he felt that the republic was solidly established by
1925. He also voiced his opinion in a 1925 publication that
the various völkisch leagues and organizations in Baden had
not really affected the political life of the state. This

view was shared by most political observers in 1925. The
organ of the Democratic party, Der Demokrat, published a note
on Hitler in late 1925 in which it concluded that the Hitler
movement was in such a decline that it was of no further interest. Hitler had disappeared from history, noted the journal.[33] Only the lonely voice of the Socialist paper of Karlsruhe, the Volksfreund, published an article in March 1925 in
which it noted that the Nazis were becoming a plague again.[34]
But in 1925 few Badenese took the Nazi party seriously.

The völkisch activists who did not support Wagner in
early 1925 turned to the Deutschvölkische Freiheitsbewegung
(DVFB). In March 1925, most of the former district leaders
of the old NSFP supported Wagner. Only three district leaders
joined the DVFB. Maasdorf, a Kaufmann, Baumann, a lawyer,
and the customs official Walther Haas were all from southern
Baden. Maasdorf and Baumann had been active in the Nazi
movement in 1923, but they had always campaigned with other
middle-class spokesmen of southern Baden. Walther Haas, the
new Gau leader of the DVFB, had been on the election slate
of the NSFP in December 1924. In general, the leadership of
the new DVFB was more middle class and professional than that
of the Nazi party and was more concentrated in southern Baden.
The socioeconomic views of the party were reflected in the
statement of its Freiburg district leader (a physician) that
farmers would never be attracted by a party which called itself "socialist workers' party."[35]

The DVFB competed with the Nazi party in all parts of
Baden. It was strongest in the southern part of the state
and in the traditional right-wing, rural strongholds of
Bretten and Wertheim in northeastern Baden. Its völkisch
message, which included attacks on Jews, Versailles, and the

Dawes Plan, could not be distinguished from that of the Nazi
movement. It cooperated with such nationalistic organizations
as the Stahlhelm, the Wikingbund, and the Jungdeutsche, and
the DVFB opposed world capitalism, banks, and parliaments.
Although the party urged an end to class wars, its middle-
class views were quite evident. The DVFB appealed to farmers
and the middle class, and it promised that in the Third Reich
the worker's quest for a pension would be converted into a
quest for property.[36] In Baden, the party seemed to identify
more with Mussolini's fascism, and Haas persistently rejected
the "black-white-red-communism" of the NSDAP. Since the
party was so strong in southern Baden, it was not surprising
that it seemed to reflect many of the old National Liberal
views. In particular, the DVFB demanded a centralized state,
and it openly attacked the Catholic party and any "capitula-
tion to the Roman clerics."[37] The Baden DVFB never attempted
to become a catch-all party as did the NSDAP.

PARTY ORGANIZATION

As the new Gau leader of the Nazi party in Baden, Wagner
faced several crucial issues in 1925. He had to establish
a Gau structure, create new party locals, and harness the
support of established local Nazi leaders. Simultaneously,
Wagner had to guide the new party through a völkisch sea
that threatened to disintegrate the Hitler movement in Baden.
Wagner had founded the new party in Karlsruhe but established
the first party business center in Pforzheim. Between June
and August 1925, he could do little organizing since he served
a term in the Bavarian Landsberg prison for insulting General

von Lossow. After his release from prison, Wagner moved the party's headquarters to Karlsruhe. The party business center was located in his apartment, where daily visiting hours were established in addition to the regular party conferences and business transactions.[38] Although Wagner was a dominating personality he was still too weak in 1925/26 to control completely the various strong local leaders. In fact, in 1926 the local and district leaders of the party, meeting in a state conference, had the power to decide Wagner's salary, and as late as January 1928, he did not have a regular one.[39]

Wagner gradually gathered a Gau "clique" that was both loyal to him and competent to handle the party's administrative affairs. Initially, the problems must have seemed insurmountable. After the first Gau business manager deserted to the völkisch Artamanen in 1926, Wagner had to administer both the Gau leadership post and the Gau business center. He was assisted only by the Gau treasurer, Peter Riedner. Neither Wagner nor Riedner received a salary in 1926.[40] Not until May 1927 was Wagner able to establish the rudiments of a permanent Gau clique. On 1 May, he named August Kramer to the full-time position of Gau business manager. In addition, Wagner acquired Karl Lenz, an extremely active agitator from the rural district of Sinsheim, as deputy Gau leader. Lenz was born in 1899 in Heidelberg to a civil servant. After public and middle school, he became a teacher. He served in the war between 1916 and 1918 and lost one eye. By 1921 Lenz had come into contact with National Socialism, and one year later he met Hitler. Between 1927 and 1931 he served as deputy Gau leader, Gau propaganda leader, and even Kreisleiter of Mannheim. All of these men had belonged to the Nazi party in 1923 (or had supported Hitler in Wagner's case),

and all were young. Kramer had been active in Liedolsheim,
Riedner was a member of the Karlsruhe local, and Lenz had led
the Heidelberg Sturmabteilung (SA) in 1923/24. All were available for full-time party work. Kramer's career as a teacher
had been terminated in 1923, about the same time that Wagner
had lost his army commission. Even Lenz, who was a teacher
in the district of Sinsheim, was suspended in 1928 because
of his völkisch activities. Only Riedner had a stable and
long-term profession. But since he lived in Karlsruhe, he
was always close to party affairs. Most important, all were
loyal to Wagner, and none had connections with the old NSFP
leadership.[41]

The first centripetal office of the Gau structure, and
one that was absolutely essential to Wagner, was the Gau
treasury. A strong treasurer was necessary not only for the
growth of the party but also to control the financial mis-
management and embezzlements of local leaders. Peter Riedner,
who took charge of the Gau treasury in 1925, was the oldest
and most settled of the early Gau clique members. He was
born in 1883 and held a steady job as a representative of a
Karlsruhe brewery. After earning the Iron Cross II in the
war, Riedner became involved with most of Baden's postwar
völkisch organizations, including the Schutz- und Trutzbund
and the Nazi party. In October 1926, Riedner began to expand the powers of the treasury by ordering locals and members to pay all September dues immediately and to present the
Gau with written proposals on how they planned to pay old
debts. He threatened to initiate exclusion procedures against
all locals that had not complied by 5 November 1926. He even
promised to initiate legal actions against members who had
been expelled but still owed dues to the party.[42]

Riedner's office helped Wagner substantially in subor-
dinating local leaders and activists to the Gau leadership.
But Riedner could do little about the party's persistent
financial plight during these early years. Gau Baden's financial position was so precarious that Munich allowed Baden until
early 1932 the privilege of sending to Munich only the dues
actually collected from party members rather than the total
amount all members were supposed to pay.[43] Only after 1929,
when the Baden membership increased rapidly, was the party's
financial situation improved.

In expanding the membership and in rebuilding the party
in general, Wagner's major task was to win the support of
established Nazi and völkisch strongholds. Throughout 1925
he issued pleas for Nazis to create locals and to send their
addresses to Karlsruhe. In addition, Wagner played an important part in the creation of locals in several major urban
centers, either by personally creating a local as in Pforzheim
in March 1925, or by presiding over the creation of a local
like Mannheim, where he allegedly "solved the disputed question of local leadership."[44] By the end of 1925, locals had
been established in many urban centers. Simultaneously locals
were established in small and even rural communities, usually
through local initiatives. In such small communities it was
Wagner's task to convince the local leader to recognize his
leadership which, after all, was sanctioned by Hitler.[45]

The primary method of spreading National Socialism in
Baden was at first the closed party meeting (Sprechabend).
These meetings converted racist clubs into Nazi locals and
introduced potential new members to the ideology of National
Socialism.[46] The most active speakers between 1925 and 1928
were Wagner, August Kramer, Karl Lenz, Friedhelm Kemper,

Walter Köhler, and Albert Roth, the rural expert of the party.
The focus of the propaganda drives, at least as revealed in
the party papers, was on the large urban and middle-sized communities of northern Baden. In addition, Albert Roth, Karl
Lenz, and August Kramer (and later Wagner) carried the party's
message to the farmers as early as 1925.[47] The party drew the
largest audiences in administrative and academic communities
like Karlsruhe and Heidelberg and in small communities like
Eberbach. In mid-1926 the Baden Nazis were even able to attract six hundred party members to a meeting held in the rural,
traditional right-wing community of Eichtersheim. On the
whole, however, the intensive party propaganda attracted few
visitors that year, and the Baden police concluded that National
Socialism's appeal in Baden was negligible.[48]

The party's main message in 1925/26 was a violent anti-
Semitism, combined with traditional völkisch rhetoric on
Versailles, banks, and "Marxist lies." Anti-Semitism always
played a primary importance in 1925/26 as Wagner and his
assistants attempted to expand the party and create new locals.
Wagner told the Mannheim local in November 1925 that the "Jewish race was the source of all ills of its host nation," while
national Nazi agitators like Arthur Dinter presented speeches
in 1925 on "the international world plague" and "the disgust-
ing activities of the Jewish poisoners of humanity." This
theme changed little in 1927 whether it was presented to an
urban audience, where the Jews were identified with Marxism,
or to a small rural community, where Jews were presented as
the traditional moneylenders. Gradually, in 1927 the Jews
were no longer painted merely as exploiters of farmers and
workers but also increasingly of the Mittelstand. The party's
propaganda began to shift attention to the "Jewish department

stores."[49]

The party's message, according to police reports and party membership figures, had limited effect in Baden in 1925/27. In fact, it presented Wagner with the problem of maintaining the party's identity since numerous völkisch clubs and organizations in Baden held similar views. Many of these völkisch groups were attracted to the Nazi meetings, and the police noted that party meetings were attended by representatives from the Frontkriegerbund and the Wehrwolf.[50] Even as early as 1925, some Baden Nazi locals had joined with paramilitary and veterans' groups to celebrate Hitler's birthday. In Freiburg, the party had established a völkisch library and invited all fatherland clubs to collaborate in the creation of a Greater Germany.[51] In order to prevent the Nazi party from being drowned in this sea of völkisch organizations, Wagner moved energetically against Nazis who had established local völkisch clubs. In 1925/26 various party members had created such organizations as the Treubund Schlageter and the Vorposten. The Gauleiter lost no time in warning party members that these movements had nothing to do with the NSDAP. Wagner also prevented any Nazi association with more powerful right-wing parties during election campaigns. When the Nazi city council member of Durlach voted with the right-wing coalition in 1926, he was expelled from the party.[52]

Wagner's determination to prevent the Nazi party from becoming a spoke on the völkisch wheel enabled the Baden party to absorb much of the völkisch energy of the state. By 1927, many of the völkisch leagues were attracted to either the Nazi party or the Stahlhelm. For example, when Hitler took a stand against the Rossbach organization, the Karlsruhe local of that group dissolved itself and joined the NSDAP. Later in 1927, both the Baden leader of the Wehrwolf, Volkert Rühle, and the Gau leader of the Frontkriegerbund, Friedrich Berlinger, joined the Nazi party. Commenting on a speech by Franz Seldte, the leader of the Stahlhelm, in Karlsruhe in December 1927, Der Führer concluded that Seldte's themes had been articulated much more effectively by Hitler. Above all, the Baden party paper noted that the Stahlhelm's methods could not bring victory since paramilitary actions were now outdated. After 1927, the Baden party boycotted rival völkisch speakers, particularly those who supported Ludendorff. By the end of 1927, the Baden NSDAP had clearly opted for the political struggle, and it declared confidently that the Nazi party was the only völkisch party in Baden.[53]

The reactivation of Nazi locals in 1925 and Wagner's offensive against the various völkisch clubs were only two aspects of the Gau leadership's tasks in 1925/26. The Gau clique also had to win control over the various party leaders and activists in the state. Wagner held his first conference with Baden's local and SA leaders after he was released from jail in August 1925. Munich sent Dr. Buttmann to support Wagner's quest for leadership. Much more important was the party conference held in Karlsruhe in October 1926. Wagner used this meeting to exclude the general membership from most of the decision-making powers. On 2 October 1926, the local and district leaders discussed the major problems of organization, finance, propaganda, the SA, and municipal elections. The following day, all party members gathered in a general assembly to hear Gottfried Feder's speech, "Volksstaat or the Rule of Banks?" The important decisions, however, had been made already. Indeed, the Völkischer Beobachter boasted that "due to the elimination of parliamentary discussion methods, the conference was concluded in a short time."[54]

The basic format of subsequent state conferences did
not change significantly. The state conferences met more frequently, and more party functionaries attended the meetings,
reflecting the expanding party organization. In 1928, for
example, three leadership conferences were scheduled. The
most important topics and party departments were controlled
by the Gau clique. This included the topics of finances,
business affairs, organization, and press and propaganda.
By 1928, the Gau leadership told the local and district leaders which policies and strategies they had to pursue. The
basic guidelines were established by Wagner with the assistance of his loyal Gau staff and then forwarded to the party
leaders.[55]

The Gau party's centralization was also reflected on
the local and district levels. Initially, local members had
elected and removed local leaders in general membership meetings. In November 1927, there were still Baden locals in
which the local leader and his assistants were elected by the
general membership. By late 1928, on the other hand, many
local leaders were not only appointed by district leaders
but in turn appointed the local functionaries.[56] In the large
urban centers of Baden, few strong local leaders emerged to
challenge the Gau's leadership primarily because of the instability of the urban leadership corps. Pforzheim had five
different local leaders between 1925 and 1928, while Mannheim
claimed three during the same period.[57] Only in the smaller
communities, where social mobility was more restricted, was
there greater continuity of leadership. These small and rural
locals, however, never posed a threat to Wagner and his Gau
clique.[58]

District leaders emerged in Baden as early as 1925. In Mannheim the district leader was elected by a district party conference that was attended by all local leaders. In the district of Karlsruhe, one of the most active district leaders of the Gau appeared as early as 1925. Albert Roth was an able agitator with a long record of völkisch activism. There is no evidence that Roth was ever elected or appointed to this office in 1925. It is most likely that Roth simply assumed the post and proceeded to help establish many rural and small-town locals in the district of Karlsruhe. As a former Landbund leader, he had the "connections" to establish his position. By 1926, he was strong enough to scold local leaders for not distributing Nazi newspapers. But Roth never challenged Wagner's leadership. First, Roth was too preoccupied with propaganda to pay much attention to administrative duties. In April 1926, he appointed Willi Worch as his assistant. One year later Willi Worch had replaced Roth as district leader of Karlsruhe. Second, Wagner saved Roth in late 1927 and early 1928 from a party court decision that would have terminated Roth's party career. Wagner made it clear to Munich that the Liedolsheim Nazi was too valuable to the party's rural propaganda drive to be sacrificed to the party court system.[59]

Gradually, in 1927 Wagner began to appoint district leaders. By 1928, most of the Gau's twenty-two district leaders were also the local leaders of the major urban centers of their districts. This reflected the growing centralization of the party structure and the erosion of local power. As Wagner gained more control over the district leaders, they in turn exercised more influence over the local leaders and the members of the Baden locals.[60] As the party became larger and more impersonal, the old <u>völkisch</u> activists were gradually being diluted by new converts who were more willing to follow than to lead.

ELECTIONS AND PROPAGANDA

In regard to voter appeal and membership expansion the Baden party represented only a small fringe of the political life of Baden. Between 1925 and mid-1927, the number of party locals in Gau Baden increased only from thirty-one to forty units (see Map 5). The growth of the party was particularly slow in 1925/26. Many locals were only temporary structures, collapsing after a few months. Often a local would vanish after its founder left the community. This instability is also revealed in a casual examination of locals listed in the <u>Völkischer Beobachter</u>. Of ten Baden locals noted in the paper in 1926, four had disappeared by July 1927.[61]

The same slow growth can be observed in the party's membership. In late 1926, only six hundred party members attended the general party conference in Karlsruhe. Some of these members may have come from other states since Hitler had urged non-Baden party members to attend the Karlsruhe meeting to bolster the image of the Baden party. The small rural local of Eggenstein near Karlsruhe had emerged in 1924 as a local of the <u>Deutsche Partei</u>. By December 1926, Eggenstein still claimed only six party members. Similarly, the local of Eberbach had been founded by thirty supporters in 1924; two years later the membership was the same.[62] Obviously, the return of political and economic stability after 1923 did little to nourish the Nazi movement in Baden.

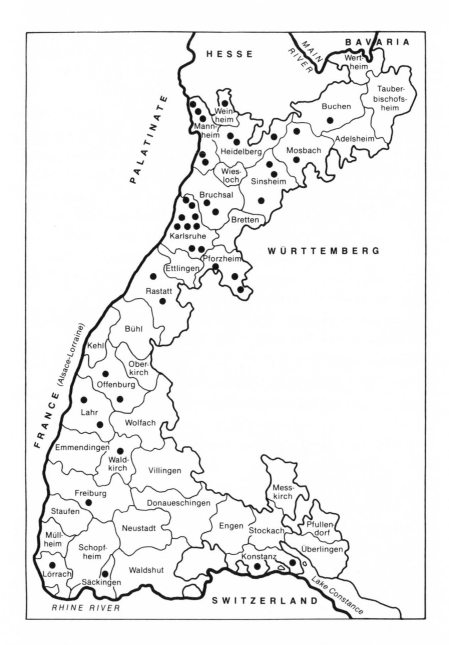

Map 5. *Nazi Locals in Baden: 8 July 1927* (According to NSDAP records)

The party's struggle in a hostile environment can be clearly illustrated by an examination of its election campaigns in 1925/26. During the presidential campaign of 1925, the Baden party was not sufficiently well organized to play a significant role. In March 1925, Ludendorff won only 513 votes in Baden. He did fare well, however, in the völkisch strongholds of Baden. During the second presidential election in April 1925, the Nazis campaigned for Hindenburg. As was to be expected, Hindenburg ran strongly in the DNVP and Landbund strongholds of Baden like Kehl, Bretten, Sinsheim, and Wertheim.[63] But these districts did not turn to the NSDAP until 1928. The election did create a Nazi martyr when party members, campaigning in Durlach on 25 April, were met by Reichsbanner men under the leadership of a union official and an off-duty police officer, Otto Reitze. In the ensuing fight, the policeman shot and killed the young Nazi apprentice Friedrich Kröber.[64]

The first major election campaign waged by the Nazis of Baden occurred during the state election of 25 October 1925. Beginning in September, the Völkischer Beobachter began to publish notices by local party leaders who urged their members to attend election meetings. On 4 October, a Gau leadership conference was held in Ettlingen, which issued the statement that the Baden party was "completely united" on the party's participation in the coming election.[65] The ensuing campaign in Baden focused primarily on national issues and specifically on the Locarno settlement. Major national political leaders such as Stresemann, Philipp Scheidemann, and Wilhelm Marx visited Baden to discuss Locarno. The Baden party naturally dealt with these national issues while continuing its attack on Jews. But the NSDAP also knew that it would have little

effect on the outcome of the election. Walter Köhler, the
local leader of Weinheim, admitted frankly in the Völkischer
Beobachter that the Nazis did not expect this election to
make the slightest contribution to the "liberation" of Germany.
Köhler reminded his readers that the party needed the "whole
man" and not just votes. The major Baden parties also neglected the Nazi party and focused instead on the dangers of the
Rechtsblock which was composed of the Nationalists and the
Landbund. Even the Socialist paper Volksfreund, which did
notice the activities of the Nazis, dismissed them as representatives of political stupidity.[66]

Only 55 percent of the electorate participated in the
October election, a fact condemned by most of the newspapers
of Baden. Despite this low voter participation, the Social-
ist-Catholic coalition maintained its clear majority in the
legislature. The Rechtsblock declined from 14 to 9 seats,
while the Communists retained only 4 seats in the legislature.
The various splinter parties, including the NSDAP, won no
seats. Since the strongest splinter party had won only 8,817
votes, the Frankfurter Zeitung had good cause to conclude
that there was no reason to change the "proven government
majority in Baden."[67]

Later Wagner admitted that the election of 1925 had been
a defeat for the new party (see Map 6). The Nazi party with
its 8,817 votes (1.2 percent) barely led its major völkisch
rival, the DVFP, which had won 6,420 votes (.8 percent). The
DVFP's list of candidates reflected a much more "respectable"
image than did the Nazi party list. Almost half of the DVFP's
candidates were civil servants and professionals (including
three lawyers and three doctors) compared to 13.5 percent for
the Nazi list. On the other hand, over 70 percent of the Nazi

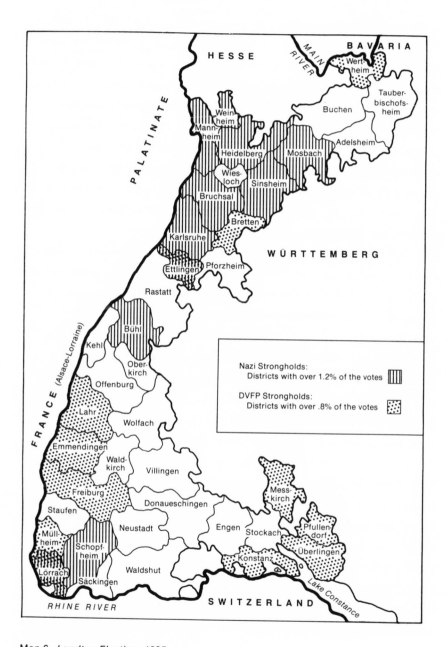

Map 6. *Landtag Election: 1925*

party's candidates were artisans, workers, craftsmen, and white-collar employees, while the DVFP's list contained only 34 percent from these same occupations. The DNVP's election themes, however, were similar to those of the Nazi party since both parties appealed to the traditional völkisch voter. Although the DVFP was strong in rural Wertheim and Bretten in northern Baden, it was much stronger than the Nazi party in southern Baden and proportionally it won more of its votes in the large urban centers than the Nazi party. The DVFP won 59 percent of its votes in urban centers with populations over ten thousand while the NSDAP won only 42 percent of its votes in those cities. The Baden voters cast 41 percent of their votes in these cities. The Nazi party was strongest in northern Baden, in both medium-sized cities and small rural communities with populations ranging between two thousand and ten thousand people.[68] Baden's moderate newspapers noted with satisfaction the weak showing of the völkisch parties and concluded that 2 percent divided between two parties was politically meaningless.[69]

The party's weak electoral showing and the close correlation between völkisch true believers, völkisch strongholds, and völkisch votes becomes even more clear when the Baden party's record in the municipal elections of November 1926 is examined. The Baden party vigorously contested both Socialist and Nationalist rallies by stressing economic ills and the Dawes Plan.[70] But the municipal election results again confirmed the party's weakness outside its völkisch strongholds or centers of activity. The Socialist and Center parties maintained their strengths while the economic interest parties drained voters away from the Democratic party. The Nazis received a total of only 847 votes in four of the sixteen

major urban centers with populations over 10,000. The party
won municipal positions in only ten Baden communities, all
in northern Baden. Three of these towns (Bruchsal, Durlach,
and Weinheim) had populations over 10,000, but they were not
the major urban and industrial centers of Baden. Only two
of the ten communities (Bruchsal and Ziegelhausen) had Catholic
majorities. Seven towns in which the Nazis won municipal seats
were small, rural Protestant communities with populations between 781 and 6,200. In all of these rural Protestant towns,
völkisch activists had been strong as early as 1923, and Nazi
locals or strongholds existed in 1926.[71]

The Baden party had to face, not only the resistance of
most of the Badenese during these formative years, but also
the hostility of the Baden government. Between 1925 and early
1927 Minister of Interior Remmele successfully controlled the
excesses of both the Communists and the Nazis in Baden. Threats
against the government, insults directed at leading statesmen,
and the carrying of weapons led immediately to arrest. According to police reports, the future of the Nazi party in 1926
did not look very bright. The völkisch ideology and the financial problems of the Nazi party in Baden threatened to condemn
it to the role of a perennial völkisch splinter group.[72] In
early 1927, Wagner attempted to invigorate the Baden party by
publishing an announcement in the Südwestdeutscher Beobachter,
demanding that party members devote themselves completely
to the movement or get out of the party. Later in the spring,
he also demanded that locals end the practice of having only
closed meetings and instead hold at least one monthly public
rally. The new direction charted by Wagner produced a more
active public propaganda and the organizational and geographic
expansion of the party in late 1927 and early 1928.[73]

When Wagner emphasized the party's public propaganda in early 1927, the Baden party was about to realize one of its most ardent desires—the public appearance of Hitler in Baden. Numerous national leaders, including Gregor Strasser, Paul Josef Goebbels, Gottfried Feder, and Hermann Esser had visited Baden between 1925 and 1927. All attempted to help the party win supporters, particularly in the urban areas of northern Baden.[74] But until 21 April 1927, the government had refused to grant Hitler permission to speak in Baden. Party members had circumvented this restriction in 1926 and early 1927 by participating in Hitler rallies in neighboring Württemberg.[75] Hitler finally came to Heidelberg and Eberbach in August and November 1927. Between March and April 1928, he appeared again in Heidelberg, Karlsruhe, and Pforzheim to campaign for the Baden party during the national election. Not until 23 November 1928 did Hitler address a rally in Mannheim, Baden's largest urban center. Hitler's themes, presented to the Baden audiences between 1927 and 1928, varied little. In August 1927, he informed a Heidelberg audience that "Aryans" had achieved culture only through constant struggle. A healthy people needed living space, and Hitler admitted frankly that Germans had to acquire this space through force. His subsequent speeches in Baden usually emphasized this same racist expansionism, united with a plea for the union of mental and physical workers to enable Germany to achieve internal peace. Hitler's message to the Badenese focused on inflated German nationalism and potential expansion, achieved by a socially cohesive but not equal "Aryan" body.[76]

According to the political police of Baden, Hitler's speeches in 1927 seemed not to have any permanent impact or produce an enlarged membership. There is no question that

Hitler's speeches did not elevate the Baden party automatically
to a position of strength. In the election of May 1928, the
Baden party did not do well in the major urban centers where
Hitler had appeared in 1927/28. But the Hitler rallies attracted huge audiences, something the Baden party had not been
able to do earlier. The Baden party benefited financially by
charging admission to the rallies. In addition, large numbers
of people in Baden were subjected to Hitler's message for the
first time. Only with deteriorating economic and political
conditions, however, did Hitler's message become palatable
to the Baden masses.[77]

Another major innovation in reaching the Baden population and in creating an information vehicle for an expanding
party was a new party paper. In 1925 the Baden party had to
rely, for the most part, on the Völkischer Beobachter for
party information and communications. One year later, Wagner
made an agreement with the neighboring Gau Württemberg to
publish jointly the weekly paper Südwestdeutscher Beobachter.
The paper was edited and published in Stuttgart by Josef Geiger,
an ethnic German from the Crimea. Wagner and Ludwig Ankenbrand
in Karlsruhe were responsible for issues and information pertaining to the Baden party. Because of its violent anti-Semitism and constant insulting of government officials, the paper
was in perpetual legal and financial difficulties in 1926/27.
The Baden party could ill afford the fines imposed by both
Baden and Württemberg courts.[78]

In late 1927, as the party began to grow and as the national elections in the spring of 1928 approached, Wagner decided
to establish his own Gau paper. On 5 November 1927, the first
issue of Der Führer, a weekly, was issued. Karl Lenz, the
deputy Gau leader, had estimated that the Gau would have to

sell at least 1,200 copies of the paper in November to remain
financially solvent. The first issue sold only 446 copies.
Advertisements at first were either free or frequently not paid.
Not until 1929 did the paper become economically viable. In
late 1927, Wagner ordered the locals of the major urban centers
of the Gau to organize street sales. The party issued constant admonitions reminding party members that every Nazi voter
must become a reader of the Nazi press. But between November
1927 and the spring of 1928, the _Führer_ editions rose only
from 446 to 800 copies. Since street sales were not very successful in 1927 and 1928, the paper was distributed mostly
to party members who used it to obtain party information.
It may also have aided in the dissemination of propaganda to
völkisch sympathizers. Little wonder that in 1928, in terms
of percentage, most papers were sold in the district of Eberbach, a hotbed of Nazi activities. In terms of actual numbers
sold, Karlsruhe was in first place.[79]

Type was set in Wagner's apartment and then carried by
train to Bretten and later to Bruchsal to be printed. Only
after June 1928 was the paper composed and printed in Karlsruhe.
The staff of the paper consisted of Wagner, Franz Moraller,
and Ludwig Ankenbrand. Among the honorary members of the
staff were Otto Wacker, Walter Köhler, and Karl Lenz. All
were trusted friends and co-workers of Wagner, and all, except
for Köhler, had been active in the Nazi movement as early as
1923.[80] Wagner decided to permit the members of the Gau
clique to write the leading article for the first edition.
Franz Moraller's draft, which became the leading article of
the paper, accused the Socialists of protecting "finance Jews."
The battle, declared Moraller, was directed against the "Marxist swindle." Jews, of course, were selected as the major

culprits who had created Germany's ills. This first issue of
the Führer initiated a journalistic style that varied little
after 1927 and which has best been characterized by Oron J.
Hale as "violent in language . . . filled with the wildest and
meanest diatribes, poisonous, bitter. . . . These Gau smear
sheets could have been the work of juvenile delinquents."
These violent and irresponsible attacks on Jews and alleged
Jewish corruption resulted in constant legal battles and
frequently forced the Führer to publish retractions.[81] But
the nature of these attacks and innuendoes did not vary much.

  Wagner's decision in early 1927 to focus the party's
energies on public propaganda was absolutely essential for
the party's efforts to break the narrow völkisch boundaries.
The party not only began to offer more public rallies, but
by the end of 1927 it had also established a newspaper. This
new party activism resulted in the expansion of locals and
a moderate increase in the total membership. It did not, however, convert the NSDAP into a mass movement. The party first
had to find a socioeconomic message that appealed to a larger
segment of society than the old völkisch appeal. Only the
deteriorating agricultural situation provided the Baden Nazis
with the opportunity to transcend these völkisch limits.

4 The Party's Social Appeals and the Rural Breakthrough, 1925-1928

THE PARTY'S APPEAL TO WORKERS

The party's decision in early 1927 to focus its energies on
public propaganda required more than Wagner's order to hold
more public rallies or the creation of a party newspaper.
Above all, the Nazis had to appeal to the specific interests
of the various socioeconomic segments of Baden society. Simultaneously, the party had to decide whether it wanted to become
a people's party (Volkspartei), which appealed to all classes,
or focus its attentions on one segment of society.

In 1920/21, the Baden party had emerged in the urban
centers of the state with the primary objective of converting
workers to the völkisch ideology in order to reverse the decision of 1918. This imperative was continued in 1925 both by
visiting "leftists" of the Nazi party from northern Germany
and by native Badenese, all calling for a national socialism.
Pamphlets issued by the Baden Nazis appealed directly to
Communists and Socialists. In speeches delivered to urban
and rural audiences, the prominent party leaders of Gau Baden
accused the state of protecting the "capitalist system of
exploitation." Even "rural" Nazis like Albert Roth actively
appealed to the workers. In an address to unemployed workers
in Heidelberg in 1926, he declared that "if the worker
doesn't come to us, we will go to him."[1] These attempts by

the Nazis to win the support of labor were noted with appre-
hension by the Communists. A Communist party leadership conference in Heidelberg in April 1926 pointed to the potential
danger of the unemployed Lumpenproletariat becoming susceptible
to the fascist propaganda. The NSDAP was identified by the
Communist party of Baden as one of the six most dangerous right-
wing groups in their appeal to the proletariat. The Communist
leadership was particularly alarmed after it discovered that
individual Nazis had established contacts with Kommunistische
Partei Deutschlands (KPD) members.[2]

The Baden Nazis used two techniques in their attempts to
pry the worker away from the Marxist parties. First, the Baden
party attempted to use anti-Semitism as the tool to convince
workers to abandon international Marxism, which was merely a
"Jewish liberal philosophy" allegedly controlled by Jews. Karl
Lenz, the deputy Gau leader and one of the party's best and
most fanatic agitators, visited Communist meetings and told
the assembled workers that Lenin was the last true Communist;
the rest were now all Jews.[3] Second, the Baden party utilized
former Socialist and Communist party members who had become
Nazis to convince the workers of the value of National Socialism. Franz Tritschler, the local leader of Freiburg and a
former Socialist, went to the local union hall to tell labor
the "truth," and another former Communist lectured about union
questions at party meetings. The Baden party was particularly
enthusiastic in reporting the occasional election of a party
member to the position of shop steward. And even after the
Baden party started to emphasize the plight of the Mittelstand
in late 1927 it continued its labor propaganda. In particular,
the party persisted in utilizing former Socialists and Communists in meetings which addressed the issue of "Workers and

National Socialism."[4]

The Nazi party's appeal to the worker's anti-Semitism
and the use of former Marxists as Nazi agitators did little
to draw the workers away from the Marxist parties. In some
cases, notorious Communist bickerers who were used by the Baden
party probably only hurt the Nazi cause. This was the case
with Hermann Friedrich, the most famous Marxist convert to
National Socialism in Baden during its formative period. He
was born in Esslingen, Württemberg, on 4 May 1901, to a father
who had been in the Social Democratic party (SPD) for most of
his adult life. A butcher by training, Hermann Friedrich
also joined the SPD in 1908 and remained in the party until
1923, when he joined the Communist party. Three years later,
he had broken with the Communists and had attracted the attention of the Gau leader of Württemberg-Hohenzollern, who recommended Friedrich to Munich.[5] After Friedrich joined the NSDAP
in 1927, he published a propaganda pamphlet, "From Hammer and
Sickle to the Swastika" (which was ordered by Wagner for all
Baden party locals), and he campaigned actively for the Baden
Nazis until August 1929. Then he broke with the party and
went on the counterattack with a new pamphlet, "Under the
Swastika," in which he tried to show the worker the new "truth"
about Nazis and the Baden party's corruption. Friedrich now
focused all of his venom on the "pretentious school masters"
who ran the Baden NSDAP.[6]

How genuine was this labor appeal on the part of the Gau
party leadership? It was clearly more than an opportunistic
attempt to win supporters, since the labor appeal alienated
potential converts who objected to the party's title of "worker
party." But this was rejected by Nazi activists like Albert
Roth, who made it clear in the Völkischer Beobachter in late

1928 that anyone afraid of the word "worker" was too immature
for the NSDAP. In addition, in May 1928, three of the six
Baden candidates for the Reichstag election were workers and
artisans, and two had belonged to the Socialist party.[7] Most
important, Gau leader Wagner vehemently supported the Handarbeiter (manual worker: industrial or artisan) Nazi over the
bourgeois Nazi. He detested intellectuals who relied on cold
reason rather than on the powers of the soul and body. In a
choice between two Nazis, one a manual worker and the other a
bourgeois, Wagner made it clear that he would choose the Nazi
with a working-class background. To Wagner, this type of
Nazi was a better and more effective fighter for the implementation of the Nazi Weltanschauung.[8] Wagner's support of
the manual laborer was based not on any socioeconomic theory
but rather on a utilitarian evaluation of who would be a more
effective Nazi. To Wagner the term Handarbeiter did not merely
mean industrial worker but rather anyone who was not an intellectual. It included artisans, craftsmen, and workers.

THE PARTY'S RURAL OFFENSIVE

The most persistent social appeal articulated by the Nazi party
in Baden was directed toward the farmer. Historians who
have focused on the national party organization have failed to
see this early effort in rural areas. They argue that National
Socialism originated in the urban areas and that until the
party shifted its appeal in 1928 (or until the emergence of
Walther Darré as the party's rural expert), the party was repugnant to much of the rural population.[9] These generalizations totally ignore the spontaneous, grass-roots origins of

National Socialism on the rural level. Baden's rural areas
had seen a variety of right-wing organizations before 1923
that promised to provide protection against potential Communist upheavals in the countryside. As early as 1920/21,
many rural Protestant districts in Baden provided the right-
wing Nationalists and Landbund with substantial support during
elections. In October 1922, the secretary of the Baden Center
party informed his fellow Badenese in Berlin, Chancellor Wirth,
that the "first recession would play into the hands of right-
wing radicals and enable them to stir up trouble in the countryside."[10] And it was in such rural völkisch centers of northern Baden as Liedolsheim that the Nazis continuously spread
the völkisch message to an agricultural population that was
beginning to feel the impact of deteriorating economic conditions.

In 1912 a report on rural debts in one Baden area concluded that the welfare of agriculture was so assured that
even a catastrophic year would not affect the prosperity of
farmers. There was little reason to question this finding,
since there was no shortage of capital, and loans could be
obtained by farmers for 4.5 percent (or even cheaper). Unfortunately, the war and the postwar era brought significant
dislocations to Baden's agriculture. The state's rural problems grew noticeably after the stabilization of the currency
in 1924 and the end of Germany's worst inflation. As early
as 1925/26, the state's professional agricultural journal,
the Badisches Landwirtschaftliches Wochenblatt, called attention to the völkisch Artamanen organization that was advocating
rural settlements in eastern Germany. In particular, the
Wochenblatt noted the rising rural debt in Baden in early
1926. And most devastating, the interest rates after 1925

were twice as high as before 1914. With high interest rates,
rising prices for industrial goods, and declining agricultural
prices, rural organizations as early as 1925/26 began to demand
cheap credit, protection from foreign competition, and a reduction of taxes.[11]

These economic problems were complicated by the failure
of farmers to heed the advice of their rural specialists.
Despite constant warnings by these specialists not to overpro-
duce, farmers continued to expand production until 1928/29.
For example, when hop prices reached a peak in 1926, farmers
increased production. Indeed, between 1925 and 1929 German
farmers raised production by one third. Consequently, prices
for hops dropped to 65 RM per Zentner (110 pounds), far below
production costs of 100 and 130 RM. A similar situation arose
in the tobacco industry, which affected Baden greatly since
half of Germany's tobacco was grown in that state. In 1927/28,
Baden's tobacco farmers were warned not to grow too much because the market could not absorb it. Despite this warning,
Baden farmers increased production in the spring of 1928 by
400 hectares over 1927. The experts had recommended a reduction of 20 percent. Finally, by early 1928 the German government had to intercede and purchase products (such as hogs)
at higher prices to prevent complete economic catastrophe in
agriculture.[12]

The rural crisis was clearly felt in Baden by early 1928.
Baden farmers cut production and harvested less in 1929, re-
versing the steady increase between 1925 and 1928. By the
summer of 1928 the Baden government had to introduce an emergency long-term loan (at 6.5 percent) to allow farmers to
meet their obligations and continue operations.[13] A special
commission also examined Baden's rural debts in the summer of

1928. The report, which focused on thirty-seven rural communities, was concluded in 1929 and then presented to the state
legislature. The study was based on communities that represented the diverse economic and geographic regions of the
state and included 8,543 farms, of which 4,141 were operated
by full-time farmers who were not employed in industry. The
statistical information was obtained from banks, city clerks,
and local informants. The report found that 43 percent of the
farmers were indebted. Interest rates varied between 5 and
13 percent, but most farmers paid from 9 to 13 percent. The
indebtedness per hectare ranged from 1,605 RM for farms under
two hectares to 457 RM for those between five and ten hectares.
The report also concluded that only three communities faced
severe economic problems, while six others had some problems
(bedenklich). But the biggest difficulties faced by all farmers were the high interest rates combined with falling agricultural prices.[14]

The deteriorating economic realities in the countryside
became more than evident in early 1928 when mass rallies were
held in Baden by farmers who pleaded with the Baden government
to provide aid and, in particular, to restrict meat imports
from France. Baden's rural organizations, from the rural
political parties to the political agricultural chambers,
called for special rallies in Karlsruhe to protest the collapse
of Baden's agriculture. Agricultural representatives from
southern Germany finally met Reich officials in Berlin in
April 1928 to plead for lower taxes, a reduction in imports,
and long-term credit.[15] The radicalization of the rural population was a reality by early 1928 and only became more extreme with time. Ultimately, Baden farmers reacted with violence. In 1932 over twelve hundred farmers near Pforzheim

threatened the police, who attempted to collect rural debts
by putting a farmer's cattle up for sale.[16]

The farmers' difficulties obviously did not go unnoticed.
But long before the Nazis began to win the support of Protestant
farmers in the election of 1928, there were several political
parties and interest groups that actively courted and claimed
to speak for farmers in Baden. The most active and for a time
the most successful was the Baden Rechtsblock, which was composed of the Nationalists (DNVP) and the Agrarian League
(Landbund). The DNVP had emerged in rural, Protestant districts (in addition to its urban strongholds) as early as the
election of 1919. Then in 1921 it had to compete with the
Landbund for rural, Protestant votes. The Landbund of Baden
emerged from two roots. First, in 1919, two thousand members
of the Bund der Landwirte established the Baden Bauernbund
in Bretten to support the DNVP in the election of 1919. Second, in Freiburg another organization, the Badische Bauernbund,
emerged to support the German People's party in the north and
the German Democratic party in the south. Although predominantly Protestant, it also had some Catholic support. In
January 1921, the two interest groups merged to form the Baden
Landbund. The organization initially had a membership of
forty thousand and was led by DNVP activists. In 1925, the
Agrarian League and the DNVP joined in an election alliance
which lasted until the election of 1928.[17] The purpose of
the Rechtsblock was to represent the conservative and antirepublican forces in Baden's cities and rural communities.

Both the Landbund and the Rechtsblock carried out a vigorous campaign among farmers in the countryside, and rural
interests were represented formally by the Landbund. The
Rechtsblock, no doubt, helped prepare the way for the Nazis

by radicalizing the traditionally conservative farmers.   In
early 1925 the Landbund delegates demanded a 6 percent interest
rate for farmers to alleviate the hardship in agriculture.
These demands were repeated in the legislature by the Rechtsblock delegates after the state election of October 1925.   As
early as November 1925, the Rechtsblock demanded protection for
domestic agriculture and relief for the "catastrophic" situation in the countryside.[18]   Even more dramatic, Landbund delegates like Fritz Hagin (who supported the Nazis in 1930/31)
led major protest rallies of up to twenty-five hundred people
in southern Protestant districts as early as 1926 to protest
taxes and the farmers' and Mittelstand's economic problems.[19]
Many of the DNVP election pamphlets, at times, sounded like
Nazi propaganda.   One Nationalist leaflet, circulating during
the May 1928 election campaign, called the farmer the nation's
backbone and fountain of youth.   It also demanded protection
for agricultural goods and lower interest and tax rates.
These themes were quite similar to the Nazi party's rural
rhetoric.[20]

In 1928, the DNVP and the Landbund faced internal crises
that eventually fragmented the political strength of both
parties.   Although both movements had helped to radicalize
the farmer, in 1928 many farmers who voted for the Nazis blamed
the DNVP for their economic difficulties since it had participated in national coalition governments.   The Landbund leadership still fought the Nazi party vigorously in early 1928 and
even accused the Nazis of being Communists in disguise.   But
its strength was dissipating rapidly.   First, more and more
Landbund members were joining the Nazi party.   Some of these
converts had advocated Nazi penetration of the Landbund as
early as 1927.   In addition, several well-known Landbund

leaders started joining the Nazi party in 1927/28. Finally,
the Landbund fragmented in May 1928 into three camps.[21] By
1930 the original membership of forty thousand had declined
to twenty thousand members. One year later, the Badische
Bauernpartei (Landbund) delegation in the Landtag dissolved
itself, with two of its delegates joining the Nazi delegation
and one joining the Zentrum delegation. Most of the former
northern and southern Protestant Landbund supporters ended
up in the Nazi camp. Only a few of the southern Catholic
Landbund members turned to the large Catholic Bauernverein.[22]

In addition to the Landbund and DNVP, the other major
"bourgeois" party that courted the farmer's vote persistently
in Baden was the German Democratic Party (DDP). Although it
could never compete with the irresponsible rhetoric of the
Rechtsblock and Nazis, the DDP was very much interested in
the support of Baden's rural population. As early as 1920,
the party's journal, Der Demokrat, published a series of
articles on rural problems and issues that affected the rural
Mittelstand. By 1925, the journal was demanding tax reform,
an end to land speculation, and even the initiation of settlement programs. In that same year, the national party organization created an agricultural committee to enlighten the
farmer about the DDP and to help the party itself understand
rural questions by formulating an agrarian program. This emphasis on rural issues, from taxes to tariffs to the cost of
fertilizer, remained constant themes in the Demokrat.[23]

The leader of the DDP in Baden after 1925, Hermann
Dietrich, was also very interested in the farmer. As early
as February 1927, in a letter to a friend, this former mayor
of Kehl wrote that he hoped he had instilled in the Baden
DDP a strong interest in the problems and issues of agriculture.

In the summer of 1928 he also became Reich minister for agriculture (until March 1930). When the DDP congress met in Karlsruhe in June 1929, it accepted the boastful resolution that "under Dietrich, for the first time a real Bauernpolitik will be implemented."[24] But Dietrich's rational approach to the problems of agriculture could no longer compete with that of the Nazis. He attempted to take the battle for agriculture out of the political arena by setting up market institutes and agricultural schools. In a radio address in late 1928, he explained the rural problems by focusing on the impact of the war, overproduction, and the credit issue. He pointed out that these roots left little room for major changes. Instead, farmers needed to cooperate and help themselves. In 1930, in a letter to the Baden tobacco guild he justified his refusal to remove the tax on tobacco by stating that "We cannot solve the reparation's problem unless we prove that we burden our people indirectly as much as the Entente states."[25] This rational approach had little chance after 1928 in the battle to capture the support of the radicalized rural voter.

In addition to the rural interest organizations and middle-class parties in Baden, the Marxist parties also attempted to establish rural bases. Obviously, the Socialists penetrated rural communities like Liedolsheim where a segment of the population was engaged in some type of industrial work (outside Liedolsheim). For example, in 1925 the SPD had ten party members in this small community, and by 1928 the membership had expanded to thirty-three. But on the whole, the Socialists failed to organize an effective rural campaign. In 1925, Remmele, the Socialist minister of interior, admitted that agriculture needed help but not at the expense of other segments of society. During the state election

campaign in late 1929, Remmele lectured on "Socialism and
Agriculture" by presenting a sobering, statistical analysis of
the rural problems and reminding his audience that a large
percentage of industrial workers, who were also truck farmers,
had agricultural interests. Remmele's speech, like the party's rural message in general, lacked both the spirit and
content that could attract a radicalized rural population.[26]

The Communists, on the other hand, had an active rural
program as early as 1926 when they called for the union of
workers and poor farmers in Baden and neighboring Württemberg.
In early 1927, the Baden KPD leadership, noting the radicalization of farmers, reflected on the party's lack of success
in rural areas. The Baden KPD concluded that its weakness
stemmed first from a shortage of rural party members, along
with a lack of organization in rural areas, and second from
a failure to understand the need to work with the small,
marginal farmer.[27] One organization the KPD tried to rely
on as early as 1926 was the Badische Pächter- und Kleinbauern-
verband, which was led by Richard Bürgi of Freiburg. This
organization had a total of 110 locals and seven thousand
members before the Communists gained control of the leadership. Bürgi issued a leaflet in 1926 that called for help
to leaseholders and small and medium-sized farmers. The
leaflet also demanded lower taxes, lower interest rates (4
percent), and lower prices for industrial goods that farmers
had to purchase.[28]

Despite this "rural" rhetoric, the Bürgi organization
was too closely tied to the Communist party to win the farmers' support. Bürgi won a seat in the Freiburg city council
when a Communist representative resigned. But when he attempted to win seats for his organization in the state's

agricultural chambers, all rural organizations from the Catholic Bauernverein to the Landbund attacked Bürgi as a Communist
and pointed out that farmers in Russia (1929) were being destroyed. And these organizations never failed to mention that
Bürgi had twice been to Russia. As early as 1927 Bürgi noted
the disintegration of his organization. By that year the
Bauern- und Pächterbund had only fifteen locals but huge debts
and a tottering newspaper. Although Bürgi tried to breathe
new life into the organization by calling it Badischer
Bauernbund and issuing a paper entitled Badischer Bauern-
anzeiger to emphasize the rural nature of the organization,
he was not successful. The Badischer Bauern- und Pächterbund
failed to run in the 1928 and 1929 elections, and by 1932
small-worker-farmer parties won only an insignificant number
of votes. The Baden farmer was much too suspicious of Bürgi's
Communist connections to support his movement.[29]

The Nazi party had to contend not only with all of these
rural competitors but also with an urban image that made it
suspect in the eyes of the rural population. But the Nazis
in Baden benefited from the fact that the "rural" Nazis of
1923 reemerged in 1925/26 to take part again in the campaign
to win not only the support of the worker but also of the
farmer. Most of the Liedolsheim and Hemsbach Nazis of 1923
(of whom many were farmers and rural artisans) joined the
party again in late 1925 or early 1926.[30] Most important,
the Liedolsheim local produced Albert Roth, a former Landbund
leader and Nazi activist, who was praised by the Völkischer
Beobachter as early as 1925 as Baden's best speaker on rural
issues and the best activist in the countryside. His preoc-
cupation with the farmer was based on a genuine belief in
the romantic rural notion of German nationalism. In articles

on "National Socialism and Agriculture" in the Völkischer
Beobachter and Führer before 1928, he clearly presented his
views on the nature of a völkisch state. The basis of a
völkisch state, according to Roth, was a healthy, debt-free,
producing peasantry. Roth, who saw the farmer as a subcon-
scious National Socialist, demanded that National Socialism
be carried to every village and even every individual farm.
Only this would provide the party with the "armies" for the
Third Reich since only a minute fraction of the degenerate
urban centers could be saved.[31]

Roth was assisted in this rural campaign, particularly
in northern Baden, by many other Nazi farmers who were also
local party leaders of small communities. Häfele in Helmsheim,
Bertold Rokar in Ziegelhausen, and Otto Bender in Eichtersheim
were only a few of these rural activists. In addition, urban
Nazis in central and northern Baden (like Köhler, Kramer,
Wagner, and Kurt Bürkle) marched to the surrounding countryside in search of followers as early as 1925/26. The urban
Nazis, with the help of Albert Roth, were particularly active
in attempting to spread National Socialism to the countryside
of southern Baden. As early as 1926 urban party leaders from
Freiburg, Bühl, and Baden-Baden sponsored campaigns in the
rural areas.[32]

The rural themes presented by these rural and urban Nazis
focused on an antiurban, völkisch, and corporate program.
In addition, vituperous attacks were launched against Jews,
and Berlin's foreign policy was blamed for causing all of the
farmers' ills. The Landbund was rejected during these early
years because it was allegedly controlled by finance capital
and because it cooperated with the parliamentary system. The
Nazis argued instead that only corporate farmers' organization

in a future Nazi corporate parliament would guarantee the farmers' economic and cultural survival and prosperity.

Although these party agitators stressed the farmers' importance in guaranteeing Germany's racial survival, they also frequently combined appeals to farmers with appeals to workers. In an address on 13 December 1925, in Stebbach (Sinsheim), Albert Roth focused on the theme "The ruin of agriculture and labor," while Walter Köhler, the local leader of Weinheim, in a speech in Weingarten in late 1926, stressed that workers and farmers were allies in a common struggle against the "exploiters." Further examples of appeals to farmers and workers between 1925 and 1927 could be presented for all parts of Baden.[33] After all, this had been the message of the Liedolsheim Nazis as early as 1923 when they attempted to reestablish social and political "homogeneity" in their community. This message continued as late as 1930 despite the fact that the party by this time was stressing its Mittelstand campaign. Wagner, Köhler, and Kraft, in speeches before businessmen in Pforzheim, declared that workers and farmers had to be saved in order to rescue the Mittelstand. And Albert Roth in early 1930 in a speech in Heidelberg was still urging the unity of farmers and workers.[34] These appeals were more than opportunistic. They reflected the conviction of the party's völkisch true believers.

The Baden Nazis also tried to win the support of the rural communities that were still relatively homogeneous and politically conservative. One example is provided by Eichtersheim, a community in the rural district of Sinsheim. This community of 781 people was predominantly Protestant (68 percent) and, unlike Liedolsheim, had no "leftist tradition." The Völkisch Block, which had won only 4 percent of the vote

in May 1924, was overshadowed in 1925 by the Rechtsblock,
which captured 55 percent of the vote in the state election.
By 1926, the Nazis had established a local under the leadership of the farmer Otto Bender and sponsored visits by Albert
Roth. The party's deference to "traditionalism" in Eichtersheim was clearly demonstrated when it held a major festival
(Bannerweihe) in August 1926. The NSDAP's activities included a city concert, required church attendance, and the
placement of a wreath on the war memorial. The Nazi festival
was concluded with an evening dance. Women and girls were
not allowed to march and youngsters under the age of twenty
were urged not to participate in the march. These tactics
enabled the Nazis to penetrate the traditional rural community
without alienating the conservative population.[35] Eichtersheim was not an isolated case in 1926. The political police
of Baden noted Nazi rural activities in late 1926, especially
in northeastern areas where Nazi speakers were received well.
Although the entry fee of 1 RM prevented many new potential
party members from joining, the police concluded that National
Socialism would grow in the rural areas.[36]

In 1927 and early 1928, the campaign to win the support
of the farmer became even more aggressive as the agricultural
depression began to be felt acutely. The party carried out a
multitude of meetings and rallies in rural areas, particularly
in northeastern Baden. In the district of Mosbach alone, the
party held eight major rallies between 24 and 29 January 1927,
which featured Karl Lenz, one of the most active and fanatic
Nazi agitators in Baden.[37] In general, the party was particularly active in the rural areas of northeastern Baden
(Hinterland), where the Nazis had established themselves as
early as 1926. In 1927 and early 1928, most of the major Gau

party figures campaigned extensively in this area. Albert
Roth presented the party's message to nine rural communities
in the districts of Mosbach and Adelsheim between 18 November
and 4 December 1927, while Wagner brought the Nazi message
to three new party locals in the district of Wertheim, a
former stronghold of the DVFB. Again the political police
noted in early 1928 that the Nazis were received well by the
rural population of the Hinterland.[38]

In 1927/28, the party expanded its rural campaign to
central Baden areas around Lahr and Bühl and to southern Baden.
The party's campaign in southern Baden in 1926 and early 1927
had been concentrated on urban areas and locals, although
minor forays were made into the countryside. But in late 1927
and early 1928, rural agitators of the party like Albert Roth
descended on southern rural districts and Black Forest villages
like Löffingen in the district of Freiburg and Bonndorf in
the southern Black Forest. The Nazis also began to work on
Protestant rural areas of southwestern Baden like Müllheim,
a future stronghold of the party. Unlike the party's campaign
in northeastern Baden, however, the Nazi rallies in the south
were still not very well attended in late 1927 and early
1928.[39]

The message spread by the party repeated many of the familiar themes. In addition, the Nazis focused increasingly on
the socioeconomic frustrations of the farmers. The party resur-
rected the old Bundschuh times to dramatize the impending rural
revolt against the "old order." In an article entitled "Bundschuh and Swastika," Friedhelm Kemper demanded the socialization
of banks and stock markets since they were responsible for
the farmer's economic plight. The farmers, according to Kemper,
would follow the Nazi party as they once had followed the

Bundschuh. Indeed, the Baden party paper in late 1927 argued that the farmer would even precede the worker and the middle class in this conversion to National Socialism. The Baden party's emphasis on economic issues and the Nazi's rural propaganda was so intense that it caught the attention of the Jewish C. V. Zeitung. In September 1927, this paper published a special report on the rural activities of the Baden Nazis.[40] The Nazis were also successful in the winter of 1927 and 1928 in converting more and more Landbund leaders who, as a result of the desperate economic problems in agriculture, had lost faith in their rural organization.[41]

The most obvious reflection of the Nazi's rural success before the election of May 1928 was the expansion of rural locals in Baden. Even a cursory survey of the Völkischer Beobachter and the Führer in late 1927 and 1928 reveals the tremendous rural expansion of the party. Of sixteen new locals reported, fourteen were in rural northern and north-eastern areas of Baden. This rapid expansion increased the number of Baden locals from forty in July 1927 to sixty-two in 1928.[42] In July 1927, 75 percent of the party's locals were concentrated in the northern urban districts of Karlsruhe, Pforzheim, Mannheim, Heidelberg, and in the rural district of Sinsheim. Eleven of the sixteen major urban centers (over ten thousand) were represented. At the same time 45 percent of all locals were in communities with fewer than three thousand people. And 73 percent of all locals had a clear Protestant majority. Much of the party's rural strength was still concentrated in the "urban" districts like Karlsruhe where socially fragmented rural communities provided the party with its major rural support. By March 1928, the party had increased to forty-eight locals, with most of the new locals

located in northeastern rural Baden. These locals were overwhelmingly Protestant, and only nineteen communities had
clear Catholic majorities. Most interesting was the fact that
the district of Mosbach now had thirteen locals and Sinsheim
claimed six. In Mosbach twelve of these locals were in communities with fewer than one thousand people. In 1927 only
32 percent of all Nazi locals had been in communities with
fewer than two thousand people; in 1928, almost 60 percent.
Clearly, the party's rural drive had been most successful in
northeastern Protestant rural communities. The NSDAP was
winning the support of the full-time farmer.[43]

THE APPEAL TO THE MITTELSTAND

In addition to the party's appeal to workers and farmers, by
1927 the Baden Nazis began to pay increasing attention to
the Mittelstand. The close association between the party's
growth and the German Mittelstand, particularly as it was
reflected in the election statistics after 1929, has already
been analyzed by several scholars.[44] Although before 1927
the Baden party had little to say about the Mittelstand as
a collective entity, numerous representatives of the lower
middle class were active party members. First the advertisements in the Führer in 1927 were mostly of small businesses,
craftsmen, artisans, and pubs that either did business with
the Nazi paper or were actually the economic enterprises or
occupations of party members.[45] Ludwig Griesinger of Eggenstein owned a small construction business. Karl Krauth
and Hans Knab of Eberbach owned quarries, which were not very
lucrative since Knab later listed his occupation as Kaufmann

and Krauth attempted to obtain government employment after
the Nazi seizure of power. Karl Berkmüller, who later became
the Gestapo chief in Karlsruhe, owned a small metal factory
in Durlach, which went bankrupt in 1929. All had joined the
party by 1925/26, and most remained with the Nazi movement
until the end. All were small businessmen who ran marginally
profitable enterprises.[46]

These obvious representatives of the lower middle class
did not feel it necessary at first to appeal to the Mittelstand
as an entity. Instead, they attempted to capture the support
of workers and farmers. One thing the party did attack with
gusto during the early years of its evolution was the solid
middle class. Karlsruhe was referred to as a typical Spiesser-
stadt or a sleepy city. As late as October 1927 Nazi speakers
reminded the party members in Rastatt and Baden-Baden of the
great guilt bourgeois society carried for the enslavement of
Germany. Little wonder that established members of the solid
urban middle class, like the father of Albert Speer, considered the Nazis as leftist representatives.[47]

In late 1927 there was a conscious shift in Nazi propaganda in Baden (and in many parts of Germany). Appeals to
farmers and workers to unite were being supplemented and in
many places replaced by appeals for farmers and the Mittelstand
to unite. As early as November 1926 three Nazis had been
elected to the city council of Weinheim. By 1927 one of these
council members, Walter Köhler, who was also the local party
leader, was demanding free medical operations for needy farmers
and members of the Mittelstand. By 1929, Köhler was advertised by the Führer as a party specialist on Mittelstand
questions.[48] In general, by 1927 a barrage of pro-Mittelstand
appeals appeared in the Führer, and special Mittelstand meetings

were held by Nazi locals. The party paper warned that in the
next generation old women would have to tell that at one time
there existed a <u>Mittelstand</u> in Germany. The culprits, according to the Nazis, were the Jews, who allegedly controlled
large department stores. The only solution, according to the
Baden paper, was to socialize the large Jewish retail stores
and replace them with small stores run by German "specialists."
During the Christmas season of 1927, Wagner and the leading
Baden Nazis focused their anti-Semitic, pro-<u>Mittelstand</u> attacks
on a large Jewish department store (Tietz) in Karlsruhe in
order, according to Wagner, to prevent the rural population
from shopping in the department stores, which were destroying
the small shopkeeper, the artisan, and the <u>Mittelstand</u>.[49]

How sincere were Wagner and the Baden leadership when
they appealed to the <u>Mittelstand</u>? The party supported the
traditional anti-Semitism and social conservatism of the
<u>Mittelstand</u>, particularly of the lower middle class. The
Baden Nazis also supported the <u>Deutschnationale Handelsgehil-
fenverband</u>, a white-collar organization, and obtained noted
conversions from <u>Mittelstand</u> groups. In public, Wagner continued to call for the salvation of the <u>Mittelstand</u>.[50] In
private, however, he indicated that much of this appeal was
opportunistic. Wagner clearly preferred the manual laborers,
whether craftsmen, artisans, or workers, over the shopkeepers
and particularly over the <u>Bürgertum</u>, the solid middle class.
In one letter in 1931, Wagner told one of his local representatives, Fucke-Michels of Rastatt, a self-proclaimed defender
of the <u>Mittelstand</u>, that it would be best if the <u>Bürger</u> lost
his economic existence as soon as possible since that would
radicalize him and help the Nazi party come to power sooner.
Fucke-Michels, aghast at this suggestion, responded that he

would expect to hear this from a Communist but not a Nazi.[51]
He forgot that for Wagner the primacy of politics was the
imperative.

THE PARTY AND INDUSTRY

Given the Nazi party's negative attitude toward the Bürger,
particularly before 1928, it was little wonder that the party
did not attract large industry. Before 1930, the largest industry (over five hundred workers) represented in the Baden
party was the textile firm of Hüssy and Kunzli of Murg, Baden.
But even this firm was only represented through the young
student Oskar Hüssy, who had joined the party in 1923 while
studying in Munich. He did not, however, become the firm's
technical director until January 1929.[52] The party did get
support from medium-sized industry (below five hundred employees) in isolated cases where the factory owners or directors
attempted to use the Nazi party to control labor. For example,
the firm of Stoess in Ziegelhausen tried in 1925 and 1926 to
employ Nazi workers whenever possible to develop a more "nation-
al-minded" labor force. Similarly, a firm like the Metallglas
A. G. in Offenburg gave permission to the Nazi labor agitator
Fritz Plattner to address the workers. And in some of the
largest firms with over one thousand workers, Nazi employees
attempted to recruit unemployed SA men before 1930.[53] But
not until 1930/31 did more representatives of medium-sized
and a few large industries join the party. There is no evidence that this involved more than a few individuals. Some
like Karl Renninger, the future mayor of Mannheim who owned
a medium-sized iron and lead-products factory, had been a

member of the Fatherland party in Mannheim in 1917. But the largest industries like Daimler and Benz were not represented. The only exception was Fritz Reuther of the Bopp and Reuther firm in Mannheim, which produced water, steam, and gas instruments and employed over one thousand workers. But there is absolutely no evidence that these few conversions of leaders of larger industries added substantial funds to the party, which obtained most of its financial support from the entry fees of new members and dues and contributions at rallies.[54]

Baden newspapers from the Socialist Volksfreund to the Catholic Badischer Beobachter published articles in 1928/29 depicting Hitler's industrial supporters. No major Baden industrial leaders, however, were listed in these articles. The Volksfreund in late 1928 did mention Kommerzienrat Stoess of Heidelberg, who was the presiding officer of the Southwestern Industrial Conference, held in Freiburg in October 1928. The paper also focused on Wilhelm Keppler, a friend of Stoess and supporter of National Socialism.[55] In both instances, the paper was absolutely correct, since the Stoess firm in Ziegelhausen preferred to hire Nazi workers, and Keppler was an active party member in Eberbach. But the Odin and the Stoess firms did not represent the largest industrial concerns in Baden. Rather the Odin case provides a good illustration of a medium-sized firm that supported National Socialism.

Eberbach had been introduced to National Socialism as early as 1923 when a small local emerged from a DNVP meeting. After the reestablishment of the Baden party in early 1925, Hans Knab became the local leader. Many of the party members who joined between 1926 and early 1928 were from the lower middle class, representing craftsmen, master artisans, and white-collar employees. This was the kind of audience that heard leading Nazis like Gottfried Feder and Hitler in 1926 and 1927.[56] The pre-1923 Nazi leadership controlled party affairs until 1927 when it was replaced by new forces that represented the interests of Keppler, the part owner of the largest firm in town. The Keppler group eventually won the support of the Gau leadership and Hitler because it was successful in attracting supporters, not because the party had shifted to industry.

Wilhelm Keppler, the future advisor of Hitler in economic affairs, was born on 14 December 1882 in Heidelberg and studied engineering at the technical universities of Karlsruhe and Danzig before the outbreak of the First World War. In 1914, he obtained a position as a chemical engineer with Stoess in Ziegelhausen (the same firm that attempted to hire only Nazi workers after 1925). Following the war, Keppler became associated with Odin Werke, whose board of directors was chaired by his uncle. He was then one of the directors until early 1932 when he sold his shares and moved to Munich. Although an important figure in Eberbach, Keppler was certainly not one of the industrial giants of Baden in the 1920s.[57]

Keppler was probably influenced by one of his chemists, Leopold Plaichinger, who was one of the first party members in Munich. Born on 14 August 1889 in Laibach, Austria, he joined the party in Munich in 1919 and again in April 1927 in Eberbach.[58] In 1926, Keppler and Plaichinger went to see Knab, the local leader of Eberbach, to request that a representative of Odin be placed on a safe slot of the Nazi party's municipal election slate. Since neither Keppler nor Plaichinger had joined the party officially, Knab refused. Keppler decided to present his own election slate, which was much more successful than the Nazi slate, winning seventeen seats compared to the Nazi party's mere three. In 1927, both Keppler and Plaichinger joined the NSDAP. They also replaced the old Nazi leadership when Plaichinger was elected local leader of Eberbach. One year later Plaichinger was not only the district leader of Eberbach but was also considered by Munich and Karlsruhe as one of the party's most effective leaders. He could also use his close "connections" with Munich to entice Hitler to schedule public and private party rallies in Baden. The Keppler group had established itself so successfully that by 1930 the old Nazi leadership of Eberbach was expelled from the party for "disobedience and rebellion."[59]

The new Nazi leadership conducted its business from Odin, where Plaichinger received party correspondence. According to a police report of March 1928, almost half of Eberbach's Nazi members were Odin employees (Arbeiter).[60] Already in November 1927, Hitler had visited Eberbach to deliver his second speech in Baden. When Hitler returned to present another speech in Heidelberg on 5 March 1928, he not only arrived in an Odin company car but he also addressed a closed meeting of 670 representatives of commerce, industry, and science, which had been arranged by Keppler. Hitler spent the night in Heidelberg with the first local leader of the city, Adolf Schroer, a white-collar employee. The police noted the presence of industrialists (but the officers did not mention any names except Stoess), civil servants, professionals, and Nazi party leaders of Baden. Hitler's speech focused on the need to preserve Germany's best blood through the growth of power and space, which would provide economic opportunities for Germany but at the same time prevent clashes with England. Hitler consciously flattered the audience by saying that the political

might of a people was reflected in its economy. And economic
conditions could be improved only through the expansion of power
and space. According to police reports, Hitler's speech was
received with strong applause by the select audience.[61] The
efforts of the Keppler Nazis in Eberbach were translated into
tireless activism, and eventually in May 1928 into 31 percent
of the total votes cast in that community.[62] Certainly Keppler's influence helped the party in Eberbach. The party's
success there, however, resulted less from the support of an
"industrialist" than traditional Nazi activism in a favorable
environment.

THE SOCIAL STRUCTURE OF THE LEADERSHIP

The party's social appeals after 1928 never varied much.
Peasants continued to be pictured as the basis of a healthy
state. Jews, banks, and high taxes were singled out as the
cancers that were eating away at the health of the agricultural
population. The only modification to appear in the Führer
was the acceptance of large estates as both economically
viable and even necessary for Germany's well-being.[63] After
1929, even more attention was focused on the Mittelstand as
it became clear that political capital could be made of this
appeal. Jews and large department stores continued to provide the major scapegoats, and economic interest parties
were rejected as economic remedies for basically political
problems. In addition, party spokesmen like Lenz began to
emphasize in 1930/31 that "German socialism" would defend
private property.[64] Yet, while the labor appeal of the party
in 1928 and 1929 was not as strong as the appeals to the

Mittelstand and farmer, the party continued to seek labor's support. In 1930, the Führer started focusing on the advancement of National Socialism in the shop council elections of Baden. With the establishment in Baden of the N.S. Betriebszellenorganization, the appeals to the workers became more profuse, although they never again reached the scope and intensity of the Mittelstand-rural appeals. In terms of its propaganda, the Nazi party of Baden was clearly a Volkspartei (people's party) which attempted to win the support of all segments of society. This was apparent as early as 1924 although it became more pronounced in 1927.[65]

How were the Baden party's social appeals reflected in the social structure of the NSDAP before 1929? The Gau had between twenty-five hundred and three thousand members in early 1928. Even if its claim is accepted that its membership increased between May and October 1928 by 50 percent, the party in late 1928 would still have had only about four thousand members.[66] The party's expansion into the rural and small-town areas of the state is reflected by the fact that family members of small communities often joined as groups in early 1928. For example, in Schollbrunn, a small community in northeastern Baden, three people with the name of Backfisch joined the party on 1 January 1928. All were young, born between 1895 and 1904. This must have been more than just a coincidence.[67] Since most of the expansion of Nazi locals in Baden between July 1928 and March 1929 occurred in rural areas (with communities under two thousand), it is obvious that the party won the support of more farmers, rural artisans and rural craftsmen. This is particularly reflected in the fact that leaders of rural locals were mostly farmers and rural artisans.[68] In medium-sized towns with populations

between five thousand and ten thousand, small shopkeepers,
artisans, and in some cases professionals dominated the local
leadership posts. This latter group, in addition to more white-
collar employees, comprised the party leadership in the largest
urban areas.[69]

The general lower-middle-class character of the leadership of the Baden party, which included few industrial workers
and educated professionals, is borne out in two documents that
reveal both the local leadership in 1927 and the district
leadership in 1928. In July 1927, the party's forty locals
were led by a relatively young group. Almost 90 percent of
all local leaders were under forty, and half were thirty or
younger. Nearly one-third had belonged to the party in 1923,
and approximately half were still active in the party after
the seizure of power in 1933. Of the occupations listed,
twelve were Kaufmänner, seven were farmers, six were artisans
and craftsmen, four were white-collar employees, and only four
were educated professionals. The list contained no industrial
worker, although two leaders were skilled craftsmen, one an
electrician, and the other a diamond polisher. The local leaders in 1927 complemented the party's appeal to the farmers and
lower middle class but did not reflect the party's appeal to
organized labor.

The Baden party's district leaders in June 1928 revealed
a similar preponderance of Handarbeiter (but not industrial
workers) farmers and Kaufmänner. Only one worker and two professionals represented labor and the solid middle class. Again
they were relatively young since 84 percent of the twenty-one
district leaders were under forty.[70] Not until after 1929
did the Baden party win increasing solid middle-class support.
By 1930 many of these well-educated members of society were

affected by the growing economic disfunctions. But the party's local, district, and even Gau positions continued to be
dominated by white-collar employees (Kaufmänner) and nonindustrial manual workers. They clearly satisfied Wagner's
predilection for the völkisch activist who was a semieducated
Handarbeiter.

THE REICHSTAG ELECTION OF 1928

The Reichstag election in May 1928 provided the Baden party
with the first major test of its organizational and public
propaganda campaigns since 1925. Although the party's newspaper on the eve of the election still maintained that the
NSDAP did not strive to enter parliament for parliament's
sake, but rather to use it as a platform from which to carry
Nazi ideas even further, the party had made elaborate preparations. In January 1928, Wagner had already prepared a speaker's list that would meet Munich's approval, and the election
campaign manager, Karl Lenz, admonished the locals to place
their orders for speakers in ample time. In early March 1928,
Wagner launched the campaign by gathering his local and district party and SA leaders, who in turn brought their propaganda, press, business, and finance officers. Under Wagner's
guidance, they planned the strategy for the election.[71]
    In March and April 1928, Hitler was the main attraction
in the Baden campaign as he presented speeches in Karlsruhe
(3 March), Heidelberg (5 March), and Pforzheim (26 April).
In Karlsruhe, he attracted a crowd estimated at about three
thousand people. In Karlsruhe and Pforzheim, Hitler stressed
the unity of the Volk over class divisions and proclaimed that

the goal of National Socialism was to educate the Volk to be
egoistical. Then he presented the traditional themes. He
pointed out that there were only three ways a nation could
adjust the relationship between its population and its soil.
It could expand its lands, it could resort to emigration, and
it could use birth control. Germany, according to Hitler,
gave up the first and only viable alternative because it lost
power. With startling frankness, Hitler promised that National
Socialism would correct this power deficiency and then solve
Germany's population problem.[72]

The nationalistic themes presented by Hitler were received favorably by the DNVP press of Baden. The Badische
Zeitung, reviewing Hitler's speech on 3 March, supported it
completely. The Führer, however, rejected the Nationalists'
theme of "marching together" because there could be no union
between youth and old age. The Nazis of Baden also rejected
the proposal to form a völkisch opposition with the DNVP because the Nazi party was, according to the Führer, the völkisch
opposition in Baden.[73] The Socialist press, on the other
hand, described Hitler's speech as a strange comical theater
presented by a worshiper of the Germanic ideology. Indeed,
the SPD of Baden predicted that the Nazis would return home
empty on 20 May, and it focused its election campaign against
the DNVP and the middle-class parties.[74]

The Nazis carried on an extensive election campaign in
Baden's rural and urban areas. Even in southern and central
Baden the party made extensive efforts to reach the rural
population. The propaganda was carried out (with the exception of Hitler), for the most part, by native Baden agitators
like Wagner, Lenz, Kramer, Roth, Köhler, Kemper, Plaichinger,
and the former Communist Friedrich. According to police

reports the rallies and meetings were well attended by the public. On the eve of the election the Nazis utilized a saturation campaign by loading SA members on trucks and driving them
through the centers of Baden's towns. All party members with
cars were urged to supply them for propaganda work between 5
and 10 May. Every Saturday and Sunday and on holidays the
cars appeared on the streets of towns and villages throughout the state.[75] These agitators presented the standard Nazi
themes. Six Baden candidates, two farmers, one master artisan,
two workers, and one teacher, were presented to the public.
Wagner and Lenz represented the Gau leadership. Geiger, a
former Landbund leader and farmer, was the district leader of
Sinsheim, and Tritschler was the local leader of Freiburg.
The two workers, Albert Schoni and Karl Weigel, the SA leader
of Mannheim, represented the workers of both Mannheim and
southern Baden.[76] The party's election slate in 1928 echoed
the party's appeals to peasants and workers between 1925 and
1928.

The Nazi party emerged with 26,330 votes or 2.9 percent
of the total votes cast on 20 May 1928. The major völkisch
rival, the Völkisch-Nationaler Block, won only 3,588 votes
and was thus eliminated for all practical purposes from the
political scene of Baden (see Map 7). The former Rechtsblock
of Baden (DNVP and Landbund) declined between December 1924
and May 1928 by almost 60,000 votes, while the Center party,
the Democratic party and the German People's party lost a
total of 83,845 votes during this same period. The Socialists and Communists, however, gained only 5,753 and 1,856
votes, respectively, between 1924 and 1928. The major bene-
ficiaries of the election were the special middle-class interest parties represented by the Badischen Mittelstand, the

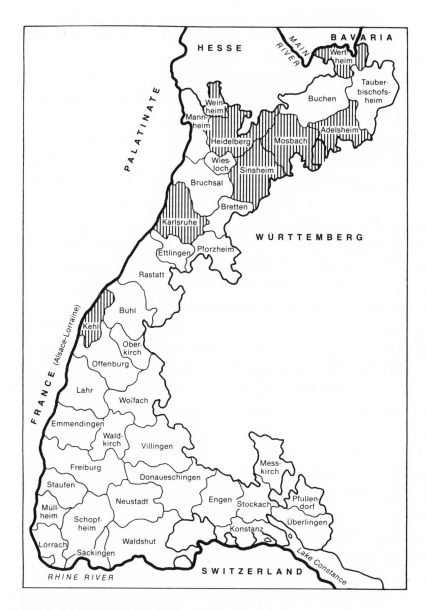

Map 7. *Reichstag Election: 1928*

Nazi Strongholds: Districts with over 2.9% of the vote

Aufwertungspartei, and the Christlich-Soziale Reichspartei.
Second, the traditional parties lost votes to political apathy
since total votes decreased during this period by 86,249.[77]

The reactions of the various parties to the results ranged
from a realistic appraisal of the political situation to wish-
ful thinking. The DVFB held a state conference after the
election in which it declared that in future elections it
would only run as the DVFB party rather than become submerged
in a völkisch coalition as in 1928. In reality, the DVFB
never ran again in Baden. The DNVP blamed its losses on the
attacks of all other parties and concluded that, in any event,
the new Reichstag would not last long. The Baden leader of
the DDP, Dietrich, was more realistic and blamed the party's
decline on the failure to carry out detail work. The Center
party concluded that the real victor of the election was the
SPD. Finally, the SPD did notice the Nazis but concluded
that Hitler's time had passed, and it predicted that the Nazis
would have no chance in the upcoming state election of October
1929. In reality, the party must have been impressed with
the Nazi party's rural success since the Volksfreund also concluded that the small farmers' problems must be relieved
through practical solutions.[78]

The Baden Nazi leadership, on the other hand, noted how
the "cowardly and indolent bourgeois parties had suffered a
new defeat at the hands of the poisonous Marxists." According to the Führer, the NSDAP was now clearly the völkisch
movement in the state. The paper also announced that the
party's goal would be to continue the battle against Marxism
and to increase the party's organization for this struggle.[79]
Wagner was absolutely right when he argued that the NSDAP
was now the only völkisch party in Baden. The DVFB lost most

of its northern support, particularly in its former rural
strongholds of Wertheim and Bretten. Over 60 percent of this
party's votes in 1928 came from five southern districts where
the party was heir to the old Protestant National Liberalism.
Above all, the party's organization was in shambles. First,
the Gau leader, Haas, had to run both Baden and Württemberg.
His deputy Gau leader lived in Ettlingen while Haas lived in
Konstanz. Worst of all, as late as 1928 the party had no
paid, full-time business manager. And in the summer of 1928
the party's locals were still holding only monthly meetings.[80]
The DVFB, with its support confined to southern Baden and an
organization that reflected neither dynamism nor structure, was
no match for the Nazis who began to penetrate southern Baden
in 1929/30.

In 1928, the Nazi party had increased its voting strength
in Baden by almost 200 percent over its 1925 state election
strength and 37 percent over its December 1924 Reichstag election strength. The Baden party, which had won votes in 885
communities, was a predominantly Protestant, rural party.
The Baden NSDAP was weak in the state's largest industrial
center, Mannheim, and very strong in the major administrative
center, Karlsruhe, and the major academic community, Heidelberg. Its strongest urban center was Protestant Weinheim,
where Köhler had carried on a strong middle-class and labor
campaign as early as 1926/27. The Nazis had been strong in
these urban centers as early as May 1924 as part of the Völkisch Block.[81] In relation to Baden's geographic regions, the
party was strongest where it had organized or campaigned most
actively. The party won 73 percent of its votes in northern
and northeastern urban and rural districts where it had campaigned and organized the most between 1925 and early 1928.[82]

Although the party exceeded or met its state average of
2.9 percent in three of the four largest urban centers of
northern Baden, and won 12.8 percent in Weinheim (population
of 14,500), its greatest advance came in rural, Protestant
communities. Most astonishing was the fact that 48 percent
of the Baden party's increase over December 1924 (or 34.5
percent over 1925) came in the five rural districts of Kehl,
Wertheim, Adelsheim, Mosbach, and Sinsheim, where only 6.2
percent of the state's votes were cast. In these districts,
43 to 54 percent of all farms were over two hectares, giving
them a rural population that consisted of full-time farmers.
Although only three districts were predominantly Protestant,
the party obtained most of its votes and had most of its
strongholds in Protestant communities. In Adelsheim fifteen
Nazi strongholds were Protestant and only one was Catholic;
and in Wertheim ten communities voted strongly for the Nazis
while two other strongholds were Catholic. In all five districts the Rechtsblock had been extremely strong in 1921,
ranging between 28 percent in Mosbach to 49 percent in Kehl.
In the radical election of May 1924, the combined Rechtsblock
and völkisch totals in the five districts ranged from 29.5
percent in Mosbach to 52 percent in Wertheim. In other words,
the Nazis, who had gained only a maximum of 1.5 percent of the
vote in these districts in 1925, had converted the former
Landbund and Rechtsblock voters by 1928 through a combination
of agitation and deteriorating economic conditions in agriculture.[83]

The importance of combined Nazi activism, Rechtsblock
tradition, and a Protestant base in the rural communities is
further illustrated by several other documents. The Baden
study of thirty-seven rural communities in all areas of the

state reveals that the Nazis did well in six communities where
they won between 6.7 percent and 48 percent of the votes. All
except Ichenheim were Protestant communities in the northern
parts of the state. Ichenheim, a Catholic community (58 percent) in the tobacco center of Baden, may have reacted to the
severe depression in the tobacco industry. All six communities had strong Rechtsblock, and particularly Landbund, activities as early as 1924. Before the election, Nazi locals already existed in three of these with locals formed in the other
three communities by mid-1928. The size of farms, the amount
of debt per hectare, and the number of workers in the six rural
communities varied greatly. The most important factors were
clearly Protestantism and a tradition of right-wing activities including, in part, Nazi locals. All were right-wing
rural communities that reacted to the agricultural depression
by accepting Nazi slogans and promises.[84]

This same pattern was evident in other areas not covered
by this study on rural debts. For example, another survey of
fifteen rural communities in the districts of Karlsruhe,
Ettlingen, and Rastatt reflects the same pattern in 1928. Six
of these towns were overwhelmingly Catholic, and nine were
Protestant. In all of these Protestant communities the DNVP
had done well in elections as early as 1919. Subsequently,
the völkisch and Nazi forces emerged strongly in the same
towns. Significantly, in five of the six communities where
the Nazis did best in May 1928, party locals existed. Although
workers existed in all of these "rural" towns, the Nazi party
did best in Protestant communities where the rural population
was the largest.[85]

Another clear example is provided by the district of
Kehl, which was not included in the study on rural debts but

which became a Nazi stronghold. It was also predominantly
Protestant and rural. Before the war, it was dominated by
the National Liberals, and in 1919 the DDP emerged with over
50 percent of the vote. By 1920 the DNVP had emerged to compete with the DDP. The expansion of DNVP and Landbund strength
in Kehl continued unabated after 1920 (until the emergence
of the NSDAP in the election of 1928). The DNVP and Landbund,
in fact, won 62 percent of the total vote in the election of
May 1924. The debt per hectare in the district was low but
this was a reflection of the failure of economic activity after
the loss of Alsace-Lorraine, a natural market for Kehl's agriculture. Land taxes based on prewar values remained high
despite economic stagnation during the period of French occupation which lasted until 1930.[86]

A final note on the importance of Nazi and völkisch activities for the party's vote in Baden is revealed by an analysis of the forty-eight party locals, existing in early 1928.
In these communities the NSDAP won 55 percent of its total vote
in May 1928. But already in May 1924 the Völkisch Block in
Baden had won 52 percent of its vote in the same forty-eight
communities (where 39 percent of the state's votes were cast).
Again, party or völkisch activism, combined with Protestantism
and a right-wing political tradition, were decisive for the
party's voting strength in 1928.[87]

In May 1928, the Baden party had realized its "take-off
potential" in its rural success. Although the party promised
to continue its battle against the Marxists, more important
for the immediate future was its realization of the potential
of the rural vote. On 3 June 1928, Wagner ordered a further
increase in propaganda, particularly in the rural communities.
Indeed, the party's intense campaign in the rural Hinterland,

and in the state in general, is revealed by the fact that the
Gau held fifteen hundred rallies in 1928 and increased its
locals to sixty-two.[88] In addition, the party followed up
its propaganda drives with organizational activities. By
June 1928, three rural experts of the party presented special
reports in Gau party leadership and strategy conferences.
Although the Gau did not set up a special rural department
until December 1931, by the end of 1928 the Gau paper already
referred to a Nazi Farmers' League. By early 1929 the party
was so strong in the rural areas that state officials were
afraid to prosecute Nazi agitators for fear of creating a
cause célèbre. In 1929, the editor of the official statistical
analysis of party movements in Baden between 1905 and 1929,
Alfred Rapp, concluded that the Nazi party in Baden had become the heir to the Landbund.[89] The persistent rural campaigns of the "rural wing" of the Baden Nazi party played no
small part in this development.

5 The Emergence of the Mass Party, 1929-1930

THE LANDTAG ELECTION OF 1929

The NSDAP of Baden had become the dominant völkisch party in
the election of 1928. In a little over a year, the Nazi party
emerged to replace both the DNVP and Landbund as the dominant
right-wing party in the state. Finally, by the fall of 1930,
the völkisch Nazi movement had evolved into a mass movement
both in terms of voter appeal and its membership. During
this period, party propaganda, party organization, and vigorous election campaigns mutually reinforced each other. The
deteriorating economic conditions, in turn, provided the fuel
that allowed the NSDAP to change from a narrow right-wing
party to a mass movement consisting of the various components
of the urban and rural Mittelstand. The Baden Nazis had accomplished their first major political breakthrough in the
state's rural areas in 1928. The next test came in the state
election of October 1929 when the party made its second important breakthrough, this time in the urban centers.[1]

Immediately after the Reichstag election of 1928, the party
stepped up its agitation. By June 1928, party functionaries
like Wagner, Kramer, and Roth, who were able to devote most of
their time to propaganda work, were again quite active in all
parts of the state and particularly in areas where the Nazis
had done well in the election. In the fall of 1928, the party

began to carry its message to all parts of the state, including the long-neglected south. For example, in the district of Neustadt, Albert Roth collaborated with Franz Merk, the recently converted Agrarian League leader and former candidate of the Farmers' party (Bauernpartei), to work in communities where the Nazis had performed well in the election of 1928. The obvious aim was to win new party members and establish locals.[2]

As early as September 1928 the Nazis began to campaign for the state election scheduled for October 1929. Two months later, Hitler finally came to Mannheim, the largest urban center of the state. At the beginning of 1929, the Völkischer Beobachter claimed that the Baden party had increased by 83 percent since the Reichstag election of 1928. It also promised that the Baden Nazis would continue the struggle with renewed vigor. By January 1929, according to police reports, the Nazis were counting on from four to six seats in the October election.[3] Two months later, the Baden party officially initiated its state election campaign. The Völkischer Beobachter declared that Baden was now under the sign of the coming state election and reported that party activists were engaged in daily rallies in all parts of the Gau. The Baden party set up a list of candidates, and in Gau leadership conferences the party's leaders were ordered to devote themselves to the election campaign, particularly in rural areas. By May 1929, the Baden police noted the party's new and energetic activism.[4]

In late September 1929, the party announced that it would hold 120 meetings between 28 September and 6 October, most of them in northeastern and central Baden where the party expected to expand its rural support. The Nazi party was clearly more

active during the election campaign than any other Baden party.
Himmler recruited rural experts and other national party
leaders for the campaign in Baden. Almost all Reichstag delegates of the party, sixteen state representatives, and ten
other well-known non-Baden Nazis visited the state during the
election drive.[5] The visiting Nazis heaped abuse on the republic, including statements that Wilhelm Gröber, the former quar-
termaster-general, should have been shot in 1918, and Gustav
Stresemann, the German foreign minister, should be incarcerated.
All of these activities were carefully monitored by Remmele's
police, and in several instances Nazi speakers were banned,
and one Nazi rally was closed.[6]

Deputy Gau leader Karl Lenz promised the population few
immediate benefits from the election. He declared on 7 September that the Nazis could do little constructive work in the
Landtag. Instead, the Nazi delegates would use immunity and
railroad passes to spread further the Nazi gospel. The actual
themes presented by both Baden and Reich Nazi agitators ranged
from attacks on banks, stock markets, Jews, Versailles, and
the Young Plan, to an appeal for assistance to farmers and
the Mittelstand. The party's election slate also reflected
this appeal to farmers and the lower middle class. The Gau
presented candidates (many of whom ran in several districts)
in twenty-one of the twenty-two electoral districts, excluding
only the southeastern rural Catholic strongholds of Messkirch,
Stockach, Pfullendorf, and Überlingen. While Gau party and
district party functionaries and activists dominated the list,
in terms of social profiles the Nazi slate presented mainly
farmers, shopkeepers, artisans, and craftsmen, with only 8
percent of the candidates representing workers and only 11
percent representing the educated or professional middle class.[7]

The NSDAP's appeal to the farmers and Mittelstand, however, was anything but unique. The Baden Nazis had to compete
with twelve political parties, many of which articulated similar
social themes. The German Democratic party (DDP) noted the
Nazis' attempt to win the support of farmers who "had been
disappointed by the Landbund." The Democrats admitted that
the NSDAP would win three to four seats in the election. At
the state congress of the DDP on 4/6 October in Karlsruhe,
Dietrich noted the plight of the Mittelstand and farmers.
He argued that both were being squeezed to death between organized labor and finance capital. Dietrich offered the
farmers higher cattle prices and tax relief.[8] In addition,
the Center party and the DNVP also appealed to the Mittelstand
and to farmers.[9] These themes differed little from the NSDAP's
socioeconomic appeals (except that the Nazis also appealed
to labor). But the Nazis, no doubt, could point out that these
very same parties had been in power during a period of deteriorating economic conditions.

The Center party and the Socialists tried to write off
the Nazis as fools who were promoting a swindle, and many of
the other parties pictured the NSDAP as a movement bankrolled
by large capitalists. Even the usually apolitical information journal of Mannheim's Jews, the Israelitische Gemeindeblatt, appealed for help and action to combat the very intense
anti-Semitic campaign of the Nazis.[10] But these parties could
not compete with the Nazis' constant propaganda and agitation,
and one might add, self-sacrifice. The police noted that the
party's tremendous election costs incurred by inviting the
various Reich and non-Baden agitators were met primarily
through collections.[11]

The election results in Baden provided the party with 7

percent of the vote (65,121) and the election of six party
functionaries to the state legislature. Walter Köhler, the
local leader of Weinheim and subsequent deputy Gau leader,
became the chairman of the Nazi delegation, and Herbert Kraft,
a Mannheim Gymnasium professor, assumed the position of vice-
chairman. Robert Wagner, the Gau leader, Karl Lenz, the deputy
Gau leader, Albert Roth, the Liedolsheim rural Nazi, and Franz
Merk, the district leader of Neustadt and a former Landbund
leader and Bauernbund candidate, represented the rest of the
Nazi delegation. A social analysis of the twenty-five alter-
nates elected also confirms that the party presented an image
of a people's party, although farmers and the lower middle
class were best represented. The list included 12 percent
workers and 16 percent professionals and well-educated members
of the middle class.[12]

The party emerged from the October election as the fourth
strongest in Baden. It was surpassed only by the Center party
(36.6 percent), the Socialists (20.1 percent), and the DDP (8
percent). The Nazis overshadowed all of the parties of the
right and all of the special-interest parties. The party's
activism in 1929 was reflected by the fact that it obtained
votes in 1,073 communities as compared to 885 in the last
Reichstag election. The NSDAP continued its rural advance,
particularly in Protestant districts and communities. For
example, in thirty-five predominantly Protestant rural communities, the Nazis won at least 50 percent of the vote and
in six villages in the rural districts of Mosbach, Adelsheim,
Tauberbischofsheim, and Kehl, and in the district of Heidelberg the Nazis won between 75 percent and 90 percent of the
vote. Again, the party expanded into rural Protestant districts like Bretten that had a history of Rechtsblock strength.

But as impressive as the party's rural advance was, reaching even 32 percent in the district of Kehl, the fact remains that the party won only 13.9 of its new votes (over 1928) in five rural districts where it advanced dramatically. This was far less of an impressive increase than had occurred in May 1928 when one third of the party's growth took place in five rural districts.

More dramatic was the party's urban advance, particularly in white-collar and middle-class strongholds like Karlsruhe and Heidelberg and in the city of Weinheim. The Nazi vote in Mannheim was still below the party's state average, reflecting the failure to convert industrial workers. But the Nazi party won 42.2 percent of its new votes in the five cities of Mannheim, Heidelberg, Karlsruhe, Weinheim, and Pforzheim, where only 28 percent of the state's total votes were cast. Almost 30 percent of the party's increase occurred in the two cities of Karlsruhe and Heidelberg, where the party was converting the middle class, which previously had voted for the DNVP and völkisch splinter parties. In Heidelberg, there was a decrease in voting participation by 798 votes and in Karlsruhe an increase of 3,327 votes, yet the Nazis increased their votes in both cities. In both towns, the Center party and the Mittelstand and Protestant political parties increased their votes while the left and the DNVP suffered losses from either desertion or apathy. Similar urban advances occurred in central Baden in Lahr, Offenburg, and Rastatt, where the party won between 7.5 and 8.1 percent of the vote.[13]

The Nazi leadership in Baden concluded that its new voters came primarily from the Marxists and only secondly from the National camp. According to the Völkischer Beobachter, most of the 32,500 voters lost by the SPD and KPD had benefited

the NSDAP. The Socialist papers of Baden agreed with this
analysis for some areas of Baden. The Volksfreund argued sadly that some of its losses had occurred because workers in
Schwetzingen and Weinheim had deserted to the Nazis. The
Catholic Badischer Beobachter also maintained that the KPD
had lost voters to the Nazis. But both the Socialist and the
Center party papers also noted the Nazis' success in rural
areas and among white-collar employees. Both party papers ran
articles on Hitler "eating Hugenberg." Since the coalition
parties still controlled over 50 percent of the vote in Baden,
they presented a calm analysis of the election. The Socialist
Volksfreund concluded that the anti-Semitic wave in Baden
would pass; the Catholic Badischer Beobachter predicted that
the Nazis, like the Landbund, would rise rapidly but also
decline with equal speed.[14] These optimistic views were echoed by much of the national press. The C. V. Zeitung saw
the future of the Weimar Coalition in Baden as more solid
than ever, as did the middle class Vossische Zeitung, Berliner
Tageblatt, and the Demokrat. All predicted the continuation
of the proven government in Baden.[15]

Much more realistic analyses came from the Communists and
from parties that were hurt directly by the Nazis. The Communist leaders admitted that they had underestimated the
influence of the Nazis and that their fight against "fascism"
had come too late.[16] The DNVP also noted the shift to the
right in Baden, which had hurt it and benefited the Nazis.
It urged serious reorganization to meet this threat. A similar view was presented by the more liberal Karlsruher Tagblatt, which blamed the growth of the Nazis on former nonvoters and a shift to the right.[17] This was also the view of
a Baden Jew writing in the C. V. Zeitung on 28 October 1929.

He lambasted the failure of Baden Jews to get involved and
to attempt to stem the tide of anti-Semitism. This writer
saw clearly that the Nazi growth was due to economic conditions, Nazi agitation, and DNVP desertions. Many of these
papers would, no doubt, have agreed with the Frankfurter Zeitung
when it declared that the Nazi success in liberal Baden should
cause serious introspection.[18]

The major reasons for the Socialist and Communist losses
was voter nonparticipation. There were only twenty-three
thousand new voters in the election of 1929 (over 1928), but
the Catholic Center party alone increased its votes by forty-
four thousand. These additional Catholic votes did not come
from a shift among Protestant parties on the right and center
but rather from new voters. Since only twenty-three thousand
new voters participated, the new Catholic votes can only be
explained if we assume that the nonparticipation of leftist
voters was compensated by the increased participation of
Catholic voters.

The Nazi increase can best be explained in terms of a
combination of new voters with a shift of middle-class and
particularly DNVP votes. In rural areas, the shift was clearly from the right. Most transient right-wing and middle-class
voters, however, still went to the emerging special-interest
parties, ranging from the Protestant Evangelische Volksdienst
to the Bauernpartei and Wirtschaftspartei. But the pattern
in all urban centers of Baden, regardless of whether there
was a slight increase or decrease in voter participation,
was the same. The Nazis, the Center party, and middle-class
special-interest parties gained votes while the Marxist parties, the DDP, DVP, and DNVP, lost voters. Of all of the
middle-class parties, the DNVP suffered the most by losing

votes to both the NSDAP and the middle-class special-interest parties.[19]

The importance of the election for the Baden party was twofold. First, it provided a group of party functionaries with Landtag salaries and privileges, which they used to further the party's expansion. In addition to the salaries and special rail passes, the Nazi delegates also won immunity from arrest during legislative sessions. Roth, Merk, and Wagner were frequently arrested before October 1929 or fined for their irresponsible and violently anti-Semitic agitation. After the Landtag election, the government had to wait until the end of the legislative period to arrest Nazi members of the Landtag. Second, the 1929 election was complementary to the 1928 rural breakthrough because now the party could also claim urban gains, particularly in the administrative, intellectual, and small-business strongholds like Karlsruhe, Heidelberg, Lahr, and Offenburg. Although the party did well in industrial Weinheim, it was still not able to win the support of the workers of Mannheim, the largest urban center of Baden. But the party's success in the rural and urban centers in 1929 gave it an impetus that caused its rapid organizational and membership expansion in 1930, long before the Reichstag election of the same year.

Immediately, however, the election did little to change the political realities in the Landtag since the Catholic-Socialist political axis continued. The party published its demands on 15 November 1929, announcing that the Baden Nazis would support any government that did not include Jews and Marxists and allowed the Nazis full opportunities of development. The government was also required to save money by using Fachminister (specialists) and to oppose the "treason" of Marxism.[20] In part this was clearly a recognition of the party's actual political impotence in the Landtag. It was also another propaganda statement intended more for the public than the other political parties.

The Baden party's legislative experience in the Landtag revolved around legislative negativism and propagandistic harassment. In early 1930, after a government had been formed that did not reflect the wishes of the Nazi delegation, Wagner greeted the new coalition of the Center party and Socialists with the declaration that "we reject the parliamentary system as demeaning." Indeed, during the first session of the new Landtag in 1930 the Nazi delegation spent most of its time outside the legislature campaigning.[21] The Nazis did use the Landtag, however, as a forum for irresponsible propaganda by introducing thirty bills and seventeen questions during the first legislative period. Most of these proposals focused first on agrarian and economic issues and second on political and administrative questions. The proposals were devoted to familiar themes. On 10 January 1930, the Nazi delegation demanded a ban on the hiring of Jews by the Justice Department. Adam Remmele, of course, received constant votes of no confidence from the Nazi delegation. The plight of the farmers, Mittelstand, shopkeepers, and laboring classes, coupled with anticapitalistic tirades, were favorite themes for the Nazi delegation's Landtag activities. All were rejected by the Baden legislature. This did not deter the Baden party leaders from announcing in late 1930 a new avalanche of proposals for the next session of the Landtag.[22] In 1931, more attention was shifted to Reich problems over which the Baden Landtag had absolutely no control. The Nazis demanded official rejection of the Versailles Treaty and the expulsion of Eastern

European Jews. Finally on 24 July 1932, the Baden party delegation attempted to solve its "legislative responsibilities"
by demanding a Reichskommissar for Baden.[23]

The Nazi party's behavior in the Landtag, which on occasion included brawls, frequently did not differ much from its
street tactics. Kraft, in particular, had a fist fight in the
legislature with the Center party and former Landbund member
Anton Hilbert after Hilbert had called Hitler an Austrian de-
serter. Often the government parties walked out of the Landtag
when the Nazis presented speeches or introduced proposals.
Finally, in May 1932, after the Nazi delegation had failed to
apologize for Kraft's insults, the president and the cabinet
agreed to have nothing more to do with the Nazi delegation.[24]

Only the right (and on occasion the Communists) supported
Nazi resolutions in the Landtag. Paul Schmitthener, a DNVP
delegate and future minister of education under the Nazis,
defended Kraft, who had called parliamentarians scum. The
DNVP (with the support of the Communists) rejected a punitive
move against Kraft. Obviously, both the DNVP and the Communist delegations had little respect for parliamentary procedures. In addition, the Bauernpartei, even before its representatives joined the Nazi delegation, voted for several Nazi
bills, including one that dealt with the reduction of ministerial salaries. Only on one occasion were the Nazis able to
add an amendment to a successful bill. The Center party had
introduced a bill banning "immoral" films in Baden, to which
the Nazis added films that violated national honor. On the
whole the experience of the Nazis in the Landtag had little
concrete impact on actual legislation. But the Nazis did
help to undermine respect for parliamentary methods.[25]

THE PARTY'S EXPANSION

Much more important for the Baden party's evolution was its
rapid organizational and membership expansion between the
Landtag election and the Reichstag election of July 1930. As
early as March 1930, the Gau announced a major spring propaganda offensive and ordered its Gau speakers (with some help
from Reich speakers) to launch over nine hundred rallies during
March. Kramer, the Gau propaganda leader, ordered that the
campaign center first on recruiting new members and second on
winning more subscriptions for the party press.[26]

Between January and June 1930 the Nazis carried out an
average of one hundred and fifty rallies per month. The police noted about sixty-two Nazis who spent a considerable
time on these propaganda drives. Later in October, the police
added twenty-two more names, which gave the party almost one
hundred devoted and fanatic permanent agitators in the state.
The social profile of these speakers was dominated by Kaufmänner and white-collar employees who apparently had the time
to campaign constantly for the party. Although no areas of
the state were neglected, the most active districts in 1930,
judged by the origins of these speakers, were still the northern urban and rural districts.[27]

The growth of the Gau apparatus was reflected in Wagner's
order in January 1930 that the Gau business center (which was
now housed in a five-room complex) was neither a warming spot
nor a debate salon. To Wagner it was the staff center for
his campaign in Baden.[28] The Gau leader, who had completely
subordinated his personal life to the party, demanded other
Nazis to follow his fanatic example. Even more important in
reflecting the party's expansion after the state election of

1929 was the growing membership and the expansion of locals
and districts. Gau Baden had forty-eight locals in May 1928
with a total membership of twenty-six hundred. The number of
locals expanded steadily after the Reichstag election of May
1928 until the Gau claimed about seventy by February 1930.
But the most rapid growth occurred between February and August
1930 when the party could rely on two hundred locals one month
before the important Reichstag election. Even the police,
which had monitored the party's activities carefully, were
surprised by the party's rapid growth after the 1929 Landtag
election. The police were quite right, however, in attribut-
ing the party's growth to Reich conditions rather than to
peculiar developments in Baden.[29]

The party's expansion can also be monitored from the
reports of the Führer, which demonstrate the constant activities of the movement in Baden even if the party's exaggerations
are taken into account. For example, according to the party
press, in the district of Heidelberg the March rallies ordered
by the Gau resulted in the creation of seven new locals and
eighteen potential locals (Stützpunkte) by April 1930. The
district's objective was to implement Kramer's order and to
win new members by converting the Nazi voters of 1929 into
party members. It also prepared for the municipal elections
scheduled for November 1930. The party's agitation and organizational expansion became interchangeable.[30] The permanent
activities can be seen in all parts of the state from the
established north and northeast to central and southern Baden.
In northern Baden the party even made an attempt to establish itself in predominantly Catholic strongholds. In central
Baden, the party concentrated on the district of Kehl and
Offenburg, where the Nazis had done well in the election

and on the surrounding districts where some communities had already revealed the party's potential during the election. In the community of Altenheim, Offenburg (later Kehl), the police counted three hundred party members as early as May 1929. By October 1929, 73 percent of the eligible voters in this small Protestant community voted for the NSDAP.[31]

The typical method of expansion was reflected by the local of Kappelrodeck in the district of Bühl, which had been formed in December 1928 by only eight men. From there the local expanded in 1929 and 1930 to the surrounding villages and by August 1930 to Achern. First, a strong local was established in a district, then the activists from that local converted neighboring communities until the district became inundated with Nazi locals. In 1930 this was also occurring in the virgin territory of the south, which was reflected in the growth of Gau districts.[32] In 1928, the Gau had twenty-three districts. In the north, the party districts corresponded with state districts (Ämter), but in the south several Ämter were combined into one party district. By February 1930, only one additional southern district had been created. But during 1930, eight new party districts appeared, primarily in southern and central Baden, giving the party greater organizational penetration of the state.[33]

The rapid expansion of the party on the district level forced the party to rely on Kreisleiters who had joined the party only recently. Of ten new district leaders appearing between 1930 and 1932, six had not joined the party until 1930. Unlike the earlier district leaders, many of these new Kreisleiters came from the educated or professional middle class. A list of twenty district leaders in 1932 included the traditional party leaders who were farmers (four), Käufmanner

(four), clerks, teachers, and lower civil servants. But the
list also contained seven well-educated professionals. Only
workers and industrial magnates were absent from the list.
Although many of these new Kreisleiters had not joined the
party until 1930 and several were dentists, lawyers, and engineers, they came from the same age group that had always
dominated this party position. The average age of ten new
leaders appointed between 1930 and 1932 was 33.9. The nine
who were born between 1897 and 1905 were of the same generation
that had founded the völkisch movement in Baden after 1925 and
contributed so heavily to the party's district leadership.
Only now more educated and professional men were attracted
by the Nazi movement. Similar to the founders of the state's
Nazi movement, many of the new Kreisleiters had participated in
right-wing and paramilitary organizations before they joined
the party.[34]

The party's constant agitation and organizational growth
after the Landtag election also resulted in the rapid expansion of its membership. For example, the party press claimed
that the local of Wertheim increased its membership between
April and July 1930 by 100 percent. Although these claims
were naturally intended for propaganda purposes, they were
not far from the truth and were often corroborated by police
reports. The expansion of the party before the Reichstag election of 1930 was both real and impressive. Heidelberg had
184 party members in the fall of 1929 and 800 members in
March 1930. By August 1930 it was, according to police reports, the largest local in Baden with 1,600 members. The
same growth between the Landtag election and August 1930 occurred in the other large locals of Baden. Between May 1929
and August 1930, the Karlsruhe local increased from 500 to

1,000 members. With this growth the large locals were forced
to subdivide into cells to handle the burgeoning membership.[35]

Both police estimates and figures published by the Führer
reveal the general growth of the Gau's membership after the
Landtag election. The party's official statistics show that
24,413 party members who were active in Baden in 1934 had
joined by January 1933. Of these, 5,259 had become members
by 14 September 1930. The Führer also published information
in 1933 which revealed that 1,500 active Baden Nazis had
joined by 1929. These two figures of 1,500 and 5,259, although perhaps not precise, do reveal the rapid expansion of
the party after the Landtag election. In fact, the 5,259
figure was probably low since the police in August 1930 estimated that 8,000 people belonged to the Baden NSDAP. In any
case, between the Landtag election and September 1930 the
party increased its membership by at least 400 percent. This
expansion contributed substantially to the party's success in
the national election of September 1930. After September 1930,
the flood of new applications caused the Baden Gau to impose
a membership freeze between 19 November 1930 and 21 January
1931, to allow for the assimilation of new members.[36]

The type of people attracted to the Nazi party did not
vary much, except that more professionals and Gebildete (educated) appeared in the party after 1930. The local leaders
appearing in 1929, the district leaders of 1930, and the
speakers listed by the police do not greatly modify the picture of a party dominated by the lower middle class. Master
artisans, skilled workers, farmers, white-collar employees,
and Kaufmänner dominated the local and district posts in 1929
and 1930. More professionals appeared after 1930. In general, the police noted that particularly in urban rallies,

the Mittelstand, civil servants, employees, and increasingly
women participated in Nazi rallies. Few workers were observed
at Nazi rallies, and as late as October 1931, the police still
concluded that the educated members (Gebildete) of society,
with few exceptions, did not participate actively in the party's public agitation.[37]

The party's expansion after the state election of 1929
resulted in the growing centralization of decision making on
all levels of the party organization. The mass of party members were gradually restricted to yearly local membership meetings, where they received activity reports and often, in the
case of larger locals, an address by Wagner. The loss of
real decision-making powers affected both local and district
structures. District leaders related Gau instructions and
programs to the local leaders and local party functionaries
at monthly district party conferences. At the very top, the
Gau section leaders presented their topical programs to the
party leadership at special Gau leadership conferences. As
the membership and locals grew, the party became more impersonal, particularly in the large urban centers. Gradually
also, Gau specialists emerged who coordinated important questions of organization, finance, propaganda, and special activities for both locals and districts.[38]

The development of a mass party organization after 1929
had the dual effect of increasing the party's finances while
simultaneously adding new burdens to the party's treasury.
From 1928/29 on, the party faced increasing costs because of
constant election and propaganda campaigns and the growing
bureaucratization of the Gau structure. At the beginning of
1930, the Gau headquarters' regular monthly financial obligations amounted to 1,000 RM. Five people on the Gau level

received salaries, including Friedhelm Kemper, the local leader
of Mannheim. Kemper's monthly salary of 150 RM, no doubt, was
intended to help advance the party in the industrial center of
Baden. In addition to these fixed costs, the party in early
1930 had to meet the debts incurred during the election of
1929.[39] Yet, by August 1930 the police noted with amazement
the sound finances of the party, with the largest source of
income coming from the Nazis' public rallies. Despite high
entrance fees, according to the police, these rallies were
always filled in 1930. This fanatic willingness to contribute
despite deteriorating economic conditions, combined with the
strong influx of new members in 1930, brought badly needed
funds into the party's coffers.[40]

THE REICHSTAG ELECTION OF 1930

All of the party's activities in 1930 reached a climax in the
national election of September 1930, perhaps the most important election for National Socialism before the seizure of
power. Although no one knew until July 1930 that the Reichstag
would be dissolved, the Nazi party had been active throughout
the year expanding its membership and preparing for the November 1930 municipal elections. In fact, as the police noted,
the Nazi party was the only one ready for the election campaign when the Reichstag was dissolved.[41] The Baden party
initiated its election campaign in August 1930 with a series
of organizational preparations. The Gau center assigned
speakers to the district leaders and demanded that all speakers follow precisely the schedule. Locals prepared by issuing
propaganda material and by demanding that all party members

be available for the election even if vacations had to be postponed. Between 23 August and 12 September, the party initiated
a mass saturation propaganda campaign that was judged to be
extremely effective even by the police. Most of the speakers
were native Badenese, although a handful of Reich and Austrian
Nazis participated in the Baden campaign.[42]

The Gau provided uniform propaganda themes by distributing
leaflets and pamphlets. The themes articulated by the Nazis
aimed at all sections of society. The workers were told that
their leaders were Jews, Catholics were reminded that no church
law existed which required a vote for the Center party, and
voters in general were warned of wasting their votes on splinter
parties, a description the Nazis used for all "bourgeois" parties. The Nazis revealed their opposition to pacifism, internationalism, and above all Jews, in addition to lamenting
frankly Germany's unfulfilled need for Lebensraum.[43]

The Baden Nazis also inspired their voters with two additional methods--mass rallies and detail work. For example,
while the district of Heidelberg initiated the election campaign with a series of mass rallies, the local of Heidelberg
was preparing for the detail work. On the eve of the election,
the local leader ordered all party members to fulfill their
voting obligations by noon and then bring their assigned voters
to the polls. The cell election steward had to make sure this
order was carried out. SA and SS men were ordered to appear
at party headquarters at 7 a.m. where they would be met by
party members who owned cars or motorcycles. One hour later,
this group proceeded to harness all possible support for the
party at the polls.[44]

The party's election slate published by the Führer on
27 August demonstrated the growing "respectability" of the

Nazi party. The first ten names on the list included five
farmers, a teacher, a shopkeeper, and three educated profes-
sionals--a lawyer, a professor, and an engineer. All of the
front-runners were either Gau functionaries or district leaders, and five were Baden Landtag members. Wagner was not on
the list, allegedly because he "considered his primary function to be still in Baden." In reality, he could not run
because had he been elected, he would have had to resign his
Landtag seat. This seat would then have gone to the first
alternate, an engineer, who joined the party in the summer of
1929 but then broke with the Nazi leadership in February 1930
after a fight with Wagner.[45]

The Nazis faced strong opposition from the government
coalition partners and the Communists. As early as May 1930,
at the party's state conference the Socialist leaders had
issued a warning not to underestimate the Nazis, who, according to the Socialists, were mostly young elements alienated
from the economic system. The party's paper, Volksfreund,
continued to picture the NSDAP as being sponsored by high
finance. The Catholic papers pointed out that the Nazis
were not real fascists. After all, the papers argued, Mussolini was not a racist and did not engage in religious fights
or anti-Semitism.[46] The Communists fought hard against the
Nazis, but they were not as well organized and lacked sufficient funds to compete effectively. After the election, the
state's KPD leader, Paul Schreck, admitted that the Nazis had
been far better prepared than the Communists, particularly in
their efforts in the countryside.[47]

The election results surprised even the Baden Nazis. The
party won 226,655 votes or a total of 19.2 percent. This
represented an increase of 161,534 votes over the state election

of October 1929. Clearly, the bulk of the new support came
from the new voters since the parties on the right and center
lost only a total of 25,000 votes. The majority of new voters
who participated in September 1930 supported the extremist
parties on the right and left. The NSDAP's activism resulted
in votes in 96.7 percent of Baden's communities, a remark-
able achievement. In many rural communities, the Nazis obtained votes without having campaigned there. Clearly, the
party's advance in the Protestant, rural strongholds continued
unabated. In Kehl, Bretten, Sinsheim, and Wertheim the party
won between 30 and 44 percent of the total vote. In all of
these districts, the Rechtsblock had been dominant since 1921.
The party's expansion to the central and southern parts of the
state was the most noticeable development in 1930. If 1928
represented a rural breakthrough and 1929 an urban breakthrough
for the Baden party, then 1930 was a southern breakthrough.
In fact, 47 percent of the party's increase came in central
and southern Baden (below the district of Ettlingen). In 1929,
only about 30 percent of the party's advance had taken place
in this area. The party began to expand into the southern
Protestant rural strongholds like Müllheim, Emmendingen, and
Lahr. In addition, it also made significant inroads into the
predominantly Catholic districts of Offenburg, Oberkirch, and
Bühl, where it won between 23 and 24 percent of the total vote.
Apparently, the party reactivated voters who for the most part
had not voted for the Center party in these districts. On the
whole, however, the Nazi party continued to be weakest in the
Catholic strongholds of southeastern Baden.[48]

In addition to the rural advance, the party did very well
in urban centers like Karlsruhe, Heidelberg, Weinheim, and
Rastatt, where it won about one fourth of the vote, primarily

because of the new voters (see Map 8). It won 19.1 percent of
its votes in urban centers with populations over 10,000. In
Mannheim, the party again did relatively poorly, getting only
13.5 percent of the vote. There is some evidence that the
Nazis captured some votes from the Communists in Mannheim.
The police noted that the Nazis did very poorly in the Socialist
strongholds. But five of the six districts in Mannheim where
the Nazis fared well were former Communist areas. Only the
sixth had been a DNVP stronghold. The Nazi-Communist rivalry
in Mannheim was clearly demonstrated by the fact that the
strongest Nazi district in the city bordered on the strongest
Communist district. Despite the Mannheim example, the Nazis'
major urban support came from the nonindustrial urban centers.
The Baden party had good cause to claim in 1930 that it had
urban and rural as well as northern and southern support.
The deteriorating economic conditions only promised the NSDAP
more potential success. In 1929, an average of 71,366 people
were unemployed in Baden. By 1930, this figure had risen to
99,813 and it continued to climb.[49]

The election gave three Baden candidates Reichstag seats.
Karl Lenz, the deputy Gau leader, Robert Roth, the founder of
the Liedolsheim local in 1923, and Johannes Rupp, a lawyer,
represented the Baden party. Rupp was the son of the Deutsch-
konservative delegate to the Reichstag from Eppingen, Sinsheim,
between 1907 and 1918. He had belonged to the Stahlhelm, and
as late as 1929 he had been on the DNVP ticket in the state
election. Rupp, who joined the Nazi party in December 1929,
was the Gau municipal office's legal advisor until 1931. Lenz
and Roth belonged to the "Gau clique," and all three of these
Baden representatives represented the interests of the Baden
Gau leadership.[50]

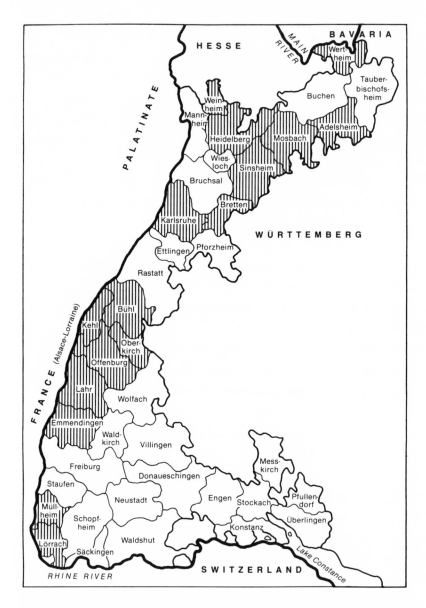

Map 8. *Reichstag Election: 1930*

Nazi Strongholds: Districts with over 19.3% of the vote

The Baden Nazis immediately demanded the dissolution of
the state legislature and new state elections in order to obtain a power base in Baden that would reflect their new political strength.[51] This was to no avail since the Socialist-
Catholic coalition held a majority in the Landtag. But for
the first time the rival Baden parties could no longer ignore
the Nazi movement. The Volksfreund lamented the "political
misery" in Baden that had resulted in the victory of lies.
It blamed the economic crisis, while the Badischer Beobachter
noted that the growth of the Nazi party was abnormal and could
not be explained rationally. All the Badischer Beobachter
could do was to attribute the Nazi vote to immaturity. Even
the organ of the DNVP, which concluded that in general the
political right was now stronger in Baden, was surprised by
the Nazi success. It attributed the Nazi growth to the shortcomings of the parliamentary system and to economic conditions.
Finally, the Communists in a postelection conference drew the
necessary conclusion from the Nazi victory. They planned to
counter Nazi activism with Communist activism, even in the
countryside and among women.[52]

The most interesting reaction to the election and one
symptomatic of the growing susceptibility of the respectable
middle class to National Socialism was an editorial in the
Karlsruher Zeitung. In 1923, this paper had not only demanded
a crackdown on right-wing activities but also scolded the judiciary for being too lax against right-wing offenders. In
1930, the paper noted that the Nazi success was not simply
the result of the activities of juvenile delinquents but rather it was due to the support the Nazis received from the
bourgeoisie (Bürgertum). It concluded that since the good
Bürgertum had now voted for the NSDAP, the Nazi party had to

be judged differently. The editorial concluded that any movement which received such strong middle-class support could no
longer be ignored or rejected. Clearly, the bourgeoisie had
fallen prey to the Nazi message by 1930.[53] The Baden leadership attempted to reassure the bourgeoisie of its legality.
The Führer in November 1930 declared that "our whole battle
was and will still be aimed at capturing political power on
the basis of a completely legal and parliamentary, democratic
path." Wagner reiterated this theme again in February 1931
when he declared that the twelfth year must belong to victory, not through force but rather through the free election
of the German Reich.[54]

MUNICIPAL ACTIVITIES

By September, the Baden party had won access to the Landtag
and Reichstag. But the most important penetration, both for
the continuous expansion of the party and for the future
seizure of power, had to occur on the local level. The party
was well prepared for the municipal election of November 1930.
It organized for the election as early as the spring and continued its agitation unabated after September 1930. Even
before the 14 September election, Gau propaganda leader Kemper
ordered all large locals to continue public rallies between
15 and 30 September, utilizing the theme "the election campaign is finished, the decisive battle goes on." Kemper reminded the party leaders that the party must arrange for future
struggles. Indeed, after the Reich election, Kemper announced
a permanent saturation campaign. No party speaker was allowed
more than fourteen days' rest because, beginning in October

1930, the Gau planned one thousand rallies monthly.[55]

The Baden Nazis had first participated in municipal elections in 1926 when the party won representation in ten (mostly medium- and small-sized) communities. But the party had no municipal program or structure until 1927 when Karl Fiehler was appointed national municipal advisor and a municipal journal (<u>Mitteilungsblatt für die N.S. in den Parlamenten und Gemeinden</u>) was issued to provide information for local Nazi delegates. Not until 1932 did Fiehler issue circulars, leaving the local battle until then in the hands of the Gau and local party structure. In Baden, this task fell primarily on two new party members who had the expertise to guide the local Nazis. Johannes Rupp, a lawyer, and Rudolf Schindler, an employee of an insurance firm in Karlsruhe, had both joined the party in 1929. Rupp was the head of the Gau municipal section until he was replaced by his assistant Schindler.[56]

The municipal campaign began in Baden in January 1930 when the party initiated a series of educational sessions for prospective candidates. The Heidelberg local, for example, scheduled up to six evening courses for February alone with lectures by Karl Pflaumer, Walter Köhler, Otto Bender, and Keppler from Eberbach, all having some municipal expertise. This was followed in March by the Heidelberg district's "March offensive for the communal elections in the fall." Also, during the same month Rupp offered training courses in several districts and special presentations on municipal affairs at Gau leadership conferences. Although these preparations were interrupted by the Reichstag election of September, they were resumed immediately afterward. In fact, the Mannheim district's municipal section warned that only Nazis with ample education and preparation could be sent to the local parliaments.[57]

In September, the Gau municipal section also prepared
lists of candidates for the election by sending questionnaires
to the local and district leaders, which had to be filled out
by the local candidates. The local leaders returned these
lists to the district leaders, who in turn sent them to the
Gau municipal section for approval. The Gau's growing centralization provided more efficiency at the cost of local autonomy.[58] During the following month, the Gau leadership announced
a program that appealed primarily to the _Mittelstand_ and farmers and espoused a "moral Christian worldview" in addition to
extreme nationalism. At the same time, the Nazis admitted
frankly that National Socialism would use every method to
strengthen itself and weaken democracy. During October, Baden
was saturated with rallies and Munich declared the Gau a major
battle area (_Grosskampfgebiet_). The climax of the election
campaign came with Hitler's visits to major urban centers in
November.[59]

The party obtained representation in about 70 percent
of Baden's communities and emerged with pluralities in Karlsruhe, Heidelberg, Rastatt, Kehl, Weinheim, Bretten, Lahr,
Bühl, and Müllheim. In numerous small communities and rural
villages, the Nazis won absolute majorities. About two thousand of the five thousand candidates presented by the party
were elected to municipal positions.[60] The Nazi candidates,
many of whom had cooperated with other bourgeois parties in
election unions, represented the various segments of the
Mittelstand. For example, in Heidelberg the thirty-one successful candidates included seven _Kaufmänner_, five farmers, and
five skilled workers who represented the lower middle class.
The rest of the list included judges, doctors, architects,
and engineers, all comprising the solid middle class. In

provincial Bühl, the party candidates reflected faithfully
the prevalent lower-middle-class occupations of the town and
included two small businessmen. Of course, in a rural community like Kappelrodeck, many Nazi municipal officials were
farmers (42 percent) or rural artisans, small businessmen,
and skilled workers. In short, the Nazi lists, except for
industrial workers and large business tycoons, represented
the communities' social structures. Many of these party representatives had joined the party only recently (1929 or 1930),
and most were older than the young Nazi activists. By 1930,
the Nazi party had not only broken into the middle-class establishment but also represented it on the local level.[61]

Even where the NSDAP was not represented, the party's
momentum in late 1930 was so great that local sympathizers
set up their own Nazi lists and candidates without ever having
officially established a Nazi local. In Sasbachried, for example, a list of Nazis was presented to the voters in the election despite the fact that the Gau did not know whether a local
or even party members existed in the village. As late as
April 1931, the Gau municipal leaders discovered Nazi electoral
lists that had been presented to the villages where no party
locals existed; and on occasion the successful candidates had
not been party members when they were placed on the lists.
While this obviously created an organizational nightmare for
the Gau's municipal leaders, it reflected the party's growing
success in presenting itself as a respectable political alternative.[62]

The Baden party's success in penetrating the Mittelstand
and even some Catholic areas is reflected in two further examples. After the election, municipalities with over 2,000
people still had to elect mayors. Again local party leaders

had to seek the approval of the Gau leadership for their candidates. In several instances the Gau granted locals permission to form coalitions with bourgeois parties. For example, when the Socialists, the Staatspartei, and the Center party of Offenburg set up a joint list for the district council elections in January 1931, the Nazis responded by forming a coalition with the middle-class Wirtschaftspartei. Even more revealing was the party's success in Catholic Bühlertal, a community (99 percent Catholic) of 5,400 people in south-central Baden. Already in May 1924 the Völkisch Block of Bühlertal had won 182 out of a total of 1,369 votes, second only to the Center party's 840 votes. By 1930 these völkisch votes, in addition to some new votes, had increased the NSDAP's vote to 260 out of a total of 1,825. This represented 14 percent of the total votes cast in this Catholic town.[63]

Of special interest is the contract drafted in January 1931 between the Bühlertal Nazi local and Karl Fauth, the party's candidate for mayor. Fauth, an accountant who was born in Bühlertal in 1885, did not join the party until 1930 (but remained active until 1945). The Nazi local's contract stipulated the usual agreement that bound Fauth to the Nazi program and to a reduced mayoral salary. But the contract also called on the Nazi candidate to protect the Catholic church and to attend church services on all religious holidays. For legal reasons, this last clause was modified to require Fauth only to carry out his office according to the basic tenets of Christianity and to protect the Christian church.[64] On 26 January 1931, Fauth was elected mayor with thirty-seven of seventy-three votes. His election, however, was declared void by the district council (Bezirksrat) because two election slips were "found" after the election, and new elections had

to be scheduled for 7 April 1931. Fauth was again elected
mayor with the support of twenty-four Nazi, twelve Bürgerliche, and three Center party votes. The party had won the
support not only of the bourgeois party but also of some
Catholics. The Center party support was related to the fact
that Fauth was a close friend of the Center party's candidate, Gustav Baumann. Apparently, Baumann urged some Center
party delegates to vote for Fauth. And even if Fauth had
lost the election, concluded one local party leader, the
party would still have had a friend in the mayoral post.[65] The
Nazi movement in Bühlertal represented not so much a revolt
of one segment of the population but rather a rallying point
for the community's majority, a majority dissatisfied with
the economic and political status quo.

After the election in November 1930, the Gau municipal
section was inundated with legal and technical questions from
the various Nazi delegations in Baden. The local Nazis frequently lacked the legal and technical knowledge required to
deal with legislative and administrative issues. Some did
not know that the mayor could vote in the executive council;
others were baffled by financial and tax issues.[66] To meet
these demands and to guide and advise the Nazi delegations in
Baden, the Gau municipal section held educational conferences. Like all sections of the party, the Gau section expanded in power and organization. Schindler, who took over
the Gau office in April 1931, was not an old party member,
but he had the solid support of Wagner, despite his personal
shortcomings (which included stealing). In the summer of
1931, he wrote the first Baden contribution to the Nazi party's municipal information bulletin, and he proceeded to
introduce municipal district leaders to thirty-one of forty

Baden districts. These leaders had the power to control publications and reports concerning the party's municipal affairs.
Above all, they had to watch over the Nazi delegations to
prevent major blunders. Finally, to enhance the Gau municipal section's influence and effectiveness, Wagner in October
1931 ordered all Nazi municipal delegates to subscribe to the
Gau party's new municipal information bulletin (Mitteilungsblatt).[67]

The legislative work of the Nazi delegations in the communities of Baden was circumscribed by Gau directives. On
occasion, local interest groups appealed to the Nazi delegations to introduce minor legislation pertaining to local matters. Much of the Nazi municipal activities revolved around
squabbles with local political opponents, but the bulk of the
party's legislative efforts were reflections of Gau directives.[68] The Gau published legislative proposals in the Führer
and in the Gau's Mitteilungsblatt, which had to be introduced
by all Nazi delegations in Baden. Most important to the Gau
were the proposals that demanded a reduction in the salaries
of mayors and officials, the elimination of positions, and
the taxation of department stores. For the most part, the
locals faithfully introduced a barrage of proposals reflecting the Gau leadership's wishes and on occasion could even
point to some successes in reducing the salaries of Nazi mayors.[69] Even in Achern, where the majority of the Nazi voters
favored the Bürgersteuer and where the Nazis had cooperated
with the Wirtschaftsbund, which also wanted this tax in order
to reduce property taxes, the Gau told the Nazi delegation
that under no circumstances could it vote for this "Negro Tax."
Instead, the Nazis were ordered to focus on the introduction
of legislation dealing with salary reductions and taxes on

chain stores.[70]

This did not mean, however, that the Nazi delegations
functioned flawlessly or that the Gau section controlled all
local affairs. Nazi council members attacked local party
leaders and in some cases voted against party bills introduced by the local Nazi municipal leader. In another instance,
the Nazi delegation leader circumvented both the party's local
leader and his own delegation and initiated legislation.[71] In
one case, a Nazi mayor even introduced the Bürgersteuer in
order to avoid losing Reich and state financial contributions.
Naturally, the Nazi delegation voted against this budget.
When the local party leader demanded the Nazi mayor's expulsion from the party, it took Wagner's personal intervention
to solve the problem. His solution was simple and typical.
Wagner declared that the Nazi delegation could not accept
the tax, hence it had to refuse the budget. But the Nazi
mayor had to support his own budget. The issue was declared
solved and the Gau leader demanded local harmony.[72]

Any evaluation of Nazi activities in the local legislatures between 1929 and 1932 must take into account the deteriorating economic and financial situation. By 1932, for
example, ten textile firms, five brush factories, four paper
shops, one machine factory, and one lumberyard had ceased to
function in Lörrach, leaving unemployed eight thousand out
of a total work force of eleven thousand. The loss of revenues
and taxes affected all aspects of local government especially
since welfare burdens escalated dramatically after 1930. Budget proposals disintegrated before they could be implemented.
In Rastatt, the budget for 1930/31 had anticipated 600,000 RM
for welfare, but by the end of December 1930 the city needed
already over 1 million RM for welfare. At the same time, one

of the city's major sources of income, the sale of lumber, declined because of the depressed wood market.[73]

The NSDAP's response to these problems was anything but constructive. The leading Gau municipal leaders and the Führer in 1931 continued to reiterate that the final collapse of the system could not be prevented and that the party had no intention of helping to preserve the government. The Gau municipal section directed the Nazi delegates, for example, in Baden-Baden to attack a budget of over 1 million RM by focusing on a minor 1,000-RM union fund and on the increase of 29,000 RM for welfare.[74] This propagandistic, but not very constructive, approach to municipal affairs by the Nazis was revealed even more by the Rastatt local. Fucke-Michels, the Nazi municipal delegation leader, had to contend with a radical local Nazi activist who had the Gau's support and who favored a blind policy of negativism and the reduction of officials' salaries. Wagner appointed this man delegation leader after Fucke-Michels voiced his disappointment with the Nazi party's municipal policy following the election of November 1930. After the election, noted Fucke-Michels, he had expected that the Nazis would show the people constructive and practical municipal accomplishments. Instead, he concluded he received only slogans (Schlagwörter) even in a private conversation with the Gau leader.[75]

Nazis like Fucke-Michels did not understand that the party's municipal policy was subordinated to the party's plan to achieve total power and was never geared to confront the problems of the time. The party's municipal program provided the party with two major benefits. First, the local Nazis could use their municipal posts for propaganda purposes and also provide the party's activists and supporters with short-range benefits in the form of positions. Second, the election of

Nazis to municipal positions gave them the experience that
facilitated both the "legal revolution" on the local level and
the consolidation of Nazi power after January 1933.

THE PARTY AND CIVIL SERVANTS

The Nazi party's success in penetrating the "establishment"
in Baden and winning support from "respectable" members of
society and the government's inability to cope with these developments is finally illustrated by the conversion of Beamte
(civil servants) to the NSDAP. Despite government bans on
the participation of civil servants in Nazi affairs and
Remmele's strict adherence to this policy, the police noted in
1930 and 1931 the increased participation of judges, teachers,
and other civil servants in Nazi rallies and activities. Three
judges from northern Baden (Roland Erb, Heinrich Bammersberg,
and Karl Fath) who had been invited to Hitler's speech in
Heidelberg in 1928 were regular and enthusiastic visitors at
Nazi rallies by 1930. Bammersberg of Mannheim, who had voiced
strong anti-Semitism and antirepublicanism as early as 1922,
denounced the police surveillance vigorously. He pointed out
that the head of the political police in Heidelberg, Gustav
Walther, was an "old SPD man" and a friend of Remmele, and he
argued that the NSDAP was not an enemy of the state. Most
of these judges simply continued to support the Nazi party
with blatant disregard for state orders.[76]

In November 1930, Gau Baden established an NS Civil
Service League, which became active on the district level by
July 1931. Civil servants from government inspectors to rail-
road and postal officials were increasingly attracted to the

Nazi movement.[77] Judicial civil servants went so far as to
sell Hitler paraphernalia in their offices, and several even
used the "Heil" greeting. Some civil servants felt secure
enough to lead Nazi rallies, while others participated in
party affairs covertly. From Heidelberg to Konstanz, the Nazi
party was converting civil servants and undermining the authority of the state.[78] In extreme cases, when lower-level
civil servants felt too much government pressure, they asked
for "withdrawal" papers from the Nazi party to protect their
jobs, although in reality they never abandoned the movement.[79]

It was much easier for the government, particularly as
long as Remmele was minister of interior, to crack down on
public schoolteachers who flocked to the Nazi movement as
early as November 1929. Wagner had received training as a
teacher before he joined the army, and Kramer and Lenz, both
key Gau officials, were teachers. When teacher participation
in Nazi activities increased dramatically in the spring of
1930, Remmele won the support of the cabinet to initiate legal
actions against several Nazi teachers. Remmele argued con-
vincingly that teachers should educate children along repub-
lican-democratic lines.[80] The three Nazi teachers attacked
by Remmele, Adolf Schuppel of Wolfach, Emil Gärtner of
Neufreistett, Kehl, and Erwin Schmidt of Pforzheim, were all
party activists. Schuppel was even a district leader, and
Schmidt was the local leader of Pforzheim. After a legal
battle, Schuppel and Gärtner each received a 100-RM fine, and
only in the case of Schmidt did Remmele insist on dismissal.[81]

Although the Führer claimed that ten Nazi teachers had
been fired by 1930, Remmele and the Baden government were totally unsuccessful in their attempts to stem the tide of the
Nazi conversion of teachers. When Remmele tried to warn Herbert

Kraft, a professor at a Gymnasium in Mannheim, that the NSDAP
was an enemy of the state and that he should be aware of the
"consequences" of belonging to this party, Kraft ignored him
and continued his party activism.[82] This was typical in
1930/31 as more and more teachers became not only members of
the Nazi party in Baden, but activists as well. For example,
between March and May 1930 alone, new Nazi converts included
three teachers who later assumed leading party posts: Wilhelm
Hartlieb, the future Gau indoctrination leader; Karl Gärtner,
the Kreisleiter of Lahr by 1931; and Wilhelm Seiler, another
future Kreisleiter. Karl Lenz also organized an NS Teachers'
League in August 1930. One month later, the Führer claimed
that 506 teachers had already joined this organization. The
political police in Baden concluded in October 1931 that in
the countryside probably most teachers (Volksschullehrer) were
actively working for the NSDAP.[83]

By the end of 1930, the Nazi party had successfully invaded the state and national legislatures and obtained significant representation in the municipal bodies of the state.
Most important, the party had succeeded in convincing middle-
class spokesmen, like the editor of the Karlsruher Zeitung
and many civil servants who used to support the Nationalists,
that the Nazi party was a viable and realistic alternative
to the established political parties, which apparently were
leading the country further and further toward economic, social, and political chaos. The deteriorating economic conditions, both in the countryside and in the cities, had played
a major part in making an increasingly large portion of the
Baden population receptive to Nazi propaganda. The overwhelming activism of the Nazis ensured that the party's themes were
disseminated to every corner of the state.

6

The Organization of the Mass Party, 1930-1932

Following the municipal election campaign late in 1930, the
Nazi party in Baden continued its massive drives to mobilize
new supporters. In December of that year, when the Gau propaganda leader decided that massive rallies would continue to
be the party's most effective propaganda vehicle, the Nazis
launched a new wave of weekend gatherings calculated to reach
a larger portion of the population. Not until April 1931 did
Kramer order a short interruption in the rallies to allow for
effective organizational consolidation.[1] Later, during the
second half of 1931, Gau Baden attempted to shift its main
efforts to the rural communities since the urban rallies
seemed to have reached a temporary saturation point. According to police reports, no rural community or village appeared
to be without a Nazi agitator. At the same time, the untiring activities of the urban party agitators again, surprisingly, increased attendance at urban rallies. Although the
NSDAP attracted few workers to these urban campaigns, the
Mittelstand and increasingly women flocked to party meetings
held in Baden's urban centers. With absolute self-confidence,
the party in September 1931 announced a "storm over Baden"
and a "storm on the factories." Deteriorating economic conditions, which pushed the unemployment up 100 percent from

1929 to 145,407, provided a fertile soil for this program.[2]

The constantly expanding program of propaganda made it imperative that the Gau leadership introduce organizational centralization, particularly since many of the new party members were not völkisch true believers. In early 1930, Kramer established firm control over the party's speakers. He prepared dossiers on all Gau speakers, and he allocated them among the various locals. One year later, local and district leaders could obtain their speakers only from a Gau speaker roster. In addition, after major saturation campaigns these speakers had to report to the Gau propaganda leader for new assignments. To control the propaganda being disseminated, the propaganda leader began to issue circulars to the Nazi speakers in Baden to provide them with information and instructions.[3] The first of these monthly circulars appeared late in 1930. They were sent to the district leaders, who in turn forwarded them to the newly appointed district propaganda leaders. These innovations ensured Gau control over both content and intensity of party propaganda themes as well as financial powers over the locals. Important rallies, particularly those featuring Hitler as a speaker, provided the locals with badly needed funds from admission fees.[4]

The same process of centralization occurred with the Gau's newspapers. Early in 1931, Wagner banned all local and district information bulletins and emphasized that thereafter the Führer would be the Gau's main vehicle for party information and instructions. The following year, he sought to control the burgeoning Nazi press, stating that the creation of a Nazi newspaper was exclusively the task of the Gau leadership.[5] Previously, various party activists had issued their own party papers, such as Schwarzwälder Flugblatt in

Donaueschingen, and the Feldberg Rundschau in Neustadt, begun
by Friedrich Sattler in 1931. After obtaining the cooperation
of the district leader, he turned out the first issue on
October 15. Sattler not only financed this weekly but he was
also its editor and publisher. Such independence could not
be tolerated by a centralizing party, and in 1932 the Gau paper
Alemanne replaced the Feldberg Rundschau. Most of the other
local newspapers gave way to the expanding Gau press. An isolated exception was the Grenzlandnachrichten of Lahr, but its
independence reflected the rebellion of a whole local against
the Gau leadership.[6]

To compensate for the loss of the local papers, the
number of Gau sheets expanded in 1931 to three and by October
1932 to five. In 1931, the Heidelberger Beobachter and the
Hakenkreuzbanner of Mannheim appeared in addition to the established Führer. During the following year, two southern
newspapers, the Alemanne of Freiburg and the Bodensee Rundschau
of Konstanz, were added to allow the party to disseminate information and instructions to its followers. All of these
papers started as weeklies and then gradually became daily
newspapers. Their editions remained modest despite noticeable increases in 1931. All of the papers were controlled
by Wagner and managed by his faithful Gau supporters.[7]

The irresponsible journalism these papers engaged in
brought them trouble with the authorities. The Führer was
banned for sixty-eight days between May 1931 and August 1932,
and its editors, Wacker and Moraller, were forced to participate during this period in sixty-five trials, twenty of
which ended in judgments against the Nazis. The Baden government prosecuted the Nazi papers for such offenses as insulting
national government leaders and accusing the Catholic Center

party of separatism. Although the party papers were irresponsible and vicious, the Baden government's limitations on the
freedom of the press was an ominous precedent for the future.[8]
These restrictions did little to inhibit the growth of the Nazi
press in Baden. Karlsruhe even published a special series
(Braune Bücherei) of Nazi "classics," which included the works
of Alfred Rosenberg and Robert Wagner's Tod dem Marxismus: Es
lebe der Nationalsozialismus, a work that related the standard
Social Darwinistic themes of the Nazi movement.[9]

THE SA AND SS

In addition to the party's press and propaganda efforts, the
Gau leadership also relied on the SA for the mobilization of
support. According to Albert Speer, for example, his mother
joined the NSDAP in Heidelberg in 1931 after witnessing an SA
parade, which "in a time of chaos gave her the impression of
energy."[10] In Baden, the SA had emerged from the Schlageterbund, which Wagner had registered with the police late in
1924. Gradually as the party organization matured, the Gau's
cadre leadership and the Gau's SA leadership evolved indepen-
dently. Early in 1929, Wagner ordered his party cadre leaders
not to join the SA in order that they might devote themselves
completely to party affairs. This separation between the SA
and the party's cadre organization was symbolized by the fact
that in 1930 the Gau's SA headquarters were not in the same
building that housed all of the other party offices.[11]

Beginning with 1929 Munich appointed and removed the
Gau's SA leaders, even over the objections of Wagner. In late
1929, Munich fired the Gau SA leader Windgassen, a retired

naval officer, for "lack of discipline" and replaced him with
another former officer, Lieutenant Fröhlich. Apparently
Fröhlich was charged with some offense against the party and
replaced in July 1930 by Marschall von Bieberstein. This former
officer had marched in Munich in 1923 and emerged in Baden in
1925 as the leader of the Schlageterbund of Freiburg. This
old Nazi was on good terms with Wagner, and in late 1930 he
became a Nazi delegate in the Baden Landtag. Bieberstein
served until the summer of 1931 when he was replaced by the
last SA leader of Baden before 1933, Hanns Ludin. None of
these Gau SA leaders were really part of Wagner's Gau clique,
and only Bieberstein received much publicity in the Führer.
Wagner did maintain close relations with the SA through his
personal friend Franz Moraller, the Gau adjutant of the Baden
SA, who became Gau propaganda leader of the party. In addition, Karl Pflaumer, a former police officer and organization
leader of the SA in Baden after 1929, eventually became the
Baden minister of interior after the Nazi seizure of power.[12]

Before the Landtag election of 1929, the Baden SA was
not very large and was plagued by conflicts. Late in 1928,
Karlsruhe had only about fifty SA members out of a total party
membership of five hundred. According to the police, the SA
leader of Karlsruhe was so militaristic that few men came to
the meetings. In Mannheim early in 1929 a major revolt broke
out that involved 25 percent of the total membership. The
conflict was between the SA leader, a worker and former Marxist, and the lower-middle-class cadre leaders of the party.
Only in 1930/31 did the SA membership expand in Baden. The
police estimated that Baden's SA membership increased from
twenty-four hundred men in mid-1930 to five thousand by October
1931. By the later date, the Karlsruhe local alone had five

hundred SA men. Although the police noted many more workers in the Baden SA than in the Nazi party, most of the SA members were Kaufmänner and Handarbeiter (manual workers). For the most part, these manual workers were artisans and skilled craftsmen rather than industrial workers. This growing SA not only helped in the new propaganda drives but also bore the brunt of the street violence in Baden after 1929.[13]

The man who assumed the leadership of the expanding SA in Baden in the summer of 1931 was Hanns Ludin, a native of Freiburg and a former army officer. He was born in 1905 to a Gymnasium teacher who had little sympathy for the military. After completing high school (Abitur) in 1924, Ludin joined the army. In the service he established close relations with two other young lieutenants of an artillery regiment. The three officers, Ludin, Richard Scheringer, and Hans Friedrich Wendt, became dissatisfied with the alleged pacifism of the government and the "bureaucratic lethargy" of senior military leaders. According to Scheringer, early in 1929 Ludin introduced his fellow Ulm officers to Nazi literature. In November of the same year, Ludin and Scheringer traveled to Munich and established contacts with the SA leadership. After returning to Ulm, the young officers attempted to convert their fellow officers to the Nazi cause. All three lieutenants were arrested and brought to trial in Leipzig in September 1930. Although the trial revealed the political discontent within the army, Hitler used it as a political platform to announce both his support of the army and his determination to adhere to legal tactics. For the young lieutenants, however, the trial resulted in shattered army careers and prison terms.[14]

In prison, Scheringer was converted to Communism, and Wendt became a supporter of Otto Strasser. Only Ludin remained

loyal to National Socialism. Since he was a native of Baden,
Ludin was sentenced to serve his prison term in Rastatt, Baden.
In May 1931, the Nazi Landtag delegation of Baden appealed
to Hindenburg to grant Ludin a pardon. After the former lieutenant finally received a pardon, he traveled to Munich and
participated in SA rallies and activities. One month later
Ludin returned to his native state and became Gau SA leader.
His relations with the party's cadre organization must not have
been very cordial since late in 1932 he was already reporting
the arrogance of the party's political leaders to his SA superiors. Wagner reacted early in 1934 by asking Robert Ley,
the national party organization leader, to use funds which
had been allocated for SA maneuvers for the purchase of party
uniforms. Despite these conflicts over spheres of influence,
Ludin worked energetically to strengthen the party's propaganda
and agitation before 1933.[15]

Violence and even death were not unknown to the party and
the SA. In April 1929, one of the largest clashes between
Nazis and Communists occurred in Karlsruhe when the notorious
Saxon Communist agitator Max Hölz held a rally. Over five hundred party members and SA men from Karlsruhe and the surrounding
communities participated in the melee.[16] In 1930 and 1931,
the violence increased dramatically. Wagner attempted to
control some of the violence by cautioning the SA to avoid
clashes and by banning Communists from Nazi meetings.[17] However, clashes ranging from individual attacks to open street
battles continued unabated. Often Communists attempted to
force their way into Nazi meetings to disrupt the NSDAP's
propaganda drives.[18] The Baden Nazis paid a heavy price by
suffering more injuries in 1931 than any other political movement. For example, in October and November 1931 the Baden Nazis

suffered 731 casualties as compared to 203 for the <u>Reichsbanner</u> Socialists and 152 for the Communists. Most of the violence against the Nazis was inflicted by the Communists, who were responsible for 543 Nazi injuries.[19]

The Baden government reacted resolutely against both Communist and Nazi violence. The various paramilitary groups associated with the Communist party were constantly monitored by the police. As late as October 1931, however, the police found neither stashes of arms nor Communist Putsch plans. In fact, the police concluded that the KPD was not a real threat to the security of the state of Baden.[20] Nor did this picture change in 1932. Despite the Communist party's opportunistic appeals to farmers and the <u>Mittelstand</u>, by late 1932 it probably did not have more than seven thousand members. According to police reports, the Communists won a majority of their new members from the ranks of the unemployed.[21]

Although the KPD did not represent a real danger to the security of the Baden state, the Nazis used the specter of an alleged Communist uprising to exploit the fears of the middle class. In mid-1932, Wagner sent a telegram to the Baden minister of interior, warning him that if the police were not ready to protect the public from the Communists, the Nazis were.[22] Wagner ignored, of course, the fact that the Baden government attempted desperately to control the activities of the NSDAP. In 1930, the police seized party uniforms from Nazis who were not even wearing them.[23]

In the spring of 1932, the state president of Baden informed Berlin that his state only had four thousand policemen to control ten thousand SA men. Karlsruhe pleaded for the introduction of more effective controls over SA activities. To strengthen its case, the Baden government ordered the police to find every possible evidence that would reveal the Nazi party's antistate activities.[24]   But when the government urged Berlin to continue the ban on the SA, Hindenburg in June 1932 informed Karlsruhe that the Nazi movement represented strong national feelings, and von Papen added that the SA ban was unfair to thirteen million Nazi voters.   After the SA ban was lifted, violence increased again in Baden.   By July 1932, the Baden minister of interior reported that on Sundays over twelve thousand Baden SA men were marching about the state.[25]   Without the support of Berlin, there was little the Baden government could do to stem the SA tide.

By 1932, the Baden SA had established work camps to meet the problem of unemployment.   Early in that year, Ludin delegated management of this program to Eduard Helff, an unemployed engineer.   Helff was born in 1891 in Freiburg and served in the war before he became an engineer.   After losing his job in 1929, he became a member of the SA and the Baden NSDAP.   As a member of Ludin's staff, Helff initiated the new program in October 1932 by enrolling fifty-nine men.   Between November and December, he opened four new camps by recruiting primarily unemployed SA men.   These camps were used almost exclusively for rural work, particularly the reclaiming of swampland. In December 1932, Helff wrote that "agriculture is and will remain the foundation for the formation and maintenance of the state."   This is precisely what the NS Labor Service of Baden did both before and after 1933 (when 80 percent of all Reich Labor Service workers in Baden were engaged in rural work).   Although the program did not really address the problem of urban unemployment, it did provide some hope for the SA faithful before 1933.[26]

Compared to the activism of the SA and its efforts to

help disseminate the Nazi message throughout the state, the contribution of the Baden SS before 1933 was only marginal. The SS was founded in Baden in March 1929 at the request of Heinrich Himmler. Wagner assigned the new task to Otto Heidt, an old party member who had joined the NSDAP as early as 1922 and the SA in 1926. Unlike the early SA leaders who were frequently manual workers (Handarbeiter) and occasionally former Marxists, the SS leadership in Baden under Heidt and his successor Hans Helwig was dominated by white-collar employees. Heidt, who was born in 1904, was a Kaufmann as was his adjutant Fritz Argus.[27] Heidt and Helwig were natives of Baden and belonged to the early Nazi movement. Only after 1933 were Baden SS leaders appointed who were not natives of the state or close to the early party activists. This reflected, of course, the growing influence of Himmler and the expansion of the SS as an organization. Before 1933, it played a small part in the Nazi party's expansion, and its own membership remained modest.[28]

YOUTH AND WOMEN

The rapid expansion of the party organization after the state election of 1929, and particularly after the national election of September 1930, was also accompanied by the NSDAP's attempt to capture both specific segments of society such as the youth and women, and representatives of pluralistic socioeconomic subdivisions of society such as labor and farmers. By 1927, the party had already prepared the groundwork for the recruitment of the youth, students, and women. Most of the socioeconomic affiliates appeared only after the national election of 1930. Party organizations devoted to the youth and women were intended to further the organizational and electoral advance of the party. On the other hand, the NSDAP's affiliates devoted to specific socioeconomic interest groups reflected a burgeoning mass party that was interested not only in expanding its electoral base but also in controlling the pluralistic segments of society and in laying the foundations for the seizure of total power.

Of all of the party's various parallel organizations, the Hitler Youth in Baden was one of the first to receive Wagner's attention. In 1926, the Baden Gau leader asked Friedhelm Kemper to organize the youth in Baden. Kemper declined, preferring to devote himself to organizational and propaganda drives, which included the district leadership of Mannheim. Kemper, who was born in 1906 in Pyritz, Pomerania, and joined the party as early as 1923, had been a member of the youth group Adler und Falken. Although Kemper refused Wagner's offer in 1926, one year later a Baden Hitler Youth was established. According to the Führer, only a handful of boys belonged to the new organization. The purpose of the Hitler Youth was stated clearly by the Führer when, in reporting the formation of a Hitler Youth local in Pforzheim in October 1927, it expressed the hope that more boys would gather in Baden "so that we can proceed as a Gau Baden and fight hand in hand with the SA."[29]

The founder of the Hitler Youth in Pforzheim, Bruno Wiesener, illustrates the close connection between the early Hitler Youth and the various paramilitary organizations in Baden. Wiesener was born in 1905. Between 1922 and 1924 he belonged to the Organization Damm and the NSDAP. After the collapse of the Nazi party Wiesener found his way to the

Schlageterbund and eventually to the SA of Baden-Baden. In October 1927, this SA leader founded the Hitler Youth of Pforzheim and led it until 1929 when he embarked on a new SS career.[30] In the spring of 1929, Wagner shifted the focus of the Hitler Youth's activities. He ordered the boys to be educated about racial issues, but he demanded that they be kept from the daily political struggle. The Hitler Youth would become a recruiting ground for the party rather than the SA.[31]

Early in 1930, the real organizational expansion of the Hitler Youth took place when the Gau ordered leadership training for all local Hitler Youth leaders. Even in communities where no Hitler Youth existed, the local party leader had to send a delegate to these courses who could then return to his community and establish a Hitler Youth local. Between January 1931 and January 1933, the Baden Hitler Youth expanded from a mere 498 boys to 5,200 members. Late in 1932, the Gau leader of the Hitler Youth, Felix Wankel, rebelled against Wagner and joined the SPD. Wankel, who had joined the Nazi party at age nineteen in 1921, was replaced by Wagner's trusted friend, Friedhelm Kemper, who held the position until 1945. Under Kemper's direction, the Hitler Youth became a mass organization that supplemented the efforts of the party's cadre organization but did not threaten it.[32]

Closely related to the party's efforts to convert the youth was its attempt to infiltrate the student organizations of the universities. In January 1926, the party created the National Socialist German Students' League (NSDStB) to further this effort. The Nazi program benefited from the nationalism that was extremely strong in German universities. For example, in 1927 students from the Technical University of Karlsruhe refused to sail on a boat in the city park because it displayed the republican colors of "black-red-gold." In addition, as a visiting New Zealander recalled, anti-Semitism was the "hourly topic of conversation" among students of the University of Heidelberg. The fact that students had to travel to Hesse to engage in duelling activities did not endear the republic to the Baden students. Finally, the deteriorating economic conditions, as the depression took a stronger hold of Baden, radicalized the student population. While university enrollments reached new heights in 1931, job opportunities for these predominantly middle-class students declined drastically.[33]

Baden had two major universities (Freiburg and Heidelberg), one Technical University in Karlsruhe, and a business school in Mannheim. The Nazis first established themselves in Freiburg in the summer of 1926. The Freiburg NSDStB built on the foundations that had been erected by the German Völkisch Student Movement in 1924, except that students had to join the party before they were admitted to the NSDStB. In the summer of 1927, the Nazi students of Freiburg decided to participate in the elections to the student council (Asta). Their platform focused on anti-Semitism, anti-Marxism, extreme nationalism, and Christian ethics and morals. Despite these efforts, the NSDStB won only 4 percent of the votes and one seat on the Asta. The Nazi expansion at the University of Freiburg was always handicapped by the fact that 44 percent of the students were Catholics. Only in the winter election of 1931/32 did the Nazis win 38 percent of the seats in the Asta. But not until the irregular election of 1932, which was boycotted by the Catholics, did the NSDStB gain control of the Freiburg Asta.[34]

The most spectacular advance of the NSDStB occurred in

northern Baden. By 1928, the Nazi students had established
themselves at the universities of Heidelberg, Mannheim, and
Karlsruhe. The NSDStB won 7.3 percent and 13.5 percent of
the votes in 1928 in the elections to the Karlsruhe and Mannheim Astas. During the following year, the Baden Nazis entered the Heidelberg Asta by capturing 605 votes in the "demo-
cratic-Marxist stronghold." The bulk of the new support came
from both new voters and the traditional right.[35] The Nazi
advance continued unabated in all of Baden's universities,
particularly in northern Baden. By the winter semester of
1931/32, the NSDStB had won 45 percent of the Asta seats in
Heidelberg, 48 percent of the seats in Karlsruhe, and 38 percent of the seats in Freiburg. Most of this support came
from the traditional right. Throughout Germany by 1931/32
the Nazi students conquered the student councils, thereby coordinating another stronghold of the German middle class.[36]

Just as important as the conquest of the Astas was the
NSDStB's involvement in major antirepublican and anti-Semitic
campaigns. The Nazi students of Heidelberg, in the "best
fashion" of the SA, to which many of the students belonged by
1930, disrupted lectures by Socialists and Jews and harassed
leftist students. In these campaigns the Nazi students usually
relied on the support of the traditional right-wing students
who also were interested in persecuting leftist and democratic
students and professors. Although many of these rallies ended
in violence, the Heidelberg NSDStB won one of its major propaganda victories in the summer of 1930 in a peaceful demonstra-
tion against the government. In that year, a new university
building was being constructed in Heidelberg and the workers
requested permission to hold the traditional celebration
(Richtfest) that followed the completion of the roof. Adam

Remmele refused the request because of the need to be frugal.
The Nazi students used this opportunity and sponsored a resolution in the Asta which provided for a student-sponsored Richtfest. Carpenters and bricklayers sat side by side with university students in defiance of the government. Even the Frankfurter Zeitung admitted that the Nazis had achieved a major
propaganda victory.[37]

Although the Nazi students sat at the same table with
workers and urged social harmony, few were willing to go beyond
this symbolic social revolution. Erwin Dittler, a former leader of the Baden Schülerbund and a student in Heidelberg in 1931,
left the Nazi party and joined Otto Strasser's movement in 1931.
Dittler and several other students did establish contacts with
the Communist party in Karlsruhe in 1931. But the police reports made it clear that they represented only an insignificant minority.[38] Most students were only interested in an
"armchair" socialism, and most Nazi students remained loyal to
the party.

The most vicious campaign waged by the Baden NSDStB, and
particularly by the Heidelberg Nazi students, was directed
against Emil Julius Gumbel. The Gumbel case illustrates the
Nazi students' successful tactics in marshaling the forces on
the right against a Jewish pacifist. Born in Munich on 18
July 1891, Gumbel assumed a position in Heidelberg in 1923.
Several years earlier, this statistician had begun to study
political murders in postwar Germany. In 1921, he published
his findings in Zwei Jahre Mord, which he expanded during the
following year into Vier Jahre Politischer Mord. In these
works, Gumbel demonstrated that the vast majority of political
murders since November 1918 had been committed by right-wing,
nationalistic groups. Continuing his study of this topic, he

published in 1925 another work which alluded to illegal army units in Germany known as the "Black Reichswehr."[39]

The Gumbel controversy existed long before the Nazis arrived on the scene. His constant derision of German nationalism, his iconoclastic attitude toward the German efforts during the Great War, and visits to Moscow created difficulties for him as early as 1924. His behavior was discussed in the faculty senate, in the Baden Landtag and in all German newspapers. Between 1925 and 1928, the Gumbel case was also presented in most European newspapers from Paris to Danzig. In Baden Gumbel faced legal and disciplinary actions after being charged with treason. Not only was he attacked by the academic community of Heidelberg, but as early as 1925 the Deutschvölkische Student Organization sent a letter to the national minister of interior demanding Gumbel's removal.[40]

The Nazis initiated an attack on Gumbel in 1930 after he was promoted to the position of associate professor of statistics by Remmele, the minister of education. The Führer greeted the appointment with the caption, "The hate apostle as professor," and the German Student Union, which was under the control of the Nazis, organized mass protests. The Nazi students of Heidelberg had found another issue that helped them gain the support of the Stahlhelm and the Nationalistic students against the republic. After the Heidelberg Asta declared that it would no longer participate in university functions if Gumbel attended, Remmele withdrew the government's recognition of the Asta and ordered it to vacate its offices at the university.[41]

Remmele's defense of Gumbel was to no avail. In 1931 the attacks on Gumbel degenerated into street brawls. The Nazis formed a permanent alliance with the nationalistic

organizations in a common offensive against the hated professor. The campaign reached a climax in 1932 under the direction
of the Heidelberg Nazi student G. A. Scheel, the future national
student leader. Over 3,500 Nazis and members of the Stahlhelm
gathered in Heidelberg to demand the departure of Gumbel.
Although some of these Nazi student leaders received reprimands
from the university, by the summer of 1932 the university senate
and the philosophy department voted to rescind Gumbel's teaching privileges. The Ministry of Education, which was no longer
under the control of Remmele, approved this decision because
Gumbel had again stirred emotions in May 1932 by calling the
German war memorial a "turnip."[42]

The Nazi tactic of joining with nationalistic organizations in a common front against the republic worked well in the
case of another candidate for a position with the University
of Heidelberg, Günther Dehn. The theology faculty rejected
Dehn because he also had made derogatory remarks about German
efforts during the First World War. Although Remmele supported
Dehn, he declined the offer to come to Heidelberg.[43] In both
Gumbel's and Dehn's cases, the Nazi students had exploited a
nationalistic issue to allow the "establishment" to destroy
itself from within. The motor behind this was a student body
that had come under the control of the Nazi party.

The party's attempt to capture the support of the youth
and the students was in harmony with both the NSDAP's image
and ideology. The Nazis' efforts to win the allegiance of
women, on the other hand, had to cope with the strong antifeminism of leading male Nazis in Germany. Before 1933, the
leaders of the German Women's Movement warned that the Nazis
would limit the role of women to childbearing, a position
that was confirmed by the statements of Nazis like Alfred

Rosenberg.[44] There were, however, many women who wanted to help the NSDAP win power. In addition, many Nazi women activists had no intention of relegating all women to the kitchen. Paula Siber, for example, warned that if policy deprived women of work, it would produce only useless mothers and teachers. In a major Nazi collective work on German women published in 1932, many Nazi women leaders encouraged the employment of women in industry, commerce, and agriculture.[45]

In Baden Nazi women had played only an insignificant part in the early history of the party. The list of over one hundred Baden Nazis who had joined by 1923 and were still active in 1933 contains the name of only one woman, the wife of Hans Knab of Eberbach. The only woman to hold an important party cadre post during these formative years was Maria Götz, the party business manager of the district of Wertheim. Götz, who married the Kreisleiter of Wertheim, Friedhelm Kemper, was even praised by Gottfried Feder in his Die Flamme.[46] Most party posts, however, were held by males. Robert Wagner, the Gau leader, clearly preferred docile housewives over political female activists.[47]

The first organized völkisch women's organization in Baden, the Königin Luise Bund, emerged in the Nazi stronghold of Neulussheim in 1925. The police noted that about forty women in that community took part in almost every Nazi rally as early as 1926. In that same year the police also began to notice that women were taking part in Nazi rallies in Karlsruhe.[48] During the following year, the NSDAP presented such themes as "NS and Women and Girls," and one thousand of twenty-five hundred spectators at Hitler's first Baden address in Heidelberg in the summer of 1927 were women.[49] It was not until January 1928 that the leader of the Nazi women's movement,

Elsbeth Zander, came to Baden to present her message in Eberbach, Weinheim, Heidelberg, and Karlsruhe. She told her audiences that women had to organize in order to help wounded SA
men who were now in the hands of Jewish doctors. By the fall
of 1928, locals had been founded in Heidelberg and Karlsruhe.[50]
It was only a small start. Commenting on the national election
of 1928, the Führer noted that women were "still swimming in
the peaceful middle." Indeed, the Nazis and the Communists
in 1928 attracted fewer female votes proportionally than any
other party.[51]

The appointment of Gertrud Klink to the Gau leadership
of the NS Women's League in 1930 was significant for the evolution of the organization. The new Gau official had been
married to Eugen Klink, a teacher in Offenburg, who was the
party's district leader in Offenburg. Gertrud was born in
1902 in Adelsheim and became a party member by 1929. The
mother of several children, she had also been the district
leader of the NS-Frauenschaft (NSF) of Offenburg. After the
death of her first husband in March 1930, Gertrud devoted
herself to the Gau organization of the NS Women's League.
By August 1930, she coordinated fourteen Baden locals and
the Gau organization's growing propaganda campaign.[52]

Gertrud Klink, who subsequently became Scholtz-Klink after
her second marriage, was appointed to lead the Reich Women's
League after 1933. Consequently, her views on the place of
women in society were of some importance. In her published
works on the role of the NS Women's League, Scholtz-Klink
stressed the duties of reviving German honor and power, and
of strengthening the Aryan race and Christian morals. She
was clearly anti-Semitic and anti-Marxist. According to
Klink, it was the function of the NS Women's League to instill

these goals into the youth. In addition, the Nazi women had
to assist the male party members in their struggle for power.
These functions were summarized in a contract signed between
Klink and the deputy Gau leader Walter Köhler in October 1931.
All women party members were required to join the NSF where
they would devote themselves to washing and sewing for SA and
party men and disseminating the doctrines of National Socialism among children.[53]

In addition to these supportive functions, the Baden NSF
assisted in the yearly winter relief program, which aided
needy party members. Nazi women gathered food in the countryside and then helped to distribute it in the urban locals to
poverty-stricken party members. However, the supervision of
the winter relief belonged to local and district party leaders
who were males. Although the NSF of Baden established an independent Nazi welfare organization in September 1932 which
was recognized by the city of Karlsruhe, after 1933 all welfare
duties came under the exclusive control of male party leaders.
Most revealing of the party's attitude toward women in Baden
was the failure of the Führer to publish a biography of Scholtz-
Klink despite her appointment in 1934 to lead the Reich Women's
League. In short, women were used to expand the electoral
base of the party and to serve the male masters of the NSDAP,
both before and after 1933.[54]

FARMERS AND WORKERS

By 1930, rapid expansion both in terms of membership and support at the polls caused the party to prepare for the future
Nazi state by establishing a variety of party-affiliated orga-

nizations devoted to specific socioeconomic segments of society.
According to a Baden party plan of December 1930, the task of
such party departments as organization and finance was to run
the party and to convert the public to National Socialism.
This would eventually help the NSDAP achieve power in Baden.
On the other hand, such departments as "culture" and the "Economic Council" were supposed to prepare the groundwork for the
future Nazi society. The SA, the Hitler Youth, the NSDStB,
and the NS Women's League were to work with both departments
in support of the party's immediate goal of achieving power
and to lay the basis for the future racial society.[55]

In 1930 and 1931, the Baden party began to establish affiliate organizations for numerous pluralistic segments of society,
many of which had already been established on the Reich level.
An avalanche of appeals appeared in the _Führer_ that urged the
creation of special-interest organizations, ranging from units
for Nazi musicians and Nazi lawyers to disabled Nazi veterans.
Whenever possible, Gau Nazi activists like the lawyer J. Rupp
and the former teacher Karl Lenz were used to lead these professional organizations.[56]

The purpose of some of these party organizations is revealed clearly in the programs of the athletic and cultural
clubs, which were led by the "old Nazis," Robert Roth and
Herbert Kraft. In June 1931, the pioneer of "racial athletics"
in Liedolsheim, Robert Roth, urged the creation of NS Athletic
Clubs. The function of these clubs was made clear by Roth in
late 1931 in an article in the _Führer_ entitled "National Socialism and Exercise." According to Roth, Germany's population of sixty million needed space, which it could only obtain
by first reestablishing Germany's power. The Nazi Athletic
Clubs would help the future Nazi state establish this power

by providing it with strong and healthy Germans. Kraft's NS
Culture Club was established in May 1931 with the express purpose of "educating" the party's political leaders about the
problems of Jewry and the value of a racial culture. The
ultimate aim of this organization, according to Kraft, was
to prepare the spiritual foundations of the future Nazi state.
These two party organizations reveal both the growing confidence of the party in 1931 that it would achieve power and
the racial, expansionistic imperative of the Nazi movement.[57]

The party also attempted to coordinate the churches.
Although the Baden NSDAP was never able to establish a party-
affiliated Catholic organization, it did utilize the services
of the noted Catholic writer Kuno Brombacher. This Catholic
figure, who supported Hitler, was used in the party's campaigns
against liberals and the political left.[58] Although Brombacher's attacks on the "atheists" may have brought the party
some additional support among a few Catholics, the movement
was much more successful in penetrating the Protestant churches. As early as 1923 Protestant ministers had been active in
the Baden party, and after 1925 more were attracted to the
NSDAP. In 1926, Wagner emphasized that the Nazis were not
heathens but good Christians. Wagner was satisfied with the
conversion of Protestant clergymen, but he did not want to
become involved in a major Kulturkampf with the churches.
Accordingly, he refused to support the German Christians in
Baden before 1933, relying instead on a NS Clergy League.
By October 1932, the Baden Nazis had won half of the seats in
the Supreme Church Council. The activism of Nazi church ministers and other party supporters within the Protestant churches
reflected the grass-roots desire of one segment of the pluralistic society to establish a relationship with the NSDAP.[59]

Of all of the party's efforts to conquer specific socioeconomic interest groups, the two most important dealt with
farmers and workers. The Baden NSDAP had appealed to both
groups as early as 1923 and continued to do so after 1925. In
1930/31 the Nazis attempted either to infiltrate the respective
interest organizations of the farmers and workers or to replace
them with Nazi organizations. In December 1930, the Führer
announced the official creation of an agricultural department
under the leadership of Walter Plesch. The function of the
new office was to provide farmers and rural locals with written advice on agricultural questions.[60] Plesch was born on
11 December 1898 in Mülhausen and received training as an
agricultural expert, although he was not a farmer. He joined
the party as early as October 1929, but he remained an outsider
to the Gau party clique.[61]

Wagner never had much confidence in Plesch. When some
of Plesch's letters were discovered among the "Boxheimer papers" in 1932, the Baden Gau leader lost all confidence in
his agricultural leader. The Boxheimer papers were discovered
on the farm of a Dr. Wagner, agricultural expert of Gau Hesse,
and had been prepared by Werner Best, the legal expert of the
party in Hesse. The papers spelled out party responses in
the event of a Communist uprising. They included SA supervision of harvesting and the regulation of private property and
incomes. Plesch's letter, which was discovered among the Boxheimer documents and subsequently read in the Baden Landtag,
was written on 29 July 1931 to Gau Baden's local agricultural
leaders. In the event of a Communist uprising, farmers were
told to withhold their harvest from the cities and sell only
enough to cover costs. According to Plesch, this would bring
the urban centers to their knees. Robert Wagner tried to

soften the potentially disastrous impact of the letter by
claiming that farmers were advised to hold back the harvest
only to prevent "Jewish capitalists" from purchasing it at
low prices. Wagner's ignorance of Plesch's activities until
1932 reveals that the Nazi party was not preparing a unified
seizure of power before 1933. It also demonstrates the centrifugal tendencies of the pluralistic party after 1930. Wagner
solved his problem, and at the same time reaffirmed his authority over the party's agrarian department, in August 1932
when he forced Plesch out of office and replaced him with the
former Landbund official Ludwig Huber, a trusted party district leader from Offenburg.[62]

Between 1930 and 1932, Plesch did make an important contribution to the Baden party by coordinating its invasion of
the Landbund. As early as 1928, some Baden party members who
also belonged to the Landbund had urged the NSDAP to infiltrate the agrarian organization, but the Baden party was still
too small to carry out this plan. By October 1930, the business leader of the Landbund, Friedrich Schmitt, had joined the
Nazis and presented their views in the Badische Bauernzeitung.
One year later Plesch told his district representatives that
the NSDAP would no longer attempt to destroy the Agrarian
League but rather conquer it from within. Nazi-Landbund
conferences were held, and Nazis were told that they could
join the Landbund. Plesch and Robert Roth also addressed
these joint conclaves and urged the farmers to organize under
Nazi guidance in order to be assured a place in the future
Nazi Corporative Parliament.[63]

The party's efforts to conquer the Landbund in Baden
were successful in 1931. The police noted that Nazis no
longer fought the Agrarian League, and all Nazi rallies in

rural villages in 1931 were well attended. Important Landbund
leaders like Hagin praised the NSDAP, and the wife of Landbund
leader Schmidt of Bretten was the local leader of the Rote
Hakenkreuz. The climax came in late 1931 at the state conference of the Landbund when leaders decided to dissolve the
legislative union between the Wirtschafts- and the Bauernpartei. Hagin and Schmidt joined the Nazi Landtag delegation
and a third member of the former Bauernpartei delegation
joined the Center party. The Wirtschaftspartei delegate became a member of the DVP Landtag delegation. For all practical purposes, the Landbund and its political party in the
legislature were absorbed by the Nazi party by the end of 1931.
Farmers had supported the NSDAP long before the dissolution
of the Landtag delegation of the Bauernpartei in 1931, but
the conquest of the Landbund prepared an important pluralistic
segment of society for the Third Reich.[64]

The party was far less effective in winning labor support.
It attempted to undermine organized labor by establishing
the NS Factory Cells in Baden in January 1931. The prime
function of this organization was to spread Nazi propaganda
in the factories and workshops. The leader of the Baden NS
Betriebszellenorganisation (NSBO) was Fritz Plattner, an
"old party" member who had belonged to a Christian union in
1922. Plattner held the first organizational meeting of the
NSBO in Karlsruhe in January 1931. By October of the same
year, the Gau claimed ninety-two factory cells. The real
advance of the NSBO of Baden, however, came only after 1933
and under duress. For example, the NSBO of Bruchsal was
organized by sixteen men in January 1931. Two years later,
the district still had only five hundred members. Only during 1933 did the Bruchsal NSBO mushroom to four thousand

members.[65]

The NSBO also attempted to advance the Nazi cause in workshop elections and eventually even during strikes. The election results in the largest factories of Baden in 1931 revealed the lack of appeal the NSDAP had with organized workers. In Mannheim's Zellstoffabrik Waldorf the Nazis won only 83 votes out of a total of 1,053. In another Mannheim factory, the Vogel Werke, the NSBO captured only 16 of the 700 votes.[66] Not only did the NSBO suffer from the lack of labor support, but it also had to face the unpopular question of strikes. In early 1931, local leaders sent Plattner reports about strikes involving Nazi workers. During the summer of the same year, Plattner ordered Nazi workers not to break strikes. Finally in February 1932, the NSBO of Baden initiated its first strike.[67] The party's hesitancy in initiating strikes was due to its fear of alienating its middle-class support. In any case, the party's belated support of strikes did not increase labor enthusiasm for National Socialism. The unemployed and radicalized workers turned instead to the Communist party. Despite Nazi efforts since 1920 to convert organized labor to völkisch nationalism, the overwhelming majority of workers continued to support the Marxist parties.

THE GAU ORGANIZATION

By 1932 the Baden party had clearly initiated a "massive effort to undermine and eventually conquer most of the economically, socially, or politically influential pluralist associations in German society."[68] Even if some organizations

like the SS and NSBO were still relatively weak, the groundwork for the coordination of German society had been well
prepared. But while the expansion of National Socialism in
Baden was advantageous to the movement, it also presented
the Gau leadership with serious organizational problems.
Who would control the various organizations and where would
the loyalties of these pluralistic party organizations be
placed? And finally, who would staff the many new party
positions?

By 1930, some Baden districts like Offenburg had full-
time, paid business managers who could absorb some of the
new responsibilities since most other party posts were
honorary.[69] But both locals and districts continued to feel
the severe lack of party leaders. In early 1930, in Heidelberg, for example, Karl Cerff was the local Hitler Youth
leader, the local business leader, and the local propaganda
leader. The situation only deteriorated as the districts
established a multitude of special-interest organizations
after 1930. In 1932, the district leader of Offenburg, Dr.
Wolfram Rombach, held three party posts, and the deputy district leader Karl Rombach was also the district's organization
and indoctrination leader.[70]

To obtain some control over this proliferation of party
offices, the Gau by late 1930 had established an elaborate
organization. The Gau offices (and subsequently the district offices) were divided into two compartments. Organization I included twenty-three sections, ranging from propaganda to party organization. It was charged with running the
party and converting people to National Socialism. Organization II was composed of the various economic and cultural
party sections. Its task was to prepare the Nazi state. In

addition to these two main departments, various organizations
such as the SS, the SA, and Hitler Youth were ordered to work
with both departments in order to prevent friction. In an
attempt to retain control over the party, Wagner staffed the
sections of Organization I with "old" party members like Karl
Lenz, Willi Rückert, August Kramer, Peter Riedner, Otto
Wacker, Walter Köhler, Fritz Plattner, and Herbert Kraft.
Most of these men had joined the party by 1923 (or 1925),
and the overwhelming majority of these loyal Gau clique members were born between 1899 and 1906. They were young,
long-term völkisch activists who were loyal to the Baden Gau
leader. Wagner also used these loyal party leaders (if they
had particular skills or training) to lead some of the special-interest departments in Organization II and several of
the affiliated or associated party organizations. Most of
the leaders of the special-interest organizations, however,
were not members of the Gau clique, and many had not joined
the party until 1930. They were also more likely to rebel
against Wagner. For example, the leader of the Hitler Youth,
Felix Wankel, and the leader of the Schülerbund, Erwin
Dittler, turned their backs on Wagner and joined rival organizations.[71]

This party structure received the approval of Munich,
and Gau Baden was named among the four best-organized Gaue
in Germany in 1931.[72] Although Gau Baden adopted Gregor
Strasser's new organization plan in August 1932, it really
changed little. On the surface the Gau was now divided into
six rather than two main sections. But Wagner's loyal men
still ran the most important Gau party posts, which controlled
the party organization. Otto Wetzel, a Kreisleiter of Heidelberg and editor of the Heidelberger Beobachter, and Robert

Roth controlled the first two sections as Gau inspectors.
Section 3, headed by Wagner, was essentially the same as
Organization I in 1930. It ran the party structure. Again
members of the Gau clique were in charge of the party's organization, finance, and propaganda departments. Sections 4
through 6 were devoted to the economy, agriculture, and labor.
They were controlled by Plattner and Jäger, who had held their
positions since 1930, and the new appointment Ludwig Huber, a
former Kreisleiter who had replaced Plesch as leader of the
agriculture department. The only other major change had occurred because Lenz, the deputy Gau leader, had become Gau
leader of Hesse and been replaced by Köhler, the Kreisleiter
of Weinheim. In addition, minor changes took place in the
special-interest organizations. Since Lenz had left Baden,
the NS Teachers' League was now led by a former teacher and
district party leader, Karl Gärtner. Of course, the rebel
Wankel had been replaced by the loyal Friedhelm Kemper.
These loyal Baden Nazis allowed Wagner to maintain control
over the expanding party departments and to limit the influence of the emerging national party leaders. The danger was
real since some of the leaders of the party's special-interest organizations, like Walter Plesch, looked to Munich or
Berlin rather than Karlsruhe for guidance. Basically Strasser's plan, which aimed at the "seizure of society," had
already been introduced by the Baden Gau leader in December
1930. Two years later, it was only refined.[73]

THE ELECTION OF 1932

The ultimate goal of the party was, of course, still the
seizure of political power. The elections in 1932 tested
the new party organization and particularly the growing centralization of the party. The nature of the campaigns and
the content of the propaganda, aside from a few tactical
changes determined by political opportunism, remained the
same as in 1930. The police had already noted late in 1931
that the Nazi party's growth had not yet come to a stand-
still. Indeed, the party continued its saturation campaign
even in districts where it was already the clear favorite.
For example, between 3 January and 7 November 1932, it held
182 rallies in the district of Sinsheim, already a solid
stronghold.[74] This activism was supported by Hitler's
visits during the July and November 1932 elections, and by
publications in the Führer which reflected the party's
organizational growth by appealing to farmers, the Mittelstand, workers, women, and the unemployed. Farmers and
workers were told that the Hindenburg parties had accepted
the Dawes and Young plans, which produced the economic disaster, and the Mittelstand was informed that the November
parties and Jews were responsible for their plight. These
themes had been presented as early as 1930. In 1932, Goebbels
sent circulars to the provincial party leaders, outlining
major campaign themes and shifting the party's tactical propaganda from issue to issue as demanded by the party's political
maneuverings.[75]

Nothing illustrated the complex new party structure more
clearly than the selection of candidates in 1932. Wagner
traveled to Munich in June 1932 to receive his instruction

for the national campaign and to discuss a list of seventeen Baden candidates he had sent Strasser. The basic problem was that Wagner wanted to protect the party's cadre organization from the various affiliated organizations that attempted to advance their interests by placing their representatives in safe positions on the election slate. Frequently, they sent their names to Strasser without the knowledge or approval of Wagner. For example, the Baden agricultural section sent three names to Darré, including the name of Plesch, whom Wagner detested and refused to accept on the list. Wagner told Wilhelm Frick that the SA, the NSBO, and the agricultural section had received ample positions including many safe slots. Wagner refused to place the Gau student leader in a safe position, and he pleaded with Frick to prevent the appointment of further SA and SS candidates. Wagner argued that the Baden party needed the election of more of its candidates to the Reichstag in order to gain financial support for the Gau's organizational apparatus.[76] The special-interest organizations, of course, argued that the same thing applied to their organizations. Darré pointed out that the election of Plesch would provide the Gau leader of the agricultural department with an income and a railroad pass. This would strengthen the ties between Berlin and Karlsruhe and benefit the agricultural department.[77] In 1932, Wagner was still influential enough that most of his wishes were respected. Plesch was not on the final list, and neither were additional SA and SS candidates. The only modification was that the list had been expanded from seventeen to twenty-six candidates, but this had no influence since the "safe positions" were not changed.[78]

The Baden NSDAP defeated Hindenburg in only six Baden

districts in the April 1932 presidential election. But in
the July 1932 national election it won 468,180 votes, representing 36.6 percent of the total votes cast. The party won
an absolute majority in the traditional Protestant, rural
strongholds of Müllheim, Kehl, Bretten, Sinsheim, and Wertheim. In sixteen other districts the party won over 40 percent
of the vote. Unlike 1930, the bulk of the Nazi growth came

Table 1. Reichstag Election Trends: 1930-1932 (in Baden)

	1930	July 1932	November 1932
New voters	+245,620	+ 90,071	−81,337
NSDAP	+161,534	+241,525	−63,638
Zentrum	+ 9,980	+ 17,454	−39,574
SPD	+ 23,462	− 38,075	−16,891
KPD	+ 57,832	+ 29,568	+26,594
DNVP	− 1,391	+ 5,782	+ 8,947
DVP/DDP	− 21,952	− 72,360	+ 8,116
Mittelstand	− 1,736	− 27,455	− 2,878
Bauernpartei	+ 2,770	− 16,257	+ 140
Evangelischer Volksdienst	+ 22,506	− 37,455	− 711

from the parties of the middle and from the right-wing special-
interest parties, and only secondly from new voters. The party in Baden increased its total votes over 1930 by 241,525,
yet only 90,071 new voters went to the polls. The middle-
class and special-interest parties lost over 150,000 votes.
The Nazi party had completed its conquest of Baden's rural

and urban middle classes (see Table 1). But its greatest
strength in terms of percentages correlated positively with
the 1921 strength of the Rechtsblock. Despite the party's
occasional inroads into Catholic strongholds and its probable
success in winning some Communist votes, the Nazi party was
heir to both the Rechtsblock and the "liberal" middle-class
parties.[79]

The election gave the party seven Reichstag seats. Robert
Roth and Johannes Rupp, who had already been elected in 1930,
and Otto Wetzel, the district leader of Heidelberg, represented
the party's cadre structure. Hanns Ludin, the Gau SA leader,
and Willi Ziegler, a Heidelberg SA leader, represented the SA.
The agricultural department was represented by Ludwig Huber,
a former party district leader who had been chosen by Wagner
to replace Plesch. The last slot, and the one dropped in
November 1932, was occupied by Hans Helwig, the SS candidate
from Weinheim. Wagner was not elected to the Reichstag until
March 1933 after the Baden delegation had expanded to eleven
members.[80]

The reaction of the Socialist press in Baden to the July
election was predictable and totally negative. The Volksfreund lamented the fact that the party of the "capitalists"
would have won forty-six Landtag seats had this been a state
election.[81] But most other newspapers in the center and on
the right raised the issue of a coalition government. As
early as March 1932, the Karlsruher Zeitung concluded that
the Nazis would never be able to form a government without
coalition partners. This was also the view of the Badischer
Beobachter, the organ of the Catholic Center party.[82]

Who would form a coalition with the Nazis? Between
August and October 1932, rumors pointed toward a Nazi-Center

coalition. Already on 1 August, the Badische Zeitung (DNVP) warned of a Nazi-Zentrum government. This same coalition, however, was favored by the Badische Presse as the only route to stability. In September and October, rumors became stronger. The SPD of Baden and the reporter in Karlsruhe of the Frankfurter Zeitung charged that the Catholic president was becoming more tolerant toward Nazis, even allowing civil servants to join the party. Then in October the state leader of the organized white-collar employees (DHV) urged that "the only salvation can be found in a Christian social front between the NSDAP and the Center party." At the state conference of the Baden Center party on 2 October in Karlsruhe, the Catholic leader Ernst Föhr declared that he still rejected the Nazi program and was not sure that the NSDAP and Zentrum could cooperate. But he also noted that a real change had occurred in the leadership of the Nazi party, and that it would be better if the NSDAP were brought into a responsible position to diffuse the revolutionary elements within the party.[83]

Nothing came of these rumors in the Reichstag, and in Baden the Catholic-Socialist coalition continued. Instead, the Nazis had to wage still another election in November and fight internal rebellion in the district of Lahr. Opposition had been voiced against Wagner in the local of Lahr as early as 1931, but the issue did not become a crisis until November 1932 when the local insisted on publishing the paper Grenzlandnachrichten despite Wagner's opposition. The response of the local to the Gau prohibition was to publish an article in the Grenzlandnachrichten (and in SPD papers) accusing Wagner and the Gau clique of corruption. Finally, on 5 November the local broke all contacts with the district and Gau leadership, and several of its members joined the SPD.

One of the leaders was the former Gau Hitler Youth leader
Felix Wankel, who had joined the Nazi party as early as 1921.
Wagner waited until after the election, and then on 7 November
he proceeded against the rebellious local by dissolving it
and assigning the trusted Robert Roth the task of reorganiz-
ing the local. Hitler's denunciation of the rebellious local,
which now called itself NS Notgemeinschaft, condemned the
movement to impotence.[84]

Even more depressing to the Gau leadership was the loss
of sixty-four thousand voters in the November election to
apathy. This was the first decline of the Nazi movement
since 1928. Only the KPD continued to grow despite the fact
that eighty-four thousand fewer votes were cast in November
in Baden. Although the NSDAP continued to have an absolute
majority in the rural Protestant districts of Kehl, Bretten,
Sinsheim, Müllheim, and Wertheim and won over 40 percent of
the vote in ten other districts, the Baden press naturally
focused on the party's losses. Only the DNVP paper, the
Badische Zeitung, urged the Nazis to cooperate. The paper
argued that most Nazis did not realize how close their views
of a "socialist economy" were to real conservatism.[85] This
suggestion of course found no echo in the Nazi camp until
December 1932. Immediately after the election Wagner attempted to soften the blow by maintaining that National
Socialism was a Weltanschauung which would not collapse just
because a sudden storm had blown away a few supporters. To
counter this trend, Wagner promised renewed battle against
the traditional enemy on the left, combined with an offensive against the "reaction."[86]

The one bright spot in the political developments in
Baden for the Nazis was the dissolution of the Socialist-

Catholic coalition on 30 November 1932. The superficial issue
leading to the collapse of the government was the Concordat
with the papacy, which was accepted by the state legislature
only because of a tie-breaking vote by the presiding officer,
who was a member of the Center party. The Nazis had also
opposed the Concordat. In principle, the NSDAP declared that
it was not against a Concordat with the churches. The Nazis'
motive was political opportunism since they had no interest
in strengthening the government. The Socialists' withdrawal
from the government was really caused by their fears of losing
more supporters to the Communists. On 9 December 1932, the
Concordat passed, supported only by the Center party, the DVP,
and Wirtschaftspartei.[87]

The breakup of the government coalition in Baden in late
1932 did not, however, solve the Baden party's problem of
political impotence in the state. No new state elections
were scheduled until the fall of 1933. What the party really
wanted was the dissolution of the Baden Landtag and new elections as soon as possible. In December 1932, the Führer presented the theme that the national parties and the two church
parties needed to cooperate in the fight against Bolshevism,
atheism, and economic desperation. This appeal found some
support among the members of the new government coalition.
Ernst Föhr, a Center party leader, and Dr. Mattes from the
DVP urged a coalition with the Nazis. But the Nazis wanted
the dissolution of the Landtag and not membership in a coalition government. Walter Köhler, the acting Gau leader of
Baden in the absence of Wagner in early 1933, rudely rejected
the offer presented by the DVP representative in January 1933.
One week later, on 10 January 1933, the Baden Landtag elected
a new state president, who would lead the last legal government

of Baden before the Nazi seizure of power. The new minority government was now composed of only the Center party and the DVP, although the Socialists refrained from open opposition.[88]

The establishment of a new government that had the tacit support of the Socialists left the Baden Nazis in a limbo. Wagner had already left for Berlin to assist the national party's organization department. Although the Baden NSDAP had prepared for the new order by establishing numerous party-affiliated interest organizations, the party was still not in power. Early in 1933, it boasted in its publications that the old order would be thrown out and the workers and Mittelstand saved. But in reality, before the appointment of Hitler as chancellor at the end of January 1933, the Baden party had little chance of gaining power in Baden. It was only after Hitler captured Berlin that the national party could rescue the Baden party from its predicament.[89]

7 The Party and the State, 1933-1945

THE NAZI SEIZURE OF POWER

By January 1933, the Baden party had obviously reached both
a political and organizational stalemate. Not only had the
party experienced a decline in electoral support but it also
had no prospect of achieving power until the next Landtag
election in the fall of 1933. At this point, the Baden party
was rescued by Hitler's assumption of power on 30 January
1933. The Nazi participation in the new Reich government
was felt immediately in Baden. First, the Baden party displayed a new self-confidence and activism, which was directed
primarily against Communists and the Center party. Intimidation and even murder became a "normal" part of this renewed
Nazi activism in February and March 1933.[1] Along with this
attack on the left and the Catholic party the state's Nazi
leaders attempted to emulate Hitler's national coalition with
the right by calling for a bourgeois-Nazi alliance against
the political left. The Baden Nazis warned that the Communists were planning a bloodbath against both the Nazis and
the bourgeoisie. To symbolize this theme, SA and SS units
held public marches with the Stahlhelm in February and March
1933.[2]

A second factor that affected the party's evolution
after January 1933 was the constant intervention of the Nazi

Reich minister of interior, Wilhelm Frick, in internal Baden
affairs. This took the form of periodic bans of Center party
and, particularly, leftist newspapers. In February alone,
fifteen papers were banned in Baden for periods between three
days and four weeks. Naturally, the Socialist and Communist
press bore the brunt of the persecution.[3] The Baden government
finally took a stand in late February after mass Catholic protests in various parts of Baden had publicly decried the
crackdown on Catholic newspapers. When Frick ordered Baden
to ban the Badische Beobachter for an article it had published
that commented on Hitler's radio address in Stuttgart, Baden
Minister of Interior Umhauer refused and appealed to the
German Supreme Court for a decision. On 22 February 1933,
the Baden cabinet also decided to ban newspapers in the state
only in exceptional cases and to meet Frick's bans with immediate appeals to the German Supreme Court.[4] On the other hand,
according to the Führer, the government did continue to dissolve Socialist rallies in some Baden cities and even arrested
Communists in Lörrach on the eve of the March election.[5]

Even more ominous for the future of democracy in southwestern Germany after January 1933 was the growing sympathy
that the Baden police displayed toward the Nazi cause. Before
1933, the Baden government had forbidden its civil servants
to join the Nazi party. A few Nazi policemen, like Karl
Pflaumer, had been dismissed by Remmele, the Baden minister
of interior in the 1920s. In early March 1933, Nazi police
officers began to organize publicly. A former police major,
with the help of the dismissed police lieutenant Karl Pflaumer,
organized a NS Police Organization in Heidelberg on 2 March
that boasted seventy members. Two days later, the Führer
published a list of three hundred and fifty names of policemen

in Baden ranging from a major to simple patrolmen, who supported the party. In one town, thirty-nine out of a force of
forty policemen announced their support of the Nazi party,
partly because of conviction but probably more because they
clearly perceived the imminent triumph of National Socialism.[6]

The party's tactic stressing a Nazi-bourgeois alliance
against the dangers of the left, aided by the Reich's pseudo-
legal interventions in Baden's internal affairs, was preparing the groundwork for the Nazi seizure of power on the state
level. This same tactic was utilized in the election campaign
in February and early March. The Baden party initiated its
campaign on 9 February with a series of election rallies and
a declaration by Köhler, the acting Gau leader, which demanded
the ruthless destruction of the Communists and promised relief
for almost all segments of society. Frick came to the assistance of regional Nazi organizations in Germany by forbidding
the Communists to engage in public activities after 2 March.
Then the party presented the Baden candidates who again represented the usual party elite and representatives from the
party affiliates. Only now, the party slate was led by Hitler,
Frick, Göring, and Robert Wagner. The party clearly attempted
to shift the Baden voter's focus on the national party and
government leaders in order to obtain maximum propaganda benefits from the theme of "national revolution." Finally, on
the eve of the election, the Nazi leaders of Baden, who were
by now the most enthusiastic and self-confident political activists in Baden, held torchlight parades in the major urban
centers of the state.[7]

The party's renewed efforts were rewarded on 5 March,
1933, when it captured 45 percent of the vote in Baden. The
party won a clear majority in eleven districts, all of them

traditional strongholds of the party since 1930. Of these
eleven districts, only one was predominantly industrial
(Pforzheim) and only one was overwhelmingly Catholic (Oberkirch). As always the Nazis were strongest in the Protestant,
rural areas of the state. But the most important reason for
the party's increase of 223,000 voters over November 1932 was
that the Nazis were able to mobilize new and "drop-out" voters.
Around 200,000 new voters went to the polls in Baden, and most
of these voted for the NSDAP. All parties with the exception
of the NSDAP, the Center party, the Socialists, and the DNVP,
lost votes. Compared to the Nazi increase of over 200,000
votes, the gains of the Catholics (21,000), the Socialists
(10,500), and the DNVP (3,000) were a pittance. The most
obvious fact emerging from this election is that the Baden
population in a still relatively free election clearly and
overwhelmingly (59 percent) rejected the Weimar Republic.
Almost three-fifths of the voters cast their votes for the
Nazi party, the Communist party, and the right-wing Nationalists.[8]

Although the Nazis, together with the Nationalists, had
won 49 percent of the total vote in Baden, the party had no
intention of waiting until the October 1933 Landtag election
to translate its voting strength into political power. Instead, the Nazis used local terrorism and Reich support to
seize power immediately in Baden. Early on 6 March, local
party leaders, with the help of the SA and in many cases the
Stahlhelm, raised swastika flags on public buildings. Franz
Moraller, a member of the Gau clique and SA leader, later admitted that a small detachment of armed police could have removed the flags and dispersed the SA hordes in the streets,
but the Baden cabinet decided to compromise with the Nazis by

allowing them to remove the flags from the public buildings inconspicuously at night.[9] The cabinet also took the initiative from the police by forcing police officials to obtain instructions from the minister of interior in case new Nazi flags were raised.[10] Even more indicative of the collapse of the republic in Baden was the reaction of the mayor of Offenburg. Although the city council of Offenburg had rejected the Nazi delegation's proposals to raise the swastika flag on public buildings, the lord mayor of Offenburg assured the Nazis that he would not oppose the raising of the flag with police power because of the "trend of the times."[11]

This "trend of the times" feeling was widespread in Baden. An independent, middle-class paper, the Karlsruher Zeitung, insisted in March that no German politics could be made without Hitler and the Nazi party, and it stated emphatically that any party winning 45 percent of the vote must have an influence on state politics. And the right-wing Badische Zeitung declared on 7 and 8 March that the Weimar Republic was now in ashes and the Center party was superfluous.[12] Even worse, when Köhler called the Karlsruhe police headquarters and demanded to see a police representative, two police officers appeared promptly at the Nazi party Gau headquarters to listen to Köhler's requests.[13] In the end, only the Socialists and the Center party in Baden defended the republic. Since the Socialists were out of power, only the Center party press could reflect the government's views. The Catholic press claimed that the "Hitler current" had crashed against the Center party barrier. Immediately after the election, the Badischer Beobachter reminded Badenese that Potsdam (Prussia) could never represent all of Germany and that Germany must remain the land of the free.[14]

On 6 March, Köhler demanded unsuccessfully that the Baden government resign and allow the formation of a new government under Nazi leadership to reflect the election results.[15] The next move was up to Berlin. On 7 March, Köhler and Moraller traveled to northern Baden and from there to Frankfurt to meet Frick and obtain instructions for further actions. In Weinheim, the two Baden Nazis discovered that Robert Wagner would return to Baden and become Reich commissar. The acting Baden Gau leader, Köhler, had been neither consulted nor even informed of this decision.[16] The next day Frick wrote to the Baden president, announcing that he was sending Wagner to Karlsruhe to maintain order. The Nazis of Baden had created the disorders that Berlin now used to justify the imposition of a Nazi commissar. Powerless, the Baden government could only protest to the German Supreme Court and to Hitler, which obviously did nothing to change the political reality.[17]

On 9 March, Wagner arrived in Karlsruhe and addressed a crowd of over three thousand SA and SS men in front of the Baden Ministry of Interior. After this show of force, Wagner assumed police powers in Baden and began to purge the police chiefs of the major urban centers and in the Ministry of Interior. At first, Wagner relied on the SA and SS to consolidate his position. The Gau's SA leader, Ludin, became the acting police chief of Karlsruhe, and Karl Pflaumer, a former police officer and party functionary in Heidelberg who had also been Gau organization leader of the SA in 1929, became personnel advisor to the Baden police. With this force, the new Reich commissar in Baden began to move against the leading left-wing functionaries. Socialist and Communist meetings were prohibited and leading "November criminals" arrested. While Wagner moved against the left, he held joint

rallies with the Stahlhelm and publicly praised Hindenburg.
The image the new leaders of Baden wanted to project was
one of a national, legal revolution against the alleged plots
of the left. This is precisely what happened throughout Baden.
In Heidelberg Hermann Röhn, the district leader of the party
and future deputy Gau leader, appeared before the state's
district office, accompanied by SS and SA men, and raised
the swastika flag. In the afternoon the police and the SS
units cooperated in searching Communist headquarters and in
purging "red mayors" of the surrounding Heidelberg communities.[18]

The Baden government was helpless against the Nazi en-
croachment on its authority. On 10 March, the government
decided to resign in order to allow the legislature to select
a new government. Since the Baden Nazis had only six delegates in the state legislature, this was the last thing Wagner
wanted. On the following day, he simply assumed complete
control of the government by claiming the positions of minister of interior and minister president. The acting Gau
leader, Köhler, became the minister of finance; Otto Wacker,
a university graduate, assumed control of the Ministry of
Education; Rupp was appointed head of the Justice Department;
and Karl Pflaumer became a special commissar for police affairs. All had been long-time Baden party members and members of Wagner's entourage, except for Rupp, who had the
legal expertise necessary for the post he occupied. The DNVP
and Stahlhelm were each granted one vice-commissar post to
preserve the image of a "national revolution." Wagner also
utilized special Nazi commissars to control all aspects of
Baden's government and society. He appointed "old" Nazis
like Kemper, Plattner, and Robert Roth to lead state offices

that duplicated their party functions. All of this was justified by the Nazi press with the usual assertion that law
and order had been jeopardized by the government's resignation
on 10 March. At the urging of Frick, Wagner even wrote
Hindenburg, defending his actions by pointing to the alleged
misconduct of the Baden government after the election of 5
March. Wagner included, of course, the charge that the government had failed to keep order.[19]

After the usurpation of all state powers, the Nazi leaders of Baden could now eliminate the last vestiges of resistance and simultaneously control the revolutionary enthusiasm
of the SA. Wagner ordered the state's district officers
(Landräte) on 11 March to remove all city police officers
who were Marxists, and the SA was ordered to guard important
state buildings.[20] But Wagner had no intention of letting
the SA and SS continue independent revolutionary actions.
On 11 March he ordered the SS and SA to let the police and
the special Hilfspolizei (auxiliary police) keep order. This
special auxiliary police formation consisted of five hundred
men of which 90 percent were drawn from the SA and SS and 10
percent from the Stahlhelm. Wagner ordered the creation of
this force, which would eventually be absorbed by the police,
to control leftist radicalism, which allegedly threatened
life and property. In reality, the Baden leader established
this force to gain further control over the police and at
the same time control the SA's spontaneous extremism. By
the end of March, about 10 percent of all Baden policemen
were newly hired auxiliaries. With the Nazi sympathizers
within the police force and with the discharge of three
hundred police officers by Wagner, the new leaders of Baden

had a solid grip on law enforcement.[21] Wagner continued
to solidify his control over the police by insisting that
only proven Nazis obtain leading police jobs in the state.[22]

The Baden Nazis had gained almost complete control over
the government of Baden in the short span of three days. Only
the SA continued to create difficulties for the party leaders.
Ludin, the Gau SA leader, issued a statement on 13 March
declaring that the state was now under the complete control
of the Nazis, and he ordered the SA to cease independent
actions against authorities, political opponents, and property.
State and municipal buildings could no longer be occupied
by the SA. Ludin's order was in response to such independent
actions of the SA as the closing of several businesses in
Karlsruhe on 13 March, steps that threatened the economic
well-being of the new Nazi state.[23] To symbolize the end
of the revolution, Wagner on 13 March ordered victory celebrations for the next day by closing schools and raising swastika
flags in the cities. This was accompanied by official rallies
in the major urban centers of Baden, all dedicated to the
successful "national revolution." In a secret cabinet meeting, Wagner told his ministers that public order had been
restored and that now the Reichskommissar had to achieve
total control over all activities in Baden. To consolidate
his power, Wagner decided to keep the Landtag from meeting,
and he admitted that he had no intention of allowing new
state elections or permitting the Communists in any future
legislature. To keep the "national movement" in motion during the next few weeks, while the Nazi ministers were consolidating their positions, was the function of the party.
It was also assigned the dual task of winning over the worker

and reducing the power of the Center party.[24]

Wagner's quest for total power in Baden was aided by the
Daniel Nussbaum affair, which may be compared to the Reichstag
fire in terms of its impact in Baden. Nussbaum, a Socialist
state delegate from Freiburg who apparently was mentally
incompetent, shot and killed a police officer who tried to
arrest him on 17 March 1933. The Nazi government used the
incident as an excuse to accelerate its seizure of total
power and its coordination of Baden society. First, Wagner
ordered a major offensive against the left. Socialist and
Communist deputies were arrested, and the leftist press,
youth, and sport organizations banned.[25] Beginning in late
March, Wagner also ordered a major purge of political opponents and Jews. The police were directed to withdraw while
the Nazis carried out the first major boycott of Jewish stores.
The Nazis usually organized demonstrations in front of the
residence of a political opponent or Jew to enable the police
to place the victim in "protective custody." As long as the
Nazis did not destroy property or physically attack anyone,
Wagner ordered the police not to interfere. Ironically, the
victims, according to Wagner's directive, had to pay for
their own incarceration.[26]

To handle these mass arrests, the new rulers of Baden
set up three concentration camps to hold the "notables of
the November Republic." Although these camps became a permanent part of the Nazi regime, financial burdens and Hitler's
decision after the election victory in late 1933 to pardon
some of the political prisoners greatly reduced the number
of inmates. In December 1933, half of the prisoners were
released, leaving only Socialist and Communist leaders

confined.[27] As the regime began to feel more secure, it
limited further protective custody to Marxists. By 1935,
the Führer could claim that most of the inmates in Baden's
concentration camps were mere tattlers (Dummschwätzer) who
had made antigovernment remarks in public.[28]

After the Nazi seizure of power, numerous opportunists,
both on an institutional and individual level, jumped on the
bandwagon. Wagner received congratulatory messages from
organizations as diverse as the Baden Turnerschaft and the
Orchester des Badischen Landestheaters, and from individual
newspaper publishers who wanted to survive in the new order.
In addition, the Nazi leaders in Baden assured the middle
class that the revolution would be orderly, that it would
respect property, and that above all it was a national movement symbolized by a meeting between Hindenburg and Hitler
on 21 March, an occasion celebrated in Baden by torchlight
parades. Finally, on 30 March, the new Nazi rulers of Baden
addressed the Baden population and reassured it that the national revolution in Baden had now been disciplined.[29]

By the end of March 1933, Wagner and his Nazi colleagues
had begun to use the various Nazi organizations to coordinate
Baden society. Only the Landtag and the political parties
remained as potential political competitors in late March.
In April, the seats in the state legislature were finally
distributed according to the March election results. Since
the Communists and the minor political parties did not obtain
representation in the new Landtag, the Nazis emerged with a
clear majority of thirty seats out of a total of fifty-seven.
A special law of coordination prepared by Wagner on 4 April
and promulgated on 7 April gave him the right to name the

government, thus usurping another important Landtag function. After becoming Reich governor of Baden on 6 May, Wagner used this power to appoint leading Nazis to the key state positions. Köhler became minister president and finance minister; Karl Pflaumer assumed the Ministry of Interior; Otto Wacker, a former Kreisleiter and member of the Gau clique and a holder of a Ph.D., was named minister of education and justice. The Nationalists were represented by Paul Schmitthenner, who became a state councilor and, after Wacker's death, the minister of education.[30]

Since most of these Nazi ministers did not have the technical experience and knowledge to handle the various ministries, they relied on professional bureaucrats who were as loyal to the new Nazi masters as they had been to the old regime. Jakob Bader, who had served in the Ministry of Interior of Baden since 1912 and as Mannheim police chief since 1921, became Pflaumer's ministerial director, while Friedrich Karl Müller-Trefzer, who also had a long career as a professional civil servant, became Köhler's expert. Both had survived the Nazi purge in 1933 to provide the Nazi ministers with the badly needed technical expertise.[31]

The final step in the Nazi consolidation of political power came between May and 5 July 1933. In May, the Nazis prepared an enabling act that would give their leaders absolute powers. Since Wagner needed the support of the Center party delegates for the two-thirds majority required to pass the enabling act, he called them together on 16 May and warned them of the consequences if they voted against the act. Wagner then attended a Landtag session on 9 June, for the first time since coming to power, no doubt to underline his threats. Köhler addressed the legislature and bluntly stated

that the new government did not really need the confidence
of the Landtag, although it desired good relations. After
these pressures the Center party voted for the enabling act,
which allowed the Nazi ministers to issue laws in violation
of Baden's constitution.[32] This act also spelled doom for
the political parties. All except the NSDAP were disbanded
between 1 June and 5 July 1933. Even the role of the Nazi
state delegates evaporated when the Landtag was dissolved in
October 1933.[33] The speed with which the Nazi ministers were
able to move against the political parties, the unions, the
Socialist party's clubs, and the Center party's Badewacht
surprised even the Nazi cabinet.[34]

With the power of the state and the grass-roots pressures from party affiliates and associated organizations, it
was equally easy to coordinate the various pluralistic bodies
of the state. The Nazi principle of the leadership concept
was introduced under a variety of different guises to facilitate this coordination. The Nazis, for example, announced
the abolition of elections to the agricultural chambers,
allegedly to save 40,000 RM but in reality to usurp control.
By October 1933, the deans of the universities were appointed
as "leaders," and the faculty senates were limited to insignificant advisory functions. These procedures were followed
with many other private social and professional organizations
that had already been infiltrated by the various party organizations.[35]

In July 1933, after having eliminated all political rivals
and initiated the coordination of Baden society, the Nazi leaders again officially declared an end to the revolution. This
was addressed particularly to the SA and other radical party
activists who wanted to reap the economic fruits of the success-

ful political revolution. In late July, Köhler, as minister of finance, addressed the Baden Chamber of Commerce and Industry and emphasized that revolutions were never productive in the economic sphere. Wagner supported this view and warned of the lack of discipline of some SA leaders who had violated both state and party discipline through their reckless actions.[36] The final elimination of all potential SA radicalism did not occur until the summer of 1934. In May 1934, Wagner again had to remind the police officers of Baden that the revolution in Baden had been terminated in 1933. He urged the police not to be intimidated by lawless party members and to move against all disruptions of state authority. Wagner emphasized that Nazis had no special privileges. After the Röhm purge, Köhler, reflecting on the removal of the SA leader, again emphatically maintained that the Nazi government wanted reconstruction, not revolution.[37]

THE PARTY AND STATE GOVERNMENT

What then was the function of the party in state affairs after the Nazis had assumed control of the leading state positions? Certainly the Nazis who flocked to the state legislature in Baden and to the Reichstag in early 1933 held no political or even functional powers. In fact, the state legislature was dissolved in October 1933, and the only function of the Reichstag seat was to provide the individual with an additional income. The party activists were also unable to penetrate the state's district offices which were headed by the Landrat. Before 1935, the Nazi leaders of the state government could purge the offices and appoint new candidates. And in Baden by September 1934, the district party leaders were designated by Wagner to be the Landräte's political advisors, particularly in personnel matters.[38] Wagner's attempt in late 1934, however, to combine the Landrat and party district posts under the direction of the party district leader failed because Hitler preferred to maintain the dualism to enhance his own powers. These Baden Landräte remained, for the most part, civil servants whose knowledge of state affairs and willing cooperation with the Nazi state made them essential to the Nazi ministries. As late as 1935, the party's official survey revealed that only fifteen of the forty Baden Landräte were party members and only two of them had joined the party before January 1933. Most of those who belonged to the party had joined only after the Nazi seizure of power in order to secure their positions.[39]

In public, Wagner declared that it was unthinkable that the state could function without the Nazi movement. He designated the party paper, Der Führer, the official organ for state and administrative news and notices.[40] But Wagner and his Nazi ministers agreed in a cabinet meeting in early 1934 that the party's influence on the state and municipalities should be restricted to personnel questions only. Later, Wagner argued that this had prevented rivalry and a dualism between the state and the party. In reality, there were constant frictions. But this arrangement did allow the party some influence over the state's personnel and at the same time enabled the Nazi ministers to rely on the administrative expertise of the traditional civil service.[41]

Only at the top were party and state positions combined. When Wagner became Reich governor of Baden in May 1933, he also assumed again his responsibilities as Gau leader of the

party. And he never tired of emphasizing that the Gau leadership of the party was an absolute prerequisite for the office
of Reich governor. This office gave Wagner considerable powers, which ranged from presiding over the meetings of the
state ministers to assigning specific tasks to the various
Baden ministers. As Reich governor and Gau leader, he could
assemble both state and party leaders and issue directives.[42]
Despite these extensive powers, in September 1933 at a Reich
governors' conference Wagner urged the transfer of more state
authority to the Reich governors, particularly in personnel
matters. Later in 1935, with the support of Frick, he attempted to combine the offices of Reich governor and minister president and relegate Köhler exclusively to the position of finance
minister. Although Hitler signed the order implementing
Wagner's plan, he never issued it, apparently preferring the
established dualism. In any case, Köhler, the minister of
finance and minister president, and Pflaumer, the minister of
interior, never challenged Wagner's powers in Baden. After
1940, when appointed chief of the Civil Administration of
Alsace by Hitler, Wagner enhanced his powers even more.[43]
These rested first and foremost on Hitler's support and second
on his control of the Nazi party in Baden.

After the Baden Nazis gained control of the state, they
tenaciously defended the interests of Baden and protected it
from Reich encroachments. To aid economic recovery, the
state's civil servants were ordered in 1933 to spend their
vacations in Baden. In a cabinet meeting, Wagner urged that
as many leading Baden civil servants as possible be placed
in leading positions in Berlin to protect the interests of
the Gau.[44] And "old" Baden Nazis who served in Berlin continued to promote provincial concerns. Franz Moraller, the

Baden Gau propaganda leader, eventually obtained a post in
the Berlin propaganda ministry, from where he advised Karlsruhe
on how the Baden Nazis could best protect the interests of the
state. In one case, he urged Karlsruhe to identify Baden with
a besieged frontier Gau in order to obtain privileges and
overcome Berlin's suspicions of provincialism. Similarly,
Otto Wacker served in the national Ministry of Education office in Berlin. He warned the Baden leaders of rival projects
by such states as Württemberg that endangered Baden's interests.[45] The Baden Nazi's loyalties to his native state remained intense, despite vehement national propaganda.

In late 1933, Minister President Köhler ordered the preparation of a Denkschrift on Baden's interests to protect the
state in the event of a major national administrative reform
(Reichsreform). No one in Baden knew what the state could
expect from any future Reich reform, but all feared the worst.
And all leading Nazi ministers in Baden, from the minister
of interior to the minister of education, argued that a special Baden Volkscharakter existed and needed to be protected.
Above all, the Baden Nazi ministers agreed that a union of
Baden and Württemberg should be resisted at all costs. Wacker
warned his colleagues that in case of such a union, Karlsruhe
would become a mere provincial city.[46]

Baden's rivalry with its neighbor Württemberg involved
a conflict over party offices and economic benefits. In June
1933, Köhler and Wagner visited Hitler to complain about the
preferential treatment of Württemberg. They claimed that
Württemberg benefited from its many national party posts and
the stationing of Reichswehr offices in Stuttgart.[47] The
next year the Gau Baden employment director complained to
the cabinet that Württemberg was still getting more new jobs

than Baden. By 1935, the Baden Nazi leaders became greatly
concerned when rumors emerged that Württemberg and Baden would
be united or that Baden would at least lose parts of its
territory to the Palatinate. The Nazi ministers in Karlsruhe
marshaled all the support they could, including testimonials
from such leading academic experts on folk culture as Metz
of the university of Erlangen, to defend the identity of
Baden.[48] In the end, there were minor territorial adjust-
ments, but Baden remained independent from Württemberg and
even acquired Alsace in 1940, which greatly enhanced its
influence in the Reich.

A much greater danger to the power of the Nazi ministers
in Baden and to the independence of Baden came from the Reich
offices after 1933. As early as the summer of 1933 the
Ministry for Public Enlightenment and Propaganda in Berlin
was assigned the task of converting the nation to the movement's philosophy. This naturally curtailed the powers of
the Karlsruhe propaganda office. Then at the beginning of
1935 the Reich Ministry of Justice absorbed the functions
of the Baden Ministry of Justice.[49] By January 1935, Köhler
was complaining bitterly to Frick about the growth of Berlin
agencies at the expense of the state's administration.
Köhler's complaints never ceased as the Reich offices continued to expand. On the eve of the outbreak of war, he
told the Baden cabinet that Berlin not only governed but
also usurped control of administration, a task that had been
reserved for the individual states.[50]

Most detrimental to the relative power base of the
Baden Nazi ministers was the loss of control over the police.
Between 1933 and 1935, Baden Minister of Interior Pflaumer
purged the state police and accepted only professional officers

who could and would accept the Nazi regime.[51] Even as late
as 1937, the Baden minister of interior and Wagner could purge
a police chief of Karlsruhe who had violated the Nazi code of
conduct by associating with Jews.[52] The Gestapo leader of
Karlsruhe until 1937, Karl Berkmüller, was a close and long-
time friend of Wagner. By 1937, things had changed drastically. After clashing with Reinhard Heydrich, the Reich
Gestapo leader, Berkmüller left the Gestapo and became the
mayor of Villingen. He was replaced by an "outsider" who
did not belong to Wagner's entourage and was not even a
native of Baden.[53] Wagner was furious because he had no influence over the political police in his own Gau. In fact,
Pflaumer had no knowledge in 1937 of the Gestapo's activities
in Karlsruhe, so, he took no responsibility for its actions.
The following year, he told Wagner that Berlin controlled the
police so strictly that it left no room for the state to
exercise its authority.[54]

In order to restrict Reich intervention as much as possible, the Baden Nazi leaders initiated administrative reforms
in Baden. In early 1935, Wagner ordered Köhler to simplify
and make more economical the administration of the state.
After a series of conferences and special reports from the
ministers of education and interior, Köhler discovered that
Baden had already carried out considerable reorganization
since 1919, even including the abolition of several ministries.[55] Despite Nazi attacks on the Baden government before
1933, the Nazi ministers subsequently adopted many of the
former government's suggestions on administrative reform.
In particular, the new Nazi masters used a 1931 study that
had recommended the reduction of districts and the abolition
of the Kreis system in order to save money and enhance effi-

ciency.[56]

Wagner approved these plans and agreed that the party could also afford to reduce its districts by eleven or twelve. Kramer, the party organization leader, was allowed to participate in the discussions of the state ministers. Finally, in May 1936, the reform program received the approval of Wilhelm Frick, the national minister of interior, and the plan was implemented first by the party and by April 1938 also by the state.[57] The following year, Baden carried out the last major administrative reform by adopting another suggestion from the Weimar era--the absorption of the duties of the self-governing Kreise by the state districts under the leadership of the Landrat.[58]

Despite the administrative simplification (which survived 1945), the Nazi ministers were unable to save much money. One reason was that the Nazis created new departments after 1933. They also pumped additional funds to such institutions as universities in order to enhance Baden's economic recovery, which was limited by the fact that the Gau was a border state which could not even host troop detachments until after 1936.[59] By 1939 Baden had exhausted its ability to initiate reforms. Pflaumer concluded that the Reich had expanded so much and controlled so many vital areas that there was little else the state could do.[60] Berlin was again the bête noire, except now it was no longer controlled by the "November criminals" but by fellow Nazis.

The leading Nazi ministers in Karlsruhe began to identify with their state functions. Köhler, who became immersed in economic and financial detail, was appointed by Göring in October 1936 to manage the allocation of raw materials in Germany within the framework of the Four Year Plan. Pflaumer

was also utilized by the Reich government for duties as an
advisor in Romania between February 1941 and March 1942.
Even Otto Wacker served in the Reich Ministry of Education
between 1937 and 1939 before returning to his Baden post.[61]
These same ministers began to defend their state prerogatives
with vigor against the interference of the party. When the
Gauamt leader for civil servants scolded the director of the
Baden State Chancellery for not allowing NS welfare membership drives in the offices, Köhler immediately set up a conference with the party leader responsible to "enlighten" him
about proper procedure when dealing with officials. Similarly, Wacker became enraged when the Führer published articles
attacking teachers, and particularly Gymnasium teachers, as
being educational Philistines. He demanded a retraction not
only because as a university-educated Nazi he resented the
educational radicalism of the Führer, but also because he was
now protecting his own fief.[62]

The national party leaders noticed a general trend by
"old party" activists who had assumed state functions to
attempt to eliminate the party's influence on state affairs.
In Baden, Minister of Interior Pflaumer was one of the most
extreme examples of this development. He made it clear to
the party's welfare organization (NSV) that it could aid the
state but that the ultimate responsibility rested with the
state.[63] Pflaumer also neglected his responsibilities as
a party member. The national party treasurer, Schwarz, had
persistent difficulties with Pflaumer between 1935 and 1944.
In 1936, he complained to Wagner that Pflaumer did not
answer his letters and had not paid his party dues for eleven
months despite repeated warnings. Wagner forced his minister
to apologize in late 1936, but by 1940 Pflaumer was again in

arrears. Schwarz was outraged at his negligence. Between November 1943 and April 1944, Schwarz wrote Pflaumer several personal letters, requesting the Baden minister's party papers for administrative procedures. On 15 April 1944, Pflaumer finally replied with a mere one-sentence note. Schwarz exploded at this lack of respect for his position and announced to Wagner that he would cease all future communications with Pflaumer. On the eve of Germany's military collapse and only days after the Allied invasion of France, Wagner instructed his deputy Gau leader Röhn to lecture Pflaumer on his party duties. Pflaumer, who served the Nazi state faithfully and had been a party district organization leader, no doubt considered his party obligations after 1933 as mere bothersome distractions from more important duties.[64]

The Nazi ministers of Baden did respond to party pleas if they did not affect vital state interests or powers. Gau party offices bombarded the Baden ministers with requests for special privileges for the party. For example, Köhler responded to a plea from the Gau propaganda leader by ordering the state agencies to grant business contracts to "old party" members. And even Pflaumer modified the orders of the state district office of Offenburg that had prohibited the party from posting party literature on houses and trees. He also obtained permission from the Reich minister of interior to grant Gau and district party offices the freedom to examine the files of Baden's state district offices relating to election campaigns between 1919 and 1935. Similarly, Wacker allowed party courts seeking documents for party court cases to be treated as any other Reich or state agency.[65] None of these issues really affected vital state affairs. Rather, the party's major efforts to influence the state below the

ministerial levels concentrated on two party affiliates, the
Office for Civil Servants (Amt für Beamte) and the Office
for Municipal Affairs (Amt für Kommunalpolitik). Both had
been founded by the party before 1933 in an attempt to infiltrate and coordinate pluralistic interest organizations.
After 1933, the party used the two affiliates to attempt to
coordinate and even control the civil service and the municipalities of Baden.

THE BADEN CIVIL SERVICE: AMT FÜR BEAMTE

Before 1933, Baden civil servants who publicly supported
National Socialism risked being fired by the government.
As late as 1932, teachers in Baden were dismissed for their
Nazi affiliation. It was not until late 1932 that the minister of interior allowed civil servants to join the NSDAP.
Despite these obstacles, lower civil servants and in particular teachers flocked to the party. Even some higher-level
civil servants became active in the Nazi movement before
1933. Several of the leading Gau Nazis like Karl Lenz and
August Kramer were former public schoolteachers. According
to official party statistics, 9.4 percent of the party's
members in Baden before the September 1930 election (and still
active in 1934) were civil servants. Considering the rapid
expansion of the membership after 1930, it is not surprising
that this figure had dropped to 8.6 percent by January 1933.
In 1935, the Baden party's membership of 13.7 percent civil
servants still exceeded the national average of 12.4 percent.
Not surprisingly, the teachers, who accounted for 25 percent
of all Baden civil servants who joined the party, represented

the largest single bloc.[66]

The Nazi ministers who assumed the leading positions in
Baden in 1933 had to rely on the technical expertise of the
civil service, whether the individual experts were Nazis or
not. Köhler immediately tried to reassure his experts in
the Ministry of Finance and State Chancellery that he did
not demand political conversion, only a total confidence.
In a cabinet meeting in March 1933, Wagner admitted that the
purge of the civil service had been slow because of financial
considerations and, most important, because the new Nazi
government could not find trained Nazi replacements. Wagner
emphasized that he wanted a reliable, nationalistic civil
service, but he also insisted on competency and performance.
He urged resistance to the growing pleas for employment in
the civil service emanating from the Nazi movement. Only
Communist civil servants, regardless of qualification, had
to be dismissed at once.[67] Despite Wagner's insistence on
competency, he took a strong personal interest in the purge
of "undesirable" civil servants, particularly those with
leftist political backgrounds or Jewish connections. The
civil service law of April 1933 allowed the Nazis to proceed
against civil servants on both political and racial grounds.
In Baden by October 1933, 415 civil servants had already
been purged from the central state administration (and only
14 of these were Jews). This process continued after 1933
in local communities where the purge of political opponents
and "non-Aryans" was pushed especially hard by the various
Nazi organizations.[68]

The Nazi rulers of Baden had to do more than purge the
civil service, particularly since very few "old" Nazi activists obtained leading state positions below the ministerial

level. One party district leader became a Landrat, and a
close friend of Wagner was appointed to the leading Gestapo
post in Karlsruhe. In addition, a few Nazis with technical
expertise also became state appointees. Most of these experts
were relatively recent party converts and not "old party"
activists.[69] As a substitute, the Nazi ministers tried to
force the civil servants to conform at least to the Nazi
rituals and participate in party rallies and activities.
In July 1933, Köhler demanded a more active participation
in party rallies, and he scolded the higher-level civil servants for refraining from these activities. He reminded
them that, after all, the NSDAP was now the state.[70]

This attack on the apolitical civil servant was led by
Hitler himself, who told his Reich governors in a meeting in
November 1934 that thousands of civil servants who opposed
National Socialism before 1933 still occupied administrative
positions. Hitler promised that in ten to fifteen years the
Nazis would have a bureaucracy which would cooperate fully.
This view was voiced publicly by Wagner in the same month
when he addressed a national conference of Gauamt leaders
of the party's office for civil servants. Wagner insisted
that he could no longer be satisfied with mere loyal civil
servants. Instead, he demanded that they pursue their responsibilities in the Nazi state with a joyful and positive acceptance of the new order.[71] This was the view that Wagner
supported in cabinet meetings in Baden with one reservation.
While he demanded that civil servants attend party functions
and civil servant recruits be introduced to National Socialism,
he also emphasized that the civil servants' party activism
could not endanger professionalism. To solve this dilemma
Wagner ordered that key personnel positions in the civil

service be filled with party civil servants who could ensure
the cooperation of the service and provide posts for loyal
and competent Nazi bureaucrats in the future.[72]

For immediate impact, the various party agencies were
utilized to ensure at least the outward conformity of the
civil servants. The civil servant who attended church services and passively accepted insults directed toward National
Socialism was warned that he would be fired. Bureaucrats
caught shopping in Jewish stores were reprimanded in public
party meetings and faced occupational threats. In an attempt
to abolish the civil service's exclusiveness, the party pressured bureaucrats to belong to its affiliate organizations,
join the party's organization for civil servants, attend NSBO
meetings, and participate in the activities of the party in
general in order to demonstrate that they were part of the
folk community.[73]

The one party organization charged with the indoctrination and conversion of civil servants to National Socialism
was the Amt für Beamte (AfB; Office for Civil Servants),
which had emerged as early as August 1932 when Wilhelm Bogs,
an inspector who had not joined the party until September
1930, took over the leadership of the new and very small organization. But this party affiliate did not really mushroom
until after 1933 under the direction of a new leader, Leopold
Mauch. Mauch, who had only an elementary education and did
not join the party until late 1931, was employed as a border
patrol officer since 1920. A poorly educated, lower-level
civil servant, Mauch strongly believed that it was his duty
to indoctrinate the civil servants and to convert them
to National Socialism. He pushed this concept with particular enthusiasm against the well-educated, higher-level civil

servants. For Mauch, who was not really one of the "old" party members, this party affiliate provided a potential tool
for social and professional mobility.[74]

The party's department for civil servants completed its
initial organizational evolution in 1935 when Wagner announced
the elimination of over sixty different civil servants'
organizations in Baden and charged the Gauamt with the conversion of civil servants to National Socialism. This party
department had seventeen full-time employees by 1935 who were
responsible for the indoctrinating and incorporating of over
fifty thousand civil servants into the new Nazi order. By
1939 Mauch boasted that of sixty thousand Baden civil servants, forty thousand belonged to the Reichsbund Deutscher
Beamte, forty-seven thousand belonged to the NSV, twenty-
three thousand held honorary positions in the party or its
affiliates, and seven thousand were active in the SA, SS,
NSKK, and NSFK. The civil servants' membership in these
organizations was interpreted by Mauch as a sign of cooperation with and acceptance of National Socialism, despite the
obvious fact that pressures were applied to force the civil
servants to join.[75]

Statistics could not, however, hide the fact that the
civil service, although purged and coordinated after 1933,
continued as a relatively cohesive body with established
privileges and procedures. This was clear as early as the
summer of 1933 when the Reich Minister of Interior Frick
issued a circular maintaining that the affairs of civil
servants would now be handled directly by the Nazi state.
He limited the functions of the Reichsbund der Deutschen
Beamten to the dissemination of propaganda and stressed
that party interference in administrative affairs would not

be tolerated. Clearly, the Nazi minister Frick was attempting to protect his fief from the encroachments of the frequently ill-prepared party activists.[76] This resistance of
Nazi ministers to the party's attempts to usurp control over
the civil service caused the AfB to become (unlike other party affiliates which represented the interest of their specific
"subculture") a party-centered organization which attempted
to bring down the protective walls of the civil service.
This can be seen in repeated examples in which the Gauamt
cooperated closely with the party cadre organization even
against the interests of civil servants.[77]

The most immediate and pressing problem faced by the
civil service after the initial purge was to ward off the
invasion of untrained party members who were seeking civil
service jobs. The Gauamt fully supported these efforts on
the part of the party members, even against the best interests
of the bureaucracy. As early as 1934, these promotions,
based on party careers rather than ability or training,
caused considerable ill feeling in the Baden civil service.[78]
The resentment became stronger in 1935 when Hitler ordered
that 10 percent of the lower- and middle-level civil service
jobs be reserved for party members who had joined the party
by September 1930 (later January 1933). Mauch supported
this policy enthusiastically. He received numerous applications from poorly educated party members, 90 percent of whom
only had an eighth-grade education, who wanted lower-level
state jobs ranging from clerks to police officers. Later
when the "old party members" date was moved to January 1933,
the educational background of at least one third of the applicants improved somewhat since they had at least a middle
school education.[79] For these Nazis, this order meant an

opportunity for social mobility, which they had "earned"
through their party careers.

This social mobility is well illustrated by the case
of Otto Pink, a customs official in Kehl and a party activist
between 1931 and 1938, who eventually became local leader of
Kehl. Since Pink's job as personnel director of the customs
office was too time-consuming for his party responsibilities,
the district leader requested that Mauch and the party's
Gau personnel leader provide a less demanding job for Pink
by promoting him despite obvious educational deficiencies.
Between December 1938 and April 1939, with the support of
the Gau personnel office the Gauamt for civil servants ac-
comodated the party's interests by obtaining Pink's promotion.[80] Little wonder that civil servants, particularly
on the lower levels, complained that they felt like second-
class citizens when compared with their colleagues who were
also party members.[81]

The civil service's resistance to party encroachments
was particularly strong in the higher levels. The lack of
interest in party affairs became clear in 1934 when the
party noticed that bureaucrats were cancelling their subscriptions to Nazi newspapers. Wagner ordered Mauch to inform the civil servants that the party press must be considered a "school." Consequently, with his usual overzeal-
ousness Mauch attempted to distribute questionnaires to all
civil servants to discover their reading habits. Even Wagner
and Köhler could not approve this procedure since it undermined the civil service's morale and efficiency. Mauch did
discover, however, that the upper civil service was especially eager to drop the party press. In 1934/35, over half
of the well-educated judicial civil servants did not subscribe

to the Nazi press as compared to one-fourth of all civil servants in twenty-six districts examined by Mauch.[82] In some
Baden districts, there were no party members among the leading
civil servants of the judiciary as late as 1936. The Gauamt
also considered most of the key civil servants in the Baden
Ministry of Interior hostile to the interests of the party.
Perhaps most detrimental to the party's influence over the
civil service was the fact that as late as 1938 the majority
of personnel departments of Baden's civil service were directed by professionals rather than party members. Since
neither the Gauamt nor the party had a systematic program
for the selection and recruitment of civil servants as late
as 1937, the Gau personnel office could only remind its district representatives that the best way to influence the civil
servant was to let him know that the party determined to some
extent his promotion.[83]

The Gauamt for civil servants tried two techniques to
obtain more influence over the civil service. First, Mauch
began an indoctrination program in 1936 by establishing a
new Gau school for civil servants. However, since the civil
servant was charged for half of the train ticket to the school
and he lost up to ten days' vacation by participating in
the two-week classes, he was less than enthusiastic about being indoctrinated by "intellectual inferiors." By early 1939
only four thousand of the nearly sixty thousand civil servants
in Baden had completed the course, and after the war broke
out, the rate of indoctrination decreased drastically.[84]
Second, early in 1938 the Gauamt and the Gau party's personnel leader devised a plan that allowed the party district
leader, with the help of the Kreisamt für Beamte, to select
civil service candidates. Every six months these names would

then be sent to the Gau personnel office, which in turn would
select final candidates to attend a two-week training session
at the civil service school of the Gauamt. After this indoctrination, which emphasized racial, cultural, and athletic
events, the Gau personnel leader sent the names of the candidates to the state administration. Mauch preferred over the
technically trained candidates those party members who had
severed their ties with the church and were also good athletes.[85]

On the surface, the new recruitment plan looked very
promising, since the Baden civil service in 1938 faced a
shortage of trained candidates. Wagner ordered Mauch to
investigate this shortage. The Gauamt leader attributed it
to the loss of civil service personnel to the army, the Four
Year Plan, and the smaller postwar generation. In addition,
civil servants had been reassigned to Austria in 1938. And
above all, Mauch blamed the poor state-party relations, and
the failure of the bureaucrats to realize that a candidate's
solid ideological and character traits were a promising foundation, even if the candidate's technical skills were wanting.
Mauch was, of course, also interested in the shortage of
civil servants because this would cause the state to release
even fewer bureaucrats for party functions and activities.
He could not understand that years after the Nazi seizure of
power leading civil servants in Baden continued to reject
the party's wishes. The recruitment plan seemed a perfect
answer to both the shortage and the Nazification problems.[86]

There were two basic weaknesses of this plan. First,
the available jobs for these Nazi candidates were limited
since 90 percent of middle-level positions were reserved for
the lower-level civil servants. In addition, the party civil

servant candidate had no legal rights to the remaining positions. All the party could do was to exert pressures on the
state personnel office. Second, the war destroyed much of
the machinery that had been charged with the ideological preparation of these candidates. The war immediately drained the
party's office for civil servants of its personnel, including
Mauch, who served in the army in 1939. After Wagner ordered
the indoctrination of civil servants resumed, the personnel
shortages limited the indoctrination of officials to twenty
minutes every three weeks. Even the Gau school of the Gauamt
was closed in early 1943.[87] In April 1943, the Gauamt and
its district offices were disbanded in an effort to eliminate
nonessential party organizations in the drive for total war
mobilization. Mauch continued to advise Wagner on civil
service affairs, and various party agencies absorbed some of
the functions of the Gauamt, but the party had to abandon
its attempts to infiltrate and control the civil service.[88]
The Gauamt always identified with the party rather than the
hostile civil service. Only through intimidation and surveillance did it exercise any significant influence over the
civil servants. Its elimination in 1943 was testimony to
its unimportance in the party hierarchy by that time.

The AfB was not the only party organization that tried
to influence or even control the bureaucracy. In 1933/34,
many party activists attempted to obtain their rewards, settle accounts with political opponents, or engage in what
Wagner in 1934 called collection mania, all of which interfered with state functions. As early as 1933/34, the Nazi
ministers Wagner, Pflaumer, and Köhler had to intercede to
protect the efficiency of the state's apparatus from the
overzealous Nazis.[89] Nazi activists were indirectly attack-

ing the Nazi ministers when they charged that the old party
civil servants of the republican era still controlled the
leading posts. Köhler, the minister president, could simply
not tolerate this attack on his alleged lack of performance.[90]
These clashes between the party and the civil service continued unabated despite warnings by Nazi ministers that admonished party functionaries not to try to order public officials to implement policies. Even the Gau staff party leader
constantly had to warn the party's district leaders, particularly after 1939, not to interfere in state affairs. The
personal conferences between party and state leaders, encouraged by the deputy Gau leader in late 1939 to enhance cooperation, had little influence.[91]

A basic reason for the party's constant clashes with
the civil service, besides mere power struggles, was the
social and educational gulf between Nazi activists who had
graduated from elementary or middle schools, and civil servants who had graduated from universities. This is clearly
illustrated by two examples that involved both teachers
and the judicial service. Otto Wacker, an old and enthusiastic Baden Nazi who became minister of education in 1933,
purged teachers who were hostile to the Nazi movement or
had actively opposed it before 1933. He also attempted to
induce teachers to participate in such party activities as
Hitler Youth meetings.[92] But when the Führer in early 1934
began to publish a series of articles questioning the teachers' ideological commitments to the new regime, and in particular focused on professors in higher education, Wacker
(who held a Ph.D.) reached the limits of his patience. He
demanded a retraction in the Führer. When the editor of
the paper refused to publish a full retraction and limited

himself to a brief note concerning a minor detail, Wacker
told the Baden cabinet that he was not satisfied. Wacker
felt that he had to protect the teachers and argued that
the humanities, instead of being merely a reflection of educational philistinism, would actually strengthen National
Socialism. By using the official Staatsanzeiger of the government, which was published by the Führer, Wacker forced
the party newspaper to publish his letter, which vindicated
the teachers. Wacker also made certain that the local papers,
which also published official news, carried the same notice.[93]
Wacker was not simply protecting his fief; he was defending
the values of higher education and traditional humanistic
studies against the party radicals.

The most bitter clashes between the party and the upper
level of the civil service involved the judiciary. The conflict was so pronounced because no leading Nazi minister was
also a legal expert and because extreme educational and social divisions separated the judicial civil service and party
leaders. Several Baden judges and prosecutors before 1933
had sympathized with the Nazi movement. After 1933, Baden's
judicial organization discovered that lawyers who did not
obtain a favorable sentence from a court would turn to the
party, to Wagner and the Führer's deputy to circumvent the
legal system. The party would even attempt to find out
which prosecutor handled cases involving party members.[94]
If the party initiated a legal case, the police would usually
overreact in fear of offending a leading party figure. In
some cases, the party tried to investigate legal cases involving party members, and in other cases the party district
leader would declare that none of his local leaders could
be arrested without his permission. If the judicial officer

attempted to press cases involving the party (even those involving moral cases), the party's response was to label the
judicial system a "bourgeois reaction."[95]

The Baden judiciary especially disliked the party district leaders, since by origin and training these Nazi functionaries understood neither law nor the work of the judges.
The state's legal representatives were delighted at the elimination in 1936 of several district leaders who had fought
the judiciary.[96] But relationships deteriorated badly during the war. Wagner did order the Kreisleiters not to pressure courts and to rely more on their legal experts, who had
legal knowledge and could communicate better with their peers.
In reality, Wagner's order, which was only issued at the
prompting of the state's chief justice mattered little. After
all, noted the same chief justice, a young prosecutor trainee
knew that his career depended on the Kreisleiter's evaluation
and veto.[97] Wagner, who relied more and more on the police
and circumvented the legal system constantly, was anything but
a good example to his district party leaders.[98] Force and
direct action were the party's answers to legal issues and
problems. Both were making the courts superfluous. The party, however, lacking the trained personnel, had no established
vehicle for control of the judiciary. As always, it relied
on intimidation and career pressures to influence the judiciary. Ultimately, Wagner could use the Gestapo, which was
beyond the courts' control.

Although the traditional Baden civil service was able
to persevere against party harassment and continue in its
traditional role, it never openly rebelled against the Nazi
state or refused to implement Nazi legislation issued by
Nazi ministers. Naturally, the civil service reacted against

the party's interference, because it threatened its established privileges and its functionalism, which was based on
competency rather than party longevity. The hooliganism and
meager education of the Nazi activists who did not obtain
leading state positions was anathema to the conservative civil
service. But the functionalism of the purged civil service
after 1933 served the Nazi ministers well. The expulsion and
persecution of Jews and political enemies, the introduction
of the Four Year Plan, and the accompanying preparations for
war and expansion would perhaps have been very difficult to
implement had the technically deficient civil service candidates of the AfB been elevated to the leading posts. The
party and its affiliates remained constant watchdogs. But
despite the party's powers of intimidation, the party on the
whole was frustrated in its attempts to gain control over the
civil service after the Nazi revolution in Baden had become
institutionalized. Only the war brought the party activists
additional functions and the state administration new competition. In the end, the war destroyed not only the Nazi
state but also the Nazi movement.

THE BADEN MUNICIPALITIES: AMT FÜR KOMMUNALPOLITIK

While the bulk of the civil servants of Baden remained in
their offices after 1933, the Nazis were able to have a much
larger impact on the leading municipal positions, which were
political posts. The new Nazi rulers began the political
revolution on the local level with the appointments of municipal commissars on 15 March 1933 in the major urban centers
of Baden, either to "restore order" or to alleviate the

"difficult financial situation." In the large urban center of Mannheim, for example, Wagner appointed as commissars the party Kreisleiter Otto Wetzel and the industrialist Karl Renninger, who had belonged to the Fatherland party in Mannheim in 1917. These Nazi commissars initiated the local purges of political opponents and municipal employees and with the help of the local party organization carried out the first "official" anti-Semitic acts.[99]

Wagner also issued a law requiring the allocation of municipal council seats according to the 5 March 1933 national election results. This gave the Nazis a clear majority in the common councils, and at least half of the seats in the executive councils of all major urban centers except Villingen, Singen, and Konstanz in Catholic southern Baden. Communist seats, of course, were eliminated.[100] As an added measure of control, in June the Nazi ministers dissolved all municipal councils where disagreements had arisen. This same coordination occurred in all other local and regional self-governing bodies. When the district party leader objected to a member of a district council (Kreisrat) and that member refused to resign in 1933, the state's district commissioner simply dissolved the Kreisrat and named new delegates to a new Kreisrat.[101]

Beginning in May 1934, the Nazi municipal commissars were replaced by appointed mayors in the major urban centers and "elected" mayors in the smaller towns. To ensure continued Nazi control over newly elected mayors, a law issued on 4 May 1933 required the approval of the minister of interior before a newly elected mayor could assume his office. There was good reason for this legislation since in small communities there was still organized opposition to the Nazis in 1933.

For example, in Staufen the German Nationalists and the Center party cooperated against the Nazi candidate and elected a mayor, and in another small community (Leinen) a Socialist was elected mayor with the help of the Nationalists and Center party. In both instances, the minister of interior immediately negated the election results and appointed Nazi mayors.[102] Finally, to complete the Nazi domination of these municipal posts, in a cabinet meeting in January 1934 Pflaumer announced the cancellation of all future mayoral elections and substituted the procedure of appointment by the minister of interior.[103]

In the major urban centers, the mayors who had occupied offices before the Nazis seized power were, for the most part, replaced by Nazi commissars. These commissars became Nazi mayors by May 1933 after having been appointed by Wagner and confirmed by the Nazi-dominated city councils.[104] Only one lord mayor who held office in a Baden town with a population of at least ten thousand people in 1932 was still in power in 1945. In June 1933, Wagner requested that Carl Neinhaus, the lord mayor of Heidelberg, who had joined the party only in 1933, retract his resignation. Neinhaus was born in March 1888, and after receiving a solid legal education he assumed a city council position in Barmen between 1920 and 1928. Then, in December 1929, he was elected lord mayor of Heidelberg as an independent. The Nazi party made it clear that Neinhaus, who did not join the party until after the Nazi seizure of power, had maintained cordial relations with the Nazis before 1933 and faithfully implemented Nazi policies after January 1933.[105] Wagner only allowed one other lord mayor, Huegel of Weinheim, who was not a party member even after 1933, to remain in office until his

retirement in 1938. By 1935, eighteen of the nineteen lord
mayors were party members, and all except two of the mayors
of these nineteen towns were party members. The Zentrum
mayor of Freiburg, for example, who had been a mayor since
1913, was allowed to remain in office until his retirement.
Of the sixteen lord mayors, four had been party activists
as early as 1923/25, four joined only during the first half
of 1933, and the rest (representing the educated middle class)
had joined the party by 1930/32. But all were active in some
party affiliate or association, even the nonparty lord mayor
of Weinheim. Finally, most of the lord mayors were relatively young, having been born in (and after) 1891.[106]

The lord mayors of Baden came from two major categories.
One group selected by Wagner represented specialists and career
bureaucrats who were also party members but usually did not
hold vital party posts. These Nazi "technicians" were appointed to posts in Mannheim, Karlsruhe, Heidelberg, Rastatt,
and Baden-Baden. They were all well-educated men who had long
experience in municipal government or in business. For example, the lord mayor of Karlsruhe, Friedrich Jäger, had joined
the civil service early in his career and the municipal service of Karlsruhe in 1903; the mayor of Rastatt, Dr. Fees,
had entered the civil service in Rastatt in 1929. In the
largest urban center of Baden, the industrialist Karl Renninger, who had not joined the party until 1930, was appointed lord mayor after having served as Nazi commissar in
Mannheim.[107]

A second type of lord mayor and mayor appointed to Baden's
largest and medium-sized cities was the party district leader.
The party Kreisleiters flocked to the mayoral posts in Baden
after 1933. Some of these Kreisleiters had both education

and training. Dr. Franz Kerber, the lord mayor of Freiburg, held a doctorate in philosophy, while Dr. Wolfram Rombach, the lord mayor of Offenburg, was a lawyer.[108] Similarly, between 1934 and 1936 the Kreisleiters of Neustadt, Buchen, and Schopfheim, to name only a few, claimed the mayoral positions of the major towns in their districts. By 1935, the lord mayors of the nineteen largest cities in Baden included three Kreisleiters, two deputy Kreisleiters, and one local leader.[109] Significantly, in 1936/37 when the party Kreisleiter post became a full-time, paid position, most Kreisleiters in Baden who held mayoral seats chose the municipal posts and relinquished their party careers. These municipal positions provided an alternative road to state power and prestige on the local level and usually better financial rewards than the party could then offer.[110]

In September, the Baden minister of interior announced that the coordination of the municipalities had been completed. The Nazi leaders had retired 127 mayors on the basis of the April 1933 civil service law and in addition had appointed trusted Nazis to vacant mayoral posts. By September 1933, about 25 percent of all mayoral posts were newly staffed with Nazis. In some cases the Nazi ministers even had to rely on former party members who had left the party because of personal disputes, but were still active in the movement's affiliate organizations, to staff mayoral posts in the smaller towns like Tauberbischofsheim and Oberkirch.[111]

Despite Pflaumer's claim that the coordination of the municipalities had been accomplished, the local party agencies continued to inundate the central offices with requests for the purge of mayors. As a result, by 1936 in some Baden districts 30 percent of the mayoral posts were occupied by new

men.[112] In the district of Bruchsal, 73 percent of its mayoral positions in early 1937 were occupied by new appointees.
Typically, the party and its various organizations provided
the new candidates. Of four new mayors appointed between
January and February 1937 in this district, one was a local
party leader, another a district press leader, and a third
a local NSV leader. By 1938 a large percentage of mayors in
Bruchsal were also local party leaders or at least held some
party office.[113]

In general, "old" party members held most of the important urban mayoral posts, while the smaller communities of
Baden were led by a sizeable bloc of post-1933 party converts. By 1935, 63.3 percent of Baden's 1,527 municipal
leaders were also party members. But most of the smaller
communities (Gemeinden) had Nazi mayors who had not joined
the party until after 30 January 1933. On the other hand,
87 of the 104 urban communities (Städte) of Baden had Nazi
mayors, of whom 64 had joined the party before January 1933.
The old Nazi activists flocked to the larger urban centers
where the mayoral posts brought financial and power rewards,
while the bulk of the smaller communities were led by recent
converts. But in both cases the Nazi penetration of the
mayoral positions continued unabated, particularly in the
communities where mayors were paid officials. By April 1937,
only seventeen full-time mayoral posts were still occupied
by nonparty mayors.[114]

The same trend occurred in the municipal councils. Most
of the new appointees were party members or representatives
of the various party affiliates who wanted a share of the
spoils. On the surface the council members appointed were
also supposed to represent the various social classes of

Baden. In Bietigheim, for example, of seven members appointed
in 1935, three were farmers, three were workers, and one was
a small businessman.[115] But the real power and function of
the councilmen had disappeared. In Baden, the mayors of the
smaller communities informed their council members of municipal affairs, but in the larger towns the Baden mayors had
neither the time nor the inclination to do this.[116] The party's influence, however, was felt in all cases. After 1935,
the district party leader had to interview a council member
before he was appointed by the state, and Kreisleiters were
constantly attempting to eliminate all council members who
had not joined the party.[117] And Baden's minister of
interior agreed in 1938 that a council member who was not a
party member was unsuited for the post. When a state district official (Landrat), who was not a party member himself,
attempted to defend a nonparty councilman, the party Kreisleiter would simply remind him that a Landrat who was not a
party member was also not qualified to hold his office.[118]

While the Nazi infiltration of the municipal leadership
posts continued unabated and the party provided leaders for
the municipalities, the role of the new mayors and their relationships with the state and the party still needed to be
defined. Wagner justified the nomination of Nazi mayors with
the argument that the party had to have a leading influence
on political questions. Yet, he also apparently agreed with
his Nazi ministers in a cabinet meeting in January 1934 that
the influence of the party and its agencies on state and municipal authorities must be restricted to pure personnel questions. These same ministers tried to protect the mayors, who
were now mostly party members, from the interference of the
various party agencies. In practice, the municipalities were

engulfed in a constant institutional turmoil and rivalry between state and party agencies.[119]

The one party organization charged with coordinating the
Nazi movement's invasion of the municipalities was the Gauamt
für Kommunalpolitik (AfK or Office for Municipal Affairs).
Before 1933, this office had supervised the Nazi participation
in municipal elections and then provided the Nazi municipal
delegates with much-needed legal and technical information.
In 1933, the Gauamt faced two tasks. First, it had to continue the Nazi penetration of the local government bodies and
it had to protect the new Nazi mayors from the unauthorized
interference of the various party organs. The Gauamt's leader until 1936 was Rudolf Schindler, who had been the business
leader of the party's municipal department until 1931, when
he assumed leadership of the agency. Born in 1903 in Karlsruhe, he had at least completed high school (Gymnasium) and
then acquired a position as a bank employee. After having
moved to South America, Schindler returned to Baden and became
a party member in 1929 and a Nazi city council member in Karlsruhe the following year. Wagner supported him before 1933,
even against a party court decision that attempted to expel
Schindler for his misappropriation of party funds.[120] As
Gauamt leader of the AfK, Schindler was also the leader of
the state's municipal agency, the Gemeindetag, although the
daily affairs of this agency were handled by the business
manager, Eduard Jäkle, a well-educated Nazi who was also one
of the mayors of Karlsruhe.[121] With control of both of these
positions, Schindler had the potential to coordinate effectively the Nazi penetration of the municipalities.

Schindler clearly believed that his Gauamt had the duty
to ensure the Nazification of the municipalities. The Gauamt

demanded that municipal council members sign a declaration
that required a delegate's resignation on the request of the
Gauamt, and Schindler tried to ensure that the personnel leaders of the towns were party members (which they still were
not in 1935).[122] To ensure the ideological indoctrination of
the new mayors, the Gauamt in cooperation with Pflaumer initiated an "educational" program for mayors in 1934. This was
followed with formal conferences, which by the middle of 1936
had introduced all mayors and municipal delegates to Nazi
leadership concepts and Nazi municipal policies, although they
provided little technical training.[123] To ensure the permanent indoctrination of the mayors, a Gau school of the party's
municipal department was established in December 1938. The
purpose of indoctrination according to the Gauamt was twofold.
It would provide the many mayors and municipal delegates, who
had emerged after 1933 without adequate prerequisites, with
substantive training, and it would ensure a force that was
solidly grounded ideologically to implement the political
and ideological goals of National Socialism.[124]

Schindler also had to meet the challenge of the party,
despite the fact that he represented a party organization.
In 1933, the various party agencies attempted numerous encroachments on the functions of the mayors and city councils.
Imbued with revolutionary fervor, party activists attempted
to interfere with municipal administrative matters. Schindler,
who was a committed Nazi and party member, believed that the
Gauamt should be independent to implement National Socialism
on the local level. By late 1934, the despondent Schindler
wrote the national Gauamt leader that every agency from the
minister of interior to the Gau leader and the party personnel office interfered in municipal affairs. No one could work

under such conditions, concluded Schindler, Instead, he maintained that only the Gauamt leader should be responsible for
the mayors. The national leadership of the AfK agreed with
Schindler and replied that the state appointed mayors in consultation with the Gau leader, who obtained suggestions from
the AfK. In particular, the national office attempted to restrain the interference of the party's personnel office and
of the local leaders.[125]

Schindler fought hard against party interference in his
domain. He admonished the party district leaders to keep the
local leaders away from the city-hall offices, and he demanded
that party district leaders refrain from interfering in non-
political municipal issues. The Gauamt leader even relied on
the support of the state in his attempts to limit the party's
interference in municipal affairs, particularly if financial
matters were involved.[126] The same conflict between the party
and the AfK occurred on the local and district level. In part,
this was due to the fact that gradually more and more district
representatives of the AfK were also mayors, which caused them
to identify with the problems of the state. And many of these
new district leaders of the municipal office had not joined
the party until after 1933. But even an old party member
like the former party district leader of Kehl, who as mayor
of Kehl was also the district leader of the AfK, was frequently not even invited to party conferences. On one occasion,
this same person was assigned a pub rather than the city hall
for a municipal conference he had planned.[127] It was basically a conflict between rival institutions rather than ideological principles.

The most important factor limiting the powers of the
Gauamt after 1935 was the growth of the power of the Kreis-

leiter over municipal affairs. Before 1935, party district
leaders had sent political evaluations of mayoral candidates
to the Gauamt and in return were informed of mayoral appointments. But in 1935 the Kreisleiter was appointed the party
delegate for municipal affairs with the privilege to review
and recommend mayoral and council candidates. In 1936, the
Kreisleiter was guaranteed private meetings with municipal
council members in order to solicit opinions and evaluations
on potential municipal candidates. No state or party agencies
were allowed to take part in these secret conferences. Trying to salvage some influence, the Gauamt reminded the party
district leaders that they could consult with the district
representatives of the AfK before the secret meetings. But
the balance of power rested now with the Kreisleiter.[128]

Wagner tried to preserve some of the Gauamt's functions
by ordering the party district leaders to exercise their
privileges only in cooperation with the Gauamt. As governor
of Baden, Wagner also invited both the party district leaders
and the Gauamt's district representatives when announcing
important municipal policies.[129] Still, the party district
leaders and the Gau personnel office continued to increase
their influence over municipal affairs. In 1936, the Gau
personnel office took a survey of Baden towns to see whether
Kreisleiters were consulted in personnel questions dealing
with municipal civil servants. Most towns did not do this
since it involved the civil service. The Gauamt for personnel immediately issued a declaration that the twelve
hundred municipal civil servants of Baden needed to know
that cities consulted the Kreisleiter first before personnel decisions were made. Several weeks later, a Kreisleiter
informed his district mayors that there would no longer be

hiring or promotion without the approval of the district leader.[130]

It was not surprising that Schindler left the Gauamt in
1936, an unpaid position, to become president of Baden's
Municipal Insurance League. He was replaced by Franz Kerber,
a former Kreisleiter and mayor of Freiburg, who served until
1942, when Oskar Hüssy, the mayor of Karlsruhe, took over the
office. In both cases, these were Wagner's candidates since
he did not even inform Fiehler, the national leader of the
AfK, of these decisions until after the appointments.[131]
Although conflicts between the Gauamt and the party did not
disappear, both Kerber and Hüssy supported the total Nazification of the municipalities. Kerber in 1937 agreed that
mayors, with the help of the district personnel leaders,
should first check the reliability of new employees. In the
same year, Kerber could claim that the party had no reasons
for complaint since most personnel leaders of the cities,
with minor exceptions, were now party members. In smaller
towns with populations below ten thousand, the mayors, who
were mostly party members, handled personnel affairs. Finally, in 1938 the Gauamt urged Hess (who complied) to obtain
the release of municipal council members who were not qualified for party membership.[132]

In addition, Wagner appointed, transferred, and promoted
mayors who could demonstrate active party careers with complete independence and disregard of the Gauamt. For example,
in April 1936 he transferred Hans Knab, one of the founders
of the Eberbach local, from his mayoral post in Tauberbischofsheim to a new post in Oberkirch. One month later, Wagner
decided to appoint Knab to the Kreisleiter post in Pforzheim
while refusing to fill the mayoral post in Oberkirch until

Knab had finally chosen the party post. As late as June
1936, one week after Knab's official appointment as party
leader of the district of Pforzheim, the Gauamt still did not
know when it could fill Knab's former mayoral position in
Oberkirch.[133] Or in the case of Fred Himmel, the former
NSDStB leader of Heidelberg before 1933, Wagner again came
to the aid of an "old" party member. Himmel held minor mayoral positions in the district of Mannheim between 1936 and
1938, which apparently did not satisfy him. He contacted
an old SA friend, who was also a Reich commissar, to address
a letter of recommendation to Wagner, pleading for Himmel's
appointment to the vacant seat of the large urban center
Bruchsal. This initiated a voluminous correspondence between
four state and party agencies, but in the end Wagner helped
Himmel obtain a mayoral post in Mosbach.[134]

These examples clearly reveal the party's and Wagner's
domination of the municipal positions. Yet, the Nazi system
also ensured that complete homogeneity was never achieved.
As late as 1941, some mayors of Baden clung tenaciously to
the Catholic church, and many were no longer active party
members. And even mayors who received positive political
evaluations from the party leaders vigorously opposed the
party's interference in municipal affairs.[135] Most typical
were the conflicts over spheres of influence rather than
deep ideological conflicts. For example, the former Kreisleiter Eberhard Sedelmeyer, who had opted for a mayoral post
in 1937, was an "old party" member and the first party district
leader of Donaueschingen. Yet, after 1937 strained relations
developed between the new Kreisleiter and Mayor Sedelmeyer.
Like many former party activists who assumed state power after
1933, Sedelmeyer wanted the party relegated to propaganda

activities rather than administrative tasks.[136]

Although the party boasted about Nazi municipal accomplishments after 1933, most of its opportunistic pre-1933
municipal programs were never implemented. In late 1936 the
Gauamt requested information from Baden's mayors about their
accomplishments as "Nazi municipal" administrators. The
replies focused on speeches, party membership meetings, and
monthly meetings with farmers to discuss problems.[137] But
in reality the Baden Nazi leaders had created a complete
volte-face vis-à-vis the party's pre-1933 municipal plans.
Before 1933, the Nazis had attacked the beer tax and the
Bürgersteuer with vituperation. By 1935, Baden citizens
were paying these taxes, which the Nazis before 1933 had
labeled "Negro taxes." And this did not even solve the defi-
cit problem of the towns. In 1935 a review of the budgets
of Baden towns with populations over three thousand revealed
that thirteen of the sixty towns reporting had budgetary
deficits. The large urban centers and the rural communities
of Baden suffered the largest deficits, and only two Baden
cities with populations over twenty thousand had balanced
budgets in 1935.[138]

The Baden Nazis before 1933 had also supported the
independence of small communities and presented themselves
as the saviors of municipal independence. They had introduced one bill in the Landtag that was specifically directed
against the "terror of municipal consolidation." By 1935,
three cities had been added to the list of towns in Baden
with populations over 10,000. In July 1935, the ministers
met to discuss municipal reforms and announced that the underlying principle must be an increase in efficiency. To accomplish this, two hundred and twenty small suburbs were incor-

porated into larger towns in 1935, and small rural communities were consolidated into larger units. Moreover, Wagner ordered that this incorporation of villages into towns be continued in 1936 and 1937.[139] On the eve of the war, the Nazi ministers had eliminated ninety Baden communities and consolidated many other smaller units to increase efficiency and save money, all in violation of pre-1933 party propaganda themes.[140] Finally, the Nazis failed to provide a solution to the housing market despite claims of massive building projects. For example, Freiburg in July 1933 faced a shortage of fifteen hundred units; by 1936 the city still had a shortage of twelve hundred housing units. After 1936, the increased German war preparations drained capital and building material from the construction industry, causing a drastic reduction of building efforts.[141]

The deficiency of housing, unbalanced budgets, and the consolidation of villages were all symptoms of municipal trends under the Nazis. The Reich's military preparations for expansion deprived the town of needed funds. This trend reached a climax in 1938 when new financial burdens were placed on German municipalities while several tax sources were severed from municipal control. The Amt for Municipal Affairs reported the dismay of Baden mayors over the reduction of municipal programs. As a result, many of Baden's communities faced growing deficits, and smaller communities were forced to increase their tax rates by 15 to 22 percent on the eve of the war.[142] After four years of Nazi coordination, mayors in Baden reported that much of the population still resented their disenfranchisement.[143]

One problem with appraising the Nazi state is complicated by the fact that the NSDAP never became an organ of the state

or commanded the state as a unified body. The Nazi state
never even received a constitution. In Baden, only Wagner
as Gau leader and Reich governor symbolized the union of party and state. The Nazis gained control of the state's ministerial posts and effectively infiltrated and manipulated the
municipal centers of power. The civil servants were forced
to pay homage, at least in public, to National Socialism.
But the conflict between party and state continued on several
levels despite Köhler and Pflaumer's constant statements that
they desired cooperation between state and party.[144] Landräte
frequently refused to support the radical measures introduced
by the party Kreisleiters, and mayors clashed with the party
leaders. In one case, the Kreisleiter of Freiburg even ordered the party to cease all communications with one of the
mayors of Freiburg because of his alleged negative attitude
toward the party.[145] Other party agencies also complained
that little was heard about National Socialism in state agencies as late as 1941.[146]

The conflict between party and state in Baden was more
than a struggle between "rational administration" and the
"totalitarian movement" although that played a part. Frequently, these conflicts were merely quarrels between rival Nazi
activists. The Kreisleiter who became a mayor intended to
implement Nazi policies through the mayoral office rather
than one of the party's agencies. Or when a Nazi mayor clashed
with a Nazi party affiliate leader, it was often a clash
over interests. Both wanted to protect their fiefs.[147] Above
all, the party was not a homogeneous structure but rather reflected diverse interests and segments of society. The AfK
was a party affiliate, yet it attempted to protect Nazi mayors
from the party, while another party organization like the AfB

fought the civil servants who had maintained a certain cohesiveness even in the face of purges and coordination. But
despite these clashes and conflicts of interest and the failure of the party to achieve monolithic organizational control
over the state, political opponents were eliminated, civil
servants purged, municipalities coordinated, and the leading
Nazi activists elevated to the state's highest ministerial
posts. The party and its affiliates played a key role in this,
and all contributed to the Nazi regime's primary goal—coordination for expansion.

8 The Party's Role in Baden: The Coordination of Society, 1933-1945

THE <u>MITTELSTAND</u>, FARMERS, AND LABOR

By 1933, the Baden party had established a multitude of organizations devoted to specific socioeconomic interest groups. The party agitators had appealed to workers and farmers as early as 1923. Four years later, the Nazis had added the <u>Mittelstand</u> to their propaganda themes. In 1930, the party organized an economic council to prepare the Nazi state by penetrating the pluralistic organizations of Baden. There were departments for artisans, farmers, white-collar employees, retail shops, civil servants, and even the unemployed.[1] Many of these party affiliates were led by Nazis who identified with the various socioeconomic segments of society. Albert Roth, a farmer, saw Germany's <u>völkisch</u> salvation only through the rural population; Fritz Plattner, a former member of a Christian trade union, believed that the worker was the key for Germany's resurrection; while Fritz Mannschott, the party's small business section leader, naturally saw and interpreted National Socialism through the eyes of the small shopkeeper. All, of course, were Nazis who accepted the basic tenets of the <u>völkisch</u>, imperialistic ideology of National Socialism.

The Gau clique around Wagner and the party's cadre organization, on the whole, manipulated all segments of society

to further their political goals. Wagner, Kramer, and full-
time völkisch activists like Lenz were probably much more
sincere in their appeals to farmers and manual workers than
in their promises to the white-collar Mittelstand. These
preferences were not based on rational economic proposals but
rather on the assumption that workers needed to be saved from
"Jewish Marxism" and that farmers represented the racial and
moral fiber necessary for the rebirth of German power. This
Gau clique was also sincere in its dislike of the comfortable
bourgeois world that had lost the war and the worker to external and internal enemies. In general, the Gau party leaders placated all segments of society during the transition
period of 1933 and then relegated them to political impotence
and coordination.

During the Nazi seizure of power in Baden in March and
April 1933, Wagner introduced several measures intended to
help the small shopkeepers. As Reich commissar of Baden, he
ordered all state agencies to purchase their supplies only
from small "German" shops, not department stores. In a cabinet meeting, Wagner also ordered an investigation of the
request of the League of Pubs to close all pubs located in
department stores in order to strengthen the business of the
small, independent owners.[2] The city council of Karlsruhe
emulated this policy by boycotting consumer cooperative organizations in order to help the small retail business.
Finally, one of Baden's new economic commissars announced an
impending law in April 1933 which promised to protect the
Mittelstand.[3]

The party's organization that was devoted to the small
shopkeepers, and the commercial Mittelstand in general, was
the Fighting League of the Commercial Middle Class. The

leaders, Fritz Mannschott and Oskar van Raay, did not belong
to the "old" Nazi activists of the party or the Gau clique,
although van Raay had held the position of legal advisor in
the party's municipal section before 1933. Like most party
"specialists" on Mittelstand questions they had not joined
the party until late 1930. Only the Kreisleiter of rural
Überlingen, Alfons Hafen, a Kaufmann who had joined the party
in October 1930, was also a member of the Fighting League.
On the whole, the party's Mittelstand affiliate was not staffed
by important and long-term völkisch party leaders.[4]

Nevertheless, in 1933, the Fighting League attempted to
implement the party's Mittelstand program. It admonished
the party Kreisleiters that its district representatives were
independent and only responsible to the Gau Mittelstand organization. Then in June 1933, the small shopkeepers' revolutionary enthusiasm came to a climax through demonstrations
in Karlsruhe and other Baden communities, which were directed
against Alfred Hugenberg, the Reich minister of economics
who was identified with large industry and business.[5] The
small shopkeepers and activists of the Fighting League who
were attacking department stores and chain stores after the
Nazi seizure of power in Baden (and Germany) were only creating new economic problems for the Nazi ministers. The disruption of department stores threatened to produce more unemployment among the department-store employees.

Early in August 1933, Hitler ordered Ley, the party's
national organization leader, to liquidate the Fighting League
since it had become a danger to the economic revival of Germany. In Baden, the day after Hitler's order, Köhler cautioned that the reduction of department stores depended on
the absorption of their personnel by the small shops.[6] The

Fighting League's successor in Baden, the NS Hago, which
was part of the German Labor Front, was put under the direction of van Raay. By March 1934, Wagner ordered the creation
of local, district, and Gau sections of the NS Hago to coordinate the small shopkeepers and commercial middle class, who
had obviously not seen the triumph of their economic dreams.[7]
Wagner and the Nazi state ministers had attempted to aid the
Mittelstand in early 1933 until they (and of course Berlin)
realized that this would only create other economic problems
for the regime. After the course was changed, it became the
task of another party affiliate to coordinate the frustrated
small shopkeepers.

In early 1935, Wagner, addressing the small retailers of
Baden, declared that the party still wanted a strong Mittelstand. Only in times of economic rebuilding, Wagner added,
one could not afford socioeconomic experiments.[8] After 1935,
even the verbal and published Mittelstand appeals of the party
receded dramatically. On occasion, the party press reminded
its readers of point sixteen of the party program, which had
promised aid to the Mittelstand. According to some party
press releases, the Gauamt for Technology was of great assistance to the Mittelstand. How technological innovation would
aid the small shopkeepers who had protested the rational
distribution of goods in department stores remained unanswered.
Rather, the war accentuated the expansion of large firms at
the expense of the small shops. Between September 1939 and
September 1940, the district of Freiburg alone reported the
disappearance of seventeen small shops, long before a total
war economy.[9] The increased urbanization and economic concentration in Baden after 1933 confronted the small shopkeepers, and the old Mittelstand in particular, with continuous

social modernization. Ironically, Köhler, who had been billed as a _Mittelstand_ spokesman in Weinheim in 1927, as minister of finance after 1933 was partly responsible for this modernization. And the only party Kreisleiter who was a member of the Fighting League ended up in the German Labor Front's "Strength through Joy" program.[10] But most revealing of the position of small business even before the war was the fact that the owner of a small café who catered to Jews could be kicked out of the party and consequently feel the brunt of persecution, while a large firm that employed the services of a Jewish lawyer could tell the party district leader to mind his own business and stop interfering in economic affairs.[11]

The "rural wing" of the Baden NSDAP was much stronger than any other socioeconomic interest group within the party. The party's rural department was led by Ludwig Huber and subsequently by Fritz Engler-Füsslin. Huber, a farmer, was born in 1889, and Engler-Füsslin, who had attended a trade school, was born in 1891. Both had been Kreisleiters and active rural propagandists before 1933. The former Landbund leader and Nazi activist Albert Roth, who had been so instrumental in spreading Nazi propaganda in rural Baden, assumed the leadership of one of the sections of the party's agrarian department.[12] In addition, Wagner in two cabinet meetings in March 1933 declared that he wanted to bring the population of Baden closer to the peasantry, and he urged that plans for economic recovery begin with agriculture.[13] The party also held harvest celebrations which were used to disseminate rural propaganda. In April 1935, August Kramer, the Gau party organization leader, finally claimed that the party had implemented its peasant program by saving the farmers from economic disaster and by elevating them to a central position in the new society.[14]

While the farmers, no doubt, benefited from the regime's interests until at least 1935, it was clear that the rural program had distinct limitations. Hitler had plainly stated in his first cabinet meeting on 31 January 1933 that although he wanted to save the peasantry, the fight against unemployment did not allow the government simply to raise agricultural prices.[15] Early in 1934, the Gauamt leader of the party's agricultural department demanded that the traditional Bundschuh flag be replaced by the new Nazi flag. One year later, farmers were becoming enraged with the Reich Food Estate (Reichsnährstand) when it issued an agricultural calendar that did not include Christian holidays and names.[16] Neither did the Reich Labor Service's help during the harvest season impress the farmers since the RAD spent precious time in indoctrination and calisthenics when weather was ideal for harvesting. Most important, in 1935/36 for the first time since 1932/33, the income of Baden's agricultural population declined, and the forced sale of farms actually increased, surpassing all years since 1933.[17] The Nazi regime, as it prepared for war, could no longer afford to allow an increase in the farmer's income since this would only result in higher wages for urban labor.

Despite Wagner's genuine interest in the farmers, the economic imperatives of the Nazi regime in Berlin, combined with the lack of a social revolution in the countryside, negated the party's efforts to initiate a major and successful rural settlement program. Wagner urged this settlement program and the reclamation of land in 1933 in order to reduce imports. He wanted to copy the Bavarian example to

settle welfare recipients on the land since job opportunities
in the cities were limited. To answer the large landowners'
hostility toward the settlement program, he ordered that a
noble be put in a leading position in the settlement office,
presumably to use positive social incentives in lieu of forced
land distributions. Even party members as early as February
1934 were skeptical about the settlement program.[18]

In July 1933, the Gauamt for Agriculture initiated a
small settlement project in the district of Mosbach, which
involved only twenty-four farms and provided for twenty-eight
more in the future. But by late 1934, Engler-Füsslin realized
that the lack of available land in Baden made the program
there impractical. The only solution, according to him, was
to convince the eastern estate owners that sparsely settled
areas could no longer be tolerated. In 1935 the Führer announced a ten-year project which, in theory, would provide
land to twenty thousand farmers, but three years later Engler-
Füsslin again admitted that only the German East would provide the solution to the settlement problem. In that same
year, he also admitted that Baden only had a few hereditary
farmers since the farms in the state were too small. This
was revealed two years earlier when almost half of all Baden
farms over 7.5 hectares were converted into Erbhöfe (hereditary family plots). This affected a mere 8,728 farms out of
a total of 170,000 agricultural units in Baden.[19]

As the Baden economy gradually improved, more rural
inhabitants flocked to the cities to find better paying jobs.
In 1935, Wagner and the party's rural representatives launched
a massive campaign against this rural exodus, which was endangering the regime's plans for economic autarchy. During
the previous year, despite the rural romanticism of the Nazi

propaganda before 1933, Wagner had urged that small industries
be established in rural Baden to provide jobs and assist economic recovery. In 1935, the unemployed were ordered to report
for agricultural work, and urban firms were supposed to return
former rural workers and farmers to the farms. Köhler announced that the employment office in Baden could demand the
release of workers for rural employment if they had engaged
in agricultural work between 1932 and 1935. The obvious problem faced by the Nazi ministers and the party's agricultural
department was that, despite rural festivals and symbolic
honors bestowed on farmers, many young farmers or sons of
farmers were attracted by the more lucrative factory jobs.[20]
The problem was never solved despite the efforts of the Nazi
ministers and the party organizations after 1935. As late
as 1943, the Gau party's rural leader lamented the fact that
Germany's agricultural population represented only 18 percent
of the population, although a healthy nation required at
least a 40 percent rural population.[21] Instead, by 1941,
southwestern Germany lacked forty thousand rural workers,
because to the problem of rural flight was now added the
drain of military service. After Baden farmers were supplied
with foreign labor (particularly Poles) and with concentra-
tion-camp inmates, the party discovered that the farmers
treated these rural laborers with considerable compassion.
Even though Baden in late 1944 needed all the human resources
it could muster, some of the party's agrarian department
leaders decided to end the assignment of Konzentrationslager
(KZ) prisoners to the farmers because they were being treated
"too humanely."[22]

Despite the prolonged efforts of the party's rural spokesmen, the economic realities after 1933 did not produce the

rural utopia promised by the Nazis before 1933. In many
small rural communities like Knielingen, near Karlsruhe,
economic modernization continued, with the consequence that
the "rural" population was little impressed by the party's
rural festivals and propaganda. Even in former Nazi strongholds in northeastern rural Baden there was a strong under-
current of protest in 1938, because the government had banned
the growth of "American grapes" used for cheap domestic wine
consumption. Some of these farmers, who probably had voted
for the Nazi party before 1933, remarked that things under
the "Remmele system" had not been worse.[23] In the Catholic
rural areas, the party became infuriated with the peasants'
dogmatic attachment to the church. During the war, party
leaders reported increased church attendance in rural communities and, above all, stubborn peasant participation in
the Catholic church festivals despite the urgencies of harvest time. Most devastating to the party's rural efforts,
by 1943 the party reported the existence of growing signs of
defeatism in rural communities.[24]

Two final examples illustrate the failure of the party's rural wing to implement its pre-1933 program, although
it must be said that the rural experts of the party persisted
in many of these efforts much longer than any other socioeconomic interest group within the party organization. First,
the evacuees from urban centers who moved to the rural communities of Baden continued to voice their preference for
urban life. The idealistic picture of "blood and soil" may
have fulfilled the romantic notions of the _völkisch_ true believer, but it found little response among the urbanized
masses who faced concrete situations. Urbanites not only considered the peasant a "pumpkin" (_G'scherter_) but also missed

the comforts of urban life. Second, the military potential
of the rural youths deteriorated consistently because of im-
proper nourishment and the adverse effect of farm work. The
Baden party's rural experts, Engler-Füsslin and Albert Roth,
had pointed this out as early as 1938/39. They had also urged
the expansion of a 1927 maternal protection law to rural
mothers who were aging prematurely. Despite the party's
rural propaganda, farm women went back to work eight to ten
days after having delivered a baby. This workload became
worse after the men were conscripted. By late 1944, the
National Office of the Landvolk lamented that the military
potential of the urban recruits far overshadowed that of the
rural youths. The Nazi leaders had managed to reverse the
nineteenth-century relationship between urban and rural military recruits to the detriment of the latter, despite the party's continuous rural propaganda both before and after 1933.
The economic and military decisions affecting the farmer, however, were made in Berlin, not in the party's agricultural
departments.[25]

The party organization charged with the coordination of
labor, the NS Factory Cells Organization (NSBO), like the party agencies devoted to the Mittelstand and farmers, attempted
to make its influence felt in 1933. Plattner, the leader of
the NSBO in Baden, had been a party convert and a member of
a Christian Trade Union as early as 1923. This völkisch activist ordered his representatives in 1933 to ascertain if employers were hiring workers according to NSBO instructions,
and beginning in May 1933 he directed the Nazi destruction
of Baden's labor unions.[26] But the party's labor wing was
limited just as the Mittelstand organization had been by the
reality that the Nazi ministers would not carry out a social

revolution. As early as August 1933, Plattner had to caution his NSBO representatives to be patient, and he warned them that he would move resolutely against dissidents.[27] Wagner made it clear that he supported private property. Although he pressured employers to hire more workers in 1933/34, he was apparently readily accessible to the spokesmen of large industry, like the directors of Bopp and Reuther and Lanz, who were allowed to air their grievances about tax and economic matters. Köhler, the minister of finance, also declared that National Socialism did not believe in state interference in economic affairs, other than to eliminate the conflict between workers and employers.[28]

The most immediate concern of the Nazi ministers in Baden was the coordination of organized labor and the drive to decrease unemployment. Wagner harnessed the machinery of both state and party agencies to carry out the employment offensive. In early 1934, Hermann Nickles, the director of the Mannheim employment office, became a member of the Gau party staff and was charged with coordinating the unemployment drive. Appropriately, he was assigned to the Gau propaganda office. In a memorandum, Nickles demanded that the employment effort be carried out without sentimentality, and that the goal must always be production. To accomplish this, women had to relinquish their jobs to men, farmers were urged to give up their aspirations to work in better-paying factory jobs, and the party leaders were assigned the task of squelching protest over work assignments. With this approach, and the fact that Germany was coming out of the depression, unemployment declined in Baden from 183,827 in January 1933 to 50,684 in January 1937. In 1937, with the growing importance of Germany's Four Year Plan, the district party leaders and farm

leaders were again admonished to combat rural exodus, and
the party's factory shop stewards were ordered to defend all
job assignments against individual preferences.[29]

In addition to the employment drive, the party played
an important part in the total coordination of labor after
1933 through the German Labor Front (DAF). By late 1934,
the Baden DAF had incorporated 483,000 workers and employees
who were directed by a massive body of 25,000 officials.
According to the national leader of the DAF, Robert Ley,
the business manager represented the company commander while
the shop steward was relegated to the position of drill ser-
geant and charged with the task of "whipping the workers into
shape." Later, the Gau leadership of the DAF in Baden emphasized that the shop steward was not an arbitrator between
management and labor (as the old system had envisioned) but
rather an arbitrator between the party and the workers. He
represented the party in the shops and was primarily responsible for the worker's political posture.[30] Since economic
revolution was out of the question, all the DAF had to
offer the workers was a symbolic incorporation in a people's
community through the cultural, athletic, and travel projects of the program "Strength through Joy" and the general
DAF indoctrination and enlightenment programs.[31]

Despite this activism, the DAF faced a serious crisis
in Baden in 1935/36. The Führer published an article in 1935
by Eduard Helff, the Gau employment leader, in which he frankly
admitted that the worker was not yet an equal link of the
folk community. Another statistic published by the Führer,
which was intended to show the progress of the DAF, actually
revealed its limitations. In elections held in 1935 to 1,747
Baden factories, only 75 percent of all eligible voters cast

affirmative votes. Compared to the over 90 percent result of
the "normal" elections and plebiscites held in Nazi Germany,
this was a weak showing.[32] In addition, Fritz Plattner was
apparently an incompetent who attempted to achieve his goals
by bullying his underlings. By 1935/36, his behavior and
lack of self-control had not only caused a serious division
within the DAF leadership in Baden but also made it apparent
to the Gau party leadership that the party's labor campaign
was in serious trouble and might not withstand the shock of
future Vertrauensrat elections in the factories. Wagner's
reaction was to transfer Plattner, despite his personal
shortcomings, to another post in the summer of 1936.[33] But
Wagner quickly discovered that the Gau party elite, and even
the Gau clique, was not interested in taking over the Gau
leadership of the DAF. The Gau Hitler Youth leader, Friedhelm
Kemper, turned down Wagner's offer, and then the NSBO leader
of Mannheim, Dr. Reinhold Roth, rejected the post. In the
meantime Plattner's former assistant, who according to Wagner
was incapable of handling the job, was directing the agency
in 1936/37. Most revealing, the Baden Gauleiter admitted in
1936 that he had paid little attention to the DAF. It obviously was not one of his priorities between 1933 and 1936.
Only the internal leadership problems caused him to focus
attention on the Labor Front. Finally, in 1937, Reinhold
Roth accepted the post of DAF Gau leader. Roth had become
attracted to the Nazi movement as early as 1929 and been the
Gau organization leader of the NS Factory Organization between 1931 and 1933. But neither his employment with I. G.
Farben as a chemical engineer nor his Ph.D. made him a representative of the workers.[34]

During the war, the function of the DAF consisted of

maintaining work discipline and increasing production. The
freeze on wages brought particular hardships to the workers,
who faced rising prices. Young workers and apprentices felt
this the most, and they responded by breaking their employment
contracts, which caused DAF officials to complain that this
was the generation produced by the Hitler Youth. But many
young apprentices had good cause to revolt since they were
required to work exceedingly long hours for the profit and
greed of their employers.[35] The Gau leadership of the DAF
held repeated production campaigns in which selected firms
were given recognition. Baden's DAF leadership discovered,
not surprisingly, that the best firms were the ones where
the party membership was two to three times higher than in
other firms. In 1940/41 over 15,000 Baden firms took part
in a production contest in which 755 businesses received
special awards. Of these 755 firms, which employed 137,374
people, 67 percent were in crafts (Handwerk) and commerce.
While only 8.8 percent of these employees were party members,
83 percent of the leaders of the firms belonged to the party
in 1941.[36] By the end of the year, the DAF had the unhappy
task of defending seventy-two hour workweeks. When the district offices of the DAF reported increased worker complaints
because of these long hours, the Gauobmann of the DAF of
Baden replied that it was not the function of the DAF to advocate the reduction of the workload. Instead, it had to
provide the political rationalization for these burdens, just
as it had assumed the duty of justifying the reduction of
food allocations in April 1942.[37]

While the DAF's burdens increased dramatically during
the war, it lost most of its best trained functionaries and
shop stewards to the army. The replacements, according to

the local DAF reports, tended to neglect their duties despite
the DAF's new indoctrination programs and attempted expansion
of the special Nazi factory brigades (Werkschare).[38] The
attack on Russia also increased labor's resistance to the
regime. As early as October 1941, for example, the Freiburg
DAF reported passive resistance in almost all shops, and some
companies faced daily, unexcused absences of 30 percent of
their workers.[39]

Although some contemporary reporters noted a new social
consciousness in Nazi Germany, and local DAF functionaries
sincerely attempted to fight social discrimination by advocating the incorporation of workers into the mainstream of
society, there was never any serious attempt to change the
economic and educational foundations of Baden society. And
the disinterest of Wagner in the DAF until 1936, combined
with the unwillingness of leading Gau Nazis to assume leadership of the DAF, does reveal the low priority the DAF enjoyed
among Gau clique members. In addition, basic socioeconomic
decisions were made not by the party but by Hitler and the
state ministries (even if they were run by leading Nazis).
Even the work rules in the plants were determined by the em-
ployer. The function of the DAF was control, not social
revolution.[40]

This coordination of the various socioeconomic segments
of society, even if it did not necessarily result in mass
conversion, did ensure that potential social grumbling would
be controlled by the party or at least circumscribed by the
party's agencies. The workers served in Hitler's armies and
worked in the factories of Baden without any major display
of public unrest. In this sense, the aspirations of the
early Mannheim and Pforzheim Nazis had found fruition.

Organized Marxism had disappeared, and the regime's vital in-
terests--power and expansion--were realized for a time at
least. But the Mittelstand was faced with growing modernization and industrialization, farmers bore a heavy load of the
labor burden, and young farmers attempted to move to the
cities. Of course, the worker lost the most important economic leverage he had previously acquired--unions.

Symbolically, the leading Nazis of Baden concluded their
careers with negative social vituperation rather than positive
plans. In 1943 and 1944, the party began again to harp on
the shortcomings of bourgeois society. Party leaders denounced
the "bourgeois straw heads" who could not understand the new
crisis. The bourgeoisie was identified with intellectualism,
individualism, and decadence. The opposition of the urban
bourgeoisie to the Volkssturm (militia) and to Himmler's appeal in late 1944 infuriated the radical party leaders of
Baden. One Kreisleiter even advocated the extermination of
the intellectuals. Wagner, who had expressed his dislike
of the bourgeois world in 1931, declared in an article in
the Führer in late 1944 that the disintegration of the old
bourgeois world was a certainty.[41] Destruction, not construction, was the leitmotif of the Baden Nazi leaders on the eve
of the Third Reich's collapse.

WOMEN, YOUTH, AND STUDENTS

Just as the party had coordinated Baden's socioeconomic groups
and submerged their organizations to party-sponsored affiliates, the Nazis infiltrated and seized control of all professional organizations and attempted to coordinate all subcul-

tures of society. Women, the youth, and a multiplicity of
professional clubs became the objects of the Nazi organizational mania even before 1933 and much more so after the
Nazis seizure. By 1933, one Baden pharmacist in Pfullendorf lamented that he and the members of his family belonged
to twenty-one party and party-affiliated professional organizations. The image the party wanted to project was best
summarized by a contemporary American student of German politics, James Pollock. He described the party as "a tremendous
social organization, constantly at work to propagate and keep
alive the National Socialist ideology--that the National Socialist party really is Germany."[42] In reality, the pluralistic segments of society continued under National Socialism,
only now they were led and coordinated by Nazi party activists who frequently identified with the various segments
they represented. As with the socioeconomic organizations
of the party, the official party attitudes toward the different components of society were modified extensively by
the pragmatic demands of an expansionistic state. This is
best illustrated by examining the party organizations devoted
to women, the youth, and students.

In 1933, there was still much confusion about women's
roles in Baden. One party faction called on women to withdraw
from the labor market while other party spokesmen advocated
the opposite and even suggested military training for women.[43]
The Nazi women had a party-affiliated organization, the NS-
Frauenschaft (NSF), which was led in Baden by Gertrud Scholtz-
Klink until she became the national Women's League leader in
1934. Many Baden women had joined the NSF before 1933 but
not the party. Some NSF district leaders did not become party members until 1937, and even the Gau NSF business leader,

Martha Kern, had not joined the NSDAP until 17 January 1933.
For many NSF activists in Baden membership was a family affair, since either their husbands or sons were active in the
Nazi movement. Most of them were wives of party activists
rather than professionals.[44] For example, Scholtz-Klink
was the wife of a party Kreisleiter before she became an
activist and party member in 1929. Her successor as Gau
leader of the Baden NSF, Elsa von Baltz, who had married
a chemist, organized the NSF in Oberkirch in early 1932 and
then joined the party in May 1932. Her two sons were already
in the SA.[45]

At least one immediate function of the NSF was perfectly
clear to Scholtz-Klink in 1933--the coordination of women's
organizations. In April 1933, she ordered the dissolution
of the Baden Women's League in order to allow the NSF to
dominate women's activities. Even Frick, the national minister
of interior, protested against this usurpation of state
authority.[46] But in May of the same year, Wagner gave her
the leadership of all women's organizations in Baden. She
immediately began to dissolve all central women's organizations, which she claimed were dominated by Jews and Democrats.
Instead, in August 1933 Scholtz-Klink formed a new umbrella
agency for Baden's women that included the NSF and all other
female clubs. Attempts at establishing other new women's
organizations were crushed. The NSF structure expanded so
rapidly that by 1936, 65 percent of Baden's communities had
NSF locals, which were actively engaged in maternal training
and home economics.[47]

The male-dominated Nazi party in Baden was willing to
see Scholtz-Klink destroy the rival women's organizations and
coordinate all women under a party-affiliated umbrella.

However, the Führer made it quite clear even before the Nazi
seizure of power in Baden that women would be given freedoms
in social and cultural areas of society but only men could
handle issues involving political, military, and diplomatic
matters, since women, who were too emotional, could never
make positive contributions in these fields. Subsequent
public pronouncements by leading Baden and Reich Nazi leaders only reiterated the theme that women should be breeders
and homemakers. Wagner, in particular, attempted to eliminate
female employees from the state administration as early as
1934 in order to provide men with jobs.[48]

The Baden party's organization leader emphasized after
the Nazi takeover that the NSF could not participate in party
marches and that female "troop building" must be avoided.
The party would simply not tolerate women in the street.
This antifeminism was carried so far that NSF representatives
were frequently not invited to local and party staff conferences in Baden, despite Gau party orders to the contrary.
Even in welfare, a field originally intended for women, the
leading posts were reserved for men. The only exception was
the NSF Gau leader who was appointed assistant Gau director
of the NS Welfare Organization in early 1934. Occasionally,
women were trusted with local and district party welfare
posts.[49] Ironically, as late as 1937 Bormann had to remind
the male party leaders that Scholtz-Klink was an important
party (Hauptamt) leader and should be treated accordingly.[50]

Gradually, because of economic imperatives and later
because of war pressures, the antifeminism of the male Nazi
leaders in Baden and Germany had to be modified. In late
1935, the Völkischer Beobachter published an interview with
Scholtz-Klink in which she declared that "the working woman

must take her place in her way and according to her capacity and her essential nature in the environment in the Volksgemein-schaft."[51] In fact, between 1933 and 1936, women factorywork-ers increased in Baden from 66,849 to 85,870, reflecting a general improvement in economic conditions. This trend con-tinued, and the Nazis also established agricultural training camps for girls to provide additional labor for the hard-pressed farmers. Eventually, in 1939 the Labor Service became obligatory for girls, again for rural projects.[52] Wagner and the Baden Nazi leaders did not hesitate to use female labor in agriculture and in the tobacco industry during the war.[53] But the publication in the Führer of an advertisement depicting the bellydancer Ursula Reinelt in a very revealing negligee in 1940 could not be justified on the grounds of war imperative.[54] The supreme volte-face in the party's attitude toward women came in the last years of the war when Baden party leaders became infuriated with women who were content with being housewives and mothers instead of volun-teering for war-related duties and work. Equally ironic was that Belgian and French workers, who were in Baden as the result of the racial expansionistic policies of the male Nazi leaders, were inseminating Baden women.[55]

Since over four hundred youth organizations existed in Germany in early 1933, it was only natural that the Nazi leaders attempted to do their best to coordinate them and to saturate the youth with National Socialist principles. In August 1933, Wagner assigned Friedhelm Kemper, an enthu-siastic party activist who had been a party district leader before becoming the head of the Hitler Youth of Baden, the task of accelerating the organization of the Hitler Youth in the Gau. By October 1935, enthusiasm, combined with party pressures, had induced 80 percent of Baden's eligible youth to enroll in the Hitler Youth.[56] In addition, a Hitler Youth leader was appointed to an honorary position in the Baden Ministry of Interior and the head of the NS Teachers' League, Karl Gärtner, another former Kreisleiter, demanded a curriculum for schoolchildren that focused on racial education and völkisch indoctrination. The aim was to produce not just a solid citizen but a political man of "heroic" spirit.[57]

The Hitler Youth's function was to provide the regime with a new generation imbued with the spirit of National Socialism. This meant that the Hitler Youth not only had to train the youth but also influence the established school system, which socialized the future adult member of society. At first, this took the form of an attack on intellectualism and higher education in Baden, which infuriated even Wacker, the Nazi minister of education. When the SD of Offenburg used boys between sixteen and seventeen for spying duties, the principal of the local high school, an old Nazi himself, became outraged at this intrusion on parental and school authority by "recent converts" to the party.[58] These attacks irritated, and at times intimidated, but they did not change the fundamental educational structure of Germany and Baden other than to help reduce the quality of education. In 1938, the children of farmers and workers in Baden still provided only 6.5 percent and 2.1 percent of the male and female students who were attending higher schools. These graduates would assume leading positions in society. To supply more indoctrinated children for leading state and party posts and to provide the potential for social elevation to children from the lower and rural classes, the party established a

variety of special schools, including one called the Adolf
Hitler Schools (AHS). But in 1943, only four of the nine AHS
graduates from Baden chose a party career; the rest opted
for traditional professional, economic, diplomatic, and military careers. This was not surprising, since only 12.9 percent of the 1940 AHS students had parents who were farmers
or industrial workers.[59]

During the war, the young workers and apprentices who
had been members of the Hitler Youth and had been told that
it was their duty to perform exemplary work frequently fell
far short of expectations. The DAF lamented the inadequate
discipline of the apprentices, particularly those between
sixteen and eighteen who had belonged to the Hitler Youth.
Some DAF officials commented that these young Hitler Youth
graduates were less willing to abide by a stringent work
ethic than the old Marxist workers.[60] The party had succeeded in eliminating rival organizations, but the conflicts
within the Nazi system, combined with the resiliency of established social patterns and the strains of war, negated many
of the ideological aspirations of such Hitler Youth activists
as Kemper.

All segments of society, from farmers to the youth,
involved a large mass of people that the party affiliates
tried to coordinate. A good example of the party's infiltration, coordination, and domination of a pluralistic segment of Baden's society, which was much smaller in size
but crucial in importance to the economic, educational,
and potential elite power structure, was the university
community. The Nazi ministers of culture and higher education
carried out a thorough purge of Jews and political enemies
in Baden after 1933. Between 18 and 24 percent of the

university faculties of Heidelberg and Freiburg were purged, leaving room for young Nazi academics like Himmel, who was Privatdozent in 1930 and a full professor by 1936.[61] As early as March 1935, hundreds of professors in Germany published testimonials supporting Hitler. The philosopher Martin Heidegger of Freiburg, who joined the party in May 1933, called for the union of all classes, and within a year he wrote that Hitler had freed Germans from "powerless thinking." In order to control professors who were not so enthusiastic, the new Nazi ministers appointed new deans to the major Baden universities in 1933, who in turn were watched closely by the leaders of the Nazi student organizations in 1933/34.[62]

The NSDStB in Baden, with the support of the National-ists, had emerged as a dominant force in the universities as early as 1931/32. This party organization had to cope with a total of 9,795 students in Baden, who were registered at the universities of Heidelberg and Freiburg and at the tech-nical and trade schools of Karlsruhe and Mannheim. The economic and social background of these students, as late as 1934, was predominantly solid middle class. Almost half of the students came from civil service families and from the academic and other professions. A fifth of the students had parents who were engaged in commercial and trade enter-prises. Only 2.3 percent of the students were children of industrial workers, and the students with parents who were farmers constituted 5.6 percent of the student body.[63]

The NSDStB in Baden tried to influence and coordinate all students and help in the purge of Jewish faculty members and students. The Jewish enrollment in the univer-sity of Heidelberg fell from 4.8 percent to 2.2 percent of the student body in the winter semester of 1933/34. Declines

also occurred in other Baden universities and technical schools
as Jewish student enrollment fell to 1.3 percent of the Gau's
student body in 1934.[64] The Nazi students' attempt to coordinate all students in Baden was complicated by the fact that
the NSDStB was not yet officially organized along party lines.
For example, district 6 had its headquarters in Karlsruhe and
technically included Baden, Württemberg, and Hesse. In reality,
the student leader of Württemberg paid little attention to
orders coming from Karlsruhe.[65] But more important than the
power conflicts between Nazi student functionaries was the
NSDStB claim in 1933 that its leaders were in charge of the
complete student body and their orders had to be followed by
all students.[66] In May 1933, the student papers were directed
to publish the NS Student Correspondence in order to produce
the complete coordination of all student papers and to provide for a uniform vehicle for the dissemination of Nazi
policies and principles. Eventually, all students were
forced to subscribe to the Nazi-controlled Deutsche Studentenzeitung, and by December the Baden NSDStB announced the
impending disappearance of the local student papers in
Freiburg, Karlsruhe, and Mannheim. When it became clear
that students could not meet the additional expense of the
Deutsche Studentenzeitung, it was distributed free by the
NSDStB.[67] The aim was to control and manipulate the students
of Baden under the guidance of the NSDStB.

After 1933, the Baden party provided two of the national
student leaders, Oskar Stäbel and Adolf Scheel. Stäbel had
been leader of district 6 of the NSDStB since 1932 and Reich
leader of the organization since 1933. He was born the son
of a farmer on 25 May 1901 in Wintersdorf, Baden. Before
completing high school in 1917, he volunteered for the army.

After the war, he completed his _Abitur_ and then joined a
variety of Free Corps movements and antileftist battles in
Central Germany, the Ruhr, and Silesia. After 1924, Stäbel
returned to the Technical University of Karlsruhe to complete
his engineering program. In 1929, he became the leader of
the NSDStB in Karlsruhe, and in the following year he joined
the party and played an active role in student and city politics in Karlsruhe.[68] Under Stäbel's leadership both as a
district and as a national NSDStB leader, the students closely
identified with the SA and at least a "spiritual" social revolution.

In May 1933, the flow of students into the SA in Baden
was so heavy that special SA student units were established
and put under the direction of regular SS and SA instructors
to inhibit the "social snobbery" of the predominantly middle-
class students. The bulk of the student leaders in Heidelberg, for example, were SA men and apparently came from a
lower social background than most students.[69] To demonstrate
the symbolic union between workers and students, the NSDStB
held joint meetings with the NS Factory Organization where
intellectuals and the bourgeoisie were attacked. The students' revolutionary responsibilities were defined by one
Heidelberg student who argued that SA experience would free
them from the "stale romanticism" of "old Heidelberg" and
allow them to become political young people who were "truly
völkisch in character."[70] The second purpose of close ties
with the SA was to provide the students with paramilitary
training during summer vacations in NSDStB-sponsored military
training camps. With this type of training, the Nazi students
became political watchdogs at the universities. But just as
with the social revolutionary enthusiasm of the other party

affiliates and organizations, the NSDStB never was able to implement real social revolution by changing the social structure of the student body.[71]

After the Röhm purge, the NSDStB was reorganized and became part of the party organization. The SA university offices were closed; Stäbel was replaced as Nazi student leader by Albert Derichsweiler, until he was in turn succeeded by Gustav Adolf Scheel. Scheel, who had come to Heidelberg in 1930 to study medicine, had been an active NSDStB leader in Heidelberg and Gaudozentenführer of Baden before assuming the national student leadership. The NSDStB became more of an elitist body and was now closely tied to the SS.[72] Hess limited the membership to 5 percent of the student body, and the Gau student leader of Baden in 1936 decreed that the NSDStB must become a Nazi elite in the universities by stressing discipline and elitism. In the same year, the Gau student indoctrination office took a stand against "barroom brawler and mercenary types," a clear rejection of the old SA image of the Nazi students.[73] The Nazi student organization began to cooperate more closely with the party cadre organization in a variety of areas, from indoctrination to special war mobilization projects, while at the same time continuing to coordinate all students.[74]

The one revolutionary task left for the NSDStB, even after the fall of Stäbel, was the coordination of the fraternities, which accounted for nearly one-half of the student body and represented a traditional subculture that the party could not tolerate. Between 1933 and 1935, the fraternities continued their snobbery and petty squabbles, including duels over insignificant matters and personal disputes.[75] The first sign of a conflict occurred in 1933 when Stäbel appointed

von Mühlen student leader of the Freiburg student body. When
the fraternity council questioned and debated the nomination,
it was promptly dissolved by von Mühlen.[76] But the real Nazi
attack came only in 1935. Despite the fact that Hans Lammers,
the chief of the Reich Chancellery, had declared in late
1934 that Hitler had no intention of destroying the fraternities, Derichsweiler in October 1935 prepared for the "voluntary" dissolution of these institutions by establishing
Fellowship Homes (Kameradschaftshäuser), which were controlled
by the Student Union. Henry Albert Philipps, in a visit to
Heidelberg in 1935, predicted the impending demise of the
fraternities and noted that the Fellowship Homes seemed to
have students who came from lower social ranks. Finally,
in 1936, Rudolf Hess forbade Nazis to join fraternities, and
Nazi students in the University of Freiburg broke into fraternity homes to vent their dissatisfaction with the exclusiveness of these organizations.[77]

The Nazi destruction of the fraternities was certainly
not caused by noncompliance with the Nazi doctrines of anti-
Semitism, extreme nationalism, and the leadership principles.
The Albingia Corporation of Freiburg, which was part of the
Miltenberger Ring, provides an example of the evolution of a
fraternity under the Nazi system. The leader of the Corps
in 1933 was Helmuth Grimm, who had studied in Freiburg after
1918 and then established a business in Hamburg, where he
joined the party in December 1931. By August 1933, he promised to mold Albingia into a tool for the Nazi education of
the youth.[78] Then the Corps complied completely with the
party's anti-Semitism. Grimm was ready as early as 1933
to sacrifice his Jewish members, which included Eberhard
Schwertfeger (whose great-grandfather had been the president

of the German National Assembly in 1849) and Rudolf Liepmann,
who had participated in the murder of Karl Liebknecht in 1919
and in subsequent actions against leftist disturbances.[79]
In comparison, the Baden Nazi Hitler Youth leader Friedhelm
Kemper, on one occasion, attempted to protect one of his
Hitler Youth activists who had a Jewish grandfather from
being purged from the NSDStB because this would have jeopardized his academic career.[80]

The final and most prolonged step in the coordination of
the old fraternity system was the attack on the alumni organizations. Beginning in 1936, Hess appealed to former students
to join the NS Student Aid Association, and Scheel after
formally establishing the NS Alumni League applied a variety
of pressures to force the former alumni groups to join the
Nazi organization. The Alumni Organization became an affiliate
of the party and was charged with the active support of the
political and cultural projects of the NSDStB Fellowship
Organization (Kameradschaften). In Baden, the superficial
organization of the NS Alumni League was completed by May
1938 and followed by constant recruitment campaigns.[81] Here
the party affiliate faced its greatest frustrations. For
example, in late 1937 the NS Student Aid Association of
Pfullendorf reported that of the forty university graduates
in its area, fifteen were clergymen, and six more had
belonged to a Catholic student union. Excluding some who
were in jail for abortion and counterfeiting offenses, and
others who belonged to duelling fraternities, only five or
six members could be recruited for the NS Student Aid Association. This was the pattern in other Baden areas when the
party attempted to recruit for the NS Alumni League after
1938.[82]

Despite these frustrations, the Nazi organizational mania
continued as long as independent alumni clubs existed. Some
traditional alumni groups survived for a time by sponsoring
NS Kameradschaften, as did the Freiburg Cimbria and Thuringia
Corps, which cooperated to support the NS Kameradschaft Müller.
But even that could not be tolerated by the Nazi student leaders, and the Corps were forced to form a NS Alumni League. The
same thing occurred in other Baden universities where similar
pressures were applied to establish conformity. By 1943, 80
percent of the former duelling alumni leagues in Germany had
joined the NS Alumni Organization.[83]

The Nazis had gained organizational control over Baden's
student and alumni associations by utilizing party affiliate
organizations. But the initial revolutionary fervor of the
Baden student leaders who had joined the SA received a set-
back in 1934 when the NSDStB became an elite SS-associated
organization. In the summer of 1930, 4,034 students attended
the University of Freiburg. By 1937, the student body had
declined to 2,187, reflecting an adjustment to economic conditions. But in 1944, the enrollment had returned to the 1930
level (4,360). Most revealing, while only 431 females attended
Freiburg in 1937, by 1944 the figure had increased to 2,500.
The same trend appeared throughout Germany where women
accounted for 33,000 of the 90,000 students in universities.
By 1944, the war had produced such a shortage of physicists,
chemists, and doctors that the Nazi student organization
was forced to plead with Gau leaders to obtain their assistance for educational training programs that had been established for war cripples and disabled veterans in an attempt
to provide trained technical personnel. Simultaneously, by
1943 half of the Reich and Gau student leaders had already

fallen in battle.[84]

In the end, despite its ability to coordinate a subculture of society, the NSDStB was unable to change the old social conflicts and tensions between students and society. The party was particularly disturbed that student church services were so well attended and that students still maintained close ties with the church. The party also lamented the lack of the spirit of folk community among students. Both party cadre leaders and DAF reports pointed out that during the war well-dressed students from "well-to-do parents" appeared in public and commanded the available restaurant accomodations. In other instances, students in Freiburg obtained many of the theater tickets the DAF had reserved for the workers' relaxation, because they were able to wait in line for hours to buy the tickets.[85] On the eve of the total collapse, there were more female students enrolled in Baden's universities, and the old social patterns of the student body continued, with children of workers and farmers vastly underrepresented. In many ways, the coordinated universities and student organizations continued as subcultures, only now under the mantle of a party affiliate.

Evaluations of the impact of the Nazi social policies have varied from Franz Neumann, who concluded that "the essence of National Socialism's social policy consists in the acceptance and strengthening of the prevailing class character of German society," to Ralf Dahrendorf, who argued that "National Socialism completed for Germany the social revolution that was lost in the faulting of Imperial Germany and again held up by the contradictions of the Weimar Republic—The substance of this revolution is modernity." Dahrendorf saw the Nazi offensive against the church, the family, regional loyalties, and social stratification as a social revolution that finally abolished the "German past as it was embodied in Imperial Germany." There is no question that Schoenbaum's conclusion-- "the cities were larger, not smaller; the concentration of capital greater than before, the rural population reduced, not increased; women not at the fireside but in the office and factory; the inequality of income and property distribution more, not less conspicuous,"--also applies to Baden.[86] After all, important socioeconomic decisions were made in Berlin, not Karlsruhe. Although this represented more "modernity," it did not greatly modify the prevailing social structure of Baden.

Wagner and his Gau clique supported the concept of private property. But most important they were devoted to völkisch political expansionism which reflected no specific economic theory--only expediency. For example, although Wagner told his cabinet that suburbs were so much more healthy than urban jungles, he also ordered the cabinet to investigate whether industry could not be relocated to the countryside to provide economic opportunities. In early 1933, Wagner had ordered his ministers to see if the pubs in large department stores could not be closed to help the small entrepreneur. But several weeks later, when it became clear that the radicalism of those who advocated the "conservative revolution" would only produce more unemployment, he changed course. Wagner and his Gau party leaders did not represent any specific socioeconomic or pluralistic interests as did some of the various party affiliates. Wagner blindly followed the Berlin policies that were intended to strengthen the movement's hold on Germany in order to implement its racial and expansionistic plans.[87]

Although a prolonged conflict such as the Second World
War could not but affect the social fabric of Baden, the
twelve-year Nazi rule did not radically alter the basic and
underlying social patterns in education, income distribution,
and even social values. During the war, the party discovered
that northern Germans and southern Germans disliked each other
as much as ever. In addition, the Nazi leaders had to acknowl-
edge the fact that the urban Germans frequently held the
rural Germans in low esteem, despite the party's "blood and
soil" propaganda. In some instances, the party's racial
policies actually perpetuated existing social stratifica-
tions. In April 1940, Karlsruhe received instructions from
Berlin to prepare homes for elderly ethnic Germans from the
Baltic states. Hilgenfeldt, the leader of the NS-Volkswohl-
fahrt (NSV) in Germany, ordered that the homes be divided
into three categories corresponding to the three Bildungs-
schichten (educational backgrounds) of the German Balts:
upper-middle-class Balts, lower-middle-class Balts, and
finally those Balts who belonged to the most "primitive"
intellectual group. Since the Nazi definition of Bildungs-
schicht was based on the Balts' facility with the German
language, the implementation of this order only perpetuated
the social inequities that had produced these educational
differences in the first place.[88]

Most of the party's pre-1933 social promises were
sacrificed to the regime's practical needs. It is true that
in 1933/34 many "old party" members benefited from a considerable social mobility. Within a short time, Nazi lec-
turers became full professors, and lower-middle-class Gau
party leaders assumed leading state positions for which
they had neither the needed educational background nor the

training. But this was not based on a social policy, only
on the length of a person's party career and on the obvious
fact that the Nazi purges had created many vacancies. The
destruction of fraternity snobbism may have eliminated one
obnoxious legacy of the Imperial Era, but it did not alter
Baden's higher education by incorporating a larger segment
of society that had traditionally been underrepresented in
the Gymnasiums and universities. Even Adolf Hitler School
graduates were attracted to traditional career patterns. In
many instances, the party affiliates perpetuated traditional
social and pluralistic loyalties. The party's agrarian department defended the interests of farmers just as other party
affiliates represented the interests of teachers and civil
servants. Most of these party affiliates interpreted National
Socialism through the eyes and interests of their particular
memberships. Even the Nazi state leaders of Baden vigorously
defended the interests of Baden against encroachments from
Berlin and neighboring Nazi states. There is no reason to
assume that this pattern would have changed after the war.
A victorious Nazi Germany could not have relinquished its
military-industrial base by deurbanizing and deindustrial-
izing the nation. Certainly, Karlsruhe would not have had
the power or will to initiate this type of a policy. Instead,
the party's most persistent themes before and after 1933,
racism and external expansion, found fruition in war, euthanasia, and concentration camps. The Baden party's major contribution had been the coordination of society that had helped
to produce the domestic strength for these goals.[89]

9 The Party's Role in Baden: The Elimination of "Alien Subcultures," 1933-1945

After 1933, Berlin determined the major social and economic policies of the Third Reich. Most of the party affiliates devoted to specific socioeconomic segments of society had to accommodate themselves to the obvious fact that Hitler had no intention of allowing a major social or economic revolution that would only endanger his powers. But all of the party agencies continued to play an active part in the elimination of "alien subcultures." In party rallies, Wagner and the leading Baden Nazis focused on Jews, Marxists, the churches, and "reaction" as the major threats to the new order. Since the police played a key role in the elimination of the Marxists and the traditional right-wing organizations were readily coordinated and eventually suppressed, the party's primary and most enduring efforts were directed against Jews and churches. With the help of the state machinery, the party succeeded in its efforts to eliminate the Jews, but it was constantly frustrated in its attempts to expurgate the influence of the churches and in particular of the Catholic church.[1]

In Baden (as in Berlin six weeks earlier), the Nazis assumed power in collaboration with the traditional political right. Both the Nationalists and the Stahlhelm, a major

veterans' organization, were represented in the new government
through Paul Schmitthenner and the retired major Hildebrand.
During the first weeks of the takeover, the Stahlhelm cooperated particularly well with the Nazi party in joint attacks
on the left.[2] By May 1933, the Nazi party and the DNVP had
established a special organization (Arbeitsgemeinschaft) to
facilitate further cooperation. Several weeks later, Wagner
also allowed the DNVP delegates to join the Nazi party (which,
however, was vetoed by the national party treasurer, Franz
Xaver Schwarz). And finally, as late as the summer of 1933,
even the rival völkisch DVFB in Baden was allowed to hold
membership meetings as long as it did not gather in public
meetings.[3]

The first signs of trouble appeared in June 1933 in a
cabinet meeting when the Minister of Interior Karl Pflaumer
reported that former members of the Catholic Center party
and other enemies of the state were joining the Stahlhelm.
The cabinet agreed to move against the DNVP and Stahlhelm
since both were becoming rallying points for enemies of the
state.[4] Although there is no question that the Nazis simply
wanted to eliminate these rival, independent organizations,
there is evidence that Marxists and Center party members did
join the Stahlhelm in an attempt to establish a new power
base. The Stahlhelm, which had 91 locals in Baden in January
1933, gained six thousand new members by mid-1935. The Gestapo
estimated that one thousand of the new members came from the
Marxist parties and another fifteen hundred from the former
Center party.[5]

Beginning in early 1934, the Gestapo moved against local
Stahlhelm organizations that were accused of harboring Marxists
and other enemies of the state. This crackdown continued even

after the Stahlhelm was converted into the NS German Front
Fighters League (NSDFB). In August 1934, the Gestapo searched
the home of Richard Wenzl (1892-1957), the state leader of
the NSDFB, and discovered some compromising letters. Wenzl,
an engineer and former member of Richthofen's air squadron,
had joined the Stahlhelm as early as 1925. In one letter to
the national Stahlhelm leader, Wenzl concluded that the veterans' organization had been tricked and cheated by the new
movement, a feeling that was apparently shared by other Baden
district leaders of the same organization.[6] In public, Wenzl
still maintained that the Stahlhelm and the Nazi party needed
each other to triumph. But in a leadership conference of
the NSDFB in October 1934, he declared that without Prussian
militarism no new Reich could be created and he demanded the
"militarization" of the new movement.[7] This obvious attachment to the values and institutions of the old order had to
be eliminated by the new Nazi masters.

By mid-1935, Wenzl had been arrested for his speeches
against the Nazi movement, and forty-five Baden locals were
dissolved in the summer of the same year. The potential
danger of the movement to the regime was illustrated by the
ruling of a Stahlhelm court, which declared Wenzl innocent
despite Gau leader Wagner's insistence that the NSDFB leader
had been working against the new Nazi order. Finally, in
November 1935 the Stahlhelm in Baden was dissolved and the
potential independence of the movement eliminated.[8] After
this destruction of the "reactionaries," the other major party
attack on the representatives of the old order came in connection with the July 1944 plot. After this event, Wagner
declared that the reactionaries had not yet realized that
their world had perished in November 1918. Although the

Gestapo was the main agency charged with the elimination of "reactionaries" after this plot, the party's evaluation of "potential" reactionaries played an important role.[9] Ironically, Wenzl's cherished Prussian spirit had given the Nazis the tools to eliminate the old order from real power in Germany.

The suppression of Marxism and illegal Marxist organizations after 1933 was, of course, the responsibility of the Gestapo. But the party organizations played an important part in attempting to generate public outrage or fear, and in informing on Marxists who inadvertently made remarks about Nazi policies. The Führer published notices about illegal Communist activities as early as August 1933, when mass arrests and the first major suppression of illegal Marxist organizations occurred. In 1935/36, the party paper's coverage of Marxist activities increased markedly. The Führer reported both the creation of illegal Marxist locals and the formation of Communist cells in RAD camps. Even some new Nazi party members were found to have distributed KPD literature.[10] In practical terms, the party and its organizations attempted to "rehabilitate" former Communists and at the same time continue the surveillance of former Marxists. For example, Karl Hermann, a carpenter and former Communist activist who had served prison terms in 1933 and 1934, received a positive recommendation from the local party leader and was thus able to become the owner of a small furniture factory. On the other hand former Socialist and Communist leaders who spoke out against Hitler and National Socialism were denounced by members of the various party affiliates to the authorities.[11]

The police responded to the increase of Marxist activities

in 1934 and 1935 with mass arrests and the destruction of
Socialist and Communist locals. The Gestapo's measures were
so successful that by late 1936, the police noted, the Marxists
were switching to Mundpropaganda (word of mouth propaganda).
Arrests, however, continued unabated and by the end of 1937
the Baden prosecutor concluded that the organizations of both
the former SPD and KPD had been destroyed.[12] Until the outbreak of war with Russia, both Gestapo and party reports
reflected no major problems with the Marxists.

Beginning in late 1941 the DAF noted an increase in passive
resistance in many shops, and by the following year, several
firms reported extremely high, daily unexcused absences.[13]
The most famous Communist resistance in wartime Baden occurred
in Mannheim in late 1941 and was led by Georg Lechleiter, a
long-time Communist functionary. Despite his internment in
a concentration camp until 1935, Lechleiter resumed his
illegal Communist activities in 1937 in the Mannheim Lanz
factory. But not until the German invasion of Russia did
the group publish and distribute issues of Der Vorbote in
an attempt to win mass labor support. The group was discovered
and subsequent arrests and executions eliminated the Lechleiter
organization. But despite the illegal activities and even
passive resistance in factories, the Baden labor movement did
not actively resist the Nazi regime even though it was never
converted to National Socialism.[14] No doubt, the party played
an important part in coordinating labor in the DAF and in providing for the constant surveillance of dissidents.

THE CHURCHES

Compared to the party's relatively minor role in the elimination of the "reactionaries" and Marxists, the various party
organizations had a crucial and continual part in the attack
on Jews and the churches. This was especially true in the
case of the churches since they could not be merely eliminated
by force. Both the Protestants and the Catholic church leaders
in Baden wanted a modus vivendi with the new Nazi masters in
1933. The Baden Nazis had succeeded in infiltrating the
Protestant churches much more effectively than the Catholic
church. Wagner basically supported the party organization
devoted to Nazi pastors (NS Pfarrerbund) but he was not enthusiastic about supporting the League for a German Church, which
had emerged in Baden about 1922/23 under the direction of
Walter Buch, the national chairman of the party's court system. Wagner did not want to be drawn into a bitter confessional dispute, nor did he want the party identified with
idol (Wotan) worshipers. After Buch left Baden, the leadership of the Deutschkirche went to Schenk, a Nazi party member
and pastor of Neulussheim, a Nazi stronghold. Before the
takeover, the NS Pfarrerbund coordinated most of the Nazi
pastors of the Protestant churches.[15]

Despite these internal bickerings, the Nazi party did
well among Protestant ministers. Some preached from the
pulpit on the value of the NS Pfarrerbund and even hid SA
equipment in church attics.[16] As early as June 1931, the
leader of Baden's Protestant political party (Christlich-
Soziale Volksdienst), Hermann Teutsch, had joined the Baden
party and was campaigning for it actively. Most significant,
the Nazis with the help of the Positiven gained control of

the church council by late 1932. Only weeks after the Nazi
takeover in Baden, the head of the Landeskirchlichen
Vereinigung in the state not only urged active support of
the new national movement but also rejected parliamentary
democracy.[17] Although the state bishop resisted complete
submission to the party as late as 1934, the Baden Nazis
gained effective control over the Protestant Church Synod
through the German Christians. This development was initially
greatly facilitated by the fact that the state leader of the
German Christians, Heinrich Sauerhöfer, was a dedicated völkisch activist. Born in Weissenburg, Alsace, in 1901,
Sauerhöfer moved to Baden after the German defeat and the
restoration of French authority in Alsace. The frustrated
Alsatian émigré joined the Baden Nazi movement in 1922,
four years before he became a vicar, and remained loyal to
the Nazi cause until 1945.[18]

The Nazi coordination of the Protestant organizations
did not eliminate all friction, particularly after the goals
of the Nazi Christians became clear. As early as 1933 the
Church Council informed the minister of culture that it
rejected the idea of having to report to party agencies who
were demanding a voice in such decisions as hiring policies.
Wacker supported this view and ordered the party to correspond with the Church Council through the Ministry of Education
and Culture.[19] The same institutional conflict occurred
between the state bishop and the Hitler Youth when the latter
attempted to encroach on church-sponsored youth organizations
in late 1933.[20] Most damaging to the unified coordination
of the Protestant churches were the internal disputes among
the German Christians and the growth of the Confessional
Church. In fact, Sauerhöfer left his post and became a mayor

and eventually a party district leader because of his frustrations with the Confessional Church. By 1937 the Baden authorities noted that the majority of the Protestant clergy in Baden supported the Confessional Church, although they presented no special problems to the Nazi state. The Nazi ministers continued to control important decision-making powers in the Protestant church, including the post of finance in the Supreme Church Council. The chief of the finance department reported to the cabinet and obtained political evaluations of prospective church appointments from the Gestapo. The conflicts continued but neither the state's prosecutor nor Wacker, a fanatic anticleric after 1935 and apparently a supporter of Bormann's church policy, noted many problems with the Protestant ministers.[21]

The real bête noire of the party and rival until 1945 was the Catholic church. There is no evidence that any priests were active in the Nazi movement before 1933. The Baden party did use Kuno Brombacher, a Catholic writer, to campaign for the party before 1933 by attacking the antireligious forces on the left. After 1933, he served for about one short year as head of the Arbeitsgemeinschaft katholischer Deutscher, a liaison office with the Catholic church. But that failed miserably, and in September 1934 he resigned because he found too strong the Catholic church's opposition to the spirit of the Third Reich.[22]

That the Catholic church in Baden and the Center party in the first months of 1933 hoped for a modus vivendi with the Nazi ministers is clearly demonstrated in the letters of the archbishop of Freiburg, Conrad Gröber. In March 1933 he revealed his fears of a Kulturkampf between the Nazi state and the Catholic church. One week after Wagner's takeover, however, he was making positive statements about the new regime. This evolution reached a climax in late 1933 after the Concordat when he informed the minister of education that he had urged the clergy to be loyal to the Nazi regime and to allow Nazi flags to be brought to church during processions. By November 1933, the archbishop was defending Germany's withdrawal from the League, and urging Germans to support this step in the plebiscite. To Gröber and many Catholics, this modus vivendi was based on opportunism rather than conversion. It lasted only as long as both sides thought they could gain more from cooperation than from conflict.[23] The overly enthusiastic comment of the Catholic professor Max Schwall of the Commercial School of Mannheim after the Concordat that it "would no longer be difficult to fly the swastika flag and introduce the Nazi salute," would soon face the reality of the party's offensive.[24]

As early as 1933, the party activists on the local level began to move against the church. From party members to Kreisleiters, speakers attacked alleged church violations of the Nazi spirit. This assault became so intense in late 1933 and early 1934 that even the Nazi ministers had to intercede.[25] But Gröber also had doubts about the Nazi intentions as early as March and April 1933 when he noted the catastrophic migration of the youth to National Socialism and his inability to intercede successfully on behalf of converted Jews in Karlsruhe. By March 1934 his speeches clearly rejected the concept of a national church and pointed out that no people or nations are eternal; only the church is eternal.[26] In local Catholic communities in early 1934, priests, supported by the population, were actively struggling against the party's expansion. In Weiher, Bruchsal, a Catholic community of two

thousand, signatures were collected for a petition to retain
the local priest, Hermann Joseph Bikel. The Catholic youth
and women's organizations were much stronger in Weiher than
the Nazi party organizations. After the Gestapo suggested
that Bikel be transferred, the minister of interior ordered
Bikel out of his community in February because he was "endangering" the youth. The same type of local Catholic resistance could be observed in other Baden communities in 1934.[27]

The party's attack on the Catholic church in 1934 and
1935 became more intense as the Führer and Hakenkreuzbanner
began publishing numerous articles on the "black reaction."
In some communities like Osterburken, the arrest of the local
priest resulted in active resistance by the population, and
additional police and SA units were called upon to restore
order.[28] But these party excesses were only in part produced
by Nazi zealots. Wagner and Minister of Education Wacker
were basically responsible for the hard line. Wagner rejected
the counsel of moderation apparently given by the Reich Church
Minister Kerrl in 1935, arguing that such a course would be
taken as a sign of weakness.[29] As a result, the Nazi ministers
began to limit the activities of the Catholic clergy and,
where necessary, of the Protestant clergy. Catholic organizations were closed and priests banned from religion classes.
The bulk of these bans were borne by Catholic priests.
Between 1934 and 1940, eighty-two Catholic priests and only
thirteen Protestant ministers were prevented from teaching
religion classes.[30]

The attack on the Catholic church reached a climax in
1935. In June Wagner declared in a Karlsruhe party meeting
that the Nazis had the courage to hang several thousand
"scum." But unlike the church, Wagner asserted, the Nazis

wanted unity. Then he demanded that the Baden ministers
introduce legislation similar to the Prussian directives which
prohibited priests from issuing political announcements from
the pulpit. In August 1935, the Baden Gau leader issued a
"last warning" to the church leaders. National Socialism
was the state, and attacks on National Socialism were attacks
on the state, according to Wagner. This warning was followed
with a saturation campaign by leading Nazi party leaders and
ministers in a common offensive against the church.[31]

The Nazi offensive against the recalcitrant church leaders
and former Center party activists in Baden was made more
vigorous by the fact that the Gestapo leader in Karlsruhe,
Karl Berckmüller, was not only an old Nazi but also an enthusiastic anticleric. He was responsible for a series of police
actions against Catholic activists. Priests and publishers
of Catholic newspapers like the Hochrheinische Volksblatt of
Säckingen, as well as former Center party leaders, felt the
brunt of this offensive. Some were arrested and others prohibited from pursuing their livelihoods. There is no question
that the Catholic clergy and laymen had attacked Nazi principles. Priests were heard to say in public that Christ would
weep over the conditions of the German fatherland, and Catholic
papers attacked the new heathendom of race and blood. Such
activities caused the Nazi press to demand the extermination
(Ausrottung) of these church leaders.[32]

The actions of the church leaders and Catholic laymen
were based not only on a genuine rejection of the Nazi racism
but also on an obvious conflict of interest. This is revealed
clearly by the youth issue. The Hitler Youth leader of Baden,
Kemper, was a zealous antichurch campaigner who demanded that
the teachers help win children for the Hitler Youth and the Nazi

movement in general. As early as 1934, the party tried to coerce and entice children to join Nazi organizations and activities. Naturally, the Hitler Youth's offensives against Catholic youth organizations led to clashes in 1934 and 1935. Even the Gestapo reported the ill feeling created by these activities among the population. In the village of Oberschopfheim, for example, the local propaganda leader was stoned by Catholic activists. At first, the Gestapo dissolved the confessional youth organizations in communities where clashes occurred, and later, in July 1935 the Baden minister of interior formally dissolved the Catholic youth organization (Deutsche Jugendkraft) in Baden.[33]

In many instances, the Hitler Youth's attack on the church resembled a Kulturkampf. In a state and party conference of teachers in the summer of 1935, Friedhelm Kemper, the Hitler Youth leader of Baden, demanded the mobilization of teachers in schools to convert the youth and build the new political man. Kemper wanted the teachers to become the preachers of the Nazi movement.[34] The Hitler Youth leader frequently used Protestant teachers and mobs to attack Catholic strongholds. For example, in Waibstadt, Sinsheim, the teacher was a party member and a Protestant in a predominantly Catholic community that was also a former Zentrum stronghold. With the support of the mayor, this teacher removed the crosses from the schools, a step that caused the parents to keep their children at home.[35] This party drive against Catholic strongholds, supported by the Nazi ministers, left the Catholic establishment little recourse except resistance. In turn, party district leaders forbade teachers to assume functions in the church, and the state and party leader of the teacher's organization ordered teachers in 1937 to leave the church when it attacked Nazi doctrines.[36]

After the massive party and Nazi ministerial attacks
on the church in the summer of 1935, the Nazi leadership
shifted to a lesser public Kleinarbeit (detail work) to
undermine the influence of the church. In late 1935 and
early 1936, Gröber wrote Wagner, asking him to moderate
Nazi policies. Wagner made it clear to the archbishop that
he would never permit antireligious and anti-Catholic circles
to assume leading positions in the party or state. But the
church was charged with being a hostile force that had disrupted the peace by its refusal to accept the Nazi state.
After the archbishop of Freiburg promised to order the clergy
to refrain from its antistate campaigns and even urged Baden's
Catholics to support the fatherland during the election of
March 1936, the Nazi ministers pardoned some of the clergy
who had been arrested.[37]

The rapprochement did not last long. In 1936, the party
urged its members to withdraw formally from the churches which
would deprive the religious institutions of financial support.
In the summer of the same year, the chief prosecutor of Baden
also noted Gröber's growing resistance in his Hirtenbriefe.[38]
Despite Wagner's public pronouncements that the church's protests against alleged party attacks were mere hysterical erup-
tions of hate, there is no doubt the party's cadre organization
pursued a rigorous campaign against the church. For example,
the district leader of Freiburg in late 1937 gathered all of
the civil service leaders of his area and warned them not to
participate in major religious marches, allegedly because
Communists and Socialists took part covertly. As a result,
few civil servants took part in these church events. Then
in August 1938 this same district leader called Gröber a scum

(Lumpenbub). When Gröber protested, Wagner replied that he was too busy to be bothered by such trivia.[39] Only as the war drew closer and during the conflict did Wagner attempt to limit the party's public disputes with the church and to eliminate the impression that the Nazis planned an antireligious offensive.[40]

When the archbishop of Freiburg attempted to use the war as a vehicle for limiting Nazi interference against the church, he failed completely. He initiated a correspondence with the Baden minister of education and culture on 2 September 1939 in which he proposed peace during Germany's period of crisis. But the correspondence resulted in only more hostility. Wacker, apparently a supporter of Bormann's church policy, simply told Gröber to restrain the clergy. After repeated complaints by Gröber about party excesses, Wacker stopped all correspondence with the archbishop, but not before he accused the church leader of being hostile to the Nazi state and party and of having illusions about the political power of the church.[41] Even after Wacker died in 1940 and was replaced by the former DNVP representative Paul Schmitthenner, relations did not improve. Responding to one of Gröber's letters, an internal memo of the Ministry of Education approved by Schmitthenner labeled the archbishop a traitor who should be in jail. Again, the new Minister of Education in late 1941 broke off all correspondence with the Freiburg archbishop, leaving Gröber only the choice of turning to Berlin agencies to voice his frustrations with Baden Nazis.[42]

Although Gröber's efforts were frustrated by the hostility of the state's Nazi leaders, on the local level the war provided the churches with unique opportunities to circumvent the party's restrictions. All party reports in Baden during the

war reveal an increase of religious activities, particularly
of the Catholic church. The church surmounted legal restrictions by creating a variety of volunteer clubs that rivaled
the Nazi welfare organization, the Nazi kindergartens and
nurses, and even the Hitler Youth.[43] The church gained control over the burial of soldiers, particularly since the party
lacked adequate personnel. In some instances, the party prepared services for fallen soldiers and assembled party representatives, only to discover that the relatives refused to
attend. Finally, the Catholic church's services for Poles
and its peace sermons convinced the party leaders that they
were dealing with a vicious enemy of the state.[44]

The party's reaction to the growing role of the church
was especially vituperous, since the pressures of war limited
its direct attacks on the religious institutions. The desire
to emulate the Bolsheviks and to exterminate the Catholic
church leaders was voiced by old Nazi activists like Franz
Merk of the district of Neustadt. In reality, the party
district leaders had to concede that the population (because
of the threat of death) feared the priests much more than
the party.[45] This did not mean that the party and its activists did not try to limit the church's influence. Farmers
were threatened that they would not receive laborers if they
continued to participate in church processions during regular
working days, and Catholic civil service pensioners were
threatened with the suspension of their pensions. War production recommendations were vetoed by party leaders because the
candidates had contributed too much money to the church while
neglecting the NSV, and whole choirs were dissolved because
they had participated in church-sponsored burials of fallen
comrades.[46] After the discovery and arrest of the Catholic

Youth organization <u>Neudeutschland</u> of Bruchsal, the party leader
of the district called a public rally in Bruchsal to focus
public attention on the youthful "criminals" and their parents.
The main physical threat to individual priests came from the
Gestapo and the state powers. The Gestapo operated a special
"Church Section" which had the sole function of supervising
confessional activities. From 1940, arrests of priests and
Catholic activists increased greatly. Finally, near the end
of the war, individual party fanatics on occasion brutally
murdered priests.[47]

The party's radical offensive against the churches had
the support of the Nazi-dominated ministries. But increasingly
during the war, party leaders reported the opposition of municipal administrative officials, and the Kreisleiter of Mosbach
estimated that 70 percent of the officials of the district
were unreliable because they still clung to church-affiliated
organizations. Local police officers were also actively
attached to the church. On some occasions a state district
official (Landrat) refused to comply with the party's demands.
For example, in Grafenhausen, Neustadt, the local leader Franz
Merk had engaged the local priest in a protracted struggle.
Merk finally induced the party district leader to urge the
Landrat to forbid the priest to present religious theater
pieces. The state officials refused, no doubt to avoid public wrath.[48]

If the party was frustrated with the public and with some
officials because of their attachments to the church and its
functions, it wanted to make absolutely sure that party members and members of party affiliates were not contaminated.
The Gau propaganda leader ordered that no reference be made
to party members engaged in church activities. After 1936,

the party activists attempted to induce party members to cut all ties with the church. Party district leaders gathered all party officials and urged mass withdrawals from the church. By 1944, nine of the ten cadre leaders of the DAF of the district of Freiburg had withdrawn from the church. The sole exception was a Protestant.[49] Those party functionaries who refused to comply were tolerated during the war because of personnel shortages, but the Nazi leaders made it clear that after the war they would be replaced.[50]

But even here the party activists and völkisch true believers faced substantial opposition. First, party leaders who withdrew experienced strong opposition from the local community. In some areas, the party leaders on the local level became outcasts. Several "old" party members also attacked the party's anti-Christian policies even before the war.[51] During the war, the Gau and district party leaders noted that some Nazis, who directed NS educational institutions, organized Christmas plays, and local party officials participated in church marriages and church choirs. Worse still, on the local level members of the party affiliates resigned these offices rather than break with their church functions. Because of the lack of personnel, these local functionaries could not be replaced.[52] When one of the local party members who was active in the church (but joined the party in 1932) protested to the Kreisleiter that he was a faithful Nazi, the reply of the party leadership was that no party political leader could accept a church position in view of the party's increasing public leadership tasks. The party district leaders of Baden frankly admitted by 1942 that after the war the local leaders and party members would have to be indoctrinated and molded all over again.[53]

The party leaders realized that the "whole man" could
never become a total supporter of the Nazi ideology as long
as he was tied to the church and its strong subcultural activities. During the war the party could do little to solve this
problem. Personnel shortages and the need to preserve domestic
tranquillity limited the party's success. That the party's
real aims, however, were only postponed, not abandoned, was
made clear by Wagner in a speech in Karlsruhe on 12 June 1941,
when he warned that after the war "we will tackle the foes at
home; there are still some running around the country in
purple and ermine."[54] The church's resistance to the Nazi
policies was based on self-interest and, in the case of the
many priests who ended up in concentration camps, on courageous
moral grounds. But above all, it was a conflict between rival
world views. Some scholars have argued that the resistance of
the Catholic church cannot be equated with resistance, but
the fact remains that the only open and popular resistance
to Nazi rule in Baden emanated from the confessional subcultures. Villages rose in defense of their priests, and
even church-affiliated party members defended their church
positions. The protest of Baden's religious leaders in late
1940 against the euthanasia of the inmates of the Grafeneck
institutions of southern Württemberg resulted in the closing
of the death camps.[55] The real tragedy was, of course, that
no similar popular outcry developed against the persecution
and eventual mass genocide of Jews and other unfortunates.

JEWS

Although the churches represented an alien subculture to the
Nazi activists and a persistent sore on the desired homo-

geneity, Jews were regarded as an expendable alien race. The national Jewish leaders in many ways were duped by the political developments as much as the Nationalists, who had made a deal with Hitler in early 1933. The C. V. Zeitung, in an article published on 2 February, only days after the Nazi takeover, noted that while Nazi participation in the government represented a danger, the Jewish community believed in the honor of the president and was convinced that no one would dare touch the constitutional rights of the German Jews. The slogan was ruhig abwarten (wait and see).[56]

Most of Baden's Jews initially also failed to understand the Nazi movement's fanatic commitment to the elimination of Jews from the nation. The lawyer Hugo Marx argued in 1932 for a Marxist solution to the Jewish problem. Since the German Mittelstand was collapsing, Marx argued, Jews must become manual workers. Among workers, they would encounter less anti-Semitism and at the same time gain more economic mobility. Jews must establish themselves as a national minority since Zionism was only associated with the capitalistic-imperialistic interests of one world power. Although Marx's solution was stillborn, he did realize earlier than most that only escape could be the final answer to the changing political situation.[57] The Israelitische Gemeindeblatt of Mannheim, the most important community paper in Baden for Jews, advised its readers of the possibility of hiring protection (Wachbereitschaft Mannheim), but on the whole it neglected politics until late February 1933. Then it reported on a meeting of the state's Centralverein, which was attended by representatives from twenty-nine Baden Jewish communities and addressed by Alfred Wiener from Berlin. In conclusion, the paper on 12 February noted that despite the seriousness of the situation, there was no reason for despair. For the

immediate future, the Baden Jews planned additional community
meetings to discuss the political situation.[58]

Understandably, the Jewish reaction changed significantly
with the Nazi takeover in Baden. On the eve of the March election, some Jewish activists presented speeches on "Political
Parties and the Jewish Question" which to no one's surprise
noted that only the small and insignificant Staatspartei and
the large Social Democratic and Center parties would support
the religious rights of the Jews in Baden. After the Nazis
seized control of the state government, the Baden rabbi Max
Grünewald concluded that the situation had changed completely,
making it imperative that Jews protect their legal rights.
Then, in May 1933 the paper published an article by the head
of the Synagogue Council, a Dr. Moses, who frankly stated that
"one feels as if one is in front of a heap of rubble." He
also called for an end to all internal disputes so that the
Jewish community might face this common danger united.[59]

Some groups such as the League of Jewish Veterans (RJF)
still clung to the illusion that the organic racism of the
Nazis could be placated by the records of Jewish war veterans.
In June, the Baden RJF issued a call to Mannheim Jews who
had participated in postwar militias or fought in the Baltic
and Upper Silesia areas against Spartacists, Separatists,
and enemies of the "national revival" to send their names to
the organization's headquarters. No doubt they hoped to
gather additional evidence of the nationalism and loyalty of
Baden's Jewish citizens. These attempts may have impressed
the public but certainly not the party activists. Nathan
Stein, an important Jewish leader in Baden until 1937, noted
in retrospect that "my experience tells me that there were many
men who thoroughly disapproved of the anti-Jewish excesses,

but could do nothing because they were unorganized."[60] It
became the function of the party to neutralize the efforts of
individuals, particularly those in the civil service and the
economy, who rose in the defense of Jews. The party was the
vanguard in the Nazi regime's efforts to eventually destroy
Baden's Jews.[61]

The offensive against Baden's Jews was launched in early
1933 by the Nazi activists who had obtained leading ministerial
posts in the state. In a cabinet meeting in March, Wagner
ordered the removal of all Jews from state and municipal positions. This order and many more dealing with the elimination
of Jewish teachers and employees of the educational system of
Baden were implemented enthusiastically by the "old" Nazi
activist and commissar of education, Wacker. By 1936, 189
Jewish teachers had been replaced and the remaining 58 had
been assigned to Jewish students. Appeals by Baden institutions, like the Senate of the University of Heidelberg, which
pleaded for moderation or the modification of these extreme
orders, were flatly rejected by Wacker and the other Nazi
commissars.[62]

Even more ominous for Jews who had still hoped in early
1933 that the Nazis would not dare touch their legal rights
were some of the court decisions emanating from the state's
leading court in Karlsruhe. A Heidelberg man had appealed
for a divorce from his Jewish wife because he had "not known
about the full concept of this race." Although the Heidelberg
court refused to grant the divorce, the court of appeals in
Karlsruhe obtained the dubious distinction on 3 March 1934
of being the first German court to grant a divorce on racial
grounds. By 1940, the state court in Karlsruhe (Oberlandesgericht) was relying on racial experts to decide legal issues.

When one mother, who had been married to a Jew in Kiev, attempted to protect her son by claiming that the father had really been a German, the Karlsruhe court used the services of Professor von Verschuer of the Institute of Heredity and Racial Hygiene in Frankfurt to examine the son. On the basis of his recommendation, the court ruled that the boy was a Jew because "he looked like a Jew."[63] The Nazi-dominated state agencies and the courts implemented racial legislation even against a Jewish veteran like Max Regenstein, who had been badly injured in the war. In addition, one of his brothers had died in the conflict and another one had been wounded. After these sacrifices, this family had to endure Max's incarceration because of alleged sexual relations with an "Aryan" girl who had already committed suicide.[64]

Not only did the Baden Jews lose their legal rights, but frequently they suffered economic strangulation. Some unscrupulous Badenese took advantage of the new state policies and attempted to blackmail individual Jews.[65] But the greatest economic danger to the Jews resulted from the party's boycott and the state's "legal" measures. Initially, in 1933 the party enthusiasts on the local level forced the closing of Jewish department stores against the desires of the Nazi ministers, who were afraid of the economic consequences during these early months of power. Then beginning on 31 March 1933, the party organized the first official boycotts against Jewish stores. Appropriately, the "action committee" that organized the boycott was directed by the party's Mittelstand affiliate and the party's Racial Policy Office.[66] But all of these measures did not prevent larger Jewish businesses in Baden from benefiting from the general economic improvements after 1933. Despite party pressures, the firm of Louis Oppenheimer in Bruchsal, which manufactured cloth (<u>Uniformtuch Gross-</u><u>handlung</u>), obtained eighteen hundred new customers between 1933 and 1936. The Nazi state's answer was to Aryanize the store and in many other cases charge Jewish businesses with tax evasion in order to facilitate Aryanization. Ironically, when the Nazis Aryanized the Bruchsal business, they emphasized in a circular that the solid tradition and quality of the firm would continue since members of the old firm were still in charge.[67] The impact of the economic moves against Jews was reflected in the fact that by 1938, 26 percent of Baden's Jews needed assistance.[68]

Many Baden Jews, particularly the <u>Ostjuden</u> (Jews from Eastern Europe), reacted to this persecution by emigrating to other European countries and to Palestine. Between 1933 and September 1935, 12 percent of Mannheim's Jews left for Palestine, France, and other European countries. After 1935, few Jews went to Palestine, and the largest percentage turned to the United States. On the whole, the Jewish population in Baden became more urban as small Jewish communities were consolidated or abolished. In addition, between 1933 and 1937 the Jewish population in Baden declined by one-third.[69]

Surprisingly, many Jews still clung to the hope that they could survive in Baden, even under the Nazi regime. Early in 1935, Wagner reported in a cabinet meeting that too many Jews were returning to Baden and argued that they should be sent to a concentration camp. The following year, the Gestapo noticed renewed Jewish activities in clubs and meetings.[70] The Jewish intellectual and romantic Jacob Piccard, who was born in 1883 in a small southern Baden community, returned for a visit in 1936 and reported that his friend Alfred Wolf was still driving about the countryside and selling his goods to the farmers.[71] This last illusion was not destroyed until the 1938 pogrom.

Until the November 1938 pogrom drove the Baden Jews out of the state in horror, the party's function revolved around the twofold attempt of supplementing the state's anti-Semitic campaign and of ensuring that there was no compromise in the population's attitude toward Jews. In fact, the party and its various affiliates acted as radical vanguards of anti-Semitic actions that frequently even clashed with the "legal" and "national" anti-Semitic moves of the Nazi-dominated state agencies. Although the socioeconomic radicalism of the party affiliates had to be shelved after 1934, the radical anti-Semitism never had to be abandoned. Kreisleiters reported to the Gestapo on women who were consorting with Jews, civil servants were threatened if they shopped in Jewish stores, and lawyers who were party members were forbidden from representing Jews in legal cases.[72]

To ensure the constant dissemination of anti-Semitism, the party and its affiliates engaged in the most primitive local education and enlightenment program, which ranged from discussions of the "Protocols of Zion" to denunciations of "Bolshevik-Jewish" culture. A special party affiliate, the Fighting League for German Culture, in 1933 promised to eliminate these alien concepts and reestablish German theater, art, and music.[73] Only the lack of party members with artistic talents and training prevented this radical party affiliate from destroying all "Jewish-Bolshevik" art. In fact, the Kreisleiter of Freiburg, who held a Ph.D., admitted that without a transition period in which one allowed such works as Franz Lehar's "Der Graf von Luxemburg" there would be no German theater.[74]

This kind of compromise was not generally the party's modus operandi. Instead, the party in most cases was far in advance of the state's more procedural anti-Semitism. For example, the Jews of Sennfeld in the district of Buchen wanted to establish an agricultural training camp for those Jews who wished to emigrate from Baden. Despite the fact the state's agricultural organization and the Ministry of Interior saw no reason to object to a project that in the end would reduce the Jewish population, the Kreisleiter of Buchen objected strenuously and predicted that he would be unable to control "public outrage." Only after the Ministry of Interior presented the party district leader with Wagner's personal approval of the project were the Jews informed that they could establish the camp if they guaranteed that the trained Jews would emigrate and not appear in public as a group.[75] The same kind of over-zealousness of the party can be observed in all areas. Wagner and the minister of interior had to caution party members to be more careful in their anti-Semitic tirades and to remove the signs "Jews not desired" in order not to endanger Germany's foreign trade and economic recovery. Individual SA violence against synagogues was still punished by Wagner in 1935, not because he wanted to protect Jews but because it represented a lack of party discipline.[76]

The party's radical anti-Semitism was obviously not opposed by Wagner, Köhler, and Pflaumer in principle; they rejected the recklessness of the party's local actions that endangered the well-being of the state. Time was crucial to Nazi ministers. In 1936, the minister of interior had ordered that the anti-Jewish signs be removed from municipal main streets in view of the impending Olympic games. But the signs could remain on secondary streets. After Germany

became less sensitive to foreign economic pressures, the anti-
Jewish actions of the state differed little from the party's
earlier activism. By 1938, the mayor of Rastatt, for example,
assured the party municipal district leader that he agreed
too many Jews were seen in public and that he had directed
the association of restaurants to post signs in all entrances
indicating that Jews were not desired.[77] This tactical shift
on the part of the Nazi ministers reached a climax in 1938.
At the beginning of that year, Wagner ordered special editions
of the Stürmer issue, entitled "Death Penalty for Racial Dese-
craters," to be distributed to all party districts in Baden.
Then during the pogrom of November 1938, the party and the SA
were allowed to vent their hate against Baden's Jews by burning and destroying synagogues in an orgy of violence. Jews
were marched through the streets of major cities and subjected
to insults and beatings. In Baden-Baden the Nazis forced
Jews, who had been assembled in the synagogue, to read selec-
tions from Mein Kampf and to sing party songs. After the
destruction of the synagogues, schoolchildren were charged
ten pfennigs to see the rubble.[78]

One especially repugnant case, which illustrates both
the extreme aspects of the party's actions in 1938 and the
attitude of the state agencies, involved the local party
leader of Eberstadt in the district of Buchen, Adolf H. Frey,
a farmer and native of the small Protestant community. Early
in the morning of 10 November 1938, the district party leader
of Buchen, Ullmer, gave Frey orders to carry out the action
against the Jews. According to Frey's testimony, Ullmer
told him that he could do whatever he wished with the Jews,
excluding only arson and plunder. Frey confronted one of the
Jews of Eberstadt, the old widow Susanna Stern (1857), and

ordered her to vacate her premises. After the old woman
refused to get dressed, Frey shot her in the chest and head.
Then, after bending over her body and detecting a murmur, he
shot the woman again. After the event, the police of Buchen
reported that the twenty-six-year-old Frey was a "decent,
solid young man" who had a good reputation, while the eighty-
one-year-old Stern was regarded as a boisterous and audacious
Jew. It also alleged that the population of Eberstadt and of
the surrounding area reacted calmly to the events. After
such reports, naturally the Reich minister of justice dropped
all proceedings against the local leader of Eberstadt.[79]

Baden's Jews reacted to the 1938 violence by mass emigration. By October 1940, only 6,437 Jews remained in Baden out
of the 20,617 when the Nazis took power. Polish Jews had
already been deported from Baden in October 1938. After the
pogrom Wagner ordered all Baden party district leaders to
prohibit further individual party actions against Jews since
the goal of the state was now to induce Jews to emigrate
through "legal" pressures.[80] Despite Wagner's order, the
local party activists proceeded against the remaining Jews
with vigor although usually not with violence. Local party
leaders attempted to prevent Jews from leaving their homes
in the fall of 1939 and to ban Jews from their towns. The
town of Breisach in the district of Freiburg, under the influence of radical Nazi activists, introduced measures to deport
its Jews to the mental hospital of Rufach, Alsace. Although
most of these measures were reversed and modified by the Gau
party leadership and the Landrat, the Baden Jews received
only a temporary reprieve.[81]

In October 1940, Hitler ordered that the Jews of Baden
and the Palatinate be expelled to France. On 22 October 1940,

seven trains from Baden carried to France 6,300 Jews who were
allowed to carry with them only a minimum of luggage and money.
The Jewish property in Baden was seized by the state, and the
synagogues in Alsace were converted into warehouses. Only
partners in mixed marriages and those Baden Jews who were
momentarily in other German states escaped deportation. After
October 1940, only 820 Jews remained in the state.[82] In the
end most of these deported Jews and the few remaining ones in
Baden were sent to extermination camps. In January 1941,
Frick ordered the Baden minister of interior to gather institutionalized Jews in Happenheim. One month later, they were
transferred to Hadamar for extermination. The party leaders
were clearly in the forefront of this extermination policy
even if Nazi state officials implemented them. For example,
the district leader of Buchen in May 1941 told the warden
of the Bruchsal jail of the necessity to exterminate all Jews
in the world. He wanted the warden to give one particular
Jewish inmate a deadly shot. By April 1942, the district
leader's wishes were fulfilled since the largest part of the
Jews remaining in Baden and the ones transferred to France
were sent to Izbica, the death camp near Lublin.[83]

The elimination of most of Baden's Jews in 1940 did not
deter the party from further anti-Semitic activities and propaganda. Most of the cases after 1940 involved Jews of mixed
ancestry (Mischlinge) or marriages. The Gau personnel office
took an adamant view and refused to moderate anti-Mischling
policies, particularly in educational and marriage matters.[84]
The party leadership also attempted to eliminate from the
economic field the last vestiges of Jewish Mischlinge or
those who were married to Jews. German small businessmen
and small entrepreneurs who were married to Jews felt the

brunt of the party's attack. In one case the owner of a construction company, who was married to a Mischling, was blacklisted by the party and consequently failed to get large contracts. In another district, a master locksmith, who was married to a Jew and emphatically declared that he would never divorce his wife, received no more apprentices and was in danger of losing the three in his employment after the Kreisleiter lodged a series of complaints with the state employment office.[85] In cases involving Mischlinge who were managers of firms, the party was totally radical even if these managers were so efficient and important that they had the support of industry and state bureaucrats. Only those industrial managers or owners who were married to Jews but ran industries vital to the war effort continued to frustrate the party fanatics. As late as 1944 the party agencies attempted to change managerial posts in vital industries because of the managers' mixed marriages.[86] Toward the end of the war, Nazi verbal attacks on Jews became more frequent and brutal. The Kreisleiter of Bühl, Hans Rothacker, candidly admitted in 1944 in the Führer the truth about the Final Solution. At the end of this war, Rothacker was quoted as saying, the Jews will have been destroyed just as Hitler had predicted in 1939.[87] Indeed, the anti-Semitism of the party's platform triumphed more completely than any other doctrine enunciated by the party activists before 1933. The Final Solution was not just a reaction to the changing fortunes of war; it was the logical outcome of the völkisch true believer's racism.

THE OFFICIAL IDEOLOGY: THE RACIAL POLICY OFFICE

The intensity of the party's opposition to the churches and
Jews was based on an aspiring totalitarian, racist Weltanschauung, which permeated most segments of the Nazi party
from the SS Race and Settlement Office to the Agrarian Section,
which established a League for Peasant Race Studies to discover the roots of the new elite of Germany. But the one
party agency that eventually emerged to supervise indoctrination and propaganda in the field of population and race politics was the Racial Policy Office (RPA). The task of this
agency, according to its national leader Walter Gross, was
to avert the downfall of civilization by increasing the population of Germany, guarding its racial excellence, and preventing, even expurgating, racial mixtures.[88]

In Baden, the agency responsible for racial indoctrination was led by the medical doctor Theodor Pakheiser, who was
also the head of the state's NS Doctors' League. In late
1933 and early 1934, no party member, in theory at least,
could present lectures on racial topics without the permission of Pakheiser.[89] Then in 1934, an independent Gau RPA
was established, but again the leading Gau and district officers were medical doctors. Although the RPA used the medical
doctors' prestige to influence the population, the various
Gau RPA sections, from propaganda to race and population
departments, were staffed by doctrinaire party bureaucrats.
No party or party-affiliated member was allowed to deliver
speeches on racial policies without being an associate member
of the RPA with an appropriate passport.[90] The RPA also
relied on the organization of the various party affiliates to
disseminate racial literature and information. The German

League for Calisthenics distributed the racist literature of
the RPA and cooperated with the RPA in racial indoctrination
programs for its officials. Similarly, the NS Teachers'
League not only urged its members to read the racist literature published by the RPA but also received racial political
outlines of German history, biology, geography, and art and
music.[91]

In addition to this basic racial propaganda, the RPA
began an active program to prevent mixed marriages between
Germans and non-German workers from Southern and Eastern
Europe. Just as important to the agency was the establishment of a breeding program within the family. Its marriage
guidelines emphasized a healthy German genetic history and
the desire of the marriage partners for numerous children.
The decline of a nation's birthrate was viewed as the biological weakening of a country's will to survive. Consequently,
the RPA arranged agreements with mayors to provide financial
and honorific benefits for mothers who produced more than
four children. All of this was intended to increase the birthrate of Baden, which, after increasing between 1934 and 1936,
had declined again in 1937, despite all of the racial propaganda.[92]

Much more ominous for some of Baden's citizens was the
RPA's call for the sterilization of people with genetic
diseases and defects. The road to euthanasia was only a
step away. As early as 1930, the Nazi Landtag delegate Franz
Merk had argued that from a racial point of view the state
could not afford to save the terminally ill while healthy
people were committing suicide because of their economic
plight. After the Nazi takeover, the party and the Nazi
ministers initiated a far-reaching sterilization program.

Frick, the national minister of interior, published a preface
in the official journal of the RPA in 1934 in which he argued
that it was the state's duty to prevent genetically damaged
people from reproducing. Nor could the state be deterred by
antiquated religious thought. In Baden by mid-1934, already
3,025 applications for the sterilization of the genetically ill
had been filed, and 572 people had been sterilized. Only 685
of these applications had been filed by the patients. Several
years later, the racial propagandists of Baden were demanding
that future generations of antisocials and subhumans be eliminated through sterilization of the genetically ill.[93]

Between October 1939 and August 1941, the Nazis substituted a euthanasia program that claimed the lives of nearly one
hundred thousand German "incurables" in six death camps. In
southern Baden alone, three thousand of thirty-two hundred
inmates of twelve institutions housing the terminally ill
and senile were murdered. Many of these were sent to the
extermination camp, Grafeneck, in southern Württemberg until
that camp was closed by popular and religious protests. Later,
some victims from Baden were shipped to the death camp,
Hadamar, in Hesse.[94] The selection and eventual murder of
these Baden inmates was carried out by "respectable" and traditional medical personnel who had for the most part not been
part of the völkisch movement before 1933. The state's health
director and leader of the party's Gauamt for Health was
Waldemar Pychlau, a medical doctor who had not joined the
party until 1933. The two doctors responsible for the selection and murder of three thousand people in southern Baden,
Ludwig Sprauer and Josef Arthur Schreck, also joined the party
in that year. Both had practiced medicine long before the
Nazi takeover, Sprauer as the state district physician in a

southern Baden district and Schreck as a physician of a nursing home.[95] Without the support of such "pillars" of society,
the racial propaganda of the RPA would have been in vain.

After the outbreak of the war, the RPA in October 1939
issued an internal circular announcing that the RPA's func-
tion--solving the Jewish and Mischling problems, supervising
foreign workers, and increasing the birthrate--would continue.[96] The RPA faced numerous new tasks after 1939 while
at the same time suffering personnel losses and the damaging
leadership of its new Gauamt leader, Paul Maass. A native
of Mühlhausen, Alsace, Maass had joined the party in 1922 and
emerged as the Gauamt leader of civil servants in Gau Düsseldorf and later in Brandenburg before coming to Alsace. He
assumed the direction of the city of Mühlhausen in Alsace and
the Gau leadership of the RPA in 1940/41. An impulsive and
brutal man who had spent much of his party career in bicker-
ing, he was almost fired by Wagner in late 1944 because of
his corruption.[97]

Maass's assistant and representative in Alsace, Otto
Freisinger, was not much better. He had started his racial
political career in 1935 in Donaueschingen and then worked
his way up to district RPA leader of Mannheim and finally Gau
propaganda leader of the RPA by September 1940. Freisinger,
who became the Gauamt representative in Alsace, completely
misunderstood the Alsatian problem and people whom he was
supposed to win over to racism. In one babbling racial speech
in Suffelweyersheim, Alsace, on 23 January 1942, he was intoxicated and nearly knocked over a column that supported the bust
of the Führer on the stage.[98] His performance was just as
dismal in other German areas. In Essen, he told a gathering
of fifteen hundred NS Frauenschaft and DAF women that Alsatians

did not like to work, they merely wanted to eat. The NS
Frauenschaft of Essen lamented that the party had spent a year
indoctrinating the population about the value of Alsatians as
Germans, and now Freisinger destroyed it with one speech. Not
until August 1944 was this incompetent drunkard removed from
office for the misappropriation of RPA money.[99]

Given this kind of leadership, it is surprising that
the RPA accomplished anything, especially since the loss of
party personnel gave the RPA difficulties in just distributing
its racist calendar Neues Volk.[100] The tasks of the agency
were staggering and ranged from the indoctrination of the
Hitler Youth to giving mayors and police officials racial
information about various ethnic Germans who were coming to
Baden. The indoctrination programs for NSV nurses, the ren-
dering of racial judgments in adoption cases, and the new
duties in Alsace after 1940 would have provided challenge
enough, even to an efficient agency.[101] In the Führer in
mid-1944 and in internal circulars, Maass proudly announced
that the RPA had accomplished its tasks splendidly and had
converted the Baden population to a racial world view.[102]
In reality, the party and police noted that the population
was consorting with foreign laborers and even conceiving
children from "inferior races." The Catholic population displayed sympathy for Eastern European workers, and the farmers,
in particular, preferred Polish workers, first, because the
Poles were good workers, and second, because they felt affinity
with the Poles' Catholicism.[103]

Despite the public's negative reaction to the racial myths
of the party and the RPA, the official racial policies were
not modified, even for the expediency of war. The party
closely monitored all legal cases involving Poles in Baden,

and the RPA circulated directives to the population to keep its distance from the East Europeans.[104] Ironically, the workers from Eastern Europe (Ostarbeiter) in Baden were considered by DAF officials to be the best laborers, on occasion even surpassing the Germans. Yet the Ostarbeiter received the worst provisions, while the Indian POWs, whose work performance was poor, were granted good provisions. In St. Blasien, the Ostarbeiter were removed from movie theaters to make room for Dutch and French war prisoners. Even the German Labor Front, which recognized the value of Ostarbeiter and on occasion demanded better provisions, viewed them as basically ignorant chattels.[105]

Racism was not merely a theory disseminated by the RPA that disappeared with the organizational collapse of this agency, but it was also an integral part of the Nazi party and its affiliates, which remained immune to reason and self-interest. This racial world view made it imperative for the party to attempt to eliminate its most dangerous and persistent rival, the Catholic church. After the coordination of "reactionaries," the suppression of Marxists, and the elimination of Jews, only the church remained to contest seriously the völkisch world view of the Nazi activists. The final, and in part inevitable, move against the Catholic church would have taken place after the successful conclusion of the war.

10 The *NS Volkswohlfahrt* and the *Winterhilfswerk*

GERMAN SOCIALISM

After seizing control of the state machinery in Baden and
coordinating various pluralistic organizations, the Nazis
still had not created a fundamentally new social order.
Instead, the party propaganda after 1933 always identified the
new order, which was described as "German Socialism," with
racial and social harmony. Party spokesmen consistently
focused on the German Labor Front (DAF) and the National
Socialist Welfare Organization (NSV) as the two agencies of
the Third Reich that would ensure the creation of a new order.
According to Erich Hilgenfeldt, the national leader of the NSV,
and his various subordinates, the NSV and the DAF were the
most important organizations in the implementation of the
"socialistic will" promised by the party program. The NSV
and in particular its Winter Relief Program (WHW) would ensure
the transition from capitalism to socialism and from individualism to a genuine Volksgemeinschaft (people's community).[1]

With this convenient definition, the Nazis could claim
that they were indeed creating a new order without ever having
to change the basic economic underpinnings of German society.
Both the NSV and the WHW were manipulated by the Nazi leaders
to facilitate the coordination of Baden society and to
strengthen their hold on that society. The relief provided

by the WHW and NSV in 1933/34 and 1934/35 was important in winning some public good will during the early years of the regime. Since these contributions came from the German public, they also helped the Nazi government reduce its welfare contributions to the states and local communities. But from the very beginning, the Nazis always described this relief as preventive aid (Vorsorge), not welfare (Fürsorge). Above all, the NSV was designed to aid only that part of German society which was racially valuable to the Nazi state. The "German Socialism" of the NSV was really only a racial breeding program and a tool for political socialization, and the WHW, which was supposed to symbolize the "socialism of deed," provided funds for the racial welfare programs of the NSV after the worst years of the depression had been overcome.[2]

Despite the party's denigration of the Fürsorge concept, public and private welfare institutions were well established in Germany before the Nazis took power. In addition to social insurance and extensive public welfare on the local level, such private organizations as the Red Cross, the Roman Catholic Caritas League, and the Protestant Innere Mission played an important role in the relief of hunger and despair.[3] After 1929, this social insurance and welfare program had to face the impact of a general economic collapse. Unemployment rose from two million in March 1930 to six million in March 1932, and welfare recipients numbered 4.5 million by December of the latter year. Between 1930 and 1933, state welfare expenditures alone increased from 1,492 million RM to 2,383 million RM. On the eve of the Nazi takeover, 57 percent of the total tax income of the German states and municipalities was consumed by welfare demands.[4] Baden was no exception to this trend. The state's welfare recipients increased from 55,395

in 1928 to 120,023 in 1933, and the total public welfare
costs rose in Baden from 52 million RM in 1927/28 to 90
million RM in 1932/33.[5]

Two methods were used before the Nazi seizure of power
to aid the public welfare institutions. First, the national
government provided subsidies to the local welfare agencies,
allocating 150 million RM in 1931 and 672 million RM in
1932. The second method used to aid and relieve pressure
from public welfare institutions was initiated by private
welfare agencies. This program, which culminated in the
first major WHW in 1931, failed miserably since only four
million RM were collected. Consequently, the national government again had to contribute subsidies, which reached 91
million RM in 1932/33.[6]

Economic conditions after 1929 and the intensity of the
political struggle also helped to produce the first Nazi-sponsored welfare organization on the local level. Before 1933,
no single party agency controlled the party's welfare efforts,
which were designed to provide aid to destitute party and SA
members. In Baden, local and district party leaders and the
NS Women's League of Karlsruhe established the NS Wohlfahrts-
dienst which was recognized by the city as a private welfare
organization.[7] It was in Berlin, however, that the roots of
the future national NSV first emerged, again due to local
initiative. In September 1931, a small Berlin party organization was organized to take care of the management of party
kitchens. With the guidance of the Gau party's municipal
advisor, Herbert Treff, a formal NSV of Berlin was established
on 8 April 1932, charged with the responsibility for the
winter relief program and the maintenance of SA and party
kitchens for the needy members of the movement. Although the

Berlin organization had expanded to 1,680 members by November
1932, the national party leadership, for technical reasons,
did not recognize it as an official party organization. The
Berlin agency continued its local relief functions, which
included the sending of children to the countryside. But
it was not until 3 March 1933 that Hitler recognized the
Berlin NSV as the party's voice on welfare. The following
month, Erich Hilgenfeldt, a party inspector of the Berlin Gau,
assumed command of the NSV, a post he held until the collapse
of the regime.[8]

At first, the NSV had no national organization, and in
fact local and Gau party leaders, unaware of the Berlin NSV
functions, made independent party welfare plans during the
first half of 1933. Then on 25 July 1933, the Führer published
a notice by the Reich party leadership ordering the creation
of the NSV on the Gau level. All party members employed
by municipal welfare departments were ordered to join the
NSV immediately. To ensure that the NS-Frauenschaft would
not dominate the new national organization, Gau leaders of
the NSV could only be men. The first Gauamt leader of the
NSV in Baden was Fritz Argus, a Nazi city council member in
Karlsruhe and the adjutant to Baden's SS leader. Argus, who
was born on 22 August 1890 in Ludwigshafen, moved to Karlsruhe
in 1921. Before 1933 he listed his occupation as Kaufmann;
by 1934 he had become a bank employee. The SS affiliation
was symbolic of the NSV's racial leitmotif. In the summer of
1933, Argus published an article in the Führer in which he
defined the three major tasks of the NSV. First, it would
aid racially healthy Germans who had temporary economic difficulties; second, it would provide for the welfare of mothers
since they guaranteed a völkisch future, and finally, the NSV

would organize the Winter Relief Program for immediate economic relief. The basic racist welfare and breeding philosophy of the NSV was thus defined as early as August 1933. In this same article the Gau NSV leader made it clear that ill and hopeless cases should be referred to religious charity or state welfare institutions.[9]

This basic premise never changed after 1933 despite temporary shifts in focus. The NSV's activities were determined by a racial Weltanschauung and the pragmatic needs of the Nazi state. Between 1933 and 1936, the NSV provided economic relief by organizing the Winter Relief Program. After 1936, the WHW collections continued unabated, but most of the funds were absorbed by the racial and political socialization programs of the NSV. Finally, after the beginning of the war, the NSV assumed additional war-related duties. The Winter Relief Program, the racial and political socialization projects, and the war-related functions of the NSV evolved simultaneously; the emphasis placed on each program, however, shifted decisively after 1936 and again after 1940. The decline in unemployment after 1936 enabled the Nazis to pursue the racial breeding programs, but the exigencies created by the war necessitated using the NSV apparatus for evacuations, air-raid protection, and the Germanization of Alsace.

NSV ORGANIZATION

At first, Wagner did not consider the NSV an important mass party organization that could convert the population to a racial world view. In early 1935, Wagner still emphasized that the NSV provided welfare for needy party members. In

addition, Fritz Argus was not one of the important Gau clique
members or even a former party Kreisleiter. Similarly, many
district leaders of the NSV, even of the important Karlsruhe
district, had only held minor party posts.[10] An important
shift occurred in late 1934 when Wagner replaced Argus with
Philipp Dinkel, a trusted party cadre leader. Dinkel was
born in Heidelberg on 28 December 1894 and joined the Nazi
party by 1926. Employed by a bank, he had advanced from a
party section leadership post in Heidelberg in 1930 to the
Kreisleiter post of the same district by 1933. Wagner must
have realized the importance of maintaining control over this
new agency, which potentially could affect more people directly
than any other single party organization.[11]

The growing importance of the party's welfare organization was reflected by the emergence of the NSV as the dominant
private welfare organization in the state. First, the NSV
absorbed the NS Women's League's welfare tasks. Wagner did
appoint the Gau leader of the NS Women's League as assistant
director of the NSV in Baden, and Dinkel demanded that district
representatives of the NSF be invited to district conferences
of the NSV. As the NSV organization grew, however, the NS
Women's League was relegated to impotence in the field of
welfare policy and administration. Later, the NSV often
ignored the Nazi women in many important campaigns and even
rejected cooperation in vital wartime programs.[12]

The national NSV also attacked the private welfare
organizations after 1933. The German Red Cross was infiltrated in 1933 with the appointment of Karl Edward Herzog von
Sachsen-Coburg-Gotha to its presidency and the nomination of
Scholtz-Klink, the former Gau Baden Women's League leader, to
the leadership of the women workers of the Red Cross. The

religious welfare institutions were not taken over by the
Nazis, but their activities, particularly public contribution
drives, were coordinated and restricted. After 1934, the
Caritas and the Innere Mission could collect only for the
Winter Relief Campaign, and in turn they received funds from
the WHW since the genetically ill and "asocial" elements were
left to the religious charity organizations. Hilgenfeldt,
the national leader of the NSV, was also the head of the Reich
Union of private welfare agencies, which included the Caritas,
Innere Mission, and NSV.[13] By 1934, the Nazi-dominated state
in Baden (and Germany) strongly supported the NSV claim to
supervise and scrutinize the non-Nazi private welfare institutions.[14]

The growing importance of the NSV was also reflected in
the party's efforts in 1934 to recruit a mass membership for
it. Membership in the party-affiliated NSV, which was open
to all adult Germans, was interpreted by the Nazis as a positive accommodation with the Nazi regime. Although the people
who joined the NSV did not have to become members of the Nazi
party, they were applauded by the Nazi activists for their
alleged approval of the regime and their public contribution
to the Volksgemeinschaft. The NSV members were required to
pay dues, which financed the growing NSV staff and eventually
the racial breeding and political socialization programs.
To the Gau NSV leadership, the membership statistics also
played a vital part in determining the effectiveness of the
Gau organization, particularly since Gaue in Germany competed
with each other to demonstrate which could enroll the most
members.[15]

In July 1934, Baden's NSV membership ranked only twenty-
sixth in the Reich. To improve the image of Baden's welfare

organization, the Gauamt leader ordered every NSV member to
bring a new member into the organization, and he directed all
districts to enroll 4 percent of the population in the NSV by
30 September 1934. The eventual goal was to expand the NSV
membership until it included 10 percent of the total population. Baden as a whole had already reached the 4 percent membership mark by the summer of 1934, although the percentage
range for the individual districts varied from 1.1 percent in
Stockach to 6.6 percent in Freiburg. The Catholic districts
in southeastern and northeastern Baden generally displayed
low percentages of NSV members, but so did the Protestant,
rural districts in southwestern and northeastern Baden,
where the party had done very well in the elections before
1933. The only generalization emerging is that the districts
of Mannheim, Karlsruhe, Heidelberg, Freiburg, and Konstanz,
which had large urban centers, boasted the largest NSV memberships in Baden. This is not surprising, given the obvious
need for welfare in the large, urban centers where unemployment had been excessive in 1933.[16]

To increase the membership, the NSV leaders resorted to
various pressure tactics. In August 1934, authorities launched
campaigns to enroll all civil servants and public employees.
Those who refused were interviewed by the NSV, and, no doubt,
the reports were sent to the party's Office for Civil Servants.
In fact, the Amt for Civil Servants declared that through his
membership in the NSV, a civil servant was expressing his willingness to cooperate with the new regime, and it urged that
all civil servants who did not belong to the organization be
induced to join. In one case, a government official who
intended to withdraw from the NSV received a personal letter
from Dinkel urging him to remain a member and to demonstrate

a positive attitude toward the Nazi regime. The Municipal
Affiliation of Baden exerted similar pressures on municipal
representatives and mayors.[17]

The party's campaign to increase the NSV membership in
the summer of 1934 raised Baden's membership within six weeks
from 99,289 to 105,964. The campaign continued into September
1934 when the Gauamt leader ordered a special saturation campaign to enlist a larger percentage of the population. Each
community created a special recruiting unit (Werbekolonne),
which was led by the mayor and included teachers and city
council members. This unit went from house to house, and
then a special campaign staff, represented by the district
party's staff, repeated the process. By February 1935, the
drive had been so successful that Baden imposed a prohibition on the admission of additional NSV members to be able
to consolidate the rapid growth of the organization.[18]

Two years later, the membership drive was renewed by
the deputy Gau leader and became a permanent institution of
the Nazi regime in Baden. This membership drive continued
during the Winter Relief campaigns when the NSV was totally
preoccupied with collection drives. Even reliable Nazis,
like the district leader of the German Labor Front of Freiburg,
were pressured by NSV leaders and the party Kreisleiter to
join.[19] In Baden, the NSV membership rose from 142,534 in
March 1935 to 336,158 in March 1939. By December 1939, 19.1
percent of the population of Baden belonged to this party
organization, with the percentages ranging from 11.3 percent
in Überlingen to 21.8 percent in Konstanz. Three years
later, 21.63 percent of the state's population had been
induced or forced to join the NSV. This represented over 76
percent of Baden's households and approached the saturation

point vis-à-vis Baden's adult population.[20]

Since theoretically the party was reserved for an elite, the NSV provided the Nazis with an organization that could reach all Germans. Persistent Nazi self-delusion could interpret the impressive statistical results as evidence of Germany's conversion to National Socialism. The real reasons for joining the NSV ranged from opportunism to political sabotage. The Gestapo of Karlsruhe noticed that former members of Marxist organizations attempted to join the NSV and obtain positions as bloc leaders in order to pursue political subversion. In Mannheim, the party locals reported that numerous former Center party women had joined the NSV and built "black cells."[21] In another instance, a civil servant, who was pensioned in June 1937 because he was married to a Jew, attempted to recapture his position by becoming a NSV bloc leader.[22] The NSV, however, was the most important party-affiliated organization that had the potential for mass political socialization and coordination from "cradle to grave." It was funded totally by the NSV membership dues and Winter Relief contributions. Regardless of the different reasons for joining the organization, the NSV was able to win the cooperation of many Badenese who would not otherwise have supported a party-affiliated organization.

One indication of the potential impact of the NSV in Baden can be seen from its organizational structure. By 1936, the NSV of Baden was the most extensively organized party affiliate, surpassing even the German Labor Front. In July 1936, 67 percent of Baden's communities claimed NSV locals. These 953 locals exceeded both the German Labor Front and the NS Women's League, the two closest competitors. Three years later, this structure had expanded to over eleven

hundred NSV locals comprising 80 percent of Baden's communities. As early as 1935, the Baden NSV had 788 political
leaders to staff these positions. Of course, with the membership and organizational expansion of the NSV, this figure
increased dramatically.[23] In terms of pervasiveness, only
the party itself could match this structure, but it had far
fewer members than the NSV.

To coordinate this vast body of members and locals, an
elaborate NSV organizational structure developed, first on
the Gau level and after 1936 on the local level. In July
1934, the Gau was divided into four geographic sections to
increase the efficiency of the NSV and to facilitate control
over the NSV districts and locals. The local and district
NSV leaders were quickly coordinated in all fields. They
lost the independent power to issue NSV information journals
and to hold district NSV conferences. But not until after
1935 was the NSV structure streamlined with that of the party's
organization.[24]

The growth of the NSV's Gau structure is reflected in the
fact that by January 1941 the NSV's 158 Gauamt functionaries
were assigned 90 rooms in the Gau party's central headquarters.
The role of the NSV is also illustrated by the five major
departments of the Gauamt: organization, finance, indoctrination, health, and welfare. According to Ley's organizational
scheme, only the welfare department of the NSV was directly
responsible to the Reich NSV leadership; all other departments
were under the control of the party's organization, finance,
health, and indoctrination leaders.[25]

On the national level, clearly Robert Ley, Franz X.
Schwarz, and Joseph Goebbels had a significant impact on the
organizational, financial, and propaganda activities of the

NSV. On the Gau level the sheer size of the organization and the multitude of different tasks soon caused the growth of centrifugal tendencies in addition to the usual Nazi rivalries. Gau section leaders devoted themselves to their specific disciplines and naturally resented other Gau section leaders' interference. For example, the Gau section leader of Welfare and Child Care bluntly told Wickertsheimer, the NSV indoctrination leader, to keep his hands off child-care centers and kindergartens. Such conflicts racked all of the NSV Gau departments.[26] Worst of all, Gau section leaders turned to Berlin in such disputes as they began to identify with their specific departments and sought to overcome the provincialism of the Gau structure.[27]

On the Gau level, the NSV Gauamt was also confronted with the growing influence of the party cadre leaders. The Baden party's finance department assumed auditing powers over all NSV and WHW activities, and the Gau personnel office had complete control over the personnel of the NSV. In one instance, the Gau personnel office ordered the dismissal of a kindergarten supervisor because of her past affiliation with a Catholic association and her correspondence with a priest, and in another case whole Gau NSV personnel appointments were voided by the Gau personnel office because the NSV had failed to consult with it.[28] In addition, the Gau propaganda leader asserted the right to evaluate both the NSV and WHW activities. Specifically, the Gau propaganda office could refuse to grant "speaker passes" to NSV officials, thus effectively limiting their functions. Although Dinkel in 1935 declared his willingness to establish formal guidelines for cooperation between the NSV and the party propaganda office, persistent conflicts remained.[29]

The influence of the Gau party offices and even district offices over the NSV was defined by the very nature of the Gau party structure. Röhn, the deputy Gau leader, had the right to adjudicate disputes between all Gau offices. The Gau personnel and organization leaders were two of Wagner's closest aides, and their directives reflected the powers of the Gau leader. Also Wagner himself circumvented Reich NSV directives with ease. On the district level, a similar relationship existed since the Kreisleiter legally (and illegally) played a dominant role in personnel policies and district party affairs.[30] Although the Reich NSV established general guidelines, the effectiveness of the NSV organization depended to a large degree on the ability of Dinkel to obtain the cooperation of the Gau cadre organization and to adjudicate internal NSV frictions. But above all, he had to have an effective local organization to implement the various programs.

Although the NSV relied to a great degree on voluntary functionaries, by 1942 the Reich NSV had eighty thousand paid employees. Beyond the Gau NSV structure, the first professionalization occurred on the district level. The Kreisamt leaders of the NSV were predominantly male party members. In 1935, there were still four female leaders, but by 1940 only men occupied this position. Also by 1937 most of the NSV districts of Baden were led by paid, full-time Kreisamt leaders.[31] The Kreisamt corps of the NSV was extremely unstable since districts were changed or reduced and people before 1937 had to choose between the NSV posts and their careers. But like all Nazi organizations, the real disruption came during the war. By March 1940, sixteen of the twenty-seven district NSV leaders had been replaced because of military assignments. This affected all district NSV sections from finance to organization. In the following war, fifteen of the twenty-seven districts had no regular NSV functionaries, and even worse to the Nazi fanatics was the fact that many of these positions were being filled by female officials. The war, while creating new tasks, consumed a large part of the districts' professional and voluntary NSV staff.[32]

On the local level, effective organization and professionalization began in 1936. Between 1933 and 1936, financial problems had prohibited the adequate equipping of local NSV offices. But more important than the structural growth of the local NSV offices after 1936 was the introduction of NSV cell and block functionaries. In many locals of the NSV, the local welfare leader had operated either alone or with only one subordinate. The introduction of cell and block functionaries promised to increase the influence and efficiency of the NSV. Consequently, Dinkel urged his leaders to staff these new positions as soon as possible before other party affiliates and organizations recruited the valuable personnel on the cell and block level.[33] It was only natural for the NSV to attempt to find people who were not burdened by other party duties. But the NSV on the local level faced another problem. Because of the sheer size of the organization, the NSV was forced to rely on a large percentage of nonparty members for its local functionaries. In 1935, Dinkel had ordered that only party members be used as NSV officials (Amtswalter), but as late as 1937 over 40 percent of the local NSV leaders were not party members.[34] While this may have diluted the party's leadership posts, it also gave the party the opportunity to involve a large part of the Baden population in party-related activities.

WINTER RELIEF

Before it could proceed with its racial and political socialization programs, the first major task of the NSV was to
organize and administer the Winter Relief Program (WHW).
Before the Nazis seized power, Goebbels had described such
aid as "socialism of deed" and urged cooperation with the
program. On 27 July 1933, in a national conference of party
and state leaders, authority decided to continue the Weimar
WHW to provide immediate assistance to those suffering from
economic distress without increasing the financial burden on
the state. The new leaders of Germany also hoped that this
program would strengthen the regime's popularity and in the
long run act as a substitute for elections and reveal popular
sentiment.[35] The theme of the first Nazi Winter Relief drive,
which was clearly stated by Goebbels, the director, was that
both national solidarity and the quest for Volksgemeinschaft
would be exemplified through this relief campaign. When the
first campaign was introduced in Baden on 30 September 1933,
all municipalities were induced to ring their town and
church bells to usher in the new era of social harmony.[36]

Every conceivable method, ranging from public collections to mandatory wage deductions, was used to collect money
and goods. The preparations started in August of each year,
and in October the first collections introduced the WHW,
which did not terminate until March of the following year.
Single-pot meals were supposed to demonstrate German homogeneity and sacrifice. On selected Sundays, Germans were urged
to prepare only single-course meals and to contribute the
savings to the WHW. The public collection drives carried
out by the various party organizations were planned to capture

the total population and provide an image of popular support for the regime.[37]

Like so much of National Socialism, the original genuine enthusiasm dissipated because of the extreme pressures of the collection tactics. On the Day of the German Police, the SS, the police, and firemen collectors dominated the street scene. Streets were partially blocked, preventing people from passing without contributing. Even one party propaganda leader admitted by 1939 that one could no longer talk about free gifts. He warned that in the future people would avoid going into the streets during collection Sundays. Often the WHW collection drives deteriorated to the point that on a normal ten-minute streetcar route eight to ten collectors descended on the captive audience. As early as 1935, the Gau propaganda leader had demanded an end to these saturation campaigns, which threatened to alienate the population. But the situation did not improve because all of the collectors were afraid that they would not meet their quotas.[38]

These public collection tactics were supplemented by various party pressures which affected all segments of society. Beginning with the first WHW in October 1933, district WHW leaders attempted to induce civil servants to collect funds. Fritz Plattner, the leader of Baden's German Labor Front, ordered each worker to contribute one hours' salary per month to the WHW and, to ensure compliance, he decreed that the "contributions" be withheld from the salaries. Contributions by firms were increased and ensured by personal party intervention, and financial contributions from the larger industries and from Reich civil servants were sent directly to the Reich leader of the WHW.[39] Finally, a special roll collection (Listensammlung) enabled the NSV functionaries

to exert pressures on individual citizens. This same kind of
individual pressure was also used by the party's political
leaders. Local leaders reported people who refused to contribute, and one Kreisleiter published a warning in the Führer,
admonishing wealthy citizens to contribute more generously.
He reminded the "culprits" that the party knew their names
and that warnings could easily be converted into acts.[40]

The collection procedure varied little even during the
war, although new ploys such as WHW tickets for free trips
to England were introduced and special collections held for
the German Red Cross. One general development that was
accentuated by the war was increased reliance on financial
"donations" in the form of salary deductions and contributions
from firms. The income of the WHW nationwide rose by 74
percent between 1939/40 and 1941/42, primarily because of
increased contributions by companies and salary deductions.
The impact of this new emphasis was reflected as early as
October 1939, when the Gau organization leader of the NSV
lamented that the party district leaders were neglecting the
concept of sacrifice and the need to activate the people in
the collection campaigns. Instead, the Kreisleiter relied
primarily on contributions from firms to fulfill their statistical obligations, neglecting active street collections.[41]

Party district leaders could hardly be blamed for their
collection techniques since Dinkel and the WHW leaders in
general constantly demanded results and the fulfillment of
quotas. In March 1940, the director of the Trick firm in
Kehl refused to contribute to the WHW, apparently because
of a dispute with the party district leader. Dinkel immediately contacted the Baden DAF to pressure the firm. By
6 April 1940, the company had allocated 2,000 RM to the WHW,

and the director personally donated 300 RM. On another occasion in 1941 when the "Day of National Solidarity" collection was omitted, the Gau organization leader of the WHW ordered his district representatives to obtain the lost funds through additional contributions from firms. Dinkel told his district representatives that he expected the Gau to achieve the results of the previous year, despite the omission of this special drive.[42] Collections for the WHW were still held as late as January 1945, but by then public exhibitions of the "socialism of deed" were replaced by predetermined deductions and houselists.[43]

While pressures were being applied to the Baden population and to the various segments of society by the WHW, the organization benefited from a lack of competition. Churches were restricted to internal religious collections, and all party agencies were ordered to allow the WHW priority and were admonished not to compete with these activities. These policies were enforced by the party and by Wagner, who, as Reich governor of Baden, used the state's police powers to move against rival collectors.[44]

Therefore, the Nazi WHW was much more effective than the Weimar WHW. Between 1933/34 and 1936/37, the Baden WHW drives produced 31.9 million RM, most of which came from salary deductions and company contributions. Only 6.7 million RM were raised from the much-publicized street collections and "one-pot" meals. Baden's WHW accomplishments placed the state in the middle of the thirty-two Gaue. During this same period, the WHW in Baden distributed 36.4 million RM to the needy. It was only in 1935/36 that the Baden WHW became self-sufficient and one year later, as economic conditions improved, that the WHW collections of Baden produced a

surplus of income over expenditures. Over half of the needy
people in Baden lived in the four major urban centers of
Mannheim, Karlsruhe, Pforzheim, and Heidelberg. The twenty-
two districts that required aid were the urban centers in
the north and the Black Forest area in the south, while the
nineteen "supply" districts were the predominantly rural
regions in the southeast and in the northeast. The impact of
the relief program can be measured from the fact that in 1935
the WHW of Baden provided aid to 14.4 percent of the state's
population. By 1938, this figure had dropped to 7 percent,
reflecting improved economic conditions.[45]

One other important function of the WHW in Baden was to
patronize the Gau's business establishments to induce economic
revival. Businessmen who were party members usually received
preferential treatment in obtaining orders. For Dinkel, the
imperative was always to obtain as many economic orders for
Gau Baden as possible and at the same time to consider the
Gau's businesses and factories first when allocating WHW
orders. The Baden WHW gave coupon orders and repair orders
to the state's industry and artisans. It also filled 90
percent of its orders in the state, and only a Reich order
induced Baden to place 10 percent of its orders in the economically depressed Gaue of Silesia and Saxony.[46] In practice,
the Nazi theme of Volksgemeinschaft did not effectively transcend the Gau barrier.

As long as unemployment remained high and large segments
of the population suffered from economic dislocation, the
purpose of the WHW was clear to most people even if they
resented the party's pressure tactics. Contemporary travelers
in Germany in 1935 and 1936 noted that "nobody was in rags,
not a single citizen . . . the impression was one of order,

cleanliness, and prosperity," and they observed that "today
the lowliest of them are faring better than the Lower Classes
of any or all of their Allied opponents." Even as late as
1938, James K. Pollock concluded that "the Winter Help is a
magnificent example of the ability of the Nazis to enlist
the support of the whole population behind a worthwhile move
to alleviate the suffering of the people."[47]

With unemployment in Baden declining from 183,827 in
January 1933 to 50,684 in January 1937, the Nazi leaders were
forced to defend the value of the WHW. Wagner praised the
WHW as a permanent institution by emphasizing its alleged
contribution to camaraderie and Volksgemeinschaft. The Winter
Relief Program would educate the Germans and convert them to
National Socialism. The more the individual contributed,
argued Wagner, the stronger the nation would be.[48] Foreign
observers and correspondents in Germany, however, presented
a different picture of the program. William Shirer in 1941
called the WHW "one of the scandals of the Nazi regime,"
and Louis P. Lochner added later that the "bulk of the annual
collections for the Winter Relief Funds went into Hitler's
war chest." Finally, the Swedish journalist Arvid Fredborg
alleged in 1943 that "people who give good leather gloves
to soldiers often find them later on some district leader in
the neighborhood."[49]

The obvious fact was that after the initial enthusiasm
of early Winter Relief drives, the WHW lost much of its value
as a true barometer of public opinion and public support of
the regime, regardless of party views. The shallowness of
Volksgemeinschaft is revealed by the hostile reaction from
the Protestants of Donaueschingen when they found out that
the potatoes collected by the WHW in the area had been given

to a local Catholic convent.[50] Since unemployment declined
and collection results increased, the obvious question is what
happened to the money? First, the Nazi armament program
probably received some funds, directly and indirectly. The
armament coffers were aided and inflation was controlled by
the simple fact that the WHW and the NSV saved the state money
by generating funds from the public to pay for public welfare
expenses.[51] In Baden alone, 14 percent of the total public
welfare between 1933 and 1937 came from the WHW. Since wages
were kept low, the WHW provided a necessary supplement, which
came from private donations. For example, in the small village
of Bürkendorf in Waldshut, small farmers depended on supple-
mentary forestry jobs, which they could not perform in the
winter months. Since the WHW provided help, the village saved
500 to 600 RM a year that otherwise it would have had to
provide from taxes or state contributions.[52] These savings
helped the Nazi ministers in Berlin, seeking military power
and eventual expansion. For the Baden party the most important contribution of the WHW after 1936 was that it provided
funds for the NSV's racial and political socialization programs, which were intended to create the new Nazi man.[53]

RACIAL WELFARE AND POLITICAL SOCIALIZATION

The NSV provided the Nazi leaders of Baden with the vehicle
to reach the whole population, particularly segments of
society that were not attracted by the party, and to extend
the racist ideology of the Nazi true believers to the masses.
The NSV was a vehicle for the racial, political socialization of the uncommitted. Dinkel repeatedly emphasized that

the NSV focused on the genetic value of man and aided those
members of society who were of value to the Volksgemeinschaft.
The function of Nazi welfare was to supplement German reconstruction through its population programs. The NSV attacked
movies that presented childless families in leading roles,
and it offered indoctrination courses that focused on race,
world Jewry, and confessional fragmentation. In practical
terms, the NSV pursued the racial and political socialization
themes in its kindergartens, community health clinics, and
its "Mother and Child" program.[54]

As early as the summer of 1933, the Gauamt leader Argus
had declared in the Führer that one task of the new organization was to provide for the welfare of mothers, since they
guaranteed the völkisch future of Germany. In March 1934,
the national NSV Mother and Child program was officially
founded expressly to aid expectant mothers and provide children
with kindergartens and summer vacations. In the summer of
1934, the first Mother and Child home was opened in Baden to
provide rest for fruitful mothers.[55] The state's district
NSV leaders were also ordered to induce the courts to allocate portions of fines to the project. By the fall of 1934,
the WHW was sponsoring special Mother and Child collections.[56]

From 1934 on, national and state party publications
emphasized the racial functions of the summer relief program
of the NSV, the Mother and Child program. While the Nazi
welfare agency helped the needy during the winter months,
in the summer the emphasis was on mothers and children, as
long as they were "genetically valuable." By propagating
genetically healthy families, Hilgenfeldt stated publicly,
the Nazis hoped to increase the population and ensure the
triumph of the Aryan race.[57] This is precisely what the

Baden population was told and what the Baden NSV leaders
emphasized. The aid to pregnant mothers would guarantee the
immortality of the German Volk.[58]

The basic purpose of the program was pursued with fanatical stubbornness by the NSV in Baden. In 1934, Dinkel ordered
that only mothers who were still fruitful and also genetically
valuable could be referred to the NSV.[59] The constant vigilance of Dinkel, who was a former Kreisleiter and völkisch
true believer, was necessitated by frequent erosions of the
Nazi welfare principles in practice. He especially attacked
the practice of granting summer welfare care to people who
were not part of the Mother and Child program. After all,
declared Dinkel, the NSV provided only preventive care
(Vorsorge), not welfare (Fürsorge). This völkisch goal,
according to Dinkel, allowed for no confessional "brotherly
love" welfare. This same criticism was directed at doctors
who used the NSV institutions as mere recuperative homes for
mothers without being aware of the racial imperative.[60]

The NSV racial welfare program that had originated during the summer of 1934 was soon expanded to encompass the
whole year. By 1935, Baden had established 1,100 consultation
centers for mothers. Two years later the NSV centers for
mothers had expanded to 1,465 units, which provided aid to
large families and sponsored the transportation of children
and mothers to the countryside. The financial commitment to
this program increased markedly from 684,000 RM in 1935 to
nearly 2 million RM in 1936. By 1939/40, the budget had
reached 8 million RM, of which only 1.4 million RM came
from state, municipal, and industrial contributions, while
the balance was funded with WHW contributions and NSV dues.[61]
This expansion of financial and personnel commitment benefited

the Mother and Child program and four other departments of the
NSV section Welfare and Child Care.[62]

The growth of the Mother and Child program after 1934
involved the NSV in a protracted struggle with confessional,
state, and municipal welfare agencies. At first, the Baden
minister of interior ordered that there would be no usurpation
of state tasks by the Mother and Child program, particularly
when it concerned family welfare issues. Relying on this
order, the state's district representatives rejected NSV
requests to appoint NSV doctors to state consultation offices
for mothers and to grant the NSV surveillance powers over the
state's district consultation offices.[63] The state did support the NSV efforts to subordinate and supervise the maternal
consultation centers of the confessional organizations and the
Red Cross. But despite NSV objections, the state as late as
1939 held maternal consultations in confessional kindergartens,
thus inadvertently supporting confessional institutions.[64]
Nevertheless, the NSV was gradually able to assume more tasks
and in some cases was even requested by state agencies to
provide support in the field of family assistance, particularly
in cases involving young mothers. But the realities of a personnel shortage produced by the war caused the NSV in July
1941 to restrict its maternal aid stations to areas where no
public health offices existed. The NSV was forced to compromise with the Nazi-dominated state agencies, at least for the
duration of the war.[65]

Although the war interrupted the structural expansion of
the Mother and Child program, the conflict burdened the NSV
with numerous new tasks. Mothers whose husbands were in the
army needed help, and women in general had to be convinced
that it was a völkisch duty to ensure Germany's population in

a time when German blood was drenching the vast lands of the
East. To honor Germany's breeders, Goebbels ordered Mother's
Day celebrations in all party locals in May 1944. The mental
agility of the Nazis produced a curious new solution to the
quest for Lebensraum. The Nazis had always argued that Germany
needed additional living space to relieve its population pressures. In 1942, a national NSV leader, Althaus, declared that
a solution to the German Lebensraum problem could only be
produced if the Mother and Child project increased the birth
rate to supply the Germans necessary for colonization.[66]
Ironically, the racial imperatives of the Mother and Child
program enabled former enemies (English, Dutch, and Danes)
to obtain aid, while citizens of Germany's allies (Italy,
Spain, and Rumania) who resided in Baden were denied NSV
benefits.[67]

Kindergartens

The Mother and Child program in Baden provided the potential
for expanding the population by reducing the infant mortality
by 25 percent between 1928 and 1938. The kindergartens and
day-care centers, on the other hand, enabled the Nazis to
launch a massive program of political socialization. The
Baden Gauamt leader of the NSV acknowledged this in 1935 when
he declared that the task of the kindergartens and day-care
centers was to rear children in the spirit of National Socialism. This view was echoed by other Nazis who saw the kindergartens as the primary educational step in the creation of the
Nazi being.[68] The Baden NSV introduced three kindergartens
in 1934, and the number was increased the following year by

the introduction of temporary kindergartens in rural areas during harvest time. By September 1937, the Gau claimed 104 permanent and 78 harvest kindergartens enrolling a total of 6,400 children. But the most massive expansion of the NSV kindergarten structure occurred between 1938 and 1940 when Baden increased its kindergartens from around 200 to 515 permanent and temporary structures, enrolling 25,199 children who were supervised by over 1,000 paid NSV kindergarten teachers and assistants.[69] The NSV expansion had reduced the gap between the 36,000 children enrolled in the 581 confessional and 206 municipal kindergartens and the 25,199 NSV children.[70]

The NSV's conflicts with the municipalities stemmed from financial and institutional issues, while the battle against the confessional kindergartens was based on a violent ideological clash. Although the NSV's major offensive against both types of kindergartens did not occur until after 1938, as early as 1935 the Nazi organization tried to encroach on both. At first, the NSV established temporary harvest kindergartens in smaller communities, which were later converted into permanent structures. The towns and villages contributed to the salaries of NSV kindergarten teachers, and they provided them with food and lodging.[71] But the NSV faced much more difficulty with the larger urban centers, especially since they were led by Nazi mayors who felt that they could disseminate National Socialism just as well with municipal institutions. In Mannheim, the mayor refused to turn over municipal kindergartens to the NSV, since they were an integral part of the city's welfare and educational system. The Gau propaganda leader of Baden attacked an article that had appeared in the Führer, depicting the availability of NSV kindergartens for all children, by pointing out that he could not send his own

children to a NSV institution in Karlsruhe because none existed
in his neighborhood. Dinkel replied that this was the fault
of the city of Karlsruhe, which refused to build NSV kindergartens.[72]

It was not until late 1940 that Wagner announced that the
NSV would assume control over all newly constructed kindergartens in the municipalities, thereby limiting the future
expansion of municipal kindergartens and assuring the NSV a
potential dominant role.[73] But during the war the municipalities used the absence of NSV district leaders who were serving
in the army or in Alsace as an excuse to avoid financial obligations to the NSV. Worse still, the NSV Kreisamt leaders
neglected their tasks to ensure that the municipalities made
their proper financial contributions. For example, in the
district of Rastatt, the towns were obligated to pay 15,000
RM for the NSV kindergartens, but they contributed only 1,700
RM in 1940. To ensure proper payments, the NSV Gau leadership in 1941 initiated written contracts with the towns.[74]
Most revealing was the response of municipalities when the
NSV tried to encroach on their kindergartens in late 1942.
The towns reminded the NSV first to "clean" its own kinder-
gartens, which still employed confessional personnel.[75]

This charge reflected the NSV's persistent personnel
problems with the confessional institutions, frustrating
its attempts to eliminate the rival subculture. The Baden
minister of interior issued a decree in May 1936 which allowed
churches to establish kindergartens if the municipalities
requested them and the NSV was unable to fulfill the town's
request. Churches could also open kindergartens that were
operated entirely with church funds. Since the Baden churches
had over twelve hundred foundations (Stiftungen), they had

ample financial resources to expand their kindergartens. The
NSV, obviously dissatisfied with this decree, began negotiations with the Baden Ministry of Interior. At a conference
on 22 January 1938, Merdes, the head of the NSV's Welfare
Section, and the representative from the Ministry of Interior
agreed on a law that had recently been passed in neighboring
Württemberg. The proposed decree would force the state youth
office to notify the NSV of all new kindergartens that were
needed to undermine the influence of the Catholic communities
which persisted in supporting confessional institutions. In
addition, the representative of the Baden Ministry of Interior
promised to investigate confessional kindergartens for building violations and subsequently to order many dilapidated
structures to be closed.[76]

These negotiations in 1938 were followed by the rapid
expansion of NSV kindergartens until 1940. The move against
the confessional kindergartens was supported by Hilgenfeldt,
the national leader of the NSV. He predicted in April 1939
that eventually over ten thousand confessional and municipal
kindergartens would be turned over to the NSV. Two years
later Martin Bormann requested Gau leaders to transfer all
confessional kindergartens to the NSV.[77] Although some Gaue,
like Hesse-Nassau, followed Bormann's request and the Baden
NSV leader Dinkel made clear to his staff that for political
and ideological considerations one of the most important
tasks of the NSV was to win control over all kindergartens,
the final decision rested with Wagner. The Gau leader, however, was interested in preserving domestic tranquillity.[78]

In addition to satisfying Wagner's wish to avoid a
Kulturkampf in wartime, the NSV's most serious problem was
to fill the staff of institutions that were to replace the

confessional kindergartens. This problem had plagued the
organization even before the war produced further personnel
demands. For example, in 1938, the Baden NSV had taken over
the eighty-four German Red Cross kindergartens, which employed
a total of 112 confessional personnel. By 1942, forty-six
of these kindergartens still employed seventy-eight confessional teachers. Since the confessional teachers had contracts with the NSV and could not be dismissed, Dinkel devised
a plan to have them transferred to army hospitals. Hermann
Röhn, the deputy Gau leader, approved this, as long as the
population was not aroused and the action did not appear as
an anticonfessional campaign.[79]

It was much easier to arrange this transfer of a small
group of confessional teachers than to prepare for the seizure
of all confessional kindergartens. In 1941, the Baden NSV
started a massive search for potential kindergarten teachers
who would replace the confessional personnel. The Baden NSV
planned to recruit a thousand teachers and another thousand
assistants at a staggering annual cost of 4.5 million RM.
Wagner had ordered a halt to the seizure of confessional and
even municipal kindergartens until the necessary NSV personnel had been recruited.[80] But by early 1942 the Baden NSV
had gathered only four hundred girls, so Röhn was forced to
postpone the takeover of the confessional kindergartens.
Even the Gau NSV leader of the kindergarten program suggested
in the summer of 1942 that the confessional kindergartens
be replaced in steps, much as the neighboring Gau Württemberg
had done despite its wish to assume complete control at once.[81]

Dinkel maintained in late 1942 that the goal of replacing
the confessional kindergartens "would be achieved because it
had to be achieved."[82] In reality, the number of Gau's NSV

kindergartens expanded only from 515 in 1940 to 567 in 1942.
In the later year, the NSV was still faced with the task of
replacing almost eight hundred confessional and municipal
kindergarten teachers in an attempt to gain complete control.[83]
Party Kreisleiters of Baden uniformly reported flourishing
confessional kindergartens as late as October 1943. Even
worse was the revelation obtained during the indoctrination
of NSV kindergarten teachers that a majority of them still
had confessional ties. These teachers were subjected to
eight-day courses which focused on racial and population
politics, Nazi welfare, and racial history. Between April
and June 1943, Baden's NSV indoctrinated 128 teachers, of
whom only 18 percent stated their religion as a Germanic racist
"God belief." Only 1.3 percent of 105 kindergarten aids, who
were also indoctrinated, professed to be adherents of this same
"God belief," while 64 percent were Catholics.[84] Clearly the
NSV still had a major obstacle to overcome before it could
claim victory over the confessional subculture, which was
still active in socializing children.

The NSV had been frustrated in its attempts to coordinate and control the confessional kindergartens, because the
Gau leader refused to become involved in a public Kulturkampf
over a very sensitive issue in wartime, and because there were
personnel shortages. Wagner wanted to continue all opera-
tional kindergartens since they provided care for an increasing number of children whose mothers had been employed by the
war effort. Despite the NSV's frustrations with the confessional kindergartens, by 1942 it controlled 42 percent of
Baden's kindergartens. Its persistent and fanatic expansion
against the rival institutions leaves no doubt that after a
successful war the NSV would have moved with even more

enthusiasm against the confessional kindergartens. Given time,
the NSV might have indoctrinated enough reliable teachers
to disseminate the new world view and to coordinate all subcultures, since völkisch indoctrination would have started in
the kindergarten. Ironically, this would have been achieved
by the least "partified" organization of the NSDAP.

Youth Homes and NSV Nurses

The racial political socialization begun in the kindergarten
was carried to all other aspects of life from free rural
vacations for urban youths to youth homes and nurses. To
maintain its influence over the older youth who either had
lost their parents or had become delinquents, the NSV revealed
its goal of obtaining total control over the lives of the
most impressionable segments of the population (as long as
they were genetically valuable).[85] Initially, Nazi Minister
of Interior Pflaumer had made it clear to his district welfare
offices that they were not allowed to relinquish youth-care
functions to the NSV. Nevertheless, the NSV opened two youth
homes, one in 1935 in Weingarten and the other in 1938 in Lahr.[86]
The NSV attempted to define its role in the Weingarten youth-
home operations in a letter to the Ministry of Interior. It
demanded that all cases of the state's youth office be sent
to the NSV. The party affiliate would then select genetically
healthy boys between ten and fourteen to attend the disciplinary
home. Pflaumer rejected the NSV's proposals and declared
that basic regulations for the operation of the home in
Weingarten would be determined by the state. Only in financial
matters was the NSV allowed to carry a large part of the burden

since the state merely supplied 1.5 RM of the daily 2.8 RM
cost per student.[87]

Even in this field the NSV gradually assumed de facto
state functions. Children who were released from the youth
homes were supervised by the NSV to ensure that they were
reared as good Aryans by their foster parents. By 1941,
most German state youth offices had delegated the care of
such foster children under the age of fourteen to the NSV.[88]
The disputes between the NSV and the state agencies did not
disappear, and many NSV leaders were convinced that the
state's opposition represented a political reaction. In some
cases, this was true but certainly not on the state level,
where an "old" Nazi was minister of interior. Here it was
an institutional conflict that involved power and influence.
Not until the regime had almost collapsed (August 1944) did
Hitler officially decree the NSV's supremacy over the state
youth agencies.[89]

The party was much less successful in trying to replace
the confessional nurses. The NSV's attempt to establish a
community nursing system to disseminate Nazi racial myths and
its effort to eliminate the rival system again demonstrates
the NSV's totalitarian aspirations. The NSV officials of
Baden were candid concerning the purpose of the NSV nurses.
As one NSV official pointed out in 1935, a successful revolution must change basic values. Only the children and grand-
children, admitted this official, would become complete Nazis.
The NSV nurses, who were responsible for health care and education, would assure the success of the Nazi revolution by
developing "racial instincts" and furthering racial care. The
racial imperative was carried to such a degree that in 1936
the Baden NSV advised the Independent Nurses not to care for

non-Aryans even if this resulted in the temporary unemployment of some nurses.[90]

The establishment of NSV community health clinics after 1935 was opposed primarily by the confessional health institutions. The confessional nurses, who played an important part in the health care of Germany, provided the NSV with both professional and ideological competition. In 1936, confessional health clinics were still being established, particularly in villages where the population rallied behind the confessional (usually Catholic) nurses. When the municipalities reduced their contributions to confessional health clinics, the priests simply founded private foundations to defray the additional costs. In the district of Wertheim alone, five "private health leagues" were organized between 1936 and 1938. These "clubs" thrived in many towns and villages where there were no NSV nurses to care for the population.[91]

In 1935, Hilgenfeldt had to admit that there existed little real prospect of replacing the Reich's 121,000 confessional nurses, particularly since there were only 4,000 party and 41,000 "sympathetic" nurses at the disposal of the NSV. Occasionally, the Gestapo dissolved confessional community nursing stations, but the great majority of these institutions continued to function despite bitter NSV and party opposition. In some Baden districts, the Catholic consultation meetings for mothers drew such a large following that only a few women visited the state's health office. Even hostile Kreisleiters and fanatic anticlerics of the party had to admit that technically the confessional nurses were performing a superb job and were frequently superior to the Nazi nurses, both in numbers and training.[92]

In Baden by 1940 the NSV controlled 290 health clinics
which were staffed by 365 NSV nurses. But the NSV's efforts
to recruit nurses were frustrated not only by confessional,
and particularly Catholic, organizations but also by competition from the state. For example, in 1941 none of the students
of the Mannheim nursing school wanted to work for the NSV,
allegedly because state service was less restricting. Even
Dinkel had to admit that the state could rely on a well-devel-
oped machinery, while the NSV was still in a developmental
stage.[93] The war only accentuated the shortage of trained
nurses, despite Hilgenfeldt's special recruiting campaigns.
In Baden, the NSV nursing staff, which was depleted by the
war tasks and the burden of serving in newly conquered Alsace,
was not only unable to replace the confessional nurses but
was also forced to accept nurses who had only been partially
trained. Of all of the NSV racial socialization attempts,
the nursing program was the weakest.[94] The Baden NSV was
much more successful with the Mother and Child program and
the kindergartens, despite some frustrations. With these
functions, the NSV pursued its racial and anticonfessional
programs which would obviously have been reinvigorated after
a successful war. Simultaneously, the NSV served the Nazi
regime's practical interests by managing the WHW, providing
kindergartens for working mothers, and by fulfilling other
war-related responsibilities.

WAR DUTIES

During the war, the vast machinery of the NSV was used for
practical purposes. Racial Germans (Volksdeutsche) were

resettled, urban dwellers evacuated, and air raid victims
aided. Finally, the NSV had to support the German occupation
of Alsace. As early as 1937, the Baden NSV had been ordered
to prepare evacuation plans in case of war. During the next
two years, the NSV established elaborate population files,
which were used during the evacuations of 1939 and 1940. The
party district leaders had also prepared local emergency
staffs, consisting of local party leaders, the NSV, the
Women's League, and mayors to help in evacuating inhabitants
of the Red Zone, a five-mile-wide strip of land along the
Rhine.[95] In practice, the NSV assumed the main tasks. The
scope of this burden can be seen in the district of Lahr,
where the Red Zone held a population of 26,407. After the
evacuation of these people and the induction of 3,560 men
into the army, the district had only 11,575 inhabitants.
The NSV's task consisted of providing shelter and nourishment
and general supervision of Baden evacuees. This task was not
made easier by the unfriendly reaction of the host population
in Württemberg and Bavaria to the "alien" German tribe.[96]

A second major duty of the NSV after 1939 concerned the
care of ethnic Germans from all parts of Europe. Gau Baden
had hosted several hundred refugees from Poland until November
1939, when most returned to their native towns. The Baden
NSV had also provided aid to a small number of Tyrolean
evacuees. But the state's real task was to provide services
for the camps of ethnic Germans from Romania.[97] The party
prepared for the arrival of ethnic Germans from Bessarabia
in October 1940 and boasted that it would provide for all
of their material and spiritual needs; they were to be gathered in camps established by the Ethnic German Office (Volksdeutsche Mittelstelle). The NSV was assigned the task of

caring for the mothers and indoctrinating the children in NSV
kindergartens.[98]

Despite the detailed preparations, no Volksdeutsche
arrived in Baden from Bessarabia or the Dobruja. Instead,
in January 1941, Dinkel ordered NSV preparations for the
arrival of ethnic Germans from Romania. After their arrival
on 12 March 1941 in Karlsruhe, the Baden NSV soon discovered
that it had to provide extensive aid to the settlers. Most
were dressed poorly, and the Baden employers paid them such
low salaries that they could not support their families.[99]
After October 1941, Himmler transferred the Romanian settlers
to the Ostmark and replaced them in Baden with Slovenes.
Since the Baden party estimated that only 20 percent of these
Slovenes were "potential" Germans, the NSV activities in the
camps were sharply curtailed. In 1942, the Baden NSV ordered
the removal of all kindergarten personnel from the camps
since the Slovenes were considered an alien race. To the
NSV, the racial imperative for welfare had to be maintained
at all costs.[100]

As the war progressed and air raids increased, the NSV
assumed a key role in the preparations for civilian evacuations and for emergency air-raid assistance. Following the
accidental German air raid on Freiburg on 10 May 1940, Rudolf
Hess ordered the NSV to care for air-raid victims. In practice, however, not until 1942 were central plans established
to deal with the problem created by air raids. Before 1942,
the police did initiate air-raid conferences with the NSV
and other party agencies, and the party assumed the task of
providing emergency camps and of calming the population after
raids.[101] But it was not until June 1942 that Wagner established a special action committee, which included state and

party representatives. It was led by Pflaumer, the minister
of interior, who was assisted by the party's Gau staff leader,
Schuppel. In addition, Wagner ordered the creation of local
committees to aid air-raid victims.[102]

The assistance of the NSV and the party was sorely
needed, because Baden had lost a large percentage of its
regular police, firemen, and RAD personnel to the army, and
because damage from air raids increased greatly. The Action
Committee also revealed that the major urban centers in Baden
and Alsace had failed to make special air-raid preparations
as late as the summer of 1942. It also pointed out that the
NSV was the best-prepared agency, rivaled only by the under-
staffed police.[103] In August 1942, Dinkel informed Pflaumer
of the NSV's readiness for air raids. Two years later, the
Gau's NSV was prepared to provide three warm meals a day for
one-half million people during emergencies. Although in
practice unexpected air raids produced panic reactions which
threw the party's preparations into disarray, the NSV did
alleviate considerable suffering and did provide emergency
relief until state agencies could resume normal activities.[104]

Closely related to the air-raid relief activities of the
NSV was the urban evacuation program. In early 1941, Wagner
delegated to Dinkel the task of evacuating children and people
who were employed in nonessential jobs from endangered towns,
particularly Mannheim and Karlsruhe. Although the minister
of interior was responsible for the plans, the NSV carried
the major burden of providing housing and care for the evacuees. By May 1943, the Baden NSV reported that it had provided
85,000 places for the Mother and Child program, 50,830 units
for evacuees from other Gaue, and 45,948 places for displaced
workers.[105] This was indeed an impressive accomplishment.

But the burden of caring for the evacuees from Westfalen-Süd tested the NSV's organizational abilities to the limit. Until early 1943, this Gau had sent its air-raid victims to the rural parts of Westfalen-Süd. After several severe air raids on Westfalen-Süd in 1943 had made Hitler and Goebbels aware of the plight of the area, Baden was forced to become the "reception region" for an additional 87,500 evacuees. The NSV and the party not only had to assist these evacuees with housing but also help overcome the inevitable frictions that developed as urban dwellers from Westfalen-Süd were placed in rural areas. The Baden population frequently refused to cooperate vis-à-vis its guests.[106] If these problems were not enough, Gau Baden was also being inundated with refugees and party notables from various Gaue. In an attempt to protect his province, Wagner in late 1943 informed Bormann that he would "throw out" several thousand people from Baden if the mass assault of evacuees who were not from Westfalen-Süd did not stop. Wagner made it clear to Pflaumer, to the NSV, and to the party that Baden was their primary concern.[107] In order to protect the Gau, Wagner ordered the NSV to circumvent or modify Reich orders. However, despite the increased war strains and dislocations which disrupted the effectiveness of the NSV's evacuation program, without such a program "confusion and demoralization of the civilian population would have been much greater than they were."[108]

ALSACE

A major new responsibility of the Baden NSV came with the German occupation of Alsace. On 20 June 1940, Hitler appointed

the Baden Gau leader chief of Civil Administration of Alsace.
The Baden NSV was immediately called on to provide relief for
the Alsatian population, which was returning from the interior
of France. By mid-June 1940, Dinkel had already ordered his
subordinates to make preparations, and he named thirteen Baden
NSV Kreisamt leaders who would lead the NSV in Alsace. The
Alsatian operation, begun by the NSV on 24 June 1940, lasted
until April 1941. The task was to reintegrate the population
into 234 Alsatian towns the French had evacuated.[109]

The NSV staff was gathered in Colmar on 24 June, and
each NSV leader was assigned to an Alsatian district. The
Baden NSV supplied field kitchens, food, and personnel, and
the Reich allocated emergency funds. At first, the NSV plundered French depots and Jewish stores in Alsace to obtain funds
for its program, but then a procedure was established that
allowed the NSV to obtain its supplies from the army quarter-
master through the chief of civil administration. Later, the
Germans planned to charge the French government for all supplies used by the NSV.[110]

On 29 June 1940, Wagner appointed the Gauamt leader of
the Baden NSV, Dinkel, director of all private welfare agencies
in Alsace. Accordingly, the NSV had three functions to perform. In order to win the support of the population, it had
to aid in the return of the Alsatian population and lead the
relief program to alleviate burdens produced by war damages.
Most important for the future of Alsace, the Baden NSV assumed
control of the private welfare organizations in order to
introduce the racial Nazi socialization program already established in Baden. To obtain the necessary personnel, the NSV
initially relied on the Baden NSV structure from Kreisamt
leaders to nurses and chauffeurs (who all neglected their Baden

duties). The NSV also negotiated an agreement with the
Alsatian Auxiliary Force (Elsässische Hilfsdienst or EHD), an
organization of sympathetic Alsatians led by Robert Ernst,
a native Alsatian who had moved to Germany after 1918. Dinkel
and Ernst agreed that the EHD would nominate Alsatians for
the NSV although the NSV assumed exclusive responsibility
for the care of all needy, and would dispense all funds collected by the EHD. [111]

With the aid of these natives, the Baden NSV provided
care for two-thirds of the returning evacuees. The train-
loads of Alsatians arriving in Alsace in August 1940 were
greeted by the Nazi party and the NSV and provided with up to
six days of assistance. The Alsatians' reaction to the NSV
was generally favorable. The evacuees appreciated the aid
and they were relieved to be able to return to their homes.
Marie-Joseph Bopp, an opponent and victim of the German occupation of Alsace, conceded in 1945 that most Alsatians in 1940
were ready to accept the NSV but not the Nazi party. The
activities of the NSV were reported to have been effective
propaganda for National Socialism, and as late as September
1940 the accomplishments of the NSV were praised by most
segments of the Alsatian population. Many Alsatians, however,
eventually discovered that the Baden NSV was an extension of
the Baden party with all the corresponding racial and political attributes. [112]

Even before the NSV's assistance program was completed
in Alsace, it began to establish an organization. On the one
hand, this was interpreted as a positive expansion of Germandom
and National Socialism. At the same time, the burden interfered with the NSV activities in Baden when major efforts were
exerted on war-related duties and on attempts to eliminate

confessional nurses and kindergarten teachers. The NSV initiated its expansion into Alsace with a wild scramble for
properties. It discovered quickly that other party, state,
and military agencies were equally anxious to seize all available properties for their purposes. The NSV was dependent
on the Gau organization leader's permission to lease or purchase a property. A typical Nazi struggle for the properties
ensued with the NSV leaders in Baden (and even in Berlin)
urging their subordinates to obtain as much as possible, as
fast as possible. Various party organizations, like the
Hitler Youth, could appeal directly to Wagner to outmaneuver
the NSV in a contest over a desired piece of real estate.[113]
Despite these squabblings, the NSV by late 1941 had enough
properties to begin an accelerated program of racial welfare
and political socialization.[114]

Between October 1940 and April 1941, Wagner issued decrees
that dissolved the private and confessional welfare organizations in Alsace. The NSV became the heir of these institutions, although it relegated the care of cripples and the
mentally ill to the state welfare institutions. Since Wagner
had ordered the introduction of the Mother and Child program
as early as June 1940, within a year the NSV had established
over one hundred centers in Alsace to provide the foundations
for the racial welfare program.[115] In addition, the NSV of
Baden was given permission almost from the beginning to take
control of the kindergartens and nursery schools. Confessional personnel were dismissed, and Baden kindergarten
teachers were assigned to supervise the NSV expansion in
this area. By May 1941, the NSV had 241 kindergartens that
enrolled twelve thousand children. Since Alsace had only
half of Baden's population, this figure compares well with

that of Baden's NSV kindergartens. It took the NSV in Alsace only ten months to accomplish what had taken seven years in Baden. Wagner ordered the continuous expansion of NSV kinder-gartens wherever they were needed since they were a prime tool in the radical elimination of French culture from Alsace.[116]

The establishment of NSV locals was not difficult; as early as October 1940 Alsace had 734 of them. But beneath this paper structure, the Baden Nazis had to find the essen-tial local support through the expansion of the NSV member-ship. All German citizens over eighteen could join the NSV. However, Alsatians were not granted automatic German citizen-ship in 1940. Consequently, by late November 1942, only 14,723 Alsatians had joined the NSV compared with over one-half million members in Baden.[117] Also many of the Alsatians had joined the NSV as the lesser evil. For example, in one Alsatian community none of the twelve NSV functionaries was willing to join the Alsatian probationary party organiza-tion (Opferring), since it prepared for admission to the NSDAP. The party's response was to apply pressure and to prepare mass campaigns in late 1942 to induce all NSV volun-teers to join the NSV. Then, in January 1943 all Alsatians were allowed and encouraged to become NSV members, with the desired result. But the Baden Nazis indulged in the illusion that this increasing membership represented a victory of Germanism and National Socialism in Alsace.[118]

Nowhere was this tactic of applying pressures to produce an image of consensus more obvious than in the Winter Relief Program introduced in Alsace in 1940. In this newly conquered area, the WHW was both a device to measure the success of the German "liberation" and to test the viability of the Nazi organization in Alsace. Kreisleiter Fritsch of Strassburg

reminded his local leaders in September 1940 that this project would provide them with the first opportunity to prove
the viability of their locals. In reality, the party leaders
pressured firms and department stores with notable success.[119]
The combination of pressures, in addition to the presence of
large numbers of German soldiers in Alsace in 1940, produced
impressive results in the first street and Opfersonntag collections, which even surpassed contemporary accomplishments
in Baden. After the first WHW, however, collection revenue
dropped precipitously in comparison with Baden and the Reich.
This reflected both the deteriorating economic situation and
the growing Alsatian dissatisfaction with the new Nazi masters.[120]

Initially, the aid provided by the NSV in Alsace between
September 1940 and March 1941 did generate positive feelings
among the Alsatians. Each month, an average of 176,000 Alsatians received some help from the NSV during this period, and
over half of this aid came from the Baden WHW funds. But
when the NSV became involved in the Germanization of Alsace
by exchanging Basque berets and helping in the distribution
of party uniforms to Alsatian formations, much of the goodwill
dissipated.[121]

To accelerate WHW collections after 1940/41, the party
in Alsace resorted to a variety of pressures that alienated
even sympathetic natives. Ironically, the party leaders
applied these pressures to increase WHW collections in order
to display the success of their policies of Germanization
and Nazification. As in Baden, recalcitrant civil servants
and mayors were reported to the party if they refused to
contribute adequately, and large firms and their owners were
forced to contribute sizeable donations in order to escape

harassment.[122] The same pressures were applied to individuals. One district leader of the WHW in an Alsatian district, in a letter to an Alsatian who had not participated in the collections, reminded the culprit that participation in the WHW was considered a "barometer of your attitude toward Nazi Germany." In another district, the WHW leader dispatched over five hundred letters to poor contributors with the admonition that they had had one and one half years now to display their support of the new Nazi Volksgemeinschaft.[123] There is ample evidence that the Alsatian refusal to participate in the WHW was a rejection of the party. For example, in the district of Altkirch, after a girl was drafted into the DAF, her family and all of her relatives refused to participate in the WHW.[124]

The Nazi leaders had to fight against declining WHW results in Alsace in order to disguise the failure of Germanization and Nazification, particularly since such a result was interpreted as the personal failure of the individual party leaders. In Molsheim, the local party leader had circulated letters warning people that they would be outside of the people's community if they did not contribute to the WHW. On 9 January 1942, inscriptions appeared on the houses of prominent citizens. The next day, the local leader ordered the leaders of the SA, SS, DAF, NS Kraftfahrerkorps (NSKK) to form small contingents of "disciplinary units." That evening (after obtaining alcoholic encouragement) the mob, which included the party's district personnel and organization leaders, descended on selected victims. One victim was a NSV cell leader who also belonged to the Opferring, and another was a sixty-one-year-old veteran of the First World War who had won the German Iron Cross, both first and

second class.[125] Even native Alsatian Nazi leaders like
Sauerhöfer, who rose to prominence in Baden after 1918 and
returned to Alsace after 1940, failed to understand the local
population. In early 1942, he gathered all of the mayors of
the district of Schlettstadt and, angered with the low WHW
collections, informed them that Wagner was planning to send
one hundred thousand Alsatians to Russia. This was precisely
what some of the mayors told their communities.[126]

The expansion of the NSV in Alsace was a mixed blessing
to the Baden NSV in another respect. The Baden NSV personnel
serving Alsace obviously had to neglect their responsibilities in their home state. In addition, numerous low-level
officials from the Baden NSV wanted to participate in the
Alsatian experience in order to advance their careers or
assume high positions.[127] To the Baden NSV leadership and
to Dinkel, the main responsibility and interest were in Baden.
Dinkel in 1940 had ordered that the number of NSV personnel
from Baden serving in Alsace must be kept to a minimum and
local Alsatians should be substituted immediately.[128] The
problem with this solution was that some of the Alsatian
personnel were still Francophile, and many of the Alsatian
nurses, according to the NSV, failed to understand the Nazi
racial Weltanschauung. Dinkel himself was forced to request
new personnel from the Reich when the Mother and Child department discovered that the personnel of some of its districts
displayed strong confessional ties. The same thing occurred
in the NSV kindergarten department, especially in areas like
the Patois where the NSV kindergarten teachers spoke inadequate
German and usually conversed with the children in French.[129]

In November 1940, the deputy Gau leader of the Baden NSV,
Merdes, urged Dinkel to close the NSV Gau branch in Strassburg.

Merdes lamented that the deployment of thirteen Baden NSV
district leaders in Alsace had resulted in the neglect of
NSV responsibilities and tasks in Baden. He also pointed
out that the constant personnel shifts between Baden and
Alsace had produced growing friction between Gau and district NSV leaders. Dinkel agreed and stated that he did
not want an expansion of the Strassburg office of the NSV
since the NSV's main focus would continue to be on Gau
Baden. But the Berlin NSV insisted that the Strassburg
office be operated separately from the Karlsruhe office
since they directed different projects. Most important, in
late 1940 Wagner had not yet given Dinkel permission to return
to Karlsruhe.[130] Wagner had no intention of returning all
Gau party offices to Karlsruhe since he planned to create
a large Baden-Alsace Gau with Strassburg as the new Gau
center. By late 1940, the NSV had established a permanent
Gau branch in Strassburg, which eventually became the main
Gau office of the NSV of Baden-Alsace after Wagner transferred
all party headquarters to Strassburg. Wagner planned to use
the NSV and the WHW to achieve the Nazification and Germanization of Alsace despite the organizational disturbances in
Baden. He was building a new empire as chief of civil administration in Alsace, where he was responsible only to
Hitler.[131]

The Alsatian experience of the NSV (and the WHW) was
typical of the evolution of this party affiliate. The NSV
used WHW funds and NSV membership dues to provide supplemen-
tary relief and comfort for "genetically" healthy Germans.
Mothers, infants, and children received additional material
support from the NSV. The underlying purpose of the NSV, however, was not welfare but rather political socialization and

a racial population program. The main concern was for the
Nazi state, not the individual, even if the individual derived
temporary benefits. Had the Nazi regime not depressed salaries
and reduced state welfare benefits while pursuing its preparations for war, the real welfare of the population would have
been much greater than anything generated by the NSV.

"German Socialism's" basic denominators were ideological coordination and Aryan multiplication. The personnel
problems and the pragmatic needs of the Nazi regime (especially during war) limited the effectiveness of the NSV in
its attempts to pursue the "basic denominators." But the
NSV was still the most important party-affiliated organization that attempted to create mass support for the Nazi regime
and to create both an image of legitimacy and eventually a
new racial order.

11 The Party Organization, 1933-1945

THE PURPOSE OF THE PARTY

During the Nazi takeover in Baden in early 1933, leading party figures flocked to the key governmental positions of the state. Köhler, Pflaumer, and Wacker assumed control of the ministries of interior, finance, and education while Wagner became the Reich governor of Baden. On the local level, the party's district and local leaders invaded the leading municipal positions. Simultaneously, a multitude of party-affiliated organizations coordinated the professional and socioeconomic interest organizations. On the surface, the coordination and gradual Nazification of Baden's government and society appeared to be only a matter of time.

In practice, there was considerable confusion among local and regional party leaders and activists concerning the purpose of the party after 1933. According to Rauschning, Hitler predicted that the party would "take over the functions of what has been society. . . . Each activity and each need of the individual will thereby be regulated by the party."[1] Lesser party spokesmen proceeded to present a variety of definitions in the 1930s concerning the party's position in German society. Some Nazis argued for a trinity composed of the people, the state, and the party; others emphasized the party's dual functions of indoctrination and leadership selec-

tion for the Nazi state.[2] But more realistic contemporary
observers like Konrad Heiden noted that "Each Nazi is left
under the illusion that the Party's only aim is to realize his
pet theory."[3] Instead of fulfilling the diverse "pet theories"
that threatened the stability and power of the Nazi system,
the Nazi ministers coordinated the diverse drives under the
umbrella of the party.

The Nazi leaders satisfied the short-term goals of many
party activists by providing them with jobs or immediate
economic benefits. Pflaumer, the minister of interior, ruled
that members of certain Nazi affiliates, like the NS Student
Organization, were eligible for vacant police positions. The
various party affiliates also played an important part in
1933 in advancing the economic interests of their members.
For example, the League of NS Jurists demanded age limitations, job placement, and the introduction of a numerus
clausus to aid the legal profession.[4] The onslaught from
party members in 1933 was so great that Wagner finally had
to publish a notice in the Führer in July, pleading with
Baden Nazis not to turn to him for employment but to use
instead the public employment office and the Gau party's
personnel office.[5]

The Nazi ministers in Baden did attempt to aid party
members as long as their requests did not endanger the social
and administrative stability of the new state. In early
1934, party district leaders were able to nominate party
delegates to the employment offices to assist "old party"
members who were seeking jobs. Municipalities, which were
controlled by the Nazis after 1933, hired a substantial number of these old party members. The process, which was coordinated by the Gau party's personnel office, was pushed

into high gear in 1935/36 when lists of applications from old
party members were collected and referred to state and party
offices for employment. Between July 1935 and September 1936
alone, the Baden personnel office placed 1,958 people, leaving
only 300 old party members who wanted employment. Many of
these later placements and applicants had joined the party
between 1930 and 1932, and most had low educational and occupational skills.[6] The job-placement function of the party
became a permanent activity, since as late as 1939 the district personnel leaders of the party still handled job placements for old party members who wanted to use their party
connections for upward social and economic mobility.[7]

The old Gau clique members and Wagner's early associates
fared especially well after 1933. Ludwig Griesinger, the
founder of the local of Eggenstein, Karlsruhe, in 1925, was
given a paying party post in 1942 after his small business
was closed as a result of the war mobilization. Wagner's
personal friends, particularly those who addressed him with
the familiar "you" (du), could always count on the party's
support if they needed assistance. Franz Moraller, the
former deputy Gau SA and Gau propaganda leader who had joined
the party in 1923, decided to join Goebbels's staff after
1934 as leader of the Reich "culture" section. Finding this
as unrewarding as his short army career in 1939, he returned
to his native Baden in 1940 and assumed a lucrative position
as editor of the Führer and subsequently of the Strassburger
Neueste Nachrichten. Similarly, in the case of the absolutely
incompetent and corrupt Fritz Plattner, Wagner continued his
support as late as 1943, despite repeated failures. Wagner
always took a personal interest in the old party members
who had been placed in state positions, and their promotions

and demotions had to be cleared with him first.[8]

While the party leaders who assumed state positions aided some Nazi activists, particularly former members of the Gau clique, many "old Nazis" after 1933 were frustrated with the new order. In some cases, individual party members had expected too much, and consequently they voiced their frustrations by alleging that "March" opportunists and even more recent party converts were obtaining the best jobs.[9] The Gau party leaders did in fact move against Nazis who were too obvious or too demanding in their requests for party support for their personal business ventures. The Gau party manager castigated party members who appeared before state officials or private employers in their party uniforms to conduct private business transactions. Also, the Gau personnel office cautioned party members continuously that it was the task of the state employment office to provide jobs, although the Gau personnel office would relay the requests of individual party members to the state office.[10] Many party members who felt slighted in their economic or professional careers either looked for new connections (Vetterchen) or turned to corruption, particularly after the outbreak of the war.[11]

Individual party members were elevated to key state positions, and many old party members received some immediate economic or professional satisfaction, but the party in 1933 was anything but a unified structure that could direct all state and economic affairs, even if it had been given the chance. Nazi organizations from the NSV and DAF to the NS Teachers' League coordinated large segments of Baden's society. Many of these party affiliates were not even organized along party cadre lines. For example, the party cadre organization

(PO) in Baden had forty districts in 1934, while the NS
Jurists' League was organized in eight districts and the NS
Doctors' Association was divided into twelve Baden districts.[12]
This development destroyed the unified image of the party.
By 1936, the Gau organization leader was decrying the centrifu-
gal tendencies of the various party affiliates and organiza-
tions.[13]

Just as perplexing to the party's cadre leadership was
the fact that Nazis who assumed state and municipal posts
often resisted the partification of these institutions to protect their new positions and to guard the operations of state
functions. Even the Nazi ministers in the Baden cabinet in
early 1934 agreed that it was desirable to restrict the influence of the party vis-à-vis the state and municipal bodies and
to limit the influence of the party to purely personnel questions. Nazification seemed possible without unified partification of Baden's society and government. Leading Nazis in
government made administrative and judicial decisions not as
representatives of the party but as Nazi functionaries of
the state. Wagner's declaration in the Führer that the party
was the root of all action was merely a verbal compensation
for the party's lack of real administrative power below the
Gau clique.[14]

The disintegration of a unified image of the party was
also furthered by the clash between the SA and the party. In
early 1934, the SA leadership in Baden noted that the relationship between the SA and the party's cadre organization
was very strained. While the SA trained seriously two days
a week during this period for "combat emergencies," the
party's cadre organization was involved solely in political
affairs.[15] Then, at the end of June 1934 when most Baden

SA men were on vacation, the SS, acting on the orders of
Berlin (and in many cases on the basis of personal grudges)
moved violently against the Baden SA and against men who had
served the Nazi cause since 1924. Although the Gestapo had
noted in late 1933 and early 1934 that the SA of Baden was
recruiting so fast that some Socialists were allowed to join
the SA, all of the evidence suggests that the Baden SA had
been totally unprepared for any uprising.[16] Understandably,
the purge crushed the spirit of many "old" SA leaders. In
addition to the psychological shock of the purge, in some
Baden SA units over half of the new SA men (according to the
old SA leaders) did not understand the spirit of the Third
Reich, and many old SA leaders had been replaced. As late
as 1935, the relations between the SA and the party's cadre
organizations were still strained severely.[17]

What then was the party's function after the takeover
and consolidation of power? According to one interpretation,
Hitler had assigned two incompatible tasks to the party.
Hitler wanted a mass membership organization with welfare
and propaganda duties (Betreuung), while at the same time he
demanded an elitist party that implemented control tasks.[18]
In Baden, the leading Nazis did have control over the top
state and municipal institutions. But they exercised these
functions not as representatives of the party but as Nazi
administrators and leaders. Much of the activity of the party
and its affiliates in Baden before the later years of the war
focused on Betreuung, first because it was vital for the
extension of racial, völkisch concepts throughout society, and
second because the party was frustrated in its attempts to win
control over economic and administrative functions. Even if

the party had become the state, the masses would still have had to be coordinated and indoctrinated to enable the Führer to implement his imperialistic and racial schemes.

This was precisely the theme articulated by the leading Nazis of Baden in and after 1935 when it became more and more essential to redefine the party's tasks. In that year, Wagner told a party meeting in Mannheim that the party had to lead the people to National Socialism and social harmony and to preserve the belief in Hitler. Two years later, he reminded the party members of Baden that the party had provided political leadership in 1933 and assumed the key state positions. Now it was the party's function to ensure that civil servants, teachers, and the general population were indoctrinated with the Nazi ideology.[19] This was precisely what the other party cadre leaders told the Baden members. The Kreisleiter of Karlsruhe, the old party activist Willi Worch, declared in 1935 that the party's Betreuung of the population ranged from cradle to grave, while the Gau organization leader demanded from the party and its affiliates the constant surveillance and indoctrination of the people. The creation of the cell and block structure of the party, which was based on the population in general rather than on party members, had the goal of enhancing the party's Betreuung duties.[20]

During the war, the party continued its Betreuung duties, and it was well aware that Hess had reminded the party leaders in September 1939 that bad public opinion only reflected incapable party leaders.[21] Wagner urged the public to turn to the local party leaders if coal supplies did not prove adequate, and the local leaders were ordered to console the relatives of fallen soldiers and to ensure the public that the party would always provide care and protection. The Baden Gau

leader wanted the party to counsel and console the public and
help it to endure the burdens of the war. Wagner even wanted
to convert local party leaders into full-time, paid functionaries who might devote themselves completely to the Betreuung
duties, and he fought rival confessional Betreuung organizations.[22]

With the advance of the German armies, vast new possibilities emerged for the various party organizations. In 1940,
the Baden party expanded into the newly conquered Alsace and
played a dominant role in the attempt to Germanize and Nazify
the Alsatians. Then on 24 June 1941, after the German invasion
of Russia, Wagner told his party leaders that the war in the
East opened up fantastic new possibilities. The party would
now have to search for people again to assume leadership positions in the state, army, or other service, although it was
not given the task of leading these institutions. As the war
continued and victory became more elusive, the party attempted
to present a picture of a fanatical, sworn elite that would
maintain public morale. Activism and the term Kampfzeit
(period of struggle) again became popular slogans after 1942.
The party was described as the political elite of the Volk,
which had the specific task of "political leadership." In
practice, this was translated into more Betreuung, although
Kreisleiters did begin to usurp as many control functions as
possible toward the end of the war.[23]

THE PARTY AS AN ELITE

To pursue its functions as a mass coordinating body that also
provided the personnel for the political leadership of the

new Nazi state, the party had to establish its exclusive
identity, create a paid staff of functionaries, and establish
a system that would guarantee the dissemination of National
Socialism among its members and later among the masses.
Ideally, the exclusive identity would guarantee the myth of
a political elite, the paid functionaries would ensure that
the party affiliates and organizations were controlled by
the cadre organization of the party, and indoctrination of the
members and the masses would further the Nazification of the
German society.

The party's cadre organization (PO) had to establish the
party's exclusive identity not only to impress the public but
also to coordinate the party affiliates and the party members.
To counteract the centrifugal tendencies of the party affiliates, the party cadre leaders initiated a series of measures
designed to subordinate the affiliates to the PO. The deputy
Gau leader in early 1934 forbade party affiliates and party
formations to hold more membership meetings than the PO. The
following year, he issued a barrage of orders designed both
to project a unified party image and to establish the supremacy
of the PO over the affiliates. In theory, the leaders of the
PO had to be consulted before the affiliates were permitted to
post public notices. In 1939, Wagner finally forbade political cadre members (PL) of the party to accept honorary leadership posts in party formations or affiliates to avoid even
the slightest detraction from the cadre leadership, which had
the task of unifying the diverse party organizations.[24]

The PO also had to coordinate the new members who either
flocked to the party or were coerced to join after 1933. In
January 1933, the Baden party probably had about 24,000 members. By 1935 it had expanded to 78,301 members, representing

3.2 percent of the population. These members, who reflected all segments of society, were predominantly young males. Only 2,536 members were women, and almost 65 percent of all members in early 1935 were between eighteen and forty. In September 1936, the district membership rate varied from 1.8 percent to 4.6 percent of the total population. There was little correlation between the strength of the party in a district and the strength of the Nazi movement in that district before 1933. Überlingen, a southern Catholic district that had provided the party with low electoral results before 1933, claimed the largest percentage of party members in 1936. On the other hand, the district Lahr had been a Nazi stronghold before 1933, but its party membership was below the 3 percent state average. The strongest districts, with membership percentages between 3.5 and 4.6, were located in both northern and southern Baden, in Protestant and Catholic districts. The membership percentages represented more the activities of the local party recruiters than Nazi sentiment in the district.[25]

After a partial lift of the membership freeze in 1937, the Baden party expanded rapidly, reaching a total membership of 168,000 by March 1938, which constituted 7 percent of the population.[26] Although Schwarz announced in early 1939 that Hitler would allow 10 percent of the population to become party members, in Baden the state's average (with regional exceptions) remained around 7 percent until 1942 when it rose to 9.3 percent, or 224,719 members.[27] Since this last figure amounted to 14 percent of the total Baden population over eighteen, the membership drives in time diluted even the appearance of an elite party organization and severely strained the party's myth of being a "tightly knit sworn community of political fighters." The emphasis on the cell and block

structure after 1936 also tended to disintegrate the exclusiveness of the party's image. Although the most active
organizational expansion of the party occurred on this level,
the cell and block structure depended on the number of households, not party members, and many cell and block functionaries were not party members. This helped in the coordination of the society of Baden but did not enhance the image
of the party as an exclusive organization.[28] As early as
1935, some party members were enrolling their children in
non-Nazi youth organizations, and by 1937 many members did
not know the new songs of the movement. Party members not
only represented diverse socioeconomic interests but also
reflected a growing generation gap. Worse still, during
the war local membership meetings, which had occurred monthly,
were reduced to one meeting every three months.[29]

Wagner and the Gau party leaders continued to attempt
to create an image of the party, and particularly of the PL,
as a disciplined and esteemed elite. Wagner insisted on a
"soldierly troop" of party leaders who could march in close
formation like the SA and SS. To fulfill Wagner's wishes the
deputy Gau leader ordered special training campaigns to
instruct the party leaders with a knowledge of their "soldierly duties," which included marching and parading. In
addition, before Gau rallies, the Gau organization department instructed every PL concerning the smallest details of
the party's uniforms and insignias. The concern of the Gau
leaders with the appearance of the party headquarters, party
flags, and even party terminology was motivated by the desire
to present the image of a unified and strong party organization. This was frankly admitted by the party leaders of
Baden when they ordered the distribution in 1935 of Leni

Riefenstahl's Triumph of the Will, which depicted the Nuremberg
Party Congress in 1934.[30]

The superficial unity of even the party leadership core
was plagued by several realities. The Baden Gau leadership
defined political leaders as all party cadre functionaries
and those affiliate functionaries who had belonged to the
party before January 1933. But the rapidly expanding party
affiliates were staffed mostly by new party members and frequently by nonparty members as in the case of the NSV. As
early as 1935, 20 percent of the local leaders and 44 percent
of the Stützpunkt leaders had joined the party after January
1933.[31] Just as devastating was the fact that many leading
party members chose municipal, state, and economic posts. By
mid-1933, one observer lamented the depletion of the party
leadership corps. The party also lost 150 PL each month due
to deaths and transfers, since most party leadership posts
were not paid positions. Wagner noted in 1935 that the best
PL were civil servants who, of course, were transferred by
the state as the need arose. Wagner could only try to miti-
gate this by ordering that the Kreisleiter had to be consulted before civil servants who were PL were transferred.[32]

The Gau leadership's attempt to professionalize the cadre
leaders by pressuring local leaders to resign from other party
offices and by urging party functionaries to devote themselves to one party function was quickly interrupted by the
realities created by the war. Party leaders were drafted into
the army and many failed to return from combat. In numerous
locals of Baden, the local leader by 1940 was also local propaganda and personnel leader. In the district of Karlsruhe,
half of the political leaders were serving in the army in
late 1940.[33] As the war continued, some locals of Baden had

only between four and six party members left, who had little
time for party activities or duties. All party organizations
experienced rapid personnel shifts and changes. In response
to the increasing loss of PL and party members to the military,
Wagner by 1942 declared publicly that the party needed 50
percent of its members as political leaders. The practical
need for agitators and political propagandists, combined
with the losses of the war, had certainly diluted the elitist
image of the PL corps.[34]

The failure of the party to develop the image of a "sworn
community of political fighters" was demonstrated not only by
the party member who sent his children to a nonparty organization or by the unstable political leadership core on the local
level, but was revealed most by the intraparty conflicts and
frictions. Party leaders made decisions against the party
press in order to protect jobs, party affiliates and local
party leaders frequently failed to cooperate with the various
Gau departments, and the NS Women's League leaders were frequently not invited to district party staff meetings. Most
symbolic of the lack of party élan was the fact that by 1944
Gauamt leaders did not even greet party district leaders unless
they were personally acquainted.[35] Each party department and
affiliate seemed to identify with its narrow special interest
or interest group, and all thought that they could best interpret National Socialism through their organizations.

GAU DEPARTMENTS

In 1934, the Gau leadership admitted that the structure of the
party was not clear to many party members, and one year later

the Führer voiced the same complaint. This was not surprising, considering the vast expansion of the party membership after 1933. The Führer decided in 1936 to initiate a series of articles on the structure of the party's Gau offices to enlighten members and the public who, according to the Nazi paper, still thought that most problems and functions were within the sphere of state and municipal activities.[36] There was good reason to enlighten the membership about the Gau sections' duties and powers, since the political cadre organization of the Gau, and to some degree of the district party departments, was the closest thing to a unified elite that the Baden party produced.

This Gau cadre structure was solidly controlled by Wagner, although he admitted in late 1933 that he had to divide his time between his duties as Gau leader and Reich governor of Baden. His staff leader, Hermann Röhn, the former Kreisleiter of Heidelberg, informed Wagner daily about all important party affairs. Röhn, born in Heidelberg in 1902, had joined the party by 1922. After a short term in the Reichswehr, he became employed in his parents' small business in Heidelberg and at the same time found his way back to the SA and then the party by 1925/26. Röhn gradually worked his way up to district organization leader and by 1931 to Kreisleiter of his native district. After 1933, he acted as the Gau staff leader until he formally was named deputy Gau leader in 1936, a position that had been held by Walter Köhler, the minister president of Baden.[37]

Since Wagner became more preoccupied with his state duties, particularly after 1939, he allowed Röhn to make party decisions after consulting with him. After 1945 Wagner noted that Röhn had practically been the party leader in Baden and

Alsace, with the power to make important Gau personnel decisions. But Röhn was never a danger to Wagner since he had no
independent power base. Officials in the national party's
central office (Partei-Kanzlei) did not like Röhn and concluded that he was a poor deputy Gau leader who should never
be considered for a Gau leadership post. The SS leadership
disliked Röhn because he had supported the primacy of the
party's cadre organization over the SS and had created problems for the SS in Baden and in Alsace. When Röhn applied
for SS membership in 1942/43, one SS leader argued that he
was only trying to insure a position for himself now that the
SS was rising in power and influence.[38] With this kind of
opposition, Röhn was clearly Wagner's tool, particularly since
Wagner maintained a warm and loyal relationship with Hitler.

After 1933, Röhn had to coordinate twenty-one Gau departments of the party. The most important ones, those that
controlled the operations of the PO, were concerned with personnel, organization, business, finance, propaganda, indoctrination, and party courts. All except the finance department
were led by Wagner's trusted colleagues, most of whom had
been members of the Gau clique since 1925. Many like August
Kramer, Willi Rückert, Franz Moraller, and Peter Riedner had
joined the party by 1923. Numerous other Gau party departments that represented party affiliates and organizations were
led by newer party technocrats and specialists. But even here,
a sizeable number of the Gau departments (encompassing party
organizations that catered to teachers, farmers, labor, municipal affairs, and the NSV) were led by former trusted Kreisleiters of Baden. This Gau clique represented the only segment
of the party that remained relatively stable.[39]

The most stable Gau department posts were led by people

close to Wagner, mostly native Badenese who defended and represented the interests of Baden. Willi Rückert, the party
manager, held the office from 1930 to 1942, when the office
was closed. A Nazi activist as early as 1925, Rückert kept
his office despite Wagner's awareness of his administrative
shortcomings.[40] Erwin Schwörer, the Gau organization leader
who had been active in the movement since 1924, was replaced
after his death in 1934 by another "old party" activist,
August Kramer, who had held a series of important Gau posts
since 1927.[41] Similarly, Peter Riedner and Oskar Hüssy, the
Gau court leaders, had joined the party by 1923 and remained
active after 1925, as had Franz Moraller, the Gau propaganda
leader in 1933. Even the few Gauamt leaders who were not
natives of Baden or had not joined the party until 1928/29
were close friends and comrades of Wagner. Adolf Schuppel,
the Gau personnel leader and Gau staff leader, had been
Wagner's regimental comrade during the war and had risen to
a party Kreisleiter post before 1933. Adolf Schmid, the Gau
propaganda leader, was born in Württemberg in 1905. He had
cooperated with Wagner as early as 1926 in preparing a Hitler
rally in Heilbronn, Württemberg. Schmid came to Baden-Baden
and assumed the post of local propaganda leader until in 1930
he was admitted to the Gau clique when he joined the editorial
staff of the Führer.[42] These Gau department leaders were
long time völkisch activists who came predominantly from the
lower middle class.

　　Wagner and Röhn protected these Gau party leaders as
well as they could against interference from Berlin. At
first, the development of a more structured party organization on the Reich and Gau level was rather haphazard. Although
after the demise of Gregor Strasser in late 1932, Wagner had

served in Berlin in the department of organization, in early 1934 the party organization was still anything but clear to Baden's leaders. Röhn found out about the Reich organization leader's reform plans through the Reich propaganda office. In early 1934 Röhn noted that party organization questions ought to be made by the Reich organization leader and not by individual Reich party offices. Röhn's motive, of course, was to limit the influence of the various Reich party offices that attempted to extend their power.[43] Naturally, the Baden Gau leadership had to follow important directives issued by Berlin agencies, particularly when they came from Rudolf Hess, Hitler's deputy. Frequently, Wagner could protect his Gau functionaries against Berlin's interference. For example, Ley pleaded unsuccessfully with Wagner to remove August Kramer and replace him with someone more flexible. Wagner refused since Kramer, a longtime Baden party activist, was "his man" who followed orders. In the macabre Nazi system, the Gau leadership could always turn to Bormann to circumvent the decrees of many Reich leaders.[44]

Two good examples of the role and function of important Gau department leaders, one loyal to Wagner and the other dominated by a Reich agency, are provided by an examination of the Gau personnel leader and the Gau treasurer. Next to Wagner and Röhn, one of the most influential Gau party leaders in Baden after 1933 was Adolf Schuppel. Born in 1895 in Waldshut, Baden, he joined the army in 1914 and then in 1917 experienced the upheavals in southern Russia. After the war, he became a teacher, first in the district of Pforzheim and then after 1924 in the Wolfach area. Before he became Gau personnel leader in 1935, Schuppel had served as Kreisleiter and Gau organization leader. According to Schuppel, the purpose of the Gau personnel office was to direct the best men of the movement toward the party, the state, and the munici-palities.[45]

The functions of this Gau office mushroomed after 1935 when, beginning with Kreisleiters in 1936 and extending to all cadre leaders in subsequent years, the party was profession-alized either by making positions full-time, paid posts or through indoctrinations. The Gau personnel office often determined the personnel policies of other Gau party offices even if these offices had the support of their respective Reich party leaders. Of course, Schuppel monitored all party leaders for corruption and competency. With Wagner's backing, Schuppel could also remove Gau party leaders.[46] In addition, the Gau personnel office after 1938 played a major role in the training and selection of potential civil servant trainees and in the selection of candidates for the Adolf Hitler Schools, which in theory would provide fanatical political leaders for the party and the state.[47]

Schuppel also assumed the position of Gau staff leader in 1942 after Wagner refused to accept the promotion of the Gau business leader Willi Rückert. One historian has argued that the introduction of the Gau staff leader by Bormann in 1942 provided for a de facto party division on the Gau level by preventing the excessive accumulation of power by the Gau leader. In Baden, this was not the case. Baden had a staff leader as early as 1933/34, and Schuppel, the new staff leader, was one of Wagner's closest associates and trusted friends. Wagner selected Schuppel and gave the Gau staff leader the tasks of coordinating all party agencies and handling all party affairs with state and Reich agencies. Wagner had already appointed Schuppel personnel director of the chief

of civil administration in Alsace, a post combining party and
state duties in personnel matters. And in Alsace Wagner was
responsible, for the most part, directly to Hitler. In Baden's
case, the Gau staff leader was simply an extension of the Gau
clique that Wagner trusted with the management of the Gau
party.[48]

The Gau personnel office was responsible for the selection
and supervision of Gau political leaders who met Wagner's and
Röhn's requirements to the last detail. Wagner told his district personnel leaders in 1937 that he wanted "political
soldiers" who were simple, uncomplicated men. He particularly
warned against the overestimation of knowledge, and above all
he rejected individualists.[49] These criteria Wagner also
tried to apply to the central Gau party center, which by May
1939 employed 52 paid political leaders and 126 party employees. The number leveled off slightly by August 1939 when the
political leaders dropped to 36 and the employees to 108. Most
of the political leaders were in their twenties and early
thirties, while the employees were mostly between the ages of
seventeen and thirty-four. Walter Gädeke, who was hired in
1934 as Wagner's adjutant, emerged after 1940 (as Wagner's
trusted personal adjutant in Alsace) with considerable responsibilities only because of the liege relationship with
Wagner.[50]

Wagner, the former army officer, ran his Gau central
headquarters ruthlessly. Affairs in the Gau house were so
closely monitored that no one was allowed to smoke there, and
all Gau functionaries were forced to participate in sports.
Gauamt leaders who missed conferences or meetings received
proper scoldings. Wagner, Röhn, and Schuppel also attempted
to coordinate the personal lives and activities of the party's

political leaders. Röhn noted in 1942 that some party employees in the Gau house did not reflect the party's racial image
and requirements, and he demanded that Gauamt leaders devote
more attention to this issue.[51] Before the war, Schuppel
had demanded that all PL of the party marry to conform to
party guidelines. In March 1944, Wagner finally ordered that
no single party member could become a full-time employee of
the party or its affiliates. During the war, the Gau leader
made certain that his professional Gau functionaries experienced military service so they might become ideal political
soldiers.[52]

One major criterion for obtaining a position as a full-
time PL of the Gau or Kreis party organization had always
been a long party career. "Old fighters" dominated the Gauamt
and the party's district leadership positions after 1933.
But in 1933, many old fighters had been attracted by state
and municipal careers while the party's functions had increased
dramatically. The party therefore established schools to
train the new German elite for both the state and the party.
Beginning in 1933 and culminating in 1940, the party established the Ordensburg, the National Political Training Institutions, the Adolf Hitler School, and Rosenberg's Supreme School.
The Adolf Hitler School (AHS) was the party's most important
attempt to transcend the traditional German elite. The early
plans of December 1936 revealed that the Nazis wanted to
attract more rural and socially disadvantaged children since
both groups contributed only an insignificant percentage to
the traditional elite-oriented German high schools. In January
1937, Ley and Schirach introduced the new AHS as a third alternative for public schoolchildren. Instead of entering a
trade school or the high school, children after six years of

public school could enroll (if nominated and selected by the
party) in the AHS, which provided a six-year course in racial
indoctrination and physical training in addition to the traditional curriculum. After graduation and fulfillment of the RAD
and military duties, the AHS student could then continue his
studies either at the Ordensburg or a regular university.[53]

In October 1937, the Gau Baden personnel office issued
five guidelines for AHS candidates. They had to be recommended by the Hitler Youth and their parents had to be active
in the völkisch movement. Other qualifications dealt with
the student's racial, genetic, and physical characteristics.
After a student had been nominated by the local party and
Hitler Youth officials, and the Kreisleiter and Kreis personnel leader had reviewed the recommendations, the Gau personnel office and the Gau Hitler Youth leadership made the selec-
tions. In the spring of 1938, the first sixty Baden AHS
candidates participated in a training camp. Of these sixty,
ten students were selected by Röhn and Schuppel to attend an
AHS.[54]

The Baden party never received AHS graduates in significant numbers to supplement its political leadership corps.
The first class was allowed to graduate early in 1942 but
all volunteered for the army. Of the nine Baden graduates
in 1943, only four chose careers as party political leaders.[55]
By late 1944, only seven AHS students graduated despite
Wagner's boast several years earlier that the party's goal
continued to be the production of ample leadership personnel
to help accelerate the mobilization of the state's resources.
By 1944, Ley had to rely on crippled war veterans who were
party members as future political leaders.[56]

The AHS also failed to provide an alternative to the

traditional German elite educational system. In 1938, only
16.6 percent of the AHS students had parents who were farmers
or rural and industrial workers, and by 1940 this percentage
had slipped to 12.9 percent. The traditional educational system had begun to feed more and more students to the AHS. By
1940, 43.5 percent of the students came from high schools and
17.5 percent from middle schools. This meant that the traditional educational elite again played a key role even in the
party's school system.[57] The increased reliance on the traditional middle-class, educational elite to furnish students for
the AHS was also reflected in the composition of the AHS's teaching personnel. In 1939, the potential AHS teacher had to have
received his Abitur (high school diploma), attended an Ordensburg for one and one-half years, and been enrolled in a university for two years. Since most AHS teachers entered the army
after 1940, the search for replacements soon focused on the
universities. By 1942, the party realized that most of the
AHS teachers would have to be recruited from the universities,
and in some instances it was even willing to modify physical
and athletic requirements to accommodate the new trend.[58]

The Nazi party simply did not replace the traditional
educational elite, and the party schools did not really provide the party with many leaders. On occasions, a party
school produced a Kreisleiter for the Gau as in the case of
Rheinhold Lawnick, a teacher at the Ordensburg Sonthofen. But
Lawnick became Kreisleiter of Weissenburg, Alsace, primarily
because he had been born in Hagenau, Alsace, in 1902. Wagner
consciously used Alsatian "emigrés" to staff some of the key
party and state posts in Alsace to facilitate the coordination of the newly conquered area.[59] For the most part, the
Baden party had to rely either on its old fighters or on the

new party functionaries and bureaucrats who had emerged after
1933.

While the personnel office provided for the coordination
of the party's political leaders, the Gau treasurer supervised
much of the party's organizational and administrative evolution
through his control of the purse strings. His position rivaled
that of Röhn and Schuppel in terms of influence and power, and,
unlike these two, after 1933 he did not belong to the Gau
clique which supported Wagner completely. In fact, he was
frequently in conflict with district and occasionally with
Gau party leaders. Until October 1933, Erwin Schwörer, a
member of the Gau clique and a völkisch activist since 1924,
was the Gau treasurer. After he became Gau organization leader
in late 1933, he was replaced by Peter Clever, who had not
joined the party until August 1931 and was by occupation a
bookkeeper. In May 1941 he in turn was replaced for reasons
of health by Franz Schwarz, the national treasurer of the
party, who merely notified Wagner of the new appointment.
The new Gau treasurer, Karl Sievers, had been Clever's assistant, and like his former chief he was a white-collar employee
who had not joined the party until early 1932. Wagner was
frequently frustrated with both of these post-1933 appointments, since they took orders directly from Schwarz. Only
on 20 March 1945 did Wagner triumph completely when he ordered
Sievers to serve in the army.[60]

Peter Clever made it clear to all party leaders in 1934
that only Schwarz could replace him and that no district and
local party treasurer could be removed without his permission.
The Gau treasury became a tightly bureaucratized agency long
before the cadre organization. For example, by 8 February
1936, the Gau treasurer had issued twelve circulars for that

year, but by the same time two years later he had circulated
twenty-three orders for the first four weeks of 1938.[61]

The Gau treasurer's powers revolved around his control
of finances. Until the Reich treasurer established firm salary
ranks in late 1937, Clever negotiated salaries with the individual employees of the Baden party. Furthermore, he simply
refused to approve party contracts unless the party departments obtained his permission prior to the conclusion of
financial contracts. All district and local party leaders had
to obtain the Gau treasurer's authorization before spending
more than 50 and 10 RM, respectively. After January 1938, the
district party treasurers received budgets each month that
they were not permitted to exceed, and even Gauamt officials
had to obtain the Gau treasurer's permission for such minor
purchases as periodicals.[62] The Gau treasurer could force
other Gau offices to comply with his directives even if these
Gau offices had received contrary instructions from Berlin.
On occasion, he refused Wagner's wishes after Schwarz had
issued contrary directives. Behind the Gau treasurer stood
one of the most powerful party leaders in the Reich, Franz
Schwarz, the national treasurer of the party.[63]

The Gau treasurer's powers are best illustrated by an
examination of his relations with Adalbert Ullmer, the district leader of Buchen. Ullmer, who was born on 26 August
1896, in Reicholszheim, Baden, became a völkisch activist
in 1926 and two years later was local leader of his native
community. A smith by occupation, Ullmer rose in the party
structure until he occupied the mayoral and Kreisleiter posts
of Buchen. Ullmer was appraised by Wagner as a good district leader for a rural district but one with limited general
knowledge. Despite these limitations, Ullmer did well finan-

cially since he received a salary as mayor of Buchen (397.5
RM) and an additional income as a member of the Reichstag
(600 RM). When Wagner urged Ullmer in 1937 to accept the
full-time district post of the party, he promised him that
he would not suffer financially. Wagner could not deliver on
this promise since the Gau treasurer subtracted Ullmer's
Reichstag salary from his salary as party Kreisleiter. In
effect, Ullmer was receiving 220 RM less a month than he had
earned as a mayor.[64]

Ullmer, furious at the Gau treasurer, reminded Clever
that he had a responsibility to the welfare of his family and
that as an "old party" member he had rights as well as duties.
Ullmer's controversy with the Gau treasurer occurred in 1938
after both Wagner and Röhn had given their support to Ullmer's
position; indeed, Röhn urged Ullmer to press his case force-
fully since he did not want him to be worse off as a Kreisleiter than he had been as a mayor. Yet all Röhn could do was
to promise that Wagner would seek Hess's intervention.[65]
When Wagner tried to order Clever to grant Ullmer a special
salary advance, Clever turned to Schwarz for approval. Schwarz
not only rejected the order and obtained Hitler's support,
but he also made it clear in an internal note that the Gau
leader had no right to order the Gau treasurer to pay money
to anyone. In 1941, the issue was settled when Schwarz established a new salary schedule for Ullmer that was 150 RM
higher than the previous one but still below what it would
have been had the treasurer recognized Ullmer's full Reichstag salary.[66]

The Gau treasurer also could interfere in the personnel
policies of the districts since he controlled the finances.
In a report to Berlin in 1937, Clever noted that he had "the

last word" in questions dealing with the employment of party
personnel. A specific example again involves Ullmer's district. In August 1938, the rural district of Buchen had lost
one of its paid functionaries to the army. Although the
Gau personnel office had requested a replacement in October
1938, Ullmer discovered that the Gau treasurer had dissolved
the district propaganda position of Buchen. Ullmer argued
that the local leader of Buchen, Erbacher, was also the district treasurer and the district propaganda leader. Should
the district propaganda post not be reactivated, Ullmer
warned, he would order Erbacher to lay down his office as
district treasurer. "I am responsible for my district, not
the Gau treasurer," declared Ullmer. The Gau treasurer merely
informed the Gau personnel leader that he would not reply to
such a letter; after all, Clever knew exactly who controlled
the purse strings.[67]

KREISLEITER

Below the Gau offices, the party's political cadre organization relied primarily on the district party leaders and the
district leaders of personnel, organization, propaganda,
finance, and indoctrination. Originally, most of the district cadre members served voluntarily, and only after 1937
did the district leaders and subsequently the key district
functionaries become full-time, paid party employees. Consequently, there were continuous personnel changes. Between
1936 and 1939, only four district organization leaders remained in their original posts. This same trend can be
found in all district cadre departments. Between January

1938 and May 1939, twelve of the twenty-seven district propaganda leaders left their original posts, and between 1937 and 1942 only 30 percent of the 1937 district leaders of the office for municipal affairs remained in office.[68] Adding to this problem of instability was the fact that the Gau leader ordered the Kreisleiters to staff their key district offices with old party members who were young, a combination that became increasingly scarce. In fact, many noncadre district leaders had not joined the party until 1933.[69]

In January 1939, in an attempt to create financial stability and strengthen the district cadre organization, Wagner announced that all district party leaders and district personnel, organization, finance, and propaganda leaders would become full-time paid, party employees. This also applied to district indoctrination leaders if the district had a population over two hundred thousand. The districts also obtained paid employees ranging between two for districts with fifty thousand people to sixteen for districts with at least three hundred thousand people.[70] By May 1939, Baden's twenty-seven districts employed 134 Kreisamt leaders and 144 employees. Most of the political leaders who earned good salaries (up to 365 RM) were between twenty-five and forty-two.[71] If the Gau leader had envisioned a permanent, young political cadre organization on the district level, he was rudely disappointed by the exigencies created by the war. For example, between September 1941 and September 1942, seven of the twenty-one district positions in the Freiburg Kreis witnessed personnel changes. This included the key party cadre posts of personnel, organization, propaganda, and indoctrination.[72]

The Kreisleiter corps reflected an even more fluid situation in Baden and in the Reich. Between January 1933

and January 1935, 35 percent of Baden's district leaders left
their posts to staff the Gau offices and to a lesser degree
Reich and state posts. In addition, after 1936 Baden's forty
districts were reduced to twenty-seven, eliminating additional
Kreisleiters. By 1937 only 25 percent of the original party
district leaders remained in office, and only seven of these
served in their original districts.[73] Although during the
war Wagner insisted that the Kreisleiters serve short terms
in the army, not one was killed in action by late 1944.
Instead, most personnel changes occurred because of reassign-
ments to other party or state offices. As a result, between
1937 and 1944 over half of the district leadership posts
received new Kreisleiters.[74]

A survey of the Kreisleiter changes between 1935 and
1938, a critical period that witnessed the professionalization of the position, reveals that only one Baden district
(Bruchsal) avoided personnel changes. After Hess had ordered
that the Kreisleiter positions would become full-time party
posts, half of the Baden Kreisleiters who decided to resign
their party posts chose to remain with their mayoral positions, particularly if they were well educated and the mayoral
post was in a major town. A third of these leaders who left
their posts selected Gauamt positions. The rest who left
opted for district agrarian posts of the Reichnährstand, and
one became the police chief of Karlsruhe. In general, then,
some of the major towns of Baden and several important Gauamt
posts, including personnel, DAF, NSV, the Office for Civil
Servants, and the Gau Agrarian Office, were occupied by former
Kreisleiters.[75]

The Kreisleiter who selected mayoral and Gauamt posts
experienced upward social and economic mobility. The example

of Ullmer has already illustrated the lucrativeness of a mayoral post, particularly if it was combined with a Reichstag
seat. Even more revealing was the example of Otto Blank, a
bank clerk apprentice who served in the army in 1917/18 and
then became manager of his parent's small textile business
in 1924. After joining the party early in 1930, his enthusiastic support of the Nazi movement enabled him by the end
of that year to become Kreisleiter of Schopfheim, his native
district. After 1933, his fanatical political zeal was converted into a quest for wealth. As mayor of Schopfheim, he
earned 8,000 RM, as president of the Chamber of Commerce he
received an additional 6,000 RM per year, and finally, as
the owner of a sawmill he earned 15,000 RM a year. The former Kreisleiter also attempted to expand his economic ventures into Alsace after the German occupation of this territory. Little wonder that the district leader of Lörrach
lamented to the Gau party leadership that Blank was no longer
active as a Nazi.[76]

The reduction in the number of districts in 1936 and
the professionalization of the Kreisleiter corps allowed
Wagner to purge the most notorious incompetents like Dr.
Theo Rehm of Emmendingen. Rehm was born in 1896 in Nethur,
British India, and became a medical doctor in 1922. Not
until 1930 did he join the party in Baden. After the Nazis
seized power, Rehm (with the help of SA leaders) beat up SA
men who missed duty, and he even ordered the local leader of
Waldkirch to collect material against the rival Kreisleiter
of Waldkirch, Maximilian Kellmayer. In 1934, the Baden party
court suspended Rehm for one year, but Wagner, who needed old
party district leaders, appealed the sentence. Not until the
reduction of Baden's districts could Rehm be eliminated and

Kellmayer moved to a mayoral post. Unfortunately, this left
the new district leader, Konrad Glas, with the problem of
coping with two former Kreisleiters in his new, expanded district.[77]

The requirement that he recruit district leaders who were
old party members after 1933 caused Wagner to resort to a
variety of tactics. He assured potential candidates that their
salaries would be equal to that of a state district official
(Landrat).[78] In at least one case Wagner turned to an old party
member who had been expelled from the party before the seizure
of power. Hans Knab, the founder of the Eberbach local and
a long-term völkisch activist, had been ousted from the party
in 1930 because of conflicts with his local superiors, although
he had never attacked Hitler or Wagner. The Baden Gau leader
was able to appoint Knab to a mayoral position. After Knab
(with the help of Wagner) was again admitted to the party in
1934, he was given a party district leadership post.[79]

For the bulk of the new Kreisleiters Wagner had to rely
primarily on local leaders and Kreisamt leaders and eventually
on former Gau clique members who had left Baden but wanted to
return to their native state. Wagner alone made the decision
who would be Kreisleiter and where he would be deployed,
although he relied on the recommendations of trusted Gauamt
leaders.[80] To prevent inbreeding, the local and district
department leaders who became Kreisleiters were usually
appointed to different districts. For example, Emil Rakow,
who was born in 1907 in Ulm and joined the party in October
1931, became local leader of Meersburg. After 1933 he became
first a Kreisamt leader in Überlingen and then in 1936 district personnel leader in Mannheim. Finally, after his military service, he was appointed district leader of Konstanz.

These new Kreisleiters included teachers, Kaufmänner, skilled artisans, and craftsmen who represented the lower middle class. No industrial workers were represented, and only one listed his occupation as Fabrikant, although he was only a small businessman. An important change after 1933 in terms of the social profile of the Kreisleiter corps was that most of the district leaders who were farmers left their posts to staff state and party agrarian offices. Half of the six well-educated professionals (doctors and Ph.D.s) had left their party district posts to become mayors. The Kreisleiter corps in many ways reflected the pre-1930 profile of moderately educated, lower-middle-class representatives except that now many of the farmers had left their posts. The new district leaders also had longterm commitments to the völkisch cause since many had belonged to various paramilitary and völkisch organizations long before they joined the party.[81]

Despite the instability of the Kreisleiter corps, the district leader was a key cadre leader of the party. Wagner scheduled more conferences with the district leaders than with the Gauamt leaders, and Kreisleiters were ordered to serve for short periods in both the Gau headquarters and on Hess's staff. The Kreisleiter coordinated party affairs on the district and local levels and directed the public campaigns of such party affiliates as the NSV.[82] The district leader's control over the cadre personnel of his district was recognized by the Gau personnel leader, who noted that district leaders were directly responsible to Wagner.[83] This allowed district leaders to purge potential rivals whom they disliked and who were a threat because they possessed more intelligence or training.[84] When a district leader decided to move against a local leader in his area, he was usually successful. For example, Fred Himmel, the local leader and mayor of Mosbach and a former Nazi student leader of Heidelberg, had received good recommendations from two Kreisleiters before 1940. After the new district leader of Mosbach in 1941, Emil Rakow, had accused Himmel of a lack of discipline, luxurious living, and of using personal acquaintances to escape military service, the Gau personnel office made sure that Himmel was drafted by the army in 1941.[85]

During the war, the influence of the Kreisleiter on party affairs and a wide variety of public affairs increased dramatically. The district leaders became responsible for increasing the public's determination to continue the war, and the various "cultural events" and political rallies were as much directed to the public as to the party members. Above all, they constantly intervened in state affairs with impunity. They supervised foreign workers and interfered in evacuations and armament production.[86] Some leaders ignored military summons with the declaration that they did not have to justify or explain their actions to the army. Others attacked military representatives in public for the failures of the army. In some instances, a Kreisleiter could scold a business manager and threaten him with confinement in a concentration camp.[87] The Baden district leaders also expanded their powers vis-à-vis the Gauamt leaders. After they had proceeded to change directives issued by Gauamt leaders, Kramer had to remind them that the Gauamt leaders issued all directives as Wagner's representatives. But as late as 1944, Gauamt leaders were complaining that their district representatives were not informed properly by the Kreisleiter.[88] During the war, district leaders appointed Kreisamt leaders over the objections of Gauamt leaders, and they ignored visiting Reich party leaders with impunity.[89]

Many of these activities were based on the Kreisleiter's initiative and frequently violated Gau directives. The records reveal persistent admonishments by the Gau staff leader and the deputy Gau leader. They warned the Kreisleiter to refrain from interfering in state affairs, to desist from interfering in court cases and to stop the deployment of workers. Röhn and Schuppel, of course, had urged the district leaders to aid in mobilization efforts, in the recruitment of labor, and in the collection of materials for the war effort. But the Kreis-leiters were supposed to report their findings to the Gau party and refrain from issuing orders to the state or the business community.[90] The problem was that the deteriorating war situation made it easy for these party leaders to act as radical agents for victory, and Wagner was inclined to support his Kreisleiters in this time of crisis.

Wagner himself had exhibited behavior that had stressed personal decisions or police power over established judicial practices.[91] This was clearly illustrated in the case of Ernst Bäckert, the Kreisleiter of Stockach. Bäckert had become a district leader in 1930 and remained in the position after relinquishing his mayoral post in Messkirch. In late 1944, he became intoxicated and wrecked a car, killing one of its occupants. The judicial forces proceeded with the legal case against Bäckert, but Wagner as defense commissar refused to permit the trial. When the prosecutor went to the scene of the crime to investigate, the Kreisleiter simply boycotted the meeting. Even the SS, which had sent a technical expert to the place of the accident, was aghast at this behavior since it turned public opinion against the Nazi leadership.[92]

Not until February 1945 did Martin Bormann finally suspend Bäckert, pending the outcome of the court case.[93]

The organization of the party reveals a complex structure of conflicting authorities and agencies. One observer, who visited the Munich party center and noted the cumbrousness of the organization, concluded that the "party today is one of the most complicated, disorderly overlapping amorphous organizations in the world."[94] In 1934 and 1935, as the party proceeded to establish its bureaucratic cadre organization, many Badenese who were willing to accept Hitler detested the "little Führers." Many of the state's party leaders escaped criticism only because of the public's fear of reprisals.[95]

Even within the party cadre organization there were violent conflicts over personal prestige and financial matters and interests. One case involved the local leader of Hettingen (also the local farm leader), who had been a party member since March 1928. In June 1933, he resigned from his party offices because of his disillusionment with the Kreisleiter, who, according to this party leader, should be hanged. In protest, he took Jews on motorcycle rides, and in his pub he displayed a sign welcoming Jews, Christians, and pagans. Another case involved the district farm leader of Oberkirch, Wilhelm Krieg, who was removed from the office in 1937 after he attacked the Kreisleiter.[96] In both cases, the party rebels had been old party members who were disappointed or disillusioned with the little Führers. "Old" party members also rebelled when their financial interests were at stake. For example, Hanns Valentine Manger, a party member since 1923 and former deputy local leader of Mannheim clashed with the new Kreisleiter, Dr. Reinhold Roth, after 1933. Roth removed Manger from the city council in 1935 because he demanded

competency, not just a party career for this post. Manger
was furious and initiated a party court case against Roth
because the loss of the post cost him 60 RM a month in benefits.[97] The party organization was riddled with such conflicts, which diminished its effectiveness. It was only the
crisis of the war that allowed the party cadre organization
to usurp functions and powers that had never been granted
legally in peacetime.[98]

PROPAGANDA AND INDOCTRINATION

Leading Nazis were political decision makers, but the party
cadre organization, as a unit, had no such function. However,
the party did have a collective responsibility in the dissemination of National Socialism to both members and the public
in general. Ernst Bramstedt has argued that in Nazi Germany
propaganda included both agitation and indoctrination. Above
all, he evaluated Nazi propaganda as a "tactical weapon to
achieve short-term rather than long-term goals."[99] Certainly
Nazi propaganda in general attempted to articulate the völkisch, racist ideology of the movement and to defend short-term
policy changes implemented by the Berlin regime. But the party
had two distinct agencies that were responsible for agitation
and indoctrination campaigns. The duties of each were poorly
defined. The party's propaganda office was concerned primarily with influencing the masses while the indoctrination
office's task was to saturate the party members and functionaries with the Nazi ideology and to act as a unifying agent
for the diverse party organizations and party affiliates.

The Gau propaganda leader was also Gau representative of

the Reich Ministry of Public Enlightenment and Propaganda,
combining the party and state agencies established to manipulate the masses. The two Gau propaganda leaders of Baden
after 1933, Franz Moraller and Adolf Schmid, had joined the
party by 1925, and both had belonged to the Gau clique before
and after 1933. The Gau propaganda office proceeded to centralize the holding of party rallies and public demonstrations,
and it issued schedules for major party celebrations. These
party events were designed to present a unified image of the
party and to inundate the public with symbolic Nazi themes.
The harvest celebration, including public marches and dances,
was intended to propagate the idea of "urban and rural entities marching hand in hand."[100] These objectives characterized
many of the party rallies and events. During the winter, the
focus of the party was often on internal affairs. Beginning
with the spring, the Gau propaganda leader initiated public
party rallies to reach citizens who usually did not attend
party events. Since most people were not able to participate
in the party's Nuremberg rallies or even the Gau rallies, the
party introduced district rallies where the leading party and
state members addressed the faithful and spread the message
to the public.[101]

The purpose of these party rallies was to impress the
public with the unity and strength of the party. But the
party's propaganda leaders were also ordered by Wagner to
focus the party's propaganda on current events. This involved
the management of "elections" and plebiscites and the defense
of the shifting Nazi foreign policy. Every party agency, from
the personnel offices to the Gau treasurer, used the party
organization to provide the desired results.[102] As Hitler's
foreign policy became more reckless, the party tried to allay

public fears and attempted to create public support. In November 1938, the propaganda campaign was directed at "Spiesser" pacifists (bourgeois pacifists) who had talked about rest and consolidation, and between 24 March and 2 April 1939, the Gau propaganda leader attempted to explain the German need for Lebensraum and the "restoration" of Germany's natural borders. Finally, when Hitler attacked Russia, the party ordered public rallies and party meetings, with the theme "Führer orders, we follow," to throw the support of the public behind this mad adventure.[103]

The party's indoctrination department (Schulung) had the task of permanently extending the völkisch, imperialistic ideology, first to the party and subsequently to the general population. Two important realities affected the function and purpose of the party's indoctrination office. First, the Nazis took over a structured German society by coordinating the technically competent teachers, civil servants, and judicial experts. And second, the party in 1933 was still concerned with eliminating alien subcultures. This made it imperative that the party membership clearly understood the party's ideology and that society was gradually converted to this Weltanschauung.[104]

In May 1933, Ley, the Reich indoctrination leader, produced an outline for the indoctrination of the party and the DAF. Ley admitted that only a few of those who had joined the party in the last few months understood National Socialism. In addition, he pointed out that the Volk still had to be converted to National Socialism by the party. Every party cadre leader (Hoheitsträger) must become both a leader and an "educator" of the people. The Gaue were advised to establish indoctrination offices and to "educate" the local

leaders once a month, using <u>Mein Kampf</u>. The DAF, which was
also controlled by Ley, was ordered to utilize the NS Factory
Cells to educate the workers, who admittedly still distrusted
National Socialism. This general draft was followed in June
with firm orders to the Gaue to establish Gau indoctrination
offices to carry out Ley's plans.[105]

The first Gau indoctrination leader was August Kramer,
who also held the post of Gau personnel leader. In late
1934, Kramer was relieved by Heinz Baumann, a native of
Pforzheim (1905) who had belonged to the <u>Wiking Bund</u> until
he joined the party in 1930. Baumann, a vicar by training,
was in turn succeeded by Wilhelm Hartlieb in 1937. Hartlieb,
a teacher, was born in the right-wing stronghold of Eichtersheim in 1898 and had joined the Free Corps movement and the
Nazi party by 1923. Although he became active again in the
Nazi party in 1927, because of the government's crackdown on
Nazi civil servants, he did not join officially again until
March 1930. All of these men were longtime <u>völkisch</u> activists.
Hartlieb, who held the office until 1945, had led the Gau
leadership school from early 1934 to fulfill Wagner's demand
for a "year of education."[106]

Since Hartlieb was involved with indoctrination from
1934 on, his views of National Socialism are particularly
revealing. In a draft curriculum for internal party indoctrination, Hartlieb in 1936 presented a clear formulation of
his concepts of the <u>völkisch</u> ideology. He started with the
<u>völkisch</u> ideas of race, blood, and soil and proceeded to the
demands for pure blood, living space, and economic autarchy.
Hartlieb declared that National Socialism was primarily a
matter of faith, not reason, although he conceded that reason
and faith were not mutually exclusive. Hartlieb was willing

to rely on "scientific" knowledge to defend the movement's racism. Once one understood the v̈olkisch racial concept, everything else followed clearly. This concept conceived settled ancient Germans, not barbarians, and it also demonstrated the evils of liberalism, Jews, Marxism, and political confessionalism. Above all, argued Hartlieb, Nazi ideology was totalitarian, encompassing all fields of human endeavor. And it was the task of the party to instill this belief into the German people and to prepare them for the unavoidable, difficult struggle for life.[107] There is no evidence that Hartlieb and his predecessor did not take this philosophy seriously.

To establish an effective indoctrination agency that could disseminate the Nazi ideology, the Gau indoctrination office first had to centralize the party's various indoctrination efforts, since the party affiliates were initiating their own programs. Early in 1934, Kramer extended the influence of the Gau and district indoctrination offices over all party affiliates and established the right to indoctrinate officials and civil servants.[108] In December 1934, Baumann, with Wagner's approval, issued directives that established the Gau Indoctrination Office's (GSA) supremacy over all political and ideological programs. The affiliates merely prepared the organizational framework for indoctrination, and no one was permitted to discuss Nazi Weltanschauung without the permission of the GSA. Only the Hitler Youth, SS, and Reich Labor Service remained exempt from these controls. The SA agreed to the GSA's supervision of its indoctrination programs. By late December 1934, the Führer could boast that unified party schooling had been established in Baden.[109]

Centralization was, however, far from complete. Rather,

it was an ongoing process, complicated by the various interparty rivalries. Baumann in 1935 forbade his district indoctrination leaders to hold other party posts, and in addition
he ordered them to attend the Gau school for training. Eventually, most of these posts were occupied by teachers since
the positions did not pay a salary before 1939. These district
indoctrination leaders were also given the power to ban affiliate indoctrination programs if they had not been approved.
The term Schulung was limited to the party's ideological indoctrination and could not be used by private clubs or other
rival organizations.[110] Despite these efforts, endemic rivalries continued. The national conflict between Rosenberg and
Ley was avoided on the Gau level since Rosenberg appointed
Baumann as his Gau representative. But disputes with such
party agencies as the SA and the Racial Political Office constantly plagued the structure. As late as 1936, Hartlieb
lamented the lack of a unified presentation of Nazi ideology
and the uncertainty about which personnel were intended for
indoctrination programs. Above all, every organization felt
qualified to indoctrinate, and indoctrination became a tool
for everything, admitted Hartlieb.[111]

Typical of the GSA's frustration was its attempt to disseminate the Schulungsbrief, the official ideological organ
of the party. In September 1936, 2 percent of Baden's population subscribed to the journal, and Baumann was determined
to increase the percentage to show the effectiveness of his
organization. Instead, he discovered that the local party
organizations, the DAF, and numerous other groups refused to
cooperate in this subscription drive. When Ley issued the
order that the Schulungsbrief was the only official ideological organ of the party and demanded that all PL and new party

members subscribe to it, Baumann joyfully concluded he now had
the authority to force the "leading men of the districts" to
cooperate.[112] But Ley's order in the Nazi party's administrative jungle gave Baumann no guarantee that the various
party organizations would obey.

The GSA had more success in running the political cadre
members through the indoctrination programs, primarily because
Wagner strongly believed in this "educational" duty of the
party. Since all Gau indoctrination plans were first submitted to Wagner for approval, they reflected the Gau leader's
authority.[113] The Gau personnel leader also demanded that
all Gau staff members attend a Gau school every two years for
refresher courses. By March 1936, Baden had established five
Gau schools and twelve district schools. Later financial problems forced the dissolution of the district schools, causing
the districts to revert to weekend courses and local evening
sessions for most of the party functionaries, but the political
cadre members who were drafted by the GSA for Gau indoctrination courses did depend on the positive evaluations from these
schools for successful party careers. In this way, the GSA
could play a part in maintaining the ideological cohesiveness
of the cadre organization.[114]

The GSA's attempt to spread the Nazi ideology to the
masses involved two techniques. First, the office supervised
a variety of clubs and organizations that disseminated parts
of the official ideology. For example, only half of the district leaders of the Reich League for Calisthenics in Baden
were party members, but the GSA had to approve the nomination
of these district leaders since they supervised "education"
rallies.[115] The GSA of Baden approved district leaders of
the League for Calisthenics even if they were devoid of

political interests, as long as they could "educate" German
citizens according to Nazi concepts. This education involved
primarily physical exercise, German songs, and discussions of
racial issues.[116]

The second technique was the establishment of public
education centers and the expansion of purged public libraries.
In 1935, Baumann stressed the importance of indoctrinating
the population by using the NS Public Education Program
(Volksbildungswerk), founded in August 1934.[117] When the
Reich Indoctrination Office in Berlin ordered indoctrination
expanded in 1937, the GSA quickly discovered that, because
of limited resources, it had to depend on the municipalities,
whose cooperation, considering their own financial problems,
was frequently withheld.[118] Instead, the party was much more
successful in making its ideological whims felt through cen-
sorship and the purge of libraries, because the police implemented these policies. The Gau literary expert advised
schools, libraries, and municipalities about books and "contaminated" libraries. The purge of Marxist and "Jewish"
literature in Germany was so effective that in 1941 Bormann
had to urge the party to search Alsatian libraries for such
literature and to safeguard it for the party. In early 1941
the party admitted that the retrieval of such material was
important since otherwise one had to travel to Moscow in order
to study Marxism.[119]

While the party naturally attacked Marxism and "Jewish"
literature, in its directives after 1936 it focused mostly
on the surviving confessional publications and libraries.
In 1937, the party's anticonfessional attack was aided by
the personnel union of the district posts of indoctrination
and Literary Supervision (Schriftumspflege). Before this

the GSA had been responsible only for the organization of the
libraries while the Literary Supervision Department had scrutinized their political and ideological content.[120] The GSA,
realizing that a direct attack on the church would merely
alienate the peasants, urged the expansion of public libraries
(Volksbüchereiwesen). The task was complicated by two factors.
First, confessional libraries could be purged but they could
not be forced to admit party literature. Second, the confessional libraries were numerous, and in 1939 the Archbishopric
of Freiburg alone spent more money on church libraries than
did all of the towns of Baden.[121] The GSA had to rely on the
party's municipal department to lead this attack. In 1936,
only six new public libraries had been established, but beginning in 1939, a massive construction effort began. Within a
year, 535 libraries had been opened, mostly in villages and
communities with populations between five hundred and two
thousand people. While the confessional libraries still far
outnumbered the party-sponsored ones, a significant beginning
had been made to undermine the confessional influence in the
small communities.[122]

These efforts by the GSA to indoctrinate the public were,
of course, supplemented by the various party affiliates like
the NS Teacher's Organization and NSV, which frequently carried the major burden for the indoctrination of the public.
But the GSA's primary function was internal schooling. The
war presented this party agency with a multitude of new tasks
in Baden and in newly conquered Alsace since Wagner ordered
the continuation of indoctrination during the war in order
to revive the spirit of the "time of struggle" before 1933.[123]
The themes never varied much, with Jews, liberalism, and
political confessionalism providing the major targets for the

party's venomous attacks.

The various new tasks after 1939 were staggering because so many regular political leaders were being replaced by new men who had usually not been active in party affairs. On occasion, the party had to rely on nonparty members as the military draft took its toll. After the party organizations for teachers and civil servants were closed in 1943, the GSA obtained the additional duty of indoctrinating the teachers and civil servants of Baden.[124] In addition, Rosenberg burdened the indoctrination office with various celebrations and commemorations that traced German history from Charles the Great to Hitler.[125] Furthermore, Himmler requested aid in the indoctrination of German settlers from Romania, who had to be introduced not only to the racial concepts of National Socialism but frequently also to proper German.[126]

On closer examination, the elaborate new indoctrination schemes of the GSA after 1939 reflected an abundance in organizational preparations and a minimum of actual implementation. The party festivals introduced by Rosenberg were not even celebrated in the majority of Baden locals, and the district weekend indoctrination conferences became merely general staff meetings where the various district staff leaders issued proposals and the Kreisleiter established general guidelines.[127] The settlers from Romania, who were much too preoccupied with work, quickly lost interest in such programs. The party's indoctrination office blamed this on "Slavic influences," despite the obvious fact that many of these settlers worked from dawn to dusk. After the Romanian Germans were replaced by the Slovene settlers in 1942, the GSA, like the NSV, officially ended its commitment to the settlers.[128]

The strain of the war caused the gradual disintegration

of the GSA. The shortage of personnel was felt as early as 1940 when the GSA lost six of its eleven full-time functionaries to the army. By the summer of 1942, only two officials were left, one of whom was Hartlieb, who had to commute between Karlsruhe and Strassburg. By August 1944, Hartlieb with the help of three female secretaries was supposed to administer district and local indoctrination, run the Gau school, and implement Rosenberg's cultural programs. Finally, in September of the same year, the Gau school was closed and the remaining personnel of the GSA assigned to other party offices.[129]

The same kind of disintegration, of course, had occurred on the local and district levels. On the district level, the GSA was administered more and more by a variety of party functionaries ranging from the NSV leader to the propaganda leader. In addition, most of the speakers of the districts who were supposed to disseminate the official ideology were in the army. On the local level, the indoctrination office remained either vacant or in effect was not administered because the local leaders carried so many other party functions. In the district of Bruchsal, in the summer of 1944, half of the locals failed to send party representatives to the district indoctrination conference where they were supposed to receive instructions.[130]

The party members and functionaries also lost interest in the indoctrination programs during the war. Party officials had dreaded attendance at the Gau school long before 1939, and during the war the GSA could only induce 50 of the 200 staff members of the Gau headquarters to attend indoctrination sessions.[131] Hitler Youth and party members were called away from important armament projects to participate in training or indoctrination programs, so many party leaders regarded

the indoctrination campaigns as futile and even destructive.
Out of desperation, party leaders began to refuse to honor
summonses for the indoctrination of their party personnel,
or they limited them to the summer.[132]

Given the constant personnel shift and burdens of war,
it is also little wonder that many district indoctrination
leaders began to report the lack of ideological homogeneity
and commitment among party members.[133] In part, this arose
from the resentment many party members felt at the GSA's violent anticonfessional campaigns. Even before the war, male
party members who had attended a GSA program encountered the
strong and determined opposition of their wives to the party's
antireligious doctrines. Religious party members were particularly offended by the coarse anticonfessionalism of
Hartlieb. The Gau indoctrination leader addressed one meeting
with a speech on the law of nature, which he defined as perpetual conflict. Hartlieb emphasized that this law could
not be overcome "by locking God up in a box and on occasion
devouring him."[134] The strains of the war had only reinvigorated the old subcultures and diluted, if not erased,
many of the GSA's accomplishments.

FORTIFICATIONS AND VOLKSSTURM

The war provided Gau party leaders with vast new powers and
responsibilities, although increasingly, party personnel had
to be relinquished to the military. Gauleiter Wagner could
legally utilize the offices of Reich governor and chief of
civil administration in Alsace to issue a great variety of
orders to state and party officials. Other party leaders

simply usurped a multitude of powers. For example, some party
functionaries planned to inspect private factories and gather
all "loafers" for special work battalions.[135] In addition, the
consolidation of newspapers in Baden, necessitated by war conditions, actually benefited the party press, since the independent papers were combined with (and subordinated to) the
party papers.[136]

In early 1942, the Baden party had to surrender 25 percent
of its political leaders who had been granted military defer-
ments.[137] Furthermore, Wagner continued to demand the release
of additional party personnel to the army and the armament
industry. The deputy Gau leader, Röhn, who relinquished personnel only reluctantly, cautioned that the party organization
first had to be simplified before personnel could be released
for war-related duties. As late as 1944, the party continued
to display little understanding for armament efforts and on
occasion refused to vacate premises needed for the war
effort.[138] The inevitable trend, however, was toward the
disintegration of the elaborate structure of the party.

These personnel problems did not deter the Gau and Kreis
party leaders from assuming new responsibilities. In 1944,
the party was ordered to build fortifications and to assist
in the establishment of a popular militia (Volkswehr). Wagner
assigned the task of coordinating the personnel and materials
necessary for the construction of fortifications to the Kreisleiter. The DAF recruited workers while the local party leaders
assembled the self-employed and professionals for fortification
duties. Before the Allied advance, these improvised defenses
did little more than hamper agricultural and armament production as early as September 1944.[139] The party's efforts to
establish a militia also failed to contribute substantially to

the German war effort. After Bormann had made Gau and district party leaders responsible for all militia activities,
Röhn appointed district staffs consisting of the district
party's staff leaders and of all wounded officers who were
party members.[140] In October, the Führer reminded the population of the holy cause of defending the Reich against the
barbarians, and it pointed to the example of the successful
German struggle against Napoleon.[141] In the same month, local
party leaders presided over a series of rallies in an attempt
to generate enthusiasm for the Volkssturm, while Wagner assured
the public that the militia would have a real military function. Although military oaths were administered to the first
units in the major urban centers of the state in November,
the party reaped few rewards. According to party reports,
the Volkssturm only produced either mass depression or apathy.[142] Both the party's efforts to create a militia and to
build fortifications had actually undermined further the
prestige of the NSDAP.

A final task of the party on the eve of the regime's
collapse was to inundate the population with propaganda campaigns in order to maintain public morale. As late as 1943,
Wagner and his Kampfzeit (period of struggle) associates,
Walter Köhler, Albert Roth, Franz Moraller, Karl Pflaumer,
and Hermann Röhn, still called for German living space in the
east, although they never failed to remind the public that
the war was a struggle against Bolshevism which threatened
social harmony and racial purity.[143] In 1944, particularly
after the invasion of the Allies in the west, the Baden party
finally noted that this was a war for survival. To convince
the public of ultimate victory, the leading Nazis promised
new weapons and new military techniques, and as the Allies

continued to advance the party stressed the advantage of "inner lines of defense." The final tactic was to remind the Badenese of Frederick the Great and even of the Thirty Years' War and to present the state's population with the alternative of total resistance against Americanism and Bolshevism or suffering a traitor's death. [144]

The population of Baden knew well the realities of the military situation, and even the party noted the collapse of the German army in 1944. German troops, returning from the west in late 1944, were often undisciplined, drunk, and frequently defeatist. In Mannheim, one soldier publicly replied to the party's claims of eventual victory with the question whether anyone had ever seen a mouse eat a cat. Wagner's attempts in September 1944 to reorganize these stragglers into effective fighting units had little practical effect. [145] Public defeatism also spread to many party members. No one wanted to participate in another Thirty Years' War, especially since the public and many party members realized that the war was ending. Letters from soldiers who served in the east (which the public trusted more than official pronouncements) revealed that all was lost. [146]

Above all, the public of Baden rejected the propaganda which was disseminated by Goebbels, Wagner, and Moraller, and one SD report noted that people bitterly complained that "if speeches could win wars we would certainly win." [147] In fact, the most persistent public criticism was directed against the party and the party's leadership as the population directed its frustrations against the visible party structure. The Baden public and even some party members began to admit that National Socialism had been Germany's momentous mistake. People also voiced their opinions that Gau district party

leaders should never have been permitted to interfere in war-
related matters. While the public esteem for the retreating
army was low, it still held the army in higher esteem than the
party.[148] As early as 1943, the public began to articulate
the view that the "small party Führers" were a collective disaster. By 1945, much of the population's criticism was
directed against Wagner, and all SD reports from Baden confirm
a general public dislike of the Gau leader. In early 1945,
while Wagner was visiting Bruchsal to inspect war damages,
people openly attacked him with "go on in and take a look you
privileged glutton [Grossfresser]." The SD branches in Baden
concluded that Wagner's removal would do much to raise public
morale.[149]

Whatever powers and prestige the party organization had
accumulated after 1933, the realities of defeat and war burdens completely discredited it. Public criticism also reveals
that the party had failed to become synonymous with German
society. Socioeconomic organizations were coordinated and the
party's affiliates penetrated social entities, but the subcultures survived and continued to disseminate their values.
Furthermore, party criticism of the public's neglecting party
functions in the 1930s reveals that many traditional patterns
of Baden life continued under the Nazi regime. The party's
long-term attempt to change basic sociocultural values by
initiating a massive system of Betreuung through such agencies
as the NSV and through indoctrination programs required time
and above all peace. The extension of the Kreisleiter's powers
in 1943/45 may have increased his control over society, but
the party now only became a target for the population's dis-
satisfactions. Yet, in reality the party never produced such
a unity. The party's cadre organization battled the affiliates

over spheres of influence, and the Kreisleiter tried to eliminate the influence of the Gauamt leaders. The party was torn
apart by both vertical and horizontal struggles, which affected
also the dissemination of the official ideology. These conflicts actually helped the survival of subcultures, from the
churches to the civil service. In the end, most symbolic of
the party's failure to become synonymous with German society
was the fact that popular discontent in Baden was directed
against Wagner the Gau leader and not against Wagner the Reich
governor.[150]

12 The Expansion and Function of the Baden Party in Alsace, 1940-1945

THE VÖLKISCH MOVEMENT

The German occupation of Alsace revealed not only the true
nature of National Socialist domination in Europe but also
demonstrated the function of the Baden party in the attempted
Nazification of the "German" Alsatians. As the party assumed
the task of absorbing the Alsatian population into the German
Reich, it was able to operate under revolutionary conditions
similar to those that had existed in Baden in 1933/34. Alsace
provided the NSDAP with vast new opportunities for renewed
party activism and the advancement of party careers. The
establishment of the Nazi party in Alsace and the admission
of Alsatians into the party could not conceal the fact, however, that even the "German" Alsatians were being dominated
and exploited by the Baden Nazis with the aid of a small group
of collaborators.[1]

Alsace had been annexed but never really absorbed by the
new German Empire after 1871. Following the First World War,
many Alsatians greeted the advancing French troops enthusiastically. The realities of French centralism, however, soon
dissipated the joy and created the Alsatian problem (malaise
alsacien), which plagued France's new territories during the
interwar period. French propaganda publications, of course,
reported confidence, optimism, and tranquillity in Alsace.[2] In

reality, the atmosphere was reflected in a letter by a French
lieutenant who was stationed in Alsace in 1933. He reported
to Paris that most French officials in Alsace found service
in the province unbearable. The lieutenant maintained that
the Alsatians were either anti-French or indifferent. Because
of the cultural isolation of French officials in Alsace, he
appealed to Paris to limit service tours in Alsace to two
years.[3]

The basic problem was the integration of Alsace into
France after 1919, and the four issues that dominated Alsace's
political life were administrative reorganization, schools,
religion, and the language dispute. The attempted centralization of Alsace began in January 1920 when the French introduced French civil servants and functionaries and declared
French the language of instruction in public schools. But
the real political explosion in Alsace was produced primarily
by the attempts of Edward Herriot to introduce the laic laws
in Alsace in 1924. After this, many Alsatian political parties, and particularly the Catholics, began to focus on the
defense of Alsatian privileges. Although these parties were
generally identified as autonomists, there were several categories. A small group of separatists around Karl Roos, Paul
Schall, Renatus Hauss, and Hermann Bickler of the Landespartei
favored union with Germany. They received support from the
two Communists, Hans-Peter Murer and Karl Hueber. Another
political group in Alsace was headed by the Abbé Haegy, who
led the Catholic group against French centralism. He had
opposed Berlin's Alsatian policies before 1918, and he continued to defend Catholic interests after 1918. Finally,
most Alsatians were probably regionalists, favoring a decen-
tralized administration.[4]

Most Alsatians wanted to maintain the religious and cultural privileges of the area. With the assumption of power by the Nazis in Germany in 1933, the Alsatian parties returned to an even stricter regionalism. The Communist paper Humanité and the bourgeois paper Strassburger Neueste Nachrichten (SNN), as was to be expected, warned the Alsatians of Hitler's designs on Alsace. In response to the Nazis' religious policies, the Alsatian Catholics naturally opposed any movement that favored union with Germany, and the Catholic spokesmen denounced the neoheathendom of National Socialism. In general, after 1933 most political parties in Alsace that favored regionalism or even autonomy clearly disassociated themselves from the principles enunciated by the Third Reich.[5]

A minority of the Alsatian political spectrum did develop and articulate völkisch themes even if pleas for annexation to Germany were not announced openly. Until 1928/29, these Alsatian "Nazis" cooperated with most Alsatian autonomists. Together with other political leaders of Alsace who had fought French centralism, the native völkisch activists were brought to trial in 1928 in Colmar. Like the early Baden party, the Alsatian Nazis developed from a "proworker" and a "propeasant" movement. After 1940 many of these Alsatian völkisch activists assumed Nazi party posts in their native state.[6]

The "prolabor" group, represented by the Communists Hans-Peter Murer and Karl Hueber, was most active in Lower Alsace (Bas Rhine). Murer, a native of Lorraine, obtained employment in Strassburg in 1918 in a train depot but was fired in 1920 for anti-French pronouncements. Between 1920 and 1928, he became active in the Communist party, and after 1928 he was elected to the French chamber as a Communist deputy. Karl Hueber, who was born in 1883 in Gebweiler, Alsace, was jailed

by the French in 1923 for his opposition to the Ruhr occupation. One year later, Hueber was elected to the French parliament as a Communist deputy, and in 1928 he also became
mayor of Strassburg. After 1929, the Communists in Alsace
split over the issue of autonomy. Hueber eventually formed
the Alsatian Worker and Peasant party (in 1935), which rejected
the internationalism of the French Communist party. One year
later Hueber's party was overshadowed by the French Communists
when it won only 5.8 percent of the vote in Lower Alsace and
.5 percent in Upper Alsace. In 1940, Murer and Hueber were
the only two Alsatian deputies from Lower Alsace who collaborated with the Nazis. Murer became a district party leader
in Alsace, and Hueber assumed the leadership of the Strassburg
local of the DAF.[7]

A much more influential völkisch wing in Alsace was the
"propeasant" movement. Like the Hueber Communist party, it
was most powerful in northern Alsace, particularly in the
rural Protestant districts, where it won 9.4 percent of the
vote in the election of 1936. The origins of the Landespartei
can be traced to the 1925 publication of the journal Zukunft
(Future), which demanded complete autonomy. In 1926, René
Hauss with the aid of Hermann Bickler's Heimatbund, a Strassburg students' organization, formed the Landespartei, which
absorbed the extreme separatists. Its most important leader
Karl Roos, who was born on 7 September 1878 in the district
of Weissenburg, had attended the universities of Freiburg and
Strassburg. After the war had interrupted his teaching career
in Cologne, he devoted himself to the separatist movement in
Alsace. In 1939, the French imprisoned and subsequently
executed Roos, providing the Nazis with an ideal martyr.[8]
Roos's associates cooperated closely with the Germans in

1940 and formed the basis for the native Alsatian Nazi movement. In 1941, Paul Schall, a völkisch activist and an associate of Roos, maintained that the Landespartei, which cooperated with the Hueber Communists, represented "naturally
evolved Nazism," particularly after the increased growth of
anti-Semitism in 1933.[9]

One of the clearest formulations of völkisch ideas in
Alsace before 1940 was articulated by Hermann Bickler and his
Jungmannschaft (Young Men's Club). Bickler was born on 28
December 1904, and obtained his primary and secondary educa-
tions in Lorraine. Between 1923 and 1927, he studied law
in Strassburg where he eventually practiced his profession.
In Strassburg, Bickler formed a student club that advocated
Alsatian autonomy. As early as September 1925, he attended
a Nazi rally in Fürth, Germany, which reinforced his völkisch
views. In 1932, Bickler not only became an active member of
the Landespartei, but he also formed the Jungmannschaft,
which was converted in 1937 into the Elsass-Lothringer Partei
(Alsace-Lorraine party). Bickler later claimed that this
group, comprising members between eighteen and forty-five,
focused first on peasants and later on workers.[10] The program
of the Alsace-Lorraine party, published in May 1938, espoused
the usual anti-French autonomy themes. But the program went
further because it attacked liberalism, capitalism, Marxism,
and Jews much as the Nazis on the east side of the Rhine had
done during the Weimar Republic. The program also stressed
favorite Nazi themes like social harmony and the unity of
blood.[11]

Bickler maintained active contacts with the German Foreign
Institute before 1940, but he did not correspond with the Baden
Nazis since in December 1940 he introduced himself to Wagner

for the first time. After 1940, Bickler like Schall and many
"Western Nazis" revealed his deep hatred of France. He supported enthusiastically a proposal by von Loesch, a notorious
Pan-German, to partition France. To these Western Nazis France
was the most opportune territory for German colonialism, surpassing even the vast lands of the east.[12]

While Bickler, Roos, and Schall prepared the groundwork
for the future public Nazi movement in Alsace, Friedrich
Spiesser voiced the first direct Alsatian appeal to Hitler for
the German annexation of Alsace. As early as the turn of the
century, the Pan-German League had supported Hans Spiesser,
Friedrich's father, in his efforts to expand and study German
culture in Alsace. The denunciations of the French influence
in Alsace and the demands for the extension of Germanization,
articulated by the Pan-Germans in 1900, could not have been
surpassed by the Nazis in 1940. They were identical in vehe-
mence and content.[13] Friedrich Spiesser, who was born in
1905, studied in Germany until 1925. After his return to
Alsace, he became associated with Bickler and later with the
Jungmannschaft. Although Spiesser's role after 1940 was
limited to the völkisch Hünenberg publication firm, he did
help to prepare the völkisch groundwork for the future collaboration with the Germans. On 10 September 1939, while
visiting in Germany, Spiesser urged Hitler to annex Alsace-
Lorraine after a victory. Later on 26 January 1940, he wrote
a letter to Robert Wagner, praising a speech the Gau leader
of Baden had presented in Freiburg on 14 January 1940, in
which Wagner had referred to the French occupation of German
soil. Spiesser approached the leader of Alsace's "brother
tribe" with requests to explain the predicament of Alsace-
Lorraine to the rest of the Reich.[14] This theme of "brother
tribe," which also had been articulated by a small but active

völkisch group in Alsace, was utilized by the Baden Nazis after
1940 to justify the Baden domination of Alsace.

THE ALSATIANS IN BADEN AND GERMANY BEFORE 1940

Baden was affected immediately by Germany's loss of Alsace in
1918. First, the new border arrangement was considered a
"Chinese Wall" by the Baden government as it proved to be so
detrimental to the economic interests of the state.[15] The
severance of economic ties between Alsace and Baden destroyed
a symbiosis that ranged from the tourist trade to agriculture.
From Kehl to Freiburg, Baden cities and communities lost former customers and markets.[16] Second, by April 1921, about one-
third of an estimated total 110,000 registered refugees from
Alsace-Lorraine had settled in Baden. This created a sizeable
and permanent audience in Baden for propaganda and literature
dealing with Alsatian issues.[17]

Many of these frustrated Alsatian émigrés became involved
with radical völkisch groups, including the Nazi party in
Baden. For example, the head of the Baden Schutz- und Trutzbund in 1921, Karl Ernst, had been born in Weissenburg, and
the leader of the Nazi local of Karlsruhe before November
1923, Hugo Kromer, was a native of Strassburg.[18] Although
most of these Alsatians were eventually absorbed by Baden's
society, many of these émigrés assumed important Nazi party
posts in Baden both before and after 1933. These "émigré
Nazis," who became active party speakers, Hitler Youth leaders,
and Kreis leaders in Baden, were for the most part young,
lower-middle-class representatives from such cities as Strassburg, Metz, Mühlhausen, and Weissenburg.[19] Two such Alsatian

émigrés, who joined the Nazi party in Baden before November 1923 and later became Kreis leaders in Baden and Alsace, were Willi Worch and Heinrich Sauerhöfer. Both served as Kreis leaders in Alsace after 1940, although Worch returned to his Baden post in 1941. Worch was born in Strassburg in 1896, and Sauerhöfer was a native of Weissenburg. The former came to Karlsruhe in 1918 to practice his trade of brewery master while the latter completed his education in Baden and then became a Protestant minister. Both of these young, displaced Alsatians, who naturally considered themselves Germans, became involved in Nazi activities by 1922/23 in order to articulate their grievances.[20]

However, there is no evidence of an active "Alsatian wing" in the Baden party. The Baden party was active in disseminating völkisch ideas in surrounding German states and even in Switzerland. In fact, in 1929 Hitler gave Wagner the task of supervising Nazi interests in Switzerland, and three years later Wagner traveled to Zürich to address a völkisch organization.[21] There is no evidence that the Baden party ever engaged in such activities in Alsace. First, the leader of émigrés from Alsace-Lorraine in Germany, Robert Ernst, did not meet Gau leader Robert Wagner until May 1934 (and again in early 1940). Second, before 1933 the Baden party paper, Der Führer, focused on Alsace only during critical moments such as the trial of Alsatian autonomists in Colmar in 1928, although on one occasion it published an article on the "unrescued brothers in Alsace-Lorraine who were under foreign domination."[22] After 1933 the Führer no longer published such articles, but in 1935 the party paper launched an attack on Alsace's German Catholic press for carrying on an offensive against the Third Reich.[23]

Both German Foreign Institute (DAI) officials and Alsatian leaders like Bickler testified in 1941 that the Baden party leaders had been unconcerned with the ethnic German movement in Alsace. Indeed, the Alsatian issue drew response in Baden primarily from a small academic circle.[24] The focal point for this concern was the Freiburg area. The Alsatian Catholic autonomist J. Rossé came to Freiburg in the fall of 1929 to attend a Catholic rally, and on 4 July 1937, French veterans from the Doubs area of France celebrated a "brotherhood" meeting with German veterans in Freiburg. The following year, Freiburg veterans returned the visit in Besançon.[25] The most important intellectual who was concerned with the unity of the upper Rhine area was Friedrich Metz, a professor. But the Baden party considered Metz an "intellectual reactionary" because of his Catholic ties.[26]

In Germany in general, the Alsatian émigré organization and the DAI were most concerned with the Alsatian problem, although the German Foreign Office also distributed limited funds to the Alsatian political parties, both before and after Hitler's seizure of power. The most important figure in the Alsatian movement in Germany, Robert Ernst, was born in Strassburg on 7 February 1887 to a vicar. Although his mother came from a pro-French patrician family, after the war Ernst moved to Karlsruhe and obtained Baden citizenship. In Germany Ernst became involved with the other émigrés from Alsace-Lorraine, and by January 1923 he issued the first edition of the journal Elsass-Lothringer Heimatstimmen. During the 1920s and 1930s he not only organized the Alsatian émigrés in Germany but also maintained contacts with political leaders in Alsace. Although he did not join the Nazi party before 1933, in April 1940 Ernst publicly called for the acquisition of German living space, and he warned that the French "would learn this and much more."[27]

In addition to Ernst, the DAI maintained active contacts with Alsatians. The institute's publication, Der Auslanddeutsche, published pleas before 1933, urging Germans not to forget Alsace-Lorraine. Personnel associated with the DAI visited the separatist Bickler in June 1938 despite Hitler's public pronouncements concerning Germany's disinterest in Alsace-Lorraine. One of these DAI visitors, who expressed his true feelings about Alsatians, noted that the largest part of Alsace's population would always cooperate with any victor. Despite this man's admiration for Bickler, he did not like the Alsatians in general. The only laudable Alsatian attribute, this observer and other German agents found, was a general anti-Semitism.[28]

This view of the Alsatians was widely shared. In fact, after 1933, the Alsatian émigrés became increasingly concerned with the public's acceptance of the fact that Alsace was lost forever.[29] Before 1933, the Völkischer Beobachter and Nazi spokesmen in Germany had attacked the Locarno settlement for sacrificing Alsace-Lorraine, but after 1933 the area became a ploy which Hitler used in his negotiations with France. After each diplomatic coup, Hitler allayed French fears by recognizing Germany's western borders.[30] Although Hitler had shown little interest in Alsace in Mein Kampf, in 1928 in a secret manuscript he had noted that in the case of a German victory over France, Germany would at least get Alsace-Lorraine.[31] But according to Speer, Hitler had declared in 1938 that a war over the insignificant strip of territory of Alsace-Lorraine would not be worthwhile. Besides, he added, "the Alsatians had become so characterless due to the constant

shifting of their nationality that it would be a gain to
neither side to have them."[32]

Not until early 1940 did a wider circle of state and
party officials in Baden and Germany focus on the future of
Alsace and publicly express the wish that Alsace be returned
to Germany. Troops were issued pamphlets dealing with the
history of Alsace-Lorraine, and Scheel, the leader of the
security police in southwestern Germany, was preparing for
his duties in Alsace by visiting Ernst. In the meantime,
Ernst met both Josef Bürckel, the Gau leader of the Saar and
the Reich commissioner for Austria, and Robert Wagner in May
1940 in an attempt to assure his position in any future settlement. Between 3 and 5 June 1940, the Gau Baden Indoctrination
leader took part in a conference in Berlin that was devoted
to a discussion of the future of Europe. The Reich Indoctrination Office presented the radical Pan-German von Loesch,
Ernst, and Metz as the main speakers of the conference, leaving
little doubt about the party's intentions. By mid-June of
1940, Ernst and other leading figures of the Alsatian émigré
movement had joined the staff of the army headquarters in
charge of the impending attack on Alsace.[33] Also in June and
July, officials of the DAI prepared a variety of plans for
the disposition of Alsace. One called for a union of Alsace,
Baden, and Württemberg, while others were reminiscent of the
German war aims during World War I in that they advocated the
German seizure of Belfort, Burgundy, Verdun, and, just to be
safe, a strip down to the Mediterranean.[34]

The decision concerning the future of Alsace rested with
Hitler alone. Ernst, who had established himself in Colmar,
heard on the evening of 20 June 1940 that Hitler had appointed
Wagner as chief of civil administration (CdZ) of Alsace, an

arrangement similar to that in Lorraine, Luxemburg, and later Lower Styria, Upper Carniola and Bialystok. In each case, the neighboring German Gau incorporated the new territory. This new status of Alsace was not defined in the armistice agreement with France. Rather, on 2 August and 18 October 1940, Hitler issued unpublished directives concerning the governing of Alsace. The CdZ received an independent budget and was made directly responsible to Hitler. Only Lammers and subsequently Bormann became the real coordinators for questions concerning the newly conquered area. Hitler also demanded that the provinces of Alsace and Lorraine be completely German in character in ten years.[35]

THE CHIEF OF CIVIL ADMINISTRATION: ROBERT WAGNER

Two factors that determined events in Alsace after 1940 must be emphasized before any discussion of the Nazi administration of Alsace. First, Wagner was not only the party leader but also the supreme state authority. His powers in Alsace exceeded even those he had exercised as a commissar in Baden in 1933. Not only did he introduce German laws and directives in his Verordnungsblatt (Ordinance Journal) for Alsace, but a special court in Strassburg also provided Wagner with powers over life and death.[36] Also, while Wagner did not become Reich defense commissar for Baden until December 1942, he exercised this power in Alsace prior to that date. In Baden, Wagner had to obtain Goebbels's permission before he could evacuate the population of Karlsruhe and Mannheim. In Alsace, he ordered the evacuation of Strassburg and Mühlhausen and made it a point to inform Berlin that he did not require

Goebbels's permission since he received his instructions
directly from Hitler. Finally, in late 1944 he was even able
to transfer his powers of CdZ to his party Kreis leaders,
enabling them to issue directives to state officials. Wagner's
position was supported by Bormann, who continued to emphasize
that Hitler would not make decisions on Alsace without confer-
ring with Wagner.[37]

Further examples revealing the CdZ's powers in Alsace are
best illustrated by the party's and state's negotiations with
two Reich agencies. One concerned the Reich rail administration, and the second involved negotiations with the Reich
general inspector for water and energy. One issue involved
the party in Alsace while the other concerned the state. The
case involving the Reich rail agency concerned the deployment
of rail employees who were also political leaders of the party.
The two hundred rail offices in Alsace employed 9,445 people,
of whom 1,446 were political leaders (PL) of the party. In
Germany, all party political leaders below the rank of local
leader could be transferred by the Reich rail office without
consultation with the party. In Alsace, however, the party
personnel leader emphasized that orders could only be issued
with the approval of the CdZ. The Baden party's personnel
leader concluded an agreement with the Karlsruhe representative
of the Reich's rail office which stated that the rail office
would present to the party personnel leader all lists of
Alsatian rail personnel scheduled to be transferred. The
lists would then be forwarded to the party district leaders
for consultation. If any party leader who was a rail employee
had to be transferred, he would be sent to Karlsruhe to ensure
his prompt return to Alsace.[38]

The second example involved negotiations concerning a

proposed Alsatian electric power complex in the Mühlhausen
area. State Secretary Schulz-Fielitz, the general inspector
for water and energy, approved the plans for an Alsatian power
complex proposed by Köhler, the economics minister of the CdZ
in Alsace. Contrary to the wishes of the civil administration
of Alsace, however, he demanded that the shareholders of the
Mühlhausen complex should continue to participate and that the
Reich control 51 percent of the project. Köhler warned Berlin
in December 1942 that Wagner would never permit these two conditions. Despite this warning Berlin insisted on a conference
in March 1943. The Berlin representative, Barth, attempted
to win his point by indicating that Speer had demanded 51 percent Reich control in all projects in the East. The CdZ's
representatives, including Köhler, refused to allow the Swiss
and Alsatian shareholders to participate and rejected the 51
percent Reich control clause.[39] In a secret memorandum, the
personal secretary of the CdZ noted that Wagner had declared
that any participation by the general inspector for water and
energy was unnecessary, since in conversations Hitler had
repeatedly emphasized that Reich offices only guided (lenken)
and Gaue administered (verwalten). Wagner emphasized that as
CdZ he was responsible only to Hitler.[40]

The vast powers that Wagner exercised as CdZ in state
affairs in Alsace he also practiced as party leader. Reich
party leaders could not hold conferences in Alsace without
his permission. Even Schwarz, the powerful Reich party treasurer, asked for Wagner's approval before he purchased Alsatian
properties desired by party agencies. Most important, the
Baden party leaders operating in Alsace were able to rely on
special party funds (Opferring) to meet party expenses that
the Gau party treasurer (acting on orders of Schwarz) refused

to recognize.[41] Schwarz did, however, successfully refuse
Wagner's demands to change Strassburg's classification to that
of a state and party capital despite the fact that all central
Baden state offices were located in Strassburg after April
1943.[42]

Wagner's relations with Himmler were dismal in 1940. At
conferences arranged by Himmler, Wagner was subjected openly
to criticism. In Alsace, the Baden Gau leader issued direct
orders to the police, and he organized his private detention
camp in Vorbruck near Schirmeck, which was independent of SS
control. In 1942 Wagner's relations with Himmler improved
considerably as both cooperated in mass deportations and
racial policies in Alsace. Of all the party (and state)
leaders, Wagner cooperated most closely with Martin Bormann,
who was Wagner's direct line to Hitler, and also served as a
counterweight to the obstinacy of Schwarz in financial matters.
By 1944, Wagner even appealed to Bormann for additional troops
to protect Alsace.[43]

The importance of the CdZ's powers in Alsace lies in the
fact that Wagner, a fanatical Nazi, could attempt to impose
Nazification on Alsace with relatively little interference.
On 3 July 1940, Wagner moved to Strassburg, and on 16 July
he held his first official conference as CdZ in that city.
He told his state and party delegates that "we came as Nazis
and can only act as Nazis." Wagner's absolute powers enabled
him again and again to introduce fanatical Nazi policies despite
the opposition of most responsible German and Alsatian officials in Alsace.[44]

The second important factor that influenced the evolution
of Alsace after 1940 was the relationship between Alsatians
and Reich Germans. The Reich Germans' enthusiasm over the

occupation of Alsace was often closely tied to expectations of
economic gain. Baden towns, as early as 21 June 1940, looked
forward to the expected economic benefits the conquest of
Alsace promised to bring. Many Baden businessmen hoped to
recover the clientele they had had in Alsace before 1919. One
Baden town even planned to increase the enrollment of its high
school by recruiting Alsatian students. These sentiments were
widespread in Germany as party offices were inundated with
requests from bank circles for information concerning invest-
ment opportunities in Alsace. Many "proper" German businesses
offered to participate in the "Aryanization" of Alsatian
firms.[45] But according to reports of Himmler's security service, which was usually well informed, most Germans in 1940
considered the Alsatians traitors and characterless Wackes
(a derogatory term Germans applied to Alsatians long before
1940).[46]

The attitude of German officials and party functionaries
threatened to create difficulties in Alsace after 1940, but
the reaction of Alsatians to the German occupation predestined
the failure of Wagner's planned Germanization and Nazification.
The Alsatians had a distinctly negative attitude toward the
German invaders, although some postwar observers have argued
that in 1940 a majority of Alsatians would have voted for
annexation to Germany and that only deportations and the introduction of military service turned the Alsatians away from
the German cause.[47]

According to the great majority of German reports on the
Alsatian situation in 1940, the Alsatians were impressed by
the German military victory, but they rejected annexation
of their province. Even Wagner later admitted to the party
chancellery in Berlin that in June 1940, the population in

Alsace was very cool toward the Germans. A report of the Gau
indoctrination office of July 1940 also lamented the lack of
acceptance of Nazi concepts in Alsace despite the efforts of
Bickler and his supporters.[48] The Alsatian population in
general was suspicious of the German occupation, but the
Catholic Alsatians were particularly opposed to the Nazis.
Upper Alsace was especially anti-German. Only in the Protestant areas of Lower Alsace were there indications of pro-German
feelings. It was in these areas that Bickler, Roos, Hueber,
and the Alsatian separatists had been most active before 1940.
But the workers who had supported the former Communist Hueber
were promptly disillusioned with the German conquerors. By
early 1941, German reports indicated that the poorest attitudes
toward the new order were held by the workers. This was the
direct result of low wages and high prices, which dominated
the Alsatian economic life after the German invasion.[49]

All German reports emphasized that unlike the joyous
entry of German troops in the Eastern European areas that were
inhabited by ethnic Germans, in Alsace little open enthusiasm
was displayed. Observers noted that "public rallies" in July
1940 were produced to a large extent by German soldiers who
were obviously ordered to attend. One DAI official noted
that from 80 to 90 percent of the Alsatians would vote for
autonomy rather than annexation to Germany. A prevailing
Alsatian attitude seems to have been the feeling that one
time "we are Germans, then French and tomorrow something
else."[50] It became the task of the Baden party functionaries
and state officials who operated in Alsace to convince the
reluctant Alsatians that they were not only Germans but German Nazis.

When Wagner moved to Colmar on 21 June 1940, he was

accompanied by the leading Baden ministers, Pflaumer, Köhler, and Schmitthenner. The ministers extended their Baden activities, which encompassed the Ministries of Interior, Economics, and Education to Alsace. In Alsace, they were completely under the control of Wagner since Reich ministries could not issue direct orders to them. Wagner also introduced two police commandos under the direction of the Baden SS leader Gustav Scheel, and he transferred Baden municipal police chiefs to Alsace.[51] All of the thirteen county and twenty-eight municipal commissars who assumed the provincial state positions in Alsace in June 1940 were from Baden. The overwhelming majority of these Baden civil servants and municipal administrators were party members.[52] Wagner and the Baden party were assured of the complete control of the personnel deployed in Alsace after Wagner established a personnel office of the CdZ in July 1940. This office, which was responsible for all basic Alsatian personnel questions concerning the state, municipalities, the party, and even the economy, was led by Adolf Schuppel, the Gau party personnel leader of Baden and one of Wagner's closest advisors.[53]

Wagner and his collaborators rationalized the use of Baden officials in Alsace in terms of racial mythology. In an interview on 14 September 1940, Wagner maintained that events in Alsace proceeded smoothly primarily because most German officials in Alsace were party members from Baden, representing a "Germanic brother tribe." To strengthen this unity, Wagner limited potential personnel to south Germans and "Old Alsatians" who were living in Germany.[54] By 1941, the Gau propaganda leader, Adolf Schmid, could boast that the "Old Alsatians" and the Baden officials deployed in Alsace guaranteed that the mistakes of the German Empire would not be repeated

in Alsace. However, one year later a more realistic picture
was given by the chief justice of Baden, who pointed out that
the "Old Alsatians" who returned from Germany after 1940 were
not recognized by the native Alsatians as true natives since
most of them had only one Alsatian parent. Most detrimental to
the German cause was the fact that Germans continued to dominate leading governmental and administrative posts in Alsace.
For example, in late 1942, the three largest courts in Alsace
were still directed by Reich Germans.[55]

Only in the economic sphere were Wagner's powers limited
by several Berlin agencies. The Hermann Göring Firms seized
most of the French-owned mines and oil wells in Alsace. Berlin
also established the conversion rate between the franc and the
Mark (20:1) which damaged the German cause since it reduced
the real value of the French franc held by the Alsatians. But
Wagner and the party could determine who was an enemy of the
Reich and whose property would be confiscated. The power to
decide which economic enterprise was hostile to the Reich
was used most effectively against Alsace's publishing enterprises. The Baden Gau press agency seized control of the
major papers in Alsace and banned the bulk of the Alsatian
press. Baden Nazi press officials were promoted to the editorial positions of the Alsatian papers: <u>Strassburger Neueste</u>
<u>Nachrichten</u>, <u>Mühlhauser Tagblatt</u>, and <u>Kolmarer Kurier</u>. This
position of strength in Alsace exceeded that in Baden, where
traditional papers were coordinated but still functioned.[56]

While Schuppel's personnel office ensured the party's
influence in the public sphere, the party also played a prime
role in the private sectors of organized activities in Alsace.
On 2 September 1940, Wagner appointed a control commissioner
for all private organizations and clubs in Alsace. Not only

did Wagner expect a portion of the funds of these organizations
to flow into a private Gauleiter account, but the party was
granted the right to review all organizations and to advise the
control commissioner whether an Alsatian organization should
be allowed to resume activities or be abolished. The district
party's organization and personnel leaders scrutinized the
Alsatian organizations and their leaders and then reported
their findings to the Gau organization leader. He in turn
advised the control commissioner. One immediate beneficiary
of this offensive against private Alsatian organizations was
of course the NS Welfare Organization, which became the sole
private welfare agency in Alsace.[57]

The influence of the party's radical stand was particularly apparent in church affairs. In July 1940, Alsatian
church leaders were summoned to the civil administration's
Department of Culture and Education and informed that the
Concordat of 1801 was not binding for the Reich. The Alsatian churches were taxed and lost their state subsidies.
Most important, the Nazis proceeded to abolish the confessional school structure in Alsace.[58] As late as 20 October
1940, Wagner was still publicly praising the numerous clerics
of both churches who had contributed to the struggle for
German identity. In secret, however, he was already preparing
further moves against the churches. As early as November
1940, the Baden Gau leader was corresponding with Bormann on
the Alsatian religious question. In a conference on 11 December 1940, Wagner had expressed his fears to Bormann that the
dissolution of confessional welfare organizations would cause
disturbances. Bormann, who had been a prime force in the
attack on the church, advised Wagner merely to produce a
plausible explanation to allay potential disturbances. Even-

tually Wagner agreed, and in March 1941 the confessional welfare organizations were dissolved and replaced by the NSV.[59]

Hitler supported these moves against the church in Alsace,
and in one of his "table talks" on 4 July 1942, he indicated
that the German Concordat indeed was not valid in Alsace. He
added that in Alsace the Gau leader could proceed against the
churches as rapidly as the population was "conditioned" or
prepared for such moves.[60] Following Hitler's suggestions,
the most ambitious and radical move was planned against the
churches in 1943. On 8 July, the CdZ held a conference that
was devoted to preparations for the dissolution of Catholic
orders in Alsace which did not work but merely prayed
(beschaulichen Orden). The 1,650 people were to be sent to
Bavaria or Württemberg on 12 and 13 July. Wagner ordered the
party to remain in the background for fear of the population's
negative reactions. But the church leaders discovered the
plans and applied pressure on Berlin while the archbishop of
Freiburg warned emphatically against provoking Catholic Alsace.
Apparently, the pressure was sufficient to cause the post-
ponement of the deportations until after the war. An order
published by the party's Gau staff office on 29 July 1943
forbade all party offices to correspond further with confessional agencies. In an attempt to control the antichurch
fervor of some local party leaders, the Gau staff office
became the central party coordinating agency in Alsace for
matters dealing with church issues. The party's radical
offensive against the churches, however, was not abandoned
but merely postponed. The party's and civil administration's
moves against the church in Alsace produced predictable responses from the Catholics, like the reactions of the Badenese.
In the end, the party paid the price since party events and

particularly Hitler Youth meetings were avoided and sabotaged.[61]

The party's most effective offensive in Alsace occurred
in the public domain. Mayors, teachers, and civil servants
were purged much more effectively than had ever been possible
in Baden. This success was possible because of Wagner's position as chief of civil administration and because the purge
was explained as a move against Francophiles and enemies of
the Reich. The party agencies responsible for the selection
and indoctrination of teachers, mayors, and civil servants
arrived in Alsace in late July 1940. Although the personnel
office of the CdZ was responsible for personnel changes in
Alsace, the detailed investigation of officials was conducted
by the party affiliates.[62]

On 21 June 1940, municipal commissars were appointed to
the twenty-eight towns in Alsace. After a period of consolidation, these commissars were replaced by Alsatian émigrés.
The party's office for municipal affairs produced a list of
three hundred Alsatians who were employed in the Reich in
municipal positions. These "Alsatians" were transplanted
back to Alsace to assume leadership positions in the major
communities. Many of the new municipal leaders had left
Alsace in 1919 and established themselves in Baden (or other
German states), where they had joined the Nazi party, frequently before Hitler's takeover. In 1940/41, they were
often appointed to lead communities in Alsace where they had
lived before 1919.[63]

Strassburg, Colmar, and Mühlhausen, the largest urban
centers in Alsace, were led by émigrés. Robert Ernst became
mayor of Strassburg, and his assistant in the Alsace-Lorraine
émigré movement in Germany after 1919, Paul Maass, became

mayor of Mühlhausen. Maass was born in Mühlhausen but had
left Alsace in 1918. By 1922, he had become a Nazi party member. Subsequently, he rose to the position of Gau (Düsseldorf)
leader of the office for civil servants. He was the only
"Alsatian" besides Ernst to occupy a Gau party office in
Baden-Alsace after 1940. Finally, the new mayor of Colmar,
L. Manny, was born in Strassburg and like many others had
left Alsace in 1918. As a lawyer in Freiburg, he had defended
Wagner in a trial in the spring of 1927.[64]

For most of the smaller towns, the Germans had to rely
on local personnel, particularly former autonomist leaders,
to full the municipal positions. In October 1940, the party
office for municipal affairs began a series of indoctrination
programs. By May 1941, 370 Alsatian mayors had attended
courses on the basic Nazi ideology and an outline of German
municipal laws. In July 1941, Wagner ordered his Kreis leaders to implement further mayoral purges and to select only
strong personalities who were totally committed to the German cause.[65] This was a continuing process and depended to
a large degree on the cooperation of Alsatian Nazis who were
familiar with the municipal leaders. As late as 1942, Bickler
was still engaged in the elimination of mayors who had "collaborated" with the French before 1940. To ensure activism
and the preponderance of the party, the mayoral positions
were frequently combined with the local party leadership post.
In 1943 for example, half of the mayors of the districts of
Strassburg were also local party leaders.[66]

The leading civil servants in Alsace who had been French
were either expelled or not permitted to return to Alsace in
1940. Their positions were usurped by Baden civil servants.
Most of the lower-grade Alsatian civil servants were allowed

to remain in office but were required to sign loyalty declarations and recognize the de facto incorporation of Alsace into the Reich. Mauch, the Gauamt leader of the party office for civil servants, finished organizing district offices by 31 July 1940 and then proceeded to initiate indoctrination courses for the Alsatian civil servants. By July 1941, over 10,000 Alsatian civil servants had been accepted for admission to the Reich's civil service. Another 5,249 had to attend further indoctrination courses and exhibit active willingness to cooperate with the Nazi cause. This usually encompassed enthusiastic participation in party affairs. A decree issued on 8 January 1942 provided the legal basis for the expulsion of all civil servants who did not obtain a positive evaluation from the party concerning their attitudes toward the Nazi state.[67]

The most radical purge in Alsace occurred among teachers. By November 1940, one-third of all public schoolteachers had either resigned or had been purged. In many cases, the teachers terminated their services rather than go to Baden to teach and submit to Nazi training programs. Under the guidance of the former Kreis leader Karl Gärtner, the Gauamt leader for teachers, the primary schools of Alsace were coordinated to parallel the German structure, and confessional education was abolished. The teachers also had to join the NS Teachers' League. In this manner, boasted the Gau propaganda leader, "German people" were being educated.[68] In secondary and higher education, the Germans reopened the University of Strassburg in November 1941, but the Nazis could not persuade the students and faculty members who had fled to Clermont-Ferrand in 1939 to return to Strassburg. Only a Gestapo raid on Clermont-Ferrand in September 1943 destroyed the exiled

University of Strassburg.[69]

The Nazi seizure of governmental control in Alsace after 1940 was complete and thorough. This did not guarantee Nazification or even Germanization beyond the structural facade. More important, by 1941 serious weaknesses had already appeared in the German position in Alsace. First, the economic situation, characterized by rising prices and low wages, proved disastrous for the German cause. In April 1941, Wagner boasted that rural Alsace would provide a natural supplement for industrial Baden. In reality, as late as 1944 Alsace was dependent on agricultural imports from the Reich.[70] The economic dislocation also permitted some of the labor force to work only a fraction of a normal workweek. Bickler complained in early 1941 that workers did not even have sufficient funds to redeem their food coupons.[71]

The economic difficulties were paralleled by administrative friction. The criticisms of the Alsatians were directed against the civil administration and particularly against Ernst, who was Wagner's general advisor. Ernst was identified by many Alsatians with the Strassburg patrician class. In July 1941 one report from the DAI estimated that only 20 percent of Alsatians supported the Reich. The criticism of the civil administration and of Reich German officials in general was pervasive and natural considering German behavior despite the racial myths of tribal unity.[72] A German police officer in Strassburg attacked Alsatian air-raid wardens in public and declared that Alsatians were only friendly to Germans to their faces. The Karlsruhe postal president, who was unable to cooperate with Alsatians, remarked in public (in Alsace) that Germans "after all came here as victors." In each instance, Bickler protested vehemently but the damage had

already occurred. By 1944, German military personnel publicly
mistreated the Alsatian public, both physically and psycholog-
ically.[73] These cases provided only a few of the many examples
of the failure of Reich Germans in Alsace to understand Alsatian people and Alsatian problems.

One case, concerning the hospital of Strassburg, best
illustrates the problems involved in the relations between
German and Alsatian officials. The private hospital of Strassburg became part of the University of Strassburg in April
1941. In early 1941, Joseph Oster, an Alsatian autonomist
leader before 1940 who had managed the hospital for two de-
cades, resigned and recommended two Alsatian doctors for the
position of president. Neither Oster nor the doctors involved
wanted a Reich German in charge. Bickler supported this
view and appealed to Schuppel, the personnel leader of the
CdZ, to intervene and consider more Alsatian doctors for important posts.[74]

Instead, H. Lemke, a Freiburg party member, became acting
director of the Strassburg hospital. Not only was he a Reich
German but he had also articulated his personal views that
the Alsatians were a lying and thieving breed. Scherberger,
the director of the University of Strassburg, had told Bickler
that Lemke was an old party member, and his transfer to Strassburg was considered a promotion. One could not simply send
him back to Freiburg. In this case, Wagner finally responded
to the barrage of Alsatian appeals and ordered the Baden minister of education to recall Lemke to Freiburg, allowing an
Alsatian to assume the leading position of the Strassburg hospital.[75] The case does illustrate the basic attitude of the
Baden party and state officials. Alsace provided them with
institutions that could be utilized for the advancement of

"deserving" party members despite the frequently hostile attitudes expressed by these same party members toward Alsatians.
Still, most of the leading administrative posts in Alsace were
held by Badenese.

THE PARTY AND NAZIFICATION

The Nazi affiliates and Wagner as CdZ ensured the establishment and supremacy of Nazi administrative norms. As had
occurred in Baden in 1933/34, the Nazi commissars purged
and coordinated the administrative and governmental posts in
Alsace. But most Alsatians had still to be Nazified and Germanized, and all reminders of the French past had to be
expunged. This became the primary function of the Nazi party
in Alsace after 1940.[76]

On 21 June 1940, Wagner and the leading Baden party and
state officials descended on Alsace. The Baden party appeared
first in the form of the NSV, which was aided by the German
Labor Service (RAD). Both relied on Alsatian collaborators
in their efforts to repair war damages and manage the return
of several hundred thousand refugees. Although the Alsatians
learned to respect the NSV, in the beginning both the NSV and
the RAD were received cooly in Alsace.[77] After the arrival of
the Baden NSV leaders on 24 June 1940, the next stage of the
Baden party's expansion involved the party district leaders.
On 3 July thirteen Baden district leaders were instructed
about their tasks and then sent to Alsace. The Kreisleiters
brought with them their closest party cadre advisors, which
included the district party's organization, personnel, and
propaganda leaders, and the district party manager. The final

stage of the Baden party's invasion of Alsace in 1940 occurred with the arrival of the affiliate representatives in late July.[78]

Alsace placed a great strain on the Baden party organization in 1940/41. In the district of Kehl, the war and service in Alsace completely depleted the party's cadre organization. The local leader of Kehl had to assume the positions of district organization and personnel leader in addition to substituting for the absent Kreisleiter. This was repeated in district after district in Baden, where party work was suspended or reduced. Later, Wagner admitted that the focus of party activities between late 1940 and early 1942 had been on Alsace. Consumed by both racial myths and the desire to further the interests of Baden, the Karlsruhe party leaders rejected assistance from non-Baden party members despite increasing tasks. Instead, the Baden party leaders placed increased reliance on Alsatian collaborators.[79]

The first political organization established in Alsace after the German invasion was the Alsatian Auxiliary Service (Elsässische Hilfsdienst, EHD). The EHD was founded in Colmar on 20 June 1940 by Ernst with the aid of twenty Alsatian collaborators. It was an attempt by Ernst to establish a functional agency in Alsace that could absorb the native collaborators. The Baden party became dependent on the EHD for both personnel and information concerning Alsatian affairs. By the end of June 1940, EHD locals had been established in most Alsatian communities, and one month later the Baden Kreisleiters in Alsace were relying on Hilfsdienst advisors.[80] The EHD became even more effective after the return of the "Nanzigers" to Alsace on 17 July 1940. The Nanzigers were a group of several hundred Alsatian autonomists who had been

arrested by the French after the outbreak of war and confined
in prison in Nancy. After the German victory, these Alsatian
autonomists returned to Alsace to play an important part in
the EHD and in general collaboration with the Nazis. The
Catholic autonomists Johann Keppi and Josef Rossé were put
in charge of the resettlement and compensation programs, and
Rossé was also appointed director of the Alsatia publishing
firm. The Communist Karl Hueber became the DAF leader of
Strassburg. The most active "Nanzig" collaborators who later
became Kreisleiters and were also selected by Himmler for SS
ranks came from the former Jungmannschaft.[81]

The first major rally of the Hilfsdienst occurred in
August 1940 when two hundred Alsatian collaborators led by
Bickler met in Strassburg. Kreisleiter Fritsch (from Freiburg)
told them that racism and the leadership concept were the two
foundations of National Socialism. The EHD, which initially
had gathered Alsatian collaborators, soon expanded to include
a larger segment of the population. Many opportunists joined
in an attempt to further their positions. Above all, segments
of the population were pressured to join the EHD in order to
display their support of the new order. Any civil servant,
for example, who had not applied for membership in the EHD
was investigated by the Nazis and risked the loss of his
career.[82]

Although the Baden Nazi leaders used the EHD in order to
facilitate the establishment of Nazi rule in Alsace, they did
not wish to perpetuate the existence of an independent Alsatian political organization. Even Ernst, the leader of the
Hilfsdienst, noted that this organization was only transitory
and preparatory to the development of the Nazi party in Alsace.
He warned that no impression must be created which would con-

vince people that the EHD would remain a permanent institution beside the NSDAP. In September 1940, after Schwarz
had decided to provide funds for the development of the party
in Alsace, the Baden party prepared to go beyond the structure of the EHD and to establish the NSDAP in Alsace. The
Baden Gau treasurer began to allocate financial support to
the party districts in Alsace, and the Gau personnel leader
directed the Baden party leaders to establish lists of full-
time party functionaries who deserved promotions. These party
officials would then be considered for future party posts in
Alsace.[83]

The first Nazi local in Alsace was founded on 26 September
1940, in Schiltigheim, Strassburg. In late 1940, a series of
mass foundations of party locals occurred. After organizational preparations for the establishment of locals had been
completed, the Baden party leaders organized public rallies.
At the rallies, the people were told about the functions of
the party and were then surprised with the information that
they had just participated in the creation of Nazi locals.
At the same time, the Baden Nazis created an Alsatian association called the Opferring (probationary association--OR),
which replaced the EHD as the preparatory agency for the eventual admission to the NSDAP. After October 1940, the EHD,
which was not abolished officially until April 1941, lost
most of its functions and important personnel to the German-
dominated Opferring.[84]

The OR enabled the Baden Nazis to enlist and control the
Alsatian collaborators who would fill the ranks of the newly
constructed Nazi party organization in Alsace. As in Baden,
civil servants were pressured to join the OR, and party leaders emphasized that membership in the OR was a prerequisite

for serving in the German administration. To ensure the progress of the Opferring, the mass party organizations such as
the NSV and the DAF could not recruit members until late
1942.[85] Although the OR members and the Alsatian party leaders called themselves Nazis, technically they were not members
of the NSDAP until 22 March 1941, when Alsatians were finally
permitted to join the Nazi party after having proven themselves
to the Opferring. Party district leaders assembled their
local leaders and affiliate leaders to inform them that they
had been recommended for admission to the Nazi party. On 3
April 1941, Wagner officially admitted five Alsatian district
leaders to the party to initiate the transition of OR members
into NSDAP members.[86]

By May 1941, the Baden Nazi leaders had established 704
party locals and a cell-block structure in Alsace. A total
of 18 percent of the population belonged to some party organization or affiliate, and 76,149 Alsatians had been enrolled
in the OR. The party's cadre organization established percentages for all party affiliates. The NS Women's League
was permitted to enroll a membership equal to 5 percent of
the total OR membership, the SA 15 percent. Popular resistance to participation in affiliate party organizations was
so strong that only the NS Women's League had achieved its
quota by May 1941.[87] As an indication of this resistance,
one-third of the Alsatian parents of potential recruits refused
to sign the admission papers during the Hitler Youth drive
in 1940/41.[88]

The Opferring and party affiliates were strongest in
northern Alsace, particularly in the districts of Zabern,
Weissenburg, and Hagenau, which had been strongholds of the
Jungmannschaft and the autonomists before 1940. In Upper

Alsace, near Mühlhausen and Altkirch, the party fared poorly.[89]
This pattern generally prevailed after 1941. Persistent
efforts by the Nazis increased the OR membership to 169,235
by June 1942, but despite purges and membership drives, the
total OR membership varied little after that year. With the
mandatory Hitler Youth membership and the expansion of the
DAF and NSV memberships after 1942, the party could boast in
June 1944 that 63 percent of the Alsatian populace was active
in party affairs.[90]

Allegedly, the most fanatical Opferring members who
became NSDAP members represented a Nazi elite in Alsace. By
February 1942, 6,283 Alsatians had become party members, and
an additional 5,701 applications had been submitted to Schwarz.
Schwarz and Bormann rejected even this modest growth, and
both demanded an elitist party membership in Alsace. In July
1941, Schwarz had urged that only Alsatians who had been
active OR leaders and fanatical Nazis should be admitted to
the NSDAP. Bormann also had told Schwarz in 1942 that Alsatian block leaders were using economic pressure to induce people
to join the party. Despite Schwarz's warnings, Wagner expanded
the NSDAP membership in Alsace to 25,000 members by June 1944.
After all, he wanted to prove that his Nazification of Alsace
was successful.[91]

The Alsatians supplied most of the local party personnel
after the accelerated expansion of the party in 1940/41. In
the district of Strassburg, half of the local leaders came
from the pre-1940 Alsatian separatist movement. The Alsatians
also occupied about 8 percent of the paid party posts, although
the top positions remained in the hands of Baden Nazis.[92] The
highest and most important party post held by Alsatians was
the district leadership position. Ten Baden district leaders

returned to their Baden party posts in January 1941 and were
replaced to a large extent by native Alsatians and Alsatian
émigrés (see Map 9). The six districts of Gebweiler, Hagenau,
Molsheim, Mühlhausen, Zabern, and Strassburg were assigned to
native Alsatians after the departure of the Badenese.[93]

The Alsatian district leaders came from the "Nanzig"
separatists who had been arrested by the French in 1939. The
Communists were represented by Hans-Peter Murer, who took over
the district Mühlhausen. Later in November 1943, H. Murschel,
another former Communist, became district leader of Gebweiler.
The former Landespartei leader, Renatus Hauss, became district
leader of Hagenau. His close collaborator, Paul Schall, was
granted the district of Molsheim in 1942 and one year later
the district of Strassburg.[94] Four of the first six Alsatian
district leaders had been members of the Jungmannschaft.
Hermann Bickler, Rudolf Lang, Edmund Nussbaum, and Alexander
Kramer were assigned to the leading party positions in Strassburg, Zabern, Molsheim, and Gebweiler. The young Alsatian
separatists who had already disseminated Nazi ideas before
1940 were clearly preferred by the Baden party leaders.[95]

Wagner later recognized the Alsatian Kreisleiter's activities as an autonomist (before 1940) as part of his official
party career. Since the district leaders' salaries in Alsace
were far below those in private industry, Wagner granted them
special compensations for the losses that had occurred when
the Germans disbanded their journals and papers after 1940.[96]
But Wagner's efforts to incorporate the Alsatian Kreisleiters
into the Reich party were always frustrated by the fact that
Alsace was not legally a part of Germany. In early 1944 he
attempted to have Alsatians nominated to the Reichstag, and
he requested the highest party honors for Alsatian party

Map 9. *Alsace: NSDAP district centers: Kreisleitungen*

leaders (<u>Blutorden</u>). The party chancellery and Schwarz, however, rejected both demands.[97] Of the six original Alsatian district leaders appointed in 1941, only Hauss and Murer remained in office in 1944. Bickler, Lang, and Kramer escaped their frustrations with German measures by opting for military service; Nussbaum was removed from office because of his corruption.[98]

Half of the twelve Alsatian party districts were led by Badenese and Alsatian émigrés. Rheinhold Lawnick was born in 1902 in Hagenau and moved to the Rhineland in 1919. He joined the party in 1928 and became SA leader and finally a teacher in the Nazi school of Sonthofen. Lawnick was named the district leader of Weissenburg, and the other Alsatian émigré, Heinrich Sauerhöfer, who had joined the party by 1923, became district leader of Schlettstadt. In theory, these émigrés were considered Alsatians by the party. In reality, they often were insensitive to Alsatian feelings. For example, when the WHW collections did not meet Sauerhöfer's expectation, he threatened mass deportations. The rest of the district leaders who were transferred to Alsace after 1940 were Baden party functionaries who "deserved" promotions. Karl Eschle, who took over the district of Thann, had joined the party in 1930 and founded the Hitler Youth in a Baden district. Later, he became Hitler Youth leader of the Villingen and Wolfach districts before joining the army in 1940. Konrad Glas was a former district indoctrination officer who became Kreisleiter of the small rural district of Emmendingen. In 1940, he was assigned the large, urban district of Colmar, a position he held until 1945.[99]

Relations between the Alsatian and Baden Kreis leaders were often strained. Frictions and jealousies pervaded the

relations even between Alsatian district leaders.[100] Baden
district leaders were particularly insensitive to Alsatian
feelings. One case involved the veterans organization of
Zabern, which in 1941 planned a commemoration on the "Hünenburg." Kreisleiter Rothacker, who was temporarily in charge
of Zabern, called a meeting of the local party leaders on that
day and forbade attendance at the Hünenburg rally. The Alsatian Nazi Bickler thought it a cruel joke that Rothacker should
impose a prohibition which even the French had never been able
to enforce.[101] Another example involved Walter Kirn, the
district leader of Donaueschingen. In January 1941, he was
transferred to the Francophile Alsatian district of Rappoltsweiler, where he made it a special point to insult and mistreat
Alsatians. His constant public drunkenness, combined with
corruption, finally led to his removal in 1942.[102]

Parallel to the development of the party structure and
the recruitment of Alsatian personnel, the Nazis in Alsace
were confronted with the never-ending task of activating an
Alsatian public who generally rejected the NSDAP. In some
instances, whole towns refused to participate in party rallies.
Although observers noted a more positive attitude among Alsatian party members, the general populace avoided party functions and party affairs. As early as August 1941, many Alsatians doubted that Germany could win and expressed the view
that eventual American participation would doom the German
war efforts.[103]

To activate both the party organization and the public,
the Nazis opened a series of purges, alternating with membership drives and public rallies. Beginning in March 1942,
the Alsatians were bombarded with appeals to participate in
party affairs. Then in August 1942, the party members were

activated. Block, cell, and local leaders visited OR and
NSDAP members and urged active participation in Nazi events.
In January 1943, Röhn, the deputy Gau leader, lifted the freeze
on OR membership to enable the party to replace the purged or
inactive members. The introduction of military service in
August 1942 had accelerated the need for permanent party activism to defend Nazi policies. The district conference became
the most important party event both in terms of activating
the party membership and in influencing the people in general.[104]

But the Alsatian party and its affiliates continued to
suffer from public indifference and open hostility. In early
1943, the party's formations (SA, SS, NSFK, NSKK) presented
an image of complete stagnation. As was common Nazi practice,
civil servants who belonged to these formations but did not
display activism were scrutinized. The Alsatian OR and NSDAP
members conformed outwardly when necessary but took every
opportunity to escape party duties. In one Strassburg rally,
which was observed by the Gestapo, the OR and NSDAP members
marched in close formation to the meeting hall. Just before
entering the hall, however, numerous marchers seized the first
opportunity to sneak away from the rally.[105] The German workers who were transferred to Alsace and did not belong to the
party or its affiliates and the Mannheim women in Alsace who
did not belong to the NS Women's League only solidified the
Alsatian resistance to the party.[106]

Even dedicated Alsatian Nazis found cooperation with
their Baden colleagues most difficult. The reaction of many
Alsatian Nazis to the Baden party is best illustrated by the
evolution of the Strassburg SA and the activities of the
party's indoctrination department (Gauschulungsamt). The SA

had established auxiliary headquarters in Alsace on 25 August
1940, and started its evolution in September with twenty men.
By March 1941, it had expanded to 2,205 men and many Alsatians
had emerged in leading positions. The Alsatian SA leader of
Strassburg saw several basic developments much clearer than
the Baden party leaders. He attributed the evaporation of
the potential enthusiasm of workers and artisans to the deteriorating economic situation, and he realized that many Reich
Germans had come to Alsace as opportunists. But most significantly, he wanted a tightly knit band of followers rather
than a large body of nonactivists who only pleased the statis-
ticians.[107] When Wagner announced quotas that the party
affiliates had to attain, Schaffer defiantly said he would
not accept such a policy and would continue to expel nonactivists without regard to numbers. Damian, the SA leader of the
southwest, however, supported Wagner's numerical offensive
and ordered his SA leaders to tell Alsatians to participate
in the SA (and party) or risk economic hardships.[108] Schaffer's experience with the "numbers mania" was common in Alsace.
Even Paul Schall, a fanatic Alsatian Nazi, expressed the hope
in late 1944 that the Baden party leaders would recognize
the futility of their obsession with numbers and percentages.
He preferred to rely upon a small group of dedicated and
fanatic party activists.[109]

The one party office that attempted to centralize and
lead the indoctrination of the Alsatian party functionaries
was the Gau indoctrination office (GSA). Since district
indoctrination officers were not paid party functionaries, the
GSA, with the aid of the Gau personnel office, had to request
the transfer of Baden teachers and civil servants to Alsace,
where they could lead the district indoctrination offices.

Then the Gau indoctrination office established two-week courses
for Alsatian local leaders, and it guided the affiliates'
indoctrination programs.[110] The courses offered in the Gau
school at Frauenalb continued year after year in an attempt
to train all Alsatian party functionaries (PL). For fourteen
days the Alsatians were subjected to exercise, German songs,
Nazi poems, and literature. Those who did not attend Frauenalb
or one of the affiliate Gau schools were indoctrinated by
district speakers in rallies and local conferences.[111] All
of this was done at the cost of neglecting the indoctrination
of Baden party functionaries.[112]

Considering the Baden party's vast efforts, how effective
was the indoctrination program? The party indoctrination
officials themselves thought the task in Alsace was most
demanding and required much idealism. Many party and affiliate indoctrination offices did not even try to recruit Alsatian personnel until late 1942 primarily because they thought
too many Alsatians were contaminated with "Western ideology."
As late as September 1943, district indoctrination leaders
reported that the circle of solid ideological followers was
very small.[113]

Alsatian PL continued to evade indoctrination courses
whenever possible. In late 1943 half of the Alsatian party
functionaries who were notified canceled their attendance at
a scheduled course in Frauenalb. But the most damaging
indictment of Nazi indoctrination policies in Alsace came
from an Alsatian local leader. He noted in late 1942 that
one of the main causes of the Nazi failure in Alsace was
the inability of Baden party leaders to understand the
"Alsatian soul." Over 75 percent of Alsatian PL who participated in Frauenalb courses suffered from low morale when they

returned to their party posts because they felt that they
received inferior treatment in Frauenalb. The constant attacks
in Frauenalb on segments of the Alsatian population irritated
even the Alsatian Nazis. The Alsatian local leader argued
that, after all, tribal hostilities still existed between
Prussians, Badenese, and Bavarians.[114] This, of course,
was exactly what the Baden Nazis felt they could not permit
in Alsace. Alsace had to be more German than the Reich, and
Alsatian Nazis had to be more Nazified than Reich Nazis. The
implementation of this dogma became the prime function of the
party. The structural organization of the party had been
established in Alsace, but Nazification had clearly failed
not only with the population but also with many Alsatian party
functionaries.

THE PARTY AND GERMANIZATION

In 1871, Treitschke had declared that the population of Alsace-
Lorraine must be made conscious of its Germandom even against
its will. This type of Germanization was repugnant even to
Alsatian separatists like Spiesser. He had warned Wagner in
early 1940 that Alsatians were German and that any Germanization mania would produce disastrous consequences. Yet, when
the party in the district of Thann summarized its initial
activities in Alsace, it emphasized its actions against French
inscriptions, books, berets, and the French language. The
party's aim was to eradicate all memories of the French past.
While some Reich German leaders were allowed to make speeches
on German-French cooperation, in Alsace such topics were
never discussed.[115]

Hitler himself was the driving force behind the Germanization of Alsace. In August 1941, during one of his "table talks," he declared that "mistakes are inevitable, but what difference do they make if in ten years I can be told that Danzig, Alsace, and Lorraine are now German." Again in May 1942, Hitler promised that the Nazis "will mercilessly wipe out bilingualism in these territories, and the racial methods to which we shall have recourse will themselves prove their efficiency, even on the population hostile to Germanization."[116] Wagner became a blind, obedient servant for the implementation of Hitler's wishes, despite the advice of his Alsatian counselors to use moderation.

Late in July 1940, French signs and inscriptions were removed from public places and structures. Later that year, Wagner made the party Kreis leaders responsible for the systematic removal of all French inscriptions, and he advised his party leaders to warn the Alsatians to remove French inscriptions from private properties or risk a tax on foreign words. The expurgation of names and inscriptions reached even the graveyards and war memorials. Not until August 1944 did the Nazis "temporarily" abandon the project of removing the last French inscription from war memorials.[117]

Most irritating to the Alsatians and requiring strong police measures were the efforts to Germanize French family names in Alsace. The ordinance that introduced German as the official language in Alsace on 16 August 1940 also urged the Germanization of first and last names. Even Bickler, who demanded the use of German clothing and hairstyles, was outraged at the Germanization of French last names in Alsace. Germain was translated as Germania rather than Hermine, and a man named Boulois, according to Bickler, received the

"African" name Bulwa. Frustrated, Bickler demanded to know
who after all was responsible for the name changes.[118]   Reich
Germans in Alsace with French names were also urged by over-
zealous officials to change their names. Although Bickler did
not approve of this practice, he saw no reason why Reich
Germans should be allowed to keep their French names and
Alsatians forced to change theirs. Despite the appeals of
Lammers, Wagner with the support of Hitler continued his
fanatical offensive against French names, excluding only Reich
German Huguenots living in Alsace.[119]

The prime responsibility for the offensive against French
names fell on the police since party and newspaper appeals
produced few applications for official name changes. In
Strassburg, for example, such appeals produced only two thousand applications. The police proceeded to contact ten
thousand people with French names until all but a handful had
complied with the directives and initiated procedures to
change their names.[120]

Besides French inscriptions and proper names, the Nazis
planned to eliminate the despised French berets. In November
1940, Wagner ordered that the Alsatian shopowners be instructed
to end the sale of French berets and French ornaments. Ironically, these berets were produced in the Reich and purchased
by Germans. Köhler advised Wagner that an embargo would prove
useless unless the berets were forbidden in Alsace by law.
Since voluntary compliance did not work, in April 1941 Wagner
ordered his Kreisleiters to ensure the arrest of people who
wore French berets. Despite the threat of a one-year concen-
tration-camp confinement, recalcitrant Alsatians continued
to wear berets as late as 1943.[121]

Similar Alsatian resistance appeared against Nazi efforts

to eliminate the French language and purge French books. In
July 1940, all Alsatian libraries were closed and subsequently
purged of French publications. The party's propaganda department was charged with investigating and purging the libraries.
Then Wagner ordered Gaupropaganda leader Schmid to supply
Alsace with German books and Nazi publications.[122] By April
1941, Alsace had been inundated with 245,629 Nazi publications,
and the Alsatian book market had been coordinated. In the
same month, Wagner ordered that all Alsatians speaking French
in public be arrested and imprisoned for three months. The
uniformed party formations were instructed to arrest such
culprits and turn them over to the police. Later, Wagner
expressed his frustration with individual Alsatians who continued to speak French by having them deported to Germany.[123]

Not only did Alsatians continue to wear berets and speak
French in public, but they also continued to read French books.
An SD report, compiled in late 1943, revealed that French
books were still read even in public facilities. Students and
schoolchildren exchanged the books on their way to school.
The German report admitted that many Alsatian students who
attended advanced schools were still able to read French more
readily than German. The major party bookstore in Strassburg
was rarely frequented by Alsatians. Alsatian workers did not
use the Nazi-sponsored shop libraries, and the peasants relied
primarily on confessional libraries.[124]

The Nazi offensive against French culture and the French
legacy not only alienated many Alsatians but proved detrimental
to German war efforts. Wagner continuously interfered with the
armament industry in Alsace. When Alsatian workers conversed
with Poles in French, Wagner ordered the removal of the fifteen
hundred "Western Poles" from Alsace. The German armament

commission in Strassburg could not understand how such a doctrine would be permitted to disrupt the production of munitions. Wagner also restricted the deployment of foreign workers in Alsace to 4 percent of the labor force, many fewer than the 13 percent permitted in Baden. In late 1943, he also ordered the exchange of Dutch and French prisoners of war (of Polish descent) for Italian workers, causing further disruptions.[125] The climax of Wagner's Francophobia was reached in early 1944 when he refused to allow Field Marshal Erhard Milch to use French, Belgian, and Dutch workers in Alsace for the air force's badly needed fighter construction program. While German cities were being reduced to rubble, Wagner worried about the influence of French on Alsatians.[126]

In addition to the anti-French campaign, Wagner's Germanization program included the introduction of military service in Alsace and the dispensation of German citizenship to "worthy" Alsatians. Wagner felt that military service would help Germanize Alsatians rapidly while German citizenship would be granted only to those who had clearly demonstrated their loyalty to the new order. The two issues became closely interwoven since the army demanded the introduction of mandatory military service. The Nazis first attempted to prepare the Alsatians for general military duty by introducing voluntary Waffen SS service, but by December 1940 only thirty-two Alsatians had volunteered. Wagner then ordered the party to aid the SS drive for recruits, but by May 1941 only 320 Alsatians had joined the Waffen SS.[127]

The Nazis failed just as miserably in their efforts to recruit young Alsatians for the Labor Service, which was another device to prepare the population for military service. Again, the Nazis initiated a voluntary program and then dis-

covered strong Alsatian resistance. In April 1941, Wagner
decided to introduce mandatory RAD service in Alsace, and in
October the first Alsatian recruits were sent to the Reich.
All Alsatians born in 1922 had to report for Labor Service
duty or face a one-year confinement in the concentration camp
Vorbruck.[128] The Alsatians reacted predictably. Young men
deserted their jobs and attempted to escape to France, and even
RAD recruits sang the "Marseillaise" or greeted the public with
"Vive la France."[129]

Wagner, who desperately wanted the introduction of military conscription in Alsace, unsuccessfully urged Bormann in
November 1941 to aid in the introduction of the military draft
in the conquered province. In an interview with Hitler on 13
February 1942, Wagner finally obtained approval for his conscription plans, but no definite date was established for the
introduction of military service in the western provinces.
Wagner then ordered two surveys in Alsace. One was conducted
by Gädeke, his personal adjutant, and the other by the Baden
party. Gädeke contacted all officials in Alsace concerning
the advisability of conscription. All replies, including those
from the military, were negative. The party was instructed
to survey all Alsatians between seventeen and forty-eight,
ostensibly to discover who would be eligible for active party
functions. In reality, the party was determining who would be
eligible for active military service. On 9 August 1942, Hitler
finally decided to introduce military service and German citizenship in the ethnic German territories.[130]

Wagner issued the decree on German citizenship on 24
August 1942 and the one on military conscription on the
following day. To allay public outrage, the Nazi leader
defended the decrees in public. German citizenship would

be granted only to military personnel and to those who had
earned it. Unlike Bürckel in Lorraine, Wagner had no intention
of granting general German citizenship. Rather, between 25
August 1942 and 15 January 1943, Wagner issued six declarations
of German citizenship. Beginning with the "Nanzigers," Wagner
granted German citizenship only to such select groups as Alsatian police personnel, party members, decorated First World
War veterans of the German army, and parents of fallen soldiers.
The bulk of the population was not admitted to German citizenship. Yet, in March 1943, Wagner declared that anyone claiming
to be French was a German traitor.[131] Ironically, in 1944
Wagner had to raise the threats of deportation to Germany to
force some Alsatians to accept German citizenship.[132]

It was far more difficult for Wagner and the party to
explain to the Alsatians that their sons would have to be sacrificed in German military operations. Before August 1942,
only twenty-three hundred Alsatians had volunteered for German
military service. On 26 August 1942, the Strassburger Neueste
Nachrichten reported that Alsace had to fight for its position
in Europe. Only through battle could Alsace assure itself of
a happy and prosperous future. Röhn, other party leaders,
and Alsatian collaborators were put into the forefront of the
futile propaganda campaign that attempted to defend the military conscription.[133] This attempt to defend the German introduction of the draft in Alsace was difficult enough. However,
when Wagner supported not only army drafts but also Waffen
SS recruitment drives (and eventually in 1944 the forced induction of Alsatians into the Waffen SS), all hopes of winning
Alsatian cooperation dissipated.[134]

It became a major function of the party in Alsace after
September 1942 to supervise and support the military conscrip-

tion efforts. On 3 September 1942, Röhn ordered the party to
supervise the physical examination of young draftees.[135] Local
leaders were advised to "counsel" draftees who refused to
sign their military identification passes, and SA units were
organized to force unwilling young men to appear at induction
centers. But even with party and police supervision many draftees appeared with French berets, departed from their relatives
with "au revoir," and even sang the French national anthem.[136]

In September 1942, Wagner demanded the exchange of Alsatian police and rail personnel for Reich German officials since
he did not trust the Alsatians, and he ordered the creation of
a from two- to three-kilometer-wide patrolled border strip to
prevent illegal emigration from Alsace.[137] Wagner also initiated plans for the deportation to Germany of families whose
young relatives had deserted military or RAD service. Beyond
this, the CdZ approved the execution of civilians who had aided
deserting Alsatian soldiers, and Wagner demanded the death penalty for Alsatians who refused to honor their induction
notices.[138] On 12 February 1943, eighteen young Alsatians from
Ballersdorf, Altkirch, attempted to escape military service by
entering Switzerland. During a clash with border guards, the
group killed one guard but was subsequently captured. The
Strassburg court, which was under Wagner's influence, sentenced
the young Alsatians to death on 16 February 1943. Even before
the court decision, Wagner had issued execution orders to the
police.[139]

If Wagner had hoped that the drafted Alsatians would be
converted to Germandom, he was sadly disappointed. The Alsatian soldiers were subjected to discrimination and harassment
in the army. Because of some Alsatian desertions, the army
refused to allow Alsatian soldiers to spend their furloughs

in Alsace. Wagner contested this rule successfully. He also
concluded special agreements with the army, air force, RAD,
and Organization Todt to assure that Alsatians were treated
as Reich Germans.[140] Despite Wagner's efforts, occasionally
Alsatians continued to receive "special" treatment. In any
case, Wagner's special arrangements with the army were not made
until mid-1944, two years after Alsatians had first been
drafted. In Alsace Wagner was also forced to take precautions
against Alsatian soldiers on leave. They had to report to the
mayors to prevent desertion, and as older age groups were
drafted, Wagner approved special three-month political training courses for Alsatian soldiers. Finally, Wagner drafted
proposals for the treatment of Alsatians in the army in which
he recommended periodic hard punishments to condition Alsatians
to military life.[141]

The belated granting of German citizenship in Alsace, combined with the introduction of military conscription, failed
to convert the majority of Alsatians to the German cause any
more than the anti-French mania had. Instead, the immediate
result of the military conscription was to produce increased
resistance accompanied by accelerated repression and deportations.[142]

VORBRUCK BEI SCHIRMECK AND DEPORTATIONS

The Alsatian opposition to Nazification and Germanization was
not produced by the introduction of military conscription
alone. It had existed as early as 1940 and was merely accelerated after 1942. The Nazis discovered this opposition immediately after the German occupation of Alsace. As early as 1940,

the Baden Nazis introduced two major techniques in their attempts to convert recalcitrant Alsatians to the German cause. The first involved the establishment of a concentration camp in Vorbruck near Schirmeck, and the second the deportation of Alsatian opponents, first to France and subsequently to the Reich.

The German security police established a detention center in Vorbruck near Schirmeck in mid-July 1940. The camp was designed as a reformatory, not a death camp, where young Alsatians would be indoctrinated (and frightened) into accepting Germanization and Nazification.[143] This camp operated under the direct control of Wagner until 1944. The chief of civil administration resisted Himmler's attempts to obtain control of Vorbruck by pointing out that the camp was for young Alsatian "thick heads." Himmler then established his own Alsatian death camp in Natzweiler, totally independent of Wagner. Between 1941 and 1943, over six thousand prisoners from various parts of Europe, including Alsace, were murdered there. Wagner's only concession to Himmler came in July 1942, when he agreed to transfer especially difficult Alsatian cases to Reich concentration camps for "permanent elimination."[144]

Wagner soon discovered that the number of Alsatian "thick heads," particularly among the Alsatian youth, was enormous. According to SD (secret police) reports, in 1940 a majority of Alsatian children over fourteen reflected the anti-Nazi sentiments of their parents and schools. These older youths, carried out persistent demonstrations against the Germanization programs and even engaged in active sabotage. Organized resistance to the Nazi occupation took hold in September 1940 in Upper Rhine and in January 1941 in Lower Rhine. The first organized public anti-Nazi activities in Alsace occurred in

1941, and they were conceived and led by young Alsatians. In
Mühlhausen, young unskilled workers (<u>Hilfsarbeiter</u>), who were
between fifteen and eighteen, formed in late 1940 a secret
"Blue Mask" association, which attacked Hitler Youth members
and destroyed party emblems and flags.[145]

The disturbances were general in Alsace in 1941, and the
introduction of mandatory RAD service aggravated the situation.
All over Alsace young people demonstrated on the eve of the
French national holiday of 14 July. In the Catholic community
of Hochfelden in the district of Strassburg, a group of 150
to 200 youths paraded on the evening of 13 July 1941. The
population applauded the youths, who sang the French national
anthem and honored the local war memorial. The security police
concluded in 1941 that the Communists were behind these demonstrations since the demonstrators were overwhelmingly workers
and artisans. The German attack on Russia in the summer of
1941, no doubt, reinvigorated the Alsatian Communists, but the
anti-Nazi rallies were just as vigorous in predominantly Catholic communities like Hochfelden. As always, Wagner resisted the
pleas of Bickler and other ethnic German leaders to show mercy.
At first, he demanded that all culprits be sent to the Vorbruck
camp in Schirmeck until the end of the war, but the chief of
the security police induced him to limit the imprisonment to
seven leaders.[146]

The increased opposition of young Alsatian "thick heads"
was not stifled by the existence of the Schirmeck concentration
camp. Wagner resorted to accelerated "legal" terrorism after
the "Weinum" group, an association of young Alsatians, bombed
Wagner's car in late 1941. Over thirty youths were arrested
and imprisoned, and Wagner demanded the death penalty for the
leader Weinum and the Pole Siratsky despite the fact that both

were minors. Bickler and the other Alsatian party members had
attempted to persuade Wagner that with the exception of the
ringleaders, most of the youths of the "Weinum" group were
merely romantic adventurers and should be freed. Wagner insisted on Weinum's death and the imprisonment of his accomplices.
In February 1942, the Reich minister of justice agreed with
Wagner that Alsatian crimes be adjudicated in Strassburg. The
special court in Strassburg, which was responsible to Wagner,
issued the death sentence against Weinum on 1 April 1942.
Increasingly, Wagner relied on this court after 1942 to supplement the Schirmeck concentration camp in his efforts to force
Germanization and Nazification on Alsace. In 1943 alone,
72 political death sentences were issued in Alsace,
and 1,086 Alsatians were sent to the concentration camp in
Schirmeck.[147]

Another method employed by the Nazis to ensure the success of Germanization was mass deportation. The first major
population purge occurred in Alsace in 1940 when "asocials,"
criminals, and gypsies were gathered and sent to France. Then
in October the Nazis deported the remaining Jews to southern
France. Finally, a total of one hundred thousand Alsatians
who had been evacuated in 1939 and 1940 by the French were
either refused readmission or failed to return. The deportations from Alsace in 1940 were completely controlled by Wagner.
Himmler had demanded in September that able-bodied criminals
and "asocials" be sent to the Reich's concentration camps.
He also emphasized that no "good racial stock" be deported
to France. Despite Himmler's desires, he had no influence
on the first deportation from Alsace in 1940.[148]

A few "French natives" (a term the Nazis applied to
non-Alsatian French) who had married native Alsatians were

permitted to remain in Alsace after September 1940 if they
signed declarations that recognized the Nazi state, Germandom,
and the Reich's claim to Alsace. Numerous Alsatian notables
and industrialists were deported because of their pro-French
sympathies. One Count Johann von Pourtales, who lost his property in Alsace, was married to a relative of the former Imperial
Reich Chancellor Theobald von Bethmann-Hollweg.[149] In fact,
most of the Alsatian noble families who were deported to France
had relatives in the Reich. By April 1941, the CdZ had
received over one hundred requests from such relatives of
deported Alsatians who attempted to salvage family archives.[150]
In addition, Alsatian émigrés who had lost their estates in
1918 attempted to return to Alsace after 1940 and claim their
properties. Many of the properties, confiscated from Alsatian
notables and Francophiles, were usurped by German party officials or agencies. The power of dispensing these properties
rested with Wagner.[151] In Alsace, Nazi racial doctrines produced concrete material advantages for the party and the chief
of civil administration.

On 20 December 1940, the SNN announced that the deportation of "harmful elements" from Alsace was complete. "Asocials" and criminals were still sent to France in 1941, but
Alsatian Francophiles were no longer deported. In 1942 Wagner
attempted to initiate another major population shift from
Alsace. In early 1942, Wagner talked to Hitler about the
necessity of cleansing Alsace of all "useless and racially
inferior" elements. Hitler approved of the plan enthusiastically. During one of his dinner conversations in May 1942,
Hitler declared that all Alsatians who could not be Germanized
must be deported. Hitler also praised Bürckel's massive deportations of Lorrainers, and he suggested that 250,000 Alsatian

Francophiles would have to be deported either to France or to
the east. The void would be filled with farmers from Baden who
needed extra land.[152]

Wagner's proposed cleansing of Alsace caused the immediate
intervention of the SS and Himmler, who demanded that the Alsatians be sent to the Reich. The SS initiated plans to have the
security police survey all Francophile Alsatians who were
scheduled to be deported. As Himmler informed Wagner in June
1942, no German blood must be lost to France.[153] Heydrich had
already established a Central Immigration Committee (EWZ) in
Paris in June 1941 to search for Germans in France. The EWZ
quickly discovered that most "Germans" living in France had
little desire to return to the Reich. This was also confirmed
by the CdZ's resettlement office, which was led by the former
Alsatian autonomist J. Keppi and charged with the task of
searching for Alsatian evacuees who had not returned after
1940. Keppi could not even induce the students and faculty of
the University of Strassburg who had fled to Clermont-Ferrand
to return to Alsace.[154] Himmler argued that only "German
blood" in France could threaten Germany in the future, and he
informed Lammers in June 1942 that he would permit no "valuable blood" to remain in France. Specifically the SS was worried that Wagner's proposed purges in Alsace would send valuable blood to France.[155]

Wagner cooperated fully with Himmler and even attempted
to surpass his racial mania. In the summer of 1942, Himmler
and Wagner met in Hitler's headquarters, and one of the topics
they discussed was the influence of Germans in France. By
November 1942, Wagner sent Hitler and Himmler a list of several
hundred French officers who had German names. Even Himmler
suggested that the "repatriation" of these officers would have

to be postponed until a final settlement was reached with
France. In March 1944, Wagner informed Himmler's representative in southeastern Germany, Hofmann, that he wanted the
return of Alsatians from France to rebuild the biological
strength of his lands. Since only 3,261 Alsatians had been
returned to Alsace from France by March 1944, Wagner, as usual,
resorted to force.[156]

Wagner and Himmler agreed not only on the return of Alsatians from France but they also decided that recalcitrant
Alsatians who resisted Germanization and Nazification be sent
to the Reich and eventually to the Ukraine. But instead of a
general deportation, which would have approached the dimen-
sions of 1940, the Nazis decided on specific categories. In
late 1942, Wagner deported Alsatian families whose sons had
deserted the army or who failed to appear for induction. He
even demanded the deportation of Alsatian "Patois" residents
who did not speak German unless they had contributed to the
Nazi and German cause in Alsace.[157] Due to the housing shortages in the Reich, Wagner was forced to cease the deportation
of Francophiles in 1943 and devote all of his attention to the
deportation of Alsatian families whose sons had refused military service. Only the growing public Alsatian resistance to
Germanization in 1944 induced Wagner again to permit the deportation of Francophiles and those Alsatians who persisted in
speaking French and wearing French berets.[158] Nothing illustrated the failure of the Nazis' Germanization efforts in
Alsace more clearly than Wagner's continuing reliance on deportations and the concentration camp in Schirmeck.

DENOUEMENT

Despite the rhetoric of tribal unity between Baden and Alsace, the German occupation of Alsace revealed two characteristics of Nazi domination in Europe. First, the Baden Nazis failed to force Nazification and extreme Germanization on Alsace. Despite the establishment of the party in Alsace, the Germans maintained power only through force. Second, the expansion of the Baden party and the Baden state ministries into Alsace represented the domination of Alsace by the leading Baden Nazis, who had immense new opportunities to acquire a degree of power and influence that they had not enjoyed in Baden since 1933/34. After a German victory, Wagner would have established himself in Strassburg in order to escape the influence of Berlin party and state agencies. As CdZ, Wagner was able to enhance both his party and his state functions. Once the Baden party and state offices had been transferred to Strassburg, the Reich party and state leaders immediately were confronted with the office of CdZ. And in Alsace only Hitler, Bormann, Schwarz, and Himmler were able to exert direct influence on party and state affairs.

In 1940, Wagner reached the apex of his party (and state) career. He was Reich governor of Baden, CdZ in Alsace, and Gau leader of both Baden and Alsace. Assuming that Hitler had remained alive after a German victory in war, Wagner would have emerged as one of the most influential Nazi leaders in Germany. Along with Wagner, the leading Gau party cadre members and several district PO leaders took part in this upward mobility. Röhn practically became Gau leader of the party in Alsace, and Schuppel handled all state and party personnel questions in Alsace. Both the party's AfB and the party's AfK

were able to control the civil service and the municipal leaders in Alsace to a degree they had never enjoyed in Baden. On
the other hand, some party and state leaders in Baden felt that
the Alsatian burden would merely disrupt both the party and
state organizations in Baden. Dinkel, the NSV Gauamt leader,
and Kerber, the lord mayor of Freiburg, expressed this view.
But Wagner's decisions had always been based on the blind
implementation of Hitler's directives rather than the organizational health of the party or the state.[159]

The Alsatians clearly perceived the Baden domination, and
they resisted the Badenese as vigorously as they had the French
centralists before 1940. In late 1942, Alsatian workers told
Eastern European laborers who were employed in Alsatian factories that they were in France, not in Germany. The Nazi
party was blamed by the Alsatians for the introduction of
military service and the war casualties. Despite accelerated
political indoctrination in schools, young Alsatians refused
to wear their Hitler Youth uniforms and in general presented
an anti-German attitude. In the rural areas of Alsace, the
party had failed to dislodge the confessional influence over
youth.[160] In general, Alsatian humor defined party member,
Parteigenosse (Pg), as having had bad luck and citizen, Volks
genosse, (Vg), as having been careful.[161] Even the fanatical
Alsatian Nazi, Paul Schall, was aware of the realities of the
political situation in Alsace when he admitted in 1943 that
Alsatians had still not discovered their Reich identity. In
September 1944, Schall concluded that the strongest argument
for the Nazi cause in Alsace had always been the realities of
German military victories. He further conceded that by late
1944 the Alsatians wanted to hear nothing more about the Nazi
party.[162] Not surprisingly, in November and December 1944

the Alsatians greeted the advancing Allied troops with jubila-
tion.[163]

Schall and the Alsatian Nazi leaders, however, continued
to support the lost cause. These Alsatian Nazis, together with
Ernst, founded the "Alsatian Liberation Front" in December 1944
in Colmar. Between late 1944 and March 1945, the Führer presented articles on Alsace, and Wagner continued to defend and
explain the Alsatians to the Badenese and the Germans. The
Stuttgart radio presented an Alsatian hour as late as March
1945, which was, however, ignored by both the Badenese and
the Alsatians in Baden.[164] The Germans and the Badenese realized that the Alsatians had rejected the German invaders. SS
leader Gottlob Berger reported to Himmler in June 1944 that
the Alsatians were scum (Sauvolk), and he suggested that half
of the population be deported. Berger noted that Stalin would
certainly accept the Alsatians.[165]

In Baden the population felt that Wagner had damaged the
German cause in Alsace more in four years than the Prussians
had in forty-five. Above all, the Badenese rejected Wagner's
defense of the Alsatians, and many expressed the wish that
Wagner should have remained with "his Alsatians." Many Badenese concluded in 1945 that the Alsatians were really useless
and not even German. How little the Baden population had
learned about European affairs in general was revealed by the
Badenese bewilderment at the knowledge that Germans were
hated so widely in Europe. With naiveté they inquired whether
this hatred was produced by German militarism or German administrative methods.[166]

The Nazi leaders of Baden were in undisputed command in
Alsace. After the war, the Baden Nazis and their Alsatian
collaborators had to account for their roles in Alsace. Some

like the Alsatian Kreisleiter Hans-Peter Murer and the SD
leader of Strassburg, Isselhorst, were shot by the French.
More important, the French tried the leading Baden Nazi leaders in 1946 in what the New York Times called "France's
Nuremberg."[167] The Gau leader Wagner, his adjutant Gädeke,
the deputy Gau leader Röhn, and the Gau staff and personnel
leader Schuppel were convicted by the French. The 1946 trial
also included the Kreisleiter of the Alsatian district of
Thann and the prosecutor and judge of the special court of
Strassburg. They were accused of forcing French citizens to
bear arms and of having committed murders. All of Wagner's
associates maintained that they merely carried out his orders.
All but the prosecutor of the special court of Strassburg
were convicted and executed. Wagner, admitting he had desired
a Nazi victory, declared that National Socialism was his faith
and Germany his religion. Before his execution on 14 August
1946, the fanatical Wagner praised a dead trinity by exclaim-
ing "long live Greater Germany, long live Hitler, long live
National Socialism."[168] Wagner's sole legacy was that Nazi
rule in Alsace probably contributed substantially to the subsequent reintegration of Alsace into France.[169]

Conclusion

Wagner's plea in 1946 for the longevity of a Greater Germany, and his praise of Hitler and National Socialism, appears absurd in view of the party's dramatic decline in prestige in Baden during the last years of the war and the total defeat of Germany. This final, futile völkisch propaganda statement may have reflected Wagner's realization that he had lost his plea before the French military court. More likely, however, it reflected his sincere commitment to Hitler and National Socialism. After all, Wagner had served the cause of völkisch German nationalism since 1918 and had been a faithful supporter of Hitler since 1923. This dedicated service to the Nazi cause continued until 29 April 1945, when he dismissed his staff at Bodmann on Lake Constance. After discovering that his wife had committed suicide, Wagner emerged from hiding and surrendered to the Americans on 29 July 1945. The American interrogator who interviewed Wagner noted the former Gau leader's "ferocious fidelity to Nazi ideology."[1]

Wagner and his Gau clique of long-term völkisch true believers had been the axis around which the Baden NSDAP had evolved before 1933. After the Nazi seizure of power, this Baden elite, functioning in both party and state positions, continued to play an important part in the coordination of society and government. Wagner's elite had guided the pluralistic party to victory and helped to maintain Hitler in power

after 1933, regardless of his shifting tactics. The Gau clique
was never connected closely with one socioeconomic world view.
In 1925 Wagner and his supporters had appealed to workers and
farmers, and two years later they had added the Mittelstand
to the list of party propaganda themes. The one theme that
remained constant in the Gau party's propaganda was völkisch
nationalism. This thematic continuity helped to coalesce a
diverse group of völkisch activists in Baden into a fanatic
movement, totally subservient to Hitler's wishes. Nor was
this total commitment unique to Robert Wagner. In an interview in Karlsruhe in June 1977, Walter Köhler, the former
deputy Gau leader and minister president of Baden after 1933,
admitted frankly that given the opportunity he would "do it
all over again."[2]

A loyal and fanatic völkisch Gau elite was imperative
because in reality the Nazi party was a "pluralistic" movement.
As early as 1923, the NSDAP had won the support of surprisingly diverse groups of völkisch activists. Former Communists
and socialists like Ulshöfer, Wittmann, and Cordier were drawn
to the Nazi movement, primarily through the middle-class
Schutz- und Trutzbund. Both the former Marxists and the
middle-class professionals who were active in the Schutz- und
Trutzbund wanted to convert the workers to völkisch nationalism. They hoped to create a new national unity that would
enable Germany to reverse the consequences of 1918. In addition to the former Marxists and middle-class völkisch activists, the Baden party by 1923 had also attracted farmers in
such communities as Liedolsheim where social homogeneity had
broken down. Since the 1890s, the Baden Socialists had
penetrated these "rural" communities and organized the part-
time farmers who had found employment in industry. In

Liedolsheim in 1923, the founders of the Nazi local appealed
to both workers and farmers in an attempt to recapture the lost
social and political homogeneity.[3]

The Baden party was also pluralistic in the sense that as
early as 1923 völkisch activists with different social backgrounds had emphasized one specific socioeconomic group in
their attempts to "rescue" Germany from defeat and social
conflict. There is no reason to question Wittmann's sincere
interest in workers. Prior to World War I, he had spent much
of his life as a member of the Socialist Party and the defeat
catapulted him into a new political milieu. Nor can there be
doubt of Albert Roth's fanatic commitment to farmers. Although
he also appealed to labor, his plan for the regeneration of
Germany called for an antiurban ruralism. Finally, the Gau
leader of the NSFP in 1924, Müller, honestly felt that Germany's social and political problems could best be solved by
the creation of a Kaufmannstand, clearly a middle-class solution that focused on one segment of the troubled Mittelstand.
These labor, farmer, and Mittelstand wings of the Baden party
were of course united by a common hatred of 1918. These
wings were most active on the local and district level after
1925, and they reflected not just opportunism but real commitment to a specific social basis for the völkisch regeneration of Germany.

The Gau clique around Wagner was less closely identified
with one specific social interest group, although until 1927
appeals to workers and peasants dominated the rhetoric of the
Gau activists. Many völkisch true believers who gravitated
to Wagner had been active in 1923/24, either in the Baden
NSDAP or in a völkisch or paramilitary organization. Like the
Baden party's leadership in general, the Gau elite was a male-

dominated, lower-middle-class group. Elementary teachers,
brewers, artisans, Kaufmänner, and white-collar employees,
with only a light sprinkling of educated members of the solid
middle class, dominated the social profile of the leadership
in Baden before and after 1933. Although there was much continuity among the "1923 Nazis" in Baden, many of the former
leftists like Ulshöfer, Cordier, and Wittmann either disappeared from the political scene or became unimportant party
members. Many of the leading Nazis after 1923 (like Walter
Köhler) came from the DNVP and the DVFB. After 1925, the
Baden party supported the white-collar employees' union (DHV)
and won the support of a growing number of Landbund leaders.
Furthermore, many small and middle-sized industries attempted
to recruit Nazi workers in an effort to undermine the influence of the Marxists. This did not mean that the Gau leadership of Baden neglected labor after 1925. In fact, as late
as 1928 the Baden candidates in the election included two
former Marxists. Despite the efforts by the Baden Nazis to
use former Communists like Friedrich to win the support of
labor, the party had little success in converting the industrial worker to National Socialism. The pluralistic social
appeals continued until 1933. The emphasis after 1927, however, was on farmers and the Mittelstand.[4]

Wagner's personal preference was for the Nazi Handarbeiter (manual laborer). The Baden Gau leader stated frankly
that if he had to choose between a bourgeois Nazi and a Handarbeiter Nazi, he would always select the latter. This view was
not based on a socioeconomic philosophy but rather on Wagner's
conviction that the Handarbeiter Nazi was a more dedicated and
fanatic party member. The Handarbeiter could be anyone working
with his hands, from the industrial worker to the artisan.

Wagner's first interest and commitment was always to the movement and particularly to Hitler. After 1933 he neglected the
DAF and discouraged the efforts of the Mittelstand to change
conditions radically in Baden. He attempted to relieve the
rural plight, but this was probably caused in part by Hitler's
emphasis on the rural problem in 1933. Instead, Wagner was
mostly concerned with consolidating the movement's political
powers. While giving lip service to rural romanticism after
1933, he also urged the industrialization of Baden's rural
areas to solve real economic problems. Wagner and his Gau
elite remained Hitler's tools until the end. Committed to
private property, racism, and völkisch nationalism, Wagner
could support nothing but a racial-political revolution.

After 1925 one of the most important functions of the
party, and particularly of the Gau party elite, was to generate
voter support for the Nazi movement and to organize the various
socioeconomic and pluralistic interest groups of society.
After the party began to prepare for the future coordination
of German society by establishing numerous affiliated organizations, the role of the Gau elite became especially crucial
since it stood above these diverse and pluralistic party
organizations. The Gau party's cadre elite provided the
organizational motor for the party's expansion after 1928,
and it guaranteed Hitler's control over the burgeoning party
structure after 1930.

In terms of voter appeal, the Baden Nazis, and the völkisch movement in general, won early support in both urban and
rural Protestant communities. Benefiting from the impact of
inflation and international crisis, the Völkisch Block did
particularly well in the election of May 1924 in urban communities like Heidelberg and Bruchsal. Even in industrial

Mannheim the Völkisch Block reached its state average of 4.8
percent of the total vote. Although the völkisch forces were
well represented in rural Protestant strongholds like Liedolsheim, the Völkisch Block's greatest strength in May 1924 lay
in the urban centers of Baden with populations over 10,000.
After 1924 the party's strength in the major urban centers
declined, as many middle-class voters returned to the DNVP or
DVP. Until 1929 the Baden NSDAP was proportionally strongest
in medium urban and small rural communities in northern Baden.
In the municipal election of 1926, the party won seats in ten
communities. Only two of these communities had Catholic
majorities and seven had populations between 781 and 6,200.
This trend reached a climax in the election of 1928 when the
Baden party's "takeoff" occurred in the rural, Protestant
communities of northern and northeastern Baden. Finally, in
the election of 1929 the party advanced again in the major
urban centers of the state, reaching in many cases the percentages achieved in the May 1924 election. The party's activism
and the deteriorating economic conditions after 1929 enabled
the Baden NSDAP to activate the large numbers of nonvoters or
former voters and eventually to gather most of the urban and
rural middle-class votes.

There was a tremendous amount of political continuity in
the völkisch and right-wing centers of Baden. Some rural
communities like Liedolsheim contained a substantial number
of people who rejected the republic from the start. The DNVP
was very strong in Liedolsheim as early as 1919. By 1924,
this DNVP base had evolved into a strong Nazi cell. In small
towns like Eberbach, the roots of the long-term Nazi cells
came from the disillusioned Democrats. In 1919, the German
Democratic party was the strongest middle-class party in

Eberbach. By 1920/21, the DNVP and DVP had emerged to rival
the Democrats. Building upon the impact of the inflation of
1923 and the frustrated nationalism of many former DNVP supporters, the Völkisch Block emerged in May 1924 and even over-
took the Nationalists in terms of voter support. This völkisch
cell became the NSDAP in 1925 and evolved into a Nazi stronghold by the fall of that year. By 1928, one third of the
voters of Liedolsheim and Eberbach cast their votes for the
NSDAP. In both instances, the Nazi party had established
itself by 1925. In the rural, Protestant district of Kehl,
the Nazis were active but not very strong before 1928. In
Kehl, the Rechtsblock was the dominant political force between
1921 and 1927. As in Eberbach, the German Democratic party
had been the strongest middle-class party in the district of
Kehl in 1919. But in this rural district the traditional right
was able to maintain itself much longer than in Eberbach or
Liedolsheim. The strong continuity of Rechtsblock politics,
however, can be seen in the overwhelming correlation between
the state election of 1921 and the national election of July
1932. The Nazi party obtained its largest percentages in the
districts and communities where the Rechtsblock had been
strongest in 1921. By July 1932, both the traditional, conservative voters and the former "liberal" voters in Baden had
been harnessed by the Nazi party. The Rechtsblock tradition
had provided the motor for this victory, while the deteriorating economic conditions supplied the fuel.[5]

By July 1932, the Baden party had reached the limits of
its voter appeal. At this stage, the national party leadership rescued the Gau party from disintegration. First,
Hitler's assumption of power in January 1933 reinvigorated
the Gau party, and second, the Nazi ministers began to inter-

fere in Baden's internal affairs. Berlin decided when the
Gau party should attempt to capture the government, and Frick
appointed Wagner Reich commissar in early 1933 without consulting Köhler, the acting Gau leader of Baden. When Wagner
returned to his native state, however, he relied on the party
and on the SA to infiltrate local governments and to usurp
state powers. In only five days (between 9 and 13 March 1933),
the Baden party leaders seized complete control of the government. It was indeed a political revolution, considering that
poorly educated members of the lower middle class, like Wagner
and Köhler, captured the leading state posts.

The Nazi seizure of power in Baden in March 1933 confronted the party organization with a series of disintegrating
forces. Leading Baden Nazis like Wagner, Köhler, Pflaumer,
and Wacker assumed the top government positions, and Kreisleiters flocked to the municipal posts. Here began one of
the first major divisions of the Baden party after 1933.
These Nazis who assumed government posts began to identify
with the new positions. Only Wagner continued to be both Gau
leader and Reich governor of Baden. While Wagner remained
attached to the party structure, Köhler and Pflaumer gradually
moved away from their former party responsibilities. Numerous former Kreisleiters who obtained municipal positions followed the examples of Köhler and Pflaumer, although they
remained loyal Nazis.

Genuine state-party conflicts persisted, particularly in
the case of the judiciary, the civil service, and the Landräte.
These state offices and positions resisted "partification"
and to some extent even Nazification. As late as 1938, many
civil servants, although loyal to Hitler, considered the party
a disruptive force. The judiciary in particular resented the

poorly educated Nazi leaders who constantly tried to interfere
in court matters. Although some leading judges had supported
the Nazi movement before 1933 and continued to support the
growth of German power after 1933, many considered the NSDAP
leaders to be social and educational inferiors.

In general, much of the state-party conflict after 1933,
both on the ministerial and the municipal levels, arose from
controversies between rival Nazis. Wagner's attempt to replace
Köhler as minister president and the efforts of Nazi mayors
to resist the encroachments of the party did not reflect basic
conflicts over policies. In these instances, convinced Nazis
held both state and party posts, and ideological conflicts
did not produce the struggles. Both groups accepted Nazification, but the "state Nazis" now had to protect their new
positions from the party activists who had not obtained such
posts. The Nazis who had risen to the state positions because
of their party careers now relied on the existing, although
purged, state apparatus and civil service. This trend was
even evident in the conflict between Karlsruhe and Berlin
after 1933. The Baden Nazis stubbornly attempted to defend
the interests of the state of Baden against neighboring states
and the encroachments of Berlin party and state agencies.

The fragmentation of the alleged monolithic party was
apparent not only on ministerial and mayoral levels, where
rival Nazis battled each other, but also in the evolution of
the party's two affiliates concerned with state affairs--the
Office for Municipal Affairs (AfK) and the Office for Civil
Servants (AfB). Before 1933, both party affiliates had pursued a common struggle against the "Weimar state." Both
party agencies represented the party's efforts before 1933
to undermine the state and to expand the party's influence in

municipalities and among civil servants. After 1933 the two
agencies pursued different tasks. The AfB saw itself as the
vanguard of the party's attack on the exclusive civil service.
It indoctrinated and attempted to coordinate the civil servants
of Baden, but it could not undermine the privileged position
of the civil service. As late as 1938, Mauch was proposing
party-sponsored selection programs for the civil service.
The failure of the AfB vis-à-vis the civil service perpetuated
the party affiliate's orientation and identification with the
party structure. The AfK, on the other hand, was much more
successful in nominating Nazis for major mayoral positions.
After the appointment of Nazis and party members to the leading municipal positions, the AfK began to identify with the
Nazi mayors and municipal administrations, and it attempted
to protect Nazi mayors from the interference of various party
agencies.

While the rival Nazis battled each other over ministerial
prerogatives and the party's affiliates began to identify with
certain subcultures in Baden's society, the party's projected
monolithic image, which had never really been achieved in practice, disintegrated even more noticeably. Of course, this does
not mean that the party had failed in its primary functions
of providing the major Nazis with governmental powers and of
perpetuating these powers. In effect, it meant the appearance of Nazi "parties," each pursuing specific functions and
interests in Nazi Germany but all charged with the ultimate
responsibility of keeping Hitler in power.

This interparty struggle was most pronounced on the socioeconomic level. The leading Baden Nazis made it clear to the
Baden party members, only three days after Wagner became Reich
commissar, that the party wanted a political revolution, not

a social one. This raised the question of what would happen
to Baden society after the Nazi seizure of political power.
Hitler had told Rauschning that the party "would take over
what had been society."[6] Later observers have echoed this
description of the functions of the party. George L. Mosse
notes that all individuals and organizations had to be nation-
alized by "making them subject to party control." He even
suggests that the "Nazi party like the spider in its web
controlled all the lifelines of the nation."[7] In reality,
the party as a unit did not control society. Rather party
affiliates and organizations, which represented diverse social
interest aggregations, coordinated different social and economic segments of society. They destroyed the pluralistic
organizations of society only to replace them with other pluralistic party organizations. Nazification was the accepted
goal and "partification" the desired mode. In practice, partification produced a variety of party affiliates which tended
(as Kramer lamented in 1936) to become independent organizations and gravitate away from the central cadre organization
of the party (PO).

In terms of implementing party programs, the Nazis fulfilled the aspirations of the early Baden Nazis of Pforzheim
and Liedolsheim by coordinating the workers and by praising
the farmers. True, most industrial workers did not become
convinced Nazis, and passive resistance was noticed, but the
Nazi leaders were able to carry on major military and extermination programs without significant labor disturbances.
Similarly, the Mittelstand and farm interests were coordinated
by party organizations, and the interests of these socioeconomic segments of society were subordinated to the needs
of an expansionistic state. In 1935, Wagner bluntly told the

Baden Mittelstand that no economic experiments would be permitted. Even the rural program of the party, despite blood
and soil propaganda, was subordinated to the interests of the
military-industrial state. The "rural flight" continued, and
many peasants remained loyal to the Catholic church. But by
eliminating the "democratic pluralism" the party affiliates
absorbed the aspirations and criticisms of the different socioeconomic segments of society without endangering the Nazi
regime's primary goals of external expansion and internal
racial purification. Party pluralism may have threatened
the cadre organization's authority, but it actually strength-
ened the Nazi rulers' control of German society by isolating
and fragmenting Baden's socioeconomic interests.[8]

This development was even more apparent in the party's
efforts to coordinate different components of society, ranging from women to students. Again a specific party affiliate
or party organization emerged to control a specific segment
of society. The evolution of the NS Student League and the
party cadre organization's discrimination against the NS
Women's League, illustrate the internal divisions of the
alleged monolithic party. But the basic purpose of both
socioeconomic and pluralistic party affiliates was to prevent
the aggregation of interests which could endanger the Nazi
regime. It was totalitarian in aspiration but not monolithic
in practice, since the diverse party organizations frequently
fought each other over spheres of influence. Also, the Nazis
did not restructure basic tenets of German society. The
social profile of students continued to reflect the educational dominance of the middle class, and the majority of
Baden's AHS graduates were still attracted to "traditional"
rather than party careers.

In one area particularly, the Nazis attempted to create
an effective monolithic milieu. This was in the party's effort
to ensure the success of the racial concepts of the völkisch
true believers. The effort entailed the elimination of alien
subcultures, particularly the church and Jews, and the establishment and perpetuation of racial norms through the Racial
Policy Office and the NSV. The party played a permanent and
important part in the persecution and supervision of both the
church and the Jews. It was the vanguard of the Nazi regime's
anti-Semitic campaigns, which continued even after most Baden
Jews had been deported to France in October 1940. While the
party eventually "triumphed" in its anti-Semitic drives,
it faced much stronger opposition from the Catholic church.
Wagner and the Gau cadre leadership supported Hartlieb's
programs, which were directed against an alien and rival view.
The Gau leadership's attitude, combined with Bormann's view
on the church, would certainly have resulted in a major church-
party conflict after the war. But it would have been a divided
party attack since Baden party leaders observed during the
war that fellow party members were placing their church positions above their party posts. As had occurred so frequently
before, Bormann and Hitler would have had to rely on the loyal
and fanatic Gau cadre leadership around Wagner to implement
the radical antichurch programs.

The völkisch-racial ideology was disseminated among party
affiliates and social organizations by the party's Racial
Policy Office, and the state provided the machinery for both
eugenics and euthanasia programs. But the most important party
agency that tried (and may in the long run have succeeded
more than any other party agency) to remold German society
along völkisch, racial lines, was the NS Welfare Organization.

Although it was led by the former Kreisleiter and fanatic
Nazi Philip Dinkel, the NSV was not an exclusive party agency
but rather a mass organization which allowed the participation
of nonparty members. The NSV allowed the Nazi regime to generate immediate support for the new regime by sponsoring the
Winter Relief Program. It also attracted the collaboration of
people who would not have supported the party's cadre organization. Finally, the NSV provided the Nazi leaders with an
organization to implement racial and political socialization
programs. Despite the cynicism associated with the WHW campaigns after 1936, and the NSV's frustrations during the war
with church-sponsored kindergartens and nursing programs, the
NSV still touched and influenced more people than any other
party affiliate with the exception of the DAF. Above all, the
NSV, unlike the other party organizations and affiliates, was
directed toward the general population rather than any specific socioeconomic or pluralist organization in society. In
this respect, the NSV provided more potential for the eventual
Nazification of Baden society than any other party-related
agency. Ironically, the NSV was one of the most nonelitist
party affiliates.

The very structure of the NSV allowed and encouraged the
participation of a large segment of the population. In this
sense, it contributed also to the "partification" of society,
especially in view of the fact that the party was not a monolithic structure. Dinkel, however, was closely connected to
the Gau cadre organization, and he relied on Wagner's support
and guidance. This type of Nazification and partification
in the long run would have been more effective in legitimizing
the Nazi regime than the expansion of the cadre organization's
"control" functions as defined by Orlow.[9] Certainly a party,

exercising control functions, still had to rely on such
Betreuung agencies as the NSV in order to establish the
regime's legitimacy.

The growth of such party affiliates and the emergence
of leading Nazis in government positions forced the party's
cadre organization to face the question of what the value and
function of the party was after 1933. The problem had mani-
fested itself clearly by 1935/36 when Wagner felt it necessary
to defend the purpose of the party. He declared that the
party would provide both Betreuung and leadership in the Nazi
state. These declarations could not hide the obvious developments. First, by 1936 the party affiliates had become independent, or aspired to become independent, from the party's
cadre organization. Second, while the party affiliates pursued "positive" functions that the population could appreciate,
the public developed a growing contempt for the cadre organization's "little Führers." Most important, the public continued
to look to state agencies for basic services. Moreover, the
party membership expanded greatly after 1933, thereby diluting
still more the elitist image of the party.

Confronted with the public reaction that continued to
look toward the state for services and the proliferation of
party agencies, the party's cadre organization (PO) began trying to project a monolithic, elitist image by emphasizing
both indoctrination and bureaucratization. The party bureaucrats and the völkisch true believers of the Gau's leadership corps had a direct interest in the efficacy of the PO
since it was their only base of power and influence. The
bureaucratization of the PO suffered from two problems. First,
the Gau clique and the Gau department leaders were the only
stable elements in the party. All other party positions,

including even the Kreisleiters, experienced constant personnel changes. The state, municipalities, and economic organizations attracted party functionaries. Second, after the
Gau had finally established a professional functionary corps,
the party faced the impact of the war. Personnel had to be
relinquished to the army, and the various party agencies and
affiliates rejected Hartlieb's indoctrination programs as
useless during the war. Confounding the situation was the fact
that the PO was not a cohesive structure, as the conflicts
between Gauamt leaders and Kreisleiters illustrated.

The war drained the party personnel and elevated the
importance of such party affiliates as the NSV that were not
elitist party agencies. But the war, and particularly the
occupation of Alsace, provided the PO and the Baden party
with opportunities that elevated the party to a position it
had not held since 1933/34. Röhn, Schuppel, and the party
organizations that coordinated the civil servants and mayors
of Alsace in 1940/41 enjoyed radical powers and influence
which they had not enjoyed in Baden since 1933. The party
and its affiliates supervised a radical purge of teachers,
civil servants, and welfare organizations.

To the Baden party, and to Baden's state and economic
interests, Alsace was a field for potential exploitation and
advancement. To Wagner, Alsace was the key to his independence from Reich interference. In Alsace, Wagner presided
over both state and party agencies with relatively little
interference from Berlin. The Baden party's cadre organization benefited from Wagner's position as CdZ, primarily because
Wagner relied on his Gau party elite and close friends to
administer Alsace. Schuppel, the party's personnel leader,
increased his powers in Alsace not because of a PO ordinance

but because he became part of Wagner's civil administrative
staff. Finally, the Baden party enhanced its position in
Alsace because it could defend its actions and new powers as
necessary to further Nazification and Germanization in the
newly conquered territories.

In the end, as the war turned against Nazi Germany,
people in Baden and in Alsace blamed an alleged monolithic
party for the hardships and for the defeat. In defeat, the
party achieved a monolithic, elitist image that it had not
deserved. In defeat, the Baden population also forgot about
the economic and military interests that had supported the
expansionistic programs of the Nazis. In June 1940, many
Baden business and municipal interests were delighted at the
economic benefits expected from the German occupation of
Alsace. The Badenese also were quick to forget their contribution to the rise of the Nazi party before 1933 and to the
support of the Nazi regime after that year.

The Nazi party has often been criticized for failing to
produce a monolithic apparatus, and Carl Friedrich even considered the Nazi one-party system a failure.[10] Yet society
had been coordinated enough for Hitler to pursue a foreign
policy that led to eventual military aggression, and the
socioeconomic segments of society were at least acquiescent
enough to prevent open mass hostility. Furthermore, the Gau
party leadership provided Hitler with a loyal group of followers who blindly implemented his programs. The Gau cadre
organization was a relatively stable party group, many of
whom had been active in the Baden party before 1923 and certainly by 1925. They were not bound by any socioeconomic
identification or connected with any specific interest other
than the party organization. This is why the Gau party

leadership was a key element in the Nazi system of government. They were reliable followers of Hitler not only because they believed in his programs but also because they depended on Hitler for their positions in the Nazi system. On the other hand, Hitler could rely on the Gau cadre organization to coordinate the diverse party interests on the Gau level. The monolithic party organization may not have materialized after 1933, but considering the Nazi party as a polymorphic party and the powers of the Nazi leaders in Berlin, the party can hardly be described as a mere failure.

Although the Gau party, and particularly the Gau elite, played a key role in both the seizure and maintenance of Nazi power, an air of impermanence surrounded the party leadership in Karlsruhe. Had Hitler died, Wagner's powers would have evaporated quickly. Wagner had no political base outside of his native state. Devoid of charisma and speaking ability, the Baden Gau leader (and Reich governor) was totally dependent on Hitler's support after 1925. In turn, of course, the Baden Gau elite was totally dependent on Wagner. Had the Gauleiter died, the influence and power of the Karlsruhe party elite would also have been greatly reduced. Only Wagner was able to resist the expanding Berlin party and state agencies. after 1933. As long as Hitler and Wagner lived, the party and the state in Baden benefited from a symbiotic relationship. After their deaths, however, Köhler's and Pflaumer's fears of the expanding Berlin agencies would have found fruition. In all probability, the most successful "expanding Berlin agency" would not have been the cadre organization of the party, but rather the SS, the various party affiliates, and the Nazi-dominated state apparatus.

Notes

INTRODUCTION

1. See for example: Eberhard Schön, Die Entstehung des Nationalsozialismus in Hessen; Geoffrey Pridham, Hitler's Rise to Power: The Nazi Movement in Bavaria, 1923-1933; and Jeremy Noakes, The Nazi Party in Lower Saxony, 1921-1933.
2. Baden, Statistisches Landesamt, Statistisches Jahrbuch für das Land Baden, 1930, pp. 1-8; Norbert Krebs, Der Südwesten, 3:70, 86.
3. Krebs, Südwesten, 3:62-63, 35; Baden, Statistisches Jahrbuch, 1930, pp. 7, 332.
4. Krebs, Südwesten, 3:55; Baden, Statistisches Jahrbuch, 1930, pp. 15-16.
5. Ibid.
6. Baden, Statistisches Landesamt, Die Industrie in Baden im Jahre 1925 auf Grund amtlichen Materials, pp. 12-13; Krebs, Südwesten, 3:53.
7. Baden, Statistisches Jahrbuch, 1930, p. 74; Baden, Statistische Landesamt, Die Landwirtschaft im Allgemeinen und in einzelnen Gauen, 1:9-19, 32.
8. Die Landwirtschaft im Allgemeinen, 1:19-30. See also Baden, Statistisches Landesamt, Die Landwirtschaft in Baden im Jahr 1925 auf Grund amtlichen Materials.
9. Baden, Statisches Landesamt, Die Religionszugehörigkeit der Bevölkerung in Baden nach der Volkszählung vom 16. Juni 1925, pp. 3-29; Baden, Statistisches Jahrbuch, 1930, p. 13.

CHAPTER ONE

1. For a general survey of the history of Baden see Rolf Gustav Haebler, Badische Geschichte, and "The State of Baden" in James K. Pollock and Homer Thomas, Germany in Power and Eclipse. For the best, short treatment of the history of modern Baden see Peter Brandt and Reinhard Rürup, eds.,

Arbeiter-, Soldaten- und Volksräte in Baden 1918/19, pp.
xv-xxxvi.
2. Loyd E. Lee, "Liberal Constitutionalism as Administrative Reform: The Baden Constitution of 1818," p. 112.
3. Beverly Heckart, From Bassermann to Bebel: The Grand
Bloc's Quest for Reform in the Kaiserreich, 1900-1914, p. 119;
Baden, Ministerium des Innern, Geschäftsbericht für die Jahre
1913-1924, 1:29, 35.
4. Carl H. E. Zangerl, "Courting the Catholic Vote: The
Center Party in Baden, 1903-1913," p. 239; see also Manfred
Stadelhofer, Der Abbau der Kulturkampfgesetzgebung im Grossherzogtum Baden, 1878-1918.
5. Heckart, From Bassermann, pp. 111, 121; Alfred Rapp,
ed., Die Parteibewegung in Baden 1905-1928: Tabellen und Text,
pp. 6-7.
6. Ibid.; Jürgen Thiel, Die Grossblockpolitik der Nationalliberalen Partei Badens 1905 bis 1914, p. 231.
7. Rapp, ed., Die Parteibewegung, pp. 15-55; Baden,
Statistisches Landesamt, Die Wahlen in Baden zur verfassungsge-
benden badischen und deutschen Nationalversammlung im Jahr
1919.
8. Stenographische Aufnahmen über die Vorgänge während
der Revolution: Staatspräsident Geiss, 6 May 1919, Generallandesarchiv Karlsruhe (hereafter cited as GLA)/file 233/
folder 27960; Joseph Becker, "Heinrich Köhler in der Politik
des deutschen Südwestens und des Reich," p. 24; Politischer
Rundbrief (Karlsruhe), 5 October 1918, in Institut für
Zeitgeschichte, Munich (hereafter cited as IfZ), Z-2047.
9. Stenographische Aufnahmen über die Vorgänge während
der Revolution: Ludwig Marum, 2 December 1918, GLA/233/27960;
Wilhelm Engelbert Oestering, Der Umsturz in Baden, pp. 46-47;
Wolfgang Benz, Süddeutschland in der Weimarer Republik: Ein
Beitrag zur deutschen Innenpolitik, 1918-1923, pp. 35-36.
10. Oestering, Der Umsturz, pp. 98-108; Heinrich Köhler,
Lebenserinnerungen des Politikers und Staatsmannes, 1878-
1949, p. 92; Hugo Marx, Werdegang eines jüdischen Staatsanwalts
und Richters in Baden, p. 126; Karlsruher Zeitung, 10 November
1918.
11. Oestering, Der Umsturz, p. 195; Benz, Süddeutschland,
pp. 37-38; Gerhard Kaller, "Die Revolution des Jahres 1918 in
Baden und die Tätigkeit des Arbeiter- und Soldatenrats in
Karlsruhe," 114:325; Gerhard Kaller, "Zur Revolution von 1918
in Baden, Klumpp-Putsch und Verfassungsfrage," 2:175-202.
Klumpp was born on 21 September 1871 in Karlsruhe. After
public school and service in the navy until 1894, he obtained
a job as an administrative clerk. He first became active in

politics as a member of the soviet movement in Hanover on 7
November 1918.

12. Benz, Süddeutschland, pp. 36–37; Reinhard Schiffers,
Elemente direkter Demokratie im Weimarer Regierungssystem, pp.
37–38; Köhler, Lebenserinnerungen, p. 92.

13. Baden, Geschäftsbericht für die Jahre 1913–1924, 1:31–
38; Baden, Statistisches Jahrbuch, 1930, p. 5.

14. Karl Joseph Rössler, Der Badische Landtag, p. 40;
Haebler, Badische Geschichte, p. 134; Baden, Geschäftsbericht
für die Jahre 1913–1924, 1:9. Adam Remmele was born in 1877
in Altneudorf, Heidelberg, and died in Hamburg in 1951. A
miller by profession, he became a Socialist editor in Mannheim
in 1908, see Wilhelm Kosch, Biographisches Staatshandbuch,
2:1026.

15. Rapp, ed., Die Parteibewegung, p. 8; Karl Gross, ed.,
Handbuch für den Badischen Landtag: IV. Landtagsperiode,
1929–1933, p. 135; Baden, Statistisches Jahrbuch, 1930, pp.
68–69; Horst Rehberger, Die Gleichschaltung des Landes Baden
1932/33, pp. 17, 43–45.

16. Politischer Rundbrief, 17 October 1919, IfZ/Z–2047;
Marx, Werdegang, p. 162; see also Reinhard Rürup, "Problems
of the German Revolution 1918–19," 3:129.

17. Oestering, Der Umsturz, p. 304.

18. Ministerium des Innern, Karlsruhe, to Amtvorstände,
10 January 1919, Staatsarchiv Freiburg (hereafter cited as
SAF)/file 317/folder 1255.

19. Der Präsident des Landesgerichts Mannheim to Präsident
Geiss, 25 February 1919, GLA/233/25985; Minister der Justiz,
Marum, "Die spartakistischen Unruhen in Mannheim am 22.
Februar 1919," 28 April 1919, GLA/233/25985; Marum to Justiz-
behörde, 6 March 1919, GLA/234/10155; Landeskommissär Konstanz
to MdI, 30 May 1919, SAF/317/1256.

20. Remmele to Staatsministerium, 25 March 1920, GLA/233/
12432; Niederschrift über die Sitzung des Staatsministeriums
vom 25 März 1920, GLA/233/12432; Bad. Staatsministerium, "An
das badische Volk," 13 March 1920, GLA/364/7745; "Auszug aus
der Niederschrift über die Sitzung des Staatsministeriums,"
27 March 1920, GLA/233/12432.

21. Remmele, telegram to Landeskommissär Konstanz, 29
March 1920, SAF/317/1257c; Remmele to Landeskommissär Konstanz,
27 March 1920, SAF/317/1257c; Landeskommissär Mannheim to
Amtsvorstände und Dienstverweser (Geheim), 30 March 1920,
GLA/364/7745.

22. Befehlshaber, Wehrkreiskommando V, Stuttgart to Bad.
Staatsministerium, 26 May 1920, GLA/233/25988; "Auszug aus

der Niederschrift über die Sitzung des Staatsministeriums vom
28. Mai 1920," GLA/233/25980; MdI to Staatsministerium, 9 July
1920, GLA/233/25988; Gemeinderat St. Georgen to MdI durch
Bezirksamt Villingen, 11 August 1920, SAF/317/1258.

23. Neue Badische Landeszeitung, 30 March 1921, GLA/233/
25988; Konstanzer Volksblatt, 15 and 19 April 1921, in SAF/
317/1257c; VKPD Bezirk Baden, "Rundschreiben," 19 March 1921,
GLA/309/1162; VKPD Baden, "Rundschreiben," 28 March 1921, in
Hauptarchiv NSDAP, Hoover Institute Microfilm (hereafter
cited as HA), roll 41, folder 811; "Auszug aus der Niederschrift über die Sitzung des Staatsministeriums vom 5. April
1921," GLA/233/25988; see also Werner T. Angress, Stillborn
Revolution, pp. 137-66.

24. Bezirksamt Heidelberg to MdI, Baden, 15 September
1921, GLA/356/2616; Arbeiter-Sekretäriat Heidelberg to
Bezirksamt Heidelberg, 1 September 1921, GLA/356/2616;
Bezirksamt Konstanz to MdI, 5 July 1922, "Ausschreitungen in
Singen, 4. Juli 1922," SAF/317/1257c; Bezirksamt Mosbach to
Zentralpolizeistelle Karlsruhe, 8 July 1922, GLA/364/7745.

25. Dr. Kaufmann, Singen to MdI, Ministerialdirektor
Leere, 28 July 1922, SAF/317/1257c. The largest firm in
southern Baden, the Maggi Werke, sent a special representative
to Karlsruhe to present the pleas of the industrial interests
of the area to the government.

26. MdI, Karlsruhe, "Erfahrungsaustausch Nr. 38," 22
October 1923 (Septemberunruhen 1923), SAF/317/1257a, part
1; Karlheinz Mundhenke, Der oberbadische Aufstand vom September 1923, pp. 57, 70; Urteil des Staatsgerichtshofs zum
Schutze der Republik in Freiburg i. Br., 27. November-2.
Dezember, 1924," GLA/234/5703; Angress, Stillborn Revolution,
p. 388.

27. Verband der Uhrenindustrie, Vorsitzende, Donauschingen
to Bezirksamt Triberg, 2 October 1923, SAF/317/1257c.

28. Frankfurter Zeitung (Morgenblatt), 26 October 1925;
Baden, Statistisches Jahrbuch, 1930, p. 64; Günter Opitz,
Der Christlich-soziale Volksdienst, p. 129; Baden, Statis-
tisches Landesamt, Die Wahlen zum Badischen Landtag am 30.
Oktober 1921, pp. 152-55; Baden, Statistisches Landesamt,
Die Wahlen im Jahr 1919. In the 1929 state election the Nazi
party won 7 percent of the vote while the Nationalists declined
to 3.7 percent and the Landbund (now running on a separate
ticket again) had to settle for 3 percent of the vote. Both
the Nationalists and the Agrarian League lost voters to the
Nazi party and to the new Protestant political party, the
Evangelische Volksdienst.

29. Flugblatt, Deutsch-Nationale Volkspartei Baden,

January 1919, in GLA/Ruge Nachlass/69N/104.

30. Landeskommissär Konstanz to MdI, Baden, 15 March 1920, SAF/317/1257c; Konstanzer Zeitung, 15 March 1920; Schwarzwalder Zeitung, 22 March 1920; Konstanzer Nachrichten, 22 March 1922, in SAF/317/1257c; DNVP and DVP leaders, Konstanz to Landeskommissär Konstanz, 19 March 1920 and Landeskommissär Konstanz to Vorstand der DNVP (and to the DVP), 22 March 1920, SAF/317/1257c.

31. Badische Post, 20 October 1921 (Flugblatt), GLA/356/ 2616; DVP, Wahlflugblatt, 1921, SAF/317/1257c; Bezirksamt Heidelberg to MdI, Baden, 15 September 1921, GLA/356/2616.

32. See the election statistics for the Landtag election in 1921 and the Reichstag election in July 1932; Deutsche Zukunft, No. 2 (1 January 1921), and No. 3 (5 July 1922), in GLA/Ruge Nachlass/69N/114; Buch to Amann, 28 June 1923, HA/ roll 16/folder 299; Baden, Statistisches Landesamt, Die Wahlen zum Landtag am 30. Oktober 1921, p. 157.

33. George L. Mosse, The Crisis of German Ideology, p. 7; Adolf Conrad, "Meine Erlebnisse im Kampf für den Führer and für ein neues deutsches Vaterland der Ehre, Freiheit und sozialen Gerechtigkeit von 1925-1933," March 1937, HA/roll 26/folder 514; see also Martin Broszat, "Die völkische Ideologie und der Nationalsozialismus," pp. 52-54.

34. Baden, Statistisches Landesamt, Die Religionszugehörigkeit in Baden in 1925, pp. 3-29; Paul Sauer, ed., Dokumente über die Verfolgung der Jüdischen Bürger in Baden-Württemberg, 1:XXVII; Franz Hundsnurscher and Gerhard Taddey, Die Jüdischen Gemeinden in Baden, p. 21. Ludwig Marum was born in 1882 in Rheinpfalz and became a lawyer in Karlsruhe in 1908. By 1911 he was a Socialist city council member of Karlsruhe. Ludwig Haas was born in 1875 in Freiburg and also studied law. Between 1909 and 1919, Haas was a Karlsruhe city council member, representing the Progressive party. After the war, he became a member of the DDP and expressed an extreme nationalistic view. In 1926, for example, in an article in the C. V. Zeitung he demanded a Grossdeutschland that included all Germans, including Austrians; see his daughter's Erinnerungen, in Leo Baeck Institute, Archives (New York); and Wer ist's?, 1922, p. 1005.

35. Remmele to Bezirksämter, 13 November 1919, SAF/317/ 1253; Mitteilungen aus dem Verein zur Abwehr des Antisemitismus, 14 May 1919; see also Hildegard Kattermann, ed., Geschichte und Schicksal der Lahrer Juden, p. 18.

36. Völkischer Beobachter, 7 and 14 February 1920; Wolfgang Kreuzberger, Studenten und Politik, 1918-1933, pp.

55, 158-60.
    37. Völkischer Beobachter, 24 January and 15 April 1920.
    38. Die Neue Zeitung, 6 (August 1924), in GLA/Ruge Nach-
lass/69N/40; Paul Bargiel, "Dr. Arnold Ruge, Ein völkischer
Typus," Abwehr-Blätter, 39 (1 September 1929):139-40.
    39. Ruge, "Das Wesen der Universitäten und das Studium
der Frauen," April 1911, in GLA/Ruge Nachlass/69N/93; Ruge,
Die Mobilmachung der deutschen Frauenkräfte für den Krieg, p.
9; Deutscher Bund gegen die Frauenemanzipation (Berlin), to
Ruge, 18 January 1917, in GLA/Ruge Nachlass/69N/7; see also
Marianne Weber, Max Weber, pp. 429-31.
    40. Flugblatt, Schutz- und Trutzbund, Karlsruhe ("Der
Fall des Privatdozenten Dr. Arnold Ruge vor dem Badischen
Landtag"), in GLA/233/24953; Badische Presse, 17 December 1920,
in GLA/233/24953; Völkischer Beobachter, 30 January 1921; Karl
Ernst to Amtsgericht Heidelberg, 26 May 1922, GLA/Ruge Nach-
lass/69N/30; Ruge, "Einige Kampfdaten aus meinem Leben," 1
January 1941, GLA/Ruge Nachlass/69N/2. Ernst was the Gau
leader of the Schutz- und Trutzbund of Baden. For Ruge's
activities in other parts of Germany see Mitteilungen aus dem
Verein zur Abwehr des Antisemitismus, 19 March and 9 May 1921.
    41. Remmele to Bezirksamt, Polizeidirektion Heidelberg,
14 October 1922, GLA/Ruge Nachlass/69N/25; Deutsche Wohlfahrt,
1 (15 May 1922), in GLA/Ruge Nachlass/69N/30.
    42. Der Demokrat, 4 (15 September 1923):155-58; Stadt-
kommissär für München Stadt und Landbezirk, 12 August 1924,
"Aufenthaltsverbot," GLA/Ruge Nachlass/69N/40; Lorenz Roder
to Oberste Landesgericht München, 18 October 1924, GLA/Ruge
Nachlass/69N/40; Prof. Fuchs, "Zur Vorgeschichte der Natio-
nalsozialistischen Erhebung," n.d., HA/roll 5/folder 113;
Ruge to Hitler, 2 June 1923, in Miscellaneous German Records,
National Archives Microcopy No. T-84 (herafter cited as
T-84), roll 6, frame 5064. For the Blücher Bund see Harold J.
Gordon, Jr., Hitler and the Beer Hall Putsch, pp. 107, 209-
10.
    43. Uwe Lohalm, Völkischer Radikalismus, pp. 11, 54-55,
89-93; Robert Waite, Vanguard of Nazism, p. 206; see also
Deutschvölkischer Schutz- und Trutzbund, "Aufnahme Gesuch,"
GLA/356/4476.
    44. Flugblatt, Alldeutscher Verband, Heidelberg, May
1919, in GLA/Ruge Nachlass/69N/104; Flugblatt, Deutsch-
Völkischer Schutz- und Trutzbund, Karlsruhe, 28 November
1919, GLA/Ruge Nachlass/69N/55; Flugblatt, Deutsch-Völkischer
Schutz- und Trutzbund (1920-21), GLA/Ruge Nachlass/69N/55.
    45. Völkischer Beobachter, 15 April, 13 May, and 6 March
1920; Lohalm, Völkischer Radikalismus, pp. 224-25.

46. Prof. Fr. Rosch, Gruppenwart of Heidelberg, to Ruge, 11 September 1920 (a Flugblatt with Rosch's note to Ruge typed on the bottom), in GLA/Ruge Nachlass/69N/55; Karl Ernst, Schwetzingen to Amtsgericht Heidelberg, 26 May 1922, GLA/Ruge Nachlass/69N/30; Nachrichtenblatt für den Schutz- und Trutzbund: Im Vertrauen, No. 8 (1921), in Records of the National Socialist German Labor Party, National Archives Microcopy No. T-81 (hereafter cited as T-81), roll 116/frame 136445; Völkischer Beobachter, 22 May 1921; Führer, 30 March 1935.

47. Deutsche Wohlfahrt, 1 (15 May 1922), GLA/Ruge Nachlass/69N/30; Lenard to Ruge, 28 March 1922, GLA/Ruge Nachlass/69N/55.

48. Remmele to Bezirksämter, 15 September 1922, GLA/377/5407; Lohalm, Völkischer Radikalismus, pp. 246, 416. By January 1923, six major völkisch organizations were outlawed in Baden: NSDAP, Schutz- und Trutzbund, Organisation Damm, Deutsch-Sozialisten, Jungdeutscher Orden, Nationalgesinnte Soldaten, see Bad. Landespolizeiamt, Abt. N. to Bezirksamt Sinsheim, 6 January 1923, GLA/377/5407; Karlsruher Zeitung, 17 January 1923.

49. Völkischer Beobachter, 6 February 1921; Führer (Sonderbeilage), 30 March 1935; Lohalm, Völkischer Radikalismus, pp. 281, 304-26; Peter G. J. Pulzer, The Rise of Political Anti-Semitism in Germany and Austria, p. 306.

50. On Buch see the correspondence between Amann and Buch in 1923 in HA/roll 16/folder 299; and Donald M. McKale, The Nazi Party Courts; for Köhler and Roth see Führerlexikon, 1934, pp. 243-44, 395.

51. Bad. Staatsanwaltschaft Karlsruhe to Landgericht Strafkammer I, 7 September 1923, GLA/234/5738; membership list of the Mannheim local for April-August 1922, HA/roll 10/folder 215.

52. Führer, 30 March 1935; Walter Buch to Amann, 17 June 1923, HA/roll 16/folder 299; for general works dealing with paramilitary activities see Waite, Vanguard, p. 281; Gordon, Beer Hall Putsch, p. 17; and James M. Diehl, Paramilitary Politics in Weimar Germany.

53. University of Freiburg, Akademisches Direktorium to Oberregierungsrat, 5 March 1919, GLA/233/25988; "Auszug aus der Niederschrift über die Sitzung des Staatsministeriums," 27 March 1920, GLA/233/12432.

54. Oberreichsanwalt, Leipzig, to Ersten Staatsanwalt Karlsruhe, 23 March 1920, GLA/309/1129. Wagener was able to recruit "respectable" people like Landgerichtsrat Fromherz to prepare publications; see Kriminalkommissär Becker, Karlsruhe, to Staatsanwaltschaft, 18 June 1921, GLA/309/1161;

Fromherz to Staatsanwalt Dr. Hafner, 18 June 1921, GLA/309/
1161. The best short account of Wagener's career is in Otto
Wagener, Hitler aus nächster Nähe, ed. Henry A. Turner, Jr.,
pp. I-XVII. Wagener, who was the regimental comrade of Robert
Wagner, the Gau leader of Baden after 1925, joined the Nazi
party in 1929 and became particularly active in the SA and in
the party's economic department.

55. Deutsche Legion, Karlsruhe, Sondermitteilung, 3 August
1920, GLA/309/1166; Deutsche Legion, Karlsruhe, 6. Mitteilung,
6 September 1920, GLA/309/1166.

56. Wagener, "Bericht," 18 November 1920, GLA/309/1166;
Robert Kessler to Oberstaatsanwalt Mehl, Mosbach, 20 June
1921, GLA/309/1161; for Remmele's fear of the Organization
Damm see Remmele to Vorsitzenden des 27. Ausschusses des
Reichstags, Landegerichtsdirektor Dr. Schletter, 22 March
1926, GLA/233/25986.

57. M. Morlacher, Hauptgeschäftsführer, Oberbayerische
Christliche Bauernverein to Bezirkssekretäre, 24 July 1919
(streng vertraulich), T-81/187/337315; Waite, Vanguard, pp.
198-201; Diehl, Paramilitary, pp. 70-93.

58. Bezirksamt Bonndorf to Landespolizeistelle beim
Bezirksamt Karlsruhe, 14 October 1919, SAF/317/1257c; Remmele
to Bezirksämter, 3 March 1920, SAF/317/1262; Hagauer Erzähler,
9 September 1920, in SAF/317/1262.

59. Remmele to Bezirksämter, 22 November 1920, GLA/309/
1161; "Ergebnis der staatsanwaltschaftlichen Ermittlungen
über Waffenfunde und Geheimorganisationen in Baden," 13 July
1921, GLA/233/27914.

60. Escherich, Baden-Nord, "Vorläufige Führerausweise,"
18 June 1920 (sent by Munich), GLA/309/1166; Escherich,
Heidelberg, "Rundschreiben," 27 April 1921, GLA/309/1162.

61. Robert Kessler vor Oberstaatsanwalt Mehl, Mosbach,
20 June 1921, GLA/309/1161; Bad. Oberlandesgericht, "Be-
schluss," 28 June 1921, GLA/309/1161; testimony of Hermann
Kessler, 17 June 1921, GLA/309/1161; Friedrich-Wilhelm v.
Wins to Oberstaatsanwaltschaft Karlsruhe, 15 February 1938,
GLA/309/1161.

62. "Personalien," 10 June 1921 (prepared by Staatsanwalt
Heidelberg); and testimony given to Polizeikommissär Becker,
June 1921; and Oswald Hartge to Staatsanwalt Hafner, 20 June
1921; and testimony of Alfred Krausse d'Avis before Staatsanwaltschaft Baden, 4 July 1921, all GLA/309/1161.

63. Testimony of Damm given to Oberstaatsanwalt Mehl,
Mosbach, 13 June 1921, and Erich Damm to Sophie Kessler,
Buenos Aires, 17 June 1921, GLA/309/1161; Walter Buch to
Amann, 17 June 1923, HA/roll 16/folder 299.

64. Polizei Wachtmeister Diener, "Zeuge: Ein Beamter, welcher mir Aufklärungen über den Fall Neiking gab," 26 November 1921, GLA/309/1161; Polizei Oberwachtmeister, Heidelberg, "Meldung," to Staatsanwaltschaft, 21 October 1921, GLA/309/1164.

65. Testimony of Pfarrer Hans Philipp given to Oberstaatsanwalt Mehl, 9 June 1921; and Polizei Wachtmeister Diener, "Zeuge," 26 November 1921; and testimony given to Polizeikommissär Becker, June 1921(?), all GLA/309/1161.

66. "Ergebnis der staatsanwaltschaftlichen Ermittlungen über Waffenfunde und Geheimorganisationen in Baden," 13 July 1921, GLA/233/27914; testimony of Landgerichtsrat Dr. Frommherz before Staatsanwalt Dr. Hafner, and Kriminalkommissär Becker, Karlsruhe, to Staatsanwaltschaft, both 18 June 1921, GLA/309/1161.

67. Versammlungsbericht, Escherich Heidelberg, 25 January 1921, GLA/309/1162.

68. "Ergebnis der staatsanwaltschaftlichen Ermittlungen über Waffenfunde und Geheimorganisationen in Baden," 13 July 1921, GLA/233/27914; Polizei Kriminaloberinspektor Stocklin, 23 September 1922, GLA/309/1161; Stocklin, "Meldung," 21 September 1921, GLA/309/1163; testimony before Polizeikommissär Becker, June 1921, GLA/309/1161; Becker, "Die Orgeschbestrebungen in Baden betreffend," 20 June 1921, GLA/309/1161. Information about the firm Stachelhaus and Buchloh may be found in Baden, Statistisches Landesamt, Handel und Verkehr in Baden, p. 129; for the Himmelbach firm see Erich Köhrer, ed., Das Land Baden, p. 190. Diehl also argues that the bulk of the financial support "appears to have come from powerful agricultural interests," although Hugo Stinnes did give 300,000 RM to the Orgesch; see Diehl, Paramilitary, pp. 328-29.

69. Testimony before Oberstaatsanwalt Mehl, Mosbach, 13 June 1921, and Süddeutsche Disconto-Gesellschaft A.G., Ettlingen, to Staatsanwaltschaft III, 24 June 1921, both GLA/309/1161.

70. Bad. Staatsanwaltschaft, "Das Verfahren wird eingestellt," 14 December 1921, ibid.

71. Damm to Heinrich Plesch, 9 October 1921, "Liste der Berichterstatter des Südwestdeutschen Zeitungsdienst"; and testimony of Hermann Kessler, 28 September 1921; and Damm's testimony before Staatsanwalt Hafner, 29 September 1921, all in GLA/309/1163; Bezirksamt Bonndorf to MdI, Baden, 17 November 1922, and Bezirksamt Bonndorf to MdI, Baden, 26 March 1923, both SAF/317/1257c.

72. Bad. Landespolizeiamt, Abtl. N., to MdI, Baden, 30 November 1922, GLA/233/27914.

73. Remmele to Staatsministerium, 16 January 1933, and Remmele to Staatsgerichtshof zum Schutze der Republic beim Reichsgericht in Leipzig, 5 July 1923, both GLA/233/27914; Remmele to Vorsitzenden des 27. Ausschusses des Reichstags, Landgerichtsdirektor Dr. Schetter, 22 March 1926, GLA/233/25986; Heinrich Winterhalter to Minister Köhler, 2 April 1934, GLA/233/27914. In 1934 Damm ended up in Argentina.

74. Volksfreund (Karlsruhe), 12 and 15 March 1921, and "Auszug aus der Niederschrift über die Sitzung des Staatsministeriums vom 18 März 1921 (and 15 March 1921)"; and Badischer Beobachter and Badische Press, 15 March 1921, all in GLA/233/27914.

75. Oberstaatsanwalt Mehl, Mosbach berichtet dem Herrn Staatspräsidenten über das bisherige Ergebnis--Osterburken, 21 May 1921; and August Hornikel testimony before Mehl, 18 May 1921; and Kriminalkommissär Becker, "Bericht," 21 May 1921, all in GLA/233/27914. For Dirlewanger's SS career after June 1940 see Hellmuth Auerbach, "Die Einheit Dirlewanger," pp. 250-63.

76. Rote Fahne, Mannheim, 8 June 1921; Karlsruher Zeitung, 21 May 1921; Volksfreund, 20 May and 13 June 1921; and Staatspräsident Trunk to Haupschriftleiter Amend, Karlsruher Zeitung, 23 May 1921; and Curt Amend to Staatspräsident, 24 May 1921, all in GLA/233/27914.

77. "Auszug aus dem stenogr. Landtagsbericht über die Orgeschdebatte," 1921, GLA/309/1164; Badische Post, Heidelberg, 30 May 1921, and Univ. Prof. Engelbert Krebs, Freiburg, to Staatspräsident, 28 June 1921, both GLA/233/27914.

78. Justizminister Bolz, Stuttgart, to Karlsruhe, 21 May 1921, and "Auszug aus der Niederschrift über die Sitzung des Staatsministeriums vom 24. Mai 1921," both GLA/233/27914; Robert Kessler to Oberstaatsanwalt Mehl von Mosbach, 20 June 1921, GLA/309/1161.

79. Deutsche Heeresfriedenkommission Verbindungsstelle Stuttgart to Zweigverbindungsstelle Karlsruhe, 25 May 1921, and Remmele to Staatsministerium, 4 June 1921, both GLA/233/27914.

80. Remmele to Staatsministerium, 27 June 1921; Bad. Staatspräsident to Reichskanzler Dr. Wirth, 13 July 1921; Oberpolizeidirektion und Vorstand der Polizeibefehlstelle in Württemberg to Oberstaatsanwalt Mehl, Mosbach, 12 July 1921; and Staatspräsident Württemberg (Hieber) to Reichskanzler Wirth (and to Bad. Staatsministerium), 3 August 1921, GLA/233/27914; Wilhelm Blos, Von der Monarchie zum Volksstaat, pp. 85-86.

81. "Aufzeichnungen über die Sitzung des Staatsministe-

riums vom 21. Sept. 1921, Vormittags, 9 Uhr, Gegenstand:
Erklärung Dr. Peters aus Berlin," and "Auszug aus der
Niederschrift über die Sitzung des Staatsministeriums vom 11.
Oktober 1921," both GLA/233/27914; Bad. Staatsanwaltschaft,
"Das Verfahren wird eingestellt," 14 December 1921, GLA/309/
1161.

    82. Walter Buch to Amann, 17 June 1923, HA/roll 16/folder
299.

    83. Gaupersonalamt Baden, "Stammbuch für Hans Knab,"
T-81/166/305423-25; Bruno Wiesener, Pforzheim, "Gesuch an
den Reichsführer SS auf dem Dienstweg," 30 January 1936,
Records of the Reichsführer SS, National Archives Microcopy
No. T-175 (hereafter cited as T-175)/roll 200/frame 2741013.
Hans Knab was born on 6 June 1887 in Eberbach and joined a
DNVP youth group; by 1923 he was a party member. Bruno
Wiesener was born in 1905 and was also a party member by 1923
while remaining active in the Organization Damm between 1922
and 1924.

    84. Walter Buch to Amann, 17 June 1923, HA/roll 16/folder
299.

    85. Führer, 7 October 1933 and 8 June 1937; Stammbuch für
Theodor Schnepf, 22 April 1939, Ortsgruppe Tiefenbach, Sinsheim, T-81/228/5010146. Gustav Oexle was born in 1890 in
Sipplingen and attended public school until the age of nine;
then he served as Dienstbube on a farm and later as a factory
worker. After serving in the navy, he returned to Baden in
1920.

    86. Karl Gropp, "Erklärung über Herrn Seitz," 30 September
1938, T-81/89/102651; Gordon, Beer Hall Putsch, pp. 95-96.

    87. Führer, 19 October 1940; Führerlexikon, 1934, p.
227. Glas was born in 1894 in Diessen, Bavaria, and learned
a printing trade. Kerber was born in 1901 in Freiburg and
obtained a university education. Both Glas and Kerber were
active in postwar actions against the left in either Munich
or Silesia.

CHAPTER TWO

    1. Dietrich Orlow, History of the Nazi Party, 1919-1945,
1:18; and Bullock, Hitler, p. 62. The influence of Munich
natives who came to Baden before 1923 and established local
Nazi cells was noted in the numerous police reports of the
political police of Baden, the Abt. N; see the reports
for Freiburg (Kurt Menger and Hans Rupprechter, both Kaufmänner), in Staatsanwaltschaft Freiburg, to Justizminister,
26 June 1923, and "Urteil gegen Hans Rupprechter et al.,"

Reichsgericht, 17 June 1924, both GLA/234/5738.

2. Führer, 4 July 1933, and 19 June 1938; Werner Maser, Die Frühgeschichte der NSDAP, pp. 315-16. On 5 November 1921, the Mannheimer General Anzeiger called Hitler the "Führer" of the Nazi movement. In Pforzheim, Heinrich Wittmann corresponded with Munich as early as 1920, and in Mannheim, Hermann Kettner, head of the Schutz- und Trutzbund, wrote to Drexler in early 1920.

3. Völkischer Beobachter, 7 February 1920 and 22 May 1921.

4. Lohalm, Völkischer Radikalismus, p. 312; Führer, 31 March 1935. Maser is incorrect when he maintains that following Dortmund, Mannheim was the oldest Nazi local outside of Bavaria; see Maser, Frühgeschichte, pp. 233, 315.

5. Mannheim had a population of 247,486, and Pforzheim claimed 78,859 inhabitants. In both cities over half of the population depended on industry. Pforzheim was 75.3 percent Protestant, and Mannheim was 50.5 percent Protestant. Jews made up 2.8 percent of the population of Mannheim and 1.1 percent of the population of Pforzheim; see Baden, Statistisches Jahrbuch, 1930, pp 332-34, 338.

6. Führer, 30 March 1935; Völkischer Beobachter, 21 November 1920; Berlin Document Center (hereafter cited as BDC), Heinrich Wittmann, Mitgliedskarte; Meldung des Polizei Inspektors Bayer und Oberwachtmeisters Ludwig to Staatsanwaltschaft Karlsruhe, 23 July 1923, GLA/234/5738. For documents and arguments linking Pforzheim with Stuttgart see Lohalm, Völkischer Radikalismus, pp. 314, 438; Franz-Willing, Ursprung, 1919-1922, p. 234; "Anschriften der Ortsgruppen," n.d. (1921), and Gustaf Seifert to Hitler, 2 December 1934, both HA/roll 6/folder 141. The Baden police reported the activities of native Pforzheim Nazis like Heinrich Wittmann and Georg Rast, but not those of Ernst Ulshöfer (at least as far as the Pforzheim local was concerned).

7. Völkischer Beobachter, 21 November 1920; Führer, 30 March 1935; BDC/Heinrich Wittmann, Mitgliedskarte. Wittmann joined the party again in August 1928 and died in 1934.

8. Völkischer Beobachter, 20 January 1921; Kriminalkommissär Karl Angstl, "Versammlungsbericht Betreff NSDAP München," 5 September 1920, HA/roll 3/folder 82. For Ulshöfer's role in Stuttgart, see Eugen Haug, "Aufzeichnung zur Vorgeschichte der Entstehung der NSDAP in Stuttgart," HA/roll 8/folder 166.

9. Völkischer Beobachter, 24 April 1921; Franz-Willing, Krisenjahr der Hitlerbewegung, 1923, pp. 226-27. Fritz Todt to Wirtschaftspolitische Abteilung der NSDAP, 26 October 1931, HA/roll 51/folder 1180; see also Alan S. Milward, The

German Economy at War, pp. 54-71, for Todt's career in the
Third Reich.

10. See the earlier section on the urban disturbances in
Baden, and Marx, Werdegang, pp. 140-45.

11. Völkischer Beobachter, 6 February 1921.

12. Ibid., 11 January, 8 March, 3 May, and 10 May 1922;
Maser, Frühgeschichte, p. 315.

13. Mannheim membership list (April-August, 1922), HA/
roll 10/folder 215; Völkischer Beobachter, 11 January, 26
April, and 10 May 1922. Maser also published the membership
list, Frühgeschichte, pp. 254-55. Maser has argued that participants of Nazi rallies in Mannheim joined on the specific
days mentioned in the document. No doubt participants of Nazi
rallies were converted to Hitler's movement. But this document
is not a chronological list of new members. Rather it appears
to be a roll of Mannheim party members who were registered
officially by Munich on these specific dates. For example,
Karl and Oskar Hensel, Paul Jansen, and Ulshöfer are listed
under the 5 May and 27 May 1922 dates. The Völkischer Beobachter and other party and police records show that Ulshöfer
was a founding father of the Stuttgart Nazi local as early
as 1920 and that Hensel was presiding at Mannheim party meetings in January 1922. The Völkischer Beobachter also reveals
that Jansen was not only a party member as early as April 1922,
but that he was also active in distributing Nazi leaflets in
Mannheim in early 1922. The list also fails to incorporate
the whole Mannheim membership until August 1922. For example,
Sporrer, the temporary leader of the Mannheim local in February
1921, and Richard Cordier, who was praised in Munich in January
1922 for his party activism, are not even listed on the membership roll.

14. Völkischer Beobachter, 12 and 26 April 1922, Führer,
20 April 1939. After the April 1922 disaster, Hitler urged
the use of smaller meeting halls that could not be dominated
by the Communists, see Mitteilungsblatt, No. 14 (25 April
1922), HA/roll 4/folder 95.

15. Neue Badische Landeszeitung (Mannheim), 2 June 1922,
in GLA/Ruge Nachlass/69N/box 73; Völkischer Beobachter, 6
February 1921; for Munich's praise of Cordier see Mitteilungsblatt, No. 12 (11 February 1922), in IfZ/file 88/folder
95 (may also be found in HA/roll 4/folder 95).

16. For Würth see Führer, 14 January 1928; and Staatsanwaltschaft Heidelberg to Justizm., 17 August 1923, GLA/234/
5738; for Jourdan see Führer, 31 March 1935; for Tritschler
see Führer, 21 April 1928. According to the Karlsruher Zeitung
in 1923, a large part of the "former Communist rowdies" were

now members of the Nazi party; see Gordon, <u>Beer Hall Putsch</u>, p. 77.

17. <u>Völkischer Beobachter</u>, 8 March 1921. An example of a long-term SPD member who became a Nazi activist outside Baden was L. Ruthmann of Hanover; see Ruthmann to R. F. Viergutz, Hellerau, 6 September 1921, <u>HA</u>/roll 6/folder 141.

18. <u>Völkischer Beobachter</u>, 8 and 25 March, 14 June 1922; Bad. Staatsanwaltschaft Karlsruhe to Landgerichtstrafkammer I, 7 September 1923, <u>GLA</u>/234/5738.

19. <u>Völkischer Beobachter</u>, 8 and 12 July 1922; <u>Führer</u>, 30 March 1935 and 2 April 1937.

20. For example, Merchingen, Adelsheim, had a free corps in 1923 but a Nazi local not until 1926, <u>Führer</u>, 24 May 1937; or Ittlingen, Sinsheim, had no party local until 1927 although the Organization Damm had been active in the community after 1920, <u>Führer</u>, 8 June 1934.

21. Baden, Statistisches Landesamt, <u>Wohnungszählung und Wohnungsbau in Baden</u>, p. 216; Max Graf zu Solms-Roedelheim, <u>Die Einflüsse der Industrialisierung</u>, p. 37; <u>Führer</u>, 9 March and 23 June 1934. For example, according to the <u>Führer</u> Kappelrodeck in the district of Bühl and Helmsheim in the district of Bruchsal had small Nazi locals by 1923.

22. Baden, Statistisches Landesamt, <u>Die Wahlen zum Reichstag am 4. Mai 1924 in Baden</u>, p. 40; John Gustav Weiss, <u>Geschichte der Stadt Eberbach am Neckar</u>, pp. 225-32, 291-95. In May 1924, the Center party won 17 percent of the vote while the DDP and DVP garnered 13.5 percent and 12 percent, respectively.

23. <u>Führer</u> (M), 8 October 1933 and 13 April 1939; Stammbuch für Hans Knab, <u>T-81</u>/166/305423-26; Gaupersonal-amtsleiter, "Bestätigung," 16 August 1938, <u>T-81</u>/166/305360; Dr. Ph. Kraft, "Meine Kampferlebnisse," 1 December 1936, <u>HA</u>/roll 27/folder 528; Baden, Statistisches Landesamt, <u>Reichs-tagswahl am 7. Dezember 1924</u>, list of candidates.

24. Solms-Roedelheim, <u>Die Einflüsse der Industriali-sierung</u>, pp. 56, 110, 179-88; <u>Führer</u>, 8 July 1933; Baden, Statistisches Landesamt, <u>Landwirtschaft in 1925</u>, pp. 24-26; Hundsnurscher and Taddey, <u>Jüdischen Gemeinden</u>, p. 180. In the election of May 1924, the Völkisch slate won 52 percent of the vote, and the DNVP and Landbund won 11 percent and 5 percent, respectively; the SPD won 22.3 percent of the vote and the KPD won 4.2 percent, see Baden, Statistisches Landes-amt, <u>Reichstagswahl, Mai 1924</u>, p. 34. After 1910 there were no Jews in Liedolsheim.

25. "Die Agrardemogogie als Vorfrucht von Spartakus," in <u>Mitteilungen</u> (Abwehr-Blätter), 18 September 1919, p. 141;

Baden, Statistisches Landesamt, Wahlen, 1919, pp. 52–53. In
the 1919 election the DNVP won 31 percent in Liedolsheim, 45
percent in Graben, and 43 percent in Friedrichstal. These
examples reflect the right-wing strength in rural areas in
1919. Many of these rural communities like Liedolsheim and
Eggenstein were described as rich and proper communities; see
Wilhelm Bergdolt, Badische Allmenden, pp. 12–13.
    26. Führer, 10 November and 4 July 1933 and 30 March
1935; Wer ist's?, 1935, p. 1332.
    27. BDC/Roth file (Hilfskasse, NSDAP to Reichsschatz-
meister, Mitgliederschaftsamt, 28 June 1939); Badische Landespolizeiamt to Staatsanwaltschaft Karlsruhe, 18 June 1930,
GLA/309/1155; Bad. Landespolizeiamt, Abt. N, "Nationalsozialistische Umtriebe in Liedolsheim," in ibid.
    28. Führer, 20 April 1939. Kramer apparently lost his
job because he misappropriated 800 RM. Obviously, the Führer
never focused attention on this, see Staatspräsident to MdI,
31 October 1929, GLA/233/27915; BDC/Kramer file.
    29. Führer, 30 March 1935 and 4 July 1933. The Turnfest
was held on 12 July 1923. It apparently helped expand National
Socialism in many parts of Germany, see HA/roll 26/folder 514
(for Ellwanger, Württemberg); and for a lower Rhine community
see Kreispresseamtsleiter Heinrich Wirths, "Kampf und Sieg
der NSDAP im Oberbergischen Land," in Kreisleitung der NSDAP
Oberbergen, ed., Buch des Oberbergischen Kreises, p. 7.
    30. Bezirksamt Waldshut, "Bericht," 21 March 1923, HA/
roll 70/folder 1515; Franz-Willing, Krisenjahr, pp. 226–27.
    31. Remmele to Bezirksämter, 15 September 1922; and Bad.
Landespolizeiamt, Abt. N to Bezirksamt Sinsheim, 6 and 16
January 1923; and Remmele to Landespolizeiamt, 28 March 1923,
all GLA/377/5407; Karlsruher Zeitung, 17 January 1923.
    32. Bad. Landespolizeiamt to MdI, 26 May 1923; and
Staatsanwaltschaft Heidelberg to Justizministerium, 14 June
1923, GLA/234/5738; and Remmele to Justizminister, 29 May
1923, all GLA/234/5738; Staatsanwaltschaft Konstanz to Justizminister, 10 July 1923, GLA/234/5738; Volkswille, 16 June
1923.
    33. Völkischer Beobachter, 4 July 1923; Adolf Schmalix
to Hitler, 29 May 1923, T-84/5/4973.
    34. Mannheimer General-Anzeiger, 7 November 1923; Justiz-
minister Baden to Bayer. Staatsministerium des Innern, 6
Dec. 1923, GLA/234/5703; Justizm. Gärtner (Bavaria) to
Justizm. Baden, 23 April 1924, GLA/234/5703.
    35. MdI, "Auszug: Entscheidung des Staatsgerichtshofs,"
19 April 1923, and Generalstaatsanwalt Baden to Oberreichsanwalt, 12 February 1923, both GLA/372/Zg 1943/40/171; Reichs-

gericht, 1. Strafsenat, "Im Namen des Reiches," 9 October 1923, GLA/234/5703; H. Kraft, "Bescheinigung," 12 January 1938, and Heinrich Kling to Kraft, 16 December 1937, GLA/235/38160; Süddeutsche Zeitung, 11 October 1923.

36. Reichsgericht, "Urteil gegen Hans Rupprechter et al," 17 June 1924, and "Urteil des Reichsgericht vom 17 Juni 1924, Hugo Kromer et al.," and Karlsruher Amtsgericht to Justizministerium, 4 February 1924, all in GLA/234/5738; see also the reports in Volkswille (Singen), 2 February 1924; Volksstimme, 1 December 1923; Volkswacht, 14 January 1924; Freiburger Zeitung, 29 November 1923, in GLA/234/5738.

37. Kraft to Gauinspekteur Brust, 8 April 1938, GLA/235/ 38160 (on Richard Schwab or Pforzheim).

38. Generalstaatsanwalt Karlsruhe to Justizminister, 4 July 1924, GLA/234/5738; Bad. Landespolizeiamt, Abt. N an sämtliche Bezirksämter, 9 December 1922, GLA/372/Zg 1943/40/ 171; Führer, 30 March 1935, 9 October 1938; Heidelberger Tageblatt, 4 June 1924; Bezirksamt Waldshut to MdI, 12 April 1923, and Bezirksamt Waldshut to Landeskommissär Konstanz, 25 April 1923, both SAF/317/1257c.

39. Remmele to Landespolizeiamt Karlsruhe, 28 March 1923, GLA/377/5407; Bad. Staatsanwaltschaft Karlsruhe to Landgericht, Strafkammer I, 7 September 1923, GLA/234/5738; Völkischer Beobachter, 25/26 March, 1923; Führer, 31 March 1935.

40. Buch to Amann, 11 May 1923, HA/roll 16/folder 299; Buch to Amann, 17 June 1923, HA/roll 16/folder 299. Walter Buch was born on 25 October 1883, in Bruchsal. A retired army major, he had been an active Baden Schutz- und Trutzbund leader; see BDC/OPG, Akten Walter Buch; Führerlexikon, 1934, p. 77.

41. Führer, 25 July 1933; Freiburger Zeitung, 29 November 1923, and Generalstaatsanwalt, Karlsruhe to Justizminister, 4 July 1924, both GLA/234/5738. Although no local was established in Eggenstein until March 1924, the Griesinger brothers who had attended the Turnfest in Munich were members by November 1923, see Landespolizeiamt, Abt. N to Bezirksamt Mosbach, 3 July 1923, GLA/364/7745; and Führer, 22 September 1933. Eggenstein was described by a contemporary as a "Musterdorf . . . wohlhabende überwiegend bürgerliche Bauernbevölkerung," see Bergdolt, Badische Allmenden, pp. 12-13.

42. Völkischer Beobachter, 3 August 1923, and 23/24 September 1923.

43. Adolf Hitler, Sekretär, "Briefeingang" and "Briefauslauf," July-October, 1923, T-84/4/2921-37; Buch to Amann, 17 June 1923, HA/roll 16/folder 299; see also the letters from individuals in Baden to the SA in Munich; for example, Emil

Danzeisen to Amann, 9 July 1923, HA/roll 16/folder 298.

44. Kurt Gottgaul to Hitler, 19 April 1923, T-84/5/4696; H. Hess (Heidelberg) to Hitler, 19 April 1923, T-84/5/4641.

45. Ernst Ulshöfer (Mannheim) to Frl. Steininger (Munich), 27 September 1923, T-84/5/4577; Wilhelm Zimmermann to Max Amann, 19 October 1923, T-84/5/4243. There were, of course, difficulties that frustrated some Baden Nazis when they attempted to communicate with Munich. The party leader of Bretten (district) in 1921/23, for example, used Liedolsheim to obtain information about Munich activities or orders. Then in late 1922, Munich sent Emil Danzeisen to Baden to act as Munich's official delegate (Beauftragter), see Karl Horn's report on Danzeisen, 18 May 1932, T-175/467/2987598.

46. Bad. Landespolizeiamt to Oberstaatsanwalt Karls., 6 December 1923, GLA/309/1158; Freiburger Zeitung, 29 November 1923, GLA/234/5738.

47. Bad. Staatsanwaltschaft Karlsruhe to Landgericht, Strafkammer I, 7 September 1923; Staatsanwaltschaft Heidelberg to Justizministerium, 14 June 1923; Staatsanwalt Marx, Heidelberg, to Bad. Amtsgericht Eppingen, "Anklageschrift," 17 August 1923, GLA/234/5738.

48. Meldung des Pol. Inspektors Bayers und Oberwacht-meister Ludwig to Staatsanwaltschaft, 23 July 1923, GLA/234/5738; Führer, 30 March 1935; Völkischer Beobachter, 3 August 1923. Worch was born in Strassburg but moved to Karlsruhe in 1918 to practice his trade of brewery master; see Strass-burger Neueste Nachrichten, 21 August 1941, in Records of German Field Commands: Rear Areas, Occupied Territories, and Others, National Archives Microfilm T-501 (hereafter cited as T-501)/roll 186/folder 344. Albert Leo Schlageter had studied in Freiburg after the war but soon devoted himself to a career of full-time völkisch activism. After being appre-hended by the French in the Ruhr, he was executed on 26 May 1923, see Waite, Vanguard, pp. 236-37.

49. Adolf Hitler, Sekretär, "Briefeingang, 11.-18. September 1923," T-84/4/2930; Adolf Hitler, Sekretär, "Brief-auslauf 16.-31. August, 1923," (and 22.-27. September), T-84/4/2935; Wilhelm Tellenbach to Hitler, 31 May 1923, T-84/5/4997.

50. Revier-Kommissär Mauss, Heidelberg to Bezirksamt-Polizeidirektion, 27 June 1922, GLA/356/2617; Pol. Oberwacht-meister Pfeiffer to Bezirksamt Polizeidirektion Heidelberg, 27 June 1922, GLA/356/2617; Marx, Werdegang, pp. 167-74. The case against Lenard was dropped, but the Socialist student Mierendorff received four months, see Staatsanwalt Heidelberg to Bezirksamt Polizeidirektion, 15 October 1922, GLA/356/

2617; and Heidelberger Tageblatt, 11 April 1923. Lenard did
not become a party member until 1937; see Alan D. Beyerchen,
Scientists under Hitler, p. 97.

51. Philipp Lenard to Prof. Stark, 27 September 1923,
"Vertraulich," T-84/5/3862; Lenard to Justizrat Class, 27
September 1923, "Vertraulich," T-84/5/3863-64. Stark was
also a Nobel Prize winner in physics (1919). Born in 1874
in Upper Palatinate, he earned a Ph.D. in 1897 in Munich.
His academic career ended in 1922 when he resigned from his
post in Würzburg; see Beyerchen, Scientists under Hitler, pp.
103-114; and Kürschners Deutscher Gelehrten-Kalender, 1928/29,
p. 2335.

52. Stark to Hitler, 29 September 1923, T-84/5/3860.
Lenard continued to correspond with leading Nazis; see T-81/
667/5475137-38; Beyerchen, Scientists under Hitler, pp.
123-67; and August Becker, ed., Naturforschung im Aufbruch.

53. Führer, 30 March 1935, 8 October 1933, 13 April
1939, 23 June 1934, and 9 March 1943; Wolfgang Schäfer, NSDAP,
p. 11.

54. Max Weber to Hitler, Sekretär, "Bericht über den
Stand der Bewegung in Württemberg, Ende Mai 1923," T-84/5/
4026.

55. Mannheim membership list, April-August 1922, HA/roll
10/folder 215; Führer, 22 September 1933 (and the BDC files
and membership cards of these party members); membership list
for September-October 1923, HA/roll 10/folder 215; about
ninety-five names appear in police and court records, see
Reichsgericht, "Im Namen des Reiches," 9 October 1923, GLA/
234/5703; Meldung des Pol. Inspektors Bayer and Oberwacht-
meister Ludwig to Staatsanwaltschaft Karlsruhe, 23 July 1923;
Freiburger Zeitung, 29 November 1923; Bad. Staatsanwaltschaft
Karlsruhe to Landgericht, Strafkammer I, 7 September 1923;
Staatsanwalt Freiburg to Justizm., 26 June 1923; Reichsgericht, "Urteil gegen Hans Rupprechter et al.," 17 June
1924; Staatsanwalt Heidelberg to Justizm., 17 August 1923;
Staatsanwalt Heidelberg to Justizm., 27 June 1923; Volkswacht,
14 January 1924; Bad. Landespolizeiamt, Karlsruhe to MdI,
26 May 1923, all in GLA/234/5738; Bad. Landespolizeiamt,
Abt. N, to Bezirksämter, 9 December 1922, GLA/372/Zg. 1943/
40/171; Bad. Landespolizeiamt to Oberstaatsanwalt Karlsruhe,
6 December 1923, GLA/309/1158; Bezirksamt Waldshut to MdI,
12 April 1923, and Bezirksamt Waldshut to MdI, 25 April 1923,
both in SAF/317/1257c. These police and court reports reveal
Nazi activities in northern and southern Baden. Of the
activists cited, 38.5 percent were born in (and after) 1900,
whereas almost 40 percent were born between 1890 and 1899.

That is, 80 percent of all Nazi activists in 1923 were at most
thirty-three years old.

56. Führer, 31 March 1935; 22 September 1933; 14 January
1928; 2 June 1928; 21 April 1928; Völkischer Beobachter, 6
February 1921; list in Führer, 22 September 1933, and BDC
files and membership cards.

57. Führer, 30 March 1935; BDC/Files of Riedner, Worch;
and Führerlexikon, 1934, p. 316. Moraller was born in 1903
in Karlsruhe, Riedner was born in 1883 in Karlsruhe, and
Worch was born in 1896 in Strassburg, Alsace. For the brewery
Schrempp-Printz see Südwestdeutsche Rundschau Baden, 10:49.
Both firms joined in 1920 because the postwar period saw a
great decline in beer consumption which endangered both companies. This may have been one of the factors that generated
the growing political radicalization of the Karlsruhe brewers.

58. Marx, Werdegang, pp. 162-63; Maser, Frühgeschichte,
p. 317. In March 1928, Heinrich Bammesberger was invited to
a Heidelberg Hitler meeting (closed), Abtl. N to MdI, 7 March
1928, GLA/234/5738.

59. Führer, 16 May 1933; 9 October 1938; Kling to Kraft,
16 December 1937, GLA/235/38160; BDC/Hüssy file.

60. BDC/Kramer file (Personalkarte, 20 March 1934);
Führer, 20 April 1939, 11 August 1933, 1 May 1936; Führerlexikon, 1934, p. 356; BDC/Röhn file.

61. Plattner to R.L., Abtl. Mitgliederschaft, 24 April
1941, BDC/Plattner file; Grossdeutscher Reichstag, 1938, p.
343.

62. On Berkmüller see MdI to Staatsministerium, 25 October
1938, GLA/233/27894; for Kemper see BDC/Kemper file; for
Kramer see BDC/Kramer file; for Plattner see BDC/Plattner file;
for Adolf Schmid see Führer, 29 August 1933; and for Röhn see
Grossdeutsche Reichstag, 1938, p. 365, and BDC/Röhn file.
See the important article by Michael Kater, "Methodologische
Überlegungen," 3:453-84 (and in particular p. 482 on "Kauf-
männer").

63. Führer, 22 September 1933; Artur Görlitzer, ed.,
Adressbuch der Nationalsozialistischen Volksvertreter, p.
424; Michael Kater, "Zur Soziographie der frühen NSDAP," 19:
137, 142.

64. Wilhelm Zimmermann, Karlsruhe, to Amann, 19 October
1923, T-84/5/42431; Völkischer Beobachter, 2 December 1925;
Rapp, ed., Die Parteibewegung in Baden, 1905-1928, p. 10.

65. For example, Hans Knab, E. Würth, and George Rast,
Führer, 20 October 1928 and 28 July 1928; Völkischer Beobachter, 17 August 1927; Gauschatzmeister Baden to Reichsschatzmeister, 20 January 1937, BDC/Würth file. Ernst Würth lost

his Kreisleiter post in 1928 and left the party in 1929; after 1933, he tried to get back into the party. Georg Rast moved to Stuttgart, and Karl Lenz became the Gau leader of Hesse after 1931. Hans Knab left the party in 1930 but was readmitted in 1934 and again became a Kreisleiter.

66. Wilhelm Marschall v. Bieberstein was active in Berlin and Munich before November 1923; Friedhelm Kemper was a native of Halle; Adolf Schmid was a party member in Heilbronn before 1925, and Josef Lidl had been a party member in Munich, see BDC/Marschall v. Bieberstein Karte; BDC/F. Kemper file; BDC/J. Lidl Karte; Führer, 6 February 1935, 29 August 1933; Emir Götz von Pölnitz, Das tapfere Leben des Freiherrn Marschall von Bieberstein, pp. 90-91, 121.

67. Hermann Röhn, Franz Moraller, Heinrich Wittmann, Hermann Schneider, Wilhelm Hartlieb, Otto Wacker(?), and Albert Schwerdel, see Grossdeutsche Reichstag, 1938, pp. 365, 438; Führerlexikon, 1934, pp. 316, 510; BDC/Wittmann Karte; BDC/W. Hartlieb file; Führer, 30 November 1933, 11 August 1933; Wer ist's?, 1934, p. 1093.

68. Based on the names listed in the Führer, 22 September 1933, and the BDC files and membership cards of these names. After 1933 the long-term völkisch activists became Kreisleiters, mayors, ministers of the departments of Interior and Education, Gau party leaders, and other important state and party office leaders. For the rise of the "plebeians" see Daniel Lerner, et al., "The Nazi Elite," pp. 230-33.

69. Bezirksamt Waldshut, "Aktennotiz," 9 April 1923; Gendarmeriekommissär Heiden, Waldshut to Bezirksamt, 10 April 1923, SAF/317/1257c; Generalstaatsanwalt to Justizminister Baden, 12 May 1923, GLA/234/10130; Volksstimme (Mannheim), 5 June 1923, in GLA/234/5703; Arbeiter-Zeitung, 21 February 1923, in GLA/356/4418.

70. Frankfurter Zeitung (Erstes Morgenblatt), 21 September 1923; F.Z. (Erstes Morgenblatt), 11 November 1923; F.Z. (Zweites Morgenblatt), 21 September 1923; OKH, Kriegsgeschichtliche Forschungsanstalt des Heeres, ed., Die Kämpfe in Südwestdeutschland, 1919-1923, pp. 111-18; Angress, Stillborn Revolution, p. 388; Gendarmeriebezirk Villingen to Staatsanwaltschaft Konstanz, 12 September 1923, SAF/317/1257c.

71. Frankfurter Zeitung (Erstes Morgenblatt), 25 September 1923; Reichstagswahl am 4. Mai 1924, p. 21; Sitzung des Kabinetts am 24 September 1923, GLA/233/27914.

72. Führer, 1/2 March 1931; Völkischer Beobachter 25, 18 September 1923.

73. Bad. Justizminister to Staatsministerium, 27 October 1924; Justizminister Karlsruhe, "Auszug aus dem Jahresbericht

der Staatsanwaltschaft Waldshut für das Jahr 1924," 11 April
1925; Sitzung des Bad. Staatsministeriums, 14 March 1925, GLA/
234/5703; Staatspräsident, Baden, to Reichswehrminister Gessler,
26 September 1923; 5. Division Stuttgart, Generalleutnant
Reinhardt, 28 September 1923 to Remmele, GLA/233/12515;
"Auszug aus der Niederschrift über die Sitzung des Staatsministeriums vom 11. Dez. 1924," GLA/233/27914. Karl Gärtner,
a teacher and future Kreisleiter, was a member of the Bauern-
wehr in 1923 in southern Baden, Führer, 30 March 1935. Dr.
Montfort was still active in the party after 1933; see BDC/
Dr. Montfort file.

    74. Emil Danzeisen to Amann, 9 July 1923, HA/roll 16/
folder 298; Emil Guttchen (Bruchsal) to SA Oberkommando
München, 6 June 1923, HA/roll 16/folder 298; H. Alfred Haueisen
to A. Hitler, 14 September 1923, T-84/6/5213; Generalstaatsanwalt, Karlsruhe to Justizminister, 4 July 1924, GLA/234/5738;
H. Kraft, "Bescheinigung," 12 January 1938; Heinrich Kling to
Kraft, 16 December 1937, GLA/235/38160.

    75. SA Oberkommando to Friedrich Ehrly, Lörrach, 9 July
1923, HA/16/298; Justizobersekretär Wilhelm Ehrly (Friedrich's
father) to Staatsministerium, 1 May 1923, GLA/233/27915.

    76. Führer, 30 March 1935; Karl Lenz, "Bestätigung,"
27 October 1938, in BDC/Heinrich Sauerhöfer file; Dr. Ph.
Kraft, "Meine Kampferlebnisse," 1 December 1936, HA/27/528;
Karl Gropp, "Erklärung über Herrn Seitz," 30 September 1938,
T-81/89/102651.

    77. "Niederschrift über die Besprechung mit den Staats-u.
Ministerpräsidenten der Länder, in der Reichskanzlei am 25
Sept. 1923," in IfZ/MA 810 (same as T-120/1690/803014-18).

    78. Frankfurter Zeitung (Erstes Morgenblatt), 10 and 11
November 1923; Führer, 30 March 1935; 8 October 1933; Karlsruher Zeitung, 9 November 1923; Sitzung des Staatsministeriums
vom 9. Nov. 1923, GLA/233/28187.

CHAPTER THREE

    1. Führer (Sonderbeilage), 30 March 1935.
    2. Pol. Sekretär Roth, Karlsruhe, to Oberstaatsanwalt, and
Bad. Landespolizei to Oberstaatsanwalt, 6 December 1923, in
GLA/309/1158; Gendarmeriebezirk Heidelberg to IV Bezirk
Heidelberg, 17 November 1923 (NS Umtriebe), GLA/356/4355.
    3. Pol. Inspektor Bayer, Karlsruhe, "Vernehmung von
Ludwig Werle," 7 December 1923, GLA/309/1158.
    4. Führer, 10 November and 30 March 1935; Bad. Landes-
polizeiamt to Oberstaatsanwalt, 30 November 1923 and to

Staatsanwaltschaft, 3 December 1923; and Pol. Inspektor Bayer, Karlsruhe, "Anzeige gegen Robert Rützler, led. Kaufmann aus Ettenheim," 3 December 1923; and Oberstaatsanwalt Karlsruhe, "Haftbefehl," 4 December 1923; and R. Rützler to Staatsanwalt-schaft Karlsruhe, 24 May 1934, all in GLA/309/1158. The Deutsche Herold was founded in 1919 by Wulle. It published the Deutsche Tageblatt.

    5. MdI, Baden, to Justizminister, 25 September 1924; and Pol. Inspektor Bayer to Bad. Landespolizeiamt, 4 September 1924; and Volksstimme, 7 August 1924; and Badische Presse, 20 March 1929, all in GLA/234/5703; Führer, 30 March 1935; Walter Sickinger, "Erinnerungen aus der Kampfzeit," 8 February 1937, HA/27/531.

    6. Bezirksamt Konstanz to Landeskommissär Konstanz, 30 January 1924, and Landespolizeiamt, Aussenstelle Konstanz to Landeskommissär, 12 March 1924, in SAF/317/1257c.

    7. Staatsanwalt Heidelberg to Bezirksamt, 11 July 1924, GLA/377/5399; Reichsbanner Schwarz-rot-gold, local Mosbach to Bürgermeisteramt, Diedesheim, 23 August 1924; and Ober-wachtmeister Obrigheim to Bezirksamt Mosbach, 21 September 1924; and Bezirksamt Mosbach to NSDAP Diedesheim, 12 February 1932, all in GLA/364/7808; Staatsanwaltschaft Mosbach to Generalstaatsanwalt Karlsruhe, 8 March 1924 and Bauländer Bote, 11 February 1924, in GLA/234/5703.

    8. Bad. Landespolizeiamt, Abt. N, "Nationalsozialistische Umtriebe in Liedolsheim," 17 March 1924; and Fraktion des Landbundes u.d. DNVP to Bürgermeisteramt Liedolsheim, 27 February 1924; and August Friedrich Göbelbecker to Bürger-meisteramt, 27 February 1924, all in GLA/309/1168.

    9. Heidelberger Tageblatt, 4 June 1924; and Volkswille (Singen), 2 February 1924; and Amtsgericht to Justizministe-rium, 4 February 1924, in GLA/234/5738; Volkszeitung (Heidel-berg), 23 June 1924, and Mosbacher Volksblatt, 4 November 1924, in GLA/234/5703.

    10. Staatsanwalt, Heidelberg to Bezirksamt Sinsheim, 11 July 1924, GLA/377/5399.

    11. Pflaumer to Staatsministerium, 9 April 1935, GLA/233/27905; Völkischer Beobachter, 21 August 1925. Two examples were Emil Schell (police) and Wilhelm Küchenmüller (teacher).

    12. Remmele, "Bekanntmachung," 11 October 1924, GLA/372/Zg. 1943/40/171; Volkswille (Singen), 2 February 1924, in GLA/234/5738; Karlsruher Zeitung, 27 October 1924.

    13. "Anzeige gegen Rechtsanwalt Dr. Edwin Müller," 11 October 1924, GLA/309/1149-50; Der Völkische Kämpfer, No. 22 (4 October 1924), GLA/309/1150.

14. Völkischer Kämpfer, 4 October 1924, GLA/309/1150; Völkischer Beobachter, 19 May 1925; for Lahr, see Oskar Wiegert, ed., NSDAP Ortsgruppe Offenburg, Festbuch, p. 12, in GLA/465d/1458.

15. Führer, 13 April 1939 and 8 October 1933; Hans Knab to Gaupersonalamt, 25 October 1937, T-81/166/305375.

16. Führer, 15 April 1934 and 25 July 1933; Ortsgruppe Eggenstein, "Stammbuch für Ludwig Griesinger," 23 September 1940, T-81/162/300532-37; Das Archiv, No. 31 (October 1936), p. 1101. Baden, unlike most southern German states, saw an increase in Nazi locals between 1923 and 1925; see Schäfer, NSDAP, pp. 11-12.

17. "Mitteilungsblatt der Völkischen Wahlverbände," 25 April 1924, in Albrecht Tyrell, ed., Führer Befiehl, p. 75; Baden, Statistisches Landesamt, Wahlen am 4. Mai 1924, pp. 62, 78. The two candidates Willy Maasdorff and Kurt Baumann had been active in the Nazi movement of Tiengen in 1923; see Bezirksamt Waldshut to MdI, Baden, 12 April 1923, and Bezirksamt Waldshut to Landeskommissär Konstanz, 25 April 1923, SAF/317/1257c.

18. Statistisches Landesamt, Wahlen am 4. Mai 1924 in Baden; Volksfreund, 5 May 1924; Karlsruher Volksblatt, 6 May 1924.

19. Heinrich Müller, testimony before Bezirksamt Bruchsal, September 1924; and MdI to Bezirksamt Bruchsal, 25 September 1924; and Landespolizeiamt, Abt. N to Landrat, Bruchsal, 13 October 1924; and Gend. Oberwachtmeister Ludwig to Landespolizeiamt, 13 October 1924; and Meldung des Polizeiinspektors Hagn to Oberbürgermeister, Bruchsal, 13 October 1924; and Volksfreund, 10 September 1924; and Bruchsaler Zeitung, 11 October 1924, all in GLA/344/6583.

20. Wahrheit, No. 1 (25 October 1924), and Pol. Inspektor Bayer to Landespolizeiamt Karlsruhe, 28 November 1924, in GLA/309/1150.

21. Baden, Statistisches Landesamt, Die Reichstagswahl am 7. Dezember 1924, p. 60; Führer, 28 April 1928 and 10 December 1927. Freiherr Schilling von Canstatt was born on 25 October 1870 in Mannheim and lived in the rural district of Sinsheim. He was Müller's assistant on the staff of the Wahrheit; see Oberwachtmeister Wilde, "Persönliche Verhältnisse," GLA/309/1150. The occupations of the candidates were: athletic director, farmer, tailor, locksmith, postal clerk, Kaufmann, customs official, retired army major, and owner of a rock quarry.

22. Ruge to Schriftleitung of the Völkischer Beobachter,

11 June 1923, T-84/6/5064; Ruge to Hitler, 1 April 1923,
T-84/5/4655. After 1933 he did get a job in the Badische
Generallandesarchiv in Karlsruhe, although he never became
the director. He also never obtained an academic position in
Heidelberg; see Ruge to Wacker, 19 April 1939, GLA/Ruge
Nachlass/69N/box 11; Ruge to Köhler, GLA/233/24953.

 23. Ruge, "Einige Kampfdaten aus meinem Leben," 1 January
1941, and Heidelberger Tageblatt, 14 June 1924, in GLA/Ruge
Nachlass/69N/box 25 and 2; "Bericht über die Tagung der
nordd. nat.soz.-en Verbände in Harburg, 7.9.1924," HA/6/141.
Both Willi Worch and Peter Riedner of Karlsruhe opposed the
leadership of the NSFP in Baden. Both joined Robert Wagner
after 1924 to build the new Nazi leadership in Baden.

 24. Statistisches Landesamt, Reichstagswahl am 7. Dezember 1924, pp. 52-61, 75; Statistisches Jahrbuch, 1930, p. 68;
Badische Zeitung, 8 December 1924. For example, in Weinheim
the party dropped from 8.7 percent to 4.1 percent while the
middle-class parties increased in strength.

 25. NSFB, Landesverband Baden to Gauleitungen und Orts-
gemeinschaften, 15 December 1924, GLA/309/1150.

 26. "Aufzeichnungen Wagener, Gen. a. D.," Heft 1, IfZ/
ED/60/1; Wer ist's? (1935), p. 1670; Führerlexikon, 1934,
p. 513; Wagner's testimony in Ludwig Voggenreiter, ed., Der
Hitler Prozess, p. 55, and in Der Hitler Prozess vor dem
Volksgericht in München, 1:88-91. Wagner was born as Robert
Backfisch but assumed the name Wagner because of "Namenspott."
His brother joined the party on 4 May 1927 as Alfred Back-
fisch; see Adolf Bach, Deutsche Nameskunde, p. 260; and
BDC/A. Backfisch file. Although Wagner apparently married
before 1929, this fact never appeared in the Führer or in any
other Baden party publication between 1929 and 1945; see Otto
Wagener, Hitler aus nächster Nähe, p. 40.

 27. Wagner to Reichsjustizministerium, Abt. Württemberg-
Baden, 6 February 1935, GLA/234/6347; Landespolizeiamt, Abt.
N to Staatsanwaltschaft, 3 July 1930, GLA/309/1176; Staatspräsident Baden to Reichswehrminister Gessler, 26 September
1923, GLA/233/12515.

 28. Führer, 20 April 1939; Staatsanwalt to Vorsitzenden
des Volksgerichts München, "Betreff: Umsturzversuch am 8./9.
November 1923," 8 January 1924, HA/5/114I; Gordon, Beer Hall
Putsch, p. 328. Lothar Kettenacker's account adds little to
the narrative above, Nationalsozialistische Volkstumspolitik
im Elsass, p. 68.

 29. Landespolizeiamt, Abt. N, to Staatsanwaltschaft
Karlsruhe, 3 July 1930, GLA/309/1176; Strafgefängnis Landsberg
a. Lech, "Verzeichnis der beim Strafgefängnis Landsberg

aufbewahrten Akten aus der Kampfzeit der N.S. Bewegung,"
HA/roll 3/folder 66; "Aufzeichnungen Wagener, Gen. a. D.,"
Heft 1, IfZ/ED/60/1; Führer, 30 March 1935.

30. Führer, 24 March 1930, 30 March 1935, 6 January 1934;
Walter Sickinger, "Erinnerungen aus der Kampfzeit," 8 February
1937, HA/27/531; "Bericht über die Tagung der nordd. nat.
soz.-en Verbände in Harburg, 7.9.1924," HA/6/141.

31. Führer, 23 September 1933, 18 April 1937, 30 March
1935; Götz von Pölnitz, Das tapfere Leben, pp. 144-45; BDC/
Wagner file; Knab to Gaupersonalamtsleiter, 24 February 1940,
T-81/166/305316.

32. Führer, 24 March 1940, 30 March 1935; Völkischer
Beobachter, 18 April 1925.

33. Der Demokrat, 6 (1 October 1925), p. 437; Adam Remmele, Staatsumwälzung und Neuaufbau in Baden, p. 162.

34. Volksfreund, 21 March 1925.

35. Das Deutsche Tageblatt, 7 October 1925; For the close
connection between the Mittelstandspartei in the Tiengen area
in 1923 and the Nazis, see Bezirksamt Waldshut to Landeskommissär Konstanz, 25 April 1923, SAF/317/1257c. The DVFB candidates in October 1925 in Freiburg were: Oberzollsekretär,
Obersteuersekretär, Kaufmann, Dr. Med., and a Werkmeister.

36. Das Deutsche Tageblatt, 15 November 1924, 5 September,
19 September, 24 October, 31 October 1925, and December
1927; Baden, Statistisches Landesamt, Badische Landtagswahl
am 25. Oktober 1925; Polizei-Präsident, Abt. I-A (Berlin) to
Bad. Landespolizeiamt, 31 January 1928, GLA/309/1142; Unsere
Waffen, Folge 23 (c. 1930), in GLA/Ruge Nachlass/69N/box 60.

37. Das Deutsche Tageblatt, 3 November, 5 July 1928;
Völkischer Herold, 22 July, 28 October 1927; Führer, 28 April
1928.

38. Völkischer Beobachter, 29 July 1927, 23 December
1925; Führer, 14 April 1928, 23 September 1933, Gaugeschäftsführung Baden to Hauptarchiv, 29 January 1937, HA/5/132.

39. Wagner to Parteiführung Munich, 14 August 1926, BDC
nonbiographical files, NA Microfilm No. T-580 (hereafter
cited as T-580)/roll 19/folder 199; Landespolizeiamt, Abt. N,
"Bericht," 20 February 1930, SAF/317/1257c; Kriminalpolizei
Karlsruhe to Staatsanwaltschaft, 28 January 1928, GLA/309/
1174.

40. Wagner to Parteiführung Munich, 14 August 1926,
T-580/19/199; Führer, 10 November 1933.

41. Karl Lenz to Reichsparteileitung, 19 May 1927, T-580/
19/199; Führer, 10 November 1933; Völkischer Beobachter, 23
September 1925; BDC/August Kramer file; Baldur von Schirach,
Die Pioniere des Dritten Reiches, pp. 143-45; Max Schwarz,

M.d.R., Biographisches Handbuch, p. 740. Kramer was born in 1900 in Lahr and joined the army in June 1918. He was trained as a teacher but was fired in the summer of 1923. By 1927 he was a full-time, paid party official. Karl Lenz (already described) was Gau leader of Hesse from 1931 until he allegedly suffered a nervous breakdown in late 1932 and returned to Baden. In Baden in 1932/33 he became active in a pro-Strasser opposition movement. He died in November 1944 in Freising, Bavaria.

42. Völkischer Beobachter, 28 October and 13 February 1926; Führer, 19 November 1927, 20 October 1928; BDC/Peter Riedner file. For corruption see BDC/Ullmer file; and BDC/Heinrich Siebach file. Munich's support of the Gau center's financial powers was ordered as early as 1925. In June 1925, for example, Munich told the local of Freiburg to stop sending membership dues to Munich directly and instead to send them to Gau leader Wagner. Munich also left it up to the Gauleitung to negotiate membership dues with the locals. In 1925, the Gauleitung had to send 10 Pfg per member, each month, to Munich. Before 1928, party members had to pay 80 Pfg each month, of which the locals sent 50 Pfg to the Gau center. In August 1928, as the party structure began to demand more funds, the locals had to send 55 Pfg to the Gau center; see also NSDAP, Munich to Ortsgruppe Freiburg i. Br. (Paul Ziegler), 17 June 1925, T-580/699/595.

43. Reichsschatzmeister to Wagner, 15 January 1932, BDC/Wagner file; Landespolizeiamt, Abt. N, "Bericht," 15 January 1929 (and 1 June 1927), SAF/317/1257d.

44. Führer, 30 March 1935; Völkischer Beobachter, 5 June, 19 May, 15 and 18 September, 18 October, 16 April, and 5 September 1925; see also Bouhler to Tritschler, 1 April 1925, T-580/699/595, for an example of how Munich helped Wagner establish his position in Baden. The local leader and founder of the Nazi local of Freiburg, Franz Tritschler, was informed that Hitler had appointed Wagner as leader of the movement in Baden. Tritschler was requested to establish contacts with Wagner.

45. Völkischer Beobachter, 18 February, 21 April 1926; Führer, 25 June 1938.

46. Landespolizeiamt, Abt. N, "Bericht," 7 September 1926, SAF/317/1257d; Völkischer Beobachter, 18/19 April, 12 February 1926. For example, the local of Karlsruhe held three Sprechabende and one public rally in January 1926. The topics were: "Rassenkunde," "Gegen Ausbeutung," "Banatparteien," "Was will der Nationalsozialismus?"

47. These names appeared in the Völkischer Beobachter and

in the reports of the Landespolizeiamt, Abt. N between 1926 and 1928, in SAF/317/1257d.

48. Landespolizeiamt, Abt. N, "Rechtsbewegung," June 1926, and Abt. N, "Bericht," 5 November 1926 (and 7 September 1926), SAF/317/1257d.

49. Völkischer Beobachter, 23 September, 1 and 28 October, 4 December 1925, and 28 October, 16 March 1926; Führer, 26 and 5 November 1927, and 21 January 1928. For example, Wagner presented six speeches during a Werbewoche in the spring of 1926, all focusing on anti-Semitism. Kemper helped found a Nazi local in Zotzenbach in October 1926 by focusing his speech on the Jewish question. See also Israelitische Gemeindeblatt, Mannheim, 20 July 1927.

50. Remmele to Bezirksämter, 1 February 1926, GLA/343/778; Volksstimme, 3 April 1925; Landespolizeiamt, Abt. N, "Rechtsbewegung," 1 August 1926 (and 1 May 1927; June 1926), SAF/317/1257d.

51. Völkischer Beobachter, 25 April, 29 December, 18 August, 2 October, 24 December 1925.

52. Ibid., 8 December, 1925, 23 January, 15 October 1926; Landespolizeiamt, Abt. N, "Rechtsbewegung," 15 January 1927, SAF/317/1257d.

53. Völkischer Beobachter, 3 March 1927; Führer, 10 December 1927, 21 and 28 January 1928, 1 and 2 March 1931; Lena Osswald, Heidelberg, "Warum ich in Ludendorff's Tannebergbund eintrat," n.d., c. 1928, GLA/Ruge Nachlass/69N/box 60; see also the reports of the Landespolizeiamt, Abt. N in 1927, in SAF/317/1257d.

54. Völkischer Beobachter, 14 September 1925, 12 October, 28 September 1926; Landespolizeiamt, Abt. N, "Bericht," 5 November 1926, SAF/317/1257d; "Erinnerungen aus der Kampfzeit, Pg. Valentin Spangenmacher aus Osthofen," HA/27/528.

55. Völkischer Beobachter, 31 August 1927; Führer, 25 February, 2 June, 13 October 1928 .

56. Völkischer Beobachter, 18 February 1926; Führer, 10 December 1927, 1 September, 3 November 1928.

57. Local leaders of Mannheim: Arthur Meyer (1926), Max Rühle (1927), and Friedhelm Kemper (1928); see Völkischer Beobachter, 12 February 1926; Führer, 28 May 1928; Ortsgruppenverzeichnis, 8 July 1927, T-580/19/199; local leaders of Pforzheim: Robert Wagner (1925), Dettlinger (1926), Rast (1927), Scholz (to July 1928); see Völkischer Beobachter, 9 February 1926, 17 August 1927; Führer, 28 July 1928.

58. For Robert Roth of Liedolsheim see Völkischer Beobachter, 7/8 August 1927; for Reinhardt of Neulussheim (1926-28) see Völkischer Beobachter, 2/3 May 1926; Führer,

1 September 1928.

59. Völkischer Beobachter, 17 and 18 February, 11 March, 29 April 1926, 23 February 1927; BDC/OPG, Albert Roth file.

60. Wagner, "Führerernennung," 2 March 1927, T-81/166/305381; Führer, 2 June 1928; Ortsgruppenverzeichnis, 8 July 1927, T-580/19/199.

61. Ortsgruppenverzeichnis, 8 July 1927, T-580/19/199; Stellv. Kreisleiter (NSDStB) to Kreisleitung NSDAP, Karlsruhe, 28 June 1933, Anlage: Schreiben des Hasso Freischlad, T-81/244/5031903; Völkischer Beobachter, 3 and 18 February, 21 April, 2/3 May, 15 July, 28 October, 17 November 1926, 7 August 1927; Führer, 24 May 1937.

62. Landespolizeiamt, Abt. N, "Bericht," 5 November 1926, SAF/317/1257d; Orlow, History, 1:111; see also Gerhard Schulz, Aufstieg des Nationalsozialismus, pp. 384-85.

63. Baden, Statistisches Landesamt, Reichspräsidentwahl 1925, pp. 36, 42-49; Volksfreund, 1 April 1925.

64. Völkischer Beobachter, 18 and 25 April 1925; Schiff, Kommissär Bezirk Durlach to Bezirksamt Karlsruhe, 27 April 1925, and Staatsanwaltschaft Karlsruhe, Abt. Ia, "Haft gegen Otto Friedrich Reitze," 22 September 1925, in GLA/309/1133. Reitze eventually received a one-year sentence while the rest of the participants went free; see Volksfreund, 8 February 1926.

65. Völkischer Beobachter, 15 and 18 September, 9 and 8 October 1925.

66. Völkischer Beobachter, 22 October, 3 November 1925; Volksfreund, 16 October 1925; Demokrat, 6 (1 October 1925), p. 437; Frankfurter Zeitung: (Abendblatt), 24 October 1925, and (Erstes Morgenblatt), 25 October 1925; Volksfreund, 23 October 1925; Badischer Beobachter, 22 October 1925. Remmele was quoted by the Frankfurter Zeitung as saying that the historical mission of the bourgeoisie had not yet been completed. He reminded his audience that a proletarian class rule could not yet cope with the capitalistic economy.

67. Frankfurter Zeitung (Abendblatt), 26 October 1925; Baden, Landtagswahl am 25. Oktober 1925, pp. 82, 93.

68. Baden, Landtagswahl am 25. Oktober 1925, pp. 82, 93; Das Deutsche Tageblatt, 24 October 1925; Führer, 30 March 1935. Albert Billich, mayor of Welmlingen, claimed that his name was placed on the DVFP slate against his wishes. He noted that he saw Hitler as the "great leader of the völkisch movement," Völkischer Beobachter, 18/19 October 1925.

69. Badische Zeitung and Karlsruher Zeitung, both 26 October 1925; C. V. Zeitung, 30 October 1925.

70. Baden, Statistisches Jahrbuch, 1930, p. 345; Landes-

polizeiamt, Abt. N, "Bericht," 1 December 1926, SAF/317/1257d;
Völkischer Beobachter, 15 October, 26 November 1926.
71. Landespolizeiamt, Abt. N, "Rechtsbewegung," 1 December
1926, SAF/317/1257d; Völkischer Beobachter, 26 November 1926;
Führer, 7 January, 14 April 1928; Der Demokrat, 7 (25 November
1926), p. 377; Frankfurter Zeitung (Abend), 15 November 1926;
Baden, Statistisches Jahrbuch, 1930, p. 345. Compared to the
SPD, the Nazis did not do well. The SPD won 42 mayoral posts,
49 Stadträte, 198 Stadtverordnete, 607 Gemeinderäte, and
3,436 Gemeindeverordnete seats, Jörg Schadt, ed., Im Dienst an
der Republik: Die Tätigkeitsberichte, p. 140.
72. MdI, Baden to Bezirksamt Mannheim, 1 August 1924,
GLA/233/12486; Landespolizeiamt to Landespolizeiamt Karlsruhe,
22 August 1927, GLA/309/1157; Remmele to Bezirksämter, 19 May
1927, and Landespolizeiamt, Abt. N, "Bericht," June 1926, and
1 May 1927, both in SAF/317/1257d.
73. Landespolizeiamt, Abt. N, "Die Nationalsozialistische
Arbeiterpartei," 25 July 1930, GLA/234/5738; Abt. N, "Rechtsbewegung," 15 November 1929, SAF/317/1257d; for the new activism that took Baden Nazis to the Pfalz and Hesse, see Führer,
3 December 1927; BDC/OPG, A. Roth file; Heinrich Haselhorst,
Friedberg, Hesse, "Meine Kampferlebnisse," 30 December 1936,
HA/27/528; Bezirksamt Kusel to the government of the Pfalz,
13 September 1927, HA/32A/1786. See also Oron J. Hale, The
Captive Press in the Third Reich.
74. Völkischer Beobachter, 8 April 1925, 30 March 1926,
8 October 1925; Führer, 19 November 1927, 13 October 1928.
75. Völkischer Beobachter, 26 May 1926, 24/25 May 1927;
Führer, 30 March 1935; Landespolizeiamt, Abt. N, to Landräte,
11 November 1925, and Remmele, "Presseabtl., Notiz," 21 April
1927, both GLA/372/Zg. 943/40/171.
76. Völkischer Beobachter, 1 May 1928, 10 August 1927,
11/12 March 1928; Führer, 24 November, 10 March 1928, 5 November 1927. Walter Köhler in a letter published in the Führer
(26 November 1927) also demanded that Germany's goal must be
"Raum für das Volk als aussenpolitische Ziel."
77. Landespolizeiamt, Abt. N, 1 November 1927, SAF/317/
1257d.
78. Wagner, "Zum zehnjährigen Bestehen des Führers,"
Führer, 28 November 1927, HA/47/1014; Joseph Geiger to Hitler,
5 August 1927; and Amtsgericht Mosbach, "Urteil," 4 January
1927; and Peter Riedner to Dr. Geiger, 1 November 1927; and
Wagner to Geiger, 22 September 1927, all HA/R31/594.
79. Wagner, "Fünf Jähre Führer," Führer, 1 November 1932;
Franz Moraller, "Erinnerungen aus der Gründerzeit," 29 July
1936, HA/47/1014; Führer, 1 November 1932, 4 November 1937,

24 and 3 December 1927, 23 June and 3 November 1928. Most
papers were sold in Karlsruhe (in terms of numbers) and in
Eberbach (in terms of percentage).

80. Führer, 1/2 January 1931, 5 November 1927; Poli.
Sekretär Buchheit to Landespolizeiamt, 22 February 1929, GLA/
309/1115. Otto Wacker was a relative of R. Theodor Wacker,
who had founded the Baden Zentrum party. He was born in 1899
in Offenburg and participated in the war in 1917/18. He was
active in the party while finishing his Ph.D. at the University of Freiburg. He also worked on the Südwestdeutschen
Beobachter in 1926 and on the Führer in 1927, see Führerlexikon, 1934, p. 510; Wer ist's? (1935), p. 1665. Ludwig
Ankenbrand, a Kaufmann by training, was born in 1889 and died
in 1928. He was succeeded as editor of the Führer by Franz
Moraller, Führer, 25 February 1928.

81. Führer, 5 November 1927; Pol. Ratschreiber to Landes-
polizeiamt, 11 July 1928, Kommissär Born to Staatsanwaltschaft
Mannheim, 24 November 1928, both GLA/309/1124; Hale, Captive
Press, pp. 50-51.

CHAPTER FOUR

1. Völkischer Beobachter, 26 March, 30/31 May 1926, 3/4
April, 26/27 May 1927, 13/14 May 1926, 16 March 1926. Some
of the speeches given in Baden articulated these views:
"Schaffendes Volk-Sozialdemokraten-Kommunisten," "Nationalsozialismus oder Grosskapitalismus?" "Nationalsozialismus-
zwei unlöslich miteinander verbundene Begriffe."

2. Bad. Landespolizeiamt, Abt. N, "Bericht," June 1926,
SAF/317/1257d. The Abt. N of the Baden police obtained KPD
documents and reports.

3. Völkischer Beobachter, 23 April 1926; Justizminister
Baden to Stresemann, 30 March 1927, GLA/234/5703; Poli. Assis-
tent Buchheit to Landespolizeiamt, 13 October 1928, GLA/309/
1170.

4. Völkischer Beobachter, 24 June 1926, 3/4 April 1927,
21 April 1928, 3 August 1926; Landespolizeiamt, Abt. N,
"Rechtsbewegung," 5 November 1926, SAF/317/1257d; Polizei
Sekretär Buchheit to Landespolizeiamt, 9 October 1929, GLA/
309/1139.

5. Friedrich's manuscript, and Gauleiter, Württemberg-
Hohenzollern to Hitler, 27 August 1926, in HA/8/166. In this
manuscript Friedrich praised Liebknecht and Luxemburg and
attacked Noske for destroying the real revolution!

6. Führer, 5 November 1927, 4 February 1928; Buchheit to

Landespolizeiamt, 9 October 1929, and Wagner to Oberstaatsanwalt beim Landgericht, 3 October 1929, both GLA/309/1139;
Hermann Friedrich, Unter dem Hakenkreuz, pp. 3-22. In late
1930, Friedrich escaped to Strassburg, see Volksfreund, 12
December 1930; and Badischer Beobachter, 15 December 1930,
in GLA/234/5738.

7. Führer, 20 October, 19 May 1928. The occupations
were: Bauernsohn (Wagner), Arbeiter, Schlosser, Schuhmacher-
meister, Lehrer, and Landwirt.

8. Robert Wagner to Fucke-Michels (Fraktionsführer in
Rastatt), 21 April 1931, T-81/173/314091-92.

9. See Orlow, History, 1:133; and Horst Gies, "NSDAP und
landwirtschaftliche Organisationen," pp. 341-42.

10. Quoted in J. E. Farquharson, The Plough and the
Swastika in Germany 1928-1945, p. 35. For traditional right-
wing strength see the election statistics for 1921 and 1925.
In 1928 and 1929 the Nazi party captured much of this support in the Protestant, rural communities. These same districts also witnessed strong anti-Semitism as early as 1848;
see Michael Anthony Riff, "The Anti-Jewish Aspect of the
Revolutionary Unrest of 1848 in Baden," pp. 22-29.

11. Badisches Landwirtschaftliches Wochenblatt, 94 (2
January 1926), pp. 1-2, and 6 February 1926, pp. 63-64,
27 November 1926, pp. 667-69; ibid., 95 (21 May 1927);
Badische Presse, 12 August 1932; Baden, Statistisches Landesamt, Die badische Landwirtschaft im Allgemeinen, 1:106;
Heinrich Hirtler, Verschuldungsverhältnisse der Kleinbauern
des Kaiserstuhls, pp. 111-12. Emigration was certainly not
the answer to Baden's rural problems. In 1927 only 550
Badenese emigrated per month, and by 1932 only twelve Baden
families had settled in Silesia as farmers.

12. Baden, Statistisches Landesamt, Die Landwirtschaft
in 1925, p. 65; Badisches Landwirtschaftliches Wochenblatt,
97 (6 April 1929), pp. 183-85, (11 August 1929), pp. 426-27;
Verhandlungen des Badischen Landtags, 1. Sitzungsperiode,
28 Oktober 1929-27 Oktober 1930, Protokollhefte, 2:299-307.

13. Remmele to Bezirksämter, 3 July 1928, SAF/317/585r;
Baden, Statistisches Jahrbuch, 1930, pp. 81-83.

14. Remmele to Statistische Landesamt, 8 August 1929;
and MdI, Baden to Präsident des Landtages, 6 November 1929
("Denkschrift über die Verschuldung der Bad. Landwirtschaft
im Jahre 1928"), GLA/380/7270/47pp; Badisches Landesökonomie-
rat, Tauberbischofsheim to Bezirksamt, 5 September 1929, GLA/
380/7270. In some areas like Kehl the low level of debts per
hectare reflected the lack of economic growth after Kehl lost
its natural markets in Alsace following 1918, see Landes-

finanzamt to MdI, 20 April 1931, SAF/358/56.

15. Badisches Landwirtschaftliches Wochenblatt, 96 (21 January 1928), p. 34, (28 January 1928), pp. 45-46, (21 April 1928), p. 229, (18 February 1928), pp. 94-96.

16. Ibid., 96 (14 April 1928), p. 218; Badische Presse, 12 August 1932. Baden used 716 Polish agricultural laborers in 1928. This journal wanted to eliminate the Polish rural workers, but it also admitted that unemployed industrial workers could not do the rural tasks.

17. Wahlhandbuch der Deutschen liberalen Volkspartei, 1921 (Badische Politik, 1918-1921), pp. 61-62, in SAF/317/1257c; Baden, Statistisches Jahrbuch, 1930, p. 214. The state's statistical yearbook for 1925 lists 50,000 Landbund members and 1,011 Landbund locals in Baden; see Baden, Statistisches Landesamt, Statistisches Jahrbuch für das Land Baden, 1925, p. 95. Although membership figures may vary slightly, the important fact to notice is the widespread organization of the Baden Landbund by 1925.

18. Bad. Landtag, Antrag, 12 January 1925, in SAF/317/636; Bad. Landtag, Antrag, 26 November 1925, in SAF/317/585r.

19. Fritz Hagen to Bezirksämter Lörrach, Schopfheim, Müllheim, 17 September 1926, and Flugblatt, Wirtschaftliche Verbände Oberbadens, 1926; and Landespolizeiamt, Aussenstelle Lörrach to Bezirksamt, 24 September 1926, all in SAF/361/289. The appeal was directed to farmers, artisans, and Mittelstand. One man carried a Werwolf sign and the KPD tried to distribute leaflets.

20. Landesgerichtsdirektor Dr. Hanemann (Mannheim), Materialien für deutschnationale Wahlredner 1928, pp. 13-14.

21. Führer, 3 December 1927, 7 January, 17 March, 19 May, 14 July 1928. The three splinter parties were: Deutsche Bauernpartei, Christlich-Nationale Bauern- und Landvolkpartei, and Völkisch-Nationale Block.

22. Abgeorndeter Hilbert to Direkt. des Bad. Landtags, 27 October 1931, GLA/231/3365; Baden, Statistisches Jahrbuch, 1930, p. 214; Deutsche Bodensee-Zeitung, 4 December 1928, in SAF/317/585r. Ernst F. Hagin was born in 1874 in Egringen to a Protestant farmer. In 1921/25 he served in the Landtag as a Landbund representative, then later as a Bad. Bauernpartei delegate. Otto Heinrich Schmidt was born in 1873 in Heddesheim, Weinheim. A lawyer, he joined the Bund der Landwirte in 1905. Between 1921 and 1925 he was a DNVP delegate and in 1929 was elected to the Landtag as a representative of the Bad. Bauernpartei; see Karl Gross, ed., Handbuch für den Badischen Landtag: 1933-37, pp. 136, 145.

23. See the articles on agriculture in Der Demokrat

between 1920 and 1929: 1 (2 December 1920), pp. 105-22; 6
(15 October 1925), pp. 443-45; 6 (5 November 1925), pp. 457-
60; 7 (4 March 1926), pp. 101-105; 10 (15 July, 25 April, 25
February 1929).

24. Adelheid von Saldern, Hermann Dietrich, pp. 20-30;
Der Demokrat, 10 (15 July 1929), pp. 366-67.

25. Wilhelm Weber, "Reichsregierung und Agrarpolitik,"
pp. 43-44; Badische Presse, 5 December 1930; Dietrich, "Rund-
funkrede: Die Landwirtschaft an der Jahresende," Badisches
Landwirtschaftliches Wochenblatt, 97 (5 January 1929), pp.
1-3.

26. Bodenreform, 34 (28 October and 22 April 1923);
Konstanzer Volksblatt, 12 and 14 October, in SAF/317/585r;
Jörg Schadt, ed., Im Dienst an der Republik, pp. 106-7, 161-62
(Landesparteitag am 29/30 Mai 1921 in Freiburg; and Landesparteitag am 17/18 Mai 1930 in Offenburg). In 1925, Remmele
agreed that agriculture needed help but not at the expense
of other segments of the economy, Staatsumwälzung, p. 177.

27. Arbeiter Zeitung (Lörrach), 22 September 1926, in
SAF/361/289; Staatspolizei Württemberg, "Kommunistische Land-
propaganda," 23 November 1927, HA/58/1400; Landespolizeiamt,
Abtl. N, "Bericht," 19 March 1927, SAF/317/1257d. As early
as 1919/20 the Communists campaigned for the support of small
farmers and rural laborers, even using the slogan "Bundschuh"
as a symbol for the union of city and country; see KPD, Das
Agrarprogramm der Kommunistischen Partei Deutschland.

28. Landespolizeiamt, Abt. N, "Linksradikalismus," June
1926, SAF/317/1257d; Bad. Pächter u. Kleinbauern Verband,
"Notprogram," 23 September 1926, SAF/361/289.

29. Landespolizeiamt, Abt. N, "Bericht," May 1927 (and
June 1928), SAF/317/1257d; Badisches Landwirtschaftliches
Wochenblatt, 97 (1 June 1929), pp. 297-99; Statistisches
Reichsamt, Hauptergebnisse der Wahlen zum Reichstag am 31. Juli
1932, pp. 66-67. In 1930 Bürgi was replaced by Ernst Gässler,
a former KPD state representative; see Landespolizeiamt, Abt.
N, "Bericht," 20 February 1930, SAF/317/1257d.

30. See the 1923/1933 list in the Führer and the corresponding BDC files. For example, most of the Liedolsheim Nazis
of 1923 joined again on 18 January 1926 (officially). There
was no generation gap, only a sociopolitical gap. Karl Friedrich Roth was born in 1877, and Julius Roth was born in 1903;
both joined on the same day--18 January 1926 in Liedolsheim,
see BDC/Karl F. Roth, Mitgliedskarte and BDC/Julius Roth,
Mitgliedskarte.

31. Führer, 26 November 1927; Völkischer Beobachter, 24
December 1925, 7 April 1926.

32. See the reports in the Völkischer Beobachter, 18 February, 10 March, 13/14 May (on Albert Roth, Kurt Bürkle, and Haselmayer), 22 January, 7 April, 17 and 18 and 26 November, 25 March 1926; see also the police reports Abt. N, "Rechtsbewegung," 7 September 1925 (and 5 November 1926), SAF/317/ 12576.

33. Völkischer Beobachter, 24 December 1925, 22 January 1926, 3/4 April 1927, 3 November 1925, 7 January 1928. Rural speeches by Albert Roth, Walter Köhler, Karl Lenz, and a Stier.

34. Polizeimeldung Pforzheim to Bezirksrat Polizeidirektion Pforzheim, 21 January 1930, GLA/234/5738; Landespolizeiamt, Aussenstelle Heidelberg to Landespolizeiamt, 20 January 1930, GLA/233/27915.

35. Ortsgruppe Eichtersheim to Amtsbezirk Sinsheim, 12 August 1926; Gend. Station Eichtersheim to Bezirksamt, 29 July 1926, GLA/377/5399; Völkischer Beobachter, 7 April 1926. In 1928 the Nazis won 43 percent of the vote in Eichtersheim.

36. Landespolizeiamt, Abt. N, "Rechtsbewegung," 15 January 1927, SAF/317/1257d. Goebbels on 21 March 1926 called Neulussheim (in the district of Mannheim) "ein NS Dorf," Helmut Heiber, ed., Das Tagebuch von Joseph Goebbels, 1925/26, p. 66.

37. Völkischer Beobachter, 3/4 April 1926; Landespolizeiamt, Abt. N, "Bericht," 5 March, 1 May, 15 August 1927, SAF/ 317/1257d. The police noted that Landbund members who attended the Nazi rallies agreed with the Nazi themes (Lohrbach, 2 April 1927).

38. Landespolizeiamt, Abt. N, "Bericht," 15 March, 15 January 1928, SAF/317/1257d; Führer, 12 November 1927, 31 March 1928; Ludwig Schwarz, Herbolzheim to Bezirksamt Mosbach, 9 December 1927, GLA/364/7810.

39. Führer, 10 December 1927, 7 April, 11 May 1928; Völkischer Beobachter, 11 May 1928.

40. Führer, 5 November 1927, 28 January, 15 September, 5 May 1928; Joseph Weil, Karlsruhe, "Von völkischer Arbeit in Baden," C. V. Zeitung, 2 September 1927. Hitler's speech in Hamburg on 11 December 1927 to rural leaders was given in the Führer, 21 April 1928 ("Bundschuh und Hakenkreuz"). The Bundschuh movement of the late fifteenth and early sixteenth century had been most active in the Upper Rhine area of southwestern Germany. Unlike most peasant risings during this period, the Bundschuh "was a highly organized movement . . . with the aim of overthrowing the existing social order and setting up a popular religious peasant society directly under the emperor," see H. G. Koenigsberger, "The Reformation and Social Revolution," p. 86.

41. Führer, 14 January, 20 October, 1928 (for Geiger and Würth); 12 November 1927 (for Landbund leader of Merchingen); 7 April 1928 (for Landbund leader of Dittishausen); and 17 November 1928 (for Merk of southern Baden).

42. Schäfer, NSDAP, p. 11; Völkischer Beobachter, 16/17 December 1925, 11 May 1928; Führer, 28 March 1928, 3 December, 5 November 1927, 8 June 1937, 9 March 1943, 11 August 1935, 26 November 1927, 7 April, 7 December 1928.

43. Landespolizeiamt, Abt. N, "Rechtsbewegung," 15 March and 15 June 1928, SAF/317/1257d; Ortsgruppenverzeichnis, 8 July 1927, T-580/19/199.

44. Hermann Lebovics, Social Conservatism and the Middle Classes in Germany; Arthur Schweitzer, Die Nazifizierung des Mittelstandes; and Heinrich August Winkler, Mittelstand, Demokratie und Nationalsozialismus.

45. Führer, 5 and 19 November, 24 December 1927. For example, in Liedolsheim a Gastwirt, a Maurermeister advertised in the party paper; in Mosbach it was a Brezelfabrik, a Gasthaus; and in Eberbach a Uhrenmacher, a Gasthaus, and Knab's Kunstein firm advertised in the Führer.

46. Ludwig Griesinger was born in 1897 in Eggenstein and entered his parents' business in 1912. A party member since 1923 (and 1926), he opened his own shop in 1921. Berkmüller ran a Metallwarenfabrik between 1920 and 1929 in Durlach. Berckmüller, born in 1895, became active in the völkisch movement in Baden by 1923 and was a close friend of Wagner after 1925. For Griesinger see Kreisl. Karlsruhe "Bescheinigung," 23 September 1941, and Max Nagel to Gauwirtschaftsberater Dr. Kentrup, 7 November 1942, both in T-81/162/300481-95. For Karl Berckmüller see MdI to Staatsministerium, 6 July 1935; and Wagner to Staatskanzlei, 19 December 1935; and Pflaumer to Staatsministerium Baden, 25 October 1938, all in GLA/233/ 27894. On Knab and Krauth see Gaupersonalamt Baden, "Rundschreiben," 30 April 1936, GLA/233/26291.

47. Völkischer Beobachter, 19 October 1927, 26 May 1926; Landespolizeiamt, Abt. N, "Rechtsbewegung," 5 November 1926, SAF/317/1257d; Albert Speer, Inside the Third Reich, p. 42.

48. Führer, 7 January, 14 April 1928, 26 October 1929; Völkischer Beobachter, 26 November 1926. Köhler, of course, also appealed to workers and farmers. In an interview in Karlsruhe in June 1977, Köhler rejected the view that he had been a Mittelstand spokesman and instead stressed the party's success in Weinheim in winning the workers' support.

49. Führer, 5 November 1927, 14 April 1928, 26 November 1927; Bezirksamt-Polizeidirektion, Karlsruhe to MdI, 29 December 1927; and Wagner to MdI, 17 December 1927; and K.

Lienhart, "Besprechung mit Beschuldigte," 30 April 1928, all in GLA/309/1174. In Baden in 1925, 38 firms were Warenhäuser (out of a total of 1,935 "Gemischtwarengeschäften"). They employed 30 percent of all people working in such businesses. The largest Warenhäuser listed in a 1925 study were dominated by Jewish firms: Geschwister Knopf and Hermann Tietz with their various branches in the state; see Baden, Statistisches Landesamt, Handel und Verkehr in Baden, pp. 7, 145-47.

50. Landespolizeiamt, Aussenstelle Offenburg to Bad. Landespolizeiamt, Abt. N, 20 January 1930, GLA/233/27915; Führer, 26 and 12 November 1927; Baden, Landtagswahl, 1921, p. 159 (Karl Pleisser, a DHV member and DNVP candidate in 1921).

51. Robert Wagner to Fucke-Michels, 21 April 1931, T-81/ 173/314091; Fucke-Michels to Wagner, 18 April 1931, T-81/ 173/314093. The primacy of politics is also stressed by Winkler, Mittelstand, p. 180.

52. Führer, 9 October 1938; BDC/Hüssy file.

53. Gauschatzmeister Baden to Hauptmitgliederschaftsamt, 19 August 1941, in BDC/Adam Wetzel file (on the Stoess firm); Oskar Wiegert, ed., NSDAP Ortsgruppe Offenburg, p. 41; Adolf Conrad, "Meine Erlebnisse," March 1937, HA/26/514.

54. Führerlexikon, 1934, pp. 379-80, 383; Landespolizei- amt, Abt. N, "Rechtsbewegung," 19 August 1930, SAF/317/1257d; Abt. N, "Die politische Lage in Baden," 5 October 1931, GLA/ 233/28388.

55. Der Volksfreund, 19 October 1928; C. V. Zeitung, 25 October 1929.

56. Stammbuch für Hans Knab; Gaupersonalamtsleiter, "Bestätigung," 16 August 1938, T-81/166/305360 and 305423; BDC/Mitgliedskarten: Fritz Backfisch, Leo Berger, Ludwig Eiermann, Josef Veith, Hermann Stumpf; Justizm. Karlsruhe to Reichsm. des Auswärtigen, 15 November 1926, GLA/234/5703; Führer, 7 November 1927; Völkischer Beobachter, 10 August 1927.

57. Grossdeutsche Reichstag, 1938, p. 274; Reinhard Vogelsang, Der Freudenkreis Himmlers, pp. 22-23; Henry A. Turner, "Grossunternehmertum und Nationalsozialismus, 1930- 1933," pp. 34-35; see the testimony in Trials of War Crim- inals Before the Nuernberg Military Tribunals, 6:285-94. Flick testified that he did not know Keppler well until after 1933.

58. BDC/Leopold Plaichinger Mitgliedskarte; Hermann Reischle, "Erinnerung an Leopold Plaichinger," Odal 7 (May 1938), 334. Plaichinger died in Munich on 27 February 1933.

59. Gau Gericht, "Beschluss," 31 May 1938; Reichsleitung,

Mitgliedschaftsamt to Gauschatzmeister, 28 July 1938, in BDC/
Hermann Stumpf file. Robert Wagner to Hess (Munich), 13
January 1928, T-580/656/folder 572. In 1930 Knab and Stumpf
rebelled against the party leadership because Keppler had put
a nonparty member on the election slate. He was a director
of the Dedi Bank branch in Eberbach, which handled the business of the Odin firm.

60. Landespolizeiamt, Abt. N, "Rechtsbewegung," 15 March
1928, SAF/317/1257d; Prop. Abtl. Munich to Fritz Reinhardt,
9 February 1929, T-580/24/206.

61. Völkischer Beobachter, 10 August 1927, 10 March 1928,
9 January 1926; Führer, 5 November 1927; Polizeiinspektor
Walther, Abt. N, Aussenstelle Heidelberg to MdI, Baden, 7
March 1928 (report on Hitler speech in March 1928), GLA/234/
5738; Aus dem Kampf der Heidelberger SA, Pfingsten 1925 bis
März 1933--Tagebuchblätter vom Oberführer Willy Ziegler, in
GLA/465d/1293. Of 800 people invited, 670 attended.

62. Polizeiinspektor Walther to Landespolizeiamt, Abt.
N, 18 May 1928; Abschrift aus Eberbacher Zeitung, 16 May
1928, in GLA/356/4835; Baden, Statistisches Landesamt, Reichstagswahl am 20. Mai 1928 in Baden, pp. 62-63.

63. Führer, 12 April, 1 March 1930; Pol. Komm. Oettinger,
Baden-Baden to Landespolizeiamt, 12 May 1930, GLA/234/5714;
Landespolizeiamt, Villingen to Landespolizeiamt, 9 February
1930, GLA/233/27915.

64. Führer, 5 April, 24/25 January, 11 September 1930
("Jede gesunde Entwicklung von Eigentum wird vom Nationalsozialismus bejaht"); Polizei Kommissär Oettinger Baden-Baden
to Landespolizeiamt, Abt. N, 16 November 1930, GLA/234/5738;
Pol. Sekretär Albrecht und Stolz, Rastatt to Landespolizeiamt,
23 March 1931, GLA/309/1151.

65. Führer, 19 April, 24 May 1930, 1 May 1936; Heidelberger Beobachter, 18 April 1931. On the party's social structure see Detlef Mühlberger, "The Sociology of the NSDAP,"
pp. 439-511, who concludes that "the NSDAP was a genuine
Volkspartei. It secured support from all social classes in
German society."

66. Landespolizeiamt, Abt. N, "Bericht," 15 March 1928,
SAF/317/1257d; Völkischer Beobachter, 23 November, 1 October
1928; Schadt, ed., Im Dienst, p. 217. The police report of
15 March 1928 listed 2,422 Nazi party members in 48 locals;
this did not include the party members in communities that had
no locals. The SPD had 46,962 party members in Baden in 1920.

67. BDC/Mitgliedskarten: Karl Backfisch (1895), Karl
Backfisch (1897), Otto Backfisch.

68. Völkischer Beobachter, 18 February, 7 April 1926;

Führer, 23 June 1934. In Ziegelhausen the local leader was
a Landwirt, and his assistants a Gärtner and a Kaufmann. In
Eichtersheim the local leader was a Landwirt, and in Helmsheim
a Gutverwalter was the local party chief. See also Abt. N,
"Bericht," 15 March 1928, SAF/317/1257d.

69. In Eberbach the first local leader was a Kaufmann
(really a Steinbruchbesitzer), and the successor was a chemist, Führer, 13 April 1939. In Konstanz the Schlageterbund
was led by a Kaufmann and a Schreiner; Völkischer Beobachter,
23 January, 26 September 1926. In Freiburg the local leader
was a Schumachermeister; Führer, 22 September 1933. In Mannheim, the local was led by a Bankbeamte in 1926, a Beamte in
1927; Völkischer Beobachter, 28 October 1926; Ortsgruppenverzeichnis, 8 July 1927, T-580/19/199.

70. Führer, 2 June 1928; Ortsgruppenverzeichnis, 8 July
1927, T-580/19/199; BDC/Mitgliedskarten and files of the
names listed above. Although only one district leader in 1928
was an "Arbeiter," two district leaders had been members of
the SPD. Of the 21 district leaders, 5 were Kaufmänner, 3
farmers, 5 artisans, 2 teachers, 2 white-collar employees,
2 Gebildete (doctor and chemist), and one worker. In 1927,
seven of the local leaders were farmers: Benjamin Heimburger
in Ichenheim, Otto Bender in Eichtersheim, Wilhelm O. Geiger
in Stebbach, Otto Biegert in Duntenheim, Berthold Rokar in
Ziegelhausen, August Häffele in Helmsheim, Ernst Vollmer in
Friedrichstal, Robert Roth in Liedolsheim; see BDC/Karten
and files.

71. Führer, 5 May 1928, 31 December 1927, 7 January,
25 February, 14 April 1928.

72. Führer, 10 and 17 and 24 March, 5 May 1928; Landespolizeiamt, Abt. N, "Bericht," 15 May 1928, SAF/317/1257d.

73. Führer, 17 March, 4 February 1928; Badische Zeitung,
14 March 1928.

74. Volksfreund, 24 March, 10 May 1928. The Volksfreund
(4 April 1928) did note the problems of the rural depression,
but it blamed them on the lack of rational production and lack
of technical improvements.

75. Führer, 2 June, 5 May, 26 May 1928; Landespolizeiamt,
Abt. N, "Rechtsbewegung," 15 June 1928, SAF/317/1257d.

76. Führer, 19 May 1928. Only Wagner and Lenz were full-
time party functionaries.

77. Baden, Statistisches Landesamt, Reichstagswahl in
Baden 1928; and Baden, Statistisches Landesamt, Statistisches
Jahrbuch, 1930, pp. 68, 86.

78. Badische Zeitung, 23 May 1928; Badischer Beobachter,
22 May 1928; Volksfreund, 25 and 21 May 1928; Das Deutsche

Tageblatt, 5 July 1928; von Saldern, Dietrich, pp. 28-29.

79. Führer, 26 May 1928.

80. Völkischer Herold, 22 July, 28 October, 30 December 1927; Das Deutsche Tageblatt, 3 November, 21 July 1928.

81. See the election statistics for May 1924, 1925, and 1928. In May 1924, the party had won the following percentages of votes in these cities: Heidelberg, 12.3; Weinheim, 8.7; Karlsruhe, 6.5; Durlach, 5.8; Bruchsal, 13.9. Hitler did not visit Mannheim until 23 November 1928; Führer, 24 November 1928.

82. Orlow has argued (History, 1:131) that "the election results and the party organization efforts showed a very high degree of negative correlations," while Thomas Childers ("The Social Bases of the National Socialist Vote," p. 18) concluded after an analysis of urban centers over fifteen thousand that the Nazi party in 1928 did not reflect a religious or social profile. Neither of these statements applies to the Baden party in 1928.

83. See Landwirtschaft in Baden, 1925; and Reichstagswahl am 20. Mai 1928 in Baden. This was, of course, similar to the developments in Schleswig-Holstein; see Rudolf Heberle, From Democracy to Nazism. Some districts like Wertheim had been strongholds of the DVFB and rural-völkisch activities. In 1968, the NPD won 9.8 percent in the election in Baden-Württemberg. Some of the real strongholds of the NPD movement were again in the Protestant, rural districts like Kehl (14.7 percent); see Rudolf Wildenmann, "Les Elections du Baden-Württemberg," pp. 117-20; A. Wiss-Verdier, "Nationaux-démocrates progrés," pp. 125-29. Childers's conclusion ("The Social Bases," p. 19), "before the Nazi breakthrough in predominantly Protestant areas in 1930, the National Socialist constituency failed to conform to the traditional confessional pattern of German electoral politics," is nonsense. By 1928 the Nazi party was strongest in the Protestant, rural districts of Germany.

84. This is based on: "Denkschrift über die Verschuldung der bad. Landwirtschaft im Jahre 1928," 6 November 1929, GLA/ 380/7270; Die Landwirtschaft in Baden in 1925; a list of Nazi locals in July 1927, T-580/19/199; and a list of Nazi locals in March 1928, Landespolizeiamt, Abt. N, "Rechtsbewegung," 15 June 1928, SAF/317/1257d. For the depression in the tobacco industry see Baden, Gewerbeaufsichtsamt, Die wirtschaftlichen, sozialen und gesundheitlichen Verhältnisse der Zigarrenarbeiter in Baden, pp. 81-97, 252-53. Most workers were women (75 percent) and came from peasant families with whom they continued strong ties. Salaries were low, and available work

was only between twenty-four and thirty-six hours a week for almost half of the workers.

85. Solms-Roedelheim, Einflüsse, pp. 9, 56-57, 63; Orts-gruppenverzeichnis, July 1927, T-580/19/199; and Landespoli-zeiamt, Abt. N, "Bericht," 15 March 1928, SAF/317/1257d.

86. Landrat Schindele, Kehl, to MdI, 12 December 1930, SAF/358/56; Badisches Landwirtschaftliches Wochenblatt, 97 (21 September 1929).

87. Based on the election statistics of May 1924 and May 1928; and Landespolizeiamt, Abt. N, "Rechtsbewegung," 15 June 1928, SAF/317/1257d.

88. Landespolizeiamt, Abt. N, "Bericht," 15 August 1928, SAF/317/1257d; Führer. 17 November, 26 May 1928; Völkischer Beobachter, 21 and 29 September, 20 October, 23 November, 16/17 December 1928, 26 January, 2 February 1929.

89. Führer, 2 June, 13 and 15 December 1928; Landrat, Mosbach, to MdI, Baden, 2 January 1929, GLA/364/7810; Rapp, ed., Die Parteibewegung in Baden, 1905-1928, p. 10. Alexander Weber ("Soziale Merkmale der NSDAP-Wähler," p. 123) argues that the Nazi party in May 1928 appealed to a new voter. This conclusion is only partially true. Although the Baden party was converting the Protestant farmer in 1928, the party continued to be strong in its old völkisch strongholds like Liedolsheim and Eberbach. In fact, the party had appealed to the small farmer as early as 1923 and continued to do so between 1925 and 1928.

CHAPTER FIVE

1. This was not peculiar to Baden, see Noakes, The Nazi Party, p. 246; and Pridham, Hitler's Rise to Power, p. 92.

2. See the reports in Völkischer Beobachter, 26 January and 2 February 1929 (for some reason the 1929 issues of the Führer, with isolated exceptions, have been lost); see also Landespolizeiamt, Abt. N, "Bericht," 1 August 1928, SAF/317/ 1257d; Staatsanwaltschaft Freiburg i. Br., to Generalstaatsan-walt, 8 March 1929, and Justizminister Baden to Reichsminister der Justiz, 29 November 1928, GLA/234/5703.

3. Landespolizeiamt, Abt. N, "Bericht," 15 January 1929, SAF/317/1257d; Völkischer Beobachter, 2 February 1929.

4. Völkischer Beobachter, 24/25 March 1929; Landespolizei-amt, Abt. N, "Bericht," 15 May 1929, SAF/317/1257d.

5. Himmler to Siegfried Kasche, 20 July 1929, HA/10/203; Abt. N, "Bericht," 15 November 1929, SAF/317/1257d; Führer, 28 September 1929. On 20 August 1929, Hitler was forced to

cancel all public rallies for several months, allegedly because
he was ill; see Hess to Gaul Rheinland, 20 August 1929, T-580/
19/203.

6. MdI, Baden, to Staatsministerium, 31 October 1929; and
Rechtsanwalt Alfred Bopp to Staatsministerium, 14 October
1929 (and 23 October 1929); and Remmele to Staatsministerium,
30 October 1929 ("Ausschreitungen bei den Vorbereitungen zur
Landtagswahl 1929"; this report was published by the Baden
Landtag on 9 November 1929), all in GLA/233/27915. The Nazis
in turn asked the government to duplicate and disseminate
Remmele's report on Nazi propaganda during the election.

7. Führer, 26 October 1929; Völkischer Beobachter, 19
and 29 October 1929; Landtagswahl am 27 Oktober, 1929, p.
22; Poliz. Assistente Knecht and Klingele, Mannheim, to Polizeidirektion Mannheim, 27 September 1929; and Pol. Oberin-
spektor Weyrauch, Freiburg, to Landesp. Freiburg, 16 October
1929; and Kriminalabteilung Mosbach to Bezirksamt Mosbach,
23 October 1929, all in GLA/233/5738.

8. J. J. Stein, "Vor der Landtagswahl in Baden," in Der
Demokrat, 10 (5 October 1929), pp. 461-63; "Demokratische
Spitzenkandidaten in Baden," in ibid. (20 September 1929),
p. 452; ibid. (20 October 1929), p. 497.

9. For the DNVP see Badische Zeitung, 22 and 26 October
1929; for the Center party see Badischer Beobachter, 23 and
26 and 27 October 1929.

10. Badischer Beobachter, 23 October 1929; Volksfreund,
5 and 25 October 1929; C. V. Zeitung, 25 October 1929; Israel-
istische Gemeindeblatt, Mannheim, 27 September 1929.

11. Landespolizeiamt, Abt. N, "Bericht," 15 November
1929 (and 15 May 1929), SAF/317/1257d. The campaign was very
expensive. As late as 1930 people like Kasche who had campaigned in Baden during the election were still trying to
obtain their fees from Baden; see Kasche to Wagner, 16 May
1930, HA/10/211.

12. "Verzeichnis der bei den Bad. Landtagsw. am 27. Okt.
1929 gewählten Abgeordneten und Ersatzmänner," GLA/231/3365;
Badische Landtagswahl am 27. Oktober 1929, p. 99; Gross, ed.,
Handbuch für den Badischen Landtag, pp. 143, 166. Franz Merk
was a farmer (and Gastwirt) from Grafenhausen in the district
of Neustadt. He was born on 26 December 1894 in Grafenhausen.
After the war he became active in politics and was even a
member of the Kreisrat (between 1922 and 1924), the Bezirksrat,
and since 1926 the Gemeinderat in Grafenhausen. The Nazi
delegation was the youngest in the Landtag; see Baden,
Statistisches Jahrbuch, 1930, p. 4.

13. Badische Landtagswahl, 1929, pp. 18, 23. In twenty-

four new communities the party obtained over twenty votes;
fifteen were predominantly Protestant and nine were Catholic
communities. In Breitenbronn, a village in Mosbach, the Nazis
ran for the first time and won 90.8 percent of the vote. In
May 1924, the Landbund and the DNVP had won 96 percent of the
vote in this rural, Protestant community of slightly over two
hundred people. This represented a continuation of the 1928
rural breakthrough in the Protestant communities of Baden.

14. Völkischer Beobachter, 30 October and 1/2 November
1929; Volksfreund, 28 and 23 October 1929; Badischer Beobachter, 28 October 1929; see also the quotations from national
papers in Wertheimer Zeitung, 29 October 1929. The SPD paper,
Volksfreund, admitted that during the campaign the Center
party and the SPD fought each other bitterly.

15. Abwehr-Blätter, 39 (1 November 1929), pp. 170-71;
C. V. Zeitung, 1 November 1929; Wertheimer Zeitung, 29 October
1929; Der Demokrat, 10 (5 November 1929), p. 529.

16. Landespolizeiamt, Abt. N, "Bericht," November 1929,
SAF/317/1257d.

17. Badische Zeitung, 29 October 1929; Karlsruher Tagblatt, 28 October 1929; Frankfurter Zeitung, 28 October 1929.

18. C. V. Zeitung, 1 November 1929; Frankfurter Zeitung,
29 October 1929 (Erstes Morgenblatt).

19. See the statistics for the 1928 and 1929 elections
in Baden; for the Evangelische Volksdienst see Opitz, Der
Christlich-soziale Volksdienst, p. 129. The Communist paper
Die Rote Fahne (29 October 1929) pointed out that the greatest
Nazi gains were registered in the largest urban centers of
Baden. The paper warned that the "Hitler party" also had an
impact on some labor voters. To the paper this represented
the real danger of this "most radical wing of the fascist
movement." Since the Catholics gained 43,936 new votes in
1929 and only 22,977 new voters appeared in 1929 (over 1928),
there must have been substantially fewer voters from the
Marxist parties, which lost 29,000 votes. Instead, the Nazi
party seems to have regained the urban völkisch voters who
had cast their votes for the Völkisch Block in the May 1924
election. Ellsworth Faris, "Takeoff Point for the National
Socialist Party," pp. 140-71, fails to see the rural breakthrough of 1928.

20. Völkischer Beobachter, 15 November 1929.

21. Führer, 1 February 1930; Landespolizeiamt, Abt. N,
"NSDAP, Entwicklung und Tätigkeit des Gaues Baden seit der
Landtagswahl vom 27. Oktober 1929," 13 August 1930, SAF/317/
1257d.

22. Führer, 18 January, 1 February, 15 March 1930, 1

November, 1931; Achern und Bühler Bote, 1 December 1930, in T-81/173/313800.

23. Führer, 1/2 January 1935; Rehberger, Die Gleichschaltung des Landes Baden 1932/33, p. 18.

24. Führer, 20 December, 15 February 1930; Badische Presse, 6 August 1930, 27 October 1932; "Auszug aus der Niederschrift über die Sitzung des Staatsministeriums vom 6. Mai 1932," GLA/233/24278.

25. Führer, 29 March, 14 February, 10 April 1930, 10 March 1931. Paul Schmitthenner, the future Nazi minister of education, defended the Nazis in the Landtag. This DNVP delegate was born on 2 December 1884 in Neckarbischofsheim, Baden. A professor at the university of Heidelberg, he was elected to the Landtag in 1925, see Alfred Rapp, ed., Die Badischen Landtagsabgeordneten, 1905-1929, p. 38; Badische Landtag, 10. Sitzung, 14 January 1930, GLA/233/27915. Other DNVP Landtag delegates like Professor Brühler allowed the publication of Nazi lead articles in DNVP-controlled papers; see Hans Georg Wieck, Christliche und Freie Demokraten in Hessen, Rheinland-Pfalz, Baden, und Württemberg 1945/46, p. 104.

26. Führer, 8 March 1930.

27. Landespolizeiamt, Abt. N, "Die NSDAP Entwicklung und Tätigkeit des Gaues Baden seit der Landtagswahl vom 27. Oktober 1929," and Abt. N, "Die Reichstagswahl vom 14. Sept. 1930 in Baden," 15 October 1930, both SAF/317/1257d.

28. Führer, 4 January 1930, 21 March 1931, 10 December 1930; Völkischer Beobachter, 24/25 March 1929.

29. Landespolizeiamt, Abt. N, "Bericht," 20 February 1930, and "NSDAP, Entwicklung und Tätigkeit des Gaues Baden seit der Landtagswahl vom 27. Oktober 1929," 19 August 1930, both SAF/317/1257d; Führer, 31 March 1935. Police reports estimated the number of Nazi locals in February 1930 at 70; by August 1930, the police noted 200 locals. The Führer (which gives no months) listed 62 locals in 1928, 228 locals in 1930, and 480 locals for 1932.

30. Völkischer Beobachter, 20/21 and 23 April 1930.

31. Führer, 30 August 1930, 30 March 1935; Landespolizeiamt, Abt. N, "Bericht," 15 January 1929 (and 15 May 1929), SAF/317/1257d; "Stammbuch für Theodor Schnepf," 22 April 1939, T-81/228/5010145; Kreisleiter Kehl to Bickler, 22 October 1942, T-81/174/315000.

32. Führer, 9 March 1943, 21 May 1938, 31 December, 30 March, 1 November, 12 December 1931; Friedrich W. Sattler, "Die Entwicklung der NSDAP in Neustadt, Schwarzwald," 19 November 1937, HA/5/132.

33. Führer, 2 June 1928, 29 November 1930; Nachrichten-blatt der Gauleitung Baden (hereafter cited as Nachrichten-blatt), 1 (1 March 1934), p. 18; Landespolizeiamt, Abt. N, "Bericht," 20 February 1930, SAF/317/1257d. In 1933 the Gau had thirty districts; one year later it had forty districts, which corresponded to the forty state districts.

34. Führer, 7 October, 3 August 1933, 19 October 1940, 27 April 1933, 29 November 1930, 18 January 1934, 7 October 1942; Kolmarer Kurier, 4 January 1941, T-81/537/5307454; Manfred Jenke, Verschwörung von Rechts?, pp. 440-42.

35. Führer, 6 August, 15 March 1930; Landespolizeiamt, Abt. N, "Bericht," 15 May 1929, and "NSDAP Entwicklung," 19 August 1930, both SAF/317/1257d.

36. Partei-Statistik, 1935, 1, p. 26; Führer, 21 January 1931, 19 November 1930, 22 September 1933.

37. Landespolizeiamt, Abt. N, "Die politische Lage in Baden," 5 October 1931, GLA/233/28388; Landespolizeiamt, Abt. N, "Bericht," 15 January 1929 (and 15 May 1929, 20 February, 19 August 1930), and "Die Reichstagswahl vom 14. Sept. 1930," both SAF/317/1257d.

38. Führer, 12 April, 8 February, 24 September 1930; Völkischer Beobachter, 2 May 1930.

39. See the reports of Landespolizeiamt, Abt. N, "Bericht," 15 January 1929 (and 15 May, 15 November 1929, 20 February 1930), SAF/317/1257d.

40. Ibid. "NSDAP: Entwicklung und Tätigkeit des Gaues Baden seit der Landtagswahl vom 27. Oktober 1929," 19 August 1930; Landespolizeiamt, Abt. N, "Die politische Lage in Baden," 5 October 1931, GLA/233/28388. Baden also had an advantage until January 1932 of having to send to Munich only the fees actually collected from the members. In January 1932 the entrance fee was raised to 3 RM, of which the Gau was able to keep 1 RM. For the party's role in another area of Germany see Horst Matzerath and Henry A. Turner, "Die Selbst-finanzierung der NSDAP, 1930-32," p. 70.

41. Landespolizeiamt, Abt. N, "Die Reichstagswahl vom 14. September 1930 in Baden," 15 October 1930, SAF/317/1257d. The Reichstag was not dissolved until 18 July 1930; see Karl Dietrich Bracher, Die Auflösung der Weimarer Republik, p. 339.

42. Führer, 16 and 2 and 23 August 1930; Landespolizeiamt, Abt. N, "Die Reichstagswahl vom 14. September 1930 in Baden," 15 October 1930, SAF/317/1257d.

43. Führer, 3 and 13 September, 23 and 20 August 1930.

44. Ibid., 8 and 1 October, 13 September 1930; Badische Presse, 17 June 1930; Landespolizeiamt, Abt. N, "Die Reichs-

tagswahl vom 14. September 1930," SAF/317/1257d. On 13 June 1930 the state had outlawed Nazi uniforms, and between 12 and 15 September public rallies were banned.

45. Führer, 27 August 1930; Statistisches Reichsamt, "Die Wahlen zum Reichstag am 14. September 1930," p. 207; Landespolizeiamt, Abt. N, "Bericht," 20 February 1930, SAF/317/1257d.

46. "Bericht für die Zeit vom 1 Jan. 1928 bis 31 Dezember 1929 zum Landesparteitag am 17/18 Mai 1930 in Offenburg," in Schadt, ed., Im Dienst, pp. 147-48; Volksfreund, 6 September 1930; Badischer Beobachter, 1 September 1930.

47. Landespolizeiamt, Abt. N, "Die Reichstagswahl vom 14. September 1930 in Baden," SAF/317/1257d.

48. Statistisches Landesamt, Reichstagswahl 1930 in Baden, pp. 10-11; Statistisches Reichsamt, Die Wahlen zum Reichstag am 14. September 1930 , p. 70. In 1928, the party won votes in 885 communities in Baden; in 1930 it won votes in 1475 communities (or 96.7 percent of Baden's communities). One Baden community that gave the party 17 percent of the vote, although the Nazis never held a rally there, is discussed in Führer, 1 November 1930.

49. Landespolizeiamt, Abt. N, "Die Reichstagswahl vom 14. September 1930 in Baden," 15 October 1930, SAF/317/1257d; Baden, Statistisches Jahrbuch, 1938, p. 213.

50. Max Schwarz, ed., M.d.R., Biographisches Handbuch der Reichstage, p. 578; Führer, 11 April 1931; BDC/Johannes Rupp file; Völkischer Beobachter, 2 May 1930. Rupp was born on 26 January 1903 in Reihen, Sinsheim.

51. Führer, 17 and 20 September 1930; Völkischer Beobachter, 18 September 1930.

52. See Volksfreund, Badische Zeitung, and Badischer Beobachter, all 15 September 1930; Abt. N, "Die Reichstagswahl vom 14. September 1930 in Baden," 15 October 1930, SAF/317/1257d (quoted Paul Schreck).

53. Karlsruher Zeitung, 15 and 16 September 1930.

54. Führer, 1 November 1930, 22/23 February 1931.

55. Ibid., 10 and 24 September 1930.

56. Ibid., 11 April 1931; BDC/Rudolf Schindler file; BDC/Johannes Rupp file; see also Horst Matzerath, Nationalsozialismus und kommunale Selbstverwaltung, pp. 35, 38.

57. Führer, 11 January, 8 and 15 March, 29 September, 15 October, 24 September, 26 April 1930; Völkischer Beobachter, 19 March, 2 May 1930.

58. Führer, 3 and 24 September 1930. The local Nazi candidate had to swear that he belonged to no capitalistic organization or enterprise, and he promised to relinquish his elected position should the Gauleitung require it; see

documents for local of Bühl, T-81/173/313793.

59. Führer, 8 and 11 October, 12 November 1930; Völkischer Beobachter, 30 November 1930; Friedrich Walter, Schicksal einer Deutschen Stadt, 2:140. The party program published in the Führer called for the following: "Local government, professional civil service, taxes on department and chain stores, reduction of the salaries of civil servants, destruction of usury, reduction of unemployment, aid to the Mittelstand, raising the German youth on the basis of Christian teachings, nationalistic enthusiasm, military training, and the concept of social justice.

60. Führer, 31 December 1931/1 January 1932, 19 November 1930; Achern und Bühler Bote, 17 November 1930, in T-81/173/ 313807; Matzerath, Selbstverwaltung, pp. 49-50.

61. Karl Maier to Gaugeschäftsstelle, 24 November 1930, T-81/173/313003-24; "Wahlvorschlagsliste 4, NSDAP Bühl," November 1930, T-81/173/318806; Völkischer Beobachter, 23/24 November 1930. In Würmersheim in the district of Rastatt the Nazis united with the Bürgerpartei to oppose the Center party; see Heinrich Hock to Wagner, 11 November 1930, T-81/173/314133.

62. Gau Baden, Gemeindepolitik to Robert Zorn (Sachbachried), 22 November 1930, T-81/173/314120; Schindler to Karl Maier (district leader of Bühl), 22 November 1930, T-81/173/ 314002; Raay to Otto Riedinger, 1 March 1931, T-81/173/ 314032.

63. Schindler to Hermann Steinle, Baden-Baden, 2 December 1930, T-81/173/313844; Führer. 29 November 1930, 14 January 1931; Wilhelm Merk, Handbuch der Badischen Verwaltung, p. 454.

64. Schindler to Fiege, 19 January 1931, T-81/173/ 313789-91; Karl Fauth, "Fragebogen," 7 October 1930, T-81/173/ 313795; Führer, 10 February 1931. There was, however, still much anti-Catholic feeling among some Nazis. Ernst Föhr, an important Center party leader in Baden, received a letter from a Nazi teacher that stated: "You black, sneaky Jesuit! You black crow! Why do you always croak in the Landtag? Shut your mouth when someone else speaks! The separation of state and church must be the goal. Wallow alone in your stinking 'Bockmist,' you black mole," quoted (my translation) in Ernst Föhr, Geschichte des Badischen Konkordats, p. 52.

65. Führer, 31 January 1931; Ortsgruppe Bühlertal to Gemeindepolitik, 20 February 1931, T-81/173/313784; Otto Koch, Bühlertal to Abt. Gemeindepolitik, April 8, 1931, T-81/ 173/313854-56.

66. Wilhelm Sutterer, Kappelrodeck to Gemeindepolitik, 14 February 1931; and Raay to Ortsgruppe Bühl, 26 January 1931; and Raay to Rathausfraktion Bühl, 8 July 1931, all in

<u>T-81</u>/173/313747-85, and 313978.

67. Raay to Dr. Fucke-Michels, Rastatt, 24 March 1931, <u>T-81</u>/173/314084; <u>Führer</u>, 2 June, 18 August 1931, 3 September 1932; <u>Mitteilungsblatt der Nationalsozialisten in den Parlamenten und Gemeindlichen Vertretungskörpern</u>, Heft 15 (1 August 1931), pp. 305-307. Wagner defended Schindler in 1932 after the party court attempted to remove Schindler for having stolen 9 RM. Wagner told the court that Schindler was too valuable for the party's municipal efforts; see <u>BDC</u>/OPG Schindler case (Wagner to R. L. Munich, 30 December 1932).

68. Some examples: Wilhelm Sutterer to Gemeindepolitik, 6 August 1931, <u>T-81</u>/173/313974; Raay to Ortsgruppe Gernsbach, 24 March 1931, <u>T-81</u>/173/313951; NSDAP Rathausfraktion Rastatt to lord mayor, 17 May 1931, <u>T-81</u>/173/3134062.

69. <u>Führer</u>, 29 April 1931, 10 December 1930, 27 February 1931; <u>Mitteilungsblatt</u>, 5 (August 1932), pp. 310-12, and (September 1932), pp. 344-51.

70. Richard Kraemer, Achern, to Gemeindepolitik, 26 September 1930, <u>T-81</u>/173/313702; Raay to Ortsgruppe Achern, 25 February 1931, <u>T-81</u>/173/313699. In 1931 Gau Baden ousted ten delegates who did not carry out Gau policy or Gau directives; see Matzerath, <u>Selbstverwaltung</u>, pp. 41-42.

71. Some examples: Fucke-Michels to Wagner, 10 February 1931, <u>T-81</u>/173/314077-80; Wilhelm Bergold, Rastatt, to Gemeindepolitik, 9 February 1931, <u>T-81</u>/173/314082; Georg Baust to Ortsgruppe Gernsbach, 11 March 1931, <u>T-81</u>/173/313958.

72. Fraktionsleiter Seebacher to Abt. Gemeindepolitik, 20 August 1931, <u>T-81</u>/173/313709; Ortsgruppe Bühlertal to Wagner, 21 August 1931, <u>T-81</u>/173/313717; Wagner to Ortsgruppe Bühlertal, n.d. (September 1931), <u>T-81</u>/173/313707.

73. Paul Rothmund, "Wirtschaftliches und soziales Leben in der Dreiländerecke," p. 155; "Aus der Stadt und Bezirk" (in an untitled Baden-Baden paper), December 1930, in <u>T-81</u>/ 173/313831. The cost of welfare in Mannheim increased from 9.8 million RM in 1930 to 16.3 million RM in 1932, while the tax base decreased from 9.15 million RM in 1928 to 4.2 million RM in 1932; see Walter, <u>Schicksal</u>, 2:151-53.

74. Raay to Kreisfraktion Baden-Baden, 5 June 1931, <u>T-81</u>/ 173/313760; "Vorlagen des Kreisrates Baden-Baden," 8 June 1931, <u>T-81</u>/173/313761-74; Raay to Richard Kraemer, 29 January 1931, <u>T-81</u>/173/313700; <u>Führer</u>, 29 April 1931.

75. Fucke-Michels to Wagner, 18 April and 10 February 1931, <u>T-81</u>/173/314077 and 314093; Raay to Karl Kepplinger, Rastatt, 8 May 1931, <u>T-81</u>/173/314112.

76. Remmele to Staatspräsident Dr. Schmitt, 21 July 1930, and Dr. Heinrich Bammesberger to Präsident des Land-

gerichts, 11 July 1930, both GLA/233/27915; Völkischer Beobachter, 23 September 1930.

77. Polizeidirektion, Bezirksamt Karlsruhe, to Justiz-
minister u. Staatsanwaltschaft, 10 August 1931, GLA/234/5738;
August Wolf to Geschäftsstelle NSDAP, Baden, 23 November 1930,
T-81/173/313838; Schindler to August Wolf, 2 January 1931,
T-81/173/313836. Some individual examples are provided by
Josef Fitterer, a Reichsbahnobersekretär who joined the party
on 1 August 1930 and became Kreisleiter of Säckingen by Janu-
ary 1932, BDC/Josef Fitterer file; Leopold Mauch, a Zoll-
inspektor, joined the party in 1931, BDC/L. Mauch Karte; and
Wilhelm Bogs, a Regierungsinspektor who joined the party in
September 1930, BDC/W. Bogs Karte.

78. Bezirksamt Donaueschingen to MdI, Baden, and Bezirks-
amt Konstanz to MdI, both 27 July 1931, SAF/317/1257b; Bad.
Justizminister "Dienststraferkenntnis," for Justizinspektor
Adolf Koch beim Amtsgericht Heidelberg (1931), GLA/234/5738.

79. Weber to Ortsgruppe Hardheim, 27 September 1938,
BDC/Julius Weber file. Weber was a Forstrat who joined the
party in 1931 but "withdrew" in May 1932.

80. Landespolizeiamt, Abt. N, "Bericht," 15 November
1929, SAF/317/1257d; "Auszug aus der Niederschrift über die
Sitzung des Staatsministeriums vom 7. Juli 1930," 8 July
1930, and Remmele to Staatsministerium, 17 July 1930, both
GLA/233/27915.

81. Rechtsanwälte K. Giehme and J. Rupp to Staatsgerichtshof f.d. Deutsche Reich, 15 July 1930; and MdK, "Disziplinarverfahren gegen den Hauptlehrer Adolf Schuppel," 29
July 1930; and MdK, "Disziplinarverfahren gegen den Hauptlehrer Emil Gärtner in Neufreistett," Amt Kehl, 30 July 1930;
and MdK, "Anklageschrift gegen Gewerbelehrer Erwin Schmidt,"
Pforzheim, 1 August 1930, all GLA/233/27915. Schuppel was
born in 1895 in Waldshut and became a party member in 1928.
He was Wagner's army comrade. Erwin Schmidt was born in 1894
in Pforzheim and taught in Kehl until September 1914. He
joined the party on 1 March 1930.

82. Remmele to Kraft, 4 July 1930, and Kraft to Privat-
sekretär W. Hess, 29 August 1930, BDC/Herbert Kraft file;
Führer, 12 July 1930, 26/27 April 1931.

83. Landespolizeiamt, Abt. N, "Die politische Lage in
Baden," 5 October 1931, GLA/233/28388; Führer, 13 August, 10
September 1930; BDC files or Mitgliedskarten for: Wilhelm
Seiler (1891) of Handschuhsheim, Heidelberg; Karl Gärtner
(1897) of Lahr; Wilhelm Hartlieb (1896) of Eichtersheim; and
Wilhelm Sandritter (1894).

CHAPTER SIX

1. Führer, 8/9 March, 3/4 April 1931; August Kramer (Gau-propagandaleiter), "Rundschreiben Nr. 1 an die Redner des Gaues Baden," 20 December 1930, T-580/19/199.
2. Landespolizeiamt, Abt. N, "Die politische Lage in Baden," 5 October 1931, GLA/233/28388; Führer, 20 September 1931; Baden, Statistisches Jahrbuch, 1938, 213.
3. Kramer to Reichspropagandaleiter, 25 February 1931; and Kramer to Reichspropagandaleitung, 14 January 1930; and Kramer, "Rundschreiben Nr. 1," all T-580/19/199; Führer, 3/4 April 1931.
4. Führer, 22 February 1930, 31 April, 13 February 1931; Landespolizeiamt, Abt. N, reports for 1931 in GLA/233/27915; Polizeimeldung Pforzheim to Bezirksrat Pforzheim, 21 January 1930, GLA/234/5738.
5. Führer, 6 March 1931, 3 January 1932.
6. Wagner, "Verfügung," in Führer, 4 and 8 and 19 November 1932; Landespolizeiamt, Abt. N, "Die politische Lage in Baden," 5 October 1931, GLA/233/28388; Friedrich Sattler, "Die Entwicklung der NSDAP in Neustadt, Schwarzwald," 19 November 1937, HA/5/132.
7. "Die Geschichte des Hakenkreuzbanner," 27 November 1936, HA/47/1024; "Bodensee Rundschau," 3 February 1936, HA/47/981; "Der Alemanne," HA/47/963; Hale, Captive Press, p. 50. Hitler suggested the name "Hakenkreuzbanner" to a Baden delegation attending a local leadership conference in Munich. By December 1932 the Führer editions amounted to 14,500 copies.
8. Franz Moraller, "Erinnerungen aus der Gründerzeit," 29 July 1936, and MdI, Baden, to Bezirksamt, Polizeidirektion Karlsruhe, 7 May 1931, both HA/47/1014; Wagner, "Fünf Jahre Führer," Führer, 1 November 1932; Führer, 26 July 1931.
9. Robert Wagner, Tod dem Marxismus, pp. 5-8, 10, 23; see also Bracher, Auflösung, p. 126, for a discussion of Nazi party propaganda.
10. Speer, Inside, p. 47.
11. Führer, 10 December 1930, 30 March 1935; Ortsgruppe Liedolsheim, "Antrag auf Verleihung des Blutordens," 12 October 1938, BDC/Robert Roth file.
12. Landespolizeiamt, Abt. N, "Bericht," 15 November 1929 (and 19 August 1930), SAF/317/1257d; Führer, 6 August 1931; Karlsruher Zeitung, 4 February 1932; BDC/SA Akten: Franz Moraller Personalkarte. According to Otto Wagener, chief of staff of the SA in 1929/30, Robert Wagner resented the independent actions of the national SA leadership; see Wagener, Hitler aus nächster Nähe, pp. 40-41.

13. Landespolizeiamt, Abt. N, "Bericht," 15 January, 15 May 1929, 19 August 1930, both SAF/317/1257d; Landespolizeiamt, "Die politische Lage in Baden," 5 October 1931, GLA/233/28388.

14. Richard Scheringer, Das grosse Los, pp. 146, 192-206; Peter Bucher, Der Reichswehrprozess, pp. 15-37; BDC/ Sonderakten No. 12: Scheringer, Ludin, Wendt: Ulmer Prozess; Reginald H. Phelps, "Aus den Groener Dokumenten, V," pp. 915-22.

15. Scheringer, Grosse Los, pp. 251-52, 280, 327; Führer, 6 August 1931; Peter Hüttenberger, Die Gauleiter, p. 72; Gau Baden, Stabsleiter to Oberste Leitung PO, Ley, 10 February 1934, T-81/121/142150. Krebs claims that Ludin surrounded himself with former soldiers and demanded strict discipline. Allegedly, he also saw the shortcomings of the party and its leaders in Baden, Albert Krebs, Tendenzen und Gestalten der NSDAP, pp. 214-15.

16. See the reports in Führer, 9 November 1932; Völkischer Beobachter, 28/29 and 24 April 1929, 24 July 1930; Bad. Landespolizeiamt to Oberstaatsanwalt, 26 April 1929, and Krim. Inspektor Funk to Oberstaatsanwalt, "Meldung der Kriminalpolizei," 24 April 1929, both GLA/309/1143.

17. Führer, 20 August, 12 July 1930, 13 January 1931.

18. Meldung der Fahndungspolizei, 8 February 1932, GLA/ 309/1123; Bad. Staatsanwaltschaft, Abtl. 2c to Generalstaatsanwalt, 15 July 1932, GLA/309/1144; Pol. Hauptwachtmeister, Karlsruhe, to Staatsanwaltschaft Karlsruhe, 5 July 1932, GLA/309/1125; Landeskommissär Mannheim, Heidelberg, and Mosbach to Bezirksamt Heidelberg, 13 August 1930, GLA/ 364/7745; "Tatbericht über den Zwischenfall am 31. Juli 1932 zwischen SA Männer and Reichswehrsoldaten in Konstanz," Führer des Sturmbann 1/114, IfZ/MA 616/20 (same as NA T-253/ 22/1472764-66); Führer, 22/23 February 1931.

19. "Zusammenstellung der in den Monaten Oktober und November 1931 vorgekommenen politischen Gewalttaten," Justizm. Baden, GLA/234/5752.

20. Landespolizeiamt, "Die politische Lage in Baden," 5 October 1931, GLA/233/28388; Abt. N, "Die kommunistische Bewegung in Baden," 7 September 1931, SAF/317/1257d; MdI to Staatsministerium, 31 October 1931, GLA/233/25860; MdI to MdJustiz, 11 May 1929, GLA/234/5739; Rote Schülerzeitung, 2 (March 1930), in GLA/309/1169.

21. MdI to Reichsm. d. Innern, 26 August 1932, GLA/233/ 25979; Bad. Landespolizeiamt, Abt. N, to MdI, 21 December 1932, SAF/317/1257aII; Bezirksamt Sinsheim to Walther Haas, 4 December 1931, GLA/377/5399.

22. Wagner to Bad. Innenminister, 27 June 1932, GLA/233/

25979.

23. MdI, Baden to Staatsministerium, 14 January 1931, GLA/233/28388; Bad. Landtag, Verhandlungen des Bad. Landtag, Amtliche Niederschrift, 7. Sitzung, 18 December 1930, GLA/233/27915.

24. "Niederschrift über die Sitzung des Staatsministeriums vom 21. April 1932," GLA/233/24317.

25. Staatssekretär Meissner to Dr. Fecht, Stellvertreter Badens im Reichsrat, 15 June 1932 (Niederschrift über die am 12. Juni 1932 im Hause des Reichspr. stattgehabte Besprechung mit den Süddeutschen Minister bezw. Staatspr.), IfZ/MA; MdI, Baden, to Staatsministerium, 21 July 1932, GLA/233/25979.

26. Eduard Helff, ed., Grenzland Baden Spaten zur Hand!, pp. 6-19; Führer, 13 December 1933; BDC/Eduard Helff file.

27. Führer, 19 June, 4 February 1938; BDC/Otto Heidt Karte; Karlsruher Zeitung, 4 February 1932; Pol. Sekretär Buchheit to Bad. Landespolizeiamt, 25 February 1931 GLA/309/1130.

28. BDC/Helwig file; BDC/Hans Adolf Prützmann file; Führer, 19 June, 4 February 1938. As early as 1932, however, Wagner lost control over the Baden SS. By September 1932, he was totally alienated from Helwig, who had Himmler's support. When Wagner suggested to Himmler to select a new SS leader, the Baden Gau leader was told to "mind his own business"; see Tom Segev, "The Commanders of Nazi Concentration Camps," pp. 108-109.

29. Landespolizeiamt, Abt. N, "Bericht," 5 March 1927, SAF/317/1257d; Führer, 1 May 1933, 10 December 1927.

30. Bruno Wiesener, "Gesuch an den RFSS auf den Dienstweg," 30 January 1936, T-175/200/2741013; Bruno Wiesener to Kamerad Henschel, 7 October 1937, T-175/200/2740102.

31. Landespolizeiamt, Abt. N, "Bericht," 15 May 1929, SAF/317/1257d.

32. Führer, 22 February 1930, 7 May 1933; Peter Stachura, Nazi Youth in the Weimar Republic, pp. 229, 262, 167.

33. Gordon Bolitho, The Other Germany, pp. 22, 47, 154; Polizeisekretär Ott to Bad. Landespolizeiamt, 31 May 1927, GLA/309/1147. For general accounts see Michael Stephen Steinberg, Sabers and Brownshirts; and Wolfgang Zorn, "Student Politics in the Weimar Republic," pp. 128-43.

34. Kreuzberger, Studenten und Politik, 1918-1933, pp. 55, 72, 109-110, 172; Völkischer Beobachter, 11 February, 30 June 1928, 24 July 1929, 12/13 June 1927; Führer, 28 July, 30 June 1928; Steinberg, Sabers, p. 92. The platform of the NSDStB in 1927 demanded the following: (1) Volk community; (2) black-white-red national colors; (3) social equality of

workers; (4) rejection of Jews, Marxism, Internationalism, and Pacifism; and (5) Christian morals and ethics.

35. See the reports in the Völkischer Beobachter, 11 February, 30 June 1928, 24 July 1929; and Führer, 28 July, 30 June 1928.

36. Steinberg, Sabers, p. 92; Führer, 12 July 1930, 9 February 1933, 21 February 1931; Kreuzberger, Studenten, p. 74; Bracher, Auflösung, pp. 148-49.

37. Frankfurter Zeitung, 16 July 1930; Führer, 26 July 1930; Völkischer Beobachter, 26 and 16 July 1930.

38. Landespolizeiamt, Abt. N, "Die politische Lage in Baden," 5 October 1931, GLA/233/28388.

39. Emil Julius Gumbel, Vier Jahre Politischer Mord, p. 81; Walter Fabian, "Vorwort," in Gumbel, Vom Femenmord zur Reichskanzlei, pp. 6-7.

40. See the Gumbel file in the Leo Baeck Institute (Archives) containing a number of Gumbel's "Scrapbooks." Gumbel collected newspaper clippings from all over the world dealing with his case in the 1920s and 1930s; see also Abwehr-Blätter, 35 (20 May 1925), and (20 June 1925); Badischer Beobachter, 11 February 1926.

41. Führer, 27 August, 6 December 1930; MdKuU to Engeren Senat der Univ. Heidelberg, 19 January 1931, GLA/233/24955.

42. Führer, 23 January 1931, 24 August 1932; Badische Presse, 27 August 1932; Heidelberger Neueste Nachrichten, 25 June 1932; and various papers from Europe and the Americas in Gumbel file, Leo Baeck Archives, New York. In August 1933, Gumbel lost his German citizenship (along with thirty-two others who had left Germany), see Berliner Morgenzeitung, 26 August 1933, in Gumbel file, ibid.

43. Eiserne Blätter, Vol. 13, No. 2, and Die Christliche Welt, No. 5 (1 March 1931), in Günter Dehn, ed., Kirche und Völkerversöhnung, pp. 39-43; Der Heidelberger Student, 19 November 1931; Herald Tribune, 15 January 1933, in Gumbel file, Leo Baeck Archives, New York.

44. Wilhelm Frick, Die Deutsche Frau im nationalsozialistichen Staat, p. 10; Alfred Rosenberg, "Der nationale Schicksalkampf der Frau," p. 169.

45. Paula Siber, Die Frauenfrage, p. 12; Toni Saring, "Berufsbilder der weiblichen Jugend," pp. 199-200; Sophie Rogge-Börner, "Der Weg in die Zukunft," pp. 338-52; see also Jill McIntyre, "Women and the Professions in Germany, 1930-1940," p. 184.

46. Führer, 29 September 1928; Die Flamme (Nuremberg), 30 January 1930, in HA/17A/1923; see also Führer, 22 September 1933.

47. Führer, 17 December 1931; Lena Osswald, "Erwiderung an die badische NSDAP," (1928?), in GLA/69N/Ruge file/60. Claudia Koonz, "Nazi Women before 1933," p. 558, is wrong in claiming that "until 1933 Nazi women were free either to sew or wear brown shirts. All activities met with a tolerant reception." This was certainly not the case in Baden or in other areas like Eutin (a part of Oldenburg but located in Schleswig-Holstein).

48. Landespolizeiamt, Abt. N, "Bericht," 1 December 1926 (and 7 September, 5 November 1926), SAF/317/1257d. To give some examples, the police noted the attendance of women at Nazi rallies: 50 out of 150 on 6 August 1926 in Karlsruhe; 13 out of 70 on 13 August 1926 in Karlsruhe; and 12 out of 65 on 10 September 1926 in Karlsruhe.

49. Landespolizeiamt, Abt. N, "Bericht," 1 June 1928 (and 1 November 1927), SAF/317/1257d.

50. Führer, 2 June, 29 September 1928; Landespolizeiamt, Abt. N, "Bericht," 15 March 1928, SAF/317/1257d.

51. Führer, 26 May, 2 June 1928. As late as September 1930, the Nazis noted that women were still drawn more to the Center and bourgeois parties; see Führer, 20 September 1930.

52. BDC/Gertrud Scholtz-Klink Karte; Führer, 12 April, 21 March, 24 May 1930; Landespolizeiamt, Abt. N, "Bericht," 15 January 1929 (and report of 19 August 1930), SAF/317/1257d; Clifford Kirkpatrick, Nazi Germany: Its Women and Family Life, pp. 66-70. The Führer published biographical notes on all types of male Baden Nazis, but never on Scholtz-Klink; her postwar recollections add little to the story. In late 1931 she also took over the NSF of Gau Hesse and combined this new duty with her Baden responsibilities; see Gertrud Scholtz-Klink, ed., Die Frau im Dritten Reich, pp. 28-29.

53. Führer, 17 December 1931; Gertrud Scholtz-Klink, ed., Was will die NS Frauenschaft? (a 4-pp. pamphlet c. 1931/32), in GLA/465d/1460.

54. Führer, 18 January, 29 November, 18 October 1930; 28 September 1932; McIntyre, "Women and the Professions," p. 196.

55. Wagner to Strasser, "Organisation der Gauleitung Baden," 30 December 1930 (Vertraulich), T-580/19/199.

56. Some examples are provided by the Führer, 11 October 1930 (for Berufsmusiker), 3 December 1930 (for NS Juristenbund), and October 1930 (for the NS Kriegsopfer). For 1931/32 see Führer, 6 January 1931, and 31 December/1 January 1932.

57. Führer, 19 June, 11 November, 23 May, 18 June 1931.

58. Nazi local Mosbach, Handzettel: "An alle Deutschen

Katholiken," January 1932, GLA/364/7805.

59. Landespolizeiamt, Abt. N, "Bericht," 15 January 1927, SAF/317/1257d; Führer, 29 November 1930; Schindler to Fritz Finkbeiner, Gernsbach, 23 May 1931, T-81/173/313945; Führer, 8 October 1932; Siegfried Heinzelman, Evangelische Kirche in Mannheim, p. 78; see also BDC/OPG, Pfarrer Schenk file, for the split within the Nazi Protestants in Baden before 1933.

60. Führer, 13 December 1930; Raay to Ortsgruppe Gernsbach, 6 May 1931, T-81/173/313890; Gies, "NSDAP und landwirtschaftliche Organisationen," pp. 342-59, 368.

61. BDC/Plesch file; Darré to Reichsorganisationsleiter, 13 June 1932, HA/29/550.

62. Wagner to Darré, 10 June 1932, HA/29/550; Führer, 7 February 1932; Karlsruher Zeitung, 5 February 1932 (published the Plesch letter). Ludwig Huber was born on 10 December 1889 in Ibach near Oppenau. A farmer and former Landesbauernführer, he joined the Nazi party in 1929 and became district leader of the Catholic district of Oberkirch. Between 1929 and May 1933, Huber spoke in 600 Nazi rural rallies, which partly explains why Oberkirch, which was 90 percent Catholic, gave the Nazis 41.6 percent of the vote in July 1932; Führer, 10 May, 10 November 1933.

63. Führer, 28 August 1931; Wagner to Darré, 10 June 1932, HA/29/550; Gies, "NSDAP und landwirtschaftliche Organisationen," pp. 561-64; Führerlexikon, 1934, p. 427.

64. Landespolizeiamt, Abt. N, "Die politische Lage in Baden," 5 October 1931, GLA/233/28388; Rehberger, Gleichschaltung, p. 18. Otto Heinrich Schmidt was born in 1873 in Heddesheim in the district of Weinheim. He was a lawyer and had a long record as a political representative, beginning in 1905 as a Landtag representative of the Bund der Landwirte. After the war he entered the Landtag as a member of the DNVP (1921-25) and later as a member of the Badische Bauernpartei. Ernst Friedrich Hagin was born in Egringen on 13 April 1874. He entered the Landtag in 1921 as a member of the Landbund, and in 1929 he represented the Badische Bauernpartei in the same legislature; see Karl Gross, ed., Handbuch für den Badischen Landtag: V. Landtagsperiode 1933-1937, pp. 136, 145.

65. Führer, 1 May 1936, 13 September 1933.

66. Führer, 19 April, 24 May 1930, 28 July 1931; Adolf Conrad, "Meine Kampfjahre in Mannheim von Mitte 1930 bis zum Umsturz 1933," March 1937, HA/26/514.

67. Führer, 25 April, 12 June 1931, 9 February 1932, 31 March 1935.

68. Orlow, History, 1:199.

69. MdI, Baden, to Staatsministerium, 6 August 1941, GLA/
233/24600. This concerns Fritz Enderle of Offenburg, Kreis-
geschäftsführer from November 1930 to August 1933.
70. Führer, 1 February, 14 June, 12 April 1930, 14 September 1932.
71. This is based on the BDC files or cards of the following leaders:

Name	Party Member	Born
Otto Wetzel	1922	1905
Erwin Schwörer	1924/28	1906
P. Munz	1929	1905
Willi Rückert	1924/25	1905
Johannes Rupp	1929	1903
Karl Lenz	1922	1899
August Kramer	1923/26	1900
Fritz Plattner	1923	1901
Herbert Kraft	1923/28	1886
Peter Riedner	1922/25	1883
Walter Köhler	1924/25	1897
Friedhelm Kemper	1923	1906
Otto Wacker	1923/25	1899
Otto Heidt	1922/25	1904

Hüttenberger is incorrect in maintaining that the majority
of the Baden Amtsleiter were new party men who joined only
after 1929; see his Gauleiter, p. 58.
72. Führer, 3 April 1931. The four best Gaue named
were Baden, Anhalt, Weser-Ems, and Mittelfranken.
73. "Neuorganisation der NSDAP im Gau Baden," in Führer,
9 August 1932 (also in T-580/19/199).
74. Landespolizeiamt, "Die politische Lage in Baden,"
5 October 1931, GLA/233/28388; MdI to Bezirksämter and Polizeidirektion Baden-Baden, 7 January 1932, and reports from
Bezirksamt Sinsheim, 11 January, 7 November 1932, both GLA/
377/5402.
75. See Führer, 2 and 6 and 8 March, 3 April, 14 June,
19 October 1932; Goebbels, "Zur vertraulichen Kenntnisnahme
an alle Parteistellen," 4 June 1932, T-81/164/303121.
76. Wagner to Strasser, 6 June 1932 (and 10 and 11 June
1932), HA/29/550; Wagner to Frick, 28 June 1932, HA/29/550.
77. Darré to Reichsorganisationsleiter, 13 June 1932,
HA/29/550.
78. Rückert to Reichswahlleiter, 13 July 1932, ibid.
79. Führer, 11 April, 3 November 1932, Reichswahlleiter,
Hauptergebnisse der Wahlen zum Reichstag am 31. Juli 1932,

p. 66.

80. Karl Lenz was now the Gau leader of Hesse. Ludin had become Gau SA leader in 1931, and Willi Ziegler was the SA leader of Heidelberg. Ziegler was born in 1899 in a small village (Epfenbach) and died in Russia in January 1942. He was a trained mechanic. Hans Helwig was born in 1881 in Hemsbach and became a party member in Weinheim in January 1927, although he had joined the SA as early as 1921. Trained as a bricklayer, he spent eighteen years in the army before becoming a clerk. Otto Wetzel, who was born in 1905 in Heidelberg, was an engineer: see Führer, 1 February 1930; BDC/Hans Helwig file; Schwarz, Biographisches Handbuch, pp. 596, 605, 667, 787, 794; and Segev, The Commanders, p. 105-106.

81. Volksfreund, 26 and 28 July 1932.

82. Karlsruher Zeitung, 14 March, 1 August 1932; Badischer Beobachter, 1 August 1932.

83. Badische Zeitung, 1 August 1932; Badische Presse, 28 September, 1 August, 3 October 1932; Führer, 9 October 1932.

84. August Kramer, "Erklärung," 2 November 1932, in Führer, 3 November 1932; Wagner, "Der Verrat in Lahr," in Führer, 8 November 1932; Stachura, Nazi Youth, pp. 82-83, 255. After the Nazis' seizure of power in 1933, they hunted the Lahr "traitors"; see Reichsstatthalter Baden, Kanzlei to Reichsm. des Innern, 24 March 1934, GLA/233/25984. Although the movement had little support in Baden after November 1932, it continued until 1933. In fact, the former deputy Gau leader of Baden, Karl Lenz, returned to his native state in December 1932 to lead the movement in Baden (after resigning his Gau leadership post in Hesse-Darmstadt). Lenz was a strong defender of Gregor Strasser and a friend of Werner Best, the author of the famous Boxheimer papers. Lenz's futile efforts continued until the NS Notgemeinschaft was disbanded in March 1933; see Udo Kissenkoetter, Gregor Strasser und die NSDAP, pp. 185-89.

85. Karlsruher Zeitung and Volksfreund, 7 November 1932; Badische Presse, 7 and 2 November 1932; Badische Zeitung, 7 November 1932; Reichswahlleiter, Hauptergebnisse der Wahlen zum Reichstag am 6. November 1932, p. 133.

86. Wagner, "Zum Wahlausgang am 6. November," in Führer, 11 November 1932; see also the explanation in Führer, 9 February 1933.

87. Rehberger, Gleichschaltung, pp. 42-45; Föhr, Geschichte des Badischen Konkordats, pp. 51-52; Föhr, Das Konkordat, p. 9; Führer, 27 October, 16 November 1932.

88. Führer, 2 December 1932; Rehberger, Gleichschaltung

pp. 48-50.
89. Führer, 3 January 1933; Hakenkreuzbanner, 6 January 1933.

CHAPTER SEVEN

1. Nazi-KPD clashes in early 1933 resulted in casualties in Baden. But the Nazis also intimidated both the Catholic Badenwacht and the Zentrum representatives who attempted to distribute political leaflets. The Baden Nazis even registered the names of people in February and March 1933 who refused to accept Nazi flags; see Gen. Kommissär Bretten to Bezirksamt Bretten, 2 February 1933, GLA/357/Zg 1973/51/No. 1777; Verlagsleiter of Pfälzer Bote, Heidelberg, to Staatspräsident Dr. Schmitt, 3 March 1933, GLA/233/25983.
2. Führer, 9 February, 2 March 1933.
3. MdI/Kommissär Wagner to RMdJ, 4 May 1933, GLA/233/25979; Führer, 22 and 24 February 1933. Of these fifteen papers, five were SPD, six KPD, three Zentrum, and one Free Union.
4. August Schreiber to Bad. Staatsministerium, 21 February 1933, GLA/233/25983; Badische Presse, 21 February 1933; "Auszug aus der Niederschrift über die Sitzung des Staatsministeriums vom 22. Feb. 1933," GLA/233/25983.
5. Führer, 24 February, 4 March 1933.
6. Ibid., 4 March 1933; Verlagsleiter of Pfälzer Bote to Staatspräsident, 3 March 1933, GLA/233/25983. According to the Führer (6 March 1933) the police searched the offices of the Volksfreund in Karlsruhe.
7. Führer, 9 February, 2 and 4 March 1933; Otto Ebbecke, ed., Die Deutsche Erhebung in Baden, p. 5.
8. Statistisches Reichsamt, "Die Wahlen zum Reichstag am 5. März 1933," pp. 235-39. The election results by percentages were: NSDAP--45.5, DNVP--3.6, Center party--25.4, SPD--11.9, and KPD--9.8.
9. Franz Moraller, "Wie ich die Revolution in Baden erlebte," in Führer, 23, 24, and 25 March 1934.
10. "Auszug aus der Niederschrift über die Sitzung des Staatsministeriums vom 6. März 1933 (10 A.M.)," GLA/233/28388; Innenminister, Baden, to Landeskommissäre, Bezirksämter, 6 March 1933, GLA/233/28388.
11. Führer, 9 March 1933.
12. Karlsruher Zeitung, 6 and 7 March 1933; Badischer Beobachter, 7 March (and 8 March) 1933. After the Nazi takeover, Wagner asked the editor of the Karlsruher Zeitung, Curt

Amend, to join the staff of the Führer; see Curt Amend to
Wagner, 5 April 1933, GLA/233/27964.
  13. Führer, 25 March 1934.
  14. Badischer Beobachter, 6 March (and 7 March) 1933;
Volksstimme, 6 February 1933.
  15. Köhler to Bad. Staatsministerium, and Staatsministerium to Gauleitung, both 6 March 1933, GLA/233/28388.
  16. Führer, 25 March 1934; interview with Köhler, 6 June
1977, in Karlsruhe.
  17. "Niederschrift über die Sitzung des Staatsministeriums
vom 9. März 1933 (and 10. März)," GLA/233/24317; Karlsruher
Zeitung, 9 March 1933; Frick's letter in Ebbecke, ed., Erhebung, p. 10. Similar letters were sent to Schaumburg-Lippe,
Württemberg, and Saxony.
  18. Führer and Karlsruher Zeitung, both 10 and 11 March
1933. On 11 March, the Führer was still announcing coalition
talks between the NSDAP and Center party.
  19. Reichsm. d. Innern to Wagner, 18 March 1933, and
Wagner to Reichsm. d. Innern, 27 March 1933, both GLA/233/
28118; Führer, 12 March 1933; Ebbecke, ed., Erhebung, pp.
12-14; Rehberger, Gleichschaltung, pp. 115-16. For the role
of Nazi commissars see "Niederschrift über die Sitzung der
kommissärischen Regierung vom März 27, 1933," GLA/233/24318;
Wagner to Bezirksämter, Polizeipräsidien, 6 May 1933, GLA/
356/5476; Kemper to Bad. Jugendherbergen, 28 April 1933,
GLA/356/4382.
  20. Wagner, "Funkspruch," 11 March 1933, GLA/233/28388;
Stabsführer SA, Untergruppe Baden, 11 March 1933, and "Im
Umlauf bei den Herren Beamten und Angestellten des Staatsministeriums," both GLA/233/26344.
  21. Wagner to Bezirksämter, Polizei, 11 March 1933,
GLA/233/25623; Führer and Karlsruher Zeitung of 11 March 1933;
Bad. Staatsministerium to Oberste SA Führer, 28 March 1933,
and Wagner to Bad. Staatsministerium, 30 March 1933, both
GLA/233/27911.
  22. "Niederschrift über die Sitzung des Staatsministeriums vom 11. Sept. 1933," GLA/233/24318.
  23. Führer and Badische Presse, 14 March 1933.
  24. Karlsruher Zeitung, 13 March 1933; "Protokoll der
Kabinettsitzung vom 14. März 1933," GLA/233/24318; Ebbecke,
ed., Erhebung, pp. 18-19.
  25. Karlsruher Zeitung, 18 March 1933; Rehberger, Gleichschaltung, pp. 121-24; Führer, 18 March 1933.
  26. Führer, 26 March, 23 August 1933; Wagner to Staatsministerium, 29 March 1933, GLA/233/28388; Wagner to Bezirksämter, Polizeipräsidien, 20 April 1933, SAF/317/1267.

27. Führer, 10 June, 19 December 1933, 23 June 1934;
MdI, Baden, to Leiter der Schutzhaftlager, 16 December 1933, SAF/
317/1267. By July 1933, 314 KZ inmates and 245 in protective
custody were victims of the Nazi purge. By July 1934 this
number had declined to 150 in KZ and 150 in protective custody;
see MdI to Bezirksämter, 31 July 1933, SAF/317/1266.
    28. MdI, Baden, to Landräte, Polizei, 8 March 1934, GLA/
233/25984; Führer, 3 November 1935.
    29. Bad. Turnerschaft to Reichsk. Wagner, 20 March 1933,
and Orchester des Bad. Landestheaters, 18 March 1933, both
GLA/233/28140; Albert Knittel (publisher of the Karlsruher
Zeitung and Karlsruher Tagblatt) to Ministerialrat Müller-
Trefzer, 2 February 1934, GLA/233/27964; Ebbecke, ed., Erhebung, p. 29.
    30. Wagner to Staatsministerium, 4 April 1933, GLA/233/
25683; Rehberger, Gleichschaltung, pp. 226-31; Badisches
Gesetz- und Verordnungs-Blatt, 12 May 1933, pp. 83-84. Wacker
held a Ph.D. in history, and Rupp was a lawyer. Rupp resigned
on 18 April 1933, allegedly because Baden was too small for
a Justice Ministry; Rupp to Wagner, 18 April 1933, GLA/233/
24283.
    31. Führerlexikon, 1934, pp. 38, 322; Wagner, "Akten-
bemerkung," 11 March 1933, GLA/235/24279. Müller-Trefzer
was born 4 October 1879 in Karlsruhe, and Bader on 20 July
1883 in Lahr. Both had studied law.
    32. "Niederschrift über die Sitzung des Staatsministe-
riums vom 13. Mai 1933," GLA/233/24318; Führer, 10 June 1933;
Karlsruher Zeitung, 9 June 1933. Since the Baden Enabling
Act was declared "urgent" by the government, it was excluded
from a plebiscite; see Köhler to Wagner, 12 June 1933, GLA/
233/28128.
    33. Karlsruher Zeitung, 23 June 1933; Gross, ed., Hand-
buch, 1933-37, pp. 1-3, 148; Rehberger, Gleichschaltung,
pp. 135-39.
    34. "Niederschrift über die Sitzung des Staatsministe-
riums vom 21. Juni 1933," GLA/233/24318; Pflaumer to Staatskanzlei, 26 May 1933, GLA/233/25979. Examples of the Nazi
purge may be found in Bezirksamt Heidelberg, "Verzeichnis
der gemäss Gesetz vom 26.5 1933 und vom 14.7 1933 in den
Landgemeinden des Amtsbezirks Heidelberg aufgelösten Vereine
und Organisationen," 27 November 1935, GLA/356/4382; Ley to
Wagner, 15 May 1933, GLA/234/5797.
    35. Führer, 4 April, 1 October 1933.
    36. Ibid., 27 and 30 July 1933; Karlsruher Zeitung, 31
July 1933. By September 1933 the special commissar positions
were abolished; Rehberger, Gleichschaltung, p. 149.

37. Führer, 8 May, 31 December 1933.

38. Führer, 30 July 1933; Karlsruher Zeitung, 31 July 1933; Nachrichtenblatt, 1 (1 September 1934); Heinrich Frick to Lammers, 28 May 1941, in Hans Mommsen, Beamtentum im Dritten Reich, pp. 233-35. Wagner did want the Landrat to represent the "gesamte Regierung"; see "Niederschrift über die Sitzung des Staatsministeriums vom 21. Juni 1933," GLA/233/24318.

39. Partei-Statistik, 1:252, 288; Peter Diehl-Thiele, Partei und Staat im Dritten Reich, pp. 176-77.

40. Führer, 8 May, 23 December 1933.

41. "Niederschrift, Sitzung des Staatsministerium vom 12. Januar, 1934," GLA/233/24318; Führer (M), 18 February 1939.

42. Führer (A), 26 June 1934, 9 May, 3 October 1933; Ministerpräsident to MdI (vertraulich), 25 February 1935, GLA/233/28084.

43. Diehl-Thiele, Partei und Staat, pp. 46-47; Rehberger, Gleichschaltung; interview with Köhler, June 1977, in Karlsruhe. In Alsace, Wagner was responsible to Hitler.

44. "Niederschrift, Sitzung des Staatsministeriums vom 24. Okt. 1933," GLA/233/24318; Führer, 8 June 1933.

45. Moraller to Bad. Staatskanzlei, 2 December 1933, GLA/233/28180; Wacker to Köhler, 11 September 1937, GLA/233/25716.

46. "Niederschrift, Sitzung des Staatsministeriums vom 17. Nov. 1933," GLA/233/24318; MdI, Baden, to Badischen Staatskanzlei, 6 December 1933; MdK to Staatskanzlei, 7 December 1933 (Streng vertraulich), GLA/233/28180.

47. "Niederschrift, Sitzung des Staatsministeriums vom 21. Juni 1933," GLA/233/24318.

48. "Niederschrift, Sitzung des Staatsministeriums vom 24. April 1934," GLA/233/24318; Leiter der Bad. Staatskanzlei to Prof. Metz, 28 February 1935 (and 22 March, 18 April 1935); Friedrich Metz to Müller-Trefzer, 28 March 1935, GLA/233/25716.

49. Hitler to Reichsstatthalter (Abschrift), 15 July 1933, GLA/233/24279; Badische Staatskanzlei, "Notiz," 3 January 1935, GLA/233/25732.

50. Köhler to MdI, Frick, 30 January 1935, GLA/233/28180; Köhler to Staatskanzlei (vertraulich), 2 May 1939, GLA/233/28090.

51. For the purges see MdI to Staatsministerium, 4 August 1933, GLA/233/29676; MdI to Bad. Staatskanzlei, 21 December 1935, GLA/233/27901; MdI to Staatsministerium, 5 April 1935, GLA/233/27905.

52. Dr. Wilhelm Heim entered state service in 1925 and police service in Mannheim in 1927. Heim, who had belonged to the Organization Damm in 1919/21, was sympathetic with

the Nazi movement since 1928/29. He was fired as police chief of Karlsruhe in July 1937 because he had two "half-Jewish" friends, see Heim to SS Oberabschnitt Südwest, 4 September 1937, Kaul to Daluege, 7 September 1937, both in BDC/ORPO file, Wilhelm Heim folder.

53. MdI, Baden to Staatsministerium, 6 July 1935; and MdI to Staatsministerium, 25 October 1938; and Heydrich to Reichsstatthalter Baden, 11 June 1937, all in GLA/233/27894; Karlsruher Zeitung, 16 September 1933. Berckmüller, who was born in 1895, was the state's deputy Schlageterbund leader in 1924.

54. Wagner to Bad. Staatskanzlei, 10 December 1937, GLA/233/27892; Pflaumer to Reichsstatthalter, 13 September 1937, GLA/235/12754; Pflaumer to Staatsministerium, 28 October 1937, GLA/233/27892.

55. Köhler to Wagner, 18 May 1935, GLA/233/28180; Köhler to MdI, MdK (vertraulich), 25 February 1935, GLA/233/28084; Köhler to Staatskanzlei, 25 April 1935, GLA/233/28084.

56. Wagner to Staatskanzlei, 25 May 1935; and Minister-präsident to Wagner, 15 October 1935; and MdI to Staatskanzlei, 14 October 1935, all in GLA/233/28084; Bühlertaler Anzeiger, 1 July 1930 (or 1931?), T-81/173/313726-28.

57. "Niederschrift über die Sitzung des Staatsministe-riums vom 6. November 1935"; and Bad. Staatskanzlei, "Notiz," 7 January 1936; and Reichsm. dI to Bad. MdI, 2 May 1936, all in GLA/233/28084; Führer (M), 23 February 1935, 2 July 1936.

58. Badisches Gesetz- und Verordnungs-Blatt, 28 June 1939, p. 93. In 1937 Frick had lamented the lack of union in Baden between the Amtsbezirk and the Kreis; see W. Frick, "Die Gemeinde in Volk und Staat," in N. S. Gemeinde, 5 (1 November 1937), pp. 646-49.

59. MdI to Staatskanzlei, 17 May 1938; and Baden, Finanz u. Wirtschaftsm. to Staatskanzlei, 27 October 1937; and MdK to Staatskanzlei, 11 April 1938, all in GLA/233/28090. The Ministry of Culture was able to save some money by cutting contributions to the priests and Oberrat der Israeliten. But this amounted to only .1 percent of the budget in 1937.

60. MdI to Staatskanzlei, 22 May 1939, ibid.

61. Das Archiv, Jahrgang 1936/37 (October 1936), p. 1076; Badischer Geschäfts- und Adresskalender, Stand Mai, 1942, p. 6; "NS Gaudienst Baden," 15 February 1940, in T-81/168/307862.

62. Mauch to Leiter der Bad. Staatskanzlei, 4 November 1936; and Bad. Staatskanzlei, "Aktenvermerk," 21 November 1936, both GLA/233/26332; Wacker to Bad. Staatsministerium, 5 July 1934, GLA/233/27969. See Daniel Horn, "The Hitler Youth and Educational Decline in the Third Reich," pp. 425-40.

63. "Niederschrift des Hauptamtsleiters Friedrichs im Stabe des Stellv. d. Führers zur Frage der Personalunion von Kreisleiter und Landrat," 1940, in Mommsen, Beamtentum im Dritten Reich, p. 229; MdI, Baden, to Gauleitung, NSV, 30 July 1935, T-81/R.87/99637-44.

64. Schwarz to Wagner, 1 October 1936, and Schwarz to Wagner, 5 January 1940, both BDC/Pflaumer file; Schwarz to Pflaumer, 26 November 1943 and 5 April 1944; and Pflaumer to Schwarz, 15 April 1944; and Schwarz to Wagner, 30 May 1944; and Röhn to Schwarz, 21 June 1944, all in T-81/120/141863-68.

65. Nachrichtenblatt, 2 (1 September 1935), pp. 66-67; and 2 (15 June 1935), p. 46; and 1 (1 March 1934), p. 19; Gaugeschäftsführer Baden, "Rundschreiben," 21 July 1937, T-81/172/312734.

66. Partei-Statistik, 1:146-48, 106-108; Badische Presse, 21 February 1933; Otto Kraft to Kreisleitung Villingen, 30 May 1933, SAF/317/494.

67. "Niederschrift über die Sitzung der kommissärischen Regierung vom 27. März 1933," GLA/233/24318; Badische Presse, 14 March 1933.

68. Führer, 17 October 1935, 21 June 1934; Wagner to Staatsministerium, 30 July 1933, GLA/233/24674; Köhler to Staatsministerium, 31 July 1934, GLA/233/27832.

69. Wagner to Staatskanzlei, 22 July 1936, and Bad. MdI to Staatskanzlei, 26 September 1936, both GLA/233/24006.

70. Köhler, "Rundschreiben," 29 July 1933, GLA/233/26332.

71. "Ausführungen Hitlers über das Verhältnis von Staat und Partei auf der Reichsstatthalterkonferenz vom 1. November 1934," in Mommsen, Beamtentum, p. 146; Das Archiv, Jahrgang 1934/35 (Nov./Dec. 1934), pp. 1151-52.

72. "Niederschrift, Sitzung des Staatsministeriums vom 8. Juni 1938" (and 24 September 1934, 7 December 1936), GLA/233/24318.

73. Führer, 26 May 1937; Nachrichtenblatt, 2 (1 July 1935), p. 51, and 1 (1 and 15 March 1934), pp. 20, 24.

74. Führer (M), 26 January 1935, 9 August 1932; BDC/Wilhelm Bogs Mitgliedskarte; BDC/Leopold Mauch Mitgliedskarte. Mauch was born in 1895 in Gosheim.

75. Führer, 18 November 1935, 18 February 1939, 26 January 1935; Gauamtsleiter, Amt f. Beamte, "Rundschreiben," 24 June 1935, T-81/42/44580.

76. Karl Bracher et al., Die nationalsozialistiche Machtergeifung, p. 504.

77. Nachrichtenblatt, 1 (1 March, 15 January 1934), pp. 20, 7.

78. MdK to Staatskanzlei, 12 September 1934, and Paula

Haar to Wagner, 25 May 1934, both GLA/233/25644.

79. Gauamt f. Beamte to Köhler, 13 June 1935, "Verzeichnis derjenigen N.S. die bis zum 14. September 1930 der NSDAP beigetreten sind," 17 July 1935, and "Übersicht A (B) über die im Geschäftsbereich des Ministerium des I. in der Zeit vom 1.8.-31.12.35 in feste Arbeitsplätze untergebrachten Altparteigenossen," both GLA/233/24005.

80. "Stammbuch für Otto Pink," November 1938, T-81/228/5010086; Kreisl. Kehl, to Gaupersonalamt, 28 November 1938, T-81/228/5010030; Gaupersonalamtsl. to Mauch, 6 January 1939, T-81/228/5010023; Mauch to Gaupersonalamt, 27 October 1939, T-81/228/5010019.

81. Direktor der Gefangenanstalten in Freiburg i.B. to Generalstaatsanwalt, "Zweimonatlicher Lagebericht," 24 January 1936, GLA/309/1211.

82. Wagner to Köhler, 3 December 1934; and Wagner to Mauch, 4 December 1934; and Staatskanzlei, "Notiz," 19 February 1935, all GLA/233/27965; Mauch to Köhler, 7 March 1935, GLA/233/26306.

83. Oberstaatsanwalt, Landgericht Waldkirch to Generalstaatsanwalt, "Lagebericht," 19 March 1936, GLA/309/1206; Gaupersonalamtsl., "Rundschreiben," 16 April 1937, GLA/465d/1090; Gauamt f. Beamte and Gaupersonalamtsl., "Rundschreiben," 7 February 1938, T-81/228/474428.

84. Führer, 25 July 1936, 18 February 1939; Mauch to Köhler, 18 February and 25 April 1936, and Köhler to Staatskanzlei, 15 May 1936, both GLA/233/26306; Prof. Fehrle, "Verwaltungsakademie Baden," to Staatskanzlei, 10 July 1936, GLA/233/26305.

85. Nachrichtenblatt, 5 (1 May 1938), p. 17.

86. Gauamt für Beamte, "Mangel an Beamten und Ausfall des Beamtennachwuchses," September 1938, T-81/220/474399-428.

87. Ibid.; Mauch, "Rundschreiben," 5 March 1940, T-81/75/86216-20; Mauch to Hauptamt f. Beamte, Reichsleitung, 11 February 1943, T-81/75/86169-70; Heimat Brief, No. 1 (1 December 1939), and No. 2 (15 December 1939), in T-81/75/86202-204.

88. Mauch to Reichsbund der Deutschen Beamten, RL, 20 April 1943, T-81/75/85948; Reichsbund d. Deutschen Beamten to Beauftragten des Gauleiters, Baden, 25 December 1943, T-81/74/85554; Mauch to Gaupersonalamt, 20 February 1943, T-81/75/86142.

89. Bad. Staatskanzlei to Leiter des Amtes f. Beamte, 30 November 1933, and to Gauleitung, 6 June 1934, both GLA/233/26332; "Niederschrift, Sitzung des Staatsministerium vom 8. Juni 1934," GLA/233/24318; MdI to Landkommissär Konstanz, 16 November 1933, SAF/317/494.

90. Kreisamtsl. Mutter, Mannheim, to Kreisleiter Roth, 31 October 1934, GLA/233/26332; BDC/Albert Mutter Mitgliedskarte; Pflaumer to Köhler, 17 July 1934, GLA/233/23992; Köhler to Kreisleiter Boos, 26 July 1934, GLA/233/23992; Bad. Staatskanzlei, "Aktenvermerk," 21 November 1936, GLA/233/26332.

91. Gaustabsamtsleiter, "Rundschreiben," 3 June (Vertraulich), 8 July 1942, and 1 December 1939, all in T-81/127/149624-47, 149666; Röhn, "Rundschreiben," 1 December 1939, T-81/119/140303; Nachrichtenblatt, 2 (1 February 1935), p. 9.

92. MdK to Kreisschulämter, 16 March 1934, GLA/497/182.

93. Führer, 28 and 8 February 1934; Wacker to Bad. Staatsministerium, 5 July 1934; and Amt f. Erzieher, Baden, to MdK, 17 July 1934; and Bad. Staatskanzlei to MdK, 19 September 1934, all GLA/233/27969; Badischer Staatsanzeiger, 10 July 1934.

94. Generalstaatsanwalt to RJM, "Lagebericht," 30 January 1936; and to Vorstand der Bad. Anwaltskammer, 15 November 1935; and in Karlsruhe, 17 February 1936, all in GLA/309/1204.

95. Generalstaatsanwalt to RJM, "Lagebericht," 18 October 1937, and Generalstaatsanwalt, "Lagebericht," 8 March 1937, both GLA/309/1204; Oberstaatsanwalt Heidelberg, "Lagebericht," 20 September 1938, GLA/309/1208; Oberstaatsanwalt Heidelberg to Generalstaatsanwalt Karlsruhe, 2 December 1935, GLA/309/1206.

96. Oberlandesgerichtspräsident to RJM, "Bericht über die Lage," 3 December 1942, and Generalstaatsanwalt to RJM, "Lagebericht," 30 June 1936, both GLA/309/1205.

97. Oberlandesgerichtspräsident to RJM, "Bericht," 30 March 1944, and Gaustabsamtsleiter, "Rundschreiben," 8 July 1942, both ibid.

98. Oberlandesgerichtspräsident to RJM, "Bericht," 2 January 1945, ibid.

99. Führer, 16 March, 11 April 1933; Friedrich Walter, Schicksal, 2:182-86; Renninger had belonged to the Deutschen Vaterlandspartei of Ludwigshafen in 1917; see General-Anzeiger (Ludwigshafen), 17 December 1917, in GLA/Ruge Nachlass/69N/54.

100. Badisches Gesetz- und Verordnungsblatt, 5 April 1933, Jahrgang 1933, pp. 55-57; Führer, 8 April 1933.

101. "Niederschrift, Sitzung des Staatsministeriums vom 12. Januar 1934," GLA/233/24318; Landeskommissär Konstanz to Heinrich Raither, Neufach, Amt Überlingen, 30 August 1933, SAF/317/492; Landeskommissär Konstanz to Kreisrat Waldshut, 20 September 1933, SAF/317/495; Führer, 9 June, 30 July 1933.

102. Landeskommissär Konstanz to Kreisrat Waldshut, 20 September 1933, SAF/317/495; Führer, 3 June 1933, 19 January 1934.

103. "Niederschrift, Sitzung des Staatsministeriums vom 12. Januar 1934," GLA/233/24318.

104. For Karlsruhe and Konstanz see Führer, 9 and 6 May 1933; for Mannheim see Friedrich Walter, Schicksal, 2:191-92.

105. Führerlexikon, 1934, p. 328; Führer, 10 June 1933; Kreisleiter, Heidelberg, "Beurteilung," 25 October 1941, T-81/126/112354.

106. "Verzeichnis der Bürgermeister in Städten mit über 10,000 Einwohner im Gau Baden," 1 March 1935, and "Fragebogen für Bürgermeister," February 1935, both GLA/465d/1094; Gauamt fK to Hauptamt fK, 19 March 1938, GLA/465d/1090. Before 1933, Kehl, Ettlingen, and Schwetzingen had fewer than ten thousand people. The "Verzeichnis der Bürgermeister" lists Neinhaus as a party member. After 1945, he became president of Baden's Landtag.

107. For biographical information see Führer, 30 July, 9 October 1938, 3 and 22 June 1933; Führerlexikon, 1934, pp. 379-80, 209-210.

108. Wer ist's?, 1935, p. 800; Führerlexikon, 1934, p. 392; Führer, 18 January 1934. Kerber was a former Free Corps member. He was born in 1901 and became Kreisleiter in 1932. Rombach was born in 1897 in Offenburg. Between 1925 and 1928 he belonged to the DVFP. He became a Kreisleiter two years after joining the party in 1928.

109. See note 106 above; Führer(M), 30 November 1935; Nachrichtenblatt, 2 (15 December, 1 September 1935), pp. 87, 65; Gaupersonalamt, "Ergänzungsblatt zum Antrag auf Besoldungsfestsetzung," 1 July 1944, T-81/228/5010156.

110. This occurred in the districts of Waldkirch, Offenburg, Engen, Freiburg, Tauberbischofsheim, Lörrach, Donaueschingen, Pforzheim, Wertheim, and Emmendingen, Nachrichtenblatt, 3 (15 April, 15 May 1936), pp. 22, 29, and 4 (15 October, 1 November 1937), p. 45; Gauleitung, "Meldung," 15 June 1936, T-81/166/305396; Kreisl. Emmendingen, "Beurteilung," 13 November 1941, T-81/126/112330; Kreisl. Hans Schmidt, "Beurteilung," 8 November 1941, T-81/126/112365.

111. Führer, 24 September 1933; "Stammbuch für Hans Knab," (c. 1936), T-81/166/315425. The Gauamt of K. noted that 254 mayors had been removed in 1933/34.

112. This is based on comparison of mayoral positions listed in 1932 and again in 1936 in Badischer Geschäfts und Adresskalender, vols. 55, 59. See also Matzerath, Selbstverwaltung, p. 88.

113. Führer, 15 January, 3 February 1937, 5 January 1938.

114. Gauamt fK, Baden, to Hauptamt fK, 1 April 1937, GLA/465d/1090; Partei-Statistik, 1:256-64; Führer(M), 4 June 1935.

115. Mayor v. Bietigheim to Gauamt fK, 21 June 1937, GLA/
465d/1147; Gauamt fK, "Niederschrift," 7 February 1936, GLA/
465d/2787.

116. Gauamt fK, Gau Württemberg-Hohenzollern to Gauamt
fK, Baden, 22 January 1937, GLA/465d/1147.

117. Kreisl. Mosbach to Gauamt fK, 15 October 1938; and
Kreisl. Offenbach to Gauamt fK, 26 January 1938; and Gauamt
fK to Kreisleiter, Offenburg, 31 January 1938, all in GLA/
465d/2787.

118. Bezirksamt Kehl to MdI, Baden, 8 July 1938; and
Gauamt fK to MdI, Baden, 16 August 1938; and MdI to Bezirksamt
Kehl, 27 September 1938, all ibid.

119. Führer, 8 June 1933, 4 June, 27 February 1935; "Niederschrift über die Sitzung des Staatsministeriums vom 12. Januar
1934," GLA/233/24318.

120. Führerlexikon, 1934, p. 414; "Fragebogen," 12 June
1934, BDC/Schindler file; BDC/OPGA, Schindler folder. Schindler's business manager, Kaufmann, was born in 1902 in Walldürn,
Baden, and practiced agriculture on his father's farm. He
joined the party in 1931 and became mayor of his native town
in 1933. He became business manager of the Amt für Kommunalpolitik in January 1935. In April 1943, he fell on the Eastern
Front; Führer, 15 April 1943.

121. Führerlexikon, p. 210; Matzerath, Selbstverwaltung,
p. 194. Jäkle was born in 1897 in Emmendingen, Baden. After
the war, and a university education, he became a business
manager of an industrial firm in Breslau (and Liegnitz and
Görlitz). After returning to Baden, he was elected mayor of
his native town in 1926. In Emmendingen he also led a paramilitary organization.

122. Nachrichtenblatt, 1 (1 April 1934), p. 28, and 2
(1 June 1935), p. 44; Matzerath, Selbstverwaltung, p. 252.

123. "Tagefolge der kommunalpolitischen Schulungstagung,"
(Feb. 1937), T-81/126/112373-74; Führer, 8 January 1935.

124. Franz Kerber, "Leistungsschau Badischer Gemeinde,"
NS Gemeinde, 5 (1 November 1937), pp. 643-44; ibid., 6 (1
September 1938), p. 533; ibid., 7 (1 February 1939), p. 80.

125. Schindler to Fiehler, 2 November 1934, and AfK,
Reichsleitung to Gauamt fK, Baden, 7 November 1934, both
GLA/465d/1090; Führer, 29 March 1933.

126. Nachrichtenblatt, 1 (1 February, 15 June, 1 April
1934, 15 November 1934), pp. 11, 45, 28, 81; and 2 (1 January
1935), pp. 3-4.

127. AfK, Baden, to Hauptamt fK, 29 April 1944, "Anschrif-
tenverzeichnis der Kreisamtsleiter für Kommunalpolitik des
Gaues Baden," BDC/Diverses, Gau Baden; AfK, Kehl, to Kreisleiter
Sauerhöfer, 11 May 1939, T-81/126/112394.

128. Diehl-Thiele, Partei und Staat, pp. 154-55; Nachrichtenblatt, 1 (1 February 1934), p. 11; ibid., 3 (1 November 1936), p. 70; Die Landgemeinde, 44 (10 January 1935), pp. 18-19; ibid., 47 (25 February 1938), p. 112.

129. NS Gemeinde, 5 (15 April 1937), p. 243, and 3 (1 January 1939), p. 18; Führer, 5 August 1936; Nachrichtenblatt, 2 (1 June 1935), p. 41.

130. Gaupersonalamt Baden to Gauamt fK, 19 December 1936, and Kreisl. Buchen to Bürgermeister des Kreises, 30 December 1936, both GLA/465d/1090.

131. NS Gemeinde, 2 (15 January 1934), p. 2; Führer, 10 February 1942; BDC/Schindler file; Fiehler to Hauptpersonalamt, 4 March 1944, and Hauptamt fK to Dr. Jobst, 28 February 1942, BDC/Hüssy file.

132. Kerber, "Rundschreiben," 29 January 1937; and Kerber to Hauptamt fK, 1 April 1937; and Gauamt f. Beamte to Kommunalpolit. Abtlg., 12 March 1937, all GLA/465d/1090.

133. Knab to Gaupersonalamt, 20 April 1936, T-81/166/305404; Wagner to Röhn, 25 May 1936, T-81/166/305399; Gauamtsleiter fK to Röhn, 27 June 1936, T-81/166/305394.

134. For Himmel's file see T-81/228/5009752-55.

135. Kreisl. Donaueschingen, "Beurteilung," 20 October 1941, T-81/126/112350; Kreisl. Heidelberg, "Beurteilung," 25 October 1941, T-81/126/112356; Kreisamtsleiter AfK, Stockach, to Gauamt fK, 25 October 1941, T-81/126/112360; Kreisamtsleiter fK, Villingen, to Gauamt fK, 8 November 1941, T-81/126/112337.

136. Kreisleiter, Donaueschingen, "Politische Beurteilung," 21 October 1941, T-81/126/112351.

137. Gauamtsl. fK to Ober-Bürgermeister der Gemeinden über 3,000, 30 December 1936; Mayor of Mosbach to Gauamt fK, 27 February 1937; and Bürgermeister von Wehr to Gauamt fK, 10 March 1937, all in GLA/465d/1147; NS Gemeinde, 5 (1 January 1937), p. 21.

138. Führer (M), 2 and 3 March, 21 April, 21 March, 1935; "Rechnungsabschluss 1934 in den badischen Gemeinden," in Gemeindetag, 29 (1 December 1935), p. 779.

139. Führer, 13 March, 14 July 1935; Nachrichtenblatt, 3 (31 January 1936), and 4 (1/15 March, 15 December 1937), pp. 15, 54. For the party's pre-1933 views on municipal affairs see Führer, 3 December 1931; and Mitteilungsblatt der Nationalsozialisten, 5 (15 January 1932), pp. 46-47.

140. MdI, Baden, to Staatskanzlei, 22 May 1939, GLA/233/28090.

141. NS Gemeinde, 7 (15 July 1939), p. 428; Kerber, "Förderung der Bautätigkeit und Wahrung der Baukultur," in Der Gemeindetag, 30 (1 May 1936), pp. 318-23; see also Arthur

Schweitzer, Big Business in the Third Reich, pp. 160, 226-27.

142. AfK, Kreis Sinsheim to Gauamt fK, "Tätigkeitsbericht," 21 August 1938, T-81/175/316312-15; NS Gemeinde, 6 (1 November 1938), p. 660, and 7 (1 April 1939), p. 208.

143. Bürgermeister von Leinen to Gauamt fK, 12 March 1937, GLA/465d/1147.

144. Führer, 26 February 1940, 12 October 1942; Bracher, Machtergreifung, p. 673; Franz Neumann, Behemoth, p. 67.

145. Kreisl. Freiburg to Kerber, 12 August 1944, T-81/646/5449022; Kreisl. Sinsheim, "Stimmungsmässiger Überblick," 22 October 1944, T-81/164/302166.

146. DAF, Kreiswaltung Freiburg, "Arbeits- und Lagebericht," 28 August 1941, T-81/69/78661-69.

147. This is Diehl-Thiele's argument, Partei und Staat, p. 32. For example, in 1936 the judicial authorities noted that former Kreisleiters who became full-time mayors gave the state (judicial) authorities no further difficulties; see Oberstaatsanwalt Freiburg to Generalstaatsanwalt Karlsruhe, "Lagebericht," 19 May 1936, GLA/309/1206. Self-interest was a major driving force behind the clashes.

CHAPTER EIGHT

1. "Organisation der Gauleitung Baden," BDC/Order 199-200, Gaue. See also Wagner to Strasser, "Organisation der Gauleitung Baden," 30 December 1930 (Vertraulich), T-580/19/199.

2. Führer, 26 March 1933; "Niederschrift über die Sitzung der kommissärischen Regierung vom 27. März," GLA/233/24318.

3. Führer, 24 March, 27 April 1933.

4. Gauamtswalterschule, "Ausweis," BDC/Alfons Hafen file and Mitgliedskarte; BDC/Oskar van Raay file. Hafen was born in 1908 and van Raay in 1903.

5. Führer, 12 April, 2 June 1933.

6. Ibid., 8 August 1933; Bracher, Sauer, Schulz, Machtergreifung, p. 192.

7. Nachrichtenblatt, 1 (1 March, 1 January 1934), pp. 17, 3.

8. Führer, 11 February 1935.

9. "N.S. Gaudienst Baden," 2 March 1940, in T-81/168/307921; DAF, Kreiswaltung Freiburg, "Tätigkeitsbericht für den Monat Oktober 1943," 27 October 1943, T-81/69/78561-63; DAF, Kreiswaltung Freiburg, "Arbeits- und Lagebericht für den Monat August 1940," 6 September 1940, T-81/69/78775.

10. For general treatments of Nazi modernization see

Lebovics, Social Conservatism, p. 219; Schoenbaum, Hitler's
Social Revolution, p. xxii. In an interview in Karlsruhe in
1977, Köhler denied that he was a representative of the party's
Mittelstand wing. Although he appealed to workers and farmers,
in 1927 the Führer and police reports noted his Mittelstand
activism. It is true, however, that after 1930 he became less
identified with any socioeconomic group and instead became a
member of the inner Gau party clique.

11. Kreis. Mannheim, "Parteiamtliches Schreiben an die
Gauleitung der NSDAP in Karlsruhe vom 30. Okt. 1936," and Kreisleiter, Weinheim, to Firma Carl Freudenberg, GMBH, Weinheim
vom 13. Feb. 1936," in Hans-Joachim Fliedner, ed., Die Judenverfolgung in Mannheim, 2:171, 371.

12. Führer, 25 January 1935, 23 April 1937; Der Grossdeutsche Reichstag, 1938, pp. 196, 256. Ironically, after the
Nazi takeover the SS discovered that Engler-Füsslin's wife was
related to a Jew. Himmler allowed the Gau agrarian leader
to remain in the SS, although Engler-Füsslin's children were
never to be admitted by the SS. After the war, Himmler planned
to decide on Engler-Füsslin's future; see RFSS/Persönl. Stab
to Chef des Rasse und Siedlungshauptamtes, 6 April 1940, T-175/
49/2562932; Chef des Rasse und Siedlungshauptamtes SS to
RFSS/Persönl. Stab, 28 March 1940, T-175/23/2529043. Wagner
must have protected Engler-Füsslin since the Gau agrarian
leader still held his post in 1943.

13. Protokoll der Kabinettsitzung vom 14. März 1933, and
Niederschrift über die Sitzung der kommissarischen Regierung
vom 27. März 1933, both GLA/233/24318.

14. Führer(M), 24 April 1935; Kreispropagandaamt Emmendingen, "Erntedankfest 1936," 19 September 1936, T-81/122/
143383-84.

15. Georg Reichart, "Politische Bedeutung und Zielsetzung
der N.S. Marktordnung," in Reichart and Hans A. Schweigert,
eds., Aufbau und Durchführung der landwirtschaftlichen Marktordnung, p. 3, in SAF/317/585s. For major policy changes
affecting farmers see Farquharson, Plough and the Swastika.

16. Führer(A), 10 February 1934; "Lagebericht Gestapo
Karlsruhe," 1 January–28 February 1935, in Jörg Schadt, ed.,
Verfolgung und Widerstand unter dem Nationalsozialismus in
Baden, pp. 138–46.

17. "Besprechungen von verschiedenen Fragen der Landes-
plannung und Gründung einer Feldberggemeinde," 1 March 1939,"
T-81/172/313423; Baden, Statistisches Jahrbuch, 1938, p. 78.

18. "Niederschrift über die Sitzung des Staatsministerium,
5. Oktober 1933," (and 24 Oct. 1934), GLA/233/24318; Landesbauernschaft Baden, II to Pg. Richard Arauner (Berlin), 2

February 1934, T-580/253/57.

19. Engler-Füsslin, Landesbauernschaft Baden to Stabsamt des Reichsbauernführer, 23 November 1934, HA/49/955; Führer, 17 November 1936, 18 January 1934, 23 January 1935; Fritz Engler-Füsslin, "Badens Bauerntum im deutschen Aufbauwerk," 7:180-85.

20. Führer (M), 6 April, 26 May, 30 April 1935; "Niederschrift über die Sitzung des Staatsministeriums vom 5. Oktober 1933," GLA/233/24318.

21. MdI, Karlsruhe, to Landräte, 31 January 1939, SAF/317/585s; Führer, 27 November 1939, 2 October 1943.

22. Der Präsident des Landesarbeitsamt Südwestdeutschland to Generalkommando VAK, 5 June 1941, T-81/665/5472667-68; Gaustabsamtsleiter to Partei-Kanzlei II, B4, "Bericht vom 21. Oktober 1944," T-81/163/3022134; Kreisamt für des Landvolk, "Bericht über die Lage," 24 October 1944, T-81/37/33732.

23. Solms-Roedelheim, Die Einflüsse, p. 181; Oberstaatsanwalt Heidelberg to Generalstaatsanwalt, "Lagebericht," 19 January 1938 (and 24 May 1938), GLA/309/1208. For general and rural opposition to the regime see the very interesting letter from Hierl to Darré, 10 February 1938, HA/46/947.

24. Kreisleitung Gebweiler, "Bericht vom 30. Juni 1943," T-81/176/324393; Kreisleitung Wertheim, "Bericht vom 8. Juli 1944," T-81/126/148536; Kreisleitung Villingen; "Bericht vom 29 Juli 1943," T-81/126/148536; Kreisleitung Villingen; "Bericht vom 29 Juli 1943," T-81/176/324366. For Swabia see Edward Peterson, The Limits of Hitler's Power, pp. 410-17.

25. Engler-Füsslin to Reichsbauernführer, 28 January 1938 and Albert Roth, "Stellungnahme zur Denkschrift 'Die bevölkerungspolitische Lage im Bauerntum,'" 3 February 1939, both BDC/Reichsnährstand file; Reichsamt für das Landvolk, "Arbeitsgrundlagen für die landvolkpolitische Ernährungs und landwirtschaftliche Aufklärungsarbeit, Januar 1945," 4 December 1944, T-81/37/33738-82.

26. Plattner to Reichsleitung/Mitgliederschaft, 24 April 1941, BDC/Plattner file; Führer, 20 April, 3 May 1933.

27. Führer, 7 August, 13 September 1933; Bracher, Machtergreifung, pp. 176-86. In September 1933, a number of NSBO and DAF men were arrested in Germany and described as "Marxist Gangsters," Schoenbaum, Social Revolution, p. 8.

28. "Niederschrift über die Sitzung des Staatsministeriums vom 17. November 1933," and 24 April 1934, 21 June 1933, 8 December 1933, GLA/233/24318; Nachrichtenblatt, 2 (15 January 1935), p. 7; Führer (M), 18 April 1935.

29. Führer, 30 March, 18 August 1935; Nickles, "Einheitliche Haltung beim Arbeitseinsatz in der Arbeitsschlacht 1936," T-81/122/143453; Nickles, "Arbeitsbeschaffung und Arbeitseinsatz

im Jahre 1937," 27 February 1937, T-81/178/327384-89.

30. Führer (M), 10 January 1935; Ley, "Anordnung Nr.
29/38," 1 May 1938, T-81/69/78937-38; Gauwaltung DAF Baden
to DAF, Kreisobmann Bender, 6 February 1942, T-81/72/82130.
See also Hans-Gerd Schumann, Nationalsozialismus und Gewerk-
schaftsbewegung, p. 160.

31. DAF, Gauwaltung Baden, Prop., "Information für Redner:
Arbeit und Leistung der 'NSG Kraft durch Freude' des Gaues
Baden im Jahre 1936," T-81/72/82638-41; Gauobmann Baden to
Gauschulungsleiter, 28 January 1937, T-81/72/82614.

32. Führer, 18 April, 1 May 1935.

33. Wagner, "Begutachtungsbogen," 15 April 1935; and
Wagner to Kanzlei des Führers, 29 December 1936; and Peter
Riedner, "Betrifft Pg. Plattner," 4 February 1936; Alfred
Rudolph to Kramer, 11 May 1935, in BDC/Plattner file. Wagner
continued to support Plattner because of his early party career
despite constant mischief. In 1940 Plattner beat up his boss
in the state labor insurance office. After Wagner ordered
that Plattner be removed from all party and state leadership
positions, he still demanded that his welfare be assured in
private industry. But Plattner only got into trouble again
in private industry. As late as November 1943, Wagner helped
Plattner with funds from a special Gauleiter account; see BDC/
Plattner file.

34. Wagner to Reichsorganisationsleiter, Hauptamt NSBO,
10 December 1936, BDC/Plattner file, and BDC/Reinhold Roth
file.

35. DAF, Kreiswaltung Freiburg, "Arbeits- und Lagebericht für den Monat Januar 1941," (and July 1941, September
1943), T-81/69/78735, 78672, 78564; Leiter des Arbeitsamt
Freiburg, "Lagebericht für die Monate Juni–Juli, 1943," T-81/
646/5449006.

36. Arbeitskammer Baden, Gauwaltung DAF, Der dritte
Leistungskampf der Deutschen Betriebe im Gau Baden: Erste
Kriegsleistungskampf, p. 5; DAF Baden, Gauwaltung, Der vierte
Leistungskampf der Deutschen Betriebe im Gau Baden: Zweiter
Kriegsleistungskampf 1940/41, pp. 26, 78, 98, 103.

37. Gauwaltung Baden, Abtl. Schulung, "Arbeitsanweisung
der Schulungsabteilung der DAF," 5 May 1941, T-81/72/82124;
Gauobmann, "Rundschreiben," 5 April 1944, T-81/69/78831;
Kreisobmann Karlsruhe to Betriebsobmänner der Werkscharbe-
triebe, 21 April 1942, T-81/72/82148.

38. DAF, Kreiswaltung Freiburg, "Arbeits- und Lagebericht
fd Monat März, 1941," 20 March 1941, T-81/69/78515; "Schulungs-
arbeit der DAF im Kreis Freiburg," T-81/65/74178; DAF Baden,
Schulung to Kreisobmänner, 12 October 1942, T-81/72/82119.

39. DAF Freiburg, "Arbeits- und Lagebericht für den Monat Oktober 1941," 29 October 1941, T-81/69/78640/43.

40. Kreisobmann Freiburg, "Stimmungs- und Tätigkeitsbericht des Kreises Freiburg für den Monat September," 29 September 1942, T-81/69/78598-602; Schoenbaum, Social Revolution, p. 160; Claude William Guillebaud, The Social Policy of Nazi Germany, pp. 59-60; Schweitzer, Big Business, pp. 361-69.

41. Führer, 14 and 22 February 1943; 11/12 November 1944; Kreisleitung Pforzheim, "Stimmungsmässiger Überblick," 21 October 1944, and Kreisleitung Freiburg, "Stimmungsmässiger Überblick über die Gesamtpolitische Lage," 14 November 1944, both T-81/164/302146-55; Kreisleitung Überlingen, "Stimmungsmässiger Überblick," 24 July 1944, T-81/126/148528.

42. James K. Pollock, The Government of Greater Germany, p. 68; Gustav Ruck to Amtsleiter der NS Studentenkampfhilfe, Gau Baden, 26 November 1937, T-81/89/102594.

43. Stellv. Kreisführer, NSDStB Karlsruhe to Bundesleiterin der ANSt., Gisela Brettschneider, 21 June 1933, T-81/244/5031942; see also Ellen Semmelroth and Renate von Stieda, eds., NS Frauenbuch (1934).

44. This information is based on the BDC files of district NSF leaders of Baden and selected Gau NSF leaders. These women were born between 1874 and 1904: Scholtz-Klink, Adeline Winter, Luise Drös, Elsa von Baltz, Erika Döther, Elisabeth Poff, Anna Perino, Lisa Moll, Romana Bäckert, Margarete Lanz, Helene Joos, Elsa Homberg, Lilli Haas. For example, the wife of the NSBO leader, and later Kreisleiter of Mannheim in 1931, was also the NSF leader of Mannheim; see Frau E. Heinle, Pforzheim to Frau Dr. Roth, 24 November 1931, IfZ/MA 454/71/170. As early as 1928, "respectable" members of the middle class who were married, like Frau Bahnhofinspektor Klein of Heidelberg and Frau Dr. Hildebrand of Karlsruhe, were leaders of Baden NSF locals; Führer, 2 June, 29 September 1928.

45. BDC/Scholtz-Klink Karte; "Mein Lebenslauf," BDC/ Elsa von Baltz file. Von Baltz was born in 1882 in Luga near St. Petersburg and grew up in Dorpat. She married in 1903, and in 1918 she experienced the Russian Revolution in the Baltic area before she moved to Baden.

46. Reichsminister des Innern to Bad. Staatsministerium, 13 May 1933, and Gaufrauenschaftsl. Gertrud Scholtz-Klink to BVfV, 27 April 1933, both GLA/233/26372.

47. MdI, Baden, to Staatskanzlei Karlsruhe, 5 August 1933, GLA/233/26372; Führer, 20 June 1934; Kreisleiter reports to Hauptorganisationsamt, July 1936, HA/10/240, Scholtz-Klink, ed., Die Frau im Dritten Reich, pp. 29-30.

48. Niederschrift über die Sitzung des Staatsministeriums

vom 3. Oktober 1934, GLA/233/24318; Führer, 3 March 1933.
Kreisleiter Rombach of Offenburg declared that breeding and
home economics were the tasks of women, Führer, 21 March 1940.
    49. Nachrichtenblatt, 1 (15 October 1934), p. 74, and 2
(15 July 1935), p. 54; Führer, 25 July 1933; Gauorganisationsleiter, "Rundschreiben," 27 June 1935, T-81/172/312933. ·
    50. Bormann, "Rundschreiben Nr. 128/37," 6 October 1937,
BDC/Scholtz-Klink file. Scholtz-Klink was arrested in March
1948 near Tübingen and received an eighteen-month prison term;
see New York Times, 2 and 24 March, 19 November 1948. For further
information see Jill Stephenson, Women in Nazi Society, pp. 194-95.
    51. Quoted in Schoenbaum, Social Revolution, p. 182. Nazi
women professionals also demanded equal opportunities; see
Ingeborg Lorentzen, "Die Frau in der Rechtspflege," pp. 417-24.
    52. Führer (L), 7 July 1936; Gaustabsamtsleiter, "Rund-
schreiben Nr. 78/44," 6 May 1944, T-81/117/137153; "N.S. Gaudienst Baden," 16 January 1940, in T-81/168/307711.
    53. "N.S. Gaudienst Baden," 20 January 1940, in T-81/168/
307778.
    54. Führer, 17 April 1940.
    55. Kreisleitung Lahr, "Stimmungsbericht," 31 July 1944,
T-81/173/313537; DAF, Kreiswaltung Freiburg, "Bericht," 25
August 1943, T-81/69/78567; DAF, Kreiswaltung Freiburg, "Tätigkeitsbericht," 27 October 1943, T-81/69/78561-63. See also
the evaluation of German war propaganda directed toward women,
Leila J. Rupp, Mobilizing Women for War, pp. 171-72.
    56. Nachrichtenblatt, 2 (15 June, 1 October 1935), pp.
4, 72; Führer, 1 January 1936. Kemper was born in 1906 in
Pyritz, Pomerania. He had joined a youth movement at age ten,
and in 1922 he belonged to the group "Adler und Falken." In
Weinheim in 1925, he led a group of boys between the ages of
ten and fourteen. He became Gau Hitler Youth leader in January 1932; see Führer, 30 March 1935; Schirach, Pioniere, pp.
127-28.
    57. Otto Mayer, Das Badische Schulwesen, p. 29. Karl
Gärtner, "Zum Geleit," Die badische Schule, 1, Folge 1 (1934),
p. 1; Badisches Gesetz- und Verordnungs-Blatt, 30 January 1934,
p. 25.
    58. Gestapo Offenburg to Staatspolizeileitstelle Karls-
ruhe, 4 November 1939, and Minister des KuU, "Aktenvermerk,"
6 December 1939, both GLA/235/35688.
    59. Baden, Statistisches Jahrbuch, 1938, p. 322; Der
Beauftragte für die Adolf Hitler Schulen to Gauschulungsamt
Baden, 3 June 1943, T-81/64/72405. See also Dietrich Orlow,
"Die Adolf-Hitler-Schulen," p. 272.
    60. DAF, Kreiswaltung Freiburg, "Arbeits- und Lagebericht,"

31 July 1941, T-81/69/78672-77; DAF, Kreiswaltung Freiburg,
"Arbeits- und Lagebericht," 25 October 1940, T-81/69/78761.
For more active resistance in Bruchsal see Arno Klönne, Gegen
den Strom.

61. Albrecht Goetz von Olenhusen, "Die nationalsozialistische Rassenpolitik und die jüdischen Studenten an der
Universität Freiburg," p. 146; Arye Carmon, "The Impact of
the Nazi Racial Decrees on the University of Heidelberg,"
pp. 134-41, 152-55, 162; Franz Heidelberger, "Leo Wohlleb als
Beamter im Badischen Kultusministerium," pp. 27-30.

62. Heidelberger Neueste Nachrichten, and Heidelberger
Tageblatt, 30 September 1933; and Andreas to Groh, 21 June
1934, both in GLA/69N/Andreas file/box 759; Alemanne, 3 May
1933, in Guido Schneeberger, ed., Nachlese zu Heidegger, p. 2.

63. Baden, Statistisches Jahrbuch, 1938, pp. 332-38.

64. See note 61 above. By June 1940, the University of
Heidelberg had also revoked 42 Ph.D.s earned by Jewish students
between 1903 and 1936.

65. NSDStB, Kreis VI, to Reichsleitung NSDStB, 28 December
1933, T-81/240/5026028.

66. Stellv. Kreisleiter, NSDStB Karlsruhe to Fachschul-
gruppenführer Mannheim, Erich Haberkorn, 28 November 1933,
T-81/244/5031427.

67. See the correspondence of NSDStB, Kreis VI, Presse
und Propaganda between June 1933 and February 1934, in T-81/
240/5026128-419.

68. Ley, "Anordnung," 20 April 1933, BDC/Stäbel file;
Führer, 29 November 1930; Freiburger Studentenzeitung, 16
May 1933, in Schneeberger, ed., Nachlese zu Heidegger, pp.
38-40; Schirach, Pioniere, pp. 212-14.

69. Stellv. Kreisführer NSDStB, Karlsruhe to SA-Gruppe
Südwest, 19 May 1933, T-81/244/5031991; Gerhard Müller, Die
Wissenschaftslehre Ernst Kriecks, pp. 116-18; Michael Kater,
Studentenschaft und Rechtsradikalismus in Deutschland 1918-
1933, p. 17. According to Müller, the leaders of the NS Stu-
dent Organization ended up in the SS.

70. "Kurzer Bericht über die Verbundenheitskundgebung
zwischen Arbeiter und Student am 5. Nov. 1933 in der Karlsruher Festhalle," T-81/244/5031555; Gerhard Krüger, "Verpflichtung der Studentenschaft zum Sozialismus," quoted in
George L. Mosse, ed., Nazi Culture, pp. 304-308.

71. Stellv. Kreisführer, NSDStB Karlsruhe to Fachschule
Pforzheim, 1 November 1933, T-81/244/5031591; Stellv. Kreisführer to Arbeitsgeberverband für Pforzheim und Umgebung,
16 August 1933, T-81/244/5031789; SA Brigadenführer Ziegler,
"Dienstleistungszeugnis" (Fred Himmel), 1 September 1937,

T-81/228/5009757.

72. Reichsstudentenbundführer, "Rundschreiben," 6 November 1936, T-81/238/5023099; Ursula Dibner, "The History of the National Socialist German Student League," pp. 173-79, 236-37; Steinberg (Sabers and Brown Shirts, p. 214) argues, "The evidence that the student shakeup had anything to do with the SA purge is merely circumstantial." There is no doubt, however, that the SA purge changed the students' close relationship with the SA.

73. Gaustudentenführung, Baden, Hauptstelle für poli. Erziehung, Abtlg. Schulung, "Anordnung W.S. 1/36," 8 December 1936, T-81/238/5023532.

74. Gaustudentenbundführung Baden, Schulung, "Ausgestaltung der Schulung," 10 May 1935, T-81/238/5023432; Gaustudentenbundführer Baden to komm. Studentenbundsgruppenführer Poling, Karlsruhe, 17 September 1936, T-81/238/5023331; Gauleiter, Baden, "Anordnung," 5 June 1944, T-81/124/145931.

75. H. Grimm to Lammers, 5 March 1935, T-81/79/91992; Benno Müller, "Tatsachenbericht," 3 June 1935, T-81/80/92035.

76. M. Otto (Albingia Corps) to Hans Lammers, 8 November 1933, T-81/79/91780-82.

77. Lammers to E. Phillippie, 8 November 1934, T-81/79/91922-23; Henry Albert Phillipps, Germany Today and Tomorrow, p. 97; Generalstaatsanwalt Karlsruhe to Reichsjustizminister, "Lagebericht," 18 June 1936, GLA/309/1204; see also Steinberg, Sabers and Brown Shirts, pp. 154-72.

78. Lammers to Helmuth Grimm, August 1933, T-81/79/91743; Grimm to Lammers, 16 August 1933, T-81/79/91748; Lammers to Grimm, 24 August 1933, T-81/79/91750.

79. Grimm to Lammers, 16 August 1933, T-81/79/91751; Grimm to Lammers, 3 February 1934, T-81/79/91839; Ulrich M. Otto to Lammers, 4 August 1933, T-81/79/91753-55; Grimm to Lammers, 13 December 1933, T-81/79/91818-19.

80. Stellv. Kreisführer, NSDStB, Kreis VI to Führer der Hochschulgruppe Freiburg, 5 July 1933, T-81/244/5031882.

81. Gaustudentenführung Baden, Amt NS Altherrenbund, "Rundschreiben," 28 May 1938, T-81/89/102452.

82. Gustav Ruck to NS Studentenkampfhilfe, Baden, 26 November 1937, T-81/89/102594; NS Altherrenbund, Bühl, to Kreisleiter Bühl, 23 June 1939, T-81/89/102484.

83. Reichsstudentenführung, Amt NS Altherrenbund to Stellv. Führer der Altherrenschaft "Weinbrenner," Karlsruhe, 18 October 1943, T-81/89/102484; R. Michaelis to Gaustudentenführer, 27 October 1942, T-81/90/102679.

84. Kreisleiter, Freiburg, "Stimmungsmässiger Überblick," 31 July 1944, T-81/173/313533; Statistisches Jahrbuch, 1938,

p. 332; Reichsstudentenführer to Wagner, 8 November 1943,
T-81/120/141946; Reichsstudentenführer to Wagner, 6 May 1944,
T-81/75/86713.

85. Kreisl. Heidelberg, "Bericht vom 7 April 1943 (and
12 Juni 1943)," T-81/165/304239, 304272; Kreisleiter Freiburg,
"Stimmungsmässiger Überblick," 31 July 1944, T-81/173/313533;
DAF Kreiswaltung Freiburg, "Tätigkeitsbericht für den Monat
Juli 1944 der Kreise Freiburg, Emmendingen und Neustadt,"
25 July 1944, T-81/69/78517-18.

86. Neumann, Behemoth, p. 366; Dahrendorf, Society and
Democracy, pp. 381, 396; Schoenbaum, Hitler's Social Revolution, p. 285.

87. The primacy of politics is also argued by T. W. Mason,
"The Primacy of Politics and Economics in National Socialist
Germany," p. 197.

88. Hilgenfeldt, "Rundschreiben," 25 April 1940, T-81/
37/34435; "Bericht über die Betreuung der Umquartierten durch
die N.S. Frauenschaft" (sent by the Gaupropagandaamt to the
head of the NSV of Baden, 18 January 1944), T-81/86/97957.

89. See also Richard Zneimer, "The Nazis and the Professors," pp. 147-56. The impact of the war can be seen in the
fact that in 1942, 40 percent of all farms in Baden were managed by women, Pirsch, "Niederschrift über die Sitzung des
Verbraucherausschusses beim Landesernährungsamt vom 21. Mai
1942 im kleinen Sitzungssaal des Dienstgebäutes des Landes-
ernährungsamtes Karlsruhe," n.d., T-81/122/143965.

CHAPTER NINE

1. Führer, 2 July 1934; Führer (L), 29 and 30 August
1935.

2. Wagner to Major a.D. Hildebrand, 30 March 1933, GLA/
233/24283; Karlsruher Zeitung, 12 May 1933.

3. Paul Schmitthenner to Präsident des Landtages, 17
July 1933, GLA/231/3365; Reichsschatzmeister to Gauleitung
Magdeburg-Anhalt, 25 July 1933, BDC/Wagner file; Bad. Staats-
kanzlei to MdI, 3 June 1933, GLA/233/28388.

4. Niederschrift über die Sitzung des Staatsministeriums
vom 21. Juni 1933, GLA/233/24318. Schmitthenner was present
at this meeting and agreed that the DNVP in no way supported
this subversive trend.

5. "Lagebericht des Gestapo Karlsruhe 1. bis 31. Juli
1935," July/August 1935, in Schadt, ed., Lageberichte, pp.
151-57.

6. "Lagebericht des Gestapo Karlsruhe, 19. Jan. bis 3.

Feb. 1934," 3 February 1934; and "Lagebericht, Gestapo Karls-
ruhe, 1. Jan. bis 28. Feb., 1935," February/March 1935; and
"Lagebericht, Gestapo Karlsruhe," 4 October 1934, all in
Schadt, ed., Lageberichte, pp. 62-67, 138-46, 120.
    7. Richard Wenzl, ed., Stahlhelm-Führer, pp. 3-8, 18.
    8. Führer (L), 12 June, 12 July 1935; Führer (M), 22
November 1935. "Lagebericht, Gestapo Karlsruhe, 1-30 November
1935," in Schadt, ed., Lageberichte, pp. 163-68. In 1938
Wenzl was again arrested by the Gestapo and taken to an "un-
known place," see Generalstaatsanwalt to RJM, "Zweimonatliche
Lagebericht," 13 September 1938, GLA/309/1204.
    9. Gaustabsamtsleiter Baden to Partei-Kanzlei II, B4,
"Stimmungsmässiger Überblick," 5 August 1944, T-81/173/313529;
Kreisleiter, Donaueschingen, "Allgemeine politische Lage,"
12 August 1944, T-81/175/316368; Führer, 28 July 1944.
    10. Führer, 6 and 27 August 1933; Führer (A), 26 February
1935; Führer, 1 March 1935; Führer (L), 13 June 1936; Generalstaatsanwalt to RJM, "Zweimonatliche Lagebericht," 30 June
1936, GLA/309/1204. See also Institut für Marxismus-Leninismus
beim Zentralkomitee der S.E.D., ed., Deutsche Widerstands-
kämpfer, 1933-1945, 2 vols.
    11. "Denunziation: Freiburg 18 Juni 1941," in Justiz und
N.S. Verbrechen, 1 (1969), 682-85; DAF, Kreiswaltung Freiburg,
"Bericht für den Monat Februar des Kreise Freiburg, Emmendingen und Neustadt," 28 February 1944, T-81/69/78543-46;
"Denunziationsschreiben von Büdenbender an die Gestapo,"
1943, in Fritz Salms, Im Schatten des Henkers, pp. 283-85.
    12. Generalstaatsanwalt, Karlsruhe, to RJM, "Zweimonat-
liche Lagebericht," 3 December 1935 (and 30 January, 18 June,
20 December 1936, 18 October 1937), GLA/309/1204; Gestapo
Karlsruhe, "Lagebericht über die illegale marxistische und
kommunistische Bewegung für das Jahr 1937," January 1938, in
Max Oppenheimer, Der Fall Vorbote, pp. 155-57. See also Erich
Matthias, "Resistance to National Socialism," pp. 118-27.
    13. DAF, Kreiswaltung Freiburg, "Arbeits- und Lagebericht,"
29 October 1941, T-81/69/78640-42; DAF, Kreiswaltung Freiburg,
"Tätigkeitsbericht," 20 February 1942, T-81/69/78613. After
the Nazi-Soviet Pact, many Communists were released from prison
in late 1939, increasing the potential for resistance after
June 1941; see Horst Dühnke, Die KPD von 1933 bis 1945, pp.
457-58.
    14. Oppenheimer, Fall Vorbote, pp. 9, 26-27, 30-43, 70-
80; Salms, Im Schatten des Henkers, pp. 195-96.
    15. Schenk to Buch, and Wagner to Buch, 17 May 1932; and
Buch to Schenk, 30 May 1932, all BDC/OPG file on Pfarrer Schenk.
Two good articles on the Baden churches are: Hugo Ott, "Mög-

lichkeiten und Formen kirchlichen Widerstands gegen das Dritte Reich," pp. 312-33; and Klaus Scholder, "Baden im Kirchenkampf des Dritten Reiches," pp. 223-41.

16. Evangelischer Oberkirchenrat to Bad. Staatspräsidenten, 30 April 1932, GLA/233/27919; MdI, Baden, to Staatsministerium, 15 June 1932, GLA/233/27919; "Auszug aus der Niederschrift über die Sitzung des Staatsministerium vom 2. August 1932," GLA/233/27914.

17. Opitz, Christlich Soziale Volksdienst, pp. 192-93; Heidelberger Neueste Nachrichten, 22 April 1933; Landeskirchliche Blätter, 23 April 1933, in GLA/235/12809. For press reports of these developments see, Volksstimme, 20 March 1931; Neue Badische Landeszeitung, 20 March 1931; Badische Presse, 6 October 1932; Führer, 4 May 1933. See also Heinzelmann, Evangelische Kirche, p. 78.

18. "Lebenslauf," BDC/Heinrich Sauerhöfer file; see also Hermann Rückleben, "Kirchliche Zentralbehörden in Baden, 1771-1958," pp. 654-61; and Kurt Meier, Die deutschen Christen, pp. 162-64.

19. Ortsgruppenleiter NSDAP, Villingen, to Evangl. Kirchengemeinderates Villingen, 17 May 1933; and Gaukampfbundführer Mannschott to Evangelische Stiftungsverwaltung, 11 May 1933; and Evangelischer Kirchenrat to Minister des Kultus, 10 June 1933, all GLA/235/12805; see also the correspondence between the MdI, Baden, and the Landesbischof Baden, and Evangelische Oberkirchenrat and between Wacker and the Evangelische Oberkirchenrat in July 1933, in GLA/235/12809.

20. Landesbischof Baden to MdK, 18 September 1933, GLA/235/12809; NS local Hoffenheim to Kemper, 26 January 1934, GLA/377/5407.

21. Generalstaatsanwalt, "Lagebericht," 27 March 1937, GLA/309/1204; MdK, Baden, to Gröber, 10 October 1939, GLA/235/12790; MdK to Gestapo Karlsruhe, 25 July 1940, GLA/235/12748; Vorsitzende der Finanzabtl., Evangelischer Oberkirchenrat to Bad. Staatskanzlei, 31 January 1941, GLA/233/25617; Generalstaatsanwalt to RJM, 30 June 1936, GLA/309/1204.

22. Kuno Brombacher to Gröber, 19 September 1934, in Stasiewski, ed., Akten Deutscher Bischöfe, 2:7.

23. Gröber to Pacelli, 18 March 1933, in Bernhard Stasiewski, ed., Akten Deutscher Bischöfe, 1:9-10; "Entwurf Gröbers zur Kundgebung," 3 November 1933, in ibid., 1:436; Gröber to Leiber, July 1933, in Ludwig Volk, ed., Kirchliche Akten, pp. 158-59; Minister des Kultus, Abt. Referent f. kath. Kultus to Gauleitung, 8 September 1933, GLA/235/12754; Führer, 28 April, 24 August 1933. Gröber was born in 1872 in Messkirch, Baden, and became Archbishop of Freiburg on 21

May 1932.

24. Matthias, "Resistance to National Socialism," p. 122.

25. Kreisleiter, Donaueschingen to Wacker, 13 May 1933; and Erzbischöfliches Ordinariat Freiburg to Wacker, 10 June 1933; and Wacker to Gauleitung, 10 August 1933; and Kramer to Generalstaatsanwalt, 16 February 1934, all GLA/235/12809.

26. Gröber to Pacelli, 18 March 1933, in Stasiewski, ed., Akten, 1:9-10; Tagblatt vom Oberrhein, 13 and 14 March 1934, in GLA/235/12805.

27. "Lagebericht des Gestapo Karlsruhe, 19. Jan. bis 3. Feb. 1934 (and 3. bis 17. März)," in Schadt, ed., Lageberichte, pp. 62-67, 80-86.

28. Hakenkreuzbanner, 24 June 1934; Führer, 3 July 1934.

29. Wagner to Wacker, 20 September 1935, and Wacker to Reichsstatthalter, 20 September 1935, both GLA/235/12789. This is only part of a voluminous correspondence on this issue.

30. MdI, Baden, to Bezirksämter, Polizei und Gestapo, 12 February 1926, SAF/317/1257f; MdK to MdI, Baden, 18 July 1934, GLA/235/12809; Wacker to Kreis u. Stadtschulämter, 25 November 1940, GLA/235/12754; Staatsanwaltschaft, Landgericht Waldshut to RJM (and Wacker), 30 January 1936, GLA/235/12789.

31. Führer (L), 8 June, 3 August 1935; Führer (A), 30 August 1935. Some of the party speakers listed were: Wacker, Pflaumer, Neuscheler, Plattner, Kerber, Schuppel, Roth, and Engler-Füsslin.

32. Berckmüller, Gestapo Karlsruhe to MdK, 18 September 1935, GLA/235/12789; Pflaumer to Wagner, 13 September 1938, GLA/235/12754; Führer (M), 24 March, 12 April 1935; Führer (A), 23 March, 30 August 1935.

33. Gestapo Karlsruhe to MdI, Baden, 9 August 1934, GLA/235/12809; Gaupropagandaleitung, Amt f. kulturellen Frieden, to MdK, GLA/235/19439; Erzbischöfliches Ordinariat to MdK, 27 March 1934, GLA/235/12809; Führer (A), 6 and 22 June 1934, 14 July 1935; Führer (L), 14 June, 24 July 1935.

34. "Arbeitstagung mit den Kreis und Stadtschulräten am 25. und 26. Juni 1935, im Unterrichtsm. Karlsruhe," GLA/235/12789.

35. Erzbischöfliche Ordinariat to Kemper, 14 June 1935, GLA/235/12809; Gendarmeriebezirk N'bischofsheim to Bezirksamt Sinsheim, 12 January 1937, GLA/309/1204.

36. Erzbischöflicher Ordinariat to MdK, 2 April 1938, GLA/235/12789; Nachrichtenblatt der Gauwaltung Baden des N.S. Lehrerbundes, 1 (11 June 1937), in GLA/497/183.

37. Wagner to Gröber, 11 October 1935; and MdI to MdK, 20 January 1936; and Erzbischof, Freiburg to MdK, 11 February 1936; and Wagner to Wacker, 3 March 1936, all GLA/235/12789;

Oberstaatsanwalt Mosbach to Generalstaatsanwalt, 18 May 1936, GLA/309/1206; "Auszug aus dem Amtsblatt für die Erzdiozene Freiburg i. Br.," 24 March 1936, GLA/235/12789; Führer, 4 April 1936.

38. Generalstaatsanwalt Karlsruhe, "Lagebericht," 30 October 1936, in Schadt, ed., Lageberichte, pp. 240-44; Generalstaatsanwalt to RJM, "Lagebericht," 30 June 1936, GLA/309/1204.

39. Der Vorstand der Gefängnisse Freiburg, "Zweimonatbericht," 24 November 1937, GLA/309/1211; Generalvikar Rösch to Wagner, 31 August 1938, and Wagner to MdK, Baden, 8 October 1938, both GLA/235/12805.

40. Stellv. Gauleiter, "Rundschreiben," 29 March 1939, T-81/119/140366; Gaustabsamtsleiter, "Rundschreiben," 1 April 1943, T-81/127/149800.

41. See the correspondence between Gröber and MdK in September and October 1939, in GLA/235/12791 and 12792; and MdK to Gröber, 1 November 1939, and Wacker to Rosenberg, 9 November 1939, both GLA/235/12790. For Wacker's views about the churches see Scholder, "Baden im Kirchenkampf," pp. 237-40.

42. Gröber to MdK, 22 July 1940; and MdK, "Aktenvermerk," 8 August 1940; and MdK to Gröber, 14 August 1940, all GLA/235/12790; MdK to Gröber, 24 November 1941; and MdI to Gröber, 9 February 1942; and Gröber to Ministerium für die kirchlichen Angelegenheiten, Berlin, 6 March 1943, all GLA/235/12789.

43. Kreisleitung, Säckingen, to Gauschulungsamt, 23 November 1943, T-81/1/11077; Kreisleiter, Heidelberg, "Bericht vom 6. Januar 1943," T-81/176/324267; Kreisleitung Villingen, "Bericht," 23 June 1943, T-81/165/304213. See also John S. Steward, ed., Sieg des Glaubens. He presents not only Gestapo reports but also party reports on confessional activities. Other reports by the party may be found in T-81/rolls 1, 126, 165, 173, and 176.

44. Kreisleitung Wolfach, "Bericht," 7 October 1943, T-81/1/11073; Kreisl. Wertheim, "Bericht," 7 October 1943, T-81/1/11089; Kreisl. Donaueschingen, "Bericht," 29 January 1944, T-81/175/316325; Kreisl. Mannheim, "Bericht," 19 June 1943, T-81/165/304217; Kreisl. Heidelberg, "Bericht," 15 September 1943, T-81/1/11103.

45. Kreisl. Villingen, "Bericht," 23 June 1943, T-81/165/304213; Kreisl. Neustadt, "Bericht," February 1943, T-81/176/324216.

46. Kreisl. Offenburg, "Bericht," 19 August 1944, T-81/126/148508; Kreisl. Wertheim, "Bericht," 5 June 1943, T-81/165/304245; Kreisleiter Fritsch, Freiburg, to Gaugeschäfts-

führer, 29 October 1940, T-81/126/148705; Kreispersonalamt
Freiburg to Gaupersonalamt, 3 March 1944, T-81/65/74034; H.
Maier to Wagner, 15 October 1942, T-81/126/148628.

47. Generalstaatsanwalt to RJM, "Zweimonatlicher Lagebericht," 28 August 1940, GLA/309/1205; "N.S. Gewaltverbrechen
in Lagern: Karlsruhe, Juni 1940-März 1945," in Justiz und NS
Verbrechen, 9 (1972), pp. 237-42; Arno Klönne, Gegen den Strom,
pp. 83-85. A series of case histories of murdered priests is
provided in August Kast, Die Badischen Martyrerpriester; see
also "Verbrechen der Endphase: Münstertal, Baden, April 15-
April 22, 1945," in Justiz und NS Verbrechen, 2.

48. See the Kreisleiter reports in 1942 and 1943 in T-81/
176/324190-328 and T-81/165/304216. They include reports from
the districts of Freiburg, Mosbach, Wertheim, Wolfach, and
Neustadt that are of interest.

49. Nachrichtenblatt, 2 (1/15 August 1938), p. 35; Kreisl.
Sinsheim, "Begutachtungsbogen," 5 July 1939, T-81/228/5010127;
Kreisleiter, Mosbach, "Kirchenaustrittbewegung," 10 December
1942, T-81/176/324318; Kreisobmann DAF, Freiburg, to Kreisschulungsamt, 9 August 1944, T-81/65/73982. Between 1933 and
1937, 11,133 Catholics and 10,628 Protestants withdrew from
the churches in Baden. After 1935, Protestant withdrawals
continued to increase while Catholic withdrawals declined
slightly in 1937; Gauschulungsamt Baden, "Wissenswertes: 16.
Sammlung," 25 July 1938, T-81/23/20597-99.

50. Amt f. Beamte, Emmendingen, "Begutachtungsbogen"
(Josef Volk), 14 December 1942, T-81/228/5010990.

51. Wieck, Christliche und Freie Demokraten, p. 104.

52. Gaustabsamtsleiter to Partei-Kanzlei, IIB4, "Aktivi-
tät der Konfessionen," 5 August 1944, T-81/173/313541; Kreisl.
Neustadt, "Bericht, Dezember 9-23, 1943," T-81/1/11066;
Kreisl. Sinsheim, "Bericht," 20 January 1943, T-81/176/324256;
Kreisl. Sinsheim, "Bericht," 8 December 1943, T-81/1/11069.

53. Hermann Mölzer to Wagner, 22 February 1942, T-81/
126/148772; Gaugeschäftsführer to Mölzer, 17 March 1942, T-81/
126/148771; Kreisl. Sinsheim, "Bericht," 30 December 1942,
T-81/176/324293; Kreisl. Wertheim, "Bericht," 24 November
1942, T-81/176/324346.

54. For Wagner's speech see Steward, Sieg des Glaubens,
p. 13; and John S. Conway, The Nazi Persecution of the
Churches, 1933-1945, pp. 256-58. The Nazis emulated many
of the procedures of the churches. For example, Baden Nazis'
"Feierstätte" were "eingeweiht", see Richard Volderauer,
"Gau Baden baut auf," p. 268.

55. "Heil und Pflegeanstalten in Baden, Februar 1940-
Juli 1941," in Justiz und NS Verbrechen, 6 (1971), pp. 479-91;

see also Bracher, The German Dictatorship, pp. 388-89; and
Conway, Nazi Persecution of the Churches, p. 337.

56. C. V. Zeitung, 2 February 1933.

57. Hugo Marx, Was wird werden, pp. 7, 15, 21. For his
flight from Baden in March 1933, see Hugo Marx, Die Flucht.

58. Israelitische Gemeindeblatt, Mannheim, 19 October, 23
November 1932, 24 January, 21 February 1933.

59. Ibid., 14 March, 4 April 1933; Dr. Moses, "In den
Tagen der Zählung," ibid., 16 May 1933. Owing to increased
interest, the paper began to appear bimonthly in February
1934.

60. Ibid., 22 June 1933; Nathan Stein, "Oberrat der Israeliten Badens 1922-1937," p. 188.

61. Oberstaatsanwalt beim Landgericht Mosbach, "Zweimonatlicher Lagebericht," 18 January 1936, GLA/309/1206.

62. Führer, 18 March 1933, 23 January 1936, 3 June 1933;
Erlass des Badischen Minister des Kultus und Unterrichts-
Staatskommissar," 6 April 1933, in Sauer, ed., Dokumente,
1:119; Hundsnurscher and Taddey, Die Jüdischen Gemeinden,
p. 24; "Erlass des Badischen M.d.K. an den Senat der Universität Freiburg," 13 April 1933, in Sauer, ed., Dokumente,
1:122.

63. Führer (M), 12 April 1938; Generalstaatsanwalt Karlsruhe to RJM, "Zweimonatliche Lagebericht," 28 August 1940,
GLA/309/1205; NS Kurier, 5 March 1934, in Sauer, ed., Dokumente, 1:20-21.

64. Direktor der Gefangenanstalten in Freiburg i. Br. to
Generalstaatsanwalt Brettle, "Zeimonatsbericht," 22 May 1937,
GLA/309/1211.

65. Generalstaatsanwalt Karlsruhe to RJM, "Lagebericht,"
18 June 1936, GLA/309/1204.

66. Führer, 14 and 31 March, 1 April 1933.

67. For the firm of Otto Oppenheimer in Bruchsal see
Leo Baeck Archives, Otto Oppenheimer file, box 2; for another
case in Bruchsal involving Raphael Bär, see Führer, 5 November 1937. Between March and November 1938, seventy-five
Jewish firms were "Aryanized" in Baden and Württemberg; see
Helmut Genschel, Die Verdrängung der Juden aus der Wirtschaft
im Dritten Reich, p. 174.

68. Israelitisches Gemeindeblatt, Mannheim, 4 March 1936;
Paul Sauer, Die Schicksale der Jüdischen Bürger, pp. 84-88.

69. Israelitisches Gemeindeblatt, Mannheim, 2 October
1935, 10 March 1938.

70. "Lagebericht, Gestapo Karlsruhe, 1-29. Februar, 1936,"
in Schadt, ed., Lageberichte, pp. 183-86; "Niederschrift über
die Sitzung des Staatsministeriums vom 21. Januar 1935," GLA/
233/24318.

71. Jacob Piccard, "Erinnerungen eigenen Lebens," in Leo Baeck Archives P-307.

72. Nachrichtenblatt, 1 (1 April, 1 July 1934), pp. 38, 50; ibid., 2 (1 October 1935), p. 72; Mauch, "Rundschreiben," 20 June 1935, in Sauer, ed., Dokumente, 1:176-78; "Erlass des Gestapo Karlsruhe an die Geheime Staatspolizeistellen in Baden," 13 August 1935, in Sauer, ed., Dokumente, 1:22.

73. Führer (M), 26 February 1935; Konstanzer Zeitung, 7 June 1933, in IfZ/MA 803/150; see also Ingeborg Görler, ed., So sahen sie Mannheim, pp. 182-83.

74. Landesgeschäftsstelle Baden, Reichsverband Deutsche Bühne, "Bericht über Badische Bühnenverhältnisse," 10 March 1934, IfZ/MA 803/150; Kerber to NS Kulturgemeinde Freiburg, 4 September 1935, IfZ/MA 803/89-90.

75. "Erlass des Badischen M.d.I. an das Bezirksamt Buchen," 30 November 1936, in Sauer, ed., Dokumente, 2:105; "Erlass des Badischen M.d.I. an den Oberrat der Israeliten," 10 March 1937, in ibid., 2:107; Kreisleitung Buchen to Bezirksamt Buchen, 3 December 1936, and Kreisleitung Buchen to mayor of Sennfeld, 14 January 1937, in ibid., 2:106.

76. Badische MdI to Bezirksämter, 28 August 1935; and "Bericht des Bezirksamt Z an den Badischen M.d.I. vom 28. September, 1934"; and "Schreiben des Bad. Ministerpräsidenten an den M. des Innern vom 26. Oktober 1934"; and Bad. MdI to Bad. Ministerpräsident, 15 November 1934, all in ibid., 1:52-55, 67; "Lagebericht für die Monate Januar bis November 1935," Generalstaatsanwalt Karlsruhe, 3 December 1935, in Schadt, ed., Lageberichte, pp. 221-27.

77. "Anordnung des Bürgermeisters der Stadt Z vom 8. Juni 1936"; "Rundschreiben des Kreisamtsleiter, A.f.K., Rastatt an sämtliche Bürgermeister des Kreises," 30 July 1938; "Bürgermeisteramt der Stadt Rastatt an den Deutschen Gemeindetag, Landesdienststelle Karlsruhe," 26 August 1938, in Sauer, ed., Dokumente, 1:55-56, 107-08.

78. Gauschatzmeister, "Rundschreiben Nr. 23/38," 8 February 1938, in Rundschreiben des Gauschatzmeisters, Jahrgang 1938; Hundsnurscher and Taddey, Die Jüdischen Gemeinden, pp. 26, 195. For some interesting pictures on Baden-Baden and the persecution of Jews see Rita Thalmann and Emmanuel Feinermann, Crystal Night, 9-10 November 1938, pp. 96-99.

79. "Aus dem Protokoll des Amtsgericht Buchen vom 10. November 1938, Aussagen des Adolf Frey"; and "Meldung der Gendarmerieabteilung Buchen vom 10. November, 1938, in Anzeigensachen gegen Adolf Frey, Landwirt von Eberstadt wegen Totschlags"; and "Erlass des Reichs Minister der Justiz durch den Generalstaatsanwalt in Karlsruhe an den Oberstaatsanwalt

in Mosbach," 10 October 1940, all in Sauer, ed., Dokumente, 2:23-28. Frey committed suicide on 1 July 1957. Eberstadt was a Protestant (91 percent) community of 470 people; by 1929 the NSDAP, DNVP, and Landbund (Bauernpartei) dominated politics in the town.

80. Wagner, "Rundschreiben an die Kreisleiter," 7 December 1938, in ibid., 2:69; Hundsnurscher and Taddey, Die Jüdischen Gemeinden, pp. 25-28.

81. Stellv. Gauleiter, "Rundschreiben," 6 November 1939, T-81/119/140320; Aussendienststelle Mosbach der Gestapo/ Staatspolizeileitstelle Karlsruhe to the Landrat in Buchen, 5 January 1940, in Sauer, ed., Dokumente, 2:188-89; Hundsnurscher and Taddey, Die Jüdischen Gemeinden, pp. 34, 52.

82. See Kurt Düwell, Die Rheingebiete in der Judenpolitik des Nationalsozialismus vor 1942, pp. 254-59; Hundsnurscher and Taddey, Die Jüdischen Gemeinden, pp. 27-28; Stellv. Gauleiter to Kreisleiters in Elsass, 16 October 1940, T-81/9/ 17033. For a personal account see Max Ludwig, ed., Aus dem Tagebuch des Hans O., pp. 11-12. For information on Mannheim Jews who committed suicide on 22 October 1940, when the Gestapo attempted to move them, see Oberstaatsanwalt Mannheim to Generalstaatsanwalt, "Zweimonatl. Lagebericht," 10 December 1940, GLA/309/1210.

83. Generalstaatsanwalt, Karlsruhe, "Lagebericht März-Mai, 1941," 3 June 1941, GLA/309/1205; Düwell, Die Rheingebiete, pp. 251, 26-64. For one specific town see Berent Schwinekörper and Franz Laubenberger, Geschichte und Schicksal der Freiburger Juden, p. 13. In 1945, Dr. Strauss was the only Jew left in Heidelberg; he had been aided by a Gestapo functionary; see Theodor Heuss, Aufzeichnungen 1945-47, p. 228.

84. Gaupersonalamtsleiter to Ministerialdirektor im Bad. Ministerium dK, Pg. Karl Gärtner, 18 March 1943, and Leiter des Gaupersonalamts to the Rektor der Univ. Freiburg, 18 May 1943, both in Sauer, ed., Dokumente, 2:371-73: Gaustabsamtsleiter, "Rundschreiben," 9 March 1944, T-81/17/137167.

85. Kreisleiter, Stockach, to Badischen Handwerkskammer in Karlsruhe, 29 October 1941, and Arbeitsamt Konstanz to Kreisleiter in Stockach, 25 November 1941, both in Sauer, ed., Dokumente, 2:375-76.

86. DAF Freiburg, Kreisobmann, to Kreisleiter, 9 February 1941 (and 14 March 1944), T-81/65/74204, 74028; DAF Freiburg, "Arbeits- und Lagebericht," 26 September 1941, T-81/69/78650-51; DAF, Freiburg, "Tätigkeitsbericht," 27 February 1942, T-81/ 69/78610-11.

87. Führer, 23 May 1943, 1 July 1944.

88. Landesbauernschaft Baden to NSV Gauleitung Baden, 14

June 1937, T-81/10/17821; Walter Gross, Rassenpolitische Erziehung, p. 8; James J. Weingartner, "The SS Race and Settlement Main Office," p. 63.

89. Nachrichtenblatt, 1 (1 and 15 January 1934); BDC/ Pakheiser file. He was born on 6 January 1898 in Mannheim and became a party member in November 1930. In January 1937, he moved to Munich to become Reichsleiter für Volksgesundheit.

90. RPA, Gau Baden, "Rundschreiben," 10 May 1939, T-81/ 9/17139; RPA, "Redner und Mitarbeiter des Gaues Baden," 15 November 1938, T-81/9/17101; RPA, Baden, "Schulungsinformationsschreiben," 24 July 1938, T-81/9/17062; RPA, Baden, "Rundschreiben," 26 June 1939, T-81/89/101779.

91. Deutscher Reichsbund für Leibesübung, Gaudietwart Baden, "Rundschreiben," 30 July 1937, T-81/89/101779; Nachrichtenblatt der Gauwaltung Baden des N.S. Lehrerbundes, 3 (24 February 1939), in T-81/74/85366.

92. RPA, Baden, "Zehn Leitsätze für die Gattenwahl," 5/7 June 1937, T-81/9/17067; RPA, Baden, "Schulungsinformationsschreiben," 15 October 1936, T-81/9/17097; RPA, Baden, "Rundschreiben," 8 July 1939, T-81/9/17170.

93. Führer, 26 April 1939; Führer (A), 21 June 1934; Knorres, "Aufgaben der Rassenpolitik," 18 April 1939, T-81/ 9/17050; Frick, "Zur Bevölkerungspolitik," in Neues Volk, 2 (1 February 1934), p. 3.

94. Klaus Dörner, "Nationalsozialismus und Lebensvernichtung," pp. 141-45; Walter Schulte, "Euthanasia und Sterilisation im Dritten Reich," p. 85. Grafeneck was closed in January 1941, and Hadamar in August 1941, but "wild euthanasia" may well have continued.

95. "Heil und Pflegeanstalten in Baden, Februar, 1940-Juli, 1940," in Justiz und NS Verbrechen, 6 (1971): 469-91; "N.S. Gaudienst Baden," 6 March 1940, T-81/168/367940. See also Alexander Mitscherlich and Fred Mielke, eds., Medizin Ohne Menschlichkeit, pp. 188, 205.

96. RPA, Baden, "Rundschreiben," 25 October 1939, T-81/ 9/17185.

97. SNN, 14 June 1941, in T-501/186/302; Wagner to Maass, 14 November 1944, T-81/228/5009865.

98. Otto Freisinger to Maass, "Denkschrift," 7 May 1942, T-81/125/148009-12; "Öffentliche Versammlung der N.S.D.A.P., Ortsgruppe Süffelweyersheim von Freitag den 23. Januar 1942," (sent by Schuppel to Maass, 17 April 1942), T-81/125/147995; Freisinger to Gaupropagandaleiter, 5 February 1942, T-81/125/ 148013-14.

99. NS Frauenschaft Essen to Gaufrauenschaftsleitung Strassburg, 6 June 1942, T-81/125/148004-5; Gaugericht Baden

to Unteroffizier Otto Freisinger, 7 January 1944, T-81/125/ 147988; Schuppel to Freisinger, 23 August 1944, T-81/125/ 147979.

100. Gauschatzmeister to RPA Baden, 17 October 1939, T-81/ 125/148074.

101. RPA, Baden, "Rundschreiben," 1 October 1940, T-81/9/ 17070; RPA, Baden, "Rundschreiben," 6 August 1943, T-81/117/ 137348-49; Röhn to Maass, 18 March 1942, T-81/9/17030; Hauptamt f. Volkswohlfahrt, "Rundschreiben," 29 September 1941, T-81/9/ 17200; HJ Baden/Elsass, III, to Führer des Bannes 737 (Zabern), 11 July 1943, T-81/100/115782.

102. Führer, 22 July 1944; Maass, "Rundschreiben, Nr. 18/43," T-81/9/16995.

103. Generalstaatsanwalt to RJM, "Zweimonatliche Lagebericht," 8 March 1940, GLA/309/1205; Arbeitsamt Freiburg i. Br., "Lagebericht für die Monate Juni-Juli 1943," T-81/646/ 5449006; DAF, Freiburg, "Bericht für den Monat Februar," 25 February 1943, T-81/69/78582-84.

104. Generalstaatsanwalt to RJM, "Lagebericht," 4 May 1940, GLA/309/1205; "Auszugsweise Abschrift aus dem Lagebericht des Oberstaatsanwalts in Mosbach vom 23. Mai 1941," GLA/309/1205; RPA Gauamtsleiter, "Rundschreiben," 22 July 1943, T-81/117/137350. In one case, Himmler ordered the public hanging of a Polish rural worker in Baden who had had sex with a German woman.

105. DAF Freiburg, Kreiswaltung, "Bericht für den Monat April 1944 der Kreise Freiburg, Emmendingen, Neustadt," 26 April 1944, T-81/69/78531; DAF, Freiburg, "Tätigkeitsbericht," 26 July 1943, T-81/69/78572; DAF Freiburg, "Bericht," 29 December 1942, T-81/69/78585.

CHAPTER TEN

1. Ludwig Walter, "Deutscher Sozialismus," pp. 10-12; Erich Hilgenfeldt, "Die Aufgabe nationalsozialistischer Wohlfahrtsplege," 17 April 1939 (a speech delivered at the Ordensburg Vogelsang to NSV Kreisamtsleiter), T-81/85/97485; Ernst Wulff, Das Winterhilfswerk des Deutschen Volkes, p. 8; Ingeborg Altgelt, Wegweiser durch die N.S. Volkswohlfahrt, p. 9.

2. The best published works on the WHW and the NSV are by Thomas E. J. de Witt, "The Economics and Politics of Welfare in the Third Reich," pp. 256-78; and "The Struggle Against Hunger and Cold," pp. 361-81. Both are based on his 1971 dissertation, see "The Nazi Party and Social Welfare,

1919-1939."

3. E. Karl Spiewok, "Der Aufbau des Wohlfahrtswesens im nationalsozialistischen Staat," pp. 8-9, 53-57; Pollock, The Government of Greater Germany, p. 165.

4. Wirtschaft und Statistik 12 (1932):292; Statistisches Jahrbuch für das Deutsche Reich 52 (1933):507-508; Otto Monckmeier, ed., Jahrbuch der nationalsozialistischen Wirtschaft, 1938, pp. 78-117; see also Dieter Petzina, "Germany and the Great Depression," p. 60.

5. Baden, Statistisches Jahrbuch, 1938, pp. 317-19.

6. Statistisches Jahrbuch für das Deutsche Reich, 52 (1933):493; ROL, Nationalsozialistische Volkswohlfahrtspflege, ihre Träger, Grundlagen und Aufgaben (1941), pp. 170-71; Spiewok, "Der Aufbau," p. 40.

7. Führer, 10 August 1933.

8. Herbert Treff, "So entstand die N.S. Volkswohlfahrt," pp. 71-72; Altgelt, Wegweiser durch die N.S. Volkswohlfahrt, pp. 14-16; Hauptamt für Volkswohlfahrt, Sozialisten der Tat, pp. 25-28. Erich Hilgenfeldt was born on 2 July 1897 in Heinitz and attended the Gymnasium for several years before becoming employed by a lumber firm. Later he found employment with the German Office of Statistics. Hilgenfeldt became a party member in August 1929, and by 1933 he had become a Nazi delegate to the Prussian Landtag and the Reichstag; see BDC/Hilgenfeldt file, and Der Grossdeutsche Reichstag, 1938, pp. 249-50.

9. Führer, 25 July, 10 August 1933; Kurt Mennecke, Ein westdeutscher NSV Kreis, pp. 17-21; Karlsruher Zeitung, 4 February 1932; Polizeisekretär Buchheit to Bad. Landespolizeiamt, 25 February 1931, GLA/309/1130; BDC/Fritz Argus file.

10. Nachrichtenblatt, 1 (1 January 1934), p. 1; Führer, 5 July 1936.

11. Nachrichtenblatt, 1 (1 March 1934), Folge 5; Nachrichtenblatt, NSV Baden, No. 7/8 (14 September 1934), in T-81/84/95868; Führer, 22 February 1930; BDC/Dinkel file.

12. Minister des Innern, Baden, to the 56 Bezirksfürsorgeverbände and the 11 Kreise, 18 May 1934, T-81/86/97861-62; Nachrichtenblatt, 1 (15 October 1934), p. 74; Dinkel, "Besprechung mit Pg. Lorenz," 22 January 1937, T-81/122/144299; "Bericht über die Betreuung der Umquartierten durch die N.S. Frauenschaft, Baden" (sent by Gaupropagandaleiter to Dinkel, 18 January 1944), T-81/86/97957-58.

13. Wulff, Winterhilfswerk, p. 81; Spiewok, "Der Aufbau," p. 53; Helmut Stadelmann, Die rechtliche Stellung der N.S. Volkswohlfahrt (1937), in T-81/86/97856.

14. Minister des Innern, Baden to Bezirksämter, 24 October 1934 (Abschrift), T-81/86/97856.

15. NSV Baden, Abtlg. Organisation, "NSV Mitglieder im Gau Baden, Statistischer Jahresbericht 1939," 1 December 1940, T-81/191/341399.

16. Nachrichtenblatt, NSV Baden, No. 1 (3 August 1934), and No. 5 (31 August 1934), in T-81/84/95834-38, and 95707.

17. Nachrichtenblatt, NSV Baden, No. 4 (24 August 1934), and No. 5 (31 August 1934), in T-81/84/95834-38, and 95816; Dinkel to Regierungsrat Osswald, Neustadt, 19 November 1934, T-81/84/98102; Gauamtsleiter, Amt für Beamte, "Rundschreiben," 24 June 1935, T-81/42/44580.

18. Nachrichtenblatt, NSV Baden, No. 7/8 (14 September 1934), No. 10 (5/19 October 1934), No. 6 (7 September 1934), and (July 1935), in T-81/84/95855-73, and 95913-96071; Nachrichtenblatt, 2 (1 February 1935), p. 12.

19. Nachrichtenblatt, 4 (1/15 May 1937), p. 21; NSV Gau-organisationswalter to Dinkel, 20 December 1938, T-81/122/144183; Kreisleiter Fritsch, Freiburg, to Kreisobmann Fritz Huber (DAF), 6 March 1941, T-81/65/74504.

20. NSV Baden, Organisationsamt, "N.S.V. Mitglieder im Gau Baden, Statistischer Jahresbericht 1939," 1 December 1940, T-81/191/341399-416; "Beim Hauptamt Berlin erfasste Mitglieder und noch unbearbeitet vorliegende Aufnahme-Erklärungen im Verhältnis zu den Einwohnern," December 1942, T-81/85/96758-59.

21. Gaupropagandaleitung, Aktive Prop. to NSV Baden, 13 June 1935, T-81/85/97532; Geheimes Staatspolizeiamt Karlsruhe, "Lagebericht," 5 January 1938, in Oppenheimer, Der Fall Vorbote, p. 157.

22. Gauamtsleiter für Beamte to Dinkel, 15 October 1937, T-81/42/44579; Dinkel to Gauamtsleiter für Beamte, 29 October 1937, T-81/42/44578.

23. Kreisleiter reports (of Baden) to Hauptorganisationsamt, July 1936, HA/10/240; Partei-Statistik, 2:148-50; NSV Baden, Organisation, "N.S.V. Mitglieder im Gau Baden, Statistischer Jahresbericht 1939," 1 December 1940, T-81/191/341399-416.

24. Nachrichtenblatt, NSV Baden, No. 11 (9 November 1934), No. 1 (3 August 1934), in T-81/84/95722, and 95935; Nachrichtenblatt, 1 (1 July 1934), p. 50; Dinkel to Merdes, 22 April 1941, T-81/172/143773; NSV Baden, Organisation to Kreisamtsleiter Karcher, 26 February 1938, T-81/122/143773.

25. Merdes to Dinkel, 13 April 1939, T-81/172/313411; NSV Baden, Organisation, "Hauptamtliche Mitarbeiter der N.S.V. Gauamtsleitung," (c. 1939), T-81/122/144163; Pirsch to Dinkel, 13 February 1942, T-81/122/1433973; Organisationsbuch der

NSDAP (1943), pp. 275-77.

26. Merdes to Dinkel, 10 June 1941, T-81/172/313164; Dinkel to Hörner, 18 January 1941, T-81/122/144056; NSV Baden, Finanzverwaltung to all Hauptstellen, 1 August 1944, T-81/40/37354.

27. Dinkel to Hauptamt für Volkswohlfahrt, Amt Wohlfahrtspflege und Jugendhilfe, 17 March 1943; Dinkel to Amt Wohlfahrtspflege, 31 July 1944, in T-81/190/317119-126; NSV Reichsschulungsbeauftragte to Dinkel, 10 August 1944, T-81/190/317113.

28. Reichsoberrevisor Sailer to Kreiswaltungen der NSV (Baden), 5 January 1943, T-81/117/137050; Dinkel to Merdes, 29 July 1940, T-81/120/141861; Gaupersonalamt to NSV Baden, 29 May 1941, T-81/121/142351; Nachrichtenblatt, 1 (15 July 1934), p. 51.

29. Dinkel to Gaupropagandaleiter, 28 May 1935, T-81/85/97533-34; Gaupropagandaleiter, Aktive Prop. to Dinkel, 27 June 1938, T-81/85/97625.

30. Dinkel to Schmid, 30 April 1941, T-81/85/97605; NSV Baden, Allgemeine Wohlfahrt to Dinkel, 3 May 1940, T-81/172/313318; Pirsch to Dinkel, 14 September 1942, T-81/122/143946; Dinkel to Pirsch, 17 September 1942, T-81/122/143943.

31. NSV, Gaupropagandawalter, "Informationen zur Unterrichtung aller Kreisamtsleiter und Redner i.d. N.S.V.," 5 January 1943, T-81/40/38147; Nachrichtenblatt, 2 (1 May 1935), p. 36; Führer, 22 July 1937; "Anschriften der Kreisamtsleitungen der N.S.V. im Gau Baden," Stand 1 April 1937 (and Stand 1 March 1940), T-81/85/96865, 96926.

32. Dinkel to NSV Gauorganisationswalter, 2 May 1941, T-81/122/144038; Pirsch to Dinkel, 6 November 1940, T-81/122/144077; Pirsch, "Aktennotiz," 8 January 1942, T-81/122/143982; Pirsch, "Protokoll des Tagesverlaufens der Arbeitstagung der Kreisorganisationswalter und deren Mitarbeiter im Haarlass in Heidelberg, 3 und 4 Oktober, 1944," n.d., T-81/122/143998-99; NSV Baden, Abtl. Wohlfahrtspflege to Dinkel, 5 July 1940, T-81/172/313290.

33. Dinkel to Hörner, 16 January 1940, T-81/122/144128; Hörner to Dinkel, 14 January 1940, T-81/122/144129; Dinkel to Stier, 20 June 1936, T-81/122/144352.

34. Nachrichtenblatt, NSV Baden, April 1935, in T-81/84/96006; Dinkel to NSV Abtlg. Organisation, 3 December 1938, T-81/122/144193; NSV Baden, "Organisationsplan 1937," n.d., T-81/85/96869-923.

35. Helmut Heiber, Joseph Goebbels, p. 217; Georg-Wilhelm Müller, ed., Wetterleuchten, entry for 20 December 1930; Witt, "The Nazi Party and Social Welfare," p. 186.

36. Nachrichtenblatt, 1 (1 December 1934), pp. 85-86;

Führer, 1 October 1933; Sozialisten der Tat, pp. 6–11.
37. NSV Baden, Abtlg. Organisation to Gauamtsleiter
Dinkel, "Termine W.H.W. 1936/37," T-81/122/144321-25.
38. Kreispropagandaleiter, Neustadt, to Gaupropagandaleitung, 1 February 1939, T-81/85/97621; Gaupropagandaleiter
Schmid to Dinkel, 11 December 1935, T-81/85/97679; Schmid to
Dinkel, 2 March 1942, T-81/85/97640.
39. Führer, 7 October 1933; Argus to Köhler, 18 October
1933, GLA/233/26332; NSV Gauorganisationswalter to Dinkel, 5
June 1936, T-81/122/144369; NSV Baden, "Kurzbericht über die
Durchführung der ersten Hälfte des W.H.W. 1935/36," T-81/
122/144456.
40. Führer (M), 7 December 1938; Pirsch to Stellv. Gauamtsleiter Stier, 17 March 1936, T-81/122/144396; Stellv.
Ortsgruppenleiter Grassmann (Eberbach) to Kreisleitung Heidelberg, 11 December 1934, T-81/86/98101.
41. "N.S. Gaudienst Baden," 5 January 1940, in T-81/
168/307664-65; Gauorganisationswalter, NSV to Dinkel, 14
October 1939, T-81/122/144152; Wulff, Winterhilfswerk, pp.
56, 111; Führer Rede zum Kriegs-Winterhilfswerk 1942/43,
p. 13.
42. Dinkel to Gauobmann Roth, 6 April 1940, T-81/88/
100577; Dinkel to Kreisbeauftragte für das WHW, 1 March 1941,
T-81/122/144125; WHW Baden, Abtlg. Organisation to Kreis-
beauftragten für das 2KWHW, February 1941, T-81/122/144124.
43. Völkischer Beobachter, 19 September 1944, Partei-
Kanzlei, Verfügungen, Anordnungen, Bekanntgaben, 4 (1943),
p. 405.
44. Nachrichtenblatt, 1 (1 January 1934), p. 1; Nachrichtenblatt, NSV Baden, No. 4 (24 August 1934), in T-81/84/
95817; NSV Gauorganisationswalter to Dinkel, 20 December 1938,
T-81/122/144183; Dinkel, "Akten Notiz für Pg. Lorenz," 26
November 1937, T-81/122/144311.
45. Statistisches Jahrbuch, 1938, pp. 318-20; Müller
to Dinkel, "Tabellenstand des Gaues Baden im Reichsvergleich
der W.H.W. Sammlungen 1937/38," T-81/122/14421; "Kurzbericht
über die Durchführung der ersten Hälfte des W.H.W. 1935/36,"
T-81/122/144455; "Hilfsbedürftige Oktober," 17 October 1938,
T-81/122/144209; Nachrichtenblatt, NSV Baden, No. 6 (7 September 1934), in T-81/84/95858-60.
46. Gaupropagandaleitung to Dinkel, 11 June 1937, T-81/
85/97576; Dinkel to Landesstelle Baden-Württemberg für Volksaufklärung und Propaganda, 19 October 1934, T-81/85/97538;
Gauorganisationswalter NSV to Dinkel, "Erfahrungsbericht des
W.H.W. 1935/36," 5 June 1936, T-81/122/144364. For the WHW's
impact on the Reich consumer market see Santoro, Hitler's

Germany, pp. 203-204.

47. Pollock, Germany, p. 164; Howard K. Smith, Last Train from Berlin, p. 9; Philipps, Germany Today, pp. 313-32.

48. Führer (M), 15 November 1935, 8 October 1937; Gaubeauftragter für Arbeitsbeschaffung, "Arbeitsbeschaffung und Arbeitseinsatz im Jahre 1937," 27 February 1937, T-81/178/327384-89.

49. Frederick L. Schuman, The Nazi Dictatorship, pp. 406-407; Stephen H. Roberts, The House that Hitler Built, p. 197; William L. Shirer, Berlin Diary, p. 495; Louis P. Lochner, What about Germany?, pp. 188-89; Arvid Fredborg, Behind the Steel Wall, p. 231. For an interesting case involving NSV corruption see Oberstaatsanwalt Offenburg to Generalstaatsanwalt, 12 February 1938, GLA/309/1208.

50. Dinkel to NSV Abtlg. Organisation, 1 December 1938, T-81/122/144194.

51. Hjalmar Schacht admitted that in 1935 all NS organisations and affiliates were examined to see if they had available funds for armament purposes; see H. Huber and A. Müller, Das Dritte Reich, p. 266.

52. Baden, Statistisches Jahrbuch, 1938, p. 318; Bürgermeister of Birkendorf, "Leistungsschau der Badischen Gemeinden 1937," 11 January 1937, T-81/175/316455.

53. See Walter Hebenbrook, "Nationalsozialistische Wohlfahrtspflege ist Gesundheitsdienst," pp. 440-46. Hebenbrook argued that "social aid can only be welfare based on völkisch racialism—the socialism of blood."

54. Nachrichtenblatt, NSV Baden, No. 2 (February 1935), and No. 5 (May 1935), in T-81/84/95988, 96022; NSV Baden, Abtl. Schulung to Gauschulungsamt, 27 March 1939, T-81/118/138498; Gauschulungsbeauftragte NSV to Gauschulungsamt, 30 May 1939, T-81/118/138478. Hans Bernsee, a Reich NSV leader, argued that the decline of the population in Germany and in the United States threatened the "white race"; see Unser Wille und Weg, 5 (April 1935), p. 135.

55. Nachrichtenblatt, 1 (1 January 1934), p. 1; Führer, 10 August 1933; "N.S. Gaudienst Baden," 29 January 1940, in T-81/168/307773.

56. Nachrichtenblatt, NSV Baden, No. 3 (3 August 1934), and No. 4 (24 August 1934), in T-81/84/95817, 96710.

57. Erich Hilgenfeldt, "Das Wohlfahrtsethos des völkischen Staates," pp. 50-54; see also Wille und Macht, 4 (July 1934):202; and Der Parteitag der Freiheit, 1935.

58. Dinkel to Gaupropagandaleiter, 28 May 1935, T-81/85/97533; Gurrath to Dinkel, 25 February 1939, T-81/172/313436; Hebenbrock, "Weltanschauliche Voraussetzungen der N.S.V.,"

19 April 1939, T-81/85/97505. In 1936 the NSV issued a monthly periodical, Ewiges Deutschland, which provided guidelines for mothers and the "breeding program."

59. Nachrichtenblatt, NSV Baden, No. 10 (5/19 October 1934), in T-81/84/95926.

60. Dinkel, "Nationalsozialistische Wohlfahrtsarbeit im Grenzgau Baden," (1938), T-81/85/97299; NSV Gauorganisationswalter Lorenz to Dinkel, 16 June 1937, T-81/122/144260; NSV Gauschulungsbeauftragte to Gauschulungsamt, 26 April 1939, T-81/118/138486.

61. Baden, Statistisches Jahrbuch, 1938, p. 320; Nachrichtenblatt, 2 (15 March 1935), pp. 23-24; NSV, Baden, Organisation, "Wohlfahrtspflege und Jugendhilfe im Gau Baden, Statischer Bericht," 1 December 1939, T-81/191/341379; "Haushaltsvorschlag 1939/40 der Abtl. III, Gauwaltung Baden," n.d., T-81/172/313448-58.

62. The five departments were: Mother and Child, Kindergartens and Day Care Centers, Juvenile Care, Youth Vacation Programs, and NS Nurses (which was not included in the budget).

63. Baden, Minister des Innern to 56 Bezirksfürsorgeverbände und die 11 Kreise, 18 May 1934, T-81/86/97861; Kreisrat Offenburg, "Abhandlung von Mutterberatungsstunden im Amtsbezirk Lahr," 25 July 1934, T-81/86/97858.

64. Baden, Minister des Innern to Bezirksämter, 24 October 1934 (Abschrift), T-81/86/97856; Dinkel to Merdes, 10 July 1939, T-81/172/313378.

65. Landesfürsorgenverband Baden, Sekretäriat to NSV, Abtlg. MuK, 15 July 1937, T-81/86/97787; Partei-Kanzlei, Verfügungen, Anordnungen, Bekanntgaben, 7 (1945), p. 37.

66. Gauleiter, "Rundschreiben," 14 February 1940, T-81/119/140122; Reichspropagandaleiter to all Gauleiter, 15 April 1944, T-81/120/141939; Führer, 8 August 1944; Althaus, "Gesunde Jugend--Gegenwartsaufgaben der N.S. Jugendhilfe," April 1942, T-81/40/38203.

67. Dinkel to NSV Kreisamtsleiter, 21 July 1942, T-81/37/34240-42.

68. Nachrichtenblatt, NSV Baden, No. 3 (March 1935), in T-81/84/96151; Der Hoheitsträger, No. 3 (1943), p. 12; Länderrat des Amerikanischen Besatzungsgebiete, ed., Statistisches Handbuch von Deutschland, 1928-1944, p. 61.

69. Baden, Statistisches Jahrbuch, 1938, p. 320; Merdes to Dinkel, 13 April 1939, T-81/172/313411; "N.S. Gaudienst Baden," 19 January 1940, p. 3, in T-81/168/307732.

70. NSV Baden, Wohlfahrtspflege und Jugendhilfe to Hauptamt fV, 14 August 1941, T-81/86/97999.

71. Bürgermeister of Birkendorf, Waldshut, "Leistungschau

der Badischen Gemeinden 1937," 11 January 1937, T-81/175/
316456; NSV Kreisamtsleitung Waldshut to Gauamtsleitung, 22
September 1936, T-81/86/97828; NSV, Hauptstelle MuK to
Pflaumer, 29 October 1936, T-81/86/97823.

72. Schmid to Dinkel, 14 August 1939, and Dinkel to
Schmid, 1 September 1939, both T-81/85/97615-16; Merdes to
Dinkel, 20 November 1940, T-81/172/313241; Gauamt für Kommunalpolitik to Stellv. Gauleiter Schuppel, 12 March 1940, T-81/
178/327297.

73. Kreisleitung Sinsheim, "Bericht vom 2. Februar 1943,"
T-81/176/324230; Bertha Finck, "Die Leistungen des Hilfswerk
MuK," 1 August 1942, T-81/40/38209.

74. Dinkel to Merdes, 21 July 1940, T-81/172/313294; Abtl.
Kindertagesstätten to Merdes, 31 March 1941, T-81/172/313193.

75. Gaureferentin für Kindertagesstätten (Müller) to
Dinkel, 30 June 1942, T-81/86/97942-43.

76. Erley, NSV Wohlfahrtspflege und Fürsorgerecht, "Akten-
Notiz," 28 January 1939, T-81/172/313474; Merdes to Dinkel, 24
January 1938, T-81/126/112305-308.

77. Hilgenfeldt, "Die Aufgabe nationalsozialistischer Wohlfahrtspflege," 17 April 1939, T-81/85/97488; Hauptamt fV,
Amt Wohlfahrtspflege und Jugendhilfe to all NSV, Gauamtsleiter,
9 July 1941, T-81/86/98010.

78. Dinkel, "Liebe Parteigenossen" (letter sent to conference of kindergarten personnel, 18 August 1941), T-81/86/
98021-22; Reichsstatthalter in Hessen to Landräte and Lord
Mayors, 23 June 1941, T-81/86/980011-12.

79. Merdes to Dinkel, 27 May 1942; and Dinkel to Hilgenfeldt, 20 August 1942; and Dinkel to Merdes, 11 July 1942,
all T-81/86/97945-47; Wohlfahrtspflege und Jugendhilfe, Baden
to Hauptamt fV, 13 May 1943, T-81/86/97948.

80. NSV, Baden Wohlfahrtspflege und Jugendhilfe to Hauptamt fV, 14 August 1941; Wohlfahrtspflege und Jugendhilfe to
Röhn, 15 September 1941, T-81/86/97996-99; Röhn to Merdes, 17
September 1941, T-81/86/97991; Merdes, "Aktennotiz," 29 October 1941, T-81/86/97984.

81. Wohlfahrtspflege und Jugendhilfe, Baden to Hauptamt
fV, 23 January 1942, T-81/86/97981; Dinkel, "Besprechung mit
dem Stellv. Gauleiter Röhn am 14.2. 42," T-81/86/97975;
Gaureferentin für Kindertagesstätten to Merdes, 4 June 1942,
T-81/86/97971-72.

82. Dinkel to Wickertsheimer, 25 November 1942, T-81/
86/97941.

83. Merdes to NSV Gaupropagandawalter Wickertsheimer,
5 June 1942, T-81/86/97949; Kreisleiter of Wolfach to Dinkel,
19 June 1942, T-81/85/97467; Dinkel to Kreisleiter of Wertheim,

18 August 1942, T-81/86/97456.

84. Kreisleitung Rastatt, "Bericht vom 25. Oktober 1943," T-81/1/11085; Kreisleitung Heidelberg, "Bericht vom 16. Dezember 1942," T-81/176/324298; Kreisleitung Sinsheim, "Bericht vom 27. April 1943," T-81/165/304265-66; NSV Gauschulungsbeauftragter to Dinkel, 27 July 1944, T-81/23/20669-70; NSV Baden, Abtlg. Schulung to Gauschulungsamt Baden, 5 July 1943, T-81/124/146345-46.

85. NSV Wohlfahrtspflege und Jugendhilfe to the Kreisleiters, 21 March 1940 (Streng vertraulich), T-81/86/96039.

86. Baden, Minister des Innern to 56 Bezirksfürsorgenverbände, 6 June 1934, T-81/86/97859-60; NSV Baden, Geschlossene Jugendhilfe," T-81/85/97507.

87. Baden MdI to Amt für Volkswohlfahrt, 30 July 1935, T-81/R.87/99737-44; Merdes to Dinkel, 20 October 1939, T-81/172/313369; Wohlfahrtspflege und Jugendhilfe to Baden, MdI, July 1935, T-81/R.87/99726-27; NSV, Abtl. III to Althaus, 3 April 1935, T-81/R.87/99754.

88. Wohlfahrtspflege und Jugendhilfe, "Rundschreiben," 9 September 1941, T-81/86/98283; NSV Offenburg, Kreisamt, "N.S.V. Jugendhilfe," 4 October 1941, T-81/122/14389-90; "N.S. Gaudienst Baden," 28 March 1940, T-81/168/308011; NSV Bühl, "Tätigkeitsbericht der N.S.V. Jugendhilfe für den Monat Januar 1937," 19 April 1937, T-81/122/143588.

89. NSV Kreisamtsleiter, Konstanz, "Tätigkeitsbericht," March-June, 1942, T-81/85/97292-93; Witt, "The Nazi Party and Social Welfare," pp. 263-64. For an interesting case involving a young man in Mannheim (b. 1922) who received NSV supervision even after he had joined the SS Totenkopfverband in November 1939 see NSV Köln-Aachen, Jugendhilfe to NSV Baden, 30 August 1939; NSV Mannheim, "Notiz," 13 July 1942, T-81/86/98614-25.

90. "Referat des Organisationsleiter Pg. Schneider zur Tagung am 17. April 1935 im Kreis Freiburg," T-81/122/144514-22; Stier to Freie Schwesternschaft, Ruth Freudenberger, 5 May 1936, T-81/122,144408.

91. Dinkel to Stier, 23 March 1936, T-81/122/144429; Bürgermeister of Ittersback to NSV Kreisamtsleitung Pforzheim, 24 August 1938, T-81/86/97743; NSV Kreisamtsleitung Wertheim to Dinkel, 19 July 1939, T-81/86/97755-56; NSV Kreisamtsleitung Kehl to Dinkel, 23 August 1939, T-81/86/97733.

92. NSV Kreisamtsleitung Emmendingen to Dinkel, 1 August 1939, T-81/86/97729; Kreisleitung Freiburg, "Bericht vom 2. Februar 1943," T-81/176/324226; Kreisleitung Donaueschingen, "Bericht vom 1. Juni, 1943," T-81/165/304247; Witt, "The Nazi Party and Social Welfare," p. 277.

93. Nachrichtenblatt NSV Baden, No. 10 (October 1935), in
T-81/84/96118; Gauvertrauensschwester to Dinkel, "Tätigkeitsbericht," November 1935, T-81/122/144474-75; "Notiz über die
Besprechung mit Frau Dr. Rocholl und den Gesundheitsfürsorge-
rinnen des Oberkurses in Mannheim am 3. März, 1941," T-81/172/
313361; Dinkel to Pgn. Gurrath, 10 March 1941, T-81/172/
313359-60.
94. Hilgenfeldt to Wagner, 30 August 1943, T-81/121/
142106; Schwesternwesen to Dinkel, 14 May 1942, T-81/172/
313035; Dinkel to Merdes, 7 November 1940, T-81/172/313264.
95. Kreisamtsleiter NSV, "Die Geschichte der Freimachung
und Wiederbesiedlung der gefährdeten Grenzgebiete am Oberrhein:
Dargestellt vom Kreis Säckingen," in Gau Archiv, c. 1940/41,
T-81/127/149930-37; Kreis Waldshut, "Bericht über die Rückführung und Betreuung der Bevölkerung aus den freigemachten
Gebieten," n.d., T-81/127/1449986-87.
96. Kreisleitung Lahr, "Bericht des Bürgermeisters Karl
Reith, Meissenheim," May 1940, T-81/127/300114; Baden, MdI,
to Gauamt für Volkswohlfahrt, 31 July 1942, T-84/257/6616816.
97. "Bericht über die Rückführung von Polenflüchtlingen
am 17.11.1939," 24 November 1939, T-81/37/33940; NSV Gauamtsleiter, Tirol-Voralber to Dinkel, 5 January 1940, T-81/37/
34423.
98. Pirsch, "Niederschrift über die Besprechung bei der
Gauleitung der N.S.D.A.P. betr. der Dobrutscha (Besserabien-
deutschen)," 5 November 1940, T-81/122/144079; NSV Finanzverwaltung to Hauptamt fV, Amt Organisation, 20 November
1940, T-81/125/147769; Reichsleitung NSV to NSV Baden, 7
November 1940, T-81/37/34320.
99. Dinkel to all Kreisamtsleiter, NSV, 28 January 1941,
T-81/125/147923; NSV Baden, Organisation to Hauptorganisationsamt NSV, 14 March 1941, T-81/125/147725; Gauorganisationswalter NSV to Hauptorganisationsamt, 3 May 1941, T-81/125/
147708; NSV, Org. Baden to Hauptorganisationsamt, NSV, 21
July 1941, T-81/125/147697.
100. NSV Baden, "Rundbrief," 25 October 1941, T-81/125/
147852; Vomi Baden, "Rundschreiben Nr. 68/41," 11 December
1941, T-81/278/2398734; Pirsch, "Rundbrief Nr. 3," 27 January
1942, T-81/37/34248.
101. H. Schlenker, "Aktennotiz," 30 August 1940, T-84/
257/6617113; Kommando der Schutzpolizei Karlsruhe, "Rundschreiben Nr. 730/41," 5 November 1941, T-84/257/6617046.
102. Baden, MdI, to Amt für Volkwohlfahrt, 18 June 1942,
T-84/257/6616748; Gaustabsamt, M-Beauftrager i.V. Weinbrecht,
"Rundschreiben," 29 June 1942, T-84/257/6616946-47; Dinkel,
"Aktennotiz über die Sitzung am 23.8.1943 unter Vorsitz des

Gauleiters," 30 August 1943 (Geheim), T-84/257/6616751.

103. Baden MdI to Gauleitung NSV, 3 July 1942, T-84/
257/6616808; Pirsch, "Niederschrift über die Besprechung des
Einsatzstabes in Kolmar am 9.7. 1942," 11 July 1942, T-84/257/
6616807; Baden MdI to Gauamt NSV, 20 July 1942, T-84/257/
6616793.

104. Dinkel to MdI, Baden, 17 August 1942, T-84/257/
6616735; Dinkel to MdI (Geheime Reichssache), 2 October 1942,
T-84/257/6616721; NSV Baden, Organisation to MdI, z.Hd. von
Schneider (Geheim), 14 January 1944, T-84/257/6616695. See
also the USSBS, report 64b, The Effects of Strategic Bombing
on German Morale, I:66-67.

105. Stellv. Gauleiter to all Gauamtsleiter and Kreisleiters, 14 May 1941, T-81/119/140209; Reichsstatthalter Baden
to Gaustabsamt Baden, 2 August 1943, T-81/165/304349; NSV
Gauamtsbeauftragter, "Aktennotiz-Betr. Unterbringung von
Fliegergeschädigten," 18 May 1943, T-84/257/6616757.

106. Wickertsheimer, "Akten Notiz über die Aussprache mit
Gauamtsleiter Hutwohl vom Gau Westfalen-Süd," T-84/257/6616755;
Gauverbindungsmann Gau W-S to Wagner, "5. Bericht über die
Umquartierten aus Westfalen-Süd im Gau Baden-Elsass," 10 August
1943, T-81/163/302038-44; Gaubeauftragter W-S to Kreisamts-
leiter NSV, Strassburg, 2 February 1944, T-81/169/309212;
Wagner to MdI, 6 June 1944, T-81/163/302064.

107. Wagner to Bormann, 25 August 1943, HA/roll 50/folder
1181; Wagner to Gaustabsamt Baden, 2 August 1943, T-81/165/
304349.

108. Dinkel to Althaus, 13 March 1944, T-81/163/302075;
Dinkel to Brust, 18 May 1944, T-81/165/304355; US report 64b,
The Effects of Strategic Bombing on German Morale, 1:70.

109. NSV Baden, Org., "Aktion Elsass: Statistischer
Bericht über die Betreuungs- und Aufbauarbeit der NS-Volkswohl-
fahrt im Elsass," (c. November 1940), T-81/40/37474-505; NSV
Baden, "Leistungsbericht der N.S.V. vom 1.4.41 bis 31.3.42,"
T-81/85/97280-82.

110. Dinkel to Merdes, 25 June 1940, and Merdes to Dinkel,
26 June 1940, T-81/172/313313-15; NSV Gauorganisationswalter to
Wulff, 16 August 1940, T-81/115/135331.

111. CdZ beim AOK7, "Anordnung," 29 June 1940, T-81/123
145232; Dinkel to Kreisamtsleiter in Alsace, 29 June 1940,
T-81/115/135338.

112. "Aktion Elsass," c. November 1940, T-81/40/37474-
505; Marie-Joseph Bopp, L'Alsace sous l'occupation allemande,
p. 101; Meldungen aus dem Reich, No. 108, 25 July 1940, T-175/
259/2752064; Meldungen aus dem Reich, No. 128, 30 September
1940, T-175/259/2752475.

113. NSV Baden, Abtl. II to Dinkel, 5 July 1940, T-81/
172/313298; Wickertsheimer to Dinkel, 27 September 1941, T-81/
167/306010; Dinkel to Merdes, 31 March 1941, T-81/172/313194;
Wickertsheimer to NSV Beauftragte in Alsace, 12 August 1941,
T-81/167/316011.

114. Komm. Gauamtskassenverwalter, NSV to Dinkel, 7 May
1942, T-81/167/306088-89.

115. Wagner, "Verfügung," 17 April 1941, T-81/88/101021;
Dinkel to Merdes, 3 July 1940, T-81/172/313299; "Leistungsbericht der N.S.V. (Baden) vom 1.4.41 bis 31.3.1942," T-81/
85/97280-82.

116. "Kurzer Tätigkeitsbericht über die Kindertagesstät-
tenarbeit im Elsass," c. November 1940, T-81/115/135237; SNN,
30 May 1941, in T-81/537/5307626.

117. NSV Gauorganisationswalter to Gaugeschäftsführung,
30 October 1940, T-81/115/135311-15; NSV Baden, "N.S.V.-Mit-
gliederstand Gau Baden und Elsass," 12 January 1943, T-81/
88/100458.

118. NSV Baden, "Leistungsbericht der N.S.V. vom 1.4.41
bis 31.3.42," T-81/85/97283; NSV Kreispropagandawalter,
Schlettstadt to all Ortsgruppenleiter, 21 December 1942,
T-81/88/100589.

119. Fritsch to all Ortsgruppenleiter, 5 September 1940,
T-81/126/112283; Brauerei Schützenberger AG to Kreisleiter
Fritsch, 7 October 1940, T-81/166/305175; Kreisleiter Fritsch
to Herrn Samuleit, Strassburg Kaufhaus Union, 11 October 1940,
T-81/166/305064.

120. "Sammlungsvergleich zwischen den 1. Sammlungen im
Gau Baden und im Elsass," 21 October 1940, T-81/189/340111;
Hilgenfeldt to Himmler, August 1942 ("1.-4. Haussammlung und
1. Strassensammlung des D.R.K."), in Library of Congress,
Manuscript Division, Himmler files, container 6, folder 14.

121. NSV Gauorganisationswalter to Gauführung WHW, 9
December 1940, T-81/189/340032; NSV Gauorganisationswalter
to Wickertsheimer, 21 May 1941, T-81/115/135261; Pirsch to
Dinkel, 22 May 1941, T-81/122/144033; Pirsch to Dinkel, 24
November 1941, T-81/122/143984.

122. Wickertsheimer to Gaugeschäftsführung, 11 February
1942; and Wickertsheimer to Amt für Beamte, 19 January 1942;
and Wickertsheimer to Gaugeschäftsführung, 5 February 1942,
all T-81/88/100464-71.

123. WHW Kreisbeauftragte, Mülhausen to Wickertsheimer,
4 March 1942, T-81/88/100500; WHW Kreisbeauftragte, Hagenau to
Wickertsheimer, 27 February 1942, T-81/88/100487.

124. WHW Kreisbeauftragte, Altkirch to Gaubeauftragte
(Wickertsheimer), 16 January 1942, T-81/88/100479.

125. Komm. Ortsgruppenleiter Rühlmann, Molsheim to Pg.
Engel, 9 January 1942 (Abschrift), T-81/179/327919; Komm.
Bürgermeister of Molsheim to Sicherheitspolizei, Aussenstelle
Molsheim, 13 January 1942, T-81/179/327922; B.d.S./Strassburg
to Wagner, 3 January 1942, T-81/179/327912.

126. Report by a Studienrat of Barr, Schlettstadt on the
situation in Barr, c. 1942, T-81/174/315837-39.

127. Merdes to Dinkel, 20 November 1940, T-81/172/313256;
NSV Org. to Kreisamtsleiter Karcher (Thann), 11 September 1940,
T-81/189/340099; Pg. Fäster (Karlsruhe) to Dinkel, 23 August
1940, T-81/189/340121.

128. Dinkel to Pg. Kempf, 3 August 1940, T-81/189/339973;
Dinkel to Pg. Otto Rink, 13 August 1940, T-81/189/340048.

129. NSV Baden, "Bericht über die Schwesternschulung in
den Monaten Juli, August und September 1943," T-81/124/146304;
SD Führer, Strassburg to Gauleitung NSV, 17 July 1944, T-81/
121/142428; Dinkel to Pgn. Gurrath, 10 July 1941, T-81/172/
313148; "Besichtigungsfahrt 22.-24. April 1942," (by Wickers-
heimer), n.d., T-81/172/313526.

130. Merdes to Dinkel, 5 November 1940, T-81/172/313267;
Merdes to Gausachbearbeiterin MuK, 6 January 1941, T-81/172/
313216-17; Dinkel to Merdes, 6 November 1940, T-81/172/313265.

131. NSV Gauorganisationswalter to Pirsch, 13 December
1940, T-81/189/339924; Gauhauptstellenleiter Baden to Zentral-
auslaufamt der Reichsleitung, 10 August 1944, T-81/120/141759.

CHAPTER ELEVEN
1. Hermann Rauschning, Voice of Destruction, p. 191.
2. Walter Ruthe, Der Nationalsozialismus, p. 13; Carl
Johanny, Partei und Staat, pp. 42-43.
3. Konrad Heiden, History of National Socialism, p. XVI.
4. Stellv. Kreisleiter, NSDStB, Karlsruhe to Bad. Poli-
zei-u. Gendarmerieschule, 12 May 1933, T-81/244/5032021; Hasso
Freischlad to Stellv. Kreisleiter, NSDStB Karlsruhe, n.d.
(sent to NSDAP, Kreisleitung Karlsruhe, 28 June 1933), T-81/
244/5031903; Führer (L), 4 June 1935.
5. Führer, 16 July 1933.
6. Führer (A), 4 September 1935; Führer (M), 3 December
1935; Nachrichtenblatt, 1 (15 April 1934), p. 31, and 2 (15
March 1935); Gaupersonalamt, Baden, 30 April 1936, "Rund-
schreiben--Betrifft Nachtragsliste zur 2. Sonderaktion," GLA/
233/26291; Schuppel to sämtliche Ministerien, Behörden, 30
September 1936, GLA/233/26291.
7. Niederschrift über die Sitzung des Staatsministeriums
vom 12. Juli 35, GLA/233/24318; Nachrichtenblatt, Baden, 6

(1/15 May 1939), p. 34; Reichsstatthalter to Ministerien, "Rundschreiben" (Vertraulich), 13 October 1941, GLA/233/26291.

8. Kreisleitung Karlsruhe to Gauschatzmeister, 13 July 1942, T-81/162/3003491; Franz Moraller to Schuppel, 7 March 1940, T-81/126/148818; Moraller to Wagner, 26 February 1940, T-81/126/148811; Strassburger Neueste Nachrichten (Abschrift), 18 November 1942, in T-81/558/5333690.

9. NSDStB Karlsruhe, Stellv. Kreisleiter to Direktor der Bad. Landeskunstschule, 29 June 1933, T-81/244/5031896; Karl Berberich to Pg. Neumann, Buchen (Gaupersonalamt fdR der Abschrift), 3 July 1934, T-81/228/5010152.

10. Gauorganisationsamt, "Rundschreiben Nr. 49/36," 27 June 1936, T-81/172/312931; Nachrichtenblatt: 1 (1 September 1934), p. 64; and 2 (15 January 1935), p. 5; and 3 (15 August 1936), p. 53.

11. Bruno Wiesener (Pforzheim) to Kamerad Henschel, 7 October 1937, T-81/200/2741012; Christian Müller to Bürgermeister Fauth (Abschrift), 18 November 1940, T-81/126/148907; Oberstaatsanwalt Waldshut to Generalstaatsanwalt, 29 March 1940 (and 16 July 1940), GLA/309/1210. For the Gau leadership's attempts to control these activities see Gauleiter, "Rundschreiben," 18 January 1943, T-81/124/146055, and Gaustabsamtsleiter, "Rundschreiben 56/42," 21 October 1942, T-81/127/149680.

12. July 1936 Kreisleiter reports to the Hauptorganisationsamt, HA/10/240; Partei-Statistik, 1935, 2:42; Nachrichtenblatt, 1 (15 January 1934), p. 7 (1 February 1934), p. 12 (15 November 1934), p. 82. In February 1933, only 16 Baden jurists and lawyers belonged to the BNSDJ, but by April 1934, this Baden party affiliate claimed 2,200 members, Führer (A), 21 April 1934.

13. Pirsch (NSV Gauorganisationsleiter) to Gauamtsleiter Dinkel, 20 June 1936, "Tagung der Kreisorganisationsleiter und der Organisationsleiter der Gauamtsleitung in Karlsruhe," T-81/122/144348.

14. Niederschrift, Sitzung des Staatsministerium vom 12 Januar 1934, GLA/233/24318; Führer (M), 20 March 1935.

15. SA Brigade 53, Standarte 250, Bruchsal, "Vierteljahresbericht der Standarte 250 über die Zeit vom 15. Januar bis 15. April 1934," GLA/465d/1357.

16. Führer, Standarte 250 to SA Brigade 153, Heidelberg, 6 July 1934, GLA/465d/1356; Lagebericht Gestapo Karlsruhe für die Zeit vom 9. bis 15. Dezember 1933 (and vom 3. bis 17. Februar 1934), in Jörg Schadt, ed., Verfolgung und Widerstand.

17. Standarte 250, Bruchsal, Vierteljahresbericht, 17

September 1934, GLA/465d/1356; Standartenarzt, Standarte 250, Vierteljahresbericht, 18 September 1934, GLA/465d/1356; Standarte 250, Vierteljahresbericht über die Zeit vom 15. Oktober 1934 bis 15. Januar 1935, GLA/465d/1357.

18. Orlow, History, 2:13-17.

19. Führer (M), 26 January, 20 March 1935, 12 February and 13 July 1937.

20. Führer (M), 26 January 1935.

21. Stellv. des Führers, "Anordnung Nr. 173/39," 18 September 1939, T-81/39/36347.

22. Führer (M), 24 January 1940; Stellv. Gauleiter to Schwarz, 17 November 1943, T-81/121/142092-94; Gaugeschäftsführer to Gauleitung Baden, 24 December 1941, T-81/119/140108; Willi A. Boelcke, ed., Kriegspropaganda 1939-41, p. 218 (3 November 1939 conference).

23. H. Bickler, "Kreisleiterbesprechung am 24.6.41 in der Reichsstatthalterei," 25 June 1941, T-81/178/327328-30; Gauorganisationsleiter, "Rundschreiben 78/43," 12 November 1943, T-81/117/137243-44; Führer, 24 May 1943.

24. Gaugeschäftsführung to all Gauamtsleiter, Kreisleiter (Vertraulich), 29 June 1939, T-81/119/14047; Nachrichtenblatt, 1 (15 April 1934), p. 29, and 2 (1 September 1935), p. 65.

25. Partei-Statistik, 1:31, 46, 148-50, 202-10; "Vergleichniszahlen über Verbreitung der Reichsschulungsbriefe der NSDAP und DAF," September 1936, T-81/64/73256-60. After 1933, the percentage of workers and farmers as party members declined while the white-collar employees, independents, and civil servants increased to encompass 52.3 percent of the party's membership in Baden.

26. Führer (M), 9 March 1938.

27. Stellv. Gauleiter, "Rundschreiben, Nr. 26/39," 13 May 1939, T-81/119/140363; Gauschatzmeister to Gauorganisationsamt, 12 January 1943, T-81/178/327528; BDC, Kreisleiter files for: Emil Epp, Fritz Senft, H. Dieffenbacher, Hans Knab, Hans Grüner, R. Burk, W. Geiger, Felix Elger, Rudolf Allgeier, and Willi Worch; these files list the total population and the number of party members in the various districts.

28. Pirsch to Dinkel, 20 June 1936, "Tagung der Kreisorganisationsleiter und der Organisationsleiter der Gauamtsleitung in Karlsruhe," T-81/122/144348; ROL, ed., Gau und Kreisverzeichnis der NSDAP, p. 72; ROL, ed., Organisationsbuch der NSDAP, p. 84; Führer (M), 15 April 1939.

29. Gauschulungsamt, "Rundschreiben Nr. 63/37," 12 November 1937, T-81/172/312705; Kreisorganisationsamt Zabern to Ortsgruppenleiter, 14 August 1942, T-81/167/306981; Führer (M), 24 January 1938.

30. Nachrichtenblatt, 1 (1 April, 15 March 1934), pp. 25, 22, and 2 (1 November 1935), p. 77; Führer, 9 June 1933; Kramer, "Richtlinien über die Wahl geeigneter Diensträume für die Kreis- und Ortsgruppenleitungen der Partei, ihren Ausbau und ihre Einrichtungen," 23 May 1939, T-81/119/140134-36; Gauausbildungsamt, "Rundschreiben Nr. 81/37," 3 November 1937, T-81/172/312685-86.

31. Nachrichtenblatt, 1 (1 February 1934), p. 10, and 3 (1 April 1936), p. 20; Partei-Statistik, 2:31, 52-60.

32. Wagner to Köhler, 10 April 1935 (and 28 December 1935), GLA/233/24007; Adolf Conrad, "Meine Erlebnisse im Kampf für den Führer 1925-1933," March 1937, HA/26/514; Führer, 1 January 1936; Nachrichtenblatt, 1 (1 November 1934), p. 77.

33. Führer (M), 21 May 1938, 7 October 1940, 29 March 1942, and 12 August 1940; Kreisleiter, Überlingen to Gaustabsamt, 25 October 1943, T-81/120/142023.

34. Gauschatzmeister, Hauptstelle Kartei to Gaupersonalamt, Hauptstelle PL, 24 November 1943, T-81/228/5009931; Amt für Kommunalpolitik, Baden to Hauptamt fK, 21 June 1937 (and 1942), "Kreisamtsleiter," in BDC/Diverses-Gau Baden; Organisationsamt Buchen, "Tätigkeitsbericht, 9.4.1943-4.6.1943," T-81/124/146213; Robert Wagner, "Zwei Jahre deutscher Aufbauarbeit im Elsass," p. 364.

35. Nachrichtenblatt, 2 (1 February 1935), p. 11; and 3 (1 August 1936), p. 50; and 1 (1 June, 15 June, and 1 December 1934), pp. 42, 44-45, 85; Gauorganisationsamt, "Rundschreiben 49/35," 27 June 1935, T-81/171/312933; Gauorganisationsamt, "Rundschreiben Nr. 45/44," 6 July 1944, T-81/93/106995-96. As early as 1935 some locals had ordered party members to address each other with the personal "Du," but Kramer promptly forbade this revolutionary attempt to change social relationships; see Nachrichtenblatt, 2 (1 December 1935), p. 85.

36. Führer, 31 March 1935, 1 January 1936; Nachrichtenblatt, 1 (1 March 1934), p. 19.

37. Partei-Kanzlei, "Lebenslauf des H. Röhn," 20 August 1943, and Partei-Kanzlei report on Hermann Röhn, July 1942 in BDC/H. Röhn file; Führer, 13 October 1933, 31 March 1935, 20 May 1933.

38. "Trial of Robert Wagner and Six Others," in Law Reports of Trials of War Criminals, 3:23-25; Gaupersonalamtsleiter to Gauamtsleiter Paul Maass, 27 April 1942, T-81/125/148017. For opposition to Röhn see Parteikanzlei, Walkenhorst, "Gauleiternachwuchs," 30 November 1943, in BDC/Akte 371; Kaul to Dr. Brandt, Persönl. Stab des RFSS (Geheim), 14 January 1943, IfZ/MA/297/frames 2573741-42; RFSS, Persönl.

Stab to Reichssicherheitsamt, SS Sturmbannführer Ploetz (Geheim), 26 January 1943, IfZ/MA/297/frame 2573739.

39. Gau Baden, "Die Dienststellen der NSDAP der Gliederungen und der angeschlossenen Verbände," 1936, HA/10/240; Gau Baden, "Liste der Gauhaupt- und Gauamtsleiter," (c. April 1944), T-81/176/324483-85; Nachrichtenblatt, 1 (1 February, 1 March 1934), pp. 12, 19. For the rise of two Kreisleiters to Gauamt positions see Führer, 27 April 1933, for Fritz Engler-Füsslin (Gauamt leader for Agriculture); and BDC/Karl Gärtner file (Gauamt leader for Teachers).

40. Walkenhorst to Reichsschatzmeister/Zentralpersonalamt, 3 April 1944; and Gauschatzmeister to Reichsschatzmeister/Zentralpersonalamt, 24 October 1944, both in BDC/Willi Rückert file; Gaustabsamtsleiter, "Rundschreiben 11/42," 4 June 1942, T-81/127/149625; Führer, 31 March 1935. Rückert was born in 1905 and obtained some high school education. Between 1923 and 1930 he was the business manager of a Karlsruhe bakery. Rückert joined the army in March 1943 and was reported missing in action in July 1944.

41. Baden, Organisationsamt to Reichsl., Organisation, 2 December 1933, and Personalkarte in BDC/Erwin Schwörer file; Führer, 13 and 17 December 1930, 30 September 1934. Schwörer was born on 18 June 1906 in Stuttgart and listed his occupation as Kaufmann. He joined the SA in 1924 and the party in January 1928.

42. Nachrichtenblatt, 1 (1 April 1934), p. 27, and 5 (1/15 November 1938), p. 63; Führer, 29 August 1933; Karl Gross, ed., Handbuch für den Badischen Landtag: V. Landtagsperiode 1933-1937, p. 146.

43. Gau Baden, Stabsleiter to Oberste Leitung PO, Robert Ley, 10 February 1934, T-81/121/142150. Diehl-Thiele argues that before 1933 there existed thirty-two party organizations, Partei und Staat im Dritten Reich, p. 202.

44. Ley to Wagner, 3 May 1944, T-81/120/141904; Rüstungsinspektion Oberrhein, Ettlingen, "Besprechungen beim Gauleiter am 6.2.45," 7 February 1945, T-73/21/3145967; Nachrichtenblatt, 3 (15 April 1936), p. 21, and 4 (1/15 March 1937), p. 13.

45. Führer, 31 March 1935, 14 December 1937; Nachrichtenblatt, 2 (15 March 1935), p. 23. The Gau personnel office declared that it was good for Nazis to enter private business but it was the movement's real task to induce the best party members to serve the party, state, and municipalities.

46. Gaupersonalamtsleiter to Hartlieb, 2 December 1937, T-81/118/138426; Dinkel to Hilgenfeldt, 9 June 1941, T-81/121/142546; Führer (M), 6 February 1937. For the removal of

one Gauamtsleiter see Gaupersonalamtsleiter to Paul Maass, 18 April 1942, T-81/125/147993, and Schuppel to Freisinger, 23 August 1944, T-81/125/147979.

47. Gaupersonalamtsleiter to Gauschulungsamt, 24 May 1938, T-81/64/72682.

48. Wagner, "Anordnung," 22 June 1942, T-81/127/149611; Orlow, History, 2, pp. 362-63.

49. Führer(M), 16 December 1937.

50. Gaustabsamt Baden, "P.L. und Angestellte der Gau-leitung, Stand Mai 15, 1939," T-81/178/326292-310; Gaustabsamt Baden, "Verzeichnis der P.L. und Angestellte der Gauleitung, Stand 15 August 1939," T-81/178/326290. The employees received salaries between 95 and 300 RM, while the party leaders earned 400 and 500 RM.

51. Stellv. Gauleiter, "Rundschreiben 12/39," 23 February 1939, T-81/119/140367; Gauausbildungsleiter Peters to Pg. Hermann, 25 July 1939, T-81/118/138597; Röhn to Hartlieb, 21 August 1942, T-81/124/146097; Röhn to all Gauamtsleiter, 7 December 1941, T-81/124/146068.

52. Gauleiter, "Anordnung," 16 March 1944, T-81/117/137324; Gaupersonalamtsleiter, "Rundschreiben 24/38," 5 July 1938 (Vertraulich), T-81/118/138421; Röhn to all Kreisleiter, Gauamtsleiter, 3 February 1941, T-81/119/140231.

53. Reichsleitung, "Die Aufbauschulen der Partei-vor-läufige Richtlinien," 8 December 1936 (Vertraulich), T-81/64/72764; Robert Ley and Baldur von Schirach, "Die Adolf Hitler Schulen," 17 January 1937, T-81/64/72731-37. See also David Schoenbaum, Hitler's Social Revolution, pp. 265-72; and Dietrich Orlow, "Die Adolf-Hitler-Schulen," p. 272.

54. Gaupersonalamt, "Anordnung Nr. 23/37," 8 October 1937, T-81/64/72756-61; Führer, 11 March 1938.

55. Beauftragte fd AHS to Gauschulungsamt Baden, 5 March 1943, T-81/155/159027-30; Beauftragte fd AHS to Gauschulungs-amt, 3 June 1943, T-81/64/72405.

56. Reichsschatzmeister to R. Wagner, 30 September 1944, T-81/120/141730-31; Gaupersonalamt, "Rundschreiben Nr. 30/40," 18 September 1940, T-81/118/138392; Kreispersonalamt Zabern, "Rundschreiben Nr. 4/44," 13 July 1944, T-81/167/306829-31.

57. Hauptschulungsamt to Hartlieb, "Berufe der Vater der A.H.S.," 1 June 1938, T-81/64/72669-77; Hauptschulungsamt, Amt AHS, "Berufe der Vater der A.H.S., Stand am 1. Oktober 1940," T-81/64/72475. Orlow ("Die Adolf-Hitler-Schulen") sees no substantial difference between the 1938 and 1940 lists. Yet the decline in the total percentage of workers and farmers was significant as was the fact that in 1940 almost half of the students came from high schools rather than public grade schools.

58. Hauptschulungsamt, Amt f. AHS to Hartlieb, 16 February

1939, T-81/64/72621-23; Gauschulungsleiter to Führer des NS
Dozentenbundes Dr. Berger, 22 February 1940, T-81/64/72520-21;
Beauftragte fd AHS to Gauschulungsleiter Baden, 27 April 1942,
T-81/64/72439-41.

59. BDC/Rheinhold Lawnick Karte; Führer, 27 September
1940; Strassburger Neueste Nachrichten, 14 August 1941, in
T-501/186/342. For Napolas in Baden see Horst Ueberhorst,
ed., Elite für die Diktatur, p. 437.

60. Organisationsamt Baden to Reichsleitung, 2 December
1933, BDC/Schwörer file; Reichsschatzmeister to Wagner, 20
August 1941, T-81/58/66572; "Personalkarte," in BDC/Clever
file; "Ausweis," in BDC/Sievers file. Clever was born in
1896 and Sievers in 1899. Clever worked in an office between
1920 and 1929, and Sievers had training in Kaufm. Lehre.

61. Gauschatzmeister, "Rundschreiben Nr. 23/38," 8
February 1938, in Rundschreiben des Gauschatzmeisters, Jahrgang
1938; Gauschatzmeister, "Rundschreiben Nr. 12/36," 8 February
1936, T-81/122/143440; Nachrichtenblatt, 1 (15 January, 1
August 1934), pp. 5, 56.

62. Nachrichtenblatt, 1 (1 November, 1 May 1934), pp. 76,
34; Gauschatzmeister, "Rundschreiben Nr. 5/38," 11 January
1938, and "Rundschreiben 121/38," 29 August 1938, in Rundschreiben, 1938; Gauschatzmeister, Baden, to Reichsschatzmeister, "Stimmungsbericht 1938," 21 January 1939, T-580/
804/239/39.

63. Gauwaltung, Amt für Beamte to Gauschatzmeister, 31
March 1943, T-81/75/86113; Gauschatzmeister to Wagner, 2
June 1942, T-81/179/328112.

64. Wagner, "Begutachtungsbogen," 15 April 1935, T-81/
228/5010179; Ullmer to Gauschatzmeister, 28 December 1937,
T-81/228/5010167-68; Gauschatzmeister to Ullmer, 22 December
1937, T-81/228/5010169; Gaupersonalamtsleiter, Ergänzungsblatt
zum Antrag auf Besoldungsfestsetzung (Ullmer), 1 July 1941,
T-81/228/5010156; Ullmer to Rudolf Hess, 7 December 1938, and
Ullmer to Schwarz, 8 February 1939, both in BDC/Ullmer file.

65. Wagner to Stellv. des Führers, 14 June 1938, and
Stellv. Gauleiter to Philipp Bouhler, 8 August 1939, both in
BDC/Ullmer file; Ullmer to Gauschatzmeister, 28 October
1938, T-81/228/5010162-63; Röhn to Ullmer, 5 January 1938,
T-81/228/5010165.

66. Schwarz, "Vortragsnotiz," 5 January 1939, and Wagner
to Schwarz, 21 December 1939, and Bouhler to Wagner, 1 February
1940, and Schwarz to Wagner, 15 January 1940, all in BDC/
Ullmer file; Gaupersonalamt, "Besoldung der Kreisleiter der
N.S.D.A.P., Anordnung des Reichsschatzmeisters Nr. 11/41
(Gehaltseinstufung Adalbert Ullmer)," T-81/228/5010154.

67. Gauschatzmeister to Gaupersonalamt, 21 November 1938,
T-81/228/5010161. Gauschatzmeister Baden to Reichsschatzmeister, "Stimmungsbericht 1938," 21 January 1939, T-580/804/
239/39.

68. Gaustabsamt, "Verzeichnis der Politischen Leiter und
Angestellte der Kreise," 15 May 1939, T-81/178/326311-40;
Nachrichtenblatt, 3 (31 January 1936), p. 10, and 5 (January
1938), p. 4; AfK, Baden to Hauptamt fK, 21 June 1937 (and
1942), in BDC/Diverses, Gau Baden.

69. Nachrichtenblatt, 2 (15 January 1935), p. 7; "Stammbuch für Walter Hensle," 6 March 1938, T-81/228/5009695.

70. Gauleiter, "Anordnung," 28 January 1939, T-81/119/
140138; Führer (M), 21 May 1938.

71. Gaustab Baden, "Verzeichnis der Politischen Leiter
und Angestellten der Kreise," 15 May 1939, T-81/178/326311.

72. Kreis Freiburg, "Liste der Kreisämter, Stand 1.
September 1942," T-81/65/74442; "Kreisämter Freiburg i. Br.,
Stand 1. September 1941." T-81/65/74486.

73. This information is based on the BDC files and membership cards of the Kreisleiters listed in the Führer and
most importantly in the Nachrichtenblatt (1, [1 March 1934],
and 4 [15 September/1 October 1937]). The Partei-Statistik
(2:278, 294, 322, 346-63) gives a profile of the Baden Kreisleiters. In 1935, 71 percent of the forty Kreisleiters were
between the ages of twenty-one and forty. Of the forty,
seven were workers (but not industrial workers), five were
farmers, and the rest were white-collar employees, civil
servants, and independents.

74. See the list of Kreisleiters in Verordnungsblatt der
NSDAP, Gau Baden-Elsass, 1 July 1943, sec. 7/p. 30, and the
reports of Kreisleiter appointments in the Verordnungsblatt
between 1942 and 1944; Führer (Ortenau), 7 October 1942.

75. This is based on the Kreisleiter changes reported
in the Nachrichtenblatt between 1935 and 1938, and on the
BDC files or membership cards of the Kreisleiters listed in
the Nachrichtenblatt on 1 March 1934 and 15 September/1
October 1937. For the promotion of one Gauleiter by Wagner,
see Wagner to Bormann, Persönlich, 28 October 1944, T-81/
178/327740-41.

76. BDC/Otto Blank file; CdZ/Personalamt to CdZ/Pers.
Abt., 28 March 1944, T-81/178/327727-29; CdZ/Pers. Abt. to CdZ/
Personalamt, 4 April 1944, T-81/178/327730. Blank was born
in 1899 in Farnau, Schopfheim.

77. Gaugericht, II.Kammer Beschluss, 3 December 1934,
BDC/Rehm file; and Oberste Parteigericht I.Kammer, 14 July
1937; and Personalkarte, 30 April 1934, all BDC/Rehm file;

Oberstaatsanwalt Freiburg to Generalstaatsanwalt Karlsruhe, "Lagebericht," 19 May 1936, GLA/309/1206.

78. Wagner to Röhn, 25 May 1936, T-81/166/305399.

79. Wagner to Schwarz, 29 October 1934, and Schwarz to Wagner, 7 November 1934, both BDC/Knab file; Gaupersonalamt to Kreisleiter Knab, 20 October 1937, T-81/166/305376. For another case see BDC/Helmut Reissner file.

80. CdZ/Adjutant to Gaustabsamtsleiter Schuppel, 23 July 1943, T-81/178/327704; Wagner to Neuscheler, 4 February 1944, T-81/178/327722-23. Neuscheler had joined the party in 1929 in Heidelberg, and eventually he was appointed editor of the Bodensee Rundschau. In 1933 he became the editor of the Führer, but in August 1940 he went to Moscow as a reporter for the Völkischer Beobachter. Then in June 1941 he moved to Vienna to manage the Völkischer Beobachter. In April 1944, he became Kreisleiter of Freiburg; see Strassburger Neueste Nachrichten, 15 April 1944, in T-81/178/327732.

81. This is based on the BDC membership cards or files of the Kreisleiters listed in the Nachrichtenblatt between 1935 and 1938, and on the Verordnungsblatt Baden, June 1941, p. 1; for Rakow see Führer, 19 October, and 27 September 1940. In 1934 there were six Kreisleiters who were either doctors or Ph.D.s and seven Kreisleiters who were farmers; by 1937, only three Kreisleiters were doctors and only two were farmers.

82. Gaupersonalamtsleiter to Gauschatzmeister, 18 November 1937, T-81/166/305374; Knab to Gaugeschäftsführung, 2 January 1939, T-81/166/305357; Partei-Statistik, 2:458; Nachrichtenblatt, 4 (1/15 May 1937), p. 21, and 5 (1/15 July 1938), p. 29.

83. Gaupersonalamtsleiter to Kreisleiter Sauerhöfer, Kehl, 8 January 1941, T-81/228/5010011. Orlow argues (History, 2:362-63) that Bormann attempted to use the Kreisleiters as potential counterweights to the Gauleiter. There is no indication that this was ever tried in Baden, nor would it have succeeded.

84. Bürgermeister of Neunkirchen, Niederdonau, to Gauamtsleiter Schuppel, 9 July 1940, T-81/126/149020.

85. Kreisleiter Senft, "Begutachtungsbogen," 30 November 1938, T-81/228/5009718; Kreisleiter Schneider, "Begutachtungsbogen," 1 July 1938, T-81/228/5009768; Kreisleiter Rakow, Mosbach, to Gaupersonalamtsleiter, 21 May 1941, T-81/228/5009741; Gaupersonalamtsleiter to Fred Himmel, 3 May 1942, T-81/228/5009736.

86. Gaustabsamtsleiter, "Rundschreiben Nr. 73/42," 2 December 1942, T-81/178/327662; Kreisleiter, Freiburg, "Rundschreiben," 29 October 1943, T-81/65/74377; Kreisleitung Freiburg, "Organisationsbefehl Nr. 3," 20 October 1943, T-81/

65/74384; Kreisleiter Rombach to Wagner, 14 December 1944, T-73/21/3145732.

87. Report of Leutnant u. Kdo. Führer Schöder, sent to Wagner by his Stellv. Btl. Kommandeur, 19 September 1944, T-81/ 178/327737; Rüstungskommando Freiburg, "Aktennotiz: Unbefügte Einschaltung von Dienststellen und Behörden," (November 1943), T-84/35/1310764.

88. Gauorganisationsleiter, "Rundschreiben Nr. 3/39," 30 October 1939, T-81/118/138584; Gaustabsamtsleiter, "Rundschreiben Nr. 41/44," 22 March 1944, T-81/117/137164; Gaustabsamtsleiter to Gauamtsleiter, 10 October 1944, T-81/137104.

89. Reichsjugendführer to Wagner, 28 September 1944, T-81/ 120/141732; Gauamt für Kommunalpolitik to Kreisleiter Rakow, 29 January 1941, T-81/228/5009745.

90. Gaustabsamtsleiter, "Rundschreiben," 8 July 1942, T-81/127/149647; Gaustabsamtsleiter, "Rundschreiben," 3 June 1942, T-81/127/149624; Stellv. Gauleiter, "Rundschreiben Nr. 121/44," 16 August 1944, T-81/124/145967; Gaustabsamtsleiter, "Rundschreiben Nr. 108/44," 12 July 1944, T-81/165/117/304163.

91. Oberlandesgerichtspräsident to RJM Thierack, "Bericht zur Lage," 13 September 1943, GLA/309/1205.

92. Partei-Kanzlei, "Besoldungsfestsetzung," 15 September 1942, BDC/Ernst Bäckert file; Reichsführer SS (draft note) to Bormann, Tgb. No. III/II 2202/44, in BDC/Bäckert file; Landgerichtspräsident Grüninger, Konstanz, to Oberlandesgerichtspräsident, 1 December 1944, GLA/309/1205. Bäckert, born in 1899 in Überlingen, listed his occupation as Magazinverwalter.

93. Gauschatzmeister to Reichsschatzmeister, Zentralpersonalamt, 3 February 1945, BDC/Bäckert file.

94. Roberts, The House that Hitler Built, pp. 72-73.

95. Karl Beberich (Buchen) to Pg. Neumann, 3 July 1934, T-81/228/5010152; Kreisleitung Waldshut, "Bericht vom 20.5.43," T-81/165/304255.

96. Gaugericht Baden, I. Kammer, Beschluss, 31 January 1939, BDC/Wilhelm Krieg file; Gaugericht Baden, II. Kammer, Beschluss, 26 October 1936, BDC/Edmund Kreuzer file.

97. Manger to Robert Ley, 4 October 1935; and Manger to Gaugericht, 2 October 1935, and Gaugericht (Hüssy), Vermittlungsversuch Manger/Dr. Roth, 19 October 1935, all BDC/ Hanns Valentin Manger file.

98. Orlow argues (History, 2:421) that in the waning days of the regime control won out over Betreuung. But we have to remember that the war situation, not the party structure, enabled the Kreisleiters to encroach on state and military prerogatives.

99. Ernest K. Bramstedt, Goebbels and National Socialist

Propaganda, 1925-1945, pp. 453-54.

100. Gaupropagandaamt Baden, ed., Richtlinien für die Propagandisten der NSDAP, Gau Baden, p. 3; Nachrichtenblatt, 2 (15 July 1935), pp. 54-55, and 3 (15 January 1936), p. 8. Kreispropagandaamt Emmendingen, "Erntedankfest 1936," 19 September 1936, T-81/122/143383.

101. Nachrichtenblatt, 4 (1 June 1937), p. 37; Führer, 19 June 1938, 15 April 1939, 18 April 1937, 25 June 1938, and 6 May 1938. The district of Karlsruhe, for example, held 500 rallies between June 1937 and June 1938. Between July 1938 and April 1939, when Nazi policies required constant defense, the district held 940 rallies.

102. Gaupersonalamt to Knab, 6 November 1933, T-81/166/ 305407; Gauschatzmeister, "Rundschreiben Nr. 55/38," 22 March 1938, in Rundschreiben, 1938; Führer, 30 October 1934; Nachrichtenblatt, 2 (1 January 1935), p. 3.

103. Führer, 17 November 1938, 25 March 1939; Schulungs- und Verordnungsblatt Gau Baden (Ausgabe Elsass), 1 August 1941, Folge 2, Blatt 4.

104. Orlow castigates Ley's schooling system as "unsuited to produce the technically competent political elite needed to bring about an able administration of German society." To Orlow the system was inadequate because it allegedly failed to create decision makers and merely produced "ideologically fanaticized officials," Orlow, History, 2:85-86, 187-88, 220- 22.

105. Reichsschulungsleiter, "Denkschrift über die Schulung der P.O. und der Deutschen Arbeitsfront," 29 May 1933, T-81/ 63/72109-117; Reichsschulungsleiter, "Anordnung Nr. 7/33," 19 June 1933, T-81/63/72102.

106. On Baumann see BDC/Baumann Mitgliedskarte; and Heinz Baumann to Rückwanderer Amt Stuttgart, 10 November 1936, T-81/155/159261; for Hartlieb see Führer (A), 15 February 1934; Gauschatzmeister to Hartlieb, 15 August 1943, and Per- sonalkarte Hartlieb, 5 January 1937, both BDC/Hartlieb file.

107. Wilhelm Hartlieb, "Entwurf eines Lehrplanes für die Schulung in Kreisen und Ortsgruppen," 16 September 1936, T-81/ 172/312885-95.

108. Führer (L), 18 April 1934; Nachrichtenblatt, 1 (15 April 1934), p. 31.

109. Führer, 22 December 1934; Nachrichtenblatt 1 (1 and 15 December 1934), pp. 84, 85.

110. Gauschulungsamt, "Anordnung," 20 October 1936, T-81/ 172/312875; Gauschulungsamt to Gaupersonalamt, 4 October 1937, T-81/118/138435; Gauschulungsleiter to Wagner, 20 Janu- ary 1936, T-81/119/140140; Führer, 1 January 1936; Nach-

richtenblatt, 3 (1 November 1936), p. 70.

111. Nachrichtenblatt, 2 (15 December 1935), p. 87; Hartlieb, "Entwurf eines Lehrplanes," 16 September 1936, T-81/172/312885-95; Gauamtsleiter, RPA, to Gauschulungsamt, 24 January 1939, T-81/118/138527.

112. Gauschulungsamt, "Rundschreiben Nr. 15/36," 26 September 1936, T-81/172/312877-80; Gauschulungsamt, "Rundschreiben Nr. 7/37," 12 February 1937, T-81/172/312863-65; Gauschulungsamt to Gauobmann, DAF, 25 March 1937, T-81/172/312986.

113. Führer (A), 27 September 1936; Gauschulungsleiter to Wagner, 1 August 1938, T-81/119/140101.

114. Gaupersonalamtsleiter to Gauamtsleitungen, 21 September 1937, T-81/118/138437; Gauschulungsleiter to Beauftragten der Parteileitung, Pg. Oechsle, 3 March 1936, T-81/155/158992; Gauschulungsburg Frauenalb, "Beurteilungsbogen für PL, Februar 12-März 1, 1939," 1 March 1939, T-81/228/5010245.

115. Gauschulungsamt to Gaudietwart, RDL, 10 December 1937, T-81/89/101758.

116. Kreispersonalamt Bruchsal, "Fragebogen zur politischen Beurteilung," 25 March 1937, T-81/89/101812; Hartlieb to Gaudietwart Richard Kraft, 19 May 1938, T-81/89/101732; "Lehrgang für Kreis- und Abschnittsdietwarte am 9. bis 12. Juni 1938," T-81/89/101729.

117. Führer, 21 and 31 March 1935.

118. Gauschulungsleiter to Schuppel, 20 March 1940, T-81/119/140286.

119. "Tätigkeitsbericht der Landesdienststelle Baden (der Reichsstelle zur Förderung des deutschen Schrifttums), über den Monat Oktober 1936," 12 November 1936, T-81/118/139199-200; "Arbeitsbericht des Gauschrifttumsbeauftragten von Baden für die Monate Juli, August, September, Oktober 1937," 26 October 1937, T-81/118/139157; Bickler to Kraemer, 27 March 1941, T-81/174/315666.

120. Gauschulungsamt, "Rundschreiben Nr. 74/37," 18 December 1937, T-81/172/312689-90; Gauschulungsamt, Hauptstelle Büchereiwesen, "Rundschreiben Nr. 9/39," 28 February 1939, T-81/117/138183.

121. "Arbeitsbericht des Gauschrifttumsbeauftragten," 26 October 1937, T-81/118/139157; Gauschulungsamt, "Borromäusbüchereien im Gau Baden," c. 1939, T-81/176/324409-10; "Arbeitsbericht des Gauschrifttumsbeauftragten," 7 January 1938, T-81/118/139150. In 1937 there were 856 Catholic and 276 Protestant libraries in Baden; by 1939 the Catholic libraries had increased to 926 units.

122. Führer (Merkur), 25 May 1940; NS Gemeinde, 7 (January 1939), p. 18; Tagepost, 24 November 1938, in T-81/118/

139110.

123. Führer, 2 April 1940; Gauschulungsamt, ed., "Grenz-gauwacht am Oberrhein," Folge 1/40 (January 1940), in T-81/23/20833-34. In Hamburg, Gauleiter Kaufmann closed the indoc-trination office after 1939; Orlow, History, 2:278.

124. Hartlieb to Röhn, "Vorschlag für die Schulung der Erzieher und Beamten," May 1943, T-81/124/146010-11; Kreis-schulungsleiter, Lahr, to Gauschulungsamt, 12 June 1943, T-81/124/146269; Kreisleitung Rastatt, "Bericht vom 24. Juni 1943," T-81/165/304208.

125. Gauschulungsleiter to Kreisleiter, 6 December 1941, T-81/21/18968-70; Gauschulungsamt, "Morgenfeier der N.S.D.A.P. zum 30.1.1943," T-81/165/304576-80; Kreisschulungsamt Wertheim to Gauschulungsamt, 5 March 1943, T-81/165/3043503.

126. Hauptschulungsamt to Gauschulungsamt Baden, 1 July 1941, T-81/63/71663; Gaubeauftragte fd geistige Betreuung der Umsiedler in den Lagern to Hauptschulungsamt, "Arbeitsbericht für Monat Juli 1941," 1 August 1941, T-81/119/139666-69.

127. Kreisschulungsamt Sinsheim to Gauschulungsamt, 26 February 1941, T-81/165/304506; Kreisleitung Freiburg, Beauf-tragte fd Wochenendschulung, "Rundschreiben," 11 January 1943, T-81/65/74090-91.

128. Kreisschulungsamt Bruchsal to Gaubeauftragten fd geistige Betreuung der Umsiedler, 29 August 1941, T-81/119/139731; Kreisschulungsleiter, Wertheim, to Gaubeauftragten fd geistige Betreuung der Umsiedler, 3 September 1941, T-81/119/139734-35; Gaubeauftragte fd geistige Betreuung der Umsiedler in den Lagern to Kreisschulungsleiter, 22 October 1942, T-81/119/139609-10.

129. Gauschulungsamt to Gauorganisationsamt, 23 January 1940, T-81/118/138578; Hartlieb to Röhn, 19 June 1941, T-81/119/140202; Hartlieb to Röhn, 13 July 1942, T-81/124/146108; Hartlieb to Röhn, 8 August 1944, T-81/124/145972; Hartlieb to Röhn, 23 September 1944, T-81/124/145959.

130. Kreisschulungsamt Lahr to GSA, 31 March 1944, T-81/124/146440-41; Kreisschulungsamt Bruchsal to GSA, 19 June 1944, T-81/124/146475-76; Kreisschulungsamt Schlettstadt to GSA, 20 December 1943, T-81/124/146393.

131. Hartlieb to Röhn, 12 February 1944, T-81/124/145999; Röhn, "Rundschreiben 32/44," 23 February 1944, T-81/117/137326; Gauschulungsleiter to Gaupersonalamt, 18 June 1938, T-81/118/138422-23.

132. Dinkel to Merdes, 23 June 1941, T-81/172/31358; CdZ/Elsass (Per. Abt.) to Röhn, 27 June 1942, T-81/121/145957; NSV Kreisamtsleiter, Konstanz, to Dinkel, 6 February 1943, T-81/86/97968.

133. Kreisschulungsamt Müllheim to Gauschulungsamt, "Tätigkeitsbericht 2. Vierteljahr 1943," T-81/124/146214.

134. Gauschulungsamt, "Dezember Bericht, 1938," T-81/118/139120-22; Georg Linder to Hartlieb, 24 November 1941, T-81/119/140080; Hartlieb to Wagner, 11 December 1941, T-81/119/14011-12; Wagner to Hartlieb, 11 March 1942, T-81/124/145920.

135. Rüst. Inspekt. Oberrhein, Ettlingen, "Besprechungen beim Gauleiter am 6.2.45," 7 February 1945, T-73/21/3145967-68; Kreisleiter, Stockach to Landrat Stockach, 15 March 1945, SAF/317/1041.

136. Amann to R. Wagner, 21 August 1941, T-81/120/141751.

137. Pirsch, "Aktennotiz, Telefonische Unterredung mit Pg. Weinbrecht vom 8. Jan., 1942," 8 January 1942, T-81/122/143982-83.

138. Stellv. Gauleiter, "Rundschreiben 123/44," 16 August 1944, T-81/124/145966; Rüstungskommando Strassburg, "Wochenbericht der Gruppe Z für die Zeit v.1.-6.6.42," 6 June 1942, T-84/35/1310804; Rüstungskommando Strassburg, "Vierteljahresbericht der Gruppe Ia PL für die Monate April, Mai, Juni 1944," 25 July 1944, T-84/35/1310660; Führer, 8 August 1944.

139. Kreisleitung Freiburg, "Rundschreiben," 10 September 1944, T-81/65/74263; Kreisleiter, Freiburg, "Rundschreiben 16/44," 28 October 1944, T-81/65/74231; Speer to Wagner (Abschrift), Fernschreiben, 14 September 1944, T-81/169/1536790.

140. Stellv. Gauleiter, "Rundschreiben," 24 October 1944, T-81/94/108262-63.

141. Führer, 26 and 27 October, 13 November 1944; Gaupropagandaleiter to all Kreispropagandaleiter, 7 November 1944, T-81/94/108231-32.

142. Kreisleitung Wertheim, "Stimmungsmässiger Überblick zur politischen Lage," 25 October 1944, T-81/165/304303; Kreisleitung Pforzheim, "Stimmungsmässiger Überblick über die Gesamtpolitische Lage," 20 October 1944, T-81/164/302146.

143. Gaupropagandaleiter to Gau and Kreisredner, 6 March 1943, T-81/65/74406; Führer, 16 and 17 August, 1 November 1943.

144. Führer, 21 November, 23 July, 30/31 December, 1944, 29 and 27 and 30 March 1945; New York Times, 31 March 1945; Kreispropagandaleiter Freiburg, "Wichtiges Rundschreiben," 14 September 1944, T-81/65/74259-60.

145. Kreisleitung Sinsheim, "Stimmungsmässiger Überblick über die polit. Lage," 4 October 1944, T-81/164/302165; Kreisleitung Offenburg, "Stimmung der Bevölkerung," 6 September 1944, T-81/165/304202; Kreisleitung Lörrach, "Stimmung

und Haltung der Bevölkerung," 1 September 1944, T-81/167/
306776; SD Hauptaussenstelle Mannheim to SD Führer Strassburg,
14 November 1944, T-175/269/2765109-27; Wagner to Bormann, 5
September 1944, T-81/R171/311213-14.

146. SD Rastatt to SD Führer Baden-Elsass, 8 March 1945,
T-175/512/9378501; SD Aussenstelle Konstanz to SD Führer
Baden-Elsass, 13 March 1945, T-175/512/9378474; Kreisleitung
Buchen, "Allgemeine Stimmung," 15 August 1944, T-81/126/
148499-500; Kreispropagandaleiter Freiburg to Ortsgruppen-
leiter, 14 September 1944, T-81/65/74256.

147. SD Aussenstelle Offenburg to SD Führer Baden, 9
March 1945, T-175/512/9378509-10; SD Hauptaussenstelle Mannheim to SD Führer Baden-Elsass, 9 March 1945, T-175/512/9378479.

148. SD Aussenstelle Villingen to SD Führer Baden-
Elsass, 7 March 1945, T-175/512/9378525; SD Aussenstelle
Lörrach to SD Führer Baden-Elsass, 14 March 1945, T-175/512/
9378538-41. One joke in the Lörrach area related that Hitler
had fallen in love with a Japanese called Sigisfutschi (victory is lost). The Baden example provides no evidence to support Orlow's suggestion (History, 2:478) that if the party
had disintegrated in January 1945, the war would have ended
sooner.

149. Kreisleitung Waldshut, "Bericht vom 20.5.43," T-81/
165/304255; Oberlandgerichtspräsident to RJM Thierack, "Bericht
zur Lage," 2 January 1945, GLA/309/1205; SD Hauptaussenstelle
Karlsruhe to SD Führer Baden-Elsass, 9 March 1945, T-175/512/
9377484-45; SD Aussenstelle Rastatt to SD Führer Baden-Elsass,
8 March 1945, T-175/512/9378499. Gauleiter Wagner confirmed
this general pessimism in a conversation with Goebbels in
early 1945, see Trevor-Roper, ed., Final Entries 1945: The
Diaries of Joseph Goebbels, p. 352.

150. A good summary of the problem faced by the Nazi one-
party system is given by Carl J. Friedrich, who concludes that
"the concessions which had to be made in building the complex
and contradictory party organization, because the country the
party was meant to rule was already a complex industrial society, the dualism of party and protective guards (S.S.) which
resulted from these concessions, the aggressive racial and
foreign policies which the search for demonstrable legitimizing successes precipitated, escalating eventually into vast
military conflict with disastrous results--all these tend to
show that a one-party system is no solution to the tensions
and breakdowns of an industrially developed country"; see
"The Failure of a One-Party System: Hitler's Germany," p. 255.
For the mood of the Gau leadership in April 1945 as reported
by the SS Captain Fritz Hockenjos, see Hermann Riedel, ed.,

Ausweglos: Letzter Akten des Krieges, pp. 188-89. Hockenjos
described the party gathering in Schönberg as a "verscheuchten,
rat- und hilfslosen Verein," (an intimidated and helpless
group).

CHAPTER TWELVE

1. For a discussion of the Nazi domination of Europe see
Lothar Gruchmann, Nationalsozialistische Grossraumordnung, pp.
119-20.
2. See, for example, Andreé Viollis [Andreé Francoise
Caroline d'Ardenne de Tizac], Alsace et Lorraine au-dessus des
Passions, pp. 145-46.
3. Lieutenant A. Rioux à Monsieur le Président du Conseil
Ministre de la Guerre, 3 May 1933, T-175/273/2770250-52.
4. For background information see Francois G. Dreyfus,
La Vie Politique en Alsace 1919-1936, pp. 265-70; Karl-Heinz
Rothenberger, Die Elsass-lothringische Heimat- und Autonomie-
bewegung zwischen den beiden Weltkriegen; Philip Bankwitz,
Alsatian Autonomist Leaders, 1919-1947; Kettenacker, National-
sozialistische Volkstumspolitik im Elsass; and Mildred S.
Wertheimer, "Alsace-Lorraine: A Border Problem," pp. 465-82.
In 1940, three of the four top judicial posts in Alsace were
in the hands of "French" officials, see Generalstaatsanwalt
Baden to Staatssekretär Dr. Schlegelberger, "Lagebericht über
die Strafrechtspflege im Elsass seit der Übernahme in deutsche
Verwaltung," GLA/309/1205.
5. SD des RFSS, Oberabschnitt Süd-West, "Pressebericht,"
14 March 1938, T-175/464/2982889-90; SD des RFSS, "Pressebericht," 2 March 1937, T-175/464/2983014-15; Eugene C.J.
Werler, Kampfmittel des Materialismus und die katholische
Aktion im Elsass, 1938, in T-175/409/2932892.
6. Wertheimer, "Alsace-Lorraine," pp. 478-80.
7. Kolmarer Kurier, 15 July 1941, T-81/538/5308931;
Strassburger Neueste Nachrichten, 21 September 1941, in T-501/
186/363; Dreyfus, La Vie Politique, pp. 259-60; Rothenberger,
Autonomiebewegungen, p. 205; Bopp, L'Alsace sous l'occupation
allemande, pp. 29-33.
8. Paul Schall, Karl Roos und der Kampf des heimattreuen
Elsass, pp. 21-26; Dreyfus, La Vie Politique, pp. 259-60.
9. Paul Schall was born in 1898 in Strassburg. He first
became editor of the Strassburger Neueste Nachrichten (SNN)
in 1941 and then in 1943 Kreisleiter of Strassburg; after 1945
he escaped to Germany and continued his right-wing activities,
see SNN, 24 June and 6 July 1941, in T-501/186/306 and 318;

Kurt P. Tauber, Beyond Eagle and Swastika, 1:178, 199.

10. Bickler to Wagner, "Lebenslauf von H.C. Bickler mit Angaben über die Nationalsozialistische Bewegung im Elsass vor September 1939," 7 December 1940, T-81/179/328005-13; Bickler to W. Scheuermann, Zeitgeschichtliches Archiv der Stadt Strassburg, 24 September 1941, T-81/166/305137.

11. Die Elsass-Lothringer Partei: Ihr Wesen und Ziel, in T-81/179/328036-51.

12. Dr. Erfurth (DAI), "Elsass-Fahrt vom 3.VI-7.VI, 1938," 19 September 1938, T-81/490/5250572-74; Dr. von Loesch to Bickler, 21 February 1941, T-81/174/315476; Bickler to von Loesch, 24 February 1941, T-81/174/315475.

13. Alldeutscher Verband to Reichskanzler Bülow (c. 1900), T-81/611/5402781-86.

14. Spiesser to Wagner, 26 January 1940, in Kampfbriefe aus dem Elsass, pp. 186-90; see also H. D. Loock, "Der Hünenburg Verlag, Friedrich Spiesser, und der Nationalsozialismus," pp. 399-417.

15. Badische Staatsministerium to RMI, 10 March 1922, GLA/233/11020. For Baden's claim on Upper Alsace during WWI see Karl-Heinz Janssen, Macht und Verblendung, pp. 208, 204.

16. For the Freiburg and Black Forest area, which suffered from a decline in tourist trade, see Badischer Verkehrsverband to MdI, Karlsruhe, December 1929, and Oberbürgermeister Freiburg to MdI, 19 October 1929, in GLA/233/11021; for Kehl see Badische Presse, 9 February 1927; Badisches Landwirtschaftliches Wochenblatt, vol. 97 (21 September 1929); and Landrat Schindele, Kehl, to MdI, Baden, 12 December 1930, SAF/358/56.

17. Badische Arbeitsministerium to Bad. Staatsministerium, 6 April 1921, GLA/233/27935; Politischer Rundbrief, 6 December 1918. For the popularity of the Elsass-Lothringer Zeitung in Baden see Generalstaatsanwalt, Karlsruhe, "Lagebericht," 7 October 1937, in Schadt, ed., Lageberichte der Gestapo, pp. 258-61.

18. Badische Staatsanwaltschaft Karlsruhe to Landgericht, Strafkammer I, 7 September 1923, GLA/234/5738; Gend. Oberwachtmeister, Schwetzingen to Staatsanwaltschaft Karlsr., 22 October 1921, GLA/309/1164. Ernst was born in October 1881 and Hugo Kromer on 2 August 1896.

19. About 4 percent of all Baden Nazis who had joined the party by 1923 and were still active in 1933 were natives of Alsace-Lorraine; this information is based on the BDC membership cards and files of the following: Kurt Gawran (1897), Fritz Skibbe (1894), Willi Worch (1896), Heinrich Sauerhöfer (1901), and on the police and judicial reports on Kurt Maier, Richard Ihm (1908), and Ferdinand Stitz (1898);

see Staatsanwaltschaft I, Freiburg, to Generalstaatsanwalt,
10 September 1929, GLA/234/5703; Landespolizeiamt Heidelberg,
Abt. N, to Landespolizeiamt Karlsruhe, 23 June 1930, GLA/377/
5399; Badische Staatsanwaltschaft Karlsruhe to Landgericht,
Strafkammer I, 7 September 1923, GLA/234/5738.

20. The biographical information can be found in SNN,
21 August 1941; 30 July 1941, in T-501/186/335-44; and Kolmarer Kurier, 4 January 1941, in T-81/537/5307454.

21. For Baden's role in Switzerland see the correspon-
dence of Kraft to Strasser, 10 December 1931, and Wagner to
Strasser, 10 December 1931, both in BDC/file 311; Wagner to
Strasser, 1 March 1932, T-580/65/folder 311.

22. Führer, 6 October, 9 June 1928, and 31 May 1930;
Ernst, Rechenschaftsbericht, p. 231.

23. Führer, 29 and 21 August 1935.

24. Bickler to Kreisleiter Lang, Molsheim, 17 September
1941, T-81/174/315889-90; Mitarbeiter des DAI, "Reisebericht
vom 4. Juli 1941: Beobachtungen und Eindrücke aus dem Elsass,"
18 July 1941, T-81/538/5308526-29.

25. Dreyfus, La Vie Politique, p. 154; Joseph M. Maitre,
"Die französischen Frontkämpfer in Freiburg i. Br.," pp.
171-77.

26. Metz to Gauleitung Württemberg-Hohenzollern, 25
November 1935, GLA/233/25693; Scherberger to Hartlieb, 15
January 1941, T-81/100/116697; Gauschulungsamt, "Dezember
Bericht 1938," T-81/118/139120-22.

27. Robert Ernst, Rechenschaftsbericht eines Elsässers,
pp. 22-28, 138-46, 209; Ernst, "Deutschland und Elsass-
Lothringen," pp. 624-27; Ernst, "Zur Ermordung von Dr. Karl
Roos," in T-81/513/5276096-97; Rothenberger, Autonomiebewe-
gung, pp. 140-41.

28. Dr. Erfurth, "Elsass-Fahrt vom 3.VI-7.VI, 1938,"
19 September 1938, T-81/490/5250572-74; Gestapo agents who
went to Strassburg disguised as émigrées noted the strong
anti-Semitism; see Gestapo Karlsruhe, "Lagebericht," 14 April
1934, in Schadt, ed., Lageberichte der Gestapo, pp. 86-96.

29. See "Deutschland und Frankreich--von einen Elsässer,"
pp. 656-58.

30. Völkischer Beobachter, 26 September 1925, 5 October,
10 December 1927, and 23/24 December 1928; Baynes, ed.,
Hitler's Speeches, II, pp. 1145, 1191, 1491, 1515, 1696;
Hitler, "Dummheiten oder Verbrechen," (c. 1922), in HA/2/46.

31. Hitler, Mein Kampf, pp. 371-72; Gerhard Weinberg,
ed., Hitlers zweite Buch, pp. 194-95.

32. Speer, Inside the Third Reich, p. 172. During such
"table talks" in 1942, Hitler did not hesitate to plan to

expel thousands of Alsatian peasants to make room for peasants
from Baden and Württemberg; Hitler's Secret Conversations
1941-1944, p. 576.

33. Ernst, Rechenschaftsbericht, pp. 227-31; Gauschulungs-
amt Baden, ed., "Grenzgauwacht am Oberrhein," Folge 6/40
(June 1940), in T-81/23/20795-96; "Aus dem Brief von Dr.
Pöschel vom 4.1.1940," DAI (Abschrift), T-81/513/5276260.

34. DAI, "Aus dem Brief Hellmut Culmann, Billigheim,"
16 July 1940, T-81/513/5276261; Dr. Karl Pöschel, "Welche
Fehler sind in der Behandlung Elsass-Lothringens gemacht
worden," 18 June 1940, T-81/514/5277252-57.

35. Ernst, Rechenschaftsbericht, pp. 232-37, 261. On
20 June 1940, Goebbels ordered that all public reports about
Alsace-Lorraine must avoid specific demands for the future
of the provinces; see Willi A. Boelcke, ed., Wollt ihr den
totalen Krieg?, p. 399. For further background information
see Eberhard Jäckel, Frankreich in Hitlers Europa, pp. 78-83.

36. Generalstaatsanwalt to RJM, "Lagebericht," 20 July
1941, GLA/309/1205; CdZ/Pers. Abtl. to Generalstaatsanwalt
Karlsruhe, 5 February 1942, T-81/179/327904; Frick to Wagner,
8 August 1940, T-77/388/1236862.

37. Wagner, "Vollmacht," 26 November 1944, T-73/21/
3145736; Wagner to Interministeriellen Luftkriegsschädenaus-
schuss im Reichsministerium für Volksaufklärung und Propaganda,
18 July 1944, T-81/165/304363; Bormann to Wagner, persönlich,
26 November 1941, T-81/R171/311330.

38. CZ/Personalamt to Reichsbahnpräsidenten, 13 March
1941, T-81/166/304979; Reichsbahndirektion Karlsruhe to CdZ/
Personalamt, 13 March 1941, T-81/166/304977.

39. Schulz-Fielitz to Köhler, 17 September 1942, T-73/1/
1045669-10; Köhler to Schulz-Fielitz, 21 December 1942, T-73/
1/1045661-4; Barth (Ministerialdiregent) to Köhler, 2 April
1943, "Ergebnisse der Besprechung vom 26.3.1943," T-73/1/
1045649-53.

40. CdZ/Pers. Abtl., "Aktenbermerkung," 13 April 1943,
T-73/1/1045647. Speer was much more successful in his attempts
to control industrial developments in Baden (over the protest
of Wagner); see Willi A. Boelcke, ed., Deutschlands Rüstung
im Zweiten Weltkrieg, p. 76.

41. CdZ/Pers. Referent to Mauch, 19 March 1941, T-81/
154/158298; Schwarz to Wagner, 15 February 1943, T-81/121/
142123; Gauschatzmeister to Paul Schall (persönlich), 29
January 1943, T-81/174/315497.

42. Röhn to Schwarz, 18 February 1944, T-81/120/141798;
Wagner to Schwarz, 9 February 1944, T-81/120/141790; Schwarz
to Röhn, 19 May 1944, T-81/120/141788.

43. Wagner to Bormann, 12 October 1944, T-81/R.171/311210; Wagner to Bormann (Geheim), 17 August 1944, T-81/178/327515; Wagner to Bormann, 11 July 1944, T-81/178/327672; Ernst, Rechenschaftsbericht, p. 270.

44. Führer, 5 and 17 July 1940.

45. Ortsgruppe Ettenheim to Gau Archiv, "Kriegsauswirkung," 21 June 1940, T-81/127/300127-28; Ortsgruppe Ettenheim to Gau Archiv, 25 June 1940, T-81/127/300129-30; Kreisleiter Karl Walther, Offenbach/aM, to Kreisleiter Fritsch, Strassburg, 25 September 1940, T-81/174/315828. The mayor of Zell, for example, was caught in Alsace with ninety-seven packages of tobacco and nine French military coats, see Generalstaatsanwalt Karlsruhe to RJM, "Lagebericht," 28 August 1940, GLA/309/1205.

46. Meldungen aus dem Reich, No. 100 (27 June 1940), T-175/259/2751859-61.

47. Ernst, Rechenschaftsbericht, p. 140; Paul Kluke, "Nationalsozialistische Volkstumspolitik im Elsass-Lothringen 1940 bis 1945," p. 627; Generalstaatsanwalt Karlsruhe to RJM, "Lagebericht," 20 July 1941, GLA/309/1205; Oberlandesgerichtspräsident, Karlsruhe, to RJM (persönlich), "Bericht über die Lage im Oberlandesgerichtsbezirk Karlsruhe, 3 December 1942, GLA/309/1205. Kettenacker (Volkstumspolitik) undermines his valuable study by omitting the numerous public opinion reports from his book.

48. Wagner to Partei-Kanzlei, 15 June 1942, T-81/R.171/311300-302.

49. Meldungen aus dem Reich, No. 108 (25 July 1940), T-175/259/2752063; ibid., No. 133 (17 October 1940), T-175/260/2752592, ibid., No. 178 (10 April 1941), T-175/260/2753632-36; ibid., No. 229 (16 October 1941), T-175/261/2755025-27; Höhere SS und PF beim CdZ, "Lagebericht," 10 October 1940, T-175/280/2774358.

50. Guido Waldman, "Bericht über die Reise im Elsass vom 29.-31. Juli 1940," T-81/273/2393533-38; Hellmut Culmann to DAI, Stuttgart, 19 August 1940, T-81/513/5276223-28.

51. CdZ beim AOK 7, Kolmar, "Bescheinigung," 30 June 1940, T-175/280/2774333; Führer, 2 July 1940. According to Ernst, who became general advisor on Alsatian affairs, both Köhler and Pflaumer warned him that he would have a most difficult task, Rechenschaftsbericht, p. 242.

52. Kettenacker, Volkstumspolitik, pp. 141-43; DAI, "Erste Ernennungen, erste Aufbauarbeit," 29 June 1940, T-81/513/5276127; Landkommissar, Zabern, to Ortsgruppe Zabern, 16 April 1941, T-81/167/307110-11. Dr. Petri, who was born in Strassburg in 1876 and had experience in Alsace in police

and state service before he moved to Baden in 1918, was the only "Alsatian" Landkommissar, see SNN, 14 June 1941, in T-501/186/303.

53. Reichsstatthalter/Personalamt, "Rundschreiben," 15 July 1940, T-81/119/140095; CdZ/Personalamt, "Rundschreiben," 11 July 1940, T-81/119/140096.

54. Ernst Günter Dickmann, "Unterredung mit Gauleiter R. Wagner," 14 September 1940, T-81/513/5276635; SNN, 8 July 1940, in T-81/513/5276153; Führer, 14 February 1941. "Old Alsatian" refers to people whose parents or grandparents were born in Alsace before 1871. By early 1941 over 8,000 applications received from the Reich were concerned with economic matters alone.

55. Adolf Schmid, "Die Lösung des elsässischen Problems," p. 312; Oberlandesgerichtspräsident to RJM, Thierack (persönlich), "Bericht," 3 December 1942, GLA/309/1205.

56. Deutsche Presse, 18 January 1941 (Abschrift), in T-81/537/5307543; Bopp, L'Alsace, pp. 197-213, 181; Kettenacker, Volkstumspolitik, pp. 162, 159; Hale, Captive Press, pp. 280-81.

57. Stellv. Gauleiter to Kreisleiters, Gauamtsleiter, 3 September 1940, T-81/119/140248; Gauorganisationsamt/Nebenstelle Strassburg, "Rundschreiben Nr. 25/41," 6 October 1941, T-81/117/306133-34.

58. Eugene Schaeffer, L'Alsace et la Lorraine, 1940-45, pp. 119-28.

59. J. Rosse to Wagner, 16 November 1940, T-81/154/158262; Bormann to Wagner, 20 January 1941, T-175/475/2997620-21; Kettenacker, Volkstumspolitik, p. 199.

60. Hitler's Secret Conversations 1941-44, pp. 516-20.

61. CdZ/Gädeke, "Notiz," 12 July 1943, T-81/179/328189; CdZ/Pers. Abtl. to BdS/Fischer, 16 March 1943, T-81/179/328219; Kettenacker, Volkstumspolitik, p. 201. For the role of the clergy and for a view of conflicts between Nazis and the church in Alsace, see Kreisleiter Fritsch, Altkirch, "Aktivität der Konfessionen, März 30 bis April 4, 1943," T-81/165/304274; Bickler to Rudolf Lang, Zabern, 6 October 1941, T-81/174/315887.

62. Amt für Beamte, Hagenau, to Kreisleiter Dieffenbacher, "Tätigkeitsbericht," 15 January 1941, T-81/127/300228; Amt für Kommunalpolitik, Hagenau, "Tätigkeitsbericht," 21 January 1941, T-81/127/300222.

63. Josef Kaufmann, "Die Tätigkeit des Amtes für Kommunalpolitik des Gaues Baden/Nebenstelle Strassburg," pp. 137-39; SNN, 6 March 1941, in T-81/537/5307419; Kolmarer Kurier, 27 January 1941, in T-81/513/5276126.

64. For biographical information see SNN, 14 June 1941,
in T-501/186/302; SNN, 18 June 1941, in T-501/186/305; Kolmarer
Kurier, 11 November 1940 (Abschrift), in T-81/513/5276129.
    65. CdZ/Pers. Abtl. to CdZ/Verwaltungs und Polizeiabtlg.,
22 July 1941, T-81/162/300331; Kaufmann, "Die Tätigkeit des
Amtes für Kommunalpolitik," pp. 137-39.
    66. Bickler to Kreisleiter Lawnick, 13 January 1942,
T-81/174/315864; Lawnick to Bickler, 23 January 1942, T-81/
174/315863; Kreisorganisationsamt Strassburg, "Rundschreiben,"
15 March 1943, T-81/178/327331-45.
    67. Mauch to Wagner, 31 July 1940, GLA/233/25704; Wagner
(Vertraulich), "Beamtenverordnung für das Elsass," 27 July
1940, GLA/233/25704; Hartlieb to Röhn, 10 September 1941,
T-81/119/140185-86; Kettenacker, Völkstumspolitik, pp. 147-49.
    68. Meldungen aus dem Reich, No. 144 (25 November 1940),
T-175/260/2752844-47. Of six thousand public school teachers
in Alsace, only four thousand remained in their positions by
November 1940.
    69. A good discussion of the University of Strassburg
after 1940 is in Kettenacker, Volkstumspolitik, pp. 184-94;
see also Wagner to Rosenberg, 5 May 1941, IfZ/MA 165/355295.
    70. Robert Wagner, "Deutsche Zivilverwaltung im Elsass,"
pp. 93-95; Persönl. Referent des Reichsm. f. Ernährung to
Persönl. Referent des RFSS/Brandt, 6 November 1944, T-175/18/
1522144-50.
    71. Rüstungskommando Strassburg, "Wochenbericht der
Gruppe Heer für die Zeit vom 9. Februar bis 14. Februar
1942," 14 February 1942, T-84/35/1311245; Bickler to Ernst,
7 May 1942, T-81/166/305216.
    72. "Reisebericht vom 4. Juli 1941: Beobachtungen und
Eindrücke aus dem Elsass" (von einem leitenden Mitarbeiter
des DAI), T-81/538/5308526-29; Ortsgruppe Blasheim, Molsheim,
"Monatsbericht," February 1942, T-81/167/307134-37. In 1941
there were about eleven thousand Reich Germans in Alsace,
see Kölnische Zeitung, 21 November 1941, in T-81/538/5308568.
    73. Bickler to Polizeipräsident Strassburg, 1 April 1941,
T-81/124/112218; Bickler to Gädeke, 27 May 1941, T-81/166/
304968; Generalmajor Vaterrodt, "Wehrmachtskommandanturbefehl,
Strassburg Nr. 2," 7 January 1944, T-84/240/6599103.
    74. Dr. Oster to Ernst, 3 February 1941, T-81/166/304853;
Bickler to Schuppel, 5 March 1941 (Vertraulich), T-81/166/
304745-48; George Metz to Kriminalpolizei, zHd von Müller,
6 April 1942, T-81/166/304894-96.
    75. Bickler to SS Oberführer Lohse (streng Vertraulich),
21 May 1941, T-81/166/304814; Kurator der Universität Strassburg to Bickler, 23 September 1941, T-81/166/304802; Kurator

der Univ. Strassburg to Bickler, 20 August 1942, T-81/166/
304779.

76. See Clifton J. Child, "The Political Structure of
Hitler's Europe," pp. 10-93.

77. "Die Aufbauarbeit der Partei im Kreise Schlettstadt,"
T-81/178/326354-74; Kreisleiter Fitterer, Altkirch, to Gau
Archiv, 17 June 1941, T-81/127/300082-86; Walter Schulz,
"Der Reichsarbeitsdienst hilft beim Wiederaufbau im Elsass,"
pp. 31-33.

78. "Das Erste Jahr Nationalsozialistischer Aufbauarbeit
im Kreise Rappoltsweiler, 1940-41," T-81/127/149894-911; Kreispersonalamt Konstanz to Kreisleiter of Strassburg, 8 December
1940, T-81/174/315795; Amt für Kommunalpolitik to Kreisleiter
Dieffenbacker, "Tätigkeitsbericht," 21 January 1941, T-81/127/
300222.

79. Gaupersonalamt to Stellv. des Führers, 6 December
1940, T-81/228/5010015; Wagner to Regierungspräsident Krebs,
Aussig, Sudetenland, 16 January 1941, T-81/154/158289; Führer,
1 January 1942.

80. Kreisleiter Rothacker, Zabern, "Bericht über die
bisher getroffenen Feststellungen im Kreise Zabern," 15 July
1940, T-81/127/149873; Kreisleiter, Zabern, "Bericht über den
Aufbau des Kreises Zabern vom 3. Juli 1940 bis zum 15.X.1941,"
T-81/127/149866-72; "10 Monate Aufbauarbeit der Partei im
Kreis Thann," n.d., T-81/127/149880-85; Ernst, Rechenschaftsbericht, p. 235.

81. For biographical information see SNN, 24 July, 24
August, 2 and 11 September 1941, in T-501/186/333 to 358;
Führer des SS Oberabschnitt Südwest to RFSS, Personalhaupt-
amt, 10 September 1940, and to SS Brigadenführer Berger, 3
September 1940, in BDC/SS Sammelliste 46A. Bopp (L'Alsace,
p. 64) blames the four hundred Nanzigers for many of the
decisions implemented by Wagner. In reality many of the
Nanzigers attempted to moderate Wagner's policies.

82. A. Schmitt to Kreisleiter of Strassburg, 7 October
1940, T-81/166/305150-51; Höhere SS und Polizeiführer Südwest
to RFSS and CdZ, "Lagebericht vom 4. Oktober 1940," 5 October
1940, T-175/280/2774354-56; SNN, 27 August 1940, in T-81/
513/5276560.

83. Ernst to Kreisleiter Willi Fritsch, 5 November 1941,
T-81/166/305001; Gauschatzmeister Clever to Kreisleiter of
Strassburg, 24 September 1940, T-81/174/315564; Gaupersonal-
amtsleiter to Hartlieb, 18 September 1940, T-81/118/138394.

84. Kreisleiter Fritsch, Strassburg, to speakers of
Versammlungswelle am 9. und 10. November, Kreis Strassburg/
Land, 6 November 1940, T-81/126/112275; Ehemaliger Kreis-

stellenleiter EHD, Hagenau, "Tätigkeitsbericht des elsässischen
Hilfsdienstes des Kreises Hagenau," 20 May 1941, T-81/127/
300197-99. For Wagner's first major address during this drive
see Der Aufbruch des deutschen Elsass, Die erste nationalsozialistische Kundgebung im Elsass, 20 Oktober 1940 in
Strassburg.

85. Schulungs- und Verordnungsblatt, Ausgabe Elsass, sec.
1/p. 1, 15 July 1941, and sec. 3/p. 3, 15 August 1941; Orga-
nisationswalter, DAF, Zabern to Ortsobmann A. Eber, Ingweiler,
25 April 1941, T-81/70/80704.

86. SNN (Abschrift), 22 March and 4 April 1941, in T-81/
537/5307443-44.

87. "Stärke der Partei im Elsass, Stand 1.5.1941," T-81/
118/138371. Many Alsatian teachers refused to join the
Deutsche Frauenwerk since Baden teachers frequently did not
participate in it; see MdUuK, Baden to Kreis- und Stadtschulämter, 10 May 1941, GLA/497/182.

88. For public opinion see Kreisobmann, DAF, Strassburg,
"Stimmung und Tätigkeitsbericht der Kreiswaltung Strassburg,
Oktober/November 1940," 28 November 1940, T-81/72/82079;
Meldungen aus dem Reich, No. 137, 31 October 1940, T-175/260/
2752677-78; ibid., No. 206, 28 July 1941, T-175/261/2754416-
17. The Hitler Youth drive was more successful in the
Protestant areas.

89. "Stärke der Partei im Elsass, Stand 1.5.1941," T-81/
118/138371. In the 1936 election Schall had won 13 percent of
the vote in Hagenau; similar successes by autonomists were
achieved in Zabern and Weissenburg; see Dreyfus, La Vie
Politique, pp. 259-60.

90. Gauschatzmeister to Gauorganisationsamt, Nebenstelle
Strassburg, 26 May 1942, T-81/178/327521-25; "Bericht über
Aufbau und Leistung der NSDAP im Elsass," June 1942, T-81/
175/316899-908; SNN, 26 June 1944, in T-81/163/301834. Most
of the funds used to establish the party organization in
Alsace between 1940 and March 1942 came from Reich party
contributions.

91. Gauschatzmeister to Gauorganisationsamt, Nebenstelle
Strassburg, 26 May 1942, T-81/178/327521-25; Schwarz to
Wagner, 15 September 1942, T-81/58/66569-71; SNN, 26 June
1944, T-81/163/301834. Many OR members who became party members benefited economically by obtaining better employment.
For example, the Buchdrucker Alfred Rudolf became an Ober-
bahnwart; see Gauschulungsamt, "Beurteilungsbogen," 1 November
1943, in BDC/A. Rudolf file.

92. Gauschatzmeister to Gauorganisationsamt, Nebenstelle
Strassburg, 26 May 1942, T-81/178/327521-25; SNN, 13 October

1941, in T-81/538/5308602. Bopp argues (L'Alsace, p. 363)
that 90 percent of the PL in Alsace sabotaged the party.
    93. Kolmarer Kurier, 4 January 1941, in T-81/537/5307454;
SNN (Abschrift), 4/5 January 1941, in T-81/513/5307453.
    94. For biographical information see SNN, 24 June and
6 July 1941, in T-501/186/306-18; Kolmarer Kurier, 15 July
1941, T-81/538/5308931; Verordnungsblatt Gau Baden, Ausgabe
Elsass, 1 December 1943, and April 1942.
    95. CdZ/Adjutant to Gaupersonalamtsleiter Schuppel, 21
September 1943, T-81/178/327707; BDC files for R. Hauss, P.
Schall, H. Bickler, and E. Nussbaum; SNN, 26 June, 3 and 8 and
17 August 1941, in T-501/186/305-43.
    96. Wagner to Bormann, 7 January and 10 February 1941;
and CdZ, "Notiz," 9 March 1942, in T-501/186/253-60, 400;
CdZ, "Notiz," 16 February 1942, T-81/179/328105.
120/141884; Partei-Kanzlei to Schuppel, 28 March 1944, T-81/
120/141884; Schuppel to Schwarz, 3 June 1944, T-81/120/141877;
Reichsschatzmeister, Amt für Mitgliederschaftswesen to Gau
Baden, 10 June 1944, T-81/120/141875-76.
    98. "Kreisleiter Verzeichnis der elsässischen Kreise"
(1944), T-81/162/300290-91; Nussbaum to Wagner, 20 December
1942, T-81/178/327693-94. Corruption must have been widespread for Ernst pleaded mercy in 1942 for Murer, Maass,
Nussbaum, and Ley "and others" who had "strayed"; see Ernst
to CdZ/Pers. Abtl., 11 July 1942, T-501/186/429.
    99. SNN, 14 August, 30 July 1941, in T-501/186/342,
335; Führer, 27 September, 19 October 1940. Kettenacker
claims that six Alsatians and one émigré became Kreisleiters.
This is not correct since it neglects Sauerhöfer; see Volkstumspolitik, pp. 125-26.
    100. Bickler to Gauschatzmeister, 26 May 1941, T-81/174/
315547-48.
    101. Bickler to Kreisleiter Lang, Molsheim, 17 September
1941, T-81/174/315889-90. Hünenburg had been a symbolic
center for Alsatian autonomists before 1940. For other frictions between Reich and Alsatian party members see Kreis-
frauenschaftsleitung, Strassburg, to Bickler, 23 October 1942,
T-81/75/86392-94.
    102. "Anonymes Schreiben an Robert Wagner," 24 April
1941, T-81/179/328086; CdZ/Gädeke, "Notiz," 27 July 1942,
T-81/178/327682; Kolmarer Kurier, 4 January 1941, in T-81/
537/5307454. Kirn, a farmer, was born in 1891 in Mühlen
near the Neckar. He became a party member in 1930 and the
Kreisleiter of Donaueschingen by 1937.
    103. Meldungen aus dem Reich, No. 178 (10 April 1941),
T-175/260/2753632-36; ibid., No. 213 (21 August 1941), T-175/

261/2754620-23; Befehlshaber der Ordnungspolizei, Stuttgart
to RFSS (and CdZ), "Lagebericht vom November 1941," T-175/
280/2774444-46.

104. Kreisorganisationsamt Zabern to local leaders, 14
August 1942, T-81/167/306987-89; Röhn, "Rundschreiben Nr.
2/43E," 28 January 1943, T-81/93/106879; Gauorganisationsleiter, "Rundschreiben Nr. 43/43," 22 July 1943, T-81/93/
106858.

105. BdS und des SD Strassburg to CdZ/Pers. Abtl., 14
January 1943, T-81/154/158450; Gaupersonalamt, "Rundschreiben,"
4 February 1943, T-81/178/327497.

106. Kreisleitung Mülhausen to Gaustabsamt, "Stimmungsmässiger Überlick über die politische Lage," 1 August 1944,
T-81/173/313554; Kreisleitung Molsheim, "Die Bombengeschädig-
ten im Kreise Molsheim," 15 October 1943, T-81/163/302035.
When Reich German workers were transferred to Alsace, KPD
activities increased; see Oberlandesgerichtspräsident to
RJM Thierack, "Bericht," 30 March 1944, GLA/309/1205.

107. SA Führer, Standarte Strassburg/Stadt, "Bericht
über den Aufbau der S.A. in Strassburg/Stadt," 17 March 1941,
T-81/93/107258-66; SA Führer, Strassburg/Stadt to Gruppenführer Damian, 1 August 1941, T-81/93/107231-36; Führer, 15
November 1942.

108. SA Oberführer Schäffer to SA Gruppe Oberrhein, 18
February 1942, T-81/93/107214-15; SA Führer Schäffer to Kreisleiter Bickler, 19 February 1942, and Gruppenführer Damian
to SA Führer, 20 March 1942, both T-81/93/107211-12.

109. Kreisleiter Schall, "Politische Lage und Stimmung,"
8 September 1943 [1944], T-81/165/304277-80.

110. Gauschulungsleiter to CdZ/Personalamt, 20 November
1940, T-81/119/140089; CdZ/Personalamt to CdZ/Abtl. Erziehung,
21 November 1940, T-81/119/140085; Hartlieb to Wagner, 19
February 1941, T-81/119/140117; Hartlieb to Röhn, 2 May 1941,
T-81/119/140213; Gauschulungsamt to Ernst, 18 December 1941,
T-81/215/367842.

111. "34. Lehrgang für elsässisch Politische Leiter auf
der Gauschulungsburg Frauenalb, 16 Juni bis 30 Juni 1943,"
T-81/661/5468587-88; Kreisschulungsamt Strassburg to Gauschulungsamt, "Tätigkeitsbericht," 25 June 1943, T-81/124/
146230-31; Hartlieb to Wagner, 2 April 1943, T-81/124/
145942-46.

112. Hartlieb to Reichspropagandaleitung, Amt Rednerwesen,
10 June 1942, T-81/155/159158-60; Gauschulungsamt, "Rundschreiben Nr. 38/43," 27 October 1943, T-81/124/145892; Hartlieb to Röhn, 23 December 1943, T-81/124/146003-4.

113. N.S. Frauenschaft, Abt. Kultur/Schulung, "Tätigkeits-

bericht f.d. Monat Juni, 1940," 16 July 1942, T-81/100/
116561; Kreisschulungsleiter Kolmar to Gauschulungsamt,
"Jahresbericht 1942/43," 1 September 1943, T-81/124/1466319.

114. Gauschulungsamt, "Rundschreiben Nr. 47/1943," 2
December 1943, T-81/124/145894; Ortsgruppenleiter of Blasheim
to Kreisleiter of Molsheim, "November Bericht," 30 November
1942, T-81/178/327413-16.

115. Hans Rothfels, "Nationalität und Grenze im späten
19. und frühen 20. Jahrhundert," p. 228; Bickler, "Kreisleiterbesprechung am 24.6.41 in der Reichsstatthalterei," 25 June
1941, T-81/178/327329-30; "10 Monate Aufbauarbeit der Partei
im Kreis Thann," T-81/127/149880-85.

116. Hitler's Secret Conversations, 1941-44, pp. 48, 444.

117. Gauleiter, "Rundschreiben Nr. 7/41E," 6 February
1941, T-81/126/148574; CdZ/Abtl. Bauwesen to CdZ/Pers. Abtl.,
11 August 1944, T-81/178/327632.

118. Bickler to CdZ/Regierungsrat Staiger, 25 September
1941, T-81/166/304945; Bickler to CdZ/Staiger, 15 May 1941,
T-81/166/304973-74; Bickler, "Rundschreiben," 2 February
1942, T-81/126/112250; Verordnungsblatt des CdZ, 1 (16 August
1940), p. 2.

119. Bickler to Polizeipräsident Engelhardt, 7 July
1942, T-81/124/112178; Kluke, "Nationalsozialistische Volkstumspolitik," p. 636; Kettenacker, Volkstumspolitik, p. 169.

120. Polizeipräsident, Strassburg to Bickler, 9 July
1942, T-81/124/112179.

121. CdZ/Finanzabl. to CdZ/Pers., 15 April 1941, T-501/
173/563; CdZ/Pers. Abtl., "Notiz," 26 April 1941, T-501/173/
568; SNN, 19 March 1943, in T-501/179/623.

122. CdZ/Verwaltungsabtl. to Landkommissäre, 20 July 1940,
T-81/163/301697; CdZ/Abtlg. Volksaufklärung to Wagner, 24 May
1941, T-81/163/301711.

123. CdZ to CdZ/Verwaltungs u. Polizeiabtl., 24 April
1941, T-175/498/9361768; CdZ/Kern, "Notiz," 27 September
1941, T-501/173/591. Half of the Alsatian population in
1940 did not even speak French, and the other half was bi-
lingual; see Berger to RFSS, "Sprachenstatistik," 7 August
1940, T-175/127/2652414. When Alsatians used French in
Baden, Wagner also ordered a crackdown.

124.BdS und des SD/Strassburg to CdZ/Pers. Abtlg., 27
October 1943, "Einstellung der elsäss Bevölkerung zum deutschen
Buch und Büchereien," T-81/163/301723-8.

125. Rüstungskommando Strassburg, "Wochenbericht der
Gruppe Z für die Zeit vom 23.-28.3.42," 30 March 1942, T-84/
35/1310891; Rüstungs-Inspektion Oberrhein, Gruppe Maschinelles
Berichtswesen, "Zusammenstellung von Zahlenergebnissen aus

den Beschäftigtenmeldungen der von den drei Rüstungskommandos der Rüs. Insp. Oberrhein betreuten A-Betriebe für das 1. Vierteljahr 1943," May 1943, T-84/29/1302532-45; Rüst. Insp. Oberrhein, "Vierteljahresbericht, Z. Abtlg. Gruppe 1b pers., Zeit 1.10 bis 31.12.43," T-84/35/1310734-35.

126. Wagner to Chef des Jägerstab, Generalfeldmarschall Milch, 27 March 1944, T-81/179/328143.

127. Staatssekretär Stuckart to Himmler, 5 August 1942, in Himmler File, folder 14, container 6, L. of C., Manuscript Division; Berger to RFSS, December 1940 (Geheim), T-175/127/ 2652261-63; Bickler, "Im Umlauf," 21 February 1941, T-81/126/ 112291; "Stärke der Partei im Elsass, Stand 1.5.1941," T-81/ 118/138384.

128. CdZ/Pers. Abtl. to Bickler, 19 April 1941, T-81/ 166/304975; CdZ/Pers. to CdZ/Verwaltungsabtl., 22 July 1941, T-175/498/9361731; Kolmarer Kurier, 6 October 1941, in T-81/ 538/5308589.

129. Rüstungskommando Strassburg, Z Gruppe Ib, "Stimmung der Bevölkerung," 30 May 1942, T-84/35/1310821; Rüstungs- inspektion Oberrhein des Reichsministers für Bewaffung und Munition, Z Abt. Ib, "Wochenbericht, v. 4.-10.10.42," T-84/ 40/1318498.

130. "Trial of Robert Wagner and Six Others," pp. 28-30; IMT, Trial of the Major War Criminals, 6:452-53; Jäckel, Frankreich, pp. 229-32; Kettenacker, Volkstumspolitik, pp. 218-22, 237.

131. SNN, 25 August 1942, in Himmler File, folder 14, container 6, in L. of C., Manuscript Division; CdZ, "Erlass," 25 August 1942, 15 January 1943, T-81/289/2413008-11; SNN, 29 March 1943, in T-81/154/158464. The failure to grant general citizenship to Alsatians was considered crucial by Reich observers in alienating Alsatians; see Oberlandes- gerichtspräsident to RJM Thierack, "Bericht," 3 December 1942, GLA/309/1205.

| 132. CdZ to SD des RFSS/Strassburg, 20 November 1944, T-175/250/2741528.

133. SNN, 26 August 1942, in Himmler File, folder 14, container 6, in L. of C., Manuscript Division; Paul Schall to Schweickhart, Adjutant beim Gauleiter, 8 March 1944, T-175/ 223/2761211-12. Wagner in 1944 ordered that injured Alsatian volunteers receive preferential treatment when paid party posts had to be filled; Gaupersonalamtsleiter to Gauschatz- meister, 16 February 1944, IfZ/MA 527/No. 5010508.

134. SS Oberabschnitt Südwest to Gädeke, 27 February 1943, T-175/159/2690426; Kreisleiter Schlettstadt, "Aktivität der Konfessionen," 15 January 1944, T-81/175/316333; HJ,

Gebiet Baden to Wagner, 22 March 1943, T-175/159/2690436.

135. Stellv. Gauleiter, "Rundschreiben," 3 September
1942, T-81/124/146090; Kreispropagandaleiter Zabern, "Rundschreiben," 14 September 1942, T-81/162/300684; SA Standarte
132, "Rundschreiben," 22 September 1942, T-81/93/107126.

136. Polizei-Revier Kolmar, "Erfahrungsbericht," 20
January 1943, published by Marie-Joseph Bopp, "L'Opinion
Publique en Alsace Occupée un Témoignage Nazi en 1943," pp.
156-59.

137. CdZ/Pers. to SS Gruppenführer Kaul, 3 September
1942, T-81/179/328319-20; CdZ/Pers. to Reichsbahndirektion,
3 September 1942, and to Pflaumer, 11 September 1942, both
T-81/179/328315.

138. CdZ/Pers. to BdS und des SD/Strassburg, T-175/223/
2761185-87; CdZ/Pers., "Vermerk," 12 May 1943, T-175/223/
2761325; CdZ to Oberlandesgerichtspräsidenten, Karlsruhe,
8 June 1944, T-175/223/2761396.

139. CdZ to Lammers, 23 February 1943, T-81/179/327944-46.
The court did work with the Chief of the Security Police in
Strassburg to moderate Wagner's actions; see Oberlandesge-
richtspräsident to RJM, 2 January 1945, GLA/309/1205.

140. CdZ to Chef des OKW, Generalfeldmarschall Keitel,
21 January 1944, T-175/155/2685687; Chef des OKW, Heeresstab I,
No. 1541/44 to Wagner, 18 July 1944, T-175/23/2761355; CdZ to
SD des RFSS/SD. Führer Strassburg, 16 August 1944, T-175/223/
2761356. On some training grounds the drill officer would use
the phrase, "stubborn pack, Alsatians to the left," see Kreisobmann DAF, Strassburg, to Paul Schall, 12 June 1943, T-81/71/
81830.

141. CdZ/Verwaltungs und Polizeiabtl. to Landkommissäre,
31 January 1944, T-175/223/2761233; CdZ/Volksaufklärung,
"Notiz," 6 May 1944, T-175/223/2761356; CdZ/Pers. Abtl. to
Ernst, 3 July 1944, T-175/223/2761372. For the role of the
Alsatians in the German army see Bopp, "Dans l'Armée Alle-
mande," pp. 104-106.

142. Wagner to Lammers, 19 January 1944, in Himmler
File, folder 14, container 6, L. of C., Manuscript Division.

143. BdS/Strassburg to Wagner, 13 August 1941, T-175/
483/9342383; BdS und des SD/Strassburg to Reichssicherheits-
hauptamt, 15 July 1940, T-175/280/2774421; Eidenstattliche
Erklärung nach 1945, 30 November 1945 von Otto Hoffmann (Hohere
SS u. Polizeiführer SW), BDC.

144. Himmler to Wagner, 17 January 1942, T-175/483/
9342431; Himmler to Wagner, 18 June 1942, T-81/179/328343;
Wagner to Himmler, 7 July 1942, T-81/179/328341; Kettenacker,
Volkstumspolitik, p. 248. Rolls 211-18 of T-175 deal with
the Natzweiler camp in Alsace.

145. Dr. Zeller, Bischweiler to SD Aussenstelle Hagenau,

24 September 1944, T-175/512/9378650-52; BdS und des SD/
Strassburg to Wagner, 16 January 1942, T-81/178/327892; BdS
to CdZ, 31 January 1942, T-81/179/327905; Eugène Mey, Le Drame
de l'Alsace, 1939-1945, pp. 67-70.

146. BdS und des SD/Strassburg to Wagner, 18 July 1941,
T-81/178/327800-804; Bickler to Wagner, 12 January 1942, T-81/
178/327885; BdS und des SD/Strassburg to CdZ/Pers. Abtl., 10
February 1942, T-81/179/327909.

147. BdS und des SD/Strassburg to Wagner, 15 October
1941, T-81/178/327851; Bickler to Wagner, 12 January 1942,
T-81/178/327880; CdZ/Per. Abtl. to Generalstaatsanwalt Karls-
ruhe, 5 February 1942, T-81/179/327904; Wagner to Lammers, 19
January 1944, in Himmler File, folder 14, container 6, L. of
C., Manuscript Division.

148. Sicherheitspolizei, Einsatzkommando 1/III Strassburg
to BdS und des SD im Elsass, 14 December 1940; and Sicherheitspolizei, Strassburg, to Staatliche Kriminalpolizei, 14 August
1940; and Sicherheitspolizei, Einsatzkommando 1/III to all
Dienststellen of EKl./III, 16 September 1940, T-175/513/
9380005-15; Kaul to Greifelt, 27 May 1942, in Himmler File,
folder 14, container 6, L. of C., Manuscript Division. Otto
Dietrich claims that Hitler gave the orders for the accelerated deportations and the Germanization after his return from
Montoire; see 12 Jahre mit Hitler, pp. 72-73.

149. BdS und des SD/Strassburg to Wagner, 18 September
1940, T-175/280/2774381-87; Landkommissar, Weissenburg, to
CdZ/Adjutant, 7 November 1940, T-77/405/1259588; LK, Weissenburg to CdZ/Pers. Abtl., 19 November 1942, T-77/405/1259584-
85.

150. CdZ/Abtl. Erziehung to Gädeke, 1 April 1941, T-77/
388/1259612.

151. Frick to Wagner, 8 August 1940, T-77/388/1236862;
CdZ to Staatssekretär Schlegelberger, 9 September 1942, T-77/
405/1259390; Reichsjugendführer to CdZ, 11 February 1944,
T-77/152/887826-27; Partei-Kanzlei to Wagner, 21 June 1944,
T-77/388/1236894.

152. BdS und des SD/Strassburg to Einsatzkommando, 1/III,
30 June 1941, T-175/513/9380025; CdZ to Himmler, March 1942,
T-81/179/328345; Hitler's Secret Conversations, 1941-1944, p.
444; SNN, 20 December 1940, in T-81/322/2454032.

153. Himmler to Wagner, 18 June 1942, T-81/179/328343;
Kaul to RFSS, 4 May 1942; Brandt to Kaul, 23 May 1942, Kaul
to Greifelt, 27 May 1942, in Himmler File, folder 14, container 6, L. of C., Manuscript Division.

154. EWZ/Paris, "Die volksdeutschen Elsässer in Frankreich und ihre Rückführung in den Verband des Grossdeutschen

Reiches," 17 July 1941, T-81/314/1444536-39; Keppi to Bickler, 9 May 1941, T-81/166/305045.

155. Dr. Best, Militärbefehlhaber Frankreich, Abt. Verwaltung to CdZ, 17 February 1942, T-175/65/2580756-62; Himmler to Lammers, 18 June 1942, T-175/65/2580876.

156. Wagner to Bormann, 5 November 1942; and Wagner to Himmler, 16 November 1942; and Himmler to Wagner, 24 November 1942, all in T-81/166/305756-59; Hofmann to RFSS, 24 August 1944, T-175/19/1523973.

157. Kaul to RFSS/Brandt, 18 August 1942; "Auszug aus dem Aktenvermerk der S.S. Gruppenf. Greifelt über seinen Vortrag beim R.F.S.S. am 10.8.1942," 2 September 1942, in Himmler File, folder 14, container 6, L. of C., Manuscript Division; CdZ/Pers. to BdS/Fischer, 8 July 1942, T-81/179/328346-47; Röhn, "Rundschreiben 6/42E," 13 July 1942, T-81/179/328324.

158. Gädeke to Schuppel, 18 August 1942, T-81/179/328178; CdZ/Pers. to Pflaumer, 18 March 1944, T-501/173/627; CdZ/Pers. to Gaustabsamt, 17 May 1944, T-81/179/328133.

159. For example, Kerber was particularly disturbed by the transfer of educational institutes from Freiburg to Strassburg, see Kerber to Reichsminister für Wissenschaft, Erziehung und Volksbildung, durch den Bad. Unterrichtsminister, 22 February 1941, T-501/195/74.

160. Kreisleitung Strassburg, "Stimmungsbericht vom 8. Oktober 1944," T-81/163/302133; SD Aussenstelle Hagenau to SD Führer Strassburg, 17 July 1944, T-175/512/9378588; Dr. Zeller to SD Aussenstelle Hagenau, 24 September 1944, T-175/512/9378650; Archbishop Gröber to Ministerium für die kirchlichen Angelegenheiten, Berlin, 6 March 1943, GLA/235/12789; Rüstungskommando Strassburg, "Kriegstagebuch," 1 January to 3 March 1943, T-84/157/1525622.

161. Kreisleitung Molsheim, "Allgemeiner Stimmungsmässiger Überblick," 1 September 1944, T-81/167/306779-80. "Pg" was translated as "Pech gehabt" and "Vg" as "vorsichtig gewesen."

162. Schall to Herta Seber, Herne, Westfalen, 11 July 1943, T-81/166/305065; Schall "Politische Lage," 8 September 1944, T-81/165/304277.

163. SD Führer Strassburg to Kaltenbrunner, 21 November 1944, T-175/281/1774534; Suhr to Hofmann, 4 December 1944, T-175/495/9357460. In November 1944, American tanks rolled into Strassburg while German courts were still in session. Wagner had not given evacuation orders; see Oberlandesgericht, Präsident to RJM Thierack, 2 January 1945, GLA/309/1205.

164. Führer, 22 and 27 December 1944; Aussenstelle

Rastatt to SD Führer Baden/Elsass, 8 March 1945, T-175/512/9378502; SD Aussenstelle Donaueschingen to SD Führer Baden/Elsass, 3 March 1945, T-175/512/9378522; SD Aussenstelle Tauberbischofsheim to SD Führer Baden/Elsass, 12 March 1945, T-175/512/9378519.

165. Berger to Himmler, 21 June 1944, in Himmler File, folder 14, container 6, L. of C., Manuscript Division.

166. SD Aussenstelle Villingen to SD Führer Baden, 7 March 1945; and SD Aussenstelle Offenburg to SD Führer Baden, 9 March 1945; and SD Aussenstelle Rastatt to SD Führer Baden/Elsass, 8 March 1945, all in T-175/512/9378502-24.

167. New York Times, 24 April 1946, p. 2; Ernst, Rechenschaftsbericht, p. 299; Führer, 30 March 1945.

168. For the trial see "Trial of Robert Wagner and Six Others," pp. 23-55; Bankwitz, Alsatian Autonomist Leaders, pp. 101-12; Schaeffer, L'Alsace et l'Allemagne, pp. 69-123; Wagner was quoted by the New York Times, 4 May and 25 August 1946.

169. See Pierre Pflimlin and René Uhrich, L'Alsace destin et volonté, p. 139; Rene Allemann, "Die Elsässer: Eine Minorität die keine sein will," pp. 9-16; and the review by Nikolas Benckiser, "Zur Sprachenfrage in einem besonderen Land," in Frankfurter Allgemeine, 13 March 1979, on Alsatian problems today.

CONCLUSION

1. See the report in Bankwitz, Alsatian Autonomist Leaders, p. 102. On 25 July 1945, Wagner went to his native community, Lindach, to meet his brother. Four days later, he surrendered to the Americans.

2. Herr Weber of the Generallandesarchiv arranged my interview with Walter Köhler, which took place in the GLA, Karlsruhe.

3. Jörg Schadt, Die Sozialdemokratische Partei in Baden, p. 195. Schadt points out that by the 1890s the SPD had already established locals in the "Arbeiterbauerndörfer."

4. See for example, "Weinheimer Allerlei," in the Führer, 26 November 1927, for the NSDAP's support of the DHV. One might also note that in the election of 1925, the Baden party presented thirty-seven candidates. Of these, sixteen were "Gewerbetreibende" and ten were "Angestellte." The other candidates were farmers, teachers, and two civil servants.

5. Alexander Weber ("Soziale Merkmale," p. 123) argues that the DVFP votes of May 1924 in Baden were quite different

from the Nazi votes of 1928. This is not completely true.
Although the Baden party did well in the Protestant, rural
districts of Kehl, where the Völkisch Block had not been
especially strong in May 1924, it also won strong support
in traditional völkisch strongholds like Liedolsheim, Eberbach, and the district of Wertheim. The biggest difference
between the May 1924 and the May 1928 election was the fact
that the Nazi party was better represented in the rural areas
in 1928. However, in the election of 1929, the NSDAP supplemented this rural strength with an urban "take-off."

6. Rauschning, The Voice of Destruction, p. 191.

7. Mosse, ed., Nazi Culture, p. xx.

8. See also Gerhard Weinberg, "Recent German History,"
p. 368. Weinberg calls for a study of "the National Socialist
consensus . . . with the care that has in recent years been
lavished on its internal rivalries."

9. Orlow, History, 2:14-16. Hitler, of course, never
supported the efforts of Hess (Bormann) and Schwarz to "remold
the PO functionaries"; see ibid., 2:489.

10. Friedrich, "The Failure of a One-Party System:
Hitler's Germany," p. 255.

Bibliography

Index

Bibliography

NOTES ON SOURCES

This book rests primarily on the files of the Baden government and police agencies, both before and after 1933, and on the surviving papers of the various agencies of the Baden NSDAP. The Generallandesarchiv in Karlsruhe contains important files pertaining to the various state agencies, ranging from the Ministry of Interior to the Staatsministerium. File 233 contains the papers of the Staatsministerium, which provide valuable information for state and party affairs before and after 1933. Folder 24318 contains the minutes of the meetings of the Baden cabinet after 1933, while folder 27914 has material on cabinet meetings before 1933. Folders 28084, 28090, 28180, 25716, 25693, and 24318 deal with the problems of Reichsreform and the role of Baden in Germany after 1933. Folders 27901-10 and 27892-94 provide information on the purge of the police after 1933, while folders 26305, 26306, 27965, and 24005 deal with the civil servants after 1933. The Nazi revolution in 1933 is covered by the following folders: 24279, 24139, 24138, 25983, 25623, 25979, 25683, 27911, 27964, 28118, and 28388. In addition, state affairs after 1933 are reflected in folders 27919, 26332, 27911, and 25984. The Nazi party's activities before 1933 are covered by folders 27914, 27915, 28388, 28187, 25979, and 25983. Of these folders the most important ones are 28388, which contains a police report on "Die politische Lage in Baden," 5 October 1931, and 27915, which contains police reports on Nazi activities between 1923 and 1930.

The papers of the Justizministerium are in file 234. Folders 5738, 5703, and 5739 contain information about court cases dealing with völkisch and Nazi activists in 1923 and 1924. The very important folder 5739 contains a police report dealing with the NSDAP's activities during the 1929 election campaign, and a March 1928 report on Hitler's meeting in Heidelberg with the "establishment." In addition, the folder contains a July 1930 Denkschrift on the Nazi party.

The documents in file 309 reflect the activities of the state's Staatsanwaltschaft. Folders 1158-68 contain much information about paramilitary and völkisch activities in Baden between 1919 and 1925. Folder 1168, in particular, deals with the activities of Liedolsheim "Nazis." Folder 1150 contains information about Nazi activities in Baden after 1925. File 309 also has the very important Lageberichte of the Oberlandesgerichtspräsident between 1936 and 1945. Folders 1204-10 provide many details about party and state affairs. Some of these documents are photocopies of originals deposited in the Bundesarchiv in Koblenz. Additional court cases, dealing with völkisch activists and police reports about such activists before 1925, may be found in file 372/Zg 1943/40/171 concerning the district of Säckingen.

Other important information came from file 237 (Finanzministerium), files 280 and 469 (Landesbauernschaft), file 231 (Landtag), and file 235 (Kultusministerium). File 235, in particular, was crucially important in dealing with church-state relations after 1933. Folders 12754, 12748, 12790, 12791, 12805, 12809, and 19439 contain the correspondence between Wagner (and Wacker) and Archbishop Gröber after 1933. In addition, folder 38160 contains Herbert Kraft's correspondence (after 1933) with various people.

Since the Baden Ministry of Interior was destroyed by the French in 1945, the files of the state district offices (Bezirksämter), which are deposited in the Generallandesarchiv (GLA), are singularly important. Particularly valuable were the files from the districts of Bruchsal, Sinsheim, and Tauberbischofsheim. File 344, folder 6583 (Amt Bruchsal), deals with the important Deutscher Tag meeting in Bruchsal in late 1924. File 377, folder 5407 (Amt Sinsheim), has information on völkisch and Nazi activities in 1922, while the papers in file 380, folder 7271 (Amt Tauberbischofsheim), provide information about rural debts in 1928/29.

The GLA, Karlsruhe, also has important NSDAP papers. Between 1963 and 1971, the Bundesarchiv in Koblenz and the Berlin Document Center returned Baden NSDAP files to the GLA. Although much of this material is available on microfilm (National Archives, T-81), the party files pertaining to the Amt für Kommunalpolitik and the SA are of special interest since some of these documents have never been microfilmed. File 465d, folders 1293, 1355-57, and 1463, contain the Baden (Amt Bruchsal) SA files, which are of special interest, particularly for 1934 and 1935. File 465d, folders 1090, 1094, 1147, and 2787 contain the files of the Amt für Kommunalpolitik after 1933.

The GLA also has important Nachlässe, of which the most important for this study was the Arnold Ruge Nachlass (69N). Most of the material in the Ruge Nachlass (organized in almost 150 boxes) had been collected by Ruge during his long career as a völkisch activist. Ruge was a GLA staff member until July 1945, which allowed him to obtain various völkisch publications. These files contain a great deal of material on völkisch and Nazi activities in Baden before 1933, and particularly before 1925. Many of these obscure völkisch papers and journals are available nowhere else.

Finally, the GLA has most of the important government publications that appeared in Baden between 1919 and 1945, and it has a good collection of newspapers, including Der Führer and the Karlsruher Zeitung (which contains the Staatsanzeiger). Newspapers not available at the GLA were found in the Stadtarchiv Karlsruhe. Thanks to the good services of Herr Weber of the GLA, I was able to interview Walter Köhler, the former deputy Gau leader and minister-president of Baden after 1933.

The Staatsarchiv Freiburg has the very important files of the Landeskommisär Konstanz, which include the crucial Baden police reports on political extremism between 1926 and 1931. File 317, folders 1253, 1255-58, and 1257c are important for völkisch and left-wing political affairs between 1919 and 1923 in Baden. Folders 1257b and 1257d contain important material on Nazi activities before 1933. Folder 1257b, in particular, contains the police reports of the political branch of the Landespolizeiamt, which deal with right-wing and left-wing political extremism in Baden between 1926 and 1930. For information dealing with rural problems in the state, folders 1262, 636, 585r, and 56 (file 355) were important. Finally, the Nazi takeover in Baden in 1933 and the consolidation of power may be followed in folders 492, 494, 1267, 1266, 1257b, and 1257e.

The Berlin Document Center (BDC) contains the files of the NSDAP and the various affiliated and associated Nazi organizations. But most important for this study were the various personal files of important Baden party leaders and activists. Where no personal files were available, I used the Central and Gau membership cards, which usually contained information about age, occupation, and party career. Additional personal information could be obtained from the party's court decisions (Oberste Partei Gericht), the SA and SS files, and the "Eidenstättliche Erklärungen." The nonbiographical files of the BDC have been microfilmed and deposited in the National Archives (US) under the designation T-580. Roll

19/folder 199 pertains to the Gau Baden files. The documents
cover the Baden party's history between 1926 and 1932, and
include a list of Baden locals in June 1927 and the Gau's
organizational reforms of 1930 and 1932. In addition, the
Hauptarchiv der NSDAP, München, which was part of the original
BDC collection, was microfilmed by the Hoover Institute.
Rolls 5, 10, 29, 47, 53, 56, 16, and 70 contain folders with
the history of the Baden party. The records of the Hauptarchiv
are most valuable for the Baden party's history before 1933.
    The Institut für Zeitgeschichte in Munich contains a large
collection of published and unpublished material dealing with
the NSDAP between 1919 and 1945. The bulk of the Microfilm
Archives used were National Archives films T-81, T-84, T-175,
T-253, and T-454. The value of the IfZ microfilm collection
lies in the fact that these files contain a "names register,"
which permitted me to search for isolated documents dealing
with Baden Nazis. The Institut also offers a wide variety of
völkisch journals and newspapers, and such important sworn
declarations (Eidenstättliche Aufzeichnungen) as Otto Wagener's
memoirs. Wagener was Robert Wagner's World War I commander.
After the war, Otto Wagener also played an important role in
the völkisch movement in Baden before he moved to Munich.
Wagener's memoirs have now been edited and published by Henry
A. Turner, Jr., see Otto Wagener, Hitler aus nächster Nähe:
Aufzeichnungen eines Vertrauten 1929-1932, (Frankfurt am
Main: Ullstein, 1978).
    A significant portion of this study is based on the files
of the Baden NSDAP and the chief of civil administration in
Alsace (who was the Gau leader of Baden). These documents
were captured by American and French forces in November 1944
in Strassburg and then shipped to Alexandria, Virginia, where
they were microfilmed. The microfilms were deposited in the
National Archives in Washington, D.C., and assigned the NA
designation T-81. All party agencies, ranging from the Racial
Policy Office to the NSV, are represented in these files.
The Gau party offices are also represented, including Wagner's
personal files, both as Gau leader and as chief of civil
administration in Alsace (CdZ). The T-81 rolls also contain
the files of local and district party agencies and the files
of party affiliates, both in Baden and in Alsace. Frequently,
important state and party documents appear in routine correspondence of party affiliates such as the NSV. In terms of
volume, the NSV, the Gauschulungsamt, the DAF, Gau party
departments, and Alsatian party agencies are most represented.
Chronologically, most of the documents pertain to the post-
1933 period, especially the late 1930s and the 1940s. Most

of the pre-1933 documents were either destroyed or deposited
in the BDC after 1945.

The Gaustab office, the Gauorganization and Gaupersonnel
offices, and Wagner's personal files as both Gau leader and
CdZ are represented in the following rolls: 117, 120-22, 126,
163, 165-66, 171, 173, 175, 178-79, and 228. These rolls contain information on the structure, evolution, and function of
the most important Gau party offices.

In addition to the CdZ files included in rolls 163, 179,
178, 154, 661, and 646, much information on Alsace and on the
party's role after 1940 appears in DAF, SA, and local party
files.   Roll 69 contains information on the DAF in Alsace;
rolls 93 and 69 reveal the SA function in Strassburg, while
rolls 99 and 100 contain the files of the Alsatian Hitler
Youth. Rolls 174 and 166, 124, and 126 provide information
about party operations in Strassburg, and roll 75 contains
the files of the NS Women's League of Strassburg. Finally,
the NSV files on rolls 40, 88, 123, 167, and 124 illustrate
the party's Germanization programs in Alsace.

The files of the Gauschulungsamt are collected on the
following rolls: 21, 23, 41, 63, 64, 72, 89, 117, 118, 119,
124, 155, 172, 176, and 215. The files include information
on party celebrations, literary purges, Gau schools and Gau
indoctrination programs, and the organization and structure
of the GSA in Baden and in Alsace. The files also contain
important information on the evolution of the Adolf Hitler
Schools between 1936 and 1944.

The NSV files are even larger than the files of the
Gauschulungsamt. They are contained on the following rolls:
38-40, 42, 85-88, R.87, 115, 121-25, 167, 169, and 189-91.
Both Baden and Alsatian operations are included. The files
contain a large amount of material on the evolution, structure, and function of the Gau and local NSV agencies, particularly during the war. The NSV was a "functional party agency"
with concrete tasks during the war. This is why the NSV files
were stored in Strassburg and included so much material.

The NSDStB files are in rolls 79, 80, 89, 90, 238, 240,
244, and 247. The documents cover the period from 1933 to
1944 and illustrate the coordination of Baden students and
alumni organizations after 1933.

Municipal affairs are reflected in the party's files on
Kommunalpolitik. Rolls 42, 126, 173, and 175 contain files
of the Amt für Kommunalpolitik. Although the files cover the
Nazi period, the most important documents, revealing the
party's municipal affairs during 1930-31, are contained on
roll 173.

Much important personnel information (and personal) may
be obtained from the files of the Gau Personnel Office and the
Stammbücher contained on rolls 162, 228, 216, and 166. The
documents reveal information on such important Baden party
activists as Griesinger, Knab, and Blank, in addition to
presenting facts about many lesser known party officials.

Important public opinion reports are contained in the
files of the DAF and the party's district offices. The rolls
65, 69, 72, and 646 contain DAF and Arbeitsamt situation and
activity reports from various Baden districts. Rolls 126,
164, 173, 163, 165, 167, 175, 178, and 179 contain Kreisleiter
and Gaustab reports on general public opinion in Baden and in
Alsace. Rolls 1, 65, 126, 127, 163, 175, 173, and 176 contain
information and activity reports by Kreisleiter and Gaustab
officials, pertaining to the role and function of the church
between 1942 and 1944.

Minor party files pertain to the Racial Policy Office
(rolls 9, 117, 228, and 125); to the Amt für Beamte (roll
220); to the Gau Archiv (rolls 167, 178, and 127); to the
NS Gaudienst (roll 168).

Among captured and microfilmed records deposited in the
National Archives, one collection of various party and state
documents was designated as Miscellaneous German Records
Collection and assigned the NA number T-84. Rolls 4, 5, and
6 contain the files of Hitler's secretariat until 1923. The
files contain important correspondence between Munich and
Baden Nazis and sympathizers. Roll 257 pertains to the NSV
files on disaster relief during the war. Rolls 29, 35, 40,
and 157 contain the files of the Rüstungskommando Strassburg
and the Rüstungsinspektion Oberrhein. The files concern
official war-production reports, situation reports, and
public opinion evaluations. Both Baden and Alsatian districts
are covered, and the documents encompass the period between
1939 and 1944.

The captured and microfilmed files of the Reich Ministry
for Armaments and War Production are deposited in the National
Archives under the designation T-73. Rolls 1, 21, and 28
concern the files of the Rüstungsinspektion Oberrhein between
1943 and 1945. Roll 1 reveals the interesting negotiation
between Köhler and the Reich Ministry for Water and Energy.
Roll 21 concerns the relationship between the Rüstungsinspektion Oberrhein and Baden party offices. It also contains a
report of an important Wagner conference on 7 February 1945.

The captured and microfilmed files of the Records of
Headquarters, German Armed Forces High Command are deposited

in the National Archives under the designation T-77. Rolls
152, 388, and 405 contain the files of the CdZ/Alsace and
reveal important property transactions and confiscations in
Alsace. The rolls also contain the files of the personal
department of the CdZ that was headed by Gädeke.

The captured and microfilmed files of the Records of
German Field Commands: Rear Areas, Occupied Territories,
and Others are deposited in the National Archives under the
designation T-501. Rolls 173, 179, 186, and 195 contain
files from the CdZ/Alsace. The documents pertain to the
party's Germanization and Nazification efforts in Alsace.
Some state documents from the Landeskommissär of Rappoltsweiler and the mayor of Freiburg are also included. The
files also contain an important Wagner-Bormann correspondence,
concerning Alsatian affairs. Finally, the rolls contain
important biographical clippings from the Strassburger
Neueste Nachrichten and the Kolmarer Kurier.

The captured and microfilmed files of the Records of
the Deutsches Ausland-Institut, Stuttgart are deposited in
the National Archives under the designation T-81. Roll 278
pertains to the Vomi in Baden and the resettlement of Ethnic
Germans from Romania. Rolls 273, 289, 314, 322, 490, 513,
514, 537, 538, 558, and 611 all concern Alsace both before
1940 and after the establishment of German domination. The
files contain CdZ ordinances, resettlement information, DAI
reports on Alsatian separatists before 1940, and a large
collection of newspaper clippings on Alsace. The clippings
are valuable for biographical information on leading Baden
and Alsatian Nazis.

The Allies captured a very large collection of Himmler
and SS files. These documents were also microfilmed and
deposited in the National Archives under the designation
T-175. Rolls 18, 19, 65, 223, 280, 281, 273, 127, 159, 475,
483, 498, and 513 pertain to Nazi Germanization efforts in
Alsace; to deportations and resettlement programs; and to the
organization of police units and the Vorbruck concentration
camp. Roll 409 contains a copy of the Catholic Die Kampfmittel
des Materialismus und die katholische Aktion im Elsass
(Strassburg, 1938). Roll 464 contains reports on the press
in Alsace between 1937 and 1939. Rolls 258-66 contain the
very important Meldungen aus dem Reich which are a mine of
information on public opinion trends. Rolls 267 and 269
also contain important Stimmungsberichte from the SD agencies
in Strassburg, Mannheim, and Konstanz. Roll 512 includes a

variety of Baden SD reports, pertaining to public opinion
in Baden in March 1945. An important folder from the Himmler
File, which concerns Alsace, is deposited in the Manuscript
Division of the Library of Congress. Folder 14, container
6 of the Himmler File, deposited in the L. of C., contains
information on Germanization in Alsace; on deportations,
drafts, and resistance in Alsace; and it includes important
Wagner correspondence. These documents are in the form of
photocopies rather than microfilms.

The Leo Baeck Institute in New York City has a large
collection of Baden and German Jewish newspapers and journals,
including the Israelitisches Gemeindeblatt, Mannheim, from
1922 to 1938. The Institute's archives contain the Gumbel
File, the Collection Baer-Oppenheimer, and various memoirs.

The Nachrichtenblatt der NSDAP Baden is in the Library
of Congress. Additional party publication, and newspaper,
were obtained from the New York Public Library, the Badische
Landesbibliothek, the Bayerische Staatsbibliothek, and the
University of Michigan Graduate Library.

UNPUBLISHED SOURCES

1.   Generallandesarchiv Karlsruhe (GLA)
     File 223: Staatsministerium
          309: Staatsanwaltschaft Karlsruhe
          234: Justizministerium
          237: Finanzministerium
          235: Kultusministerium
          280: Landesbauernschaft
          469: Landesbauernschaft
          231: Landtag
          500: Gestapo, Leitstelle Karlsruhe
          505: Arisierungsakten
     Files of Bezirksämter: 364 (Mosbach); 377
               (Sinsheim); 361 (Schopfheim); 357 and 343
               (Bretten); 356 (Heidelberg); 380 (Tauber-
               bischofsheim); 344 (Bruchsal); 372
               (Säckingen); 345 (Buchen); 357 (Karlsruhe)
     File 465d: NSDAP Baden files
               Ruge Nachlass
               Willy Andreas Nachlass

2. Staatsarchiv Freiburg (SAF)
   File 317: Landeskommissär für die Kreise Konstanz,
             Villingen und Waldshut
        358: Amtsbezirk Kehl

3. Institut für Zeitgeschichte, Munich (IfZ)
   Microfilm Archives of the Institut, files: 87; 131;
        137/1; 141/11; 144/3; 297; 442/1; 441/2; 527;
        616/20; 606; 803; and 1165
   Otto Wagener, "Eidenstättliche Aufzeichnungen"

4. National Archives Microfilm Collection (NA)
   T-81: Records of the National Socialist German Labor Party
   T-81: DAI Records
   T-84: Miscellaneous German Records Collection
   T-175: Himmler and SS Files
   T-73: Reich Ministry for Armaments and War Production
   T-77: Records of Headquarters, German Armed Forces
          High Command
   T-501: Records of German Field Commands: Rear Areas,
          Occupied Territories
   T-580: Berlin Document Center files, nonbiographical
          materials

5. Library of Congress, Manuscript Division
   Himmler file

6. Hauptarchiv NSDAP: Microfilmed by Hoover Institution (HA)
   Rolls: 5, 10, 29, 47, 53, 56, 16, 70

7. Leo Baeck Institute, New York City
   Gumbel file
   Collection Baer-Oppenheimer
   File E146: Judith Schrag-Haas, "Erinnerungen an meinen
               Vater"
   File P-307: Jacob Piccard, "Erinnerungen eigenen Lebens"

8. Berlin Document Center (BDC)
   Personal files of Baden Party Members and Leaders
   Zentral- and Gaumitgliederkartei
   Oberste Partei Gericht
   SA files
   Diverses: Gau Baden
   ORPO file

Sonderakten Nr. 12
Reichsnährstand
Sammellisten: 61, 46A 45 (SS)
Orders: 239 (Hitler Youth); 371 (Parteikanzlei); 400
     (Namenliste); 311 (Schweiz); 266 (Reichsschatz-
     meister); 392 (Goldene Ehrenzeichen)
Blutordenliste
Eidenstättliche Erklärung (1945)

PUBLISHED DOCUMENTS, STATISTICAL GUIDES, GOVERNMENT PUBLICA-
TIONS, PARTY DIRECTIVES AND STATISTICS, AND BIOGRAPHICAL
INFORMATION

Arbeitskammer Baden, Gauwaltung der DAF. Der Dritte Leistungs-
     kampf der Deutschen Betriebe im Gau Baden. Karlsruhe,
     1940.
     _____. Der Vierte Leistungskampf der Deutschen Betriebe im
     Gau Baden. Heidelberg, 1942.
Der Aufbruch des deutschen Elsass: Die erste national-
     sozialistische Kundgebung im Elsass, 20 Oktober 1940
     in Strassburg. Kolmar: Alsatia, 1940.
Baden, Bericht des Gewerbeaufsichtsamts. Die wirtschaft-
     lichen, sozialen und gesundheitlichen Verhältnisse
     der Zigarrenarbeiter in Baden. Karlsruhe: Macklotsche,
     1925.
Baden, Ministerium des Innern. Geschäftsbericht für die Jahre
     1913-1924. 2 Vols. Karlsruhe: G. Braun, 1926.
Baden, Statistisches Landesamt. Die Wahlen in Baden zur
     verfassungsgebenden badischen und deutschen National-
     versammlung im Jahr 1919. Karlsruhe: E. F. Müllersche
     Hofbuchdruckerei, 1920.
     _____. Die Wahlen zum Badischen Landtag am 30. Oktober
     1921. Karlsruhe: E. F. Müller, 1922.
     _____. Die Wahlen zum Reichstag am 4. Mai 1924 in Baden.
     Karlsruhe: J. Boltze, 1924.
     _____. Die Reichstagswahl am 7. Dezember 1924 in Baden.
     Karlsruhe: Macklotsche, 1925.
     _____. Badische Landtagswahl am 25. Oktober 1925.
     Karlsruhe: Macklotsche, 1925.
     _____. Die Reichstagwahl am 20. Mai 1928 in Baden.
     Karlsruhe: Macklotsche, 1928.
     _____. Badische Landtagswahl am 27. Oktober 1929.
     Karlsruhe: Macklotsche, 1930.

Baden, Statistisches Landesamt. Reichspräsidentenwahl 1925 in Baden. Karlsruhe: Macklotsche, 1925

_____. Handel und Verkehr in Baden. Karlsruhe: Badischer Kommunalverlag, 1927.

_____. Die Badische Landwirtschaft im Allgemeinen und in einzelnen Gauen. 3 Vols. Karlsruhe: Macklotsche, 1932-36.

_____. Die Landwirtschaft in Baden im Jahr 1925 auf Grund amtlichen Materials. Karlsruhe: Badischer Kommunalverlag, 1927.

_____. Die Industrie in Baden im Jahr 1925 auf Grund amtlichen Materials. Karlsruhe: G. Braun, 1926.

_____. Der Stand der Industrie und Industriearbeiterschaft im Amtsbezirk Lörrach in der Nachkriegszeit. Karlsruhe: Badenia, 1925.

_____. Die Religionszugehörigkeit der Bevölkerung in Baden nach der Volkszählung vom 16. Juni 1925. Karlsruhe: Macklotsche, 1926.

_____. Statistisches Jahrbuch für das Land Baden, 1925. Karlsruhe: Macklotsche, 1925.

_____. Statistisches Jahrbuch für das Land Baden, 1930. Karlsruhe: Macklotsche, 1930.

_____. Statistisches Jahrbuch für das Land Baden, 1938. Karlsruhe: Macklotsche, 1938.

_____. Volksbegehren und Volksentscheid über den Gesetzentwurf "Enteignung der Fürstenvermogen." Karlsruhe: Macklotsche, 1926.

_____. Wohnungszählung und Wohnungsbau in Baden. Karlsruhe: Volksfreund, 1928.

Badischer Geschäfts- und Adresskalender. Vols. 55-59. Karlsruhe: J. Lang, 1932-36. Vol. 65. Karlsruhe: G. Braun, 1942.

Badisches Gesetz- und Verordnungsblatt. 1933-1942.

Boberach, Heinz, ed. Meldungen aus dem Reich: Auswahl aus den geheimen Lageberichten des Sicherheitsdienstes der S.S., 1939-1944. Neuwied/Berlin: Hermann Luchterhand, 1965.

Boelcke, Willi A., ed. Deutschlands Rüstung im Zweiten Weltkrieg: Hitlers Konferenzen mit Albert Speer, 1942-1945. Frankfurt: Akademische Verlagsesellschaft, 1969.

_____, ed. Wollt ihr den totalen Krieg? Die Geheimen Goebbels Konferenzen 1939-1943. Stuttgart: Deutsche Verlags-Anstalt, 1967.

Boelcke, Willi A., ed. Kriegspropaganda 1939-1941. Geheime
    Ministerialkonferenzen im Reichspropagandaministerium.
    Stuttgart: Deutsche Verlags-Anstalt, 1967.
Bopp, Marie-Joseph. "L'Opinion Publique en Alsace Occupée un
    Témoignage Nazi en 1943." Revue d'Alsace 96 (1957):156-
    59.
Büro des Reichswahlleiters. Hauptergebnisse der Wahlen zum
    Reichstag am 20. Mai 1928. Berlin: Reimar Hobbing, 1928.
Das Deutsche Führerlexikon. Berlin: Otto Stollberg, 1934.
Ebbecke, Otto, ed. Die Deutsche Erhebung in Baden. Karlsruhe:
    G. Braun, 1933.
Fliedner, Hans-Joachim, ed. Die Judenverfolgung in Mannheim,
    1933-1945: Dokumente. 2 Vols. Stuttgart: W. Kohl-
    hammer, 1976,
Gaupropagandaamt Baden, ed. Richtlinien für die Propagandisten
    der NSDAP Gau Baden. Karlsruhe: Südwestdruck, 1937.
Gauschatzmeister Baden. Rundschreiben des Gauschatzmeisters,
    Jahrgang 1938. Karlsruhe, 1938.
Görlitzer, Artur, ed. Adressbuch der Nationalsozialistischen
    Volksvertreter. Berlin: Verlag Die Deutsche Tat, 1933.
Gross, Karl, ed. Handbuch für den Badischen Landtag: IV.
    Landtagsperiode, 1929-1933. Karlsruhe: Badenia, n.d.
    _____. Handbuch für den Badischen Landtag: V. Landtags-
    periode, 1933-1937. Karlsruhe: Friedrich Gutsch, n.d.
Der Grossdeutsche Reichstag, 1938. Berlin: R. V. Deckers,
    1938.
Der Hitler Prozess vor dem Volksgericht in München. Munich:
    Knorr and Hirth, 1924. Reprinted by Verlag Detlev
    Auvermann: Glashütten im Taunus, 1973.
International Military Tribunal. Trial of the Major War
    Criminals Before the International Military Tribunal,
    Nuremberg 14 November, 1945-10 October, 1946. 42 Vols.
    Nuremberg: International Military Tribunal, 1947-49.
Justiz und NS Verbrechen: Sammlungen Deutscher Strafurteile
    gegen Nationalsozialistischer Tötungsverbrechen 1945-1966.
    9 Vols. Amsterdam: University Press, 1969-72.
Kosch, Wilhelm. Biographisches Staatshandbuch, Lexikon der
    Politik, Presse und Publizistik. Vol. 2. Bern:
    Francke, 1963.
Krebs, Norbert. Der Südwesten. Vol. 3 of Landeskunde von
    Deutschland. Ed. Norbert Krebs. 3 Vols. Leipzig and
    Berlin: B. G. Teuber, 1931.
Kürschners Deutscher Gelehrten-Kalender, 1928/29. 3rd. ed.
    Berlin: Walter de Gruyter, 1928.

Länderrat des Amerikanischen Besatzungsgebiete, ed.
Statistisches Handbuch von Deutschland, 1928-1944.
Munich: Franz Ehrenwirth, 1949.

Monckmeier, Otto, ed. Jahrbuch der nationalsozialistischen
Wirtschaft. Munich: Eher, 1937.

Nachrichtenblatt der Gauleitung Baden. 5 Vols. Karlsruhe:
Gau Baden Verlag, 1934-38.

Partei-Kanzlei. Verfügungen, Anordnungen, Bekanntgaben.
Munich: Eher, 1942-44.

Der Parteitag der Freiheit, 1935. Munich: Eher, 1935.

Rapp, Alfred, ed. Die Badischen Landtagsabgeordneten, 1905-
1929. Karlsruhe: Badenia, 1929.

_____. Die Parteibewegung in Baden 1905-1928: Tabellen und
Text. Karlsruhe: Badenia, 1929.

Reichsorganisationsleiter, NSDAP, ed. Gau und Kreisverzeichnis
der NSDAP. Munich: Eher, 1938.

_____. Nationalsozialistische Volkswohlfahrtspflege, Ihre
Träger, Grundlagen und Aufgaben. Munich: Eher, 1941.

_____. Organisationsbuch, NSDAP. 5th ed. Munich: Eher,
1938.

_____. Partei-Statistik, 1935. 2 Vols. Munich, Eher, 1935.

Reichswahlleiter. Hauptergebnisse der Wahlen zum Reichstag
am 6. November 1932. Berlin: Reimar Hobbing, 1932.

Sauer, Paul, ed. Dokumente über die Verfolgung der Jüdischen
Bürger in Baden-Württemberg durch das Nationalsozial-
istische Regime 1933-1945. 2 Vols. Stuttgart: W.
Kohlhammer, 1966.

Schadt, Jörg, ed. Im Dienst an der Republik. Die Tätigkeitsberichte des Landesverbands der Sozialdemokratischen
Partei Badens 1914-1932. Stuttgart: W. Kohlhammer, 1977.

_____, ed. Verfolgung und Widerstand unter dem National-
sozialismus in Baden. Die Lageberichte der Gestapo und
des Generalstaatsanwalts. Stuttgart: W. Kohlhammer,
1976.

Schulungs- und Verordnungsblatt, Ausgabe Elsass. 1941-43.

Schwarzmaier, Hansmartin, et al., eds. Der deutsche Südwesten
zur Stunde Null. Zusammenbruch und Neuanfang im Jahre
1945 in Dokumenten und Bildern. Karlsruhe: Harschdruck,
1975.

Stasiewski, Bernhard, ed. Akten Deutscher Bischöfe über die
Lage der Kirche 1933-1945. 2 Vols. Mainz: Matthias-
Grünewald, 1968, 1976.

Statistisches Reichsamt. "Die Wahlen zum Reichstag am 5.
März 1933." Statistik des Deutschen Reichs. Vol. 434.
Berlin: Verlag für Sozialpolitik und Statistik, 1935.

Statistisches Reichsamt. Hauptergebnisse der Wahlen zum
    Reichstag am 31. Juli 1932. Berlin: Reimar Hobbing,
    1932.
_____. "Die Wahlen zum Reichstag am 14. September 1930."
    Statistik des Deutschen Reichs. Vol. 382. Berlin:
    Reimar Hobbing, 1932.
_____. Statistisches Jahrbuch für das Deutsche Reich.
    Vol. 44. Berlin: Reimar Hobbing, 1924/25.
Statistisches Jahrbuch für das Deutsche Reich. Vol. 52.
    Berlin: Reimar Hobbing, 1933.
Steward, John S., ed. Sieg des Glaubens: Geheime Gestapo
    Berichte über den Widerstand der Kirchen. Zürich:
    Thomas, 1946.
Südwestdeutsche Rundschau. Baden: Monographien seiner Städte
    und Landschaften. Vol. 10. Karlsruhe: G. Braun, 1958.
"Trial of Robert Wagner and Six Others." U.N. War Crimes
    Commission, ed. Law Reports of Trials of War Criminals.
    Vol. 3. London: Majesty's Stationery Office, 1948.
Trials of War Criminals Before the Nuernberg Military
    Tribunals. Vol. 6, The Flick Case. Washington, D.C.:
    Government Printing Office, 1952.
Verhandlungen des Badischen Landtags 1. Sitzungsperiode
    28 Oktober 1929 bis 27 Oktober 1930, Protokollheft,
    II. Karlsruhe: Aktiengesellschaft Badenia, 1930.
Verordnungsblatt der NSDAP Baden. 1941-42.
Verordnungsblatt der NSDAP Gau Baden-Elsass. 1942-43.
Verordnungsblatt des Chef der Zivilverwaltung. 5 Vols.
    Strassburg: Oberrheinischer Gauverlag, 1940-44.
Voggenreiter, Ludwig, ed. Der Hitler Prozess: Das Final
    zum Erwachen Deutschlands. Potsdam: L. Voggenreiter,
    1934.
Volk, Ludwig, ed. Kirchliche Akten über die Reichskonkor-
    datsverhandlungen. Mainz: Matthias-Grünewald, 1969.
Volz, Hans, ed. Dokumente der deutschen Politik: Das Reich
    Adolf Hitlers. Vol. 8, Part 2. Berlin: Junker and
    Dünnhaupt, 1943.
Wer ist's? Berlin: H. Degener, 1922, 1935.

NEWSPAPERS AND PERIODICALS

Das Archiv, 1936/37
Badische Presse
Die Badische Schule
Badische Zeitung
Badischer Beobachter

Badisches Landwirtschaftliches Wochenblatt
Bodenreform
C. V. Zeitung (Central-Verein Zeitung)
Der Demokrat
Das Deutsche Tageblatt
Deutschlands Erneuerung
Ewiges Deutschland
Frankfurter Zeitung
Der Führer
Der Gemeindetag
Der Hoheitsträger
Israelitisches Gemeindeblatt (Mannheim)
Karlsruher Tagblatt
Karlsruher Zeitung
Die Landgemeinde
Mitteilungen aus dem Verein zur Abwehr des Antisemitismus
Mitteilungsblatt der Nationalsozialisten in den Parlamenten
    und gemeindlichen Vertretungskörpern
Nationalsozialistische Gemeinde
NS Partei-Korrespondenz
New York Times
Odal
Politischer Rundbrief
Rote Fahne (Berlin)
Völkischer Beobachter (Munich)
Völkischer Herold
Volksfreund
Wirtschaft und Statistik

GENERAL (BOOKS, ARTICLES, DISSERTATIONS, MEMOIRS, AND DIARIES)

Allemann, Rene. "Die Elsässer: Eine Minorität die keine sein
    will." Der Monat 7 (November 1962):9-16.
Allen, William S. The Nazi Seizure of Power: The Experience
    of a Single German Town, 1930-1935. Chicago: Quadrangle,
    1965.
Altgelt, Ingeborg. Wegweiser durch die N.S. Volkswohlfahrt.
    Berlin: Weidemann, 1935.
Angress, Werner T. Stillborn Revolution: The Communist Bid
    for Power in Germany, 1921-1923. Princeton, N.J.:
    Princeton University Press, 1963.
Auerbach, Helmuth. "Hitlers Politische Lehrjahre und die
    Münchener Gesellschaft 1919-1923." Vierteljahrshefte für
    Zeitgeschichte 25 (January 1977):1-45.

Auerbach, Helmuth. "Die Einheit Dirlewanger." Vierteljahrs-hefte für Zeitgeschichte 10 (July 1962):250-63.

Bach, Adolf. Deutsche Namenkunde. Heidelberg: C. Winter, 1952.

Badische Politik, 1918-1921. Heidelberg: Heidelberger Verlagsanstalt, 1921.

Bankwitz, Philip Charles Farwell. Alsatian Autonomist Leaders 1919-1947. Lawrence, Kansas: Regents Press of Kansas, 1978.

Baynes, Norman H., ed. The Speeches of Adolf Hitler, April 1922 - August 1939. New York: Howard Fertig, 1969.

Becker, August, ed. Naturforschung im Aufbruch. Munich: Lehmann, 1936.

Bender, Helmut. Baden 1000 Jahre europäische Geschichte und Kultur. Konstanz: Friedrich Stadler, 1971.

Benz, Wolfgang. Süddeutschland in der Weimarer Republik: Ein Beitrag zur deutschen Innenpolitik, 1918-1923. Berlin: Duncker and Humbolt, 1970.

Bergdolt, Wilhelm. Badische Allmenden: Eine Rechts- und Wirtschaftgeschichtliche Untersuchung über die Allmendverhältnisse der badischen Rheinhardt insbesondere der Dörfer Eggenstein, Liedolsheim und Russheim. Heidelberg: J. Hörning, 1926.

Bernsee, Hans. Aufgaben der N.S.-Volkswohlfahrt im Kriege. Berlin: Zentralverlag der NSDAP, 1941.

_____. "N.S. Volkswohlfahrt in der Welt voran." Unser Wille und Weg 5 (April 1935):133-36.

Besson, Waldemar. Württemberg und die deutsche Staatskrise 1928-1933: Eine Studie zur Auflösung der Weimarer Republik. Stuttgart: Deutsche Verlags-Anstalt, 1959.

Beyerchen, Alan. Scientists under Hitler: Politics and the Physics Community in the Third Reich. New Haven: Yale University Press, 1977.

Bickler, Hermann. "Verschwörung des Blutes." Unser Wille und Weg 10 (April 1941):1-8.

Birker, Karl. "Die badischen Arbeiterbildungsvereine vor dem Ersten Weltkrieg." Internationale wissenschaftliche Korrespondenz zur Geschichte deutscher Arbeiterbewegung 18 (April 1973):11-13.

Blachly, Frederick F.; and Oatman, Miriam E. The Government and Administration of Germany. Baltimore: Johns Hopkins Press, 1928.

Bloch, Erich. Geschichte der Juden von Konstanz im 19. und 20. Jahrhundert: Eine Dokumentation. Konstanz: Rosgarten, 1971.

Blos, Wilhelm. Von der Monarchie zum Volksstaat: Zur Geschichte der Revolution in Deutschland insbesondere in Württemberg. Stuttgart: Bergers Literarisches Büro und Verlagsanstalt, 1922.

Bolitho, Gordon. The Other Germany. London: Lovat Dickson, 1934.

Bopp, Marie-Joseph. L'Alsace sous l'occupation allemande. 2nd ed. Le Puy: Xavier Mappus, 1947.

_____. "Dans l'Armée Allemande, 1940-45." Revue Historique de l'armée 4 (September 1948):104-106.

Bracher, Karl Dietrich. Deutschland zwischen Demokratie und Diktatur: Beiträge zur neueren Politik und Geschichte. Bern/Munich: Scherz, 1964.

_____. Die Auflösung der Weimarer Republik: Eine Studie zum Problem des Machtverfalls in der Demokratie. 4th ed. Villingen: Ring Verlag, 1964.

_____. The German Dictatorship: The Origins, Structure, and Effects of National Socialism. Trans. Jean Steinberg. New York: Praeger, 1970.

_____; Sauer, Wolfgang; and Schulz, Gerhard. Die National-sozialistische Machtergreifung: Studien zur Errichtung des totalitären Herrschaftssystems in Deutschland 1933/34. Köln and Opladen: Westdeutscher Verlag, 1962.

Bramstedt, Ernest K. Goebbels and National Socialist Propaganda, 1925-1945. East Lansing: Michigan State University Press, 1965.

Brandt, Peter; and Rürup, Reinhard, eds. Arbeiter-, Soldaten- und Volksräte in Baden 1918/19. Düsseldorf: Droste, 1980.

Breuning, Klaus. Die Vision des Reiches, Deutscher Katholizismus zwischen Demokratie und Diktatur, 1929-1934. Munich: Max Hueber, 1969.

Broszat, Martin. "Die völkische Ideologie und der National-sozialismus." Deutsche Rundschau 84 (January 1958): 53-68.

Bry, Gerhard. Wages in Germany, 1871-1945. Princeton: Princeton University Press, 1960.

Bucher, Peter. Der Reichswehrprozess: Der Hochverrat der Ulmer Reichswehroffiziere, 1929/30. Boppard am Rhein: Harold Boldt, 1967.

Bullock, Alan. Hitler: A Study in Tyranny. Rev. ed. New York: Harper and Row, 1962.

Carmon, Arye. "The Impact of the Nazi Racial Decrees on the University of Heidelberg: A Case Study." Yad Vashem Studies 11 (1976):134-62.

Carsten, Francis L. The Reichswehr in Politics, 1918-1930. London: Oxford University Press, 1966.

Carsten, Francis L. The Rise of Fascism. Berkeley and Los
Angeles: University of California Press, 1969.
Cecil, Lamar. Albert Ballin, Business and Politics in Imperial
Germany, 1888-1918. Princeton, N.J.: Princeton University
Press, 1967.
Cecil, Robert. The Myth of the Master Race: Alfred Rosenberg
and Nazi Ideology. New York: Dodd and Mead, 1972.
Child, Clifton, J. "The Political Structure of Hitler's
Europe." In Hitler's Europe: A Survey of International
Affairs, 1939-1946, ed. Arnold and Veronica M. Toynbee.
London: Oxford University Press, 1954.
Childers, Thomas. "The Social Bases of the National
Socialist Vote." Journal of Contemporary History 11
(October 1976):17-31.
Conway, John S. The Nazi Persecution of the Churches 1933-
1945. London: Weidenfeld and Nicolson, 1968.
Dahrendorf, Ralf. Society and Democracy in Germany. New
York: Doubleday, 1969.
Dehn, Gunter, ed. Kirche und Völkerversöhnung, Dokumente
zum Halleschen Universitätskonflikt. Berlin: Furche,
1931.
"Deutschland und Frankreich--von einen Elsässer." Deutschlands
Erneuerung 18 (November 1934):656-58.
Dibner, Ursula Ruth Brockert. "The History of the National
Socialist German Student League." Ph.D. dissertation,
University of Michigan, 1969.
Diehl, James M. Paramilitary Politics in Weimar Germany.
Bloomington: Indiana University Press, 1977.
Diehl-Thiele, Peter. Partei und Staat im Dritten Reich:
Untersuchungen zum Verhältnis von NSDAP und allgemeiner
innerer Staatsverwaltung 1933-1945. Munich: C. H. Beck,
1969.
Dietrich, Otto. 12 Jahre mit Hitler. Munich: Isar, 1955.
Dörner, Klaus. "Nationalsozialismus und Lebensvernichtung."
Vierteljahrshefte für Zeitgeschichte 15 (April 1967):
120-52.
Dreyfus, Francois G. La Vie Politique en Alsace 1919-1936.
Paris: Armand Colin, 1969.
Dühnke, Horst. Die KPD von 1933 bis 1945. Cologne:
Kiepenheuer and Witsch, 1972.
Düwell, Kurt. Die Rheingebiete in der Judenpolitik des
Nationalsozialismus vor 1942: Beitrag zu einer
vergleichenden zeitgeschichtlichen Landeskunde. Bonn:
Ludwig Rohrscheid, 1968.

Die Elsass-Lothringer Partei: Ihr Wesen und Ziel. Strassburg:
    Frei Volk, 1938. This work may be found in T-81/179/
    328036-51.
Engler-Füsslin, Fritz. "Badens Bauerntum im deutschen Aufbau-
    werk." Odal 7 (March 1938):180-85.
Erbacher, Hermann, ed. Vereinigte Evangelische Landeskirche
    in Baden 1821-1971. Karlsruhe: Evangelischer Pressever-
    band, 1971.
Ernst, Robert. "Deutschland und Elsass-Lothringen." Deutsche
    Politik 6 (2 July 1921):642-47.
_____. Rechenschaftsbericht eines Elsässers. 2nd ed.
    Berlin: Bernard and Graeffe, 1954.
_____. "Zur Ermordung von Dr. Karl Roos durch die Franzosen."
    Elsass-Lothringer Heimatstimmen 18 (25 April 1940). This
    work may be found in T-81/513/5276096-97.
Evans, Richard J. The Feminist Movement in Germany, 1894-
    1933. London: Sage, 1976.
Faris, Ellsworth. "Takeoff Point for the National Socialist
    Party: The Landtag Election in Baden 1929." Central
    European History 8 (June 1975):140-71.
Farquharson, John. "The NSDAP in Hanover and Lower Saxony,
    1921-26." Journal of Contemporary History 8 (October
    1973):103-20.
_____. The Plough and the Swastika in Germany 1928-1945.
    London: Sage, 1976.
Fellmeth. "Religionsstatistik in Baden." Deutschlands
    Erneuerung 12 (September 1928):540-42.
Fittbogen, Gottfried. Was jeder Deutsche von Grenz- und
    Auslanddeutschtum wissen muss. 8th ed. Munich/Berlin:
    R. Oldenburg, 1937.
Florinsky, Michael T. Fascism and National Socialism: A
    Study of the Economic and Social Policies of the
    Totalitarian State. New York: Macmillan, 1936.
Föhr, Ernst. Geschichte des Badischen Konkordats. Freiburg:
    Herder, 1958.
_____. Fünf Jahre Schulpolitik und Schulkampf in Baden
    1918-1923. Karlsruhe: Badenia, 1923.
_____. Das Konkordat zwischen dem Heiligen Stuhle und dem
    Freistaate Baden 12. Oktober 1932. Freiburg im Breisgau:
    Herder, 1933.
Franz, Erwin. Der jüdische Marsch zur Macht: Eine Quellen-
    sammlung als Beitrag zur Judenemanzipation in Baden
    1806-1933. Karlsruhe: Karl Moninger, 1944.
Franz-Willing, Georg. Krisenjahr der Hitlerbewegung 1923.
    Preussisch Oldendorf: K. W. Schütz, 1975.

Franz-Willing, Georg. Ursprung der Hitlerbewegung, 1919-1922.
2nd ed. Preussisch Oldendorf: K. W. Schütz, 1974.

Fredborg, Arvid. Behind the Steel Wall: A Swedish Journalist
in Berlin, 1941-43. New York: Viking, 1943.

Frick, Wilhelm. Die Deutsche Frau im nationalsozialistischen
Staat. Langenslaza: Hermann Beyer and Sons, 1934.

_____. "Die Gemeinde in Volk und Staat." N.S. Gemeinde 5
(November 1937):646-49.

_____. "Zur Bevölkerungspolitik." Neues Volk 2 (February
1934):3.

Friedrich, Carl J. "The Failure of a One-Party System:
Hitler's Germany." In Authoritarian Politics in Modern
Society: The Dynamics of Established One-Party Systems,
ed. Samuel P. Huntington and Clement H. Moore. New
York: Basic Books, 1970.

Friedrich, Hermann. Unter dem Hakenkreuz. Meine Erlebnisse
als Agitator bei der Nat. Soz. Dt. Arbeiterpartei.
Karlsruhe: Selbstverlag, 1929.

Fritsch, Willi. Neues Bauen in Baden. Karlsruhe: Führer
Verlag, 1936.

Führer-Rede zum Kriegs-Winterhilfswerk 1942/43. Berlin:
Eher, 1942.

Genschel, Helmut. Die Verdrängung der Juden aus der Wirtschaft
im Dritten Reich. Göttingen: Musterschmidt, 1966.

Gies, Horst. "NSDAP und landwirtschaftliche Organisationen
in der Endphase der Weimarer Republik." Vierteljahrshefte für Zeitgeschichte 15 (October 1967):341-76.

Giese, Friedrich; Neuwiem, Erhard; and Cahn, Ernst.
Deutsches Verwaltungsrecht. Berlin/Vienna: Industrieverlag Spaeth and Linde, 1930.

Glockner, Hermann. Heidelberger Bilderbuch: Erinnerungen.
Bonn: H. Bonvier, 1969.

Görler, Ingeborg, ed. So sahen sie Mannheim. Stuttgart:
Konrad Theiss, 1974.

Gordon, Harold J., Jr. Hitler and the Beer Hall Putsch.
Princeton, N.J.: Princeton University Press, 1972.

Gross, Walter. Rassenpolitische Erziehung. Baden: Junker
and Dünnhaupt, 1935.

Gruchmann, Lothar. Nationalsozialistische Grossraumordnung:
Die Konstruktion einer deutschen Monroe Doktrin.
Stuttgart: Deutsche Verlangs-Anstalt, 1962.

Guillebaud, Claude William. The Social Policy of Nazi
Germany. Cambridge, England: Cambridge University
Press, 1941.

Gumbel, Emil. Vom Femenmord zur Reichskanzlei. Heidelberg:
Lambert Schneider, 1962.

Gumbel, Emil. Vier Jahre Politischer Mord. Berlin/Fichtenau: Verlag der Neuen Gesellschaft, 1922.

Gutt, Arthur. "Bevölkerungs- und Rassenpolitik." Grundlagen, Aufbau, und Wirtschaftsordnung des nationalsozialistischen Staates. Vol. 1. Berlin: Spaeth and Linde, 1936.

Haebler, Rolf Gustav. Badische Geschichte. Karlsruhe: G. Braun, 1951.

Hale, Oron J. The Captive Press in the Third Reich. Princeton, N.J.: Princeton University Press, 1964.

Halperin, S. William. Germany Tried Democracy: A Political History of the Reich from 1918 to 1933. New York: W. W. Norton, 1965.

Hanemann, Landesgerichtsdirektor. Materialien für deutschnationale Wahlredner. Freiburg in Breisgau: Emil Gross, 1928.

Haselier, Günter. "Baden." In Geschichte der deutschen Lander: Territorien Ploetz, ed. Georg W. Sante and A. G. Ploetz Verlag. Vol. 1. Würzburg: Ploetz, 1971.

Hauptamt für Volkswohlfahrt. Sozialisten der Tat; Das Buch der unbekannten Kämpfer der NSV. Berlin: N.p., 1934.

Hebenbrock, Walter. "Nationalsozialistische Wohlfahrtspflege ist Gesundheitsdienst." Der Schulungsbrief 5 (1938): 440-46.

Heberle, Rudolf. From Democracy to Nazism: A Regional Case Study on Political Parties in Germany. 1st ed. 1945. New York: Grosset and Dunlap, 1970.

_____. Landbevölkerung und Nationalsozialismus: Eine soziologische Untersuchung der politischen Willensbildung in Schleswig-Holstein, 1918-1932. Stuttgart: Deutsche Verlags-Anstalt, 1963.

Heckart, Beverly. From Bassermann to Bebel: The Grand Bloc's Quest for Reform in the Kaiserreich, 1900-1914. New Haven: Yale University Press, 1974.

Heiber, Helmut. Joseph Goebbels. Berlin: Colloquium, 1962.

_____, ed. Das Tagebuch von Joseph Goebbels, 1925/26. Stuttgart: Deutsche Verlags-Anstalt, 1960.

Heidelberger, Franz. "Leo Wohleb als Beamter im Badischen Kultusministerium." In Humanist und Politiker, Leo Wohleb der letzte Staatspräsident des Landes Baden, ed. Hans Maier and Paul-Ludwig Weinacht, pp. 27-30. Heidelberg: Kerle, 1969.

Heiden, Konrad. A History of National Socialism. Reprinted and translated from Geschichte des Nationalsozialismus (1932) and Geburt des Dritten Reiches (1934). New York: Octagon, 1971.

Heinzelman, Siegfried. Evangelische Kirche in Mannheim: Aus der Kirchengeschichte einer leidgeprüften Stadt. Mannheim: Dr. Haass, 1965.

Helff, Eduard, ed. Grenzland Baden Spaten zur Hand! Karlsruhe: E. F. Müller, 1936.

Hellpach, Willy. Wirken und Wirren, Lebenserinnerungen. Eine Rechenschaft über Wert und Glück, Schuld und Sturz meiner Generation. 2 Vol. Hamburg: Wegner, 1948/49.

Heuss, Theodor. Aufzeichnungen 1945-47. Edited and introduced by Eberhard Pikart. Tübingen: Rainer Wunderlich, 1966.

Hilberg, Raul. The Destruction of the European Jews. Chicago: Quadrangle, 1967.

"Hilfswerk Mutter und Kind in der Praxis." Der Gemeindetag 28 (1 July 1934):401-402.

Hilgenfeldt, Erich. "Das Wohlfahrtsethos des völkischen Staates." In Deutsche Sozialisten am Werk: Ein sozialistisches Bekenntnis Deutscher Manner, ed. Friedrich Christian, Prinz zu Schaumburg-Lippe. 2nd ed. Berlin: Deutscher Verlag für Politik und Wirtschaft, 1936.

Hirtler, Heinrich. Verschuldungsverhältnisse der Kleinbauern des Kaiserstuhls. Karlsruhe: G. Braunsche Hofbuchdruckerei, 1912.

Hitler, Adolf. Mein Kampf. Annotated translation. New York: Reynal and Hitchcock, 1939.

Hitler's Secret Conversations 1941-1944. Trans. Norman Cameron and R. H. Stevens. New York: Signet, 1953.

Hoch, Anton. "Der Luftangriff auf Freiburg am 10. Mai 1940." Vierteljahrshefte für Zeitgeschichte 4 (April 1956): 115-44.

Horn, Daniel. "The Hitler Youth and Educational Decline in the Third Reich." History of Education Quarterly (Winter 1976):425-40.

Horn, Wolfgang. Führerideologie und Parteiorganisation in der N.S.D.A.P., 1919-1933. Düsseldorf: Droste, 1972.

Huber, H.; and Müller, A. Das Dritte Reich: Seine Geschichte in Texten und Dokumenten. Munich: Kurt Desch, 1964.

Hüttenberger, Peter. Die Gauleiter: Studie zum Wandel des Machtgefügs in der N.S.D.A.P. Stuttgart: Deutsche Verlags-Anstalt, 1969.

Hundsnurscher, Franz; and Taddey, Gerhard. Die Jüdischen Gemeinden in Baden: Denkmale, Geschichte, Schicksale. Stuttgart: W. Kohlhammer, 1968.

Institut für Marxismus-Leninismus bein Zentralkomitee der
S.E.D., ed. Deutsche Widerstands-Kämpfer, 1933-1945.
2 Vols. Berlin: Dietz, 1970.

Jacobsen, Hans-Adolf. Nationalsozialistische Aussenpolitik,
1933-1938. Frankfurt am Main and Berlin: Alfred Metzner,
1968.

Jäckel, Eberhard. Frankreich in Hitlers Europa: Die Deutsche
Frankreichpolitik im Zweiten Weltkrieg. Stuttgart:
Deutsche Verlags-Anstalt, 1966.

Janssen, Karl-Heinz. Macht und Verblendung, Kriegszielpolitik
der deutschen Bundesstaaten, 1914-18. Göttingen:
Musterschmidt, 1963.

Jenke, Manfred. Verschwörung von Rechts? Ein Bericht über
den Rechtsradikalismus in Deutschland nach 1945. Berlin:
Colloquium, 1961.

Jeserich, Kurt, ed. Die Deutschen Landkreise: Material zur
Landkreisreform. Stuttgart and Berlin: W. Kohlhammer,
1937.

Jong, Louis de. Die Deutsche Fünfte Kolonne im zweiten
Weltkrieg. Translated by H. Lindemann. Stuttgart:
Deutsche Verlags-Anstalt, 1959.

Johanny, Carl. Partei und Staat. Königsberg: Grafe and
Unzer, 1937.

Kaller, Gerhard. "Die Revolution des Jahres 1918 in Baden
und die Tätigkeit des Arbeiter- und Soldatenrats in
Karlsruhe." Zeitschrift für die Geschichte des
Oberrheins 114 (1966):301-50.

_____. "Zur Revolution von 1918 in Baden, Klumpp-Putsch
und Verfassungsfrage." Oberrheinische Studien 2:175-202.

Kast, Augustin. Die Badischen Martyrerpriester: Lebensbilder
Badischer Priester aus der Zeit des Dritten Reiches.
Karlsruhe: Badenia, 1947.

Kater, Michael. "Methodologische Überlegungen über Grenzen
und Möglichkeiten einer EDV-Analyse der NSDAP-Sozial-
struktur von 1925 bis 1945." Geschichte und
Gesellschaft 3 (1977):453-84.

_____. Studentenschaft und Rechtsradikalismus in Deutschland
1918-1933. Hamburg: Hoffman and Campe, 1975.

_____. "Zur Soziographie der frühen NSDAP." Vierteljahrs-
hefte für Zeitgeschichte 19 (April 1971):135-59.

Kattermann, Hildegard, ed. Geschichte und Schicksal der
Lahrer Juden. Lahr: Stadtverwaltung, 1976.

Kaufmann, Josef. "Die Tätigkeit des Amtes für Kommunalpolitik
des Gaues Baden/Nebenstelle Strassburg." NS Gemeinde 9
(1 May 1941):137-39.

Kele, Max H. Nazis and Workers: National Socialist Appeals to German Labor, 1919-1933. Chapel Hill: University of North Carolina Press, 1972.

Kemper, Friedhelm. "Unser Kampf um die Jugend." Die badische Schule 2 (1935):224-25.

Kerber, Franz. "Leistungsschau Badischer Gemeinden." NS Gemeinde 5 (1 November 1937):643-44.

_____. "Förderung der Bautätigkeit und Wahrung der Baukultur." Der Gemeindetag 30 (1 May 1936):318-19.

_____, ed. Das Elsass, Des Reiches Tor und Schild. 3rd ed. Strassburg: Hüneburg Verlag, 1940.

Kettenacker, Lothar. Nationalsozialistische Volkstumspolitik im Elsass. Stuttgart: Deutsche Verlags-Anstalt, 1973.

Keyser, Erich, ed. Badisches Stadtebuch. Stuttgart: W. Kohlhammer, 1959.

Kirkpatrick, Clifford. Nazi Germany: Its Women and Family Life. Indianapolis and New York: Bobbs-Merrill, 1938.

Kissenkoetter, Udo. Gregor Strasser und die NSDAP. Stuttgart: Deutsche Verlags-Anstalt, 1978.

Klönne, Arno. Gegen den Strom: Bericht über den Jugendwiderstand im Dritten Reich. 2nd ed. Hanover and Frankfurt: O. Goedel, 1960.

Kluke, Paul. "Nationalsozialistische Volkstumspolitik im Elsass-Lothringen 1940 bis 1945." In Zur Geschichte und Problematik der Demokratie. Festgabe für Hans Herzfeldt, ed. Wilhelm Berges and Carl Hinrichs. Berlin: Duncker and Humbolt, 1959.

Kneip, Rudolf. Jugend der Weimarer Zeit, Handbuch der Jugendverbände 1919-38. Frankfurt am Main: Dipa, 1974.

Kocka, Jürgen. "The First World War and the Mittelstand: German Artisans and White-Collar Workers." Journal of Contemporary History 8 (January 1973):101-23.

Koehl, Robert Lewis. R.K.F.D.V., German Resettlement and Population Policy 1939-45: A History of the Reich Commission for the Strengthening of Germandom. Cambridge, Mass.: Harvard University Press, 1957.

Köhler, Heinrich. Lebenserinnerungen des Politikers und Staatsmannes 1878-1949. Ed. Josef Becker. Stuttgart: W. Kohlhammer, 1964.

Köhrer, Erich, ed. Das Land Baden: Seine Entwicklung und seine Zukunft. Berlin: Deutsche Verlags-Aktiengesellschaft, 1925.

Koenigsberger, H. G. "The Reformation and Social Revolution." In The Reformation Crisis, ed. Joel Hurstfield. New York: Harper and Row, 1966.

Kolb, Eberhard; and Schönhoven, Klaus, eds. Regionale and lokale Räteorganisationen in Wurttemberg 1918/19. Düsseldorf: Droste, 1976.

Koonz, Claudia. "Nazi Women before 1933: Rebels against Emancipation." Social Science Quarterly 56 (March 1976): 552-63.

KPD. Das Agrarprogram der Kommunistischen Partei Deutschland. c. 1919/20 Hoover Microfilm Publication: KPD Pamphlets.

Krause, Fritz. "Die Arbeit der N.S. Volkswohlfahrt im Sommer 1934." Wille und Weg 4 (July 1934):201-203.

Krebs, Albert. Tendenzen und Gestalten der NSDAP. Stuttgart: Deutsche Verlags-Anstalt, 1959.

Kreuzberger, Wolfgang. Studenten und Politik, 1918-1933: Der Fall Freiburg im Breisgau. Göttingen: Vandenhoeck and Rupprecht, 1972.

Laqueur, Walter, ed. Fascism: A Reader's Guide. Berkeley: University of California Press, 1976.

Lebovics, Hermann. Social Conservatism and the Middle Classes in Germany 1914-1933. Princeton, N.J.: Princeton University Press, 1969.

Lee, Loyd E. "Liberal Constitutionalism as Administrative Reform: The Baden Constitution of 1818." Central European History 8 (June 1975):91-112.

Lerner, Daniel; de Sola Pool, Ithiel; and Schueller, George K. "The Nazi Elite." In World Revolutionary Elites: Studies in Coercive Ideological Movements, ed. Daniel Lerner and D. Lasswell. Cambridge, Mass.: Mass. Institute of Technology Press, 1966.

Lochner, Louis P. What about Germany? New York: Mead and Company, 1943.

Lohalm, Uwe. Völkischer Radikalismus: Die Geschichte des Deutschvölkischen Schutz- und Trutz-Bundes, 1919-1923. Hamburg: Leibnitz, 1970.

Loock, H. D. "Der Hünenburg Verlag, Friedrich Spiesser und der Nationalsozialismus." Gutachten des Institut für Zeitgeschichte. Vol. 2. Stuttgart: Deutsche Verlags-Anstalt, 1966.

Loomis, Charles; and Beegel, J. Allen. "The Spread of German Nazism in Rural Areas." American Sociological Review 11 (December 1946):725-34.

Lorentzen, Ingeborg. "Die Frau in der Rechtspflege." In Unsere Zeit und Wir; Das Buch der deutschen Frau, ed. Elsbeth Unverricht, pp. 417-24. Gauting: Heinrich A. Berg, 1935.

Ludwig, Max. Aus dem Tagebuch des Hans O. Documente und
  Berichte über die Deportation und den Untergang der
  Heidelberger Juden. Heidelberg: Schneider, 1965.
Mager, Syndikus. "Aus Heidelberg." Deutsche Selbstverwaltung:
  Kommunalpolitische Monatsschrift der D.N.V.P. 1 (1927):
  No. 1.
Maier, Hans; and Weinacht, Paul-Ludwig, eds. Humanist und
  Politiker, Leo Wohleb der letzte Staatspräsident des
  Landes Baden. Heidelberg: Kerle, 1969.
Maitre, Joseph M. "Die französischen Frontkämpfer in Freiburg
  i. Br." In Alemannenland, Ein Buch von Volkstum und
  Schulung, ed. Franz Kerber. Stuttgart: J. Engelhorns,
  1937.
Marx, Hugo. Die Flucht, Jüdisches Schicksal 1940. Düsseldorf:
  Verlag Allgemeine Wochenzeitung der Juden in Deutschland,
  1955.
_____. Was wird werden: Das Schicksal der Deutschen Juden
  in der sozialen Krise. Wiesbaden: Westdruckerei, 1932.
_____. Werdegang eines jüdischen Staatsanwalts und Richters
  in Baden 1932-1933: Ein soziologischpolitisches Zeitbild.
  Villingen: Neckar, 1965.
Maser, Werner. Die Frühgeschichte der NSDAP, Hitlers Weg
  bis 1924. Frankfurt am Main: Athenaum, 1965.
Mason, T. W. "The Primacy of Politics: Politics and Economics
  in National Socialist Germany." In Nazism and the Third
  Reich, ed. Henry A. Turner, Jr. New York: Quadrangle,
  1972.
Matthias, Erich. "Resistance to National Socialism: The
  Example of Mannheim." Past and Present 45 (November
  1969):118-27.
Matzerath, Horst. Nationalsozialismus und kommunale Selbst-
  verwaltung. Stuttgart: W. Kohlhammer, 1970.
_____; and Turner, Henry A. "Die Selbstfinanzierung der
  NSDAP, 1930-1932." Geschichte und Gesellschaft 3
  (1977):59-92.
Mayer, Otto. Das Badische Schulwesen. Munich: M. Müller,
  n.d. (1938).
McIntyre, Jill. "Women and the Professions in Germany,
  1930-1940." In German Democracy and the Triumph of
  Hitler, ed. Anthony Nicholls and Erich Matthias.
  London: George Allen and Unwin, 1971.
McKale, Donald. The Nazi Party Courts: Hitler's Management
  of Conflict in His Movement, 1921-1945. Wichita:
  University Press of Kansas, 1974.

Meier, Kurt. Die Deutschen Christen: Ein Bild einer Bewegung im Kirchenkampf des Dritten Reiches. Halle: Max Niemeyer, 1964.

Mennecke, Kurt. Ein westdeutscher NSV Kreis. Seine Entstehung und sein Menschengefuge vom 15. September bis zum 30. November 1934. Cologne: Georg Zimmermann, 1936.

Merk, Wilhelm. Handbuch der Badischen Verwaltung. 2nd ed. Heidelberg: Adolf Emmerling and Son, 1930.

Merkl, Peter H. Political Violence Under the Swastika: 581 Early Nazis. Princeton, N.J.: Princeton University Press, 1975.

Mey, Eugène. Le Drame de l'Alsace, 1939-1945. Paris: Éditions Berger Levrault, 1949.

Milward, Alan. The German Economy at War. London: Athlone, 1967.

Mitscherlich, Alexander; and Mielke, Fred, eds. Medizin Ohne Menschlichkeit. Dokumente des Nürnberger Ärzteprozesses. Frankfurt am Main: Fischer, 1960.

Moers, Martha. Der Fraueneinsatz in der Industrie: Eine psychologische Untersuchung. Berlin: Duncker and Humbolt, 1943.

Mommsen, Hans. Beamtentum im Dritten Reich: Mit Ausgewählten Quellen zur nationalsozialistischen Beamtenpolitik. Stuttgart: Deutsche Verlags-Anstalt, 1966.

Mosse, George L. The Crisis of German Ideology: Intellectual Origins of the Third Reich. New York: Grosset and Dunlap, 1971.

_____, ed. Nazi Culture: Intellectual, Cultural and Social Life in the Third Reich. New York: Grosset and Dunlap, 1968.

Mühlberger, Detlef. "The Sociology of the NSDAP: The Question of Working-Class Membership." Journal of Contemporary History 15 (July 1980):493-511.

Müller, Georg-Wilhelm, ed. Wetterleuchten: Aufsätze aus der Kampfzeit von Joseph Goebbels. Munich: Eher, 1939.

Müller, Gerhard. Die Wissenschaftslehre Ernst Kriecks. Motive und Strukturen einer gescheiterten nationalsozialistischen Wissenschaftsreform. Freiburg: Johannes Krause, 1976.

Mundhenke, Karlheinz. Der oberbadische Aufstand vom September 1923. Heidelberg: Bündischer Ring, 1930.

Neesse, Gottfried. Die Nationalsozialistische Deutsche Arbeiterpartei: Versuch einer Rechtdeutung. Stuttgart: W. Kohlhammer, 1935.

Neumann, Franz. Behemoth: The Structure and Practice of
    National Socialism, 1933-1944. New York: Harper, 1966.
Nilson, Sten S. "Wahlsoziologische Probleme des National-
    sozialismus." Zeitschrift für die Gesamte Staatswissen-
    schaft 110 (1954):303-11.
Noakes, Jeremy. The Nazi Party in Lower Saxony, 1921-1923.
    London: Oxford University Press, 1971.
Nolte, Ernst. Three Faces of Fascism. Trans. L. Vennewitz.
    New York: Mentor, 1969.
N.S. Lehrerbund Sachsen, ed. Bekenntnis der Professoren an
    den deutschen Universitäten und Hochschulen zu Adolf
    Hitler und dem nationalsozialistischen Staat. Dresden:
    N.p. (1933).
Nyomarkay, Joseph. Charisma and Factionalism in the Nazi
    Party. Minneapolis: University of Minnesota Press, 1967.
Oestering, Wilhelm Engelbert. Der Umsturz in Baden.
    Konstanz: Reuss and Itta, 1920.
OKH, Kriegsgeschichtliche Forschungsamt des Heeres, ed.
    Die Kämpfe in Südwestdeutschland, 1919-1923. Berlin:
    E. S. Mittler, 1939.
Olenhusen, Albrecht Goetz von. "Die nationalsozialistische
    Rassenpolitik und die jüdischen Studenten an der
    Universitat Freiburg, 1933-45." Freiburger Universitäts-
    blätter 3 (1964):71-80.
O'Lessker, Karl. "Who Voted for Hitler? A New Look at the
    Class Basis of Nazism." American Journal of Sociology
    74 (July 1968):63-69.
Opitz, Günter. Der Christlich-soziale Volksdienst: Versuch
    einer protestantischen Partei in der Weimarer Republik.
    Düsseldorf: Droste, 1969.
Oppenheimer, Max. Der Fall Vorbote: Zeugnisse des Mannheimer
    Widerstandes. Frankfurt am Main: Roderberg, 1969.
Orlow, Dietrich. The History of the Nazi Party, 1919-1945.
    2 Vols. Pittsburgh: University of Pittsburgh Press,
    1969-73.
_____. "The Conversion of Myth into Power: The NSDAP
    1925-26." American Historical Review 72 (April 1967):
    906-24.
_____. "Die Adolf-Hitler-Schulen." Vierteljahrshefte für
    Zeitgeschichte 13 (July 1965):272-84.
Ott, Hugo. "Möglichkeiten und Formen kirchlichen Widerstandes
    gegen das Dritte Reich von Seiten der Kirchenbehörde und
    des Pfarrklerus: Dargestellt am Pfarrklerus: Dargestellt
    am Beispiel der Erzdiözese Freiburg am Breisgau."
    Historisches Jahrbuch 92 (1972):312-33.

Peterson, Edward N. The Limits of Hitler's Power. Princeton, N.J.: Princeton University Press, 1969.

Petzina, Dieter. "Germany and the Great Depression." Journal of Contemporary History 4 (1969):59-74.

Pflimlin, Pierre; and Uhrich, René. L'Alsace destin et volonté. Paris: Calmann-Lévy, 1963.

Phelps, Reginald H. "Aus den Groener Dokumenten, V: Der Fall Scheringer-Ludin-Wendt." Deutsche Rundschau 76 (November 1950):915-22.

Phillipps, Henry Albert. Germany Today and Tomorrow. New York: Dodd, Mead and Company, 1936.

Pölnitz, Emir Götz von. Das tapfere Leben des Freiherrn Marshall von Bieberstein. 3rd ed. Munich: Callwey, 1938.

Pollock, James Kerr. The Government of Greater Germany. New York: D. Van Nostrand, 1940.

_____; and Thomas, Homer. Germany in Power and Eclipse: The Background of German Development. New York: D. Van Nostrand, 1952.

Pridham, Geoffrey. Hitler's Rise to Power: The Nazi Movement in Bavaria, 1923-1933. New York: Harper and Row, 1973.

Pulzer, Peter G. J. The Rise of Political Anti-Semitism in Germany and Austria. New York: John Wiley and Sons, 1964.

Raible, Eugen. Geschichte der Polizei, Ihre Entwicklung in den alten Landern Baden und Württemberg und in dem neuen Bundesland Baden-Württemberg. Stuttgart: Boorberg, 1963.

Rauschning, Hermann. The Voice of Destruction. New York: G. P. Putnam's, 1940.

Rehberger, Horst. Die Gleichschaltung des Landes Baden 1932/33. Heidelberg: Carl Winter, 1966.

_____. "Die Gleichschaltung des Landes Baden 1932-1933." In Oberrheinische Studien, vol. 2, ed. Alfons Schafer. Karlsruhe: Kommissionsverlag G. Braun, 1973.

Reischle, Hermann. "Plaichinger." Odal 4:58.

Reitlinger, Gerald. The S.S., Alibi of a Nation, 1922-1945. New York: Viking, 1968.

Remmele, Adam. Staatsumwälzung und Neuaufbau in Baden. Karlsruhe: G. Braun, 1925.

Reuter, Alfred. "Vom Fürsorgeamt zum Sozialamt." NS Gemeinde 6 (15 March 1938):168-69.

Riedel, Hermann, ed. Ausweglos: Letzter Akt des Krieges im Schwarzwald in der Ostbaar und an der oberen Donau Ende April 1945. 2nd ed. Villingen: Albert Wetzel, 1975.

Riff, Michael Anthony. "The Anti-Jewish Aspect of the
    Revolutionary Unrest 1848 in Baden and its Impact on
    Emancipation." Leo Baeck Institute, Year Book 21 (1976):
    22-29.
Roberts, Henry Stephen. The House that Hitler Built. New
    York: Harper and Brothers, 1938.
Rössler, Karl Joseph. Der Badische Landtag. Freiburg im
    Breisgau: Rombach, 1949.
Rogge-Börner, Sophie. "Der Weg in die Zukunft." In Unsere
    Zeit und Wir: Das Buch der deutschen Frau, ed. Elsbeth
    Unverricht, pp. 338-52. Gauting bei Munich: Heinrich
    A. Berg, 1932.
Rosenberg, Alfred. "Der nationale Schicksalkampf der Frau."
    In Unsere Zeit und Wir: Das Buch der deutschen Frau,
    ed. Elsbeth Unverricht, pp. 169-72. Gauting bei Munich:
    Heinrich A. Berg, 1932.
Rothenberger, Karl-Heinz. Die elsass-lothringische Heimat-
    und Autonomiebewegung zwischen den beiden Weltkriegen.
    Frankfurt: Peter Land, 1975.
Rothfels, Hans. "Nationalität und Grenze im späten 19. und
    frühen 20. Jahrhundert." Vierteljahrshefte für Zeit-
    geschichte 9 (July 1961):225-33.
Rothmund, Paul. "Wirtschaftliches und soziales Leben in der
    Dreiländerecke." In Der Kreis Lörrach, ed. Konrad
    Theiss. Stuttgart: Theiss, 1971.
Rückleben, Hermann. "Kirchliche Zentralbehörden in Baden,
    1771-1958." In Vereinigte Evangelische Landeskirche in
    Baden 1821-1971, ed. Hermann Erbacher, pp. 654-61.
    Karlsruhe: Evangelischer Presseverband, 1971.
Rürup, Reinhard. "Problems of the German Revolution 1918-19."
    Journal of Contemporary History 3 (October 1968):109-35.
Ruge, Arnold. Das Wesen der Universität und das Studium der
    Frauen. 1911. This pamphlet may be found in GLA/Ruge
    Nachlass/69N/box 93.
_____. Die Mobilmachung der deutschen Frauenkräfte für den
    Krieg. Berlin Verlag Kameradschaft, 1915.
Rupp, Leila J. Mobilizing Women for War: German and
    American Propaganda, 1939-45. Princeton, N.J.:
    Princeton University Press, 1978.
Ruthe, Walter. Der Nationalsozialismus in seinen
    Programmpunkten, Organisationsformen und Aufbaumassnahmen.
    Frankfurt am Main: Moritz Diesterweg, 1937.
Santoro, Cesare. Hitler's Germany as Seen by a Foreigner.
    Trans. from the 3rd German edition. Berlin: Inter-
    nationaler Verlag, 1938.

Saldern, Adelheid von. _Hermann Dietrich. Ein Staatsmann der Weimarer Republik._ Boppard am Rhein: Boldt, 1966.

Salms, Fritz. _Im Schatten des Henkers: Vom Arbeiterwiderstand in Mannheim gegen faschistische Diktatur und Krieg._ Frankfurt am Main: Röderberg, 1973.

Saring, Toni. "Berufsbilder der weiblichen Jugend." In _Unsere Zeit und Wir: Das Buch der deutschen Frau_, ed. Elsbeth Unverricht. 4th ed. Gauting bei Munich: Heinrich A. Berg, 1935.

Sauer, Paul. _Die Schicksale der Jüdischen Bürger Baden-Württembergs während der Nationalsozialistischen Verfölgungs zeit 1933-1945._ Stuttgart: W. Kohlhammer, 1969.

_____. _Württemberg in der Zeit des Nationalsozialismus._ Ulm: Süddeutsche Verlagsgesellschaft, 1975.

Sauer, Wolfgang. "National Socialism: Totalitarianism or Fascism?" In _Adolf Hitler and the Third Reich_, ed. Robert E. Herzstein. Boston: Houghton Mifflin, 1971.

Schadt, Jörg. _Die Sozialdemokratische Partei in Baden von den Anfängen bis zur Jahrhundertwende 1868-1900._ Hanover: Verlag für Literatur und Zeitgeschehen, 1971.

Schaeffer, Eugène. _L'Alsace et la Lorraine, 1940-1945: Leur occupation en droit et en fait._ Paris: R. Pinchon and R. Durand-Auzias, 1953.

Schaeffer, Patrick J. _L'Alsace et l'Allemagne de 1945 à 1949._ Metz: Centre de Recherches Relations Internationales de l'Université de Metz, 1976.

Schäfer, Wolfgang. _NSDAP, Entwicklung und Struktur der Staatspartei des Dritten Reiches._ Hanover and Frankfurt: Norddeutsche Verlags-Anstalt, 1957.

Schall, Paul. _Karl Roos und der Kampf des heimattreuen Elsass._ 3rd ed. Kolmar: Alsatian, 1941.

Scheringer, Richard. _Das Grosse Los: Unter Soldaten, Bauern und Rebellen._ Hamburg: Rowohl, 1959.

Schiffers, Reinhard. _Elemente direkter Demokratie im Weimarer Regierungssystem._ Düsseldorf: Droste, 1971.

Schindler, Rudolf. "Gedanken zur Verwaltungsreform in den Gemeinden." _Mitteilungsblatt der N.S. in den Parlamenten und gemeindlichen Vertretungskörpern_ 5 (September 1932):344-51.

Schirach, Baldur von. _Die Pioniere des Dritten Reiches._ Essen: Zentralstelle für den deutschen Freiheitskampf, 1933.

Schirmer, Rudolf. "Die Verwirklichung des Systems der repräsentativen Demokratie in der badischen Gemeindeverfassung insbesondere der Gemeindeordnung vom 5. Oktober 1921." Ph.D. dissertation, Albert-Ludwigs University of Freiburg, 1933.

Schmid, Adolf. "Die Lösung des elsässischen Problems." In Elsass und Lothringen, Deutsches Land, ed. Otto Meissner. Berlin: Otto Stollberg, 1941.

Schneeberger, Guido, ed. Nachlese zu Heidegger: Dokumente zu seinem Leben und Denken. Bern: Selbstverlag, 1962.

Schön, Eberhard. Die Entstehung des Nationalsozialismus in Hessen. Meisenheim am Glan: Anton Haim, 1972.

Schoenbaum, David. Hitler's Social Revolution: Class and Status in Nazi Germany. Garden City, N.Y.: Doubleday, 1967.

Schofer, Joseph. Mit der Alten Fahne in die neue Zeit, Politische Plaudereien aus dem Musterländle. Freiburg im Breisgau: Herder, 1926.

Scholder, Klaus. "Baden im Kirchenkampf des Dritten Reiches: Aspekte und Fragen." In Oberrheinische Studien, vol. 2, ed. Alfons Schäfer. Karlsruhe: Kommissionsverlag, G. Braun, 1973.

Scholl, Inge. Die Weisse Rose. Frankfurt: Verlag der Frankfurter Hefte, 1961.

Scholtz, Harald. "Die N.S. Ordensburgen." Vierteljahrshefte für Zeitgeschichte 15 (July 1967):269-98.

Scholtz-Klink, Gertrud. Verpflichtung und Aufgabe der Frau im Nationalsozialistischen Staat. Berlin: Junker and Dünnhaupt, 1939.

_____, ed. Die Frau im Dritten Reich: Eine Dokumentation. Tübingen: Grabert, 1978.

Schulte, Walter. "Euthanasia und Sterilisation im Dritten Reich." In Deutsches Geistesleben und Nationalsozialismus: Eine Vortragsreihe der Universität Tübingen, ed. Andreas Flitner. Tübingen: Rainer Wunderlich, 1965.

Schulz, Gerhard. Aufstieg des Nationalsozialismus: Krise und Revolution in Deutschland. Frankfurt am Main: Ullstein, 1975.

Schulz, Walter. "Der Reichsarbeitsdienst hilft beim Wiederaufbau im Elsass." In Jahrbuch des Reichsarbeitsdienstes, vol. 6, ed. Oberstarbeitsführer Müller, pp. 31-33. Berlin: Volk und Reich, 1942.

Schulz, Werner, ed. Bibliographie der badischen Geschichte. Vol. 6, part 2. Stuttgart: W. Kohlhammer, 1973.

Schulze, Hagen. Freikorps und Republik 1918-1920. Boppard
    am Rhein: Harald Boldt, 1969.
Schumacher, Martin. Mittelstandfront und Republik: Die
    Wirtschaftspartei, Reichspartei des deutschen Mittel-
    standes. Düsseldorf, Droste, 1972.
    _____. "Stabilität und Instabilität. Wahlentwicklung und
    Parliament in Baden und Braunschweig 1918-1933." In
    Gesellschaft, Parlament und Regierung, ed. Gerhard A.
    Ritter. Dusseldorf: Droste, 1974.
Schuman, Frederick L. The Nazi Dictatorship: A Study in
    Social Pathology and the Politics of Fascism. New York:
    Alfred A. Knopf, 1935.
Schumann, Hans-Gerd. Nationalsozialismus und Gewerkschafts-
    bewegung. Hanover and Frankfurt: O. Goedel, 1958.
Schwarz, Jürgen. Studenten in der Weimarer Republik: Die
    deutsche Studentenschaft in der Zeit von 1918 bis 1923
    und ihre Stellung zur Politik. Berlin: Duncker and
    Humbolt, 1971.
Schwarz, Max, ed. M.d.R., Biographisches Handbuch der
    Reichstage. Hanover: Verlag für Literatur und
    Zeitgeschehen, 1965.
Schweitzer, Arthur. Big Business in the Third Reich.
    Bloomington: Indiana University Press, 1964.
    _____. Die Nazifizierung des Mittelstandes. Stuttgart:
    Ferdinand Enke, 1970. Schwinekörper, Berent; and
    Laubenberger, Franz. Geschichte und Schicksal der
    Freiburger Juden. Freiburg: Rombach, 1963.
Segev, Tom. "The Commanders of Nazi Concentration Camps."
    Ph.D. dissertation, Boston University, 1977.
Semmelroth, Ellen; and Stieda, Renate von, eds. NS Frauen-
    buch. Munich: J. F. Lehmann, 1934.
Shirer, William L. Berlin Diary: The Journal of a Foreign
    Correspondent 1934-41. New York: Alfred A. Knopf, 1941.
Siber, Paula. Die Frauenfrage und ihre Lösung durch den
    Nationalsozialismus. Wolfenbüttel/Berlin: Georg
    Kallmeyer, 1933.
Smith, Howard K. Last Train from Berlin. New York: Alfred
    A. Knopf, 1943.
Sohms-Roedelheim, Max Graf zu. Die Einflüsse der Industriali-
    sierung auf 14 Landgemeinden bei Karlsruhe. Heidelberg:
    Heinrich Fahrer, 1939.
Speer, Albert. Inside the Third Reich. Trans. Richard and
    Clara Winston. New York: Avon, 1971.
Spiesser, Friedrich. Kampfbriefe aus dem Elsass. Berlin:
    Volk und Reich, 1942.

Spiewok, E. Karl. "Der Aufbau des Wohlfahrtswesens im nationalsozialistischen Staat." Grundlagen, Aufbau, und Wirtschaftsordnung des Nationalsozialistischen Staates. Vol. 2. Berlin and Vienna: Industrieverlag Spaeth and Linde, 1936.

Stachura, Peter D. Nazi Youth in the Weimar Republic. Santa Barbara, Calif.: Clio, 1975.

Stadelhofer, Manfred. Der Abbau der Kulturkampfgesetz gebung im Grossherzogtum Baden, 1879-1918. Mainz: Matthias-Grünewald, 1969.

Stegmann, Dirk. Die Erben Bismarcks: Parteien und Verbande in der Spätphase des Wilhelminischen Deutschlands, Sammlungspolitik 1897-1918. Cologne and Berlin: Kiepenheuer and Witsch, 1970.

Stehling, Jutta. Weimarer Koalition und SPD in Baden: Ein Beitrag zur Geschichte der Partei und Kulturpolitik in der Weimarer Republik. Frankfurt am Main: Haag-Herchen, 1976.

Stein, Nathan. "Oberrat der Israeliten Badens 1922-1937." Leo Baeck Institute of Jews from Germany, Year Book, vol. 1. London, 1956.

Steinberg, Michael Stephen. Sabers and Brownshirts: The German Students' Path to National Socialism 1918-1935. Chicago: University of Chicago Press, 1977.

Steiss, Hans., ed. Der Stahlhelm: Bund der Frontsoldaten, Landesverband Württemberg-Hohenzollern, Unser Marsch. Stuttgart: Theodor Kommer, 1937.

Stephan, Werner. "Grenzen des nationalsozialistischen Vormarsches." Zeitschrift für Politik 21 (1931):571-78.

Stephenson, Jill. Women in Nazi Society. New York: Barnes and Noble, 1975.

Ströbel, Engelbert. "Land und Städte in Baden." In Badisches Städtebuch, ed. Erich Keyser. Stuttgart: W. Kohlhammer, 1959.

Tauber, Kurt P. Beyond Eagle and Swastika: German Nationalism since 1945. 2 vols. Middletown, Conn.: Wesleyan University Press, 1967.

Thalmann, Rita; and Feinermann, Emmanuel. Crystal Night, 9-10 November 1938. Trans. Gilles Cremonesci. New York: Coward, McCann and Geoghegan, 1974.

Thiel, Jürgen. Die Grossblockpolitik der Nationalliberalen Partei Badens 1905 bis 1914. Ein Beitrag zur Zusammenarbeit von Liberalismus und Sozialdemokratie in der Spätphase des Wilhelminischen Deutschlands. Stuttgart: W. Kohlhammer, 1976.

Thomas, Homer L.; Pollock, James K.; Ramsdell, Willett; and
    Trow, W. Clark. A Survey of Land Baden. Michigan
    Survey, no. 10. Ann Arbor, Michigan, 1944.
Tinnemann, Ethel Mary. "Attitudes of the German Catholic
    Hierarchy towards the Nazi Regime: A Study in German-
    Political Culture." The Western Political Quarterly
    22 (June 1969):333-49.
Treff, Herbert. "So entstand die N.S. Volkswohlfahrt."
    NS Gemeinde 10 (1 May 1942):71-72.
Trever-Roper, Hugh, ed. Final Entries 1945: The Diaries of
    Joseph Goebbels. New York: Avon, 1979.
Turner, Henry A., Jr. "Fascism and Modernization." World
    Politics 24 (July 1972):547-64.
_____. "Grossunternehmertum und Nationalsozialismus, 1930-
    1933." Historische Zeitschrift 221 (1975):18-68.
Tyrell, Albrecht, ed. Führer Befiehl, Selbstzeugnisse aus
    der Kampfzeit der NSDAP: Dokumente und Analyse.
    Düsseldorf: Droste, 1969.
Ueberhorst, Horst, ed. Elite für die Diktatur: Die National-
    politischen Erziehungsanstalten, 1933-1945. Ein
    Dokumentarbericht. Düsseldorf: Droste, 1969.
Uhlig, Heinrich. Die Warenhäuser im Dritten Reich. Cologne:
    Opladen, 1956.
United States Strategic Bombing Survey. Report 64b. The
    Effects of Strategic Bombing on German Morale. Vol. 1.
    Washington, D.C.: U.S. Government Printing Office,
    1947.
Viollis, Andrée. Alsace et Lorraine au-dessus des Passions.
    Paris/Neuchâtel: Editions Victor Attinger, 1928.
Voelkel. "Die systemtreuen Bürgermeister." Mitteilungsblatt
    der Nationalsozialisten in der Parliamenten und
    gemeindlichen Vertretungskörpern 5 (August 1932):
    310-312.
Voelkel. "Hakenkruez über Kappelwindeck." Mitteilungsblatt
    der Nationalsozialisten in den Parliamenten und
    gemeindlichen Vertretungskörpern 6 (March 1933):120-22.
Vogelsang, Reinhard. Der Freudenkreis Himmlers. Göttingen:
    Musterschmidt, 1972.
Vogelsang, Thilo. Reichswehr, Staat und NSDAP: Beiträge
    zur deutschen Geschichte 1930-1932. Stuttgart:
    Deutsche Verlags-Anstalt, 1962.
Volderauer, Richard. "Gau Baden baut auf." Buch der
    deutschen Gaue: Fünf Jahre nationalsozialistische
    Aufbauleistung. Bayreuth: Gauverlag Bayerische
    Ostmark, 1938.

Vollmer, Bernhard. <u>Volksopposition im Polizeistaat: Gestapo und Regierungsberichte</u>. Stuttgart: Deutsche Verlags-Anstalt, 1957.

Volz, Hans. <u>Daten der Geschichte der NSDAP</u>. Berlin and Leipzig: A. G. Ploetz, 1938.

Wagener, Otto. <u>Hitler aus nächster Nähe: Aufzeichnungen eines Vertrauten 1929-1932</u>. Ed. Henry A. Turner, Jr. Frankfurt am Main: Ullstein, 1978.

Wagner, Robert. "Deutsche Zivilverwaltung im Elsass." <u>NS Gemeinde</u> 9 (1 April 1941):93-95.

_____. <u>Tod dem Marxismus: Es lebe der Nationalsozialismus</u>. Karlsruhe: Führer Verlag, 1932.

_____. "Zwei Jahre deutscher Aufbauarbeit im Elsass." <u>Strassburger Monatshefte</u> 6 (July 1942):364-68.

Waite, Robert G. L. <u>Vanguard of Nazism: The Free Corps Movement in Postwar Germany, 1918-1923</u>. New York: W. W. Norton, 1969.

Walter, Friedrich. <u>Schicksal einer Deutschen Stadt: Geschichte Mannheims, 1907-1945</u>. 2 Vols. Frankfurt am Main: Fritz Knapp, 1950.

Walter, Ludwig. "Deutscher Sozialismus." In <u>Kreis Freiburg i. Br. an der Arbeit</u>, ed. Dr. Fritsch, pp. 10-12. Freiburg im Breisgau: Der Alemanne, 1939.

Weber, Alexander. "Soziale Merkmale der NSDAP-Wähler. Eine Zusammenfassung bisheriger empirischer Untersuchungen und eine Analyse in den Gemeinden der Länder Baden und Hessen." Ph.D. dissertation, Albert-Ludwig University in Freiburg, 1969.

Weber, Marianne. <u>Max Weber; A Biography</u>. Trans. Harry Zahn. New York: John Wiley, 1975.

Weber, Wilhelm. "Reichsregierung und Agrarpolitik." <u>Berichte über Landwirtschaft</u> 45 (1967):41-44.

Weinberg, Gerhard. <u>The Foreign Policy of Hitler's Germany, Diplomatic Revolution in Europe, 1933-36</u>. Chicago: University of Chicago Press, 1970.

_____. "Recent German History: Some Comments and Perspectives." In <u>Festschrift für Fritz T. Epstein</u>, ed. Alexander Fischer, Günter Moltmann, and Klaus Schwabe. Wiesbaden: Franz Steiner, 1978.

_____, ed. <u>Hitlers zweite Buch: Ein Dokument aus dem Jahr 1928</u>. Stuttgart: Deutsche Verlags-Anstalt, 1961.

Weingarten, James J. "The SS Race and Settlement Main Office: Towards an Orden of Blood and Soil." <u>The Historian</u> 24 (November 1971):62-77.

Wenzl, Richart, ed. Stahlhelm-Führer-Spiegel des L.V. Baden. Freiburg im Breisgau: Poppau and Ortmann, 1934.

Werler, Eugene C. J. Kampfmittel des Materialismus und die katholische Aktion im Elsass. Strassburg: N.p., 1938.

Wertheimer, Mildred S. "Alsace-Lorraine: A Border Problem." Foreign Policy Association Information Service 5 (19 February 1930):465-82.

Wieck, Hans Georg. Christliche und Freie Demokraten in Hessen, Rheinland-Pfalz, Baden, und Württemberg 1945/46. Düsseldorf: Droste, 1958.

Wiegert, Oskar, ed. NSDAP Ortsgruppe Offenburg, Festbuch zur 10 jährigen Gründungsfeier am 17. und 18. März 1934. Offenburg: Franz Burda, 1934.

Wilcox, Larry Dean. "The National Socialist Party Press in the Kampfzeit, 1919-1933." Ph.D. dissertation, University of Virginia, 1970.

Wildenmann, Rudolf. "Les Élections du Baden-Württemberg." Documents: Revue des questions Allemandes 23 (May-June 1968):117-29.

Winkler, Heinrich August. Mittelstand, Demokratie und Nationalsozialismus: Die politische Entwicklung von Handwerk und Kleinhandel in der Weimarer Republik. Cologne: Kiepenheuer and Witsch, 1972.

_____. "Extremus der Mitte? Sozialgeschichtliche Aspekte der nationalsozialistischen Machtergreifung." Viertel-jahrshefte für Zeitgeschichte 20 (April 1972):175-91.

Wirths, Heinrich. "Kampf und Sieg der NSDAP im Oberbergischen Land." In Buch des Oberbergischen Kreises, ed. Kreisleitung der NSDAP Oberbergen. Gummersbach: Gauverlag Westdeutscher Beobachter, 1939.

Wiss-Verdier, A. "Nationaux-démocrates progrés." Documents: Revue des questions Allemandes 23 (May-June 1968): 125-29.

Witt, Thomas E. J. de. "The Economics and Politics of Welfare in the Third Reich." Central European History 11 (December 1978):256-78.

_____. "The Nazi Party and Social Welfare, 1919-1939." Ph.D. dissertation, University of Virginia, 1971.

_____. "The Struggle against Hunger and Cold: Nazi Winter Relief, 1933-39." Canadian Journal of History 12 (February 1978):361-81.

Wulff, Ernst. Das Winterhilfswerk des Deutschen Volkes. Berlin: Eher, 1940.

Zangerl, Carl H. E. "Courting the Catholic Vote: The Center Party in Baden, 1903-1913." Central European History 10 (September 1977):220-40.

Zeman, Z. A. B. *Nazi Propaganda*. London: Oxford University Press, 1964.

Ziegler, Willy. *Aus dem Kampf der Heidelberger S.A., Pfingsten 1925 bis März 1933: Tagebuchblätter von Oberführer Willy Ziegler*. This typed diary may be found in GLA/465d/1923.

Zneimer, Richard. "The Nazis and the Professors: Social Origin, Professional Mobility, and Political Involvement of the Frankfurt University Faculty, 1933-39." *Journal of Social History* 12 (Fall 1978):147-56.

Zorn, Wolfgang. "Student Politics in the Weimar Republic." *Journal of Contemporary History* 5 (1970):128-43.

Index